Please return items on or before the Due Date printed
on your receipt.
Register your email address and you will receive a
reminder before your books are due back.
You can register your email address, check the Due
Date and renew your loans online at
www.dublincitypubliclibraries.ie
Have your Library Card Number and PIN to hand.
You can also renew your loans in person or by phone.

ᵣrlanna Poiblí Chathair Bhaile Átha Cliath
' ibraries

Dueling Dragons

The Struggle for Ireland
1849 – 1875

Marjorie Harshaw Robie

with

William D. Harshaw

ISBN- 13:978-1722422943

Published July, 2018

Cover designed by David Robie

For further information on the subjects in this book see the blog
https://duelingdragonsireland.blogspot.com.

Dedication

Dedicated to friends and family, Irish and American.

Table of Contents

List of Illustrations

Acknowledgements

The companion book, *Dwelling Place of Dragons*, was finished ten years ago. Many of those who helped with that project generously continued to help during the additional ten years that passed before *Dueling Dragons* was finally ready for publication. Karen Hickey who started this project with a single phone call and who trusted me with the Harshaw Diaries has remained an integral participant over the twenty-five years that followed her first call. Suzanne Ballard and I continued to share family information. She edited my transcription of the Harshaw Diaries and indexed them so they could be searchable at the Mormon website.

Irish researchers stood by. David Huddleston works now at the lovely modern PRONI research facility at the Titanic Center. He has continued to watch over the Harshaw Diaries. They have been of such interest to historians that the condition of the diaries has deteriorated. To protect them from further damage, the originals are only available with David's special permission. Tom Desmond, head of the Manuscript section of the National Library in Dublin, continued to assist in finding all John Martin writings.

Jan Fortado, a good friend from Ipswich, has shared my great interest in family history for many years. Through much of the research for *Dueling Dragons,* she has traveled with me to Ireland, sharing the adventures of our many weeks in Dublin. She introduced me to Helen Martin at Montrose Lodge where we were always welcomed. Thanks to her companionship, researching in such a large city was never a lonely operation. We always had much to talk about over lunch. Through a great stroke of luck, we were in Dublin when President Obama and Queen Elizabeth visited there.

Maud Hamill continued to help and support my research. She planned the book events for *Dwelling Place of Dragons,* which included a very special launch in Newry as well as a book signing in the Linen Hall Library in Belfast where I was fortunate enough to meet some of the members of the Henderson family. She also allowed me to use one of her photographs on the front cover of this book, for which I am very grateful. Adrian Murdoch has remained a great friend, contributing pictures I needed for this new book, as well as continuing to find new cousins living in the Donaghmore area.

My home in Northern Ireland has been Cedar Haven in Donaghmore, the home of Joan and Walter Malcomson. They have always treated me as family, and have provided a welcome to the steady stream of my friends and relatives who have heeded my advice that Donaghmore was a place that must be visited. Walter's Sunday morning rambles have become a most special treat. On one of them, he was able to bring me to the site of my Harshaw family's home in Loughgilly Parish.

Though my husband Gene died before the first book was published, my family has continued to be extremely supportive, listening patiently as I recounted my exciting discoveries and offering support when my spirits lagged. And another family member, my cousin Bill Harshaw, appeared just when I most needed his advice on managing new technology, and keeping readers always in mind. Without his help, this book would never have been published.

Ron Donaghe not only edited my first book, but traveled to Ireland to participate in the launch, an act much above the call of duty. He signed on again to edit this book as well. Though this book is longer than the first, this time, he didn't recommend any cuts.

My son David Robie has designed the cover for this book, as he did for my first one. He has also created the maps that will help familiarize readers with the area. I'm very grateful that he interrupted other projects so I could get this book into print. My son Stephen has assumed the very support role that my husband once occupied, giving me weekly pep talks, and financial assistance.

I want to pay special tribute to the family and friends who have died since this adventure began. Sadly, I now remember our special times when I visit Irish graveyards. Hugh Harshaw and his wonderful wife Maisie have died, along with Hugh's brother James and his wife big Myrtle. Wee Myrtle Harshaw and her son-in-law Maurice Hillis are gone as well.

One of my special friends, Dr. Maurna Crozier, died far too young. As I was writing this book, I missed her enthusiasm and wise advice. Maurna and I should never have met at all. She lived in a large country house down a long narrow lane, a place I would never have ventured. Except for one thing. Her home, Lisnacreevy House, had once belonged to a relative named Elizabeth Harshaw Corbett. Maurice Hillis drove me down Maurna's lane so I could take a picture. Her husband greeted us, and graciously allowed me to take my photographs. Before we left, he insisted that I go into the kitchen to meet his wife.

This should have been a passing meeting, but that wasn't Maurna's way. The next day she invited me to go with her to a play in Belfast. By intermission, she was introducing me as her "friend from America." That is what we had become on a short drive. We kept in touch by email. Whenever I went to Ireland, she saved as much time as she could for us to adventure together. I saw the Glens of Antrim with Maurna and the mountains of Fermanagh. We shared cake cooked over an open fire in Margaret Gallagher's thatched cottage and simple suppers at her kitchen table. When she retired, she would clear her calendar so we could spend the days together. Whenever friends and family visited me there, she entertained us all at Lisnacreevy.

I hope this book would make all these very special people proud.

Marjorie Harshaw Robie

Ipswich MA 2018

John Martin
1812-1875
Young Irelander, exile, writer, and eventually the first Member of Parliament of the Home Rule League. He was respected by both extremes of Irish opinion, but he always worked for an end to English rule over the island.

James Harshaw
1797-1867

James Harshaw was a farmer, employer, Presbyterian elder, Poorhouse guardian, dispensary overseer, friend, neighbor and diarist. Most of all he was father and grandfather to a large family in Ireland, America, and Australia.

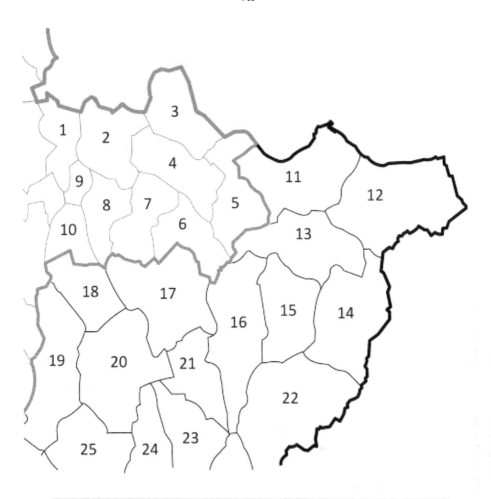

Townlands in Donoghmore and Newry Parishes

1: Buskhill
2: Ringclare
3: Annaghbane
4: Ringolish
5: Ardkeeragh
6: Ringbane
7: Cargabane
8: Tullymurry
9: Glebe
10: Augnacavan
11: Ouley
12: Gransha
13: Curley
14: Ardarragh
15: Lisnaree
16: Shinn
17: Loughorne
18: Lisserboy
19: Corcreeghy
20: Carnacally
21: Castleenigan
22: Finnard
23: Savamore
24: Savalbeg
25: Turmore

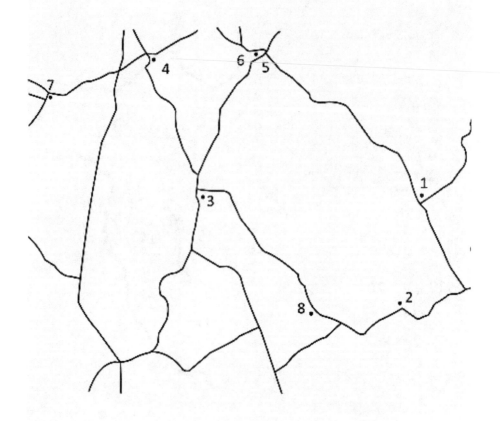

Donaghmore Locations

1: Harshaw House
2: Loughorne House
3: Donaghmore Meetinghouse
4: St. Bartholomew's Church
5: McGaffin's Corners
6: Donaghmore School
7: Four Mile House
8: Presbyterian Manse

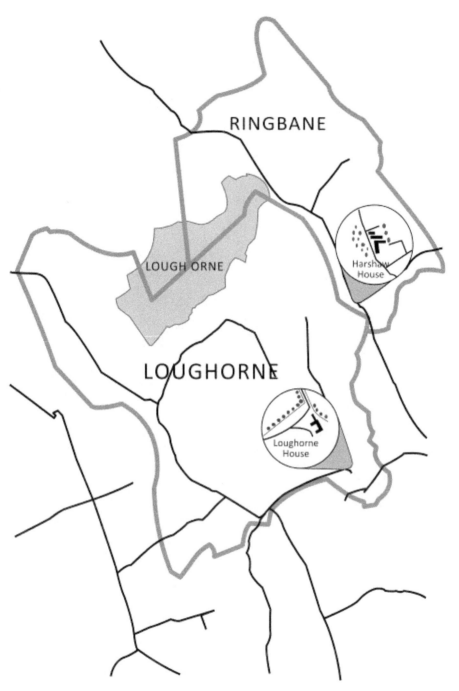

Homes of John Martin and James Harshaw

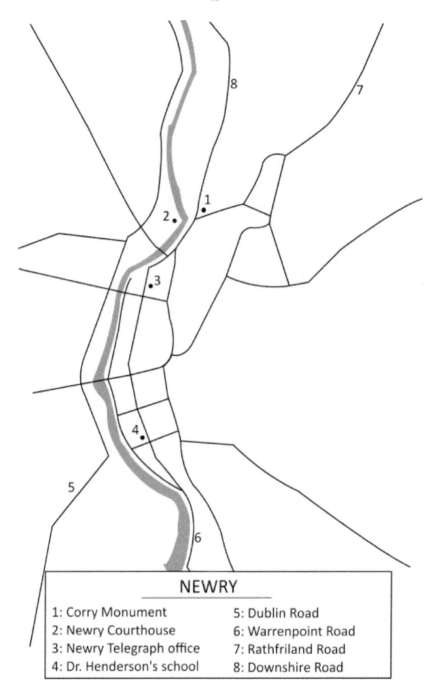

NEWRY

1: Corry Monument
2: Newry Courthouse
3: Newry Telegraph office
4: Dr. Henderson's school

5: Dublin Road
6: Warrenpoint Road
7: Rathfriland Road
8: Downshire Road

Introduction

My two books, *Dwelling Place of Dragons*, and now *Dueling Dragons*, exist only because of modern technology and a wild set of unlikely events. I never intended to write either of them, or any other book on Irish history for that matter. My interest in Ireland was limited to learning about my Irish ancestors and the places in Ireland they left over several centuries to make their homes in America. I had no expectation that I would find long-lost relatives there.

I was vaguely aware that there were old Irish diaries that might help my search for family history. However, any interest in history was confined to an intense interest in local Ipswich history, honed by two decades of service on our local Ipswich Historical Commission. All that changed in 1992 when I reluctantly entered the modern technological era. My son Stephen sent me his old computer when he upgraded. He also sent me a printout of the addresses of all Harshaws in America. I could potentially contact many possible cousins using my new old computer.

Soon after, my children gave me and my husband a trip to Ireland. I could now possibly find more genealogical information, if I could find those diaries. Finding them seemed suddenly important. I decided to use my new technology to create a form letter, requesting information about the diaries from some of the Harshaws on my list of names and addresses. When the job was finished, I carried the large bundle of letters to our post office and waited for results.

Many of the letters were just returned as undeliverable. But soon, I had a few actual responses, some of them very interesting. But no one knew anything about the Harshaw diaries. I thought that most likely they would be in the Public Record Office in Belfast, so I planned several days in Belfast to search for them.

Everything in my life changed one Friday evening, not long before my husband and I were leaving for Ireland. My phone rang just before supper. A woman whose voice I didn't recognize responded to my "hello." "Hello, you don't know me, but I'm a cousin. My name is Karen Hickey. I live in Keokuk, Iowa. I have the Harshaw diaries." I can't recall a more stunning surprise. I would certainly have never hunted for Irish documents in Keokuk, Iowa.

Then Karen explained to me how they had made their way from a farm in Ringbane Parish, County Down, Ireland to the farmland of mid-America. She had been searching for a Harshaw ancestor of her own named James Harshaw, the same name as the diarist. Through the use of old technology, Karen soon was on the phone with Sally Harshaw Lowing of Grove City PA. She told Karen that she had some diaries with that name on them.

Sally explained that she had gotten the journals from the bank across the street. An employee there had discovered a package containing the diaries in a basement section that was undergoing renovation. If Sally didn't want them, they would be discarded. Sally agreed to take them, thinking that the proper owner would someday come to claim them. Had the diaries been discovered just a bit later, Sally would have been gone, and so the diaries would have been lost forever. Having a long-time interest in history, I was stunned at the thought that this family story, this Irish national treasure, was nearly lost forever. My interest in Irish history catapulted from casual to intense. I could hardly wait to get to Ireland.

The first shock of my trip to Northern Ireland was finding that I had entered a war zone. Every car entering Newry had to drive into a metal cage where police and British soldiers carefully checked for weapons or bombs. Just beyond the checkpoint, British soldiers dressed in full camouflage, machine guns at the ready, provided reinforcements in case of trouble. Rather than convince me never to come there again, the scene enhanced my desire to understand what historic events had led to this frightening result.

Once out of Newry, we seemed to be in a totally normal and very beautiful Irish countryside. After a fruitless search for my family origins, we headed into the small town of Poyntzpass where a possible cousin, Hugh Harshaw, lived.

No one answered my knock, and I was turning away dreadfully disappointed, when a car pulled up in front of the house. Hugh Harshaw got out and asked if he could help. I explained who I was, and he invited the American strangers in for tea. While we chatted, he pulled out a book from his shelf, opened it to a certain page, and handed it to me. It was a book my father had once owned, a history of Donaghmore Parish written almost a century before by a local clergyman.

"This man," he said pointing to the reference in the book of James Harshaw and his diaries, "was my great grandfather." He went on to tell me that he and his brother James had hunted for years for the diaries without success.

One of the greatest joys of my life was to be the privileged person who got to respond to Hugh and see the look on his face. "Hugh, I know where they are." The memory of that moment still produces misty eyes every time I remember it. I knew at that moment, I would pursue this adventure wherever it led me.

Over tea, I explained where they were and how they narrowly escaped destruction. I also promised him that I would do everything I could to make sure he would get to hold them in his hands and read them by his home fire.

Thanks to Karen Hickey, I was able to keep my promise. She sent the diaries to me, entrusting me with the job of ensuring that the contents were preserved. When I opened the box, I discovered that the diaries weren't at all what I expected. They were large bound books, with dark red covers, the pages all handwritten on ledger paper. I turned to the New England Historic and Genealogical Society in Boston for advice. Historians there recognized their great historical value and had the entire contents preserved on microfilm.

After transcribing them myself, I put them in my carry-on and took them home to Ireland. By then, I had learned that after James died, the diaries were passed on to his oldest surviving son John. After John died in 1896, his family sent them to his brother Willy in Paterson NJ. At some point, Willy shared the diaries with a cousin in Grove City. Then they were stored in the bank for safety, and ultimately forgotten when both men died not long after. I returned them to Ireland late in 1996, after almost exactly a century in America. After Hugh and his brothers had read them, an historian from the Public Record Office in Belfast, came to Poyntzpass to take them to Belfast where they could be properly protected for generations.

Through his diaries, my cousin James introduced me to another cousin, his nephew John Martin. I had never heard his name before, but some reading in existing Irish histories provided brief but intriguing accounts of his life. I yearned to know more about him, and the history of the part of Ireland James and John lived in. I discovered that there was a local newspaper, *The Newry Commercial Telegraph,* which could certainly provide me a good exploration of this southern part of Ulster. I bought a second-hand microfilm reader, and began to buy, read and take notes on all the available newspapers.

When I finished, I had carefully read the newspaper, edition by edition, from 1828 to 1875. I knew I had discovered the foundations of an important new history. But a problem remained. I realized that James Harshaw and John Martin had political opinions that differed from many residents of southern Ulster. To offer a complete history, I needed a person who shared the prevailing political point of view. George Henderson who was the editor of the *Telegraph* was a great candidate. When I discovered that he and John Martin were actually friends, I knew I had my third character.

I wrote *Dwelling Place of Dragons* when I had completed the necessary research. More years and many hours reading John Martin's letters owned by the National Library in Dublin, and existing in newspapers on film there passed before I was ready to complete my history of these men and this part of Ireland. *Dueling Dragons* completes the history that James, John, and George left behind for me to find.

Marjorie Robie Harshaw   July 23, 2018

Young Irelanders in Van Diemen's Land

William Smith O'Brien

Kevin O'Dogherty

    Several of the Young Irelanders who supported the repeal of the Act of Union were arrested in 1848 for felony treason and related charges, convicted, and exiled to Van Diemen's Land. O'Brien and Martin left VDL together, receiving pardons, and returning to Ireland. O'Dogherty (aka O'Doherty) was pardoned and had a varied life. Meagher, McManus, and Mitchel left VDL without permission, settling in the United States. McManus died in San Francisco, Meagher led Union troops in the Civil War, while Mitchel supported the Confederacy. Mitchel, Martin, and O'Dogherty were all elected to the House of Commons. For more see the University of Tasmania website: http:// www.utas.edu.au/young-irelanders/home.

Terence McManus

Thomas Meagher

John Mitchel

Prologue

The 19th century brought many challenges for Ireland: deep divisions of religion and class, peasants without jobs, adequate food or health care, an undereducated population, government imposed by England to benefit English interests, and the daunting difficulty of surmounting these obstacles to form one society and one country. Many of these challenges still echo today both in Ireland and across the world today.

The town of Newry and the farming areas and small towns surrounding it were locations where Catholic and Protestant populations lived side by side. When conflicting interests of the two religions were increased by English legislation and Irish political movements, confrontations of man on man or group on group often led to harassment or violence. Newry became an epicenter of Irish struggles during this critical century.

Newry was an ancient Irish town when the Act of Union, passed with great corruption by the English and Irish Parliaments in 1800, transformed Ireland from a semi-independent country into a third section of greater England, along with Scotland and Wales. Reactions to this legislation varied in Newry and across neighboring South Down and South Armagh. Protestant citizens of the area were proud to have fought to create a Parliament in Ireland almost two decades before. Most wanted to maintain it. The perspective of the Catholic majority of Newry was different. They supported the union with England as they had been promised the same equality under law that Catholics enjoyed in England.

However, Catholics soon discovered that the promises that led to their support were immediately disavowed and consigned to oblivion. Protestants realized that the loss of their own Parliament was more than compensated for by assurances that their privileged position in Ireland was secure, and they would enjoy a position of importance in England's expanding empire. Their previous opposition quickly shifted to enthusiastic support. The stage was set for trouble.

For the first years of the Union, Ireland was quite prosperous as England needed Irish food during its long war with France. Prices for farmers' produce increased more rapidly than their rents. Newry ships plied the Irish sea every fall carrying the Irish harvest to England. However, when the war ended in 1815, prices for farm produce plummeted while rents remained near their wartime highs. A terrible depression settled over Ireland.

Much of Irish land was owned by rich men in England. They had little interest in helping their impoverished laborers maintain access to land, which was essential for their survival. Instead, when rents were unpaid, laborers and their families were forcibly ejected from their simple cottages, thrown out into the road with their meager possessions heaped about them. Most had no money to emigrate. They were left to beg or starve.

In 1830, religious leaders of Newry did something remarkable to end the problematic religious intolerance. Catholic, Church of Ireland and Presbyterian clergy and lay leaders met to establish religious peace in Newry. This is the point where the first book in this series, *Dwelling Place of Dragons,* began to reveal Newry's important story. Beginning with the peace conference, it covered the Tithe Wars resulting from laws that required Catholics and Presbyterians to provide financial support for the official government church, the Church of Ireland, the creation of the poorhouse system, and the first steps toward Irish independence with the founding of the Repeal Association and the Young Irelanders in the 1840s. While the Irish famine was most devastating across southern and western Ireland, it had great impact in Ulster as well. *Dwelling Place of Dragons* ended in 1849 when religious hostilities erupted again with the battle between local Catholics and Orangemen on parade through the tiny Catholic village of Dolly's Brae.

The two books, *Dwelling Place of Dragons,* and now *Dueling Dragons,* recount the history of Newry, the town serving as an exemplar of the history of Ireland during most of the century. The history is written in a somewhat untraditional manner. Its story is related mainly through the writings of three interconnected citizens as year followed year for a quarter of a century. When the Newry peace conference was taking place, John Martin and George Henderson, were still teenagers. John's father and his brothers were prosperous owners of the townland (an area of approximately 350 acres) of Loughorne, and linen mills in the town of Rostrevor. George's family owned the *Newry Commercial Telegraph,* the most influential Conservative newspaper in southern Ulster. By 1836, John had become manager of the family farms in Loughorne, Newry Parish. George had become the editor of the family newspaper in Newry.

The third narrator is James Harshaw. His sister Jane was John Martin's mother. In 1830, he was helping his brother William manage land they leased in the parish of Ringbane. He had married Sarah Kidd before he reached majority. In his early 30s, they already had seven children. That same year, William died, and James inherited management of the family property. Ordinarily, Irishmen labored on farms across Ireland, married, had children, and when they died, they were buried in unmarked graves and their existence forgotten. But James kept a journal through most of his life, providing a valuable accounting of the struggles of Irish farmers.

Dueling Dragons picks up the story of the three men in 1849, concluding in 1875 when John Martin died. The struggle between supporters of the union with England and those supporting Irish independence, between Whig and Conservative, between Protestants and Catholics, between George Henderson and John Martin, unfolded during the intervening years and provided a prologue for the events of the 20th century. Farmers like James Harshaw were often collateral damage, caught in the swirl of historical forces over which they had little influence.

These men may have been Newry men, but the account of their lives informs the history of Ireland for those with an interest in Irish history across the globe.

Churches

Donaghmore Presbyterian Church, where James Harshaw was an elder for much of his life

St. Bartholomews Church (CofI), where John Martin is buried.

Chapter 1

A World Apart

1849 – 1850

John Martin's world was blue, when it should have been green. As he stood by the railing of the ship Mountstewart Eliphinstone, all he could see was blue ocean and blue sky. Only in his imagination could he see the green meadows and green hedges of his much-loved home in Ireland. His reality and his dreams were thousands of miles apart. The ship with its cargo of Irish prisoners was nearing Australia where it would soon be spring. In Ireland, the tenants on his farm in Loughorne, County Down would be bringing in the autumn harvest.

This dramatic turn in his life was something that John could never have foreseen. But the great Irish Famine had seared his soul and prompted him to take political action on behalf of his dying countrymen. The English government moved quickly to prevent the desperate Irish from rebelling by passing a law that made even writing against English policies a crime of felony treason. When John refused to be silenced by this new law, he was arrested, tried and convicted by a jury carefully chosen from a list of his enemies. His sentence to ten years transportation to Van Diemen's Land was being implemented in September 1849. Australia lay not far beyond the horizon.

Each Irish harvest followed a routine so familiar that John knew what was happening at home almost as clearly as if he had been walking the fields himself. The grains would have been cut. Flax would have been pulled rotting from the flax holes and tied up in stooks after drying. However, there was one unknown that John could only worry about, the status of the potato crop. Without a good crop, free of the deadly blight, many more poor Irish laborers would die.

The health of the potato crop was also of great concern to John's uncle James Harshaw. He planted many potato ridges to feed his large family and the farm laborers who worked the land he leased. Every morning, James rose with the dawn, and went to his potato drills hoping that the lovely green potato leaves and stems he left the previous evening hadn't been transformed by the blight into a black, stinking mess. This year James and the farmers of Ulster were lucky. Their potato crop remained healthy. This year there would be enough to eat in Ulster

James and John had always been particularly close. John's mother was James's sister Jane. The land John owned in Loughorne was next to the land that James leased in Ringbane. From the desk where James wrote the daily entries in his journal, he could see the row of trees in front of Loughorne House where John had lived, fields, trees and cottage still clear in John's memory.

James had other concerns, which he mentioned in his journal entry for September 20th. "Another fine dry morning & dryer day then yesterday. Stacked some oats off the far-cow-park. The wind stil north...Oats 8 ½ pir stone in Newry. Willy first asked my permission."

Farming in Ireland was becoming an increasingly risky way to earn a living. So James had attempted to find non-farming occupations for his six living sons. Willy, or William Kidd, had been apprenticed to the linen industry in nearby Banbridge to take advantage of the one growing industry in the northern part of Ireland. But now Willy was asking James for permission to emigrate to America. Similar requests had plunged the hearts of many Irish families into despair. From the moment Willy uttered those words, James knew that too soon, Willy would walk away from a final embrace, and that he would experience that same heartbreaking loss. Despite James's intense heart pain, he knew at once that he couldn't keep his son chained to a land of despair and death when a future of hope lay on the other side of the Atlantic Ocean. He gave Willy the "permission" he requested.

While Willy was leaving Ireland for a more promising economic future. John had been forced to leave Ireland for a far less positive reason. He had been exiled for his political beliefs, his intense wish for Irish independence. The fact that his conviction was pleasing to many other Irishmen, particularly those in Ulster, was a clear indication that many others cherished intense hopes directly contrary to John's dreams. Indeed, many of John's friends and neighbors wished to maintain the Irish connection to England forever.

One such person was George Henderson. He was the editor of the most important newspaper in southern Ulster, the *Newry Commercial Telegraph*. He had been a friend of John's from the time they were students at Dr. Henderson's School on Hill Street in Newry. He was distinctly a loyalist, loyal to the authority of England and its laws, always ready to vigorously oppose any effort to weaken England's management of Ireland.

That support for England didn't prevent George from criticizing English actions when he thought they were unfair to the Protestants of Ulster. In July, marching Protestants had attacked a small Irish community at Dolly's Brae, resulting in the deaths of four Catholics and the destruction of several cottages. Trials had followed without convictions. Usually, none of the Orange leaders risked any penalty either. But this time, Lord Robert Roden and two Orange leaders had had their positions as Justices of the Peace revoked by Lord Clarendon, the Lord Lieutenant of Ireland. Their crime was inciting the perpetrators with their speeches at the Orange gathering at Lord Roden's estate before the deadly march to Dolly's Brae.

George was a skilled writer, his words more powerful than those that resulted in John's conviction. His customary strong support for the English government ensured that he would escape the same severe penalty that John endured when he criticized government actions. "The sacrifice desired in order to satiate Faction has been made. Our readers will, we are sure, be as wholly unprepared as we ourselves have been to receive the astounding intelligence, that the EARL OF RODEN AND THE MESSERS BEERS HAVE BEEN DISMISSED FROM THE COMMISSION OF THE PEACE." For powerful people to be punished for the actions of the mobs their words unleashed was certainly as astounding to the Catholic victims as it was to Orange supporters like George.

§

John Martin, James Harshaw and George Henderson were men of Newry, a town both favored and cursed by geography. Located at the end of Carlingford Lough, it provided sanctuary for mariners imperiled by storms raging on the Irish Sea just beyond the entrance. Bronze age craftsmen found the area to their liking and settled there around 4,500 B. C. For centuries, they lived in relative safety, building their ring forts, digging burial caves and crafting bronze tools and jewelry. When Saint Patrick came to Ireland to convert the pagan population to his Catholic faith, the Newry people embraced the new religion.

Unfortunately, Newry's prime location attracted other invaders as well. Viking raiders sailed down the Lough to pillage Newry and the rich monasteries the Catholic Church had established farther inland. King William of Orange, invaded Ireland in 1689 to establish the supremacy of England and its Protestant religion. His army marched through Donaghmore, Newry, and the pass between the mountains south of town to the decisive battle at the River Boyne.

Many of King William's soldiers were given property in the fertile land around Newry in return for their military service. The Newry area became a religious battleground between early Catholic and more recent Protestant residents for the centuries that followed. The population of Newry was always predominantly Catholic while the leaders, merchants and elected officials were members of the Church of Ireland. These leaders were originally opponents of English efforts to gain control of Ireland through the passage of the Act of Union in 1800. However, passage of law after law by the English Parliament that followed the Union had different effects on adherents of the different religions and prompted strong Protestant support or vehement Catholic opposition. Partisans on each side organized, Protestants into the Orange Order, Catholics into various groups, each celebrating their heroes in processions, and sometimes in actual fighting, as at Dolly's Brae.

§

The days that followed Willy Harshaw's request for permission to emigrate to America were long and painful ones. Not only was Willy to risk a long ocean voyage, but son James Jr., whom James had nicknamed Joseph, decided to give up his grocery business in nearby Mountnorris to accompany his younger brother on his great adventure. James and his wife Sarah Kidd were losing two more sons having already watched two sons and a daughter die. Emigration was another form of death for James and Sarah to endure.

The two young adventurers had much to do once they had booked passage on the Janet, out of Warrenpoint. Young Protestant men emigrated with references to ease their transition to life in a new country. James and Willy obtained statements of character from the ministers of the churches they attended. Willy also received a letter of endorsement from the linen company he worked for. There was also a round of visits to friends and neighbors to say their goodbyes.

Irish farmers cherished many old Irish traditions. One of these was that swallows brought good luck to those at sea. So James was watching for swallows as he worked. In several diary entries, he mentioned that some were flying about. On Tuesday, October 9th, James wrote, "Frost, fine day. Joseph and Willy busy preparing for New York. Several friends visited them...No swallows. Slept little."

The next day, Willy and James left for America. James couldn't bring himself to put his pain into words. He hugged them one more time as they boarded the cart that would take them to Warrenpoint. He didn't join the sad procession of friends and relatives who accompanied them to the dock, where the ship Janet was waiting to transport them to New York City. Instead, as the cart clattered up the lane, James walked through the back gate and headed to the fields.

The Janet actually didn't pull away from the pier at Warrenpoint until late the next day to catch the evening tide. At that time, James reported that he had seen two swallows which then disappeared. He hoped that they were flying west with the Janet.

Besides ongoing farm work, James started a civic project to help pass the long days before he could expect to hear of the boys' safe arrival. James leased land in Donaghmore Estates. Almost ten years had passed since the previous landlord had died, during which time the tenants remained in an unsettling limbo. Finally the estate had been freed of legal encumbrances and sold. The new owner was Hill Irvine, a Newry merchant. Having this good local man buy the property was the best of fortune for local farmers. A benevolent owner was essential to maintain access to land which, in Ireland, was tantamount to access to life.

So James and his fellow tenants began preparations for a dinner to be held to honor their new landlord and ensure that this critical relationship began in a positive way. On Saturday September 22nd, James had sent Willy into Newry to meet Mr. Todd who was Hill Irvine's land agent. Following Irvine's positive response, James sent one of his workers around the area to distribute a flyer he had created inviting all the tenants to attend. Next, he went to Newry to distribute tickets to the businessmen of the town.

On October 20th, a ceremony took place to formally turn Donaghmore Estates over to Mr. Irving. The local sheriff, Mr. Nelson, was on hand to manage the formalities. Mr. Todd acted for the new owner. The small ceremony took place on the forthfield, with James and his son John present. The transfer was formalized by "a clod & branch of a poplar." Then James was off to the Four Mile House for a meeting of the planning committee.

The dinner took place three days later. George Henderson covered the event extensively in the *Telegraph*, knowing the high esteem in which Mr. Irvine was held in Newry. Such events followed a well-established pattern. After the meal was finished, a series of toasts and responses took place, often far into the night as in this case. James was the chairman and offered the first toast to the new landlord.

In his response, Mr. Irvine outlined some of the problems facing Irish farmers. "This demonstration of good feeling and kindly regard towards me is doubly enhanced by the fact of your all holding, under leases giving a permanent interest in the soil; and, therefore, free from any obligation beyond the mutual good will and proper understanding that should always exist between parties whose interests are so identical as landlord and tenant. (Cheers.) In fact, Gentlemen, I consider that this satisfactory relationship which you have so heartily manifested to-night, and which it is so desirable should be established in all parts of Ireland, can only properly exist, when the tenure of the land is legally secured to the tenant, where he has a direct and permanent interest in improving his farm, and when he feels secure that he will reap the full benefit of his own labor and capital. (Tremendous applause, which lasted for several minutes).

"But, though your interest in the land is so valuable, and your industry and perseverance so great, as to enable you thus far to meet all your engagements with such credit to yourselves, yet believe me, gentlemen, unless tenants and landlords, and all others interested in the welfare of the country, speedily make a united effort to have the burthens upon land reduced, so as to meet the present low prices of Irish produce, and a more equitable adjustment of taxation generally established, it will be impossible for men holding, even under your favorable tenures, to bear up against the burthens under which the country is now laboring. (Hear)." This chilling warning matched the deep worries of the Donaghmore farmers.

After toasts and discussions of education and religious liberty, Mr. Greer of Buskhill rose to discuss the problems facing Irish farmers that fall from the perspective of tenants: "His recollections went back at least forty years, and in the course of that time he had seen many depressions, some greater and some less, but he had seen none like the present. (Hear). The farmers had now to pay rates, and other imposts, altogether unknown before, and these, together with the depression in the prices of produce, weighed them down to the ground. The poor-rate, in that division, would amount to 4s on the acre, if not more, which constituted a very large tax on the industry of the farmer. (Hear, hear).

"The causes of the present depression were, in his opinion, three-fold— 1st, the repeated failure of the potato crop; 2d, the repeal of the Corn Laws; and, 3d, rack-rents...The blight continued to work its evil effect, notwithstanding all the efforts that could be made to the contrary. (Hear). The repeal of the Bill, abolishing the Corn Laws, we need not look for, he believed. It was idle to expect it. As to rack-rents, what would have been a fair rent from 1800 up to the battle of Waterloo, would be a rack-rent when war had ceased, and a fair rent before the repeal of the corn laws and potato failure, poor-rate, and rate-in-aid–(hisses), would be a rack-rent now. He trusted, however, that the landlords would take this circumstance into their serious consideration, demanding from their tenantry only such an amount as the altered state of affairs warranted, and such as the farmers of the country could fairly pay. Of course he did not apply these observations to this estate, where the rents were exceedingly low. (Hear, hear, and cheers)."

Mr. Greer was so clear in his analysis of the perilous situation of Irish farmers that George reprinted this speech, knowing that it would be of intense interest to his readers. Without some redress, many Ulster farmers would also leave Ireland, just as Willy and James Jr. had done. George would continue to report on the danger and any actions by the English government to solve the unbearable squeeze between high rents and taxes and low prices for Irish farm products

More toasts followed, each accompanied by a "raising of the cup." The linen industry was saluted along with the trades of Newry, good landlords who were lowering their rents, the press, legal profession, the Donaghmore Farming Society, and finally the chairman. George considered the whole evening a great success, and an example of proper landlord and tenant relations. There was general agreement that James's leadership had set the new relationship between owner and tenants of Donaghmore Estate off on a positive footing.

§

As the year 1849 neared its close, the absence of any word of James's loved ones became, day by day, a more painful silence. There had been no news of John Martin who had last been heard from before his prison ship had cast off its moorings at Spike Island and sailed into the mist the end of June. There hadn't been any news from the Harshaw boys either. With the passage of every day, fears for their safety increased. By the time the New Year came and went, fears became near panic.

The weather on January 2nd must have matched James's mood. "Gray morning, it continues to thaw." He was on the road above the farbray when he saw someone approaching. The "postWoman" was hurrying toward him. She handed him "a letter from Joseph & Willy dated Newyork 18th Decr 1849…The letter informed us that they had reached Newyork in good health." The ocean crossing had taken 65 days. "The news of theer arrival in Newyork spread rappedly over the country and a good manney people called through the day to make enquirey about them."

James continued his farm work with a much lighter heart. Once the wall of silence had been broken, letters from his lost sons in America would arrive more often. About a week later, there was more news. Winter wheat was being thrashed on January the 10th when a second letter arrived. This one was dated on Christmas day. "The letter informed us that they were well, the city large & dirty, and none of the people so purty as Miss Jones." A few days later, Miss

Jones herself visited James to hear about the latest news from Willy and James Jr.

There was still no word from John Martin.

§

There was so much farm work for James to attend to that he didn't often mention the poverty and destitution that was too often a feature of Irish life. But George frequently reported on the reality of life for the Irish. He shared the story of Margaret Gallagher with his readers. Margaret lived in Clones in County Monaghan with three sons and a daughter. She had no access to land or job to buy even a bit of bread there. So she decided to walk to Belfast with her children to find work. Despite long days plodding through wind and cold, the whole family arrived safely in Belfast.

Margaret scoured the shops of Belfast begging for work. Her haggard appearance and ragged clothes didn't make her an attractive job candidate, so she trudged around Belfast in vain. Her older sons left her hoping for better luck on their own. When her meager funds ran out, Margaret decided that she must take a most desperate step to find help for her two younger children. She would enter the poorhouse.

The poorhouse with its high dark walls was easy enough to find. Fearfully, Margaret crept along in the shadow of the wall until she reached the main door where an entrance official was always on duty. The most important job for this official was to ensure that no one from beyond the boundaries of the Poor Law District was allowed to enter to become a burden on local rate payers. After a few questions, the admitting officer was sure that Margaret and her children belonged within the jurisdiction of a different poorhouse. Her appeal for help was rejected and she was instructed to return to Clones.

So on Saturday January 5th, she started the long walk back to Clones with her two older sons joining in for the long painful journey. By evening, the desperate family had arrived in Lisburn. There they sold some of their remaining clothes and begged in the street to obtain enough money for some shelter, and bread and coffee to provide a meager breakfast the next morning.

Before continuing their painful journey, the family separated again. The older sons went to friends in Armagh for help. Margaret, her youngest son, and daughter walked on alone. By nightfall, they had arrived in Moira. There the kind wife of a local clergyman gave them enough money for shelter and bread. The effort was becoming too taxing for the family to cover many miles. The next night they had reached Portadown where they met one of the sons returning with a shilling that he had been given.

The next morning, the family started out yet again. But about a mile and a half out of Portadown, Margaret sank down beside the road to rest. She huddled silently in the cold. Soon, the children noticed that she was growing ever more pale. In fact, she had quietly died. An inquest on the body was held that same day. Mr. Atkinson, the district coroner, gave his verdict. "Death from destitution."

One of the solutions to such deadly poverty was a law strengthening access to land for farmers and laborers across Ireland. In a country where there was little money in the hands of most laborers, access to land was essential. A movement to achieve more access to land had begun to sweep across the island. One such tenant rights meeting took place in nearby Banbridge. James mentioned the meeting in his entry for Monday January 28th. "Tennant right meeting at Banbridge."

This was an effort that George strongly opposed, as he made clear in his extensive coverage of this meeting. As usual, the meeting was publicized by printing placards that were placed in visible locations throughout the steep streets of the town. The meeting was to be held in a field at the "upper end" of town at 11 a.m. But the crowd then was so sparse that the start was delayed for two hours. George described the audience as lacking respectable men of the town. There were only a few shop owners, and just two local ministers, Rev. Rogers of Glascar and Rev. Doran of Loughbrickland. Joseph Carswell was in the chair. The goal of the meeting was to get a reduction in local rents necessitated by the losses from the potato blight and the repeal of the Corn Laws. For many years, the Corn Laws had placed tariffs on competing grain imports, increasing the return Irish farmers received for Irish crops. When Parliament revoked these laws in 1846, the income of Irish farmers plummeted.

The two main speakers were Presbyterian ministers from other parts of Ulster. One of them, Rev. William Dobbins, expressed his belief in and support of the class-based social structure existing in Ireland. He wasn't a revolutionary. He wasn't opposed to the wealth of landlords. "They are born to the enjoyment of superior privileges; and, if improving their advantages, they would exhibit themselves, as they should, patterns of high intellectual attainment, generous benevolence, and Christian justice, I believe they would go far to dignify their order, and they would reap a rich reward in the respect and gratitude of a warm-hearted and generous people."

But he didn't stop there. "The English language affords me no term to express my abhorrence of heartless rack-renting, and the unfeeling exercise of landlordism's irresponsible power. These are indeed, the enemies of your country, their creed is spoliation, their practice robbery, spoliation and ruin ever mark their progress, and their bloody history is a record of fearful wrong to the Irish people."

Rev. Dobbins recognized that the people of Ulster had a legitimate grievance against the actions of the upper classes. The landowners were living their good lives on the collection of unfair rents. Rents had risen greatly when times were good, and they hadn't fallen to account for consequences of the potato blight, death from hunger and emigration of the young and fit. Farmers couldn't labor longer or sell enough of their meager treasures to earn enough to pay them. To them, this rack-renting was a moral outrage.

Rev. Rutherford was another speaker who made a forceful case against the practice of rack-renting. "While the landlords were lying reclining on couches of velvet, or spending their time and their wealth in profligacy in foreign lands, the tenant had drained the swamps, quarried the stone, formed the roads, and, after all this his labor, who would dare to assert that he had no property in the soil, or attempt to wrench it from him by rack-renting and oppression?"

The actions of the English government had served to intensify the farmers' burdens through oppressive layers of taxes. The county cess funded the cost of local governments, but it also included the costs of maintaining the English troops that were always stationed in Ireland to maintain the peace. Poor rates supporting the poorhouses were rapidly increasing, as the desperate poor sought help within them. Most annoying of all these taxes was the rate-in-aid. This was an extra tax levied on the farmers of Ulster to provide funds for the poorhouses in southern parts of Ireland where too many people were too poor to support their own poorhouses.

There were solutions to rack-renting, which Rev. Rutherford explained to the audience. First, the government should be the entity that established the value of land, not the landlord. Second, since so many large estates were in financial distress, the government should take advantage of the situation and buy the land at the current depressed value, and then sell the land to the tenants to be paid for by their rents. Should Parliament take this action, land issues in Ireland would surely vanish.

These improvements wouldn't take place unless farmers united and acted, dangerous though such actions would be. Every farmer understood that their protests might result in their being ejected from the land they leased. They had to ensure that landowners understood that any punishment ejectments would result in a boycott that would leave their land to turn to wasteland.

Rev. Rutherford ended his speech and the meeting on a hopeful note. "Though the country was passing through a furnace of trial, if every man was sure of his labor, and had the opportunity of earning his bread by the sweat of his brow, he thought there was hope for it (Ireland) yet, it would rise out of its ashes with more splendor and brilliancy."

§

While January had begun with good news from Willy and Joseph, it ended with news from John. James and his laborers had begun "plowing the marsh at the far side where there were a good many stones." He ended his journal entry with news that he had long awaited. "Saw a leter from John Martin." Three months had passed since John had finished writing it and brought it to the Post Office in Bothwell. Finally the letter had reached its destination in Loughorne.

This letter was most welcomed by the family, eager to learn about long trip and safe arrival at his prison. John was an interesting writer, and an astute observer of even the most minor events of his journey. He and Kevin O'Dogherty proved to be good sailors, encountering only the most minor complaints from the motion of the ship. Kevin was a stranger to John when they came on board. He had been convicted of the same crime as John, publishing editorials the Lord Lieutenant Clarendon found objectionable. By the time their long journey ended, they had become lifelong friends.

The political prisoners were segregated from the other transported prisoners as much as possible. John and Kevin shared a comfortable cabin, were allowed the freedom of the ship, and because they paid for the privilege, were allowed to eat the same diet as the officers. "The Captain is quite polite, but we have hardly any intercourse with him. The Doctor has been growing more polite and rather attentive since we got to sea. The Chaplain has never addressed a word to either of us. We have agreed to learn German together and to read Homer in Greek. O'D seems determined to pay close attention to his medical studies. I wish to read History and to make myself acquainted with some of the thousand subjects of which I am shamefully ignorant. I have a fine opportunity now, if my health continues so good."

Finally, after three months at sea, they passed the mouth of Sydney Harbour on October 3rd. However, the final stage of the trip from Sydney to Hobart Town in Van Diemen's Land turned out to be unexpectedly complicated.

Almost two weeks passed without progress, leaving John still confined to the Mountstewart Elphistone, pacing around the deck in frustration. British officials were struggling to find a ship to take John and Kevin to Van Diemen's Land, their final destination. The first ship officials found was inspected and deemed unsatisfactory. Finally, John received the good news that a replacement had indeed been found. They would soon make the final passage to Hobart Town on the brig Emma. It belonged to an Irish settler named McNamara who had prospered in Australia. It had finally arrived in Sydney Harbour on Sunday, October 14th. John was delighted to see that an Irish harp surrounded by a wreath of shamrocks had been painted on the side. Certainly a good omen. But another week of formalities would pass before the Emma could actually sail.

Convicts had to be carefully inspected physically to make sure that they could be easily identified should they try to escape. This involved not only looking carefully at their head including opening their mouths to inspect inside, but also a partial strip search. John greatly objected to such treatment, as he disliked showing his chest deformity, "pigeon breast," to anyone. He resolved to refuse to undergo the same examination as the ordinary convicts.

When John's turn for inspection came, he informed the clerk that he would refuse any such inspection and would protest in writing to the government. He maintained that all the Young Irelanders who had participated in the revolt against English rule in 1848 had been promised that they would be spared any indignity. Head inspector McLean assured John that he would experience no embarrassment. The inspecting clerk would visit them in their cabin to take the most basic information of height, hair and eye color etc. The report on John stated that he was 5'8" tall, had dark brown hair and hazel eyes, and a ruddy complexion. He was missing a canine tooth on the upper right side of his jaw.

John still had one other problem to overcome. He was very short of money. The £40 he had brought with him had dwindled to less than £10. That amount was insufficient to cover his remaining expenses, tips to the steward and other crew members who had been kind and helpful during the long voyage. The food bill had also ballooned during the long delay in Sydney. Finally, there would be additional costs for the last part of their trip. John faced the humiliation of more debt than money.

The captain had been very kind to him, so he resolved to ask him for a loan which could be repaid by his relatives when the captain next visited Ireland. This was a terrible embarrassment for John, but he saw no other option. He put the request in the form of a letter and waited for results. When none came, he assumed that the Captain had refused, and he would need to search for other options.

Chief Inspector of Convicts McLean visited the two prisoners a couple of days later and asked if they needed anything. Both men took the opportunity to explain their financial difficulties. John told McLean that he wished to be treated like the rest of the convicts and would repay the government for that poor diet as soon as he was able. McLean wasn't able to help, but he told John and Kevin that the Deputy Commissioner of the Commissary could, and he was currently on board.

John described the meeting that followed. "So down came Mr. Dept. Commissary General Ramsay, his long gilt spurs clanking against the steep steps of our hatchway ladder. Ramsay is a rather tall man some 50 to 60 years old, very stout and healthy looking with strong bright eyes, a ruddy round plump weather beaten face, a head of snow white hair, an erect carriage and bluff haughty & military manner." Despite his appearance, he treated John courteously. He explained that John would need to put his request in writing before any action could be taken.

The next day, John had completed the note and handed it to the doctor to be delivered. The note restated their financial difficulties resulting from unplanned delays and his plan to repay any money advanced to aid him. The response came quickly. The next day, October 18th, McLean and Ramsey visited again. Mr. Ramsey informed John that he and Kevin were to share the ladies cabin on the Emma, that they would mess with the officers at no charge. The captain also gave each of them six sovereigns, the answer to his request of a loan. He also delivered a letter from a Mr. McCurtayn. The letter was fulsome in its praise for John and his fellow Young Irelanders and contained an offer of whatever cash John might need.

With the financial problems behind him, John relaxed for the last part of his long trip to exile, anticipating his new life as a ticket-of-leave convict somewhere on Van Diemen's Land. He was delighted when the Emma finally nosed out of Sydney Harbor. The last 150 miles of his long trip took a short time. So a few days later, the Emma with John and Kevin on board, arrived in Hobart Town. The town didn't appear too different from many harbor towns in other parts of the world that nestled between water and mountains.

When the government officials came on board, John and Kevin were informed that they would serve their sentences confined to different districts. John would be assigned a district in the highlands about 45 miles north of Hobart Town. Kevin would be in a district to the east. John was shocked to learn that Terrance McManus and Smith O'Brien who had said goodbye to John as he left Richmond Prison had arrived before him along with another convicted felon Thomas Francis Meagher. O'Brien had refused to accept a ticket-of-leave believing that it would be considered accepting a favor from the English government. He had been confined under close watch on an island south of Van Diemen's Land. Meagher was confined to a district just north of John's Bothwell district.

John boarded a stagecoach for his trip to his new home. As the coach bounced along, John had ample time to observe features of the very different place he now lived. Gone were the oak and ash trees of County Down, replaced by pungent eucalyptus and black gum trees. Mimosa trees with their rich fragrance grew on the lower slopes of the mountains.

The wildlife was very different as well. There were no foxes or magpies or swallows. Instead, brightly colored parrots swooped about or perched on the trees, bright spots against gray clouds or dark vegetation. Kangaroo hunts replaced the fox hunts of home.

Bothwell was very different from Newry though many of the settlers had come from Scotland, England or Ireland. It was in a valley several miles wide, and about eight miles long. A small river, the Clyde, flowed through the valley, carrying some of the run-off from the tree-covered mountains that surrounded it.

Bothwell did have many of the amenities of Irish towns, as it served the settlers who lived in more remote areas surrounding it, many of them emigrants from Great Britain. There was a church, four hotels with pubs, a post office, and the police quarters to which John had to report every month. It was a much more pleasant setting than Dublin's Richmond Prison, where John had spent the previous year. The clear highlands air and different vegetation proved very beneficial to John's always fragile health. He might even survive his ten-year sentence.

§

James was still preparing his fields for planting as January ended, still plowing and still removing stones from the marsh. This was unpleasant work as the weather had been dark and rainy. Plowing was difficult for the horse teams and the laborers who guided the heavy beam plows even when the weather was sunny and dry. The harsh weather made plowing the straight rows needed for a bountiful harvest even more difficult. Still the work continued all day. In his journal, James gave a listing of the work that was underway. Then he mentioned that "Parliament meets."

Parliamentary sessions always began with Queen Victoria's speech, which George usually printed in the *Telegraph*. However this year, her speech was read by the Lord Chancellor. The Prime Minister actually wrote the speech laying out the agenda for Parliament for the year. This year's speech referred to the pleasure the Queen felt over her recent trip to Ireland. While it was still possible to see the effects of the scarcities of recent years, food now seemed abundant and the country seemed at peace. She was, however, distressed by the conflicts between owners and occupiers of the land.

The speech called on Parliament to enact several measures that would make the Irish more content. First there should be an end to "the mischiefs of Party processions." Next, she called for new laws that would lessen the problems between landowners and those who leased the land. Finally, she noted the decline in the number of Irish men entitled to vote for members of Parliament due to famine deaths and emigration. The government would solve this problem as well. This was much more attention to Irish issues than the Irish were used to. But the Irish well understood that promises made in the Queen's speech didn't necessarily translate into laws that actually benefited the surviving Irish population.

Early in February, James reported that a severe storm had swept across Ireland. His entry for Tuesday the 5th reported. "An almost wet day, with a high gale from the west. The glass falls to stormey and the gale encreses to a hurricane after nightfall and all night." The bad weather continued for two more days, but James and his workers returned to the fields.

George gave a graphic account of the storm in the next edition of his paper. The storm was the most severe to strike the area since the great storm of 1839. There was extensive local damage, trees down and slates stripped from rooftops. In Belfast, the wind blew down a chimney which then fell through the ceiling of a boys' dormitory, killing three young boys.

The most severe weather passed in a couple of days, but it remained rainy for a week. Only then could James report, "Fine dry morning. The thrush on the tree. The river has overflowed its banks." James was referring to the Shinn River that flowed across his property.

That same day, more news arrived from John. "James Martin, [John's brother] breckfasted here and while at it a letter from John Martin was handed to him for Anna [John's youngest sister]. He opned & read it to us in the parlor."

The first of the Queen's promises to the Irish people was quickly translated into legislation designed to end the contentious issue of sectarian marches that had caused so much anger and bloodshed across the years. When the text of the Processions' bill was made public, George printed it in the Telegraph, at the same time making sure his readers understood his displeasure. He believed that all legislation should favor the virtuous and penalize the malcontents, but that this bill seemed to treat both sides the same. Under this legislation, Justices of the Peace were to read an order to disperse whenever a procession took place. Participants had fifteen minutes to do so before they would be arrested and fined five pounds for the first offense. If the marchers had no money for the fines, they would spend a month in jail. Penalties would be doubled for the second offense.

Despite the fact that George considered the bill unfair, its passage through Parliament was fairly routine. The fallout from the confrontation at Dolly's Brae helped shape the resulting legislation, which included added gun restrictions. Every gun found would be confiscated. Despite George's opposition, the bill was enacted in time to prevent any Catholic marches on St. Patrick's Day.

Another bill that had been on the Queen's list of legislation for Ireland was the bill to increase the number of voters. George was even more upset by this bill than by the Processions Act. He saw the legislation as a plan "To enfranchise the ignorance and poverty of Ireland." It would give the priests of the Catholic Church the power to return Catholics as members of Parliament. "The influence of the Priesthood would be irresistible, their will paramount. For, Popery being the essence of despotism, alike in doctrine and discipline, taking away from the laymen freedom of action as of thought, the privileges and liberties, with which legislation would thus invest the Roman Catholic population, would be sure to be turned to advantage by those whom the laws of their Church enable arbitrarily to exert from the laity implicit obedience."

In Ireland, at that time, only men could vote and only if they owned or leased land assessed at a specified value. When property values dropped, the number of men entitled to vote dropped as well. The voters most likely to have access to sufficient property were mainly Protestants. The hard part of all legislation relating to Irish voting was to set property requirements at a level where most Protestants could vote, and most Catholics couldn't. Clearly George didn't believe that this legislation achieved the proper balance.

§

James was a man who believed his religious obligations extended beyond church walls and into his community. He fretted over the lack of medical attention for the poor laborers in his neighborhood. Therefore, he set about helping to create a local dispensary to solve this problem, taking a leadership role in a local dispensary committee. The first action of the new committee was to apply for a grant of money to help establish a dispensary in Donaghmore. On Wednesday, March 13th, James recorded a major step forward. "John left about <u>one</u> oclock to go on the post-care to Downpatrick for the sum of 70 19 6 granted by the Grand Jury to the Donaghmore Dispensary." The next day "John in Newry to cash the dispensary cheque." When the dispensary opened, the poor people of the area, for the first time, would have access to some medical care.

Without this local initiative, destitute families had to enter the workhouse, as it was officially called, to receive medical care. These facilities were quite like prisons in appearance, and in the harshness of their rules, the most hated of them being the separation of families, husbands from wives, and children from their parents. But inmates would have access to food, and health care, no matter how meager the help might be. Not surprisingly, Newry residents referred to the Newry Workhouse, as the "poorhouse." It loomed over Newry from its elevated location just south of town. The workhouse/poorhouse was managed by a Board of Guardians elected by voters in each poor law district or appointed from among Newry's most prominent citizens.

Every year, on April 1st, the Board of Guardians assembled for an organizational meeting with new members sitting for the first time. James was present at the meeting of 1850, as the elected representative of Donaghmore. Meetings were held every Saturday in a comfortable room in the reception building of the workhouse. That arrangement enabled members to perform their duties without actually entering the prison-like complex or encountering any of the paupers.

A contentious subject occupied James's first meeting, involving a family from Donaghmore. Four orphaned children named Campbell were admitted to the poorhouse. According to the rules, each child had to have a recorded religion, the religion of the father. This information determined which church service the inmates would be required to attend. Two of the children wanted to attend the Catholic Church of their mother rather than the church of their father.

Efforts to find a compromise began at once. A motion was made to allow the children to be entered according to the religion they wanted to follow. James voted against this motion. As this motion failed to pass, all the children were entered as members of their father's Presbyterian religion.

The problem of the Campbell children returned to the Guardian's agenda a second time. This time James wasn't at the meeting. A new report from the children's grandfather informed the Guardians that his son had allowed the children to be raised as Catholics. With this new information, the Guardians decided to hold a full hearing in a couple of weeks. This discussion never took place, as the children left the poorhouse before then.

§

While James was settling into his new responsibilities, John was continuing to adjust to his new life in exile. He rented a room, which suited his needs and his scant financial resources. John was a friendly person, open to chatting with the citizens of Bothwell. Though he was a prisoner, he was welcomed by the people of Bothwell and treated kindly.

Once he had a place to live, he set out to find a pony he could rent. He found a grey pony that seemed both docile and strong. With transportation at the ready, John set about exploring his new home. John enjoyed investigating this very beautiful place, riding around the valley and venturing into the mountains. He found one trail especially to his liking, that had an opening from which he had a great view of the valley below, which was now home.

Soon he was sufficiently familiar with the area to arrange a trip north to meet Meagher, and his shipmate Kevin at the intersection of their prison territories. The three men reveled in this first joyous reunion, friends experiencing a feeling of home in very foreign surroundings. Since no official complained, these secret meetings continued on a weekly basis, and brought John great pleasure. All in all, his health was excellent, and life was pleasant in his new home, but he never forgot that he was still a prisoner, a man without freedom, a man far from home.

One day, John made a special effort to meet the stagecoach from Hobart. By the time he heard the clatter of coach approaching, his heart was pounding. He was there to meet a special passenger. His best childhood friend John Mitchel was on the coach, having been moved from prison in Bermuda to Van Diemen's Land in hopes that his failing health would improve. And knowing that John had had medical training, Mitchel had been assigned to the same penal territory.

The two friends had last met in the Green Street Courthouse in Dublin, when Mitchel was sentenced to fourteen years in exile for felony treason, under a law passed for the express purpose of silencing all the opposition press. Now in a very different place, the two men were about to meet again.

John was shocked when Mitchel climbed down from the coach. His already poor health had declined even more during the year that it took for him to travel from Bermuda to Van Diemen's Land. Mitchel was gaunt, and his face an unhealthy color, his breathing labored. As the two men embraced for the first time in two years, the strange circumstances of the reunion didn't dampen their great joy.

John was confident that Mitchel would soon regain his good health in this most beneficial climate and established a routine that he expected to restore Mitchel to the rigorous good health of their youth. The two men settled into a room in a cottage near the village. It was owned by an immigrant, who was very kind to the two strangers. There was much for the two friends to discuss, as John had later information on the affairs of Ireland, and Mitchel told John of his experience as a captive. These conversations accompanied walks about Bothwell and the surrounding territory. The lovely air and exercise were a tonic for Mitchel, bringing color to his pale cheeks and ease to his labored breathing. Mitchel described his feelings in a book he wrote later, his popular *Jail Journal*. "Opposite sits John Martin, sometime of Loughorne, smoking placidly and gazing curiously on me with his mild eyes."

The treatment that John prescribed of rest, and good food, followed by slowly increasing activity produced the rapid improvement that he had hoped for. He found a horse to rent that Mitchel could use to travel ever farther away from Bothwell, understanding that Mitchel's love of nature would be a powerful medicine. As soon as he felt that Mitchel was ready to undertake a more arduous adventure, he arranged for a trip to Lake Sorrel where a reunion with his good friends would be yet another important step on Mitchel's road to good health

When the day for the planned reunion arrived, the weather had turned rainy, and cold, much too much like winter for their liking. So they delayed their departure from Bothwell in hopes that the weather would improve. So unpleasant was the thought of a long ride through the cold rain that the two men thought of cancelling the trip. But knowing that there was no way to send word of a change of plans, they decided to keep to their plans despite the risk to Mitchel's health.

John and Mitchel set off about noon, though the weather had in no way improved. While rain was falling in the valley, snow was falling in the mountains they would have to cross. To make matters more hazardous, much of the trek was uphill, across streambeds and up steep inclines that had become dangerously slippery.

Both men were wet and cold when the woods finally opened to expose the high central plateau where traveling would be easier despite the strong winds swirling about them. The plateau was open enough to make two large lakes, Lake Sorrel and Lake Crescent, fully visible. These lakes were connected by a small stream. Along that stream, a recluse named Cooper lived in a primitive cabin. By the time they caught sight of the cabin, Mitchel was bent over his horse's mane, his face white from the strain of the long ride. John had watched Mitchel carefully during the ride and recognized from his face and posture that Mitchel could go no farther. He turned his pony into the yard and helped Mitchel dismount. He supported his friend as they opened the door and entered the rustic cabin.

Mitchel would later describe the events that followed. Mr. Cooper knew who John was and greeted the two men warmly, settling Mitchel near the warm fire. Though the meeting site was only four miles away, it was clear that Mitchel would not be able to travel nearly that far. So Cooper volunteered to make the final leg of the trip and bring O'Dogherty and Meagher back with him.

The two men were still resting by the fire, when they heard the clatter of horses' hooves on the hard ground outside the cabin. The door burst open and O'Dogherty and Meagher rushed into the room. The four men did not speak when they met, but just began to laugh so that the room echoed. As they ate a meal of lamb and damper, a cake of flour and water baked on a fire, the words began to flow, there was so much to talk about. Though the food was simple and eaten with their fingers, no grand banquet could have been more enjoyable.

Cooper made the Irishmen comfortable through the night. When they awoke, they found that the weather had improved greatly, and Mitchel was sufficiently strengthened by the warmth, rest, and good food to travel farther. Together, they set off to introduce Mitchel to his strange new home. They explored the lake areas and rowed to a small island with a lovely beach. They talked of Ireland and the divisions between the Irish in America, and of Smith O'Brien who was suffering greatly for his gallant refusal to take a ticket of leave. The friends parted the next day, still savoring their time together.

§

The long, dark days of the Irish winter had given way to brighter skies and longer days in which to do the jobs required to complete planting for a new season. As April ended, plowing was still underway. And James noted signs of spring that he always listened for. "Heard the coocoo from the plantin, on Kiddstown trees for the first time, this <u>morning</u>." Soon after, James reported the return of the corncrake for another season.

Despite the hard work required to get planting done, James had responsibilities as an elder of the Donaghmore Presbyterian Church as well. One of these duties was to visit the sick and dying. The first parishioner to slip away with the spring was Betty Donley. James took time from his work to pay her several visits. "Visited Betty Donley. She died about 2 oclock aged about 80 years. She was a good natured well wishing woman."

Another death occurred in Carnically, the townland that abutted Loughorne. Catherine McKeown was a much younger woman, and her death was suspicious enough to warrant an inquest. The autopsy showed that a bone in her neck had been broken though there were no external marks on the body. Her lungs had been badly affected, her body an odd red color. The jury returned a verdict, "Died by the visitation of God."

Just ten days before Catherine died, her husband had died. These deaths, so close together, left three small children orphans. The oldest of these children was seven years old, the youngest just a few months old. They had all been infected with the fever that killed their father. Authorities went to the McKeown cabin to retrieve the children and take them to the Fever Hospital in Newry. When they arrived at the hovel, they reported that they had found the youngest child "endeavoring to suck the breast of the poor mother when lying dead! The family were in extreme poverty."

§

Another death occurred before May ended. This one attracted much more attention than the passing of Betty or Catherine, and occupied George's attention for months. This time the cause of death was obvious. George deemed it an act of "agrarian murder."

The murder took place just south of Crossmaglen, a town southwest of Newry, in County Armagh. The victim was a land agent named Robert Lindsay Mauleverer. He was in Crossmaglen to deal with the business issues of property, which was owned by his brother-in-law.

Friends were shocked to learn that Mauleverer had suffered such a horrible death. They viewed him as "a man of undaunted bravery, and of a liberal and generous disposition, and by every person by whom he was known, he was beloved. He scorned, however, to court popularity and his manner was, perhaps, not altogether calculated to make him a favorite with the peasantry."

Tenants on the property viewed his unwillingness to "court popularity" as unfair treatment. When rents were in arrears, Mr. Mauleverer resorted to another common practice to obtain the money he felt was due. He would restrain [seize] cattle or crops, often selling them for far less than their value, leaving no money to pay for a year of hard work for struggling farmers

While he was in the area, Mr. Mauleverer stayed at the O'Donnell Inn in Crossmaglen. After he had collected rents from the tenants, and attended to other estate business, he prepared to return to his home in County Derry. While waiting for the jaunting car he had ordered to take him to the nearest train station, he chatted with the owner of the hotel. The conversation was interrupted with the slow opening of the front door. An old woman, poorly dressed, head down to acknowledge her low position, entered and approached Mr. Mauleverer. She held out a worn and calloused hand on which lay four pennies. She wished to purchase a turf ticket, which would allow her to dig turf in the local bog. Without that ticket, she would have no turf and no heat for the next winter.

Despite the show of respect from his poor tenant, Mauleverer wasn't moved. Without a shred of human empathy, he informed her that turf tickets cost six pence each, and he was unwilling to sell one for even a penny less. Mr. O'Donnell assured Mr. Mauleverer that the intruder was indeed a very poor woman in need of help. But this assurance produced no change of heart. The dejected pauper turned sadly away and left even more desperate than when she had come.

Certainly, word of Mauleverer's actions spread quickly around the back alleys of Crossmaglen, triggering rising anger. What wasn't passed so quickly around the village was the strange thing Mauleverer had done after his scornful treatment of the pauper. Mr. Mauleverer handed his remaining turf tickets to O'Donnell, giving him permission to dispose of them as he wished, by selling them or giving them away.

The two men continued their conversation until shortly after noontime, when the clunk of horses' hooves and the rattle of a cart indicated that the transportation O'Donnell had engaged for Mauleverer had finally arrived. When the driver, Pat McNally, had placed the luggage in the jaunting car, Mr. Mauleverer climbed on the seat facing left. McNally mounted the driver's seat and set the horse along the road to Castleblaney.

They had traveled about a mile when a sudden attack took place. Someone protected from view by the hedge along the verge of the road hurled a large stone at Mauleverer's head, stunning him and causing him to fall from the cart. Mauleverer had survived two previous attacks on his life, but he didn't survive this one. Once he was prostrate on the ground, the murderer apparently took hold of Mr. Mauleverer's cane, and beat him with it repeatedly. Then he disappeared behind the hedge.

McNally reported later to the police that his horse had been startled by a gunshot and had galloped off down the road in a panic, while he struggled to regain control. The cart had travelled a mile farther before he was able to slow the frantic horse and turn it back to the spot where Mauleverer had fallen. His bloody body lay alone by the side of the road. Rather than stopping, McNally hurried back to Crossmaglen for help. He rushed into the hotel to tell O'Donnell what had happened. O'Donnell called on the local policeman, Mr. Holmes, and they hurried back along the Culloville Road together.

The two men found Mauleverer about a mile down the road. He was lying with his head in the road and his feet in the ditch beside it. His head had been so severely battered that his brains were oozing out of his ruined skull and mingling with the dust in the lane. His walking stick was found nearby, the head of it covered with blood and hair.

This was a murder with a potential eye witness, so it should have been easy to solve. After all McNally was at the scene, as the murder was taking place. Even if he had to fight to control the horse, a quick glimpse to the side would have allowed him to make an identification. That turned out not to be the case. McNally claimed he heard Mr. Mauleverer shout out the words "Murder," but hadn't turned his head to see what was happening. He used the runaway horse story to explain this odd behavior. Holmes, the lead policeman at the scene, didn't believe McNally and arrested him on the spot.

At the inquest that followed, John McParlon, the coroner, reported that there were nine fractures on the victim's skull, but no sign of a bullet wound. The local bailiff, Michael Morgan, testified as to the activities of Mr. Mauleverer that might have served as a motive. He had attempted to seize two heifers from Sarah Hale, and seven cows from another farmer, David Jackson. Sarah got her cattle back as she was able to prove that she wasn't the owner of the heifers. Jackson's cattle had been rescued by neighbors who then intermingled them with their own animals making identification impossible. Still, Mauleverer had gone to court in an attempt to acquire them.

Ejectments were the most feared landlord action. Mauleverer had issued numerous ejectment orders and more notices to quit. Losing access to land was a death sentence in Ireland. So given this record, Mauleverer was an exemplar of a hated land agent. His death wasn't a surprise, and it brought pleasure to local farmers.

One of these local farmers testified that he had come upon the scene soon after the assault. He saw first Mauleverer's coat. A bit farther down the road, he saw a hat, and finally the body. He claimed to see two men running away across the fields. Police had immediately pursued the two suspects over fields and through hedges for three miles. By then Sub-constable Benjamin Darlington was too exhausted to continue the chase. When he reached a County Louth police station, he stopped to get help. Sub-constables Steward and Farrell were able to catch up to the fugitives, and after a struggle were able to make an arrest. The suspects were named Hanratty and McAtavery

George wrote a scathing editorial on the tenant rights movement and its influence on the Mauleverer murder. He maintained that the murder wasn't surprising since the "rebel and revolutionary" press had been pretending that their concern was to provide the "weak protection against the strong." Instead they were pandering to "the worst passion of ignorance," and goading them to "commission of crimes." Then they could use any murder like that of Mauleverer "as proof of the injustice" under which the people of Ireland were living.

There was another element contributing to the danger to landlords and their agents which George had detected, and with which he ended his editorial. Catholic Priests were leading the effort to secure the overthrow of "landlordism," as that was the basis for the wealth of the official governmental church, the Church of Ireland. George warned that all legal land rights of landlords were in grave danger.

The trial of the three men accused of murdering Mr. Mauleverer didn't begin until July. Brian Hanratty was accused of committing the murder with a rock, the murder weapon of choice for the Catholic population who were forbidden by law to own guns. Two other men, John McAtavery and Patrick McNally were accused of "aiding and abetting." The government assigned some of its best legal best prosecutors to officiate over the trial. All of the accused pleaded "not guilty."

This was the first time that most of the people who had crowded into the court room had seen the accused. Hanratty had a "cold and cunning eye; crossing his arms he leant on the front of the dock, and looked round the Court with an air almost of defiance. He seems about forty years of age." The other men seemed disinterested.

The first witness added a few new details to those provided at the inquest. When Hanratty was arrested, he was very sweaty as though he had just undergone great exercise. His clothes were covered in blood. He had a couple of wounds on his head, which matched the end of Mr. Mauleverer's walking stick. Hanratty's hair was also found on the bloody cane.

Jeremiah O'Donnell was the next witness. He told the court that he had arranged for McNally to take Mauleverer to the train station in a jaunting car. He waited beside the door of the inn several minutes for Mauleverer to come out. McNally sat on the right side of the car, Mauleverer on the left when they drove out of town. Only about fifteen minutes passed before McNally returned with news of the attack. At that time, O'Donnell saw fresh blood on the car. When asked what he knew about Brian, O'Donnell reported that Brian was a blacksmith, who lived with a brother beside the road that Mauleverer was due to take.

The prosecution questioned several additional witnesses, including the policemen who had participated in the chase and had made the arrest. Then they turned the trial over to the defense.

The chief lawyer for the accused was Mr. O'Hagan from Newry. He first maintained that there was no evidence against McNally. He had been the driver by chance. There was no blood evidence against McAtavery, or any other evidence beyond his proximity to Hanratty at the time of his arrest. When O'Hagan spoke of Hanratty, he maintained that he was just strolling along, had made no effort to disguise himself or remove the blood the policemen had seen. The only evidence that the jury had to consider was the stick and hair. O'Hagan pointed out one witness had seen no hair on the stick, nor did one of the policemen. With the critical evidence in dispute, there was no evidence on which to convict any of the accused.

Having pointed out those important discrepancies in the testimony, the defense rested. The jury retired to consider their verdict. After deliberating for a couple of hours, they returned to the court and the foreman delivered a verdict of "Not guilty" for Hanratty. He explained the jury's thinking. They did believe that Hanratty was implicated in the murder, but they hadn't had enough evidence to conclude that he had caused Mauleverer to die.

When the crowd gathered outside the courthouse heard the verdict, there was "great cheering." Hanratty was also roundly cheered as he walked down the steps of the courthouse. However, both McNally and McAtavery were bound over to the next court session. Mr. O'Hagan requested that the two men be released on bail, given the fact that there was no evidence that they had participated in the murder, and the chief suspect against whom there was the strongest evidence had already been acquitted. The government lawyer protested this request, and the judge ruled that the two men should be held in jail until the next Assizes.

Before the next court appearance, a new witness appeared that authorities believed would link both McNally and McAtavery to the crime. A young woman claimed to have seen the crime being committed and had told a friend what she had seen. The friend had alerted authorities, and the potential witness, who had fled to America, was brought back to Ireland. There was new hope that a conviction might be obtained.

The second court appearance didn't occur until March of 1851. By that time, the two men had spent nearly a year in prison, ironically, vastly more time than the accused murderer had spent behind bars. When the case was called in the Armagh Court, the government did not produce the new witness. Under questioning, she had offered such varied accounts of what she had seen, that she could not be presented as a witness. So the only issue at the court hearing was whether the two men should now be released on bail. O'Hagan asked for a low bail, as the two men were men from the poorest segment of Irish society. This time the judge did allow the men to leave jail on bail, but he set a high bail for their release. Neither man could raise the sum ordered, but O'Hagan said that he would attempt to raise the necessary money. When he was able to provide the required £50, the men were released pending further action.

But there was no further action. No one was ever convicted for Mr. Mauleverer's murder.

Chapter 2

Unrest

1850 - 1851

Snow had fallen over the highlands of Van Diemen's Land when Brian Hanratty, the man accused of murdering Robert Mauleverer, was tried and freed. It was just about this time that John Martin first learned that the murder had even taken place. Brutal murders such as that which had taken place on the quiet road out of Crossmaglen were all too frequent occurrences throughout Ireland. So as John read his first accounts of the killing in the old issues of the *Telegraph*, he was certainly saddened, but not surprised.

At the same time, John had a most welcome visitor. John and Mitchel were in their room in Bothwell, when a message was sent up to them that a Mr. Smith was waiting to see them. For the length of time it took them to make their way to the entrance, they must have thought that their visitor was actually Smith O'Brien, who had recently been released from his island prison upon agreeing to accept a ticket of leave. However, Mr. Smith turned out to be a different Young Irelander, Terrance McManus. He had traveled away from his assigned district in New Norfolk, in violation of the conditions of his ticket of leave. The penalty for this crime would be a revocation of his limited freedoms and immediate confinement in one of the nearby Australian prisons where he would be subjected to hard labor beside thieves and chronic drunks.

Recognizing the risk that McManus was taking, John was especially happy to see him. McManus had been imprisoned in Richmond Jail with John after they were both convicted at separate trials. After a year together in their Dublin prison, the government had finally arranged for both men to be removed from Ireland.

John had known nothing of the arrangements for his transportation until he was awakened early one morning in June 1849. He was instructed to pack his belongings, and when he had completed the task as required, he was escorted down the stairs to the main floor. This activity produced enough noise from the banging about of John's trunks and the clump of the soldiers' boots, that other prisoners were awakened. Several of them rose to see what was afoot. Most of them were driven back up the stairs. Only McManus and O'Brien were allowed to give John what might well have been a final embrace.

The guards were so concerned that a rescue attempt had been planned, that John was hustled quickly out of the prison and into a prison van waiting just outside. He had only a quick glimpse of the mounted soldiers arranged around the van, before he was pushed inside, and the door locked behind him. The barred windows had been covered, so John could see nothing of Dublin as he was driven south to the port in Kingstown. Three months at sea lay ahead.

John had shared another exceptional moment with McManus. Both men were in the Green Street Courthouse when Mitchel had been sentenced. The Courthouse was so crowded, that Mitchel would have had difficulty catching a last sight of McManus before being forced into prison garb, secured by heavy chains and dispatched to the prison hulks in Bermuda. But both men responded positively to the call for patriots to stand with Mitchel.

And now, in wintry Bothwell, the three men held a very happy reunion. The conversation was so pleasant that the two men prevailed on McManus to risk staying longer, enabling them all to make the trip north to visit Meagher and O'Dogherty, affectionately nicknamed St. Kevin. Under English law in Ireland, a gathering of five rebels in one place would constitute a riot, subjecting them to arrest and severe punishment. Their risks would have been greatly enhanced had they been home in Ireland because some of the rebels carried an item that few Irishmen could possess legally, a gun. In this part of Australia, there was little worry that guns would be used to promote revolution, so little attention was paid to who possessed them. Guns in the area around Bothwell were used for hunting. In fact, the Young Irelander "mob" went duck hunting around the upland lakes.

None of the men wanted the visit to end. So McManus extended his visit for an entire week. John and Mitchel stood together as they watched McManus climb onto the coach. Mitchel and McManus would meet again, but for John, that farewell was final. However, John and McManus would cross paths again in the strangest way, one that would have an important impact on Irish history.

§

For the five springs that followed the arrival of the potato fungus in Ireland, farmers continued to plant potatoes. Each of those years, farmers feared that the day would come when they would visit their fields to discover that the dreaded disease had struck yet again. The stench the disease produced in the dying potatoes was so intense that it conveyed the bad news before farmers reached the potato drills.

The dreaded day in 1850 arrived on the first of August. James Harshaw was forced to report, "Potatow disease progresses on the tips." This was a devastating loss for James. Though he planted a variety of crops and wouldn't starve, the loss of yet another crop would bring financial hardship for James and his workers. The shocks to the Irish economy would continue to drag out for yet another year.

The session of Parliament was nearing an end, as Irish potatoes began to die. Members.completed a piece of legislation that the conservative government had promised to deliver when the Parliamentary session began with the passage of the Parliamentary Voters (Ireland) Bill. It addressed the problem of the shrinking number of Irish voters. The bill reduced the value of property holdings required to enjoy the right to vote from £15 to £12. Anyone who believed that his property was worth that much money could declare his desire to vote.

However, a substantial barrier remained before the newly eligible voters could find their names officially recorded in the poll books. A special meeting would be held in the Newry Courthouse attended by applicants, local party leaders and lawyers. These were often raucous affairs. Applicants nervously waited for their names to be called, hoping only silence would follow. Very frequently, lawyers shouted their opposition and engaged in shouting matches with opposing lawyers about the value of a single room. Party lawyers had a single goal, to increase the number of their voters and to limit those of the opposition party. The judge presiding at these presentment sessions made the final determination. If the judge concurred with any challenges, the applicant could not vote.

This process was a traditional part of the voting laws for Ireland, but now ran counter to efforts to increase the number of voters. Given the uncertainty of the process, no one knew if the reduction of the property test by £3 was sufficient to reach Parliament's desired number of voters. When the new voting law passed through Parliament, only two percent of the Irish population had the right to vote. Parliament hoped the newly expanded eligibility would increase the number of voters to ten percent. Newry officials quickly acted to revise local voting lists. When the last approved name had been added to the list of electors, 618 Newry men were entitled to vote in the next election. This legislation was one act of Parliament that was appreciated in Ireland.

There was another problem in Ulster upon which Parliament took no action. This was religious antagonism between Catholics and Protestants in the Newry area following the murders at Dolly's Brae. Newry was a predominantly Catholic town, as Ireland was predominately a Catholic country. But famine deaths and emigration, which were particularly devastating in the areas where Catholics lived, had certainly reduced the numerical gap between Catholics and Protestants. A growing number of Protestants, including the Protestant men who governed Newry, had come to believe that when members of the Church of Ireland and Presbyterian Church were unified, they nearly equaled the Catholic population.

The men who labored in the farmlands that surrounded Newry were less concerned with the rivalry of the two main churches than with maintaining their connections with the land. Catholics and Protestants alike rose at dawn to labor in the fields that James leased and looked to the setting sun to signal the end of a day of arduous drudgery. Sunday was their only day of rest. Still, this was the life they knew and a life they intensely wished to preserve. These farmers and their laborers would be more interested in strengthening their attachment to the land than in religious confrontations.

So it wasn't surprising that the growing agitation for increased tenant rights to the land they worked would attract adherents without reference to religion. The farmers of Donaghmore had made their feelings on the subject clear in the dinner they held to honor their new landowner the previous fall. For George Henderson and many other leaders of the Newry community, the willingness of the farm community to work together without reference to religion was an alarming development. From his office on Hill Street, George viewed the cooperation between Presbyterians and Catholics as a great threat to Protestant unity and a far greater threat to Ireland than the unfair expulsion of a few lower-class farmers from their land. Because the tenant right agitation united Presbyterians and Catholics, the Tenant Right League must be defeated.

The linkage between the two issues was clearly stated in a letter from an Alexander Chevne of Killinchy, which George published in the *Telegraph* on August 25th. Chevne had also noticed that Presbyterian ministers had become part of the agitation for the rights of Irish tenants. He was appalled at the possibility of any cooperation between Presbyterian ministers and Catholic priests. He excoriated the "culpable negligence of those whose duty it was to have crumbled it in its infancy."

What was reported a month later in the *Telegraph* would provide Chevne no comfort. A tenant-rights meeting was held in Kilkenny at which a Presbyterian minister, Rev. Rogers, spoke. He wanted to assure the people of the South of Ireland that Ulster wasn't "Orange." At least the Presbyterian portion wasn't. "*Presbyterianism is incompatible with, and destructive of, Orangeism.*" He concluded his speech this way. "*Orangesm is intolerance,* but Presbyterianism has ever been foremost to rebuke intolerance, and to vindicate and defend civil and religious liberty."

George quickly responded. "We would…hope that we shall find the Presbyterian Ministers of Ulster not slow…to reprehend the proceedings and renounce the principles of those clerical charlatans who are polluting the sanctity of their cloth and creed by such daring villainy as marked their demagogism."

The relationship between Presbyterians and Catholics in Ulster traditionally wavered between cooperation and confrontation. Irish Catholics leaders had long enjoyed some autonomy within the Church, allowing them to maneuver and sometimes collaborate with moderate Protestants. A leader in these efforts was Rev. Crolly, Archbishop of Armagh. In 1846 Pope Pius IX became the new head of the Roman Catholic Church intending to reverse Crolly's policies and to strengthen the position of Rome and the Papacy within the Irish church ("ultramontanism"). Archbishop Crolly died of cholera in 1849. Instead of accepting one of the candidates offered by the Irish bishops, which was the usual procedure, Pius IX appointed Paul Cullen, who had been the head of the Pontifical Irish College in Rome for twenty-eight years, as the new Archbishop of Armagh and Apostolic Delegate (representing Ireland to the Papacy). When Cullen returned to Ireland, the land of his birth, he convened the Synod of Thurles in August 1850, an important first step in bringing the Irish church into conformity with Rome and building walls against Presbyterian proselytizing. Cullen also planned to create a new system of Catholic colleges, separate from the new nondenominational Queens Colleges but also government funded. His success in reforming the church, including founding the Catholic University of Ireland, was rewarded by elevation to Cardinal in 1856.

Meanwhile, across the Irish Sea Catholics in England and Wales were still organized in districts rather than dioceses and led by vicars apostolic rather than archbishops, just as they had been since the days of Queen Elizabeth I. In 1850, Pius IX seized on the influx of Irish fleeing the famine to reinstitute the hierarchy, changing the organization to dioceses and archbishops and naming an Irishman Nicholas Wiseman, as Cardinal. The conjunction of these events raised the fear of Protestants in both Ireland and England about the spread of Popery.

§

George took his responsibilities as the editor of an important loyalist newspaper and as an analyst of the most critical issues of the day very seriously. He made sure that his readers were well aware of the rising threat posed by the expansionist Pope in Rome. He needed to first warn and then arouse the passions of those farmers and laborers who were accustomed to live in peace with their Catholic friends and neighbors. James Harshaw subscribed to the *Telegraph,* but not to its concern about Catholic power. He needed to focus on more pressing problems, despairing thoughts of famine, falling farm prices and rising taxes. However, every morning, he reinforced his Presbyterian faith by conducting morning prayers for family members and laborers before tackling his day's work.

James now had a new problem that deeply concerned him. At the Presbyterian gathering in Belfast in July, Rev. Samuel Moore, the current minister of James's church, received a call to become the minister of a small church in Ballymena. He was very popular in the Donaghmore Presbyterian Church, and his departure would place an additional burden on James as a ruling elder and clerk of the session.

Rev. Moore reported the news to the congregation on July 14th. Leading members of the congregation met in the session room the next day to see what could be done to keep Rev. Moore from leaving. They decided to present a formal plea for him to stay at a special meeting at the home of a parishioner named Parker in Buskhill. After tea was served to the deputation, Parker attempted to read the address that James and his fellow elders had prepared. However, "the shades of evening" made the room too dark for Parker to see what was written. So James was called upon to read the address to Rev. Moore. Then Rev. Moore responded with remarks that lasted "eight or ten minutes" in a "most solemn manner." James sadly concluded that the efforts of the church to keep their minister hadn't been sufficient. Rev. Moore indicated that his decision "pointed to Ballymena."

Sunday August 11th, James reported in his journal entry, was the "44th Sabbath" since he had last seen sons Willy and James Jr. The two young men wrote frequent letters home to Ireland, which made their absence a bit less painful. James also reported that this sermon at this service would be the last Rev. Moore would preach as their minister. When the service was over, Rev. Moore requested non-members to withdraw, so he could speak to the congregation. He explained why he had decided to leave and expressed great appreciation to the people of the nearby townlands who had supported him and his ministry. Then he offered special thanks to "this one." He implored forgiveness for any offenses and urged the members to live in such a way that they could all meet at "the right hand of Christ."

Two days later, James and his son Robert Hugh visited Rev. and Mrs. Moore at Buskhill. After worship, they traveled together under gray skies to 2nd Drumbanagher Church where the Presbytery was meeting. There, the formal call for Rev. Moore to transfer to the church in Ballymena was presented. James Martin, John's brother, spoke in opposition to the transfer. He pointed out the good work Rev. Moore had performed in Donaghmore, how highly he was thought of by the members. This church was a larger and more important church than the one in Ballymena. For the good of the church, Rev. Moore should stay where he was most needed. Robert Craig and Robert Jeffrey also spoke with a similar request.

After dinner with the Presbytery, Rev. Moore spoke of his own feelings. He said, "he saw the finger of God directing him to Ballymena, and he considered it his duty to accept the call." The Presbytery voted unanimously to delay approval for a week. A new meeting would then be held to allow both sides to present their best arguments. When the second meeting ended, it was clear to James that the Newry Presbytery would approve Rev. Moore's transfer. All James could do was wish him well and request the Newry Presbytery to assign ministers to fill their empty pulpit each Sunday. This practice allowed the congregation to audition ministers who might provide a permanent replacement.

Whether it was a blessing or a curse, James always had a range of issues to deal with that sometimes overlapped. So it wasn't surprising that James couldn't attend every meeting of the workhouse Guardians. But he went to as many as he could manage. Being a Guardian was a complicated job. Under the Poor Law that established the workhouse, expenses voted by the Guardians resulted in an increase in the poor rates that farmers would immediately have to pay. Keeping the poor rates to a minimum would greatly benefit taxpayers. On the other hand, depriving the workhouse of the necessary funds constrained the already impoverished lives of the inmates.

One such issue was raised soon after James became a Guardian. The original plans in 1838 for the Newry poorhouse had included a residence for 400 girls. However, just creating the most basic institution had been very difficult for the farmers to afford. But the idea resurfaced while James was a Guardian. Supporters argued that this new expenditure would save money spent in outdoor relief. James joined all the other Guardians in supporting this proposal.

There were other issues as well. The Commissioners of National Education had found the education offered in the workhouse school deficient during a previous inspection. They enumerated for the Guardians the needed improvements. However, when the Commissioners returned for their next inspection, this time while James was a Guardian, they found no improvement.

The goal was to have one teacher for each 50 students. In order to meet this goal, the Newry Guardians would have to hire eight new teachers, a costly new expense for local farmers. Staffing levels were still far below the mandate. As a result, the girls weren't being properly taught plain and fancy sewing, and the boys weren't being prepared to go to sea on merchant ships or join the British Navy. Improvement might have been demanded, but none was delivered.

Adding to the financial problems of the workhouse was the failure of collectors to squeeze the taxes from cash strapped farmers. The Guardians had hired several of these collectors for each area of the Poor Law district to canvass their districts demanding full payment on the spot. However, all too often the collectors were leaving farmhouses either with a few pence on the pound or nothing at all. This situation had led to a frightening deficit. Farmers were £4,300 behind in their payments. Expenses of the workhouse would have to be reduced and quickly

James attended the meeting where this critical discussion took place. To save money, Guardians voted to eliminate one of the relieving guardians, whose job it was to identify which applicants were really eligible to enter workhouse in Newry. As a result of the vote, the workhouse would have just three relieving officers, making it more difficult for the most desperate paupers to gain admission. However, reducing the population was another effective way to reduce costs. That effect, along with salary reductions for the workhouse staff would allow the poorhouse to stay within their existing budget without adding to the taxes collectedfrom farmers.

But there was other bad news for local rate payers. Even though the British government was aware of the terrible destitution in Ireland, they announced that they would begin to collect the money that had been loaned to Ireland to fund the workhouse system ten years earlier, a system few people in Ireland wanted. Newry was expected to begin repaying their loan of £15,000. In order to collect this large additional sum of money, the Guardians were expected to levy yet another tax of "2d in the pound on the valuation for 25 years." The Newry Guardians said "no," voting to refuse to strike this new rate for a year. British tax collectors would have to extract the money from existing workhouse funds.

At each meeting, a report was given on the people who had been admitted the previous week. If the new tax were to be paid by reductions in the existing budget, the pauper residents of the poorhouse would face reduced amounts and quality of food, more filth, and more preventable disease. On the day that the Board refused to pay the additional rate, the story of one such sad pauper inmate was told. A young woman, very pregnant, was admitted. Her husband had worked on the local railway extension, and had been one of the workers, navies as they were called locally, who had gone on strike. As a result, he had been fired. He left her in total destitution and went off to Derry in hopes of finding work.

All too often, pregnancy was an unbearable burden for poor families. Newborn infants were frequently abandoned along roadsides or in barns. The Guardians were told that one such infant had been abandoned at the gate of the poorhouse. He was named James Arnold after the guard who found him. However, the name was changed when it was discovered that the mother was named Anderson and was ill in the fever hospital. James certainly found this meeting very depressing.

§

While James was attending to his responsibilities in Newry, and George was fuming about Presbyterian participation in the Tenant Right movement, John was experiencing his first spring in Van Diemen's Land with his friend Mitchel. Despite having his best friend with him in exile, John felt alienated from his home in Ireland. News from Newry arrived very slowly. But fortunately, news did finally arrive, as someone in Newry sent each copy of the *Telegraph* to a friend in Bothwell. So each edition of the paper was eventually passed on to John. He read every word of every new newspaper with great interest, including George's leaders. His reading was accented by various faces as he read about familiar names and places, and the current issues of the town he loved. He knew Mitchel didn't like hearing news of activities he could not influence, but sometimes John shared items he thought would be of particular interest.

Fellow captive Thomas Meagher described the situation of the two men in their new lives in exile. When Mitchel had arrived, he looked near death. His cheeks were sunken, his eyes blood-shot. Each breath was thick and rasping. He was bent, his steps slow and difficult. But he soon rallied, and good health returned. In describing John's new life, Meagher reported that since John had arrived in Bothwell, he had been living a quiet life, "reading, writing, walking and riding in the quietest and gentlest manner possible, and hurting no…creatures, not even the black and diamond snakes, nor suffering a single word against any thing or any body, passing away his days."

John's health was always of concern to his friends. So Meagher took particular note of that worry to calm these anxieties. "His health all the while has been excellent, he has in fact grown quite strong–and is able to take real exercise without suffering any great fatigue. I have known him to walk frequently from this cottage of mine down to Bothwell (a distance of 24 mi) in 5 hours and a half and experience no exhaustion whatever."

Unfortunately, John's morale was unsettlingly different. Generally, his spirits "have been very low." He was restless and felt the loss of purpose. Meagher felt that this situation resulted from the fact that he was the oldest of the prisoners, and therefore less likely to recover his sense of purpose than the rest of the Irish friends. "Sometimes indeed, he has been in utter misery– brooding over the horrible conditions of our wretched country, and the hopelessness which seems to have taken possession of it."

There was a remedy at the ready. John often ventured out from Bothwell into the surrounding highlands of Van Diemen's Land to enjoy their beauty.

When out on his pony, John's spirits seemed to improve. On April 24th, John and Mitchel had received a letter from O'Brien. His health had declined under his strict captivity, and both men feared that their good friend would die soon. They were thinking of their friend as they rode in the countryside, late one afternoon. They dismounted, and sat on a ruined gum tree, pondering this sad problem.

The two men lit their pipes and sat silently together. The scene was breathtakingly beautiful. The setting sun turned the wood purple, crimson and gold. A white magpie called out as it circled overhead. As the Irish exiles watched the sun disappear, Mitchel informed John he had decided that he must invite his family to risk the long trip and join him in his long years of exile.

In October, George finally reported news of Newry's political exiles. He printed an account in the *Telegraph* of Mitchel's arrival in Van Diemen's Land, his reunion with John in Bothwell, and their adventurous reunion with the other Young Irelanders. The two Newry men might be on the other side of the earth, but they hadn't been forgotten at home.

§

John hated being disconnected from events in Ireland. Had he been home, he would have written and spoken in support of tenant rights. He would have argued vehemently against the anti-Catholic prejudice that was sweeping over Ulster following the transfer of Archbishop Cullen from Rome to lead the Catholics of Ireland

George continued to follow the actions that the new Irish Archbishop was pursuing. Besides appointing this pro-Rome prelate, Pope Pius directed Irish clergy to adopt titles to match those already held by the leaders of the Church of Ireland. This action produced an outcry of rage in Parliament and the prompt creation a new bill to ensure that such a bold move wouldn't succeed. In leader after leader, George made his opinions clear as did other Irish organizations. This controversy raged through the declining days of 1850.

The editor of the Presbyterian newspaper of Ulster, the *Banner of Ulster*, had a different perspective, He saw the action of the Catholic Church as a simple matter of renaming bishops, which it certainly had a right to do. George responded by quoting a different Presbyterian newspaper, the *Edinburgh Witness*. The writer of this leader agreed that the Catholic Church had a right to provide titles for its bishops, as did all religious denominations. However, he claimed that the Catholic Church was both a religious and temporal organization. That being the case, nothing that the Catholic Church did was purely spiritual, but was also a temporal action. In this situation, renaming Catholic bishops was purely a temporal issue. Therefore, the Church was attempting to intrude its temporal authority into England. This was a Presbyterian view with which George happily agreed.

Soon afterwards, George published another letter designed to change Presbyterian minds about the issue, this one from the Earl of Enniskillen, the Grand Master of the Orange Order. The Earl claimed that his organization was the only one in Ireland strong enough to defeat "this Popish plot." He begged all Irish citizens "by all you hold dear and sacred, to enroll yourselves in our order." He implored everyone who read his letter "to perpetuate your efforts, and to secure the future integrity of our glorious Constitution in church and state, by becoming members of that loyal body, that has never ceased to proclaim no peace with Rome, and whose watchword ever has been, and ever will be, no surrender!" To this, George might well have shouted "Amen."

This anti-Catholic movement was not limited to newspaper articles. Soon, Presbyterian leaders pronounced their strong opposition to the Catholic actions. The organized Presbyterian Church took its first actions at a meeting of the Belfast Presbytery. The main speaker was Rev. Cooke, who had been a mentor for James's son Robert Hugh during his ministerial studies. Rev. Cooke claimed that the Catholic Church viewed all other churches as non-religious institutions. Therefore, they were free to convert Presbyterians and members of the Church of Ireland to Catholicism. That being the case, Protestants were free to convert Catholics as well. This effort to convert the Irish from adherence to their Catholic faith and to persuade them to join a Protestant religion had been going on for years. Rev. Cooke denounced Archbishop Cullen's attempts to quell Protestant proselytizing and urged increasing efforts to reduce Catholics' numerical advantage.

Several meetings on the rising Catholic threat took place in Newry as well. One was organized by Major Waring, one of Newry's well-known leaders. Major Waring spoke to the large crowd that had gathered at Sugar Island for the event. He claimed the dispute wasn't so much a dispute between churches as it was a dispute "between error and truth." This reality should immediately bring all Protestants together. He claimed that this position had nothing to do with limiting the rights of the Catholic citizens. They were free to pursue whatever religion they wished. But "there is a wide difference between religious freedom and political power." He agreed that the Pope's actions were temporal, and as such were a threat to Protestant freedom.

The Newry Presbytery was next to take action. James often attended these meetings, but on the important meeting on December 10th, James was involved in a meeting in Donaghmore to discuss reactions to the ministers that had preached before the Donaghmore congregation. But his son John was on hand. This meeting repeated many of the opinions previously presented by Rev. Cooke and like-minded Presbyterian ministers. But the purpose of this meeting went beyond venting. This time, attendees wished to make their feelings heard beyond Sugar Island. They chose to submit resolutions to the Queen to make their discontent clear to London leaders. The Presbytery claimed Catholic actions by the imperious Pope were an insult to the Queen and a threat to Irish religious freedom. Rev. Moran, a leader of the Newry Presbytery, argued that the time had come for the Presbyterian Church to make clear to their members the danger the Catholic Church presented to their own church. The time had come to recognize that "war, not with carnal but spiritual weapons should be waged against this enemy of their temporal and eternal interests."

Five resolutions were passed unanimously and were signed before being sent off to Queen Victoria by the Moderator and the Clerk. The clerk at that time was Rev. Robert Lindsay who was the minister of the nearby Drumbanagher Presbyterian Church. When John Harshaw voted to support the resolutions, he could not know that this same Rev. Lindsay would become a great threat to his father.

The new year 1851 began for George with his customary New Year leader in the *Newry Telegraph,* with some optimistic words. "A happier future we trust is in store for her [Ireland]; and more confidently might we look forward to the realization of our hope, were there sure tokens of a disposition on the part of our fellow countrymen generally, to renounce abortive agitations and betake themselves to work together, in social harmony, for the accomplishment of, not Utopian, but substantial and practical projects."

George believed "*the* grave national and political question of the time" was the advance of "Popery." It was the duty of all Protestants to be vigorous in their counter actions. "Silence and supineness should no longer characterize us, as a people…We owe it to ourselves, to our Sovereign, to our religion, that we be out-spoken." He didn't recommend large-scale gatherings, but rather a flood of petitions to Parliament to make clear the position of Irish Protestants. This action was the responsibility of each Protestant of every denomination. "Let us continue silent or practically indifferent, and Ireland may be handed over to the galling despotism of the Papal tyranny, the most fearful calamity that could befall a nation."

Then George echoed a blistering attack on the new head of the Catholic Church, Rev. Paul Cullen, pronounced by the Church of Ireland Primate of Armagh. For centuries, the Catholic leaders of Ireland had resisted the imposition of control over them by the Pope in Rome. Now it was clear that the new actions of the Pope had placed the relative Irish Catholic independence in great danger.

There was nothing to like about this new head of the Catholic Church. George saw Rev. Cullen as a stranger, "a man of meager intellect, of foreign tastes, foreign sympathies, trained up to admire arbitrary and oppressive rule, and to regard the people as abject slaves of powers, to whom shouldn't be allowed either liberty of action or of thought." His arrival in Ireland was an ominous turn in the wrong direction, a bad omen for the new year.

An issue that George didn't mention in his New Year greeting loomed not far in the future. Every ten years, a census took place in Ireland. Eighteen fifty-one was the year designated for the next one to be taken. This counting of the Irish people would supplant opinions about the cost of years of famine and emigration with concrete data. George might not have mentioned the census, but he knew the official counting would soon take place, and he would publicize the results.

§

James subscribed to two Irish newspapers, George's *Newry Telegraph,* and the Presbyterian newspaper, the *Banner of Ulster.* He closely followed

George's attacks on the Catholic Church, as well as the more liberal beliefs of the Presbyterian Church that the *Banner* represented. But he remained focused on finding a new minister for Donaghmore. James hosted each minister, and often provided some detail on the sermon. On October 20, 1850, a new candidate had attracted particular attention, the Rev. Patrick White. He based his most effective sermon on references from Isaiah and Ezekiel.

Most of the candidates came, preached and left shortly after the service. This time Rev. White stayed over Sunday night at Ringbane. Rev. White followed up his time with James and his family with two days of visits to other important members of the church. Wednesday was "Sackremental fast day." After that official duty had been completed, Rev. White stayed on yet two more days as James's guest. There was a particular reason for the congregation's interest in young Rev. White. He was one of six sons of the Rev. Patrick White of the Corglass Church in Ballieboro, County Cavan. One of the older White sons, Verner, had already been a much loved and respected minister in Donaghmore.

Early in December, the Newry Presbytery took the next step to fill the church vacancy in Donaghmore. The Presbytery charged Rev. Moran and Rev. Lindsay with the responsibility of verifying the list of male members qualified by character and consistent church attendance to vote in the upcoming election of a new minister. Approved voters then met to select ministers for a second hearing. They invited four men, Revs. Johnston, Steel, White and Field, to return.

George had published his New Year's leader before the last candidate was heard for the second time. The next day, voters met to select the new minister. Rev. Moran of Newry began by preaching a unifying sermon. Next, members decided to offer the new minister a yearly salary of £40 pounds hoping to entice the winner to accept Donaghmore's call. Then nominations were accepted, each being moved and seconded. The first names placed in nomination were Rev. Smith, and Rev. Fleming Then James's son-in-law Archy Marshall nominated Rev. White. Rev. Field was the final nominee. When Ross Todd of Newry, John Martin's brother-in-law, and James's son John Harshaw, reported the official count, Rev. Fleming had three votes, Rev. Smith nine votes, Rev. Field nine votes, and Rev. White 43. The final action was a vote to make the call unanimous. Rev. White would be the next minister of the Donaghmore Presbyterian Church.

The transition of a minister from one church to another took some time. So it was the first Sunday in March before Rev. White preached his first sermon in Donaghmore. The formal installation took place even later on March 11th. Rev. Moran of the Newry Presbytery preached a very able and eloquent discourse, according to George. Rev. West, explained, and the new minister's father Rev. Patrick White offered the prayer. The ceremony ended with a charge by Rev. McCleen. The new minister was introduced by his brother Verner of Liverpool. George also mentioned that Rev. White would preach the following Sunday in the Downshire Road Church. The day after the ceremony, both White brothers visited James.

Once the festivities surrounding the installation ended, Rev. White began a systematic visit to all the members of his new congregation. James described the visits in his journal. "Mr. White commenced a regular visitation of the congregation about <u>ten, this day</u> in the touneland of Ardkeragh and began with <u>Joe Duff</u>." Joe was one of James's favorite laborers. He lived in one of a cluster of small cabins that James provided for some of his long-term laborers.

James was well loved and respected in Donaghmore in part because he was endlessly ready to help in any civic project. In early January of 1851 while he was still working to find a new minister for his church, he led another project in an area he felt strongly about, education. He helped arrange for a farewell dinner at the Four Mile House, for John Irvine, the Principal of the Select Boarding and Day School in Anaghbane. James described the event in his journal. "Dined at <u>five</u>. Was in the chair. Dinner very substancial, & good punch &c. very good & very abundant. 27 dined, all cheerful, but none drunk."

Given James's position as chairman of the event, he was responsible for offering the toast to the honored guest. "We are assembled here this evening to testify our regard and esteem for my worthy friend Mr. Irvine. You all know him to be a learned, talented, warm-hearted, kind gentleman.

"He has educated the young people of the neighbourhood in the precepts and divinity of the Bible and in Classic literature, He has prepared many of your sons for the rooms of the College and the halls of the University in all of which he has been so eminently successful that he deserves the gratitude of the country."

James went on to report that Mr. Irvine was moving to Ballynahinch where he was certain to again be very successful. Then he offered the official toast. "I have much pleasure in giving the health of our esteemed guest Mr. Irvine, may health and happiness attend him."

George was one of the guests and wrote a report for his paper. He complimented Mrs. Woods, whose husband owned the Four Mile House, on the dinner and all the arrangements. George concluded, "The toast was enthusiastically received by the company, and Mr. Irvine replied in a very feeling and affectionate manner. The removal of Mr. Irvine, and that of his amiable and excellent lady, is felt to be a public loss. They carry with them the best wishes of all who know them for their success in their new sphere of labor, and it is hoped that they will receive, from an intelligent public, that patronage and encouragement which they so deservedly merit."

§

The dinner for Mr. Irvine had been a diversion for both James and George. James returned to his farm work, George continued his crusade against the Catholic Church and the tenant rights movements. The *Telegraph* provided extensive coverage of a major gathering of Protestants that had taken place early in the new year in Belfast. The principal speaker was Lord Roden whose extensive property lay east of Donaghmore in County Down. Despite his involvement in the killing of four Catholics in the battle between Catholics and Protestants in Dolly's Brae, he was still greatly admired by many in Ireland. This was his first major speech since the horrid events there.

Lord Roden made clear what he thought about the new moves of Pope Pius IX. "Gentlemen, it appears to me that those who have paid any attention to passing events, must have perceived that, during the last few years, more than ordinary efforts have been made by the Church of Rome to establish her doctrines and dogmas and tyranny within our land." He continued, "If I am led to look for a reason for all those events we deplore; and I think I am not saying too much when I say it is because the Protestants of England and Ireland are surrounded by enemies within and without, because there is treachery going forward and being done, which has brought these things to pass which now we so deeply deplore."

These words certainly seemed most intolerant. But Lord Roden explained why that wasn't the case. "It cannot be considered intolerance to disable the intolerant from carrying any evil purpose into effect, while we leave them all liberty for good."

This was a conversation that George wanted to be part of. So he issued his own strong statement on the subject. "Turn where you will, if Popery be predominant, there is degradation, if Popery be powerful, there is discord: if Popery be absent, or its evil influence be counteracted by the active presence of Protestantism, there are prosperity and peace."

As a counter to these efforts to unite and activate the Protestant minority of Ireland, the new Archbishop of Ireland called a meeting of the Catholic clergy of the Diocese of Armagh to assemble in Dundalk. George reported on the event and published the Archbishop's speech. But he couldn't resist publishing a warning to all his readers first. He explained that Catholic actions in England were an effort to reestablish the power of Catholic hierarchy whose "fraud, violence and tyranny" had resulted in its loss of power three centuries earlier.

George scolded the church for extorting money from its poor members rather than mounting efforts to help their suffering. This was a sign of their great weakness. "They see that their establishment is not founded on the rock of truth–they see it breaking into pieces–they know that it has no vitality–that it is a deformed corpse without any attractions. It is not to the free exercise of individual judgments–it is not to the private interpretation of the Scriptures–it is not to the doctrines of individual judgment–it is not to reason or arguments– no, it is to penal laws they now appeal. They have no foundation to stand on but brute force and violence."

Still George had hope that Protestant actions would end the threat. "May we not trust that their want of charity–their want of confidence in truth and justice, will react upon themselves, and make reflecting men see the folly of upholding an establishment whose mission it is to disturb the harmony of the inhabitants of this country? Are we to sacrifice without a struggle those rights we prize so highly and which we sighed for so long!"

Before George returned to the subject of tenant rights, he published a brief note that the wife and children of John Mitchel had been escorted to Liverpool and had soon sailed for Australia on the *Condor* to rejoin Mitchel for the remaining years of his sentence.

After that brief mention, he provided a detailed report on a tenant rights meeting held in Armagh City on January 28th. The chairman of the meeting was Rev. D. G. Brown. He stressed the reality that land was the "natural source of wealth, and, this being so certainly the tillers of the soil are entitled to food and raiment...The man who tilled the land had a right to be supported by the land—or in other words, to a fair remuneration for his labor."

Rev. Brown argued that attaining this "fair remuneration" was the sole purpose of the tenant right movement. Tenant farmers, like James, expected that this right would be accepted by the land owners. Attaining this goal was of grave importance to all Irishmen.

As usual, George felt impelled to comment first on the failure of the meeting. He doubted that the meeting had been well attended, though he hadn't himself been an eyewitness. More importantly, he knew the leading clergymen of Armagh weren't present; that alone substantiated his judgment. Their absence clearly indicated opposition to the Tenant Rights League.

George attempted to make clear that despite his intense opposition to the tenant rights agitation, he had great sympathy for the farmers. "Certain are we that both the clergy and laity of the Archiepiscopal City sincerely commiserate the hard fate of an industrial and independent-minded class, whose circumstances, calamitous visitations and ill-devised legislative actions have latterly tended so materially and lamentably to impair. Concern for the true interests of the farmer would prompt men of sense to repudiate the unsound principle of the League."

According to George, farmers would be in a better position if the tenant rights movement just disappeared. It was this confederation's actions that prevented the government from passing any legislation that would actually help Irish farmers. He went on to warn farmers that the government would never enact any law that would interfere in the "equal negotiations" between landlord and tenant over what constituted a fair rent. George didn't mention that "equal negotiations" could never exist when landlords held the power of life and death over their tenants. Until there was a disinterested power to judge rent disputes, Irish farmers would face power from a position of weakness.

Despite the many articles that George published on the subject, Tenant Rights League meetings continued, and came ever closer to Newry. On February 3, 1851, another tenant rights meeting took place, this time in Banbridge. The main speaker was Rev. William Dobbin. He recounted the many problems Irish farmers faced as a result of current laws, such as rack renting (rent charges above the value of the land or produce) and ejections.

George was ready with a quick response. First, he highlighted the poor attendance, declaring that whatever the number, it was far less than the 3,000 claimed, indeed it was a "beggarly" amount. The meeting wouldn't warrant a mention at all were not it necessary to "examine the construction and contortion of mischievous, poisonous reptiles."

The Presbyterian leaders, George claimed, who led this rally were "all hypocrites, sporting their fantastic tricks for a selfish purpose. Many of them are mere simpletons. They have neither head nor heart to be rogues; and yet they have not either head or heart to stand up as honest public men. They swim with a local current, as ships and rotten leaves do." This organization, representing a union between Presbyterian and Catholic interests, could not stand. He viewed it as "an unhallowed confederacy."

Tenant rights speakers deplored the actions of the great Irish landowners. George knew many of them personally, and vigorously defended them and their actions, maintaining that they treated their tenants fairly. The main evil of the Irish land system was the "jobbers." Such middlemen were the "curse of Ireland." These men leased large amounts of land, which they parceled out in small amounts to impoverished laborers, ringing out from them their last pence. Not only did this evil practice allow too many people access to ever smaller bits of land, it kept them from moving to more productive manufacturing jobs. "Strange that, while the landowner is denied liberty to 'do what he will with his own,' the land-jobber should experience immunity."

George claimed that middlemen participated in the tenant rights movement for self-protection, to hide the evils of their own selfish actions. He concluded his screed with this ominous warning. "Though we be forbearing now, we may be tempted yet, to smite hypocrisy of this cast. Let us just hint that there are certain parties we have an eye upon–Donaghmore in particular– who since they will not keep at home we may possibly compel us to look at home."

James was one of the largest land holders in Donaghmore. And he was a middleman who supported tenant rights. James was clearly one of the middlemen George had put on notice.

Despite George's continuous warnings, tenant rights meetings, led by Presbyterians, continued. The next major meeting was held the end of March in Dromore before a crowd of about 3,000 people.

Rev. Dobbins of Annaghlone returned fire after George's attacks on Presbyterian ministers. "It [the *Newry Telegraph*] is presided over by a genius facetiously called a man, and sometimes, for the sake of euphony, styled an Editor, who, on the principle that two negatives make an affirmative, derives his qualification to be the landlord's advocate from neither common sense or common honesty."

The main speaker, Rev. Rutherford, made clear the philosophical underpinnings of the league that all rights to the land belonged to the farmer tenants. First, landlords were involved in a chain of ownership that began with the false premise that someone had had title to the wilderness land of Ireland. Without a clear right of ownership in the first place, no succeeding person had a right to sell what he had no right to own.

The second fundamental premise was that the farmers who had turned land from wilderness to valuable farmland owned all the value of the land thus created. "The draining of marshes, the quarrying of rocks, the fencing, clearing, fertilizing, and draining of fields, the constructing of roads, the building of houses–in a word–all the differential value of the land, in the state of a wilderness, when it is tenanted only by the beasts of the forest, and a state of cultivation such as Ireland presents at this day, is unquestionably the property of the man who, by his skill, labor, and capital has, called it into existence."

As the supporters of the tenant rights movement saw it, the resolution of this terrible injustice was simple. The dispute over ownership of this value was the basis for the dispute between landlords and tenants. The solution to the problem would come when the government bought out the landlords' limited interest in the land, and legally transferred ownership to the tenants.

§

On March 15, 1851, James neared the end of his term as Donaghmore's Guardian. He would be replaced at the beginning of April by John Bradford of Ardkeragh. But on March 18th, James was still faithfully attending to his responsibilities. He recorded the major item on the agenda. "A rate of 3d on the pound voated for 15 years, to pay for the building the poorhouse &c, &c." George added a bit more explanation. This new rate was in addition to a 2d increase in the rate-in-aid tax levied by the British government the day before the laws expiration would have prevented its imposition. This additional 5d impost would make the financial situation of local farmers even grimmer.

On March 31st, the greatly anticipated census took place. Police fanned out across the area to collect the forms every family had already received. One of the policemen knocked on the door of Ringbane House to collect the Harshaw information. One form focused on personal family information. Other forms collected data about buildings and people who were sick or were lunatics. Hospitals, schools, and gaols had their own unique forms to file.

Form A requested personal information for every person who was present in the home. Naturally, they asked for the names. But they also asked for ages, marriage status, occupations, literacy, and finally place of birth. James handed the official census form to the police, but he copied his family data into his journal first.

Census Form A

Name and Age	Marital Status	Occupation (Literacy)	Place of Birth
James Harshaw - 54	Married 1816 - farmer	R & W	Down
Sarah Harshaw - 52	Married	None**	Down
John Harshaw - 30	Unmarried	None **	Down
Andrew Harshaw – 21	Unmarried	None **	Down
Sarah Anne Harshaw – 11	Unmarried	None attending school	Down
John Thompson – 34	Unmarried	Gardner R	Armagh
James Wright – 18	Unmarried	Plowman R	Down
John Ward – 14	Unmarried	Cowkeeper R	Down
Eliza McDowell – 19	Unmarried	Housemaid R	Down
Mary Duff – 16	Unmarried	Housemaid R	Down

In the next section, the government requested information about people belonging in the residence but who were living elsewhere

People Belonging in the Residence – Living Elsewhere

Name and Age	Marital Status	Occupation	Living Elsewhere
James Harshaw – 22	Unmarried	None	New York
William Kidd Harshaw – 20	Unmarried	None	New York
Robert Hugh Harshaw – 19	Unmarried	Attending College	Belfast
Samual Alexander Harshaw – 14	Unmarried	None	Mountnorris

The final question asked who had died since they were recorded in the last census, plus the cause of death. James had two entries to make in this final category. But it was clear that the famine wasn't the cause of death.

Deceased Since Last Census

Name	Age	Cause of Death	Date of Death
Elizabeth Martin Harshaw	10 Months	Inflamation	Summer 1842
Hugh Harshaw	27	Epilepsy	Winter 1845

James explained the process in his journal entry for the day: "Fine dry morning. The cences taken of all those who had slept or remained in or about the difrent dwellings last night." James didn't list an occupation for John or Andrew, but they were the sons who worked the farms with their father.

The policeman left Ringbane with James's documents. His report was gathered together with the other returns from Donaghmore, and, combined with those of other parishes, were hurried to Dublin to begin the official counting. The anxious waiting for the results began.

While the census was taking place across Ireland, James was still involved in the time-consuming process of reinventing the Donaghmore Dispensary to comply with a new law regulating Irish dispensaries. This preliminary work was finally completed on March 31st. "Attended a meeting of Dispensary committee in the fourmile house where I was derected to advertice for a medical officer. Election to be on the 14th of April in the fourmile house."

The advertisement appeared in the *Telegraph* three days later. Candidates for the position were requested to apply before noon on Monday the 14th. The election would take place in the Four Mile House. James Harshaw was the treasurer to whom the "Testimonials" should be sent.

This effort didn't go smoothly. On the appointed day, James arrived for the meeting early giving time for him to have breakfast with Mrs. Woods, the wife of the owner. After a preliminary discussion, the committee met at the announced time, with James again chairing the meeting. Two candidates were present, Quinn and Derby. Apparently, the committee wasn't satisfied with either candidate. They voted to begin the process again with another advertisement.

April ended without a new doctor for the dispensary. Though the dispensary wasn't yet running, James was required by law to account to the managing committee for all financial transactions. The members of the committee were Wilson, Bryson, David Woods, Archy Marshall, James Martin, and John McMaster. They checked his records and signed for their accuracy. James then sent the records as required to Downpatrick.

On May 8th, James wrote eighteen personal notes to the other members of the Dispensary Committee, advising them that there would be yet another meeting of the committee at the Four Mile House the following Monday.

Monday was a fine day. James left early to go to the Dispensary Committee meeting. There were applications from new candidates, Drs. Saunderson, McClelland, Barr, Davidson, Parry, McKaine, and Mitge. Attendance was small for such an important meeting. Still the Committee began to review the candidates. The committee had read the documents for two of the candidates, Barry and Mitge, when the validity of the meeting was challenged. The meeting was then adjourned after James was directed to write to all the original dispensary subscribers and absent members requesting their presence at yet another meeting that Friday.

The weather on Friday was not nearly as fine, but the necessary work of the committee was finally accomplished. Dr. Sanderson was elected the new doctor for the poor of the Donaghmore area. Dr. Sanderson got fourteen votes, Dr. McClelland four. James paid Dr. McKaine £6, 10, 0 for his services after Dr. Bryson's death. James then placed the dispensary in the care of Dr. Saunderson, who would remain the area doctor until he died some years later.

§

A tenant rights meeting held in Dromore before the end of March remained very much on George's mind. Not surprisingly he attributed an attack on a sub-sheriff and two helpers who were serving an ejectment notice on a tenant four years behind in his rent to the tenant rights agitation. The officials observed a crowd of perhaps two hundred people converging on the officials. A volley of shots was then fired, some striking as close as the trees above their heads. However, the men were able to safely withdraw and return to Banbridge.

Though George was well aware of the tenant rights activities in the area, he professed to be unprepared for the attack "in a district that has hitherto been in so good repute, of moral disorganization, and of that total disrespect for the rights of property with which it is ordinarily accompanied." He expected that he would soon hear of the area being in a state of war. But he also expected that the executive would promptly bring the full weight of the law into play. Surely there would be no tolerance for "agrarian outrage." There must be a quick end to the idea "that no matter what the conduct of the tenant may have been, no matter what arrears of rent he owes, for the landlord to evict him is a crime, justifying an immediate recourse to the 'wild justice of revenge?'"

George had no doubt that attacks like this were inspired by the actions of the Tenant Rights League and the Presbyterian ministers who were preaching against the long-established rights of property. The principles that tenant rights advocates were endorsing were "worse than Communism." Then George challenged authorities again. "It is for the Government of the country to determine whether, while the rights of property are said to be guaranteed by law, the exercise of those rights is to be...rendered impossible" because agitators, claiming to be upholding the rights of the weak against wrongdoing were actually spouting "the most delusive and mischievous representations, thus 'sowing dragons' teeth that may spring up armed men?'"

§

The Whig administration which had been in power since replacing the Conservative party in 1846 was in trouble. The administration was hanging on to power by a thread, which George hoped would soon break. So he was very happy to publish remarks that were delivered by Sir H. W. Barron on the floor in Parliament on the temporary resignation of the Whig government. Barron provided his colleagues with a critique of Whig policies toward Ireland from the perspective of a Whig supporter. After an introduction to his remarks, Barron pronounced his pleasure that the Whig administration was ending and concluded with a description of the horrid situation in Ireland which James and George were witnessing and enduring.

This was Ireland in 1851, after five years of famine and Whig governance. "Trade is smashed, the land ruined, the tenants broken, the laboring portion of the people, who have the means, are fleeing the kingdom by whole parishes. The Irish nation is totally wrecked, devoured by its own paupers; cities and towns are desolate, villages are leveled to the ground, and their former occupiers are wandering about the country, beggars or thieves. The gaols are full of criminals, who are no sooner discharged for one offence, than they commit another in order to get again into prison. Housebreaking is more common than picking pockets in London. Emigration is rife."

Conservatives in Parliament, led by Benjamin Disraeli, attempted to provide some relief to Irish farmers, not by interfering with free trade, but by adjusting the taxes farmers had to pay. His bill was defeated by fifteen votes.

George reacted angrily to the news. He thought it represented a complete disconnect between Parliament and the rest of the country. Even the *London Times,* a strong supporter of free trade, acknowledged the problem facing Ireland. This was something that George liked so much, he quoted a section of it. "'There is no doubt that a large proportion of our farmers at this moment are losing money, and that if their payments and their receipts continue long at the present rate, they must be utterly ruined.'" As long as the Russell Whig administration remained in power, nothing positive to help Irish farmers could pass.

Given this kind of analysis, it wasn't surprising that the tenant rights movement continued to hold meetings as the spring progressed. A large one was held in Belfast, with some support from the business community there. One of those present was John's fellow Young Irelander, Charles Gavan Duffy. George commented, "Heartily sympathizing with the industrious and sorely-discouraged farmer, we sincerely rejoice that the intelligence of Belfast has so significantly forborne from fraternizing with a cabal whose existence constituted the greatest barrier in the way of the equitable adjustment of the relations between landlord and tenant."

Naturally George couldn't resist commenting on the part of the tenant right movement that bothered him the most, the cooperation between Presbyterians and Catholics. He pointed out that Catholics in the movement wanted to regulate rents, which was worrisome enough. But they also wanted to regulate wages so that "'the laborer, in Summer, shall not receive less than one shilling per day, nor less than tenpence in Winter.'" The idea of a government regulated minimum wage had led to ruin wherever it had been tried, as George saw the issue. Clearly this was an idea no Presbyterians could endorse.

All too soon, George had another agrarian murder to report. This murder took place about a mile away from the site of Mauleverer's murder. The victim was Samuel Coulter who had left his home to go to the fair in Crossmaglen. He was found leaning against a stone wall, his head terribly mangled. It was obvious from the scene that he had put up a strong resistance. Evidence collected by the police at the scene included "a brass pistol, a bayonet, the lock of an old gun, and a leaden bullet." While Mr. Coulter was alive when he was found, he died soon after.

George had a no doubt as to the cause of this new murder. "The assassination of Samuel Coulter has its origin in what are designated 'agrarian causes' may be, as we judge, fairly assumed."

Within a few days, there was another attack for George to report. This time, an elderly couple who lived between Castleblayney in County Monaghan and Keady in County Armagh were attacked and severely beaten by a group of eleven invaders. Before the assailants left, they warned their battered victims to give up the land they had recently taken, or they would return and kill both of them. Such intimidation was a common tactic used to prevent landlords from re-renting land from which the former occupants had been ejected.

Police arrived quickly and noticed dogs barking in the distance. The police followed the sound to a cabin near a bog. They peered into the window and saw a group of men, with one kneeling as if taking an oath. The police entered and quickly arrested all the men without incident. George was sure that the police had detected a Ribbon ceremony (a Catholic secret society supporting agrarian reforms) under way. He greatly hoped that the arrest of these men would put an end to Ribbon activity in the area.

The leader George wrote on the news of this last attack on helpless elders made clear the depth of his anger and frustration. "What is there that a landlord can do which [Tenant Rights] League Moralists will not condemn and arraign him for? Under all circumstances and for all manner of causes the landowner is denounced and put under ban. His tenants may be reducing him to beggary by declining to pay their engagements but let him attempt to enforce his rents and his denunciation as a tyrant rings in men's ears, and is sure to bring upon him popular odium, if not to subject him to bitter experience, in his property or person, of 'the wild justice of revenge.'"

Clearly, at least to George, prompt action was required to put a quick end to current laws that made convictions slow and hard to obtain. This was a time for a renewed push for law and order, for quick and sure convictions. Recognizing that convictions for Irish crimes were difficult to obtain, George recommended quick passage of a new law establishing the Scotch system of justice into Ireland. There, defendants were convicted by just a majority vote by the jurors.

There would be another benefit as well. "This would effectually silence objections on the score of 'packing,' which, whether well or ill founded, do certainly detract from the moral weight of convictions." This, of course, was the system used to obtain convictions against John and his fellow Young Irelanders.

§

As George composed the *Telegraph* for publication in mid-May, an interesting notice caught his eye. It was an article from a Hobart Town newspaper in Van Diemen's Land reporting that three of the Irish convicts had been arrested for violating their parole. And indeed, they had risked just this outcome by leaving their assigned districts to visit Smith O'Brien who had just been freed from severe captivity having finally accepted a ticket of leave. Only profound deterioration of his health had induced him to accept what he saw as a favor from the British. When his health improved, he intended to renounce it.

Each of the three men, Kevin O'Dogherty, Terrance McManus and Patrick O'Donoghue, had been convicted of violating their tickets of leave and were sentenced to three months at hard labor in a penal station. O'Dogherty had been dressed in a gray prison uniform and marched through the streets of Hobart Town with other prisoners. He and McManus were placed on board a steamer and sent to the Cascades. O'Donoghue was sent to Salt Water River.

Though the gentlemen, not used to such hard physical work, suffered greatly, McManus had a great benefit when he was released. No official required him to sign another ticket of leave, as they did his fellow prisoners. So he just walked to the harbor and safely boarded a ship heading away. McManus reached California and made his home there.

Neither John nor Mitchel had violated their paroles in this instance.

§

Early in May, Newry's member of Parliament, Lord Newry, died, making a new election necessary to replace him. The first person to express an interest in standing for election inserted that information in the *Telegraph* on Tuesday May 20th. Edmond G. Hallewell let potential supporters know what he saw as the most important issues. He supported protecting capital and industry, and opposed infringement on civil and religious liberties, from whatever quarter. He signed his letter "A true conservative."

George was very pleased with this candidate. He was happy that no one would have to "cast about" for any other candidate. Hallewell was a fine candidate. "We believe …that his principles are such as will render him with the preponderating class of the constituency an acceptable candidate." He went on to claim many people of different politics and parties would unite to support this candidate.

Within a few days, George reported that the election was proceeding well. Hallewell had been around the area conducting his canvass. Local voters seemed willing to support his election in such numbers that no other candidate had declared for election. Voters of all political beliefs were indeed flocking to his support.

However, there was one small cloud in George's sunny picture. Objections to his candidacy had been "afloat." One accusation was that Mr. Hallewell had personal interests that differed from those of the community. He was, after all, an Englishman. He was also charged with being an Orangeman.

As this was an anathema to the Catholic majority of Newry, George quickly dismissed these charges. There was a potential conflict of interest issue as well. Hallewell was the owner of the Newry Gas and Water Works. But he had pledged that he would abstain from any legislation that might affect his business.

The charge of being an Orange Order member arose from campaign cards that he had printed. On each of them were printed the words. "Hallewell. Fear God–Honor the Queen–Love the Brotherhood." It was the part about "Brotherhood" that fostered the spread of the Orange charge, but George claimed that it was a misinterpretation of the word "Brotherhood." It was Biblical, not an Orange reference. Hallewell flatly denied that he was a member of the Orange Order, which, to George's mind, should end the issue.

George defended Hallewell against additional charges that he had taken advantage of the financial problems of the local Gas Works at the time of the famine. When the Newry Gas Works went bankrupt, Hallewell had invested his own money to turn the critical local industry into a profitable one as well. This was a hard sell, as the alleged poor gas service received many complaints from Newry residents. Few people saw his move from Gloucestershire an important sacrifice either.

No other candidate stepped forward, so the results of the election were already known before the election took place on May 30th at the Newry Courthouse. James recorded the results in his journal for that date. "Fine morning, and dry day. Eleven men making mud in Ringbane. Mr. Hallewell elected in Newry." Newry would remain in good Conservative hands.

§

Citizens of both England and Ireland were waiting anxiously for the results of the census, the release of which was expected daily. With that unveiling drawing ever closer, George kept the terrible problem of Irish poverty in mind. In mid-June, he wrote a leader on the topic. He hated that the costs of the labor-rate and out-door relief for the poor were "not only threatening to swamp individual and National resources, but, also rapidly eating into the vitals of the lower classes of our community." Farmers like James and his neighbors in Donaghmore were forced to pay more money to support the poor than they could afford to spend on their own families.

George believed that this impossible situation was clearly obvious to everyone. By so heavily taxing farmers, the government had forced many of them into poverty themselves. Yet "public functionaries are infatuated enough to set themselves against patriotic endeavors [Orange Order] to stay the plague, and the Government of the day abets its subordinates in this insane and impolitic course."

Everyone expected that the census data would be released at the beginning of July, three months having elapsed since the census was taken in late March. Indeed, the results of the census count for the England, Scotland and Wales had already been released. But for some strange reason the reports for Ireland were still secret though supposedly the results were already in the hands of the Lord Lieutenant. George reported that there was great anxiety about the results. He believed that the "revelations will destroy for ever the pretension that the Whigs were friends to Ireland."

An early report leaked out of Dublin claiming that the population of Ireland had fallen to 6.5 million. George was skeptical. "This is almost incredible; and yet, when we remember the horrible sufferings through which we have passed–the famine, the fever, and the cholera–and bear in mind the extent of the emigration from our shores, we should not be surprised if it turned out to be true." The population at the time of the last census had been 8.2 million. "No explanation can do away with a fact so tremendous and appalling, as that, in time of peace, this country should have lost nearly one third of its entire population." That said, George didn't believe that the population had fallen below seven million. But given the fact that the population should have risen, that difference was truly alarming.

When it came to Newry, George believed that the population was about the same as it had been during the 1841 census when the population had been slightly above 13,000. The population measured then had surely dwindled, but the loss had been compensated for by a large number of strangers present in the town, and the number of men working on the railroad nearby.

§

The days of waiting for the official census report dragged on. But James had another matter on his mind. He had been selected by the Donaghmore congregation to attend the General Assembly of the Presbyterian Church. James left early in the morning, this time bringing his wife Sarah with him. This was the first time she had ever been to Belfast or ridden on the ever-expanding network of trains. They arrived safely in Belfast around noon. Then James took Sarah to the train leaving for Ballymena to visit their former minister, Rev. Moore.

Once Sarah was safely on her way, James made his way to the meeting. The first item on the agenda was the location of the next Assembly meeting, in Armagh or Derry. James voted for Armagh and it was chosen by forty votes. In the evening, he listened to Dr. Dell give a three-hour speech on the issue of British support for Irish colleges.

The next morning, July 3rd was a fine sunny day. He went to an early session of the Assembly, listening to a response to the speech the night before. Then he met Sarah to make sure she was safely on the train heading south. He "Dined with Mr. White. Sat in the Assembly at seven. Listened to the English and then the Scotch Deputations. And then the famous Dr. Duff, moderator of the free church of Scotland who was received with great applause. He spoke on missions for about two hours & a half with energy & great effect and sat down amidst great applause." Dr. Duff was the first missionary from the Free Church to India. For years afterward, people claimed to have been present at this sermon, long considered one of the finest sermons in Presbyterian history.

There were more sessions on Friday that James attended. A committee was appointed, but "little business of a public nature gone into up to 4 oclock when I left Belfast and arrived home about ten oclock."

§

The day after James returned from Belfast, George received the long-awaited results of the census and began to publish the stunning results for his readers. The reason behind the reluctance to release the results became clear. "The astounding fact is now before the world that, within the last decennial period, the very short space of ten years, the population of Ireland has DECREASED *more than a million and a-half!* Nay, it is now a plain matter of statistics that, in 1851, the number of persons is in the island less by 300,000 than in 1821–that is, thirty years ago. What a fearful proof of the havoc made by famine, pestilence, and flight from our shores!"

Other statistics were also devastating. The number of houses that had gone empty exceeded 280,000. George wondered, "Where are the people that, but ten years ago, occupied and enlivened those homes?" The local population statistics were also depressing. Ulster's population had declined by 14 percent. Still that was the best result after Leinster which lost 12 percent of its population. Munster lost 25 percent, and Connaught 29 percent. Strangely some towns had gained in population, as starving country laborers fled there to beg. If one calculated what the population should have been given the starting point of 1796, when the population was just over four million, and given the standard amount of population growth, the population "should this year have proved to be upwards of ELEVEN MILLION."

George was well aware that the Tenant Right League would make good use of these statistics, blaming the British government for misrule of the country. "We impeach not the motives or designs of those in authority. We render to landowners, all the sympathy which their privations and losses deserve at the hands of all unbiased and judicious observers of public events. Our principle is, submission to the Divine will–a humble recognition of an all-disposing Hand. Our trust is, that the melancholy crisis in human events, as connected with our country, may finally prove the dawning of a happier day for Ireland."

Because of the intense interest, George published the total population figures as well. In 1841, the population of Ireland was 8,175,124. In the new census, the population was 6,515,794, proving the population had actually dropped further than George had been willing to admit.

On the day after these first census reports appeared in the *Telegraph,* George's wife Isabella Barclay died after a long illness at their home in Emyvale. She was the daughter of the late Alexander Williamson of Lambeg in Lisburn. She was buried in the family plot there two days later. George and Isabella had happily welcomed four children, only to watch them die one by one before their mother. George stoically absorbed yet another painful loss and was quickly back at work, returning to more fallout from the Irish census, including the reaction in England.

Interest in the shocking results of the Irish census prompted extensive coverage in English newspapers as well. The *London Morning Herald* carried a British perspective that George liked so much that he reprinted it in his paper. The title was "'What Hope is There for Ireland?'" The data clearly indicated that 1.5 million Irish citizens had died. The general British reaction was that this horrid tragedy was a divine act, which they had tried valiantly to mitigate. The editor of the *Herald* wasn't about to let the government escape responsibility. To get the proper prospective of the calamity, the government should examine the situation in Ireland when the famine struck. "Had we not constantly had before us their wretched condition in official reports, in the testimony of travelers, and in the wailings and complaints of the poor sufferers themselves?" The British had seen partial losses of the potato crop off and on for years. Surely it wasn't beyond imagination that should a complete loss of the crop occur during some future autumn the results would be dreadful.

The editor hoped that now that the appalling news of what had happened to Ireland could be proven statistically, perhaps the government would look closely at what was going on there and fix the problems. "The state of Ireland is neither one of actual prosperity, nor one which affords the slightest ray of hope that, for years, anything approaching to a state of prosperity awaits her, unless a total change in the system of government adopted in that country can be accomplished." People were still dying in the poorhouses. "Large districts of Ireland…which used to be cultivated, are left untouched, and are covered with worthless weeds. There is no stock to consume what may chance to grow on these deserted lands, the gable ends of her desolate cottages look as if the country had been sacked by an hostile army, the gentry are, with few exceptions, with their lands diminished to one-half, in many instances to one-third their former values, are selling at that reduced value, the most solvent and valuable of the tenant farmers are taking all their money and fleeing the stricken land–Popery…is rampant nearly throughout the country, encouraged and favored by the Government…Protestantism is discouraged, and the most able and sincere of her champions are placed under the ban of the Government murderers, tenant right agitation, Synod of Thurles, and a poor-rate in many places more than the whole produce of the soil complete the picture of Irish 'prosperity!'"

Still there must be some hope for Ireland "*Now* is the time to work, *now,* with far less of effort than ever, we might restore something like prosperity to Ireland. There are upwards of two millions of her children gone forever; let us prove our repentance by saving the remainder."

Handwriting Samples

Portion of a page of James Harshaw's diary.

A rent receipt written by John Martin

Chapter 3

Protestant Fractures

1851 - 1852

George watched dispatches from Australia for any news of his friends John and Mitchel. As he prepared a newspaper in mid-July, he discovered a letter from Mitchel in the *Freeman's Journal.* Mitchel had written it four months earlier to the publisher, Mr. Gray, a personal friend. George published the entire letter.

Officials in Van Diemen's land had noticed the meetings that the Young Ireland exiles were having at the place where their areas intersected and had published articles that accused them of "a breach of faith." Mitchel saw this as an attempt to blacken their reputations for no reason. He explained that it would be easy to escape if that should be their goal. He wanted to make sure that people in Ireland understood the situation.

The letter had some news of John as well. John had joined Mitchel and some of the young people of an Irish family, the Connells, on a visit to one of the many fast flowing rivers in the highlands. On the way home, all of the adventurers raced through the woods, frightening the local wildlife. After the wild and exhilarating ride, the party clattered up to a house and farm that appeared to be transported from a familiar Irish landscape. The house was built like an Irish two-storied house, the farm buildings and fields laid out just like the farms of County Down. This was the home of the Connells, an Irish family from Cork. They had been early settlers of this remote island, a world away from Ireland.

John dismounted and happily entered this special place knowing that he would feel transported home to Ireland. Since the feel of the coming winter was strong in the brisk air, the roaring fire inside was most welcome. Julia Connell was ready to serve them a proper Irish tea. After the riders had eaten, they assembled around the piano to sing the songs of home. Small wonder that John cherished the hours he spent at this special place at the foot of the Sugar Loaf Mountain.

Shortly after this visit, which George had reported for John's family and friends, John sent a songbook to the three Connell daughters. In August, Mrs. Connell wrote a "thank you" letter to John. It gave the Connell's address as Connellville, Macquarie River. She reported to John that her daughters had been delighted with his gift and would join him in singing the songs when he again visited them at the Sugar Loaf. She hoped the visit would come soon. She closed by reporting. "All the family unites in affectionate remembrances."

John's time as Mitchel's solo roommate was nearing an end as snow began to dust the mountains around Bothwell in June 1851. The Mitchel family was expected to arrive almost any day. Mitchel left Bothwell for the reunion. However, due to difficulties in finding a ship to bring the family to Van Diemen's Land, the reunion was considerably delayed. Six weeks passed before the joyous family reunion took place on July 18th. For the first few days, the Mitchel family lived in a hotel in Bothwell. Soon they found a small home, the Nant cottage, that was suitable for the family, plus John, to live in. The cottage stood high enough for the new residents to get a good view of the valley. There were 200 acres attached, the eastern end of their land reaching the river Clyde. This was certainly enough acreage for Mitchel to be a successful farmer. John would be the official teacher for the five Mitchel children, spending four hours every day fulfilling his teaching responsibilities.

This was no chore for John, as he had known the children since they were born. The oldest of the children was John, who had been born when Mitchel and Jennie lived in Banbridge. Along with James, Henrietta, Mary and William, they had come often to visit John in Loughorne, roaming about the lawn while John and Mitchel talked. So the days when John was in charge of the children were very special to him.

Once Mitchel had established his family in Van Diemen's Land, he was permitted to roam around the island as he wished. So in October 1851, Mitchel and Jennie left John in charge of the children while they visited Smith O'Brien in his new residence in Avoca. When the Mitchels' horses galloped into view on their return, John and all the children ran to greet them, laughing and exclaiming over the baby kangaroo the Mitchels brought back with them.

§

James worried as the harvest approached in August. This was the time the blight might return. So while he watched and waited, his responsibilities toward the Dispensary were likely a welcome distraction. Parliament had passed new legislation to regulate Irish dispensaries, which would affect the local dispensary James had worked diligently to create. "A fine dry day with bright sun. Attended a meeting of Dispensary in the Four-Mile-House where a number of accounts were passed & ordered to be paid. The meeting was adjourned to the 1st September till a copy of the Medical Charities Bill be received."

When the day arrived for the next meeting, the weather was quite different, rainy and blustery, making the walk to the Four Mile House distinctly unpleasant. The directions from the government had yet to arrive, but there was another issue to deal with. While Dr. Saunderson had recently been voted to the post of dispensary doctor, he didn't seem to be fulfilling the promises he made when he was hired, spending less time in Donaghmore than the Donaghmore Committee expected. After a new meeting with Dr. Saunderson, James reported "Dr. Sanderson continued on his promising to live in the fourmile house every Wednesday, Thursday, & Saturday, Day & Night."

James and the other members of the Dispensary Committee would have to wait weeks more for the official directions explaining the new law to arrive. It was almost the end of November before they were able to take any action. Under this new law, all local dispensaries would be placed under the direction of the Board of Guardians, but the local committee would continue to manage day-to-day operations of the Donaghmore Dispensary. "Dark fogy day. Mild thaw. Met Mr. Greer in Newry with a view to a settlement of the Dispensary by the board. Donaghmore, Oully, & the Glen appointed a Dispensary District by the board. The medical officer for the Dispensary would now get £50."

As August progressed, so did a new attack by the blight. There seemed to be little hope that there would ever be a healthy potato crop. But despite the terrible loss of income to farmers like James, the loss of the main source of food for poor laborers and their families was a matter of life and death. Still to linger over such losses instead of pushing forward to harvest other corps when they were ripe only intensified the losses of income.

Yet that same week, James had an unusual interruption in his work. He was visited by a policeman, who was conducting an inventory of Irish farms for the government. James was expected to provide an official report on his crops: "Wheat 6½ acres, Oats 11, Potatows 7, Turnips 1½, Mangel ¼, Carrots ½, Flax 8, Meadow & clover 8, Remainder Grass." James also owned 4 horses, 11 cows, 10 heifers, 5 sheep, 5 pigs, and 100 fowl.

§

The Irish Catholic Church intended to resist the new Ecclesiastical Titles Act that Parliament had passed, restricting titles for the Catholic leaders. Archbishop Cullen immediately began to bestow the forbidden titles. This was an action that George couldn't ignore. "While the loyal Orangemen of Ireland have been slighted and grievously oppressed, our Rulers have fawned upon the most disloyal, traitorous system."

George then reported that the Catholics had gathered in the Rotunda in Dublin in early September to create a new organization called the Catholic Defense Association, to lead the fight against the English temporalities law. Dr. Henry Cooke and a couple of other Presbyterian leaders obtained tickets and attempted to infiltrate the meeting. However, Rev. Cooke was so well known, he was easily intercepted before he could enter the meeting. Instead of writing his own leader describing the events, George published excerpts from the *Daily Express*. "'An organized assault upon the Protestant Church and Constitution of the land, such as we are threatened with from this misnamed Defence Association, must be met in a different way than by mild expostulation. It will have to encounter national rebuke and brave defiance.'"

Meetings like this heightened George's concern about the future Catholic plans for Ireland. After all, this religion was practiced by the vast majority of Irish citizens. Even when the Protestants of the Established Church and the Presbyterians acted together, they represented only a minority of the Irish population. Now the Tenant Rights League seemed to be enticing Presbyterians to unite in political actions with the Catholic majority. Should this union continue, or strengthen, the Established Church, the Church of Ireland, would be in great danger. So George kept repeating his warnings whenever a possible trigger attracted his attention.

George issued another warning to Presbyterians after the Dublin meeting. These were dangerous times due to the expansion of the Catholic Church led by Pope Pius and Archbishop Cullen and its attempts to "realize the delusive dream of the complete subjugation of the British Empire to her sway." Catholics are the enemies of the "Established Church and the Presbyterian Churches." For these reasons, the entire Protestant population of Ireland should be tightly aligned.

For years, George would advocate for Protestant unity. He was sure that the Catholic religion could not be defeated without it. Disunity between the Protestant religions would result in them devouring each other, and the Catholic Church would gobble up the remnants. "If however, side by side they push forward, in a determined and united movement, to spread their Protestantism over all the land, they will be crowned, ultimately, with triumphant success."

§

No man in Donaghmore was a better example of living one's religion through good works than James Harshaw. Another project he was very much interested in was a charity that helped children who were deaf, dumb and blind or who had some combination of these terrible disabilities. So not surprisingly, James led a meeting of this organization in the Meeting House schoolroom. He reported that Rev. Moran of Newry and a Mr. Kingon were part of the charity leadership who attended the meeting. According to James's report, one hundred twenty additional people were present to support this cause.

George however, added considerable detail to James's account. He reported that the classroom was "crowded to excess by a respectable audience." James conducted the meeting due to the absence of the president Rev. John C. Quinn, who was the minister of St. Bartholomew Church of Donaghmore, the local Church of Ireland church. The focus of the meeting was the questioning of two students who were benefiting from the charity. One was deaf and dumb, one was blind. The gathering seemed impressed that they scarcely missed a single question.

Having demonstrated what carefully taught students could achieve, Rev. Moran of Newry and other members of the delegation appealed to the audience to help fund this valuable organization. The audience seemed greatly impressed. Then, as was his custom, George mentioned by name attendees he considered important, among whom were the misses Marshall of Tullymurry House and John's brother James Martin of Loughorne.

§

In the October 1st edition of the *Telegraph*, George reprinted a paragraph from a Catholic newspaper stating the Catholic point of view in such stark terms that even George must have been somewhat surprised. "'Religious liberty, in the sense of a liberty possessed by every man to choose his own religion is one *of the most wicked delusions ever foisted upon this age by the father of all deceit...No man has a right to choose his religion.*'"

Later, George found an article in the *Britannia* that he thought provided a very fitting response to the Catholic statements. The author discussed the somewhat shocking benefit of the outmigration of so many Irish Catholic citizens. He didn't care much about the causes, but certainly applauded the results. "'As an Irish or rather Romish Exodus, it is a mercy rather than otherwise. It rids that unhappy land of a race who seem to defy...all the influences of civilization...The Protestant Saxon will soon occupy the forsaken settlements of the Irish Papist, and English industry find a home where, for nearly three centuries, Irish indolence had endured a purgatory...It is barbarism fleeing before civilization, superstition before Christian truth, and mediaeval night at the approach of the rising sun of social and national regeneration...God has taken the nation out of the hands of quacks, and placed it immediately in his own. He is now subjecting it to a process alike disinfecting and restorative.'"

The long Irish winter lay ahead, when George noted that the English government had attempted to throw a sort of life preserver to the Irish farmers who were being overwhelmed by the taxes Parliament had placed on the land. The British government had begun to collect taxes to repay England for the costs of building the Newry workhouse, a scheme Newry residents hated. The outcry over this perceived injustice was so intense the government attempted to soften the blow, by declaring that any Poor Law Union which paid a poor rate of 4s on the pound, would be excused from the tax. Other unions would just have to pay the difference between their poor rate and 4s on the pound. No additional repayment would be required.

George was not impressed. He thought this proposal was totally inadequate, when compared with the terrible need for major tax relief.

§

The harvest in Donaghmore was over by November, providing a break in the usual farm activities. And there was a Christmas celebration to look forward to. There was even time for farmers to engage in a fox hunt on December 9th. "A dry day, Men scraped the street, & road. A fox hunt. He was killed in the bog."

As Christmas neared, James's family began to gather for the celebration. Son Robert Hugh came home from Belfast where he was nearing the end of his ministerial education. Joe Duff "cut up a hog & salted it" for their Christmas dinner.

James recorded the events of the day. "Christmass day. Dry, cloudy, damp day: like some rain. Breakfasted with James Martin and [Robert] Hugh at my sisters old house in Loughorne. Visited Master Brown. Walked thrugh the fields. Dined with the family, had A. Douglass for tea."

Eighteen fifty-two began with cold weather, frosty ground and some snow. Still James plowed the ground to prepare for spring planting. His sons Samuel [Absalom] and Robert Hugh returned to Belfast after the holiday celebrations. On January 3rd, James traveled into Newry to meet Maxwell Simpson at the home of Robert Ross Todd. These two men were married to two of John's sisters, Mary to Maxwell, and Elizabeth to Robert Ross Todd. They were charged with supervising John's property in Loughorne while he endured his exile He had deeded the land to Simpson before he began publishing the *Felon* in May 1845 to escape one of the law's penalties. The Felony Treason Act, which had been passed to stifle any dissent published by any Irish paper, had another provision that Parliament designed to further punish any nationalist daring to criticize the government. A conviction for felony treason would also result in confiscation of all their assets, leaving their families destitute. This was indeed what happened when Mitchel was convicted. However, John made sure that the government would not seize any of the Martin assets. John signed over all his possessions to Simpson before he published the first edition of his paper. Todd was the lawyer who had drawn up the documents that ensured that John had no assets to seize. Following the first day of discussions, the men met again the next morning in Loughorne, before Maxwell returned to Dublin.

A few days later, James had another task to attend to in Newry. He attended Court in Newry on behalf of his neighbor Sarah Jorden. She had charged John McMaster with seduction. The case was settled for a payment of £21 and costs. She may well have been the daughter of Jonathan Jorden as James stopped there after he returned to Donaghmore.

George might well have covered a story of such unacceptable conduct in his paper. However, this case and its settlement passed unnoticed as a much more pressing story appeared. George published some additional raw data from the census on local parishes. In 1841, 2453 people had lived in Donaghmore. The census for 1851 showed that the population had dropped to 1744. Two of those missing citizens were James's dead children, Hugh and Elizabeth Martin. Two more were sons Willy and James who had emigrated to America. Similar loss of population occurred in the other parishes around Newry.

§

In January 1852, a second Young Irelander escaped from Van Diemen's land, McManus having simply walked away the previous year. Thomas Meagher had married a young local woman named Catherine Bennett. At first, John thought her unworthy, lacking the graces that were taught to young Irish women. However, as they came to know her, they found her an admirable young woman.

Despite his new link to Van Diemen's Land, Meagher turned in his ticket of leave, and fled, as Catherine was about to deliver their first child. In fact, she did give birth just a few weeks later. The baby, named Henry Emmet Fitzgerald Meagher, only lived four months, and was buried in Australia. His father never saw him. A few months later Catherine left to travel alone to Ireland to live with Meagher's father.

Thomas's escape was the subject of some controversy, as there was a question as to whether his actions conformed to the Young Irelanders' sense of honor. O'Dogherty and O'Brien thought that he had acted honorably, there being no obligation for Meagher to remain once he had announced that he was renouncing his ticket. If the authorities were unable to effect an arrest, that wasn't Meagher's fault.

John explained in a letter to O'Dogherty, that he and Mitchel didn't agree with their friends. He disputed Meagher's claim that his ticket expired as soon as he renounced it. But that aside, Meagher hadn't actually walked into the police station to announce his intentions. Instead, he handed the policeman on duty a letter and walked quickly away, mounting the horse he had waiting outside and riding away. By the time the police had time to read the letter, Meagher was gone. Only if the police had attempted to arrest him was he free to escape, according to John's thinking. However on reflection, John decided Meagher's escape met honorable standards.

Meagher had little difficulty completing his escape. Without interference from authorities, he was able to book passage away from Van Diemen's Land traveling safely to New York City. Now there were only four Young Irelander leaders still serving their terms in Van Diemen's Land.

§

Another agrarian attack in County Louth returned George's attention to the danger to property owners in the area. He remained convinced these frequent attacks were being caused by the Ribbonmen, a despicable Catholic group that the government had done little to suppress. This time, Lord Clarendon did act, ordering more police to the area, the costs for which would be extracted from the people that were most in danger. A new gun confiscation followed. George thought these measures were useless. The Ribbon killers came from other areas, not necessarily near the residents of their intended victims. They could carry guns to the scene of the intended murder with complete impunity.

On January 22nd, agrarian attacks hit very close to home. The victim this time was an important figure in Newry, a man that George knew well through his work as a local magistrate. Meredith Chambre was a large landowner who lived a short distance outside of Newry. On January 22nd, he had attended the Forkhill Petty Sessions where he served as one of the magistrates. Darkness had fallen before he headed home to his estate at Hawthorn Hill. As usual, on such routine trips, he was riding in a car accompanied this time by his brother Hunt and his butler. He had reached the Meigh section of Killeavy unaware that danger lurked behind a wall not far from the entrance to his estate. Five men were waiting unseen, guns at the ready.

For Chambre, there would be no warning. He felt the sting of eight bullets before he realized he was in grave danger. Though badly hurt, Mr. Chambre sprung from the car in an attempt to restrain the assailants. He took several steps toward the wall, his own gun now in his hand ready to give battle. However, he was losing large amounts of blood, so instead of capturing the shooters, he collapsed across the wall. His brother Hunt with his own gun in hand, rushed to help his brother.

The horse, which had also been wounded in the attack, was terrified. Dragging the car behind him, it raced toward Hawthorn Hill. Mrs. Chambre had already dressed for dinner, saw the horse and knew that something terrible had happened. Along with some staff, she hurried along the road, retracing the route of the panicked horse.

By the time she arrived at the scene of the crime, Chambre had been taken inside a nearby house. The tenant had refused to open his cottage to the injured man until the butler pulled out his own pistol and put it to the occupant's head. Police were quickly at the scene. Chambre was placed on a door and carried the rest of the way to Hawthorn Hill. As the procession passed by, not one person left their cottages to lend a hand. Surprisingly, Chamber was still alive when he was carried into his home.

Doctors were quickly summoned to attend the wounded man. Dr. Stronge was the lead doctor. They found that the pellets had entered obliquely. After some probing, doctors were able to extract two of them. Despite the help they were able to provide, the doctors held little hope that Chambre would survive the attack.

Meanwhile, the police were pursuing the assailants. They successfully captured two men they believed were responsible for the attempted murder. The motive for the shooting was assumed to be related to landlord and tenant strife, though, according to George, Chambre seemed to exemplify a benevolent landlord. Chambre had never ejected any of his tenants, most of whom were Catholics. That fact alone should have endeared him to his tenants. He had a substantial number of tenants whom he paid with money, another unusual occurrence. He had endowed a school for the tenants' sons, while his wife had endowed a second school, this one for daughters. He had built a great mansion with lovely grounds, hiring locals for the work who were described as "miserable & semi-barbarians, almost strangers to civilization." Rumors circulated that the trigger for the shooting had little to do with his relations with his tenants, but instead resulted from stern actions as a magistrate, especially toward any suspected Ribbonmen who appeared before him.

George was furious at the shooting of this good man, his friend, and searched for explanations and people to blame. The first villain George deemed culpable was the government. For years officials had done nothing to curb violence in a widespread area. It had been a "slaughter-house for banded assassins" yet the government had taken no actions to crush this "viperous brood." "Are THE MEN of a doomed community to be left at the mercy of the dagger, the bludgeon, or the bullet? Are they, while they stand to their post of duty, to society and state, to feel night and day, that they are marked for extermination, and that their hour may be close at hand?"

The next villain was the Tenant League agitation. In George's eyes, they had supplied the spark that set off the rash of agrarian murders. They had never expressed the least regret at the result of their actions, no support for the dead landlords or their families. Despite the carnage, the League continued to plan new meetings, a major one to take place soon in Belfast.

As the facts connected to the attack became known, George reported them to his readers. Police had begun to make good progress in their attempts to locate the attackers. They had found a sort of nest where the men had waited for Chambre to approach. There were remnants of oaten bread and carrots at the site. Also, the police found a blunderbuss, which was loaded but not fired.

George sought out any information on the condition of Chambre. The first medical update that George provided for his readers was indeed ominous. Chambre had lost the sight in one eye. Even more grim, his doctors again reported there was little hope that he would survive his wounds.

In the next edition of the *Telegraph*, George updated the situation. Chambre was still suffering from delirium. However, doctors had removed another pellet that had entered his mouth, knocking out two teeth and then lodging in his palate. The wound behind his eye had become infected, and since the site of the infection was near the base of the brain, doctors feared that the infection would soon travel into his brain. Several days after the shooting, they could see no improvement.

But just two days later, George reported better news. Chambre had an improved night, his infection was decreasing, his delirium lessoning as well. Perhaps, Chambre would survive the attack after all.

There was news on the investigation as well. The suspect, now identified as Francis Berry, had been delivered a meal with some butter, wrapped in newspaper. This newspaper fragment, along with a fragment of paper that had wrapped the pellets found in the blunderbuss at the scene of the shooting, matched a newspaper found in the cottage of the suspect. He had also been identified by a Newry merchant who had sold him the percussion caps. So a strong case seemed to promise a conviction of the assailant.

George broadened his list of entities that had contributed to the rising danger to resident landlords, strongly attacking a rival newspaper, the *Banner of Ulster*, a Presbyterian newspaper that supported the Tenant Rights League. The editor of the paper had expressed sympathy for Chambre, but George found this expression devoid of sincerity. George also claimed that the League meeting in Belfast was a total failure. There might have been a fair-sized crowd on hand, but there was certainly no person of importance among them. Then George issued his own warning. If the League wasn't careful, they would find themselves wearing a "hempen halter." (hangman's noose)

Mr. Chambre continued to improve. Soon George was able to report that the pellet behind his eye was now located harmlessly behind his ear. At this point, Chambre began to improve quickly. First, he was able to sit in his parlor. Then he was able to walk around the grounds. By the second week in February, his supporters in Meigh saluted his recovery by lighting barrels on fire. Mrs.

Chambre invited them to Hawthorn Hill for tea. The accused shooter, Francis Berry, remained locked in gaol awaiting trial in the next Assizes.

§

For James, February began with the sad news that the wife of his good friend had become very ill. James recorded her death. "Mrs. James Todd died about half past <u>two</u> oclock <u>this</u> morning. She was an active, kind woman." James spent much of the day with his friend, helping where he could. Son John went to Newry to buy the casket and make the necessary arrangements. The next day, James and Sarah spent much of the day with the Todds greeting visitors at the wake. The following day, they participated in the funeral and burial.

But James could not linger in his grief. There was much work to do that couldn't wait. At the dinner for new landlord Hill Irvine in the fall of 1849, James had discussed the importance of improving the heavy, wet Irish soil by installing proper drainage. Before planting this year, James had his laborers working to improve drainage on another field. This was backbreaking work requiring laborers to shovel the heavy soil aside to create trenches across the fields. These channels drained toward the ditches at the edges of the fields in which hedges were planted. When a trench was completed, workers filled it with stones, and covered the stones with soil. This system allowed planting in fields that would otherwise have been too wet. This year's ditching took most of February to complete. Then James was ready to start planting, and again, he planted several fields with potatoes. despite the continuing blight. James didn't record the reason for such a risky undertaking. Perhaps he hoped that the blight had finally run its course. If his crop survived, his work would return a good profit.

§

George continued his attacks of the Tenant Rights League in articles and leaders. He was delighted to report that his flow of anti-League articles and leaders had attracted the attention of League supporters. He was pleased to be personally attacked by the hated League, writing that he was delighted to be "enjoying the sweet and savory abuse of the whole tribe of Leaguers. We are truly proud of this distinction."

The landlord and tenant dispute soon rose to a higher level with the prospect of a new by-election where this was sure to be a major issue. One of the current MPs for County Down resigned. A new candidate, William Sharman Crawford, immediately stepped forward to stand for the seat. Crawford was already a sitting MP from an English constituency and a leader in the Tenant Rights League. He had introduced a bill in Parliament designed to solve some of the major problems between landlords and tenants. As a large property owner in County Down, the issue was one with which he had considerable personal experience and expertise.

Crawford's support of the League wasn't the only reason that George would deploy his writing skills and newspaper in an intense effort to ensure that Crawford would lose. Crawford supported democracy. George saw this movement as a threat to the monarchy, which must be vigorously fought. After all, Crawford believed in such radical ideas as voting by ballot, household voting eligibility, and yearly elections to Parliament. Furthermore, he opposed government support of religion, even the Regium Donum, which provided stipends to Presbyterian ministers. George found it strange that Crawford would find any support among the Presbyterian ministers who were so active in the League.

Soon there were several potential candidates, most of whom George really liked. But he urged them to withdraw from the race to concentrate support for David Ker to make defeat of Crawford less complicated and more certain.

While the Down election would soon take place, the general election awaited the adjournment of Parliament. This election was mandated by law as parliamentary terms expired after six years. The last general election had taken place in 1846 when the Whigs had taken power from the Conservatives. Though no date had been established for the election, early preparations were already underway across Ireland including Newry.

George was a strong supporter of the current MP for Newry, Edward Hallewell, who was an Englishman, and a proper Conservative. He had been elected unopposed the previous year in a special election. This time there was a new candidate running against the incumbent, William Kirk. Kirk was a Presbyterian businessman. Presbyterians weren't elected to Parliament from Ireland. Non-Catholic seats were always held by members of the Church of Ireland. George admitted that Kirk was a fine person and a good businessman, but he strongly suggested to his readers that Kirk was supported for election by unsavory people.

In his address to voters, Kirk promised them that he supported ending hostilities between landlords and tenants. He also favored the National School Board position supporting integrated schools. These statements weren't persuasive to George. So as May began, George turned his attention away from the League to focus on this Presbyterian challenge to the Church of Ireland.

First George reviewed the positions of Hallewell and Kirk. They seemed very much the same to him at first glance. So what could be the reason for Kirk to run at all? George concluded that it had to be for party reasons. Kirk had to be a Whig supporter. And he must have been influenced to run by the Presbyterian ministers who had come to Newry to support tenant rights.

In the next edition of the paper, George was even more direct in his opposition, claiming that he had "No misgivings, not withstanding the vaporings indulged in on the part of the factious organizations opposing the Honourable Gentlemen's reelection." George found no reason to assume that Kirk would represent Newry's interests better than Hallewell. In fact, Kirk had always been of a liberal bent. He would therefore be in opposition to the expected Conservative government, and therefore of little use to the people of Newry.

Then George issued a challenge to Mr. Kirk. To satisfy George, Kirk must answer two important questions. What did Kirk think of the recently passed Ecclesiastical Titles bill? Next, what was Kirk's opinion on the Maynooth grant? This was a donation voted yearly by Parliament to support Maynooth College where many priests were educated. This money was meant to balance in a small way the donations that the British government gave the Presbyterian church. George was well aware that any answer that Kirk might give would risk splitting his Catholic and Presbyterian supporters. Despite George's continued pushing, Mr. Kirk remained wisely silent.

George also reported on the progress of Kirk's canvas of local voters. He was assisted by his election manager Robert Ross Todd and supporter Hill Irvine. Todd was John's brother-in-law through his marriage to John's sister Elizabeth. Hill Irvine owned both the Dromalane Mills in Newry and Donaghmore estate where James Harshaw farmed. These were hardly "unsavory" people. With leaders of this caliber, George had to report that the Kirk canvass had gone well. He also had support from Bishop Blake who headed the local Catholic diocese. So presumably the 180 electors who had pledged themselves to support Kirk were a blend of Presbyterian and Catholic, a blend that George greatly feared.

In the next edition of the *Telegraph*, George pounded on another sharp distinction between the two candidates. Hallewell had stated his positions clearly when he ran for Newry's seat in Parliament the year before. George proclaimed himself unable to decipher Kirk's positions and repeated his challenge to answer the two questions on the Ecclesiastical Titles bill and Maynooth Grant. Two other newspapers, the *Northern Whig* and the *Banner of Ulster* had studied the results of the Kirk canvass and predicted that Kirk would win by a large margin. They pointed out that Hallewell had gone back to England after completing his canvass, a clear sign to them that he didn't think he would win. That was an interpretation that George angrily rejected.

§

While Ireland waited for Parliament to dissolve, James kept busy with his farm work and support of the local dispensary, though he had other responsibilities as well. As time neared for Communion Sunday at church, James ensured this solemn event would be conducted efficiently. Four tables were set up in the church aisles, covered with their best linen and the appropriate vessels for the service. James was pleased that 355 members attended this quarterly celebration.

The weather wasn't particularly good in May. In fact, on one day there was a fall of hail, but work continued. One day, everyone at Ringbane was up before dawn, filling carts with flax that son John would drive to the flax market in Tandragee. Preparations for "making mud," the first step in harvesting turf to heat cottages for the winter, began in the bog in Loughorne which John had previously owned. Though most animals were born in March, there were still some animals giving birth to watch over and some born in previous years to be sold as well.

James also supervised some building upgrades. He sent workers Davy Boyd and Joe Duff to repair Jo Dell's old cottage at Loughorne. They were adding windows, so it could be occupied by Tommy Rainey. Work continued for several days. There was a special assignment for another laborer, John Wright, a worker that James had a nicknamed "nobleman," who was set to work thatching the upper house at Ringbane. This was an extension to Ringbane house that was used as a barn, as well as a place for large dances and religious services.

On May 19th, James walked through the rain to another meeting of the new Donaghmore District Dispensary Committee necessitated by the new dispensary legislation. At this meeting, the committee read the official reappointment of Dr. Saunderson as the Donaghmore doctor. The other important item of business was acquiring a building to house the new dispensary. One building, just north of the Four Mile House, seemed to fit their needs nicely. It could be rented for £10 a year. Besides having space to treat patients, there was a room large enough for the dispensary committee meetings. This space was made available by David Woods, owner of the Four Mile House.

James attended another meeting of the dispensary committee later in May. This time at issue were charges brought against Dr. Saunderson for his treatment of "Bedy" O'Hare during her recent labor. Bridget, her baptismal name, subsequently died. Bridget O'Hare was the wife of a local cottier. When Bridget went into labor, she appealed to one of the local dispensary officials, perhaps James, for a ticket that would allow her to see Dr. Saunderson.

However, when Bridget appeared at the Dispensary and presented her ticket, Dr. Saunderson refused to honor it. After considerable delay, another doctor was found. But by that time, help was of no use. Bridget gave birth to a stillborn child and soon died herself.

The committee held a lengthy discussion. They suggested that midwives might be used to provide delivery help if the doctor was unavailable. Was this acceptable under the new legislation? Some members of the committee were charged with finding the answer and reporting back to the full committee.

James began the month of June with a trip to Dublin to resolve financial issues involving his guardianship of the two young children of the former owner of Donaghmore Estates. He started out at 6 a.m. For the first time, he made his way to the new railroad station that had recently opened at Goragh Woods located on the road between Newry and Poyntzpass. He could now catch the train between Belfast and Dublin in Newry, instead of making the longer trip to Dundalk. By half noon, he was in Dublin.

There he met a Mr. Cooper who went with him to the Four-Courts where he signed two books and had five different officials sign to indicate his right to £14-11-7. This represented 2½ years interest on bonds that were due to James as guardian for the minor children James and Ralph Vaughan.

James took the mail train out of Dublin after 7 p.m. and headed home to Donaghmore. He arrived in Dundalk around 10 p.m., and then traveled on to

Newry with Mr. and Mrs. Hill Irvine. It was midnight when they arrived in Newry after a long and tiring day. But he still faced a long, dark walk home to Ringbane, finally arriving around 2 a.m.

The money he received was kept by Mr. Cooper. James also paid him £1-17-0 for his legal fees and the cost of the trip to Dublin. James itemized his expenses: cost of his seat from Newry to Dublin, 9s 6d, breakfast 1s 6d, dinner 1s 9d, seat on the mail train 8s 0, trip from Dundalk to Newry 2s 6d, for a total cost of £1-3-2.

§

While the general election continued to await the dissolution of Parliament, George kept a keen eye on the County Down election that would take place before the general voting. His opposition to the candidacy of Crawford and hopes for his defeat remained an imperative during the wait. His preferred candidate was David Ker. George was happy to report in early June that Ker's canvass was well underway in the area. Crawford on the other hand, had returned to England and seemed to have no interest in working for his election. James's son John was one of the local volunteers in Donaghmore who was supporting Ker in his area canvass.

George also noted that the Dublin papers were less enthusiastic in their support of the League now that its rallies and potential violence were inching closer to Dublin. This news offered George a good chance to attack the League again. He accused members of "betraying the ignorant and credulous, fleecing their dupes" while working for their own goals "at the expense of sore and lasting damage to many a tenant-farmer."

A couple of papers later, George reported on a Tenant League meeting in nearby Kilkeel. He was happy to note that there were no important Presbyterians present, and no notable Catholics either. Only Crawford was there to speak for the League. In George's eyes, Crawford and his supporters were separating tenants from their benevolent landlords, a division that George found very dangerous. After all, who had tenant interests more at heart than landlords?

This was a relatively bland account of the Kilkeel meeting from George. But he corrected that impression soon enough. In a leader on June 8th, George went on a full rant against the Tenant League. He called them "the latest edition of the Young Ireland cabal."

Some of the news outlets supportive of the League had renewed their personal attacks on George for his opposition to their cause. George had a reply to this latest attack. "We are determined to make this journal a sledge-hammer for the annihilation of all League hypocrisy and deception." He concluded with a threat. "To scourge them everywhere and on all occasions, we have firmly resolved."

§

When George had first begun to notice William Kirk as a candidate, he didn't see him as a serious threat to his preferred candidate. George felt free to offer a positive assessment of the man. But as time passed, the Kirk candidacy seemed to be a growing threat to Hallewell. Positive comments ceased.

The first evidence for this shift occurred in an article that recounted testimony that Kirk had previously given before the Crime and Punishment Commission. In his testimony, Kirk had said that he thought the Ribbonmen had evolved over the past twenty years from their founding as an organization designed to oppose the Orange Order to one more committed to protecting tenants who faced seizures or ejectments when they were behind in their rents. This perspective on the Ribbonmen was disturbing to George. He wasn't much reassured when Kirk said he thought that the Ribbon practice of sending laborers from one area to another to attack landlords, who hadn't wronged them personally, was wrong. This was a man that George would keep a watchful eye on.

Hallewell held his constituent meeting first in mid-June in the meeting room of the Savings Bank. He announced that he had supported the Ecclesiastical Titles bill and the recent vote on the Maynooth Grant, the very issues on which George pressed Mr. Kirk for an answer. Of great local interest, Hallewell opposed requiring local farmers to pay for the loans given by the British government for the strongly opposed construction of the Irish workhouses. This loan along with interest would worry Irish ratepayers for many years. Hallewell took credit for at least getting these interest payments reduced from 5s 4d% to 4%. This was small comfort to financially strapped farmers.

On the issue of tenant rights, Hallewell stated that he thought that farmers should be paid for all their work and improvements made to the land they leased. He did admit that this hadn't always been the practice of landlords. His solution was to have an impartial jury decide what was fair compensation. In an effort to attract more Presbyterian voters, he pledged to continue to support the Regium Donum. He warned voters that he didn't think Kirk did. When he asked for a show of support, everyone attending the meeting pledged to support Mr. Hallewell on election day.

The *Banner of Ulster* claimed that Hallewell didn't support the issues of interest to Presbyterians. George responded with an angry leader in the next edition of his paper. He used Hallewell's support of Regium Donum as proof that Hallewell had demonstrated his support for Presbyterians. George wasn't at all convinced that Kirk did. And since the column was about Kirk, George repeated his demand that Kirk inform voters what party he could support and respond to his two questions.

Less than a week after Hallewell met his supporters, Kirk had a meeting in the Savings Bank meeting room as well. Among his supporters there were Hill and William Irvine, and Robert Ross Todd. Kirk wasn't a party man, so felt he might be able to find common ground with members of both parties. He had been urged by many local people to stand for the seat, even though he didn't live in Newry, but in Keady, a town south of Armagh City. He was a strong supporter of free trade, believing that it had been a big benefit to the businessmen and shippers of Newry. Trade barriers across Europe were also beginning to fall as other countries saw the benefits of free trade.

Opposition to free trade had been fierce locally. But Kirk felt that the dire warnings of the opposition hadn't actually come true. Wages hadn't fallen, People weren't starving, and gold wasn't flowing out of the country. For Newry, free trade, and repealing the Corn Laws, had been a great benefit.

His view of tenant rights was much stronger than Hallewell's position. He believed that farmers were entitled to the value of everything on their land, buildings, ditches etc. Furthermore, they were the men who had paid for all the infrastructure, not the landlords. So they were entitled to recoup the costs laid out for those improvements as well. The value of this debt could be determined at each November Assizes.

Kirk was a strong supporter of the National Board's view of education. He saw no reason that religious education should be barred from the National Schools, referencing schools that had instituted Bible readings and prayer twice a day in their schools without any problem.

Following this Kirk meeting, George had a new issue to upset him. Denis Brady, a prominent local Catholic businessman, had appeared at the Kirk meeting. This was another sign of the continuing alliance between Presbyterians and Catholics that George so feared. He claimed that everyone going to Parliament must be a member of a religion that supported the Reformation and the results of the invasion of Ireland by William of Orange in 1689. Furthermore, George argued that Kirk belonged with a radical group with a radically different point of view. "It is the natural instinct of a tribe of vulgar, half-educated, self-conceited Radicals to deal in wholesale slander against the party the herd bitterly Hates."

While the election waited in limbo for Parliament to act, the Tenant Rights League continued to hold meetings. At the end of June, the Tenant Rights agitation came to Donaghmore. The organizers had offered to pay £5 to rent a field, but no one came forward to accept the offer. So a platform was erected in the center of the intersection at McGaffin's Corners. Those who attended were largely either laborers or "drifters" from out of town. None of the local farmers or ministers were there. To cap off the event, the stage collapsed sending the people on it tumbling down the slope in a most undignified way. James did not mention the event in his journal.

The election drama was interrupted by an unusual natural one. James described it on June 13th this way. "The day was heavy with occasionally cloud & sunshine with some element fire and like thunder." "About <u>six</u> there was a weting shower, and clouds continued with flashes of fire, and thunder in the southwest which continued at a distance until about one." Early in the next morning, the storm worsened. "A terrific storm burst overhead which alarmed this part of the country."

This was such a significant storm that George included a write-up on the event in his paper. There was heavy rain along with lightning and thunder all night, closely matching the report that James had written. George concurred with James that it was the worst storm in many years. A man named Patrick Mooney from Milltown was on his way home from Newry in a mule cart when he was struck by lightning. He was struck in the foot; the lightening apparently being attracted by the nails in his boot. He lost all feeling in his foot and his mule was killed, leaving Moony to limp a half mile to reach his cabin.

§

As July entered the second week, election dates were being set in surrounding areas, but there was no word on when the Newry election would take place. But George was confident that he knew what the outcome would be. That didn't keep him from continuing his attacks on the publications put out by the Kirk campaign. He felt that they proved that local Presbyterians were ashamed of their heritage. George claimed that there were ninety-two local Presbyterians entitled to vote. Of those, only thirteen were pledged to Kirk. Most of his support came from Catholic voters.

Finally, Newry election officials were notified that the election would be held on July 14th. The day before the Newry election, the trial of Francis Berry for shooting Chambre took place at the Armagh Assizes with Baron Green presiding. The lead prosecutor was Thomas Staples; the defense was led by Mr. Joy. A jury was selected with relative ease, the Crown using seven of their challenges, the defense twenty.

The defendant was neatly dressed in a tweed jacket, and dark pants. He was twenty-seven years old, of medium height. And he was illiterate. Much of the testimony that followed had been presented at the inquest. But this time, Chambre could testify in person. He said he knew Francis Berry and had seized his goods the previous fall for non-payment of rent. He went on to describe the shooting and the scene where it took place. But he remembered nothing of what had happened from the moment he collapsed for three days. On cross-examination, he said that Berry leased about five acres of land, which he had held for a long time. His father was dead, and he lived with his widowed mother and some sisters, having no brothers. Meredith's brother confirmed the testimony that he had given previously.

The family butler David Cole also testified for the first time. He had started an immediate pursuit of the shooters. He jumped over the wall, gun in hand, but saw no one. He did know Francis Berry and had seen him hanging about a few days earlier when Chambre was hunting on the bog. Various policemen testified to finding the tracks that matched one of the boots taken from the accused. They had quickly secured the scene of the crime to ensure its integrity. The prosecutors seemed to be building a strong case against the accused. They linked the percussion caps found in a newspaper at the scene of the shooting to a newspaper that came from Berry's house.

But there was stunning new testimony as well, provided by another new witness at this trial, George Scott who was a businessman in Newry. He testified that he had sold the caps to Berry, whom he identified. Berry had come into his shop with a male companion a few days before the shooting, seeking to purchase some small shot. The two men had to wait for some minutes before the clerk who handled that product arrived. After the clerk weighed out the pellets, Berry signed the sales book, removing any doubt as to identification. Scott produced the book in court for the jury to examine. Scott had also been able to pick Berry out in the gaol yard, though his face was swollen as though he was trying to hide his identity. With this dramatic testimony, the prosecution rested its case.

Joy mounted a long defense. He maintained that there was no evidence that Berry was part of the Ribbon conspiracy or had religious motives. There was no evidence that he actually shot the gun at Chambre. They couldn't convict on mere suspicion. But the jury saw the evidence differently. It took them about twenty-three minutes to return with a guilty verdict, but also with a recommendation for mercy, since Chambre hadn't died.

The judge wasn't interested in the recommendation of mercy from the jury. He immediately warned Berry to prepare to meet his maker. Then he donned the black hood and ordered Berry to be executed on August 7th.

Berry was contemplating his fate in a dark prison cell the next morning, when the voters of Newry gathered to elect their new Member of Parliament. The Seneschal conducted the meeting, held as usual in the Court House. He faced a crowd of agitated voters. Hallewell's supporters were on one side of the center aisle, Kirk's on the other. Each man would be nominated and seconded, and then get a chance to speak to his supporters. Then a voice vote would be taken, and the Seneschal would declare the winner. The loser could appeal by requesting a poll vote.

The meeting was stormy from the beginning. Hallewell was nominated first by W. N. Thompson. He began by stating that Ireland was fortunate to have religious liberty. The room immediately erupted in loud shouts and catcalls. Nothing Thompson could say then could be heard above the din. It took one of Kirk's supporters to quell the noise. He warned his fellow Kirk supporters that if they wished to be heard, they would have to allow the other side to be heard. The noise decreased enough for Thompson to finish his remarks.

Thompson claimed that Ireland had such religious liberty only because it was a Protestant nation. He accused Kirk's supporters of making this election a matter of religion. That alone should disqualify Kirk's candidacy.

Denis Maguire, a prominent Catholic businessman, nominated Kirk. He claimed that Ireland had been slow to advance because of religious antagonism. Kirk supported the Maynooth grant and would continue to do so long as both Catholics and Presbyterians had to support the Established Church. When that requirement ended, there would be no need for the Maynooth grant. On the subject of education, he favored a mixed education. If that should happen in Ireland, and continued for a generation, many of the religious problems of Ireland would improve. He would also continue to favor free trade, as he saw that would be of great benefit for the people and businesses of Newry.

Hallewell began his acceptance speech by reaffirming that he and his twelve children lived in England, and that he hadn't really wanted to run in a contested election. But because of the new changes in law, he felt the election would be fair. He had a different point of view on free trade than Kirk. He was supportive of some moves toward free trade like the repeal of the Corn Laws. But if all the tariffs and quotas were eliminated, there would be a loss of revenue to England, which would have to be regained through other taxes.

His position on the National Board and education was simple. There were some subjects that could be taught in a secular way, like art, science and literature. But religion had to be taught through the use of the Protestant Bible. It should be a textbook in all schools. He did support tenant rights, thought that the value added to farms should be applied both retroactively and into the future. However, he didn't believe Crawford's tenant rights legislation would solve outstanding issues.

The speech that Kirk gave proceeded in a very different way. Instead of explaining his policy views, he began by discussing some contradictions between dates on a letter that he had written to Lord Downshire, which George had made the subject of some dispute. At that point, George interrupted and began a dialogue with Kirk. This caused so much additional uproar that little that Kirk said could be heard by anyone in the courtroom. In the chaos, there could be no meeting of the minds.

Then the Seneschal announced that the vote would be called. Great shouting erupted from all corners of the room. But the Seneschal declared that Kirk had gotten the most shouted votes. Hallewell supporters immediately requested an official poll. This was agreed to, and the date was set for two days later.

George predicted that Saturday would be a great day for "us and our great cause." He praised Kirk for being a good man but charged him with being a terrible candidate. He and his supporters had ignored the good men who were landlords and neglected to consider their needs. Voting on Saturday would begin at 8 a.m. and end at 5 p.m. George urged the Hallewell voters to vote early and administer a great defeat to the "unholy alliance."

Election day began with rain, but by the time the voting began, the weather had turned fair. James wasn't able to vote in this election, so he and his family enjoyed an outing together. James left Ringbane about 7 a.m. when son Andrew, nicknamed "Chiefton," drove him and daughter Mary to Newry where they caught the train to Warrenpoint. There they joined Mary's husband, Alex Douglas, Sarah Anne, Weechile as James referred to her, Samuel, nicknamed "Absalom," and his wife for breakfast. The family spent the day together in Warrenpoint. When they headed home around 6 p.m., Sarah ended her visit to Warrenpoint and came home with her family.

They would have arrived in Newry about the time that election results were announced. Supporters of both candidates gathered again in the Court House to hear the Seneschal announce the official count. Kirk had 233 votes, Hallewell had 204, giving Kirk a 39-vote win.

While George was greatly disappointed at the results, he was proud that his candidate had waged an honorable campaign, something that Kirk and his evil supporters couldn't claim. Despite the Conservative failure in Newry, party candidates were doing well around the country.

Swallowing his great disappointment, George still had high hopes that the County Down election would have results more to his liking. There, three candidates were competing for the two allotted seats. The much-despised Crawford was competing against Sir Edwin Hill, and David Ker. George greatly hoped for an ignominious Crawford loss. James and his son John were working hard to ensure that at least George could celebrate a Ker victory.

§

The County Down election took place two days later. On Sunday, July 21st James's son John was busy making arrangements to support Ker over the two days of voting. While James was in church, John was hiring jaunting cars to carry voters into Newry.

Election day dawned sunny and pleasant. James was up by 5 a.m. preparing to travel to the Ker Committee rooms in Newry. John drove him that far and then took the train to Warrenpoint to get Samuel who had remained there after the family visit. Robert Wilson, another strong Ker supporter, was already in the committee rooms when James arrived. All was going smoothly in Ker headquarters until around 8 a.m. when a mob that James described as a "riotous party" arrived. They were quickly "checqued by the military."

George provided additional information about the riotous event that James had described. Approximately fifteen hundred men from the area around Hilltown had gathered together under the leadership of several Catholic priests. They attempted to interfere with voters in Rathfriland before marching on Newry.

A warning about the mob's activities reached Captain Warburton before their arrival in Newry. He alerted the Colonel commanding the 71st Lancers. When the mob, shouting loudly for Crawford entered Newry, the Lancers were on station on one side of the Rathfriland Road, the Highlanders on the other. Local constabulary were lined across the road to prevent the mob from nearing the Corry monument and the polling booths that were on the main road in Newry just beyond.

With the mob surrounded by Newry forces, they could progress no further. Their arsenal of bludgeons, knives and guns were quickly seized by the British troops. Then Magistrate Warburton shouted a warning that anyone arrested and convicted for their unlawful assembly would be subject to a penalty of transportation for seven years. This was a sufficient threat to the Crawford supporters to turn them back toward Hilltown.

Both James and Mr. Wilson voted for Hill and Ker. When the work in the committee rooms was over for the day. James reported that there was a happy celebration during which James drank some beer. He reported afterwards that "he felt poorly."

The next day James was back at work on the election. He met early with several of his neighbors and arranged to transport them to Newry to vote. Late in the day, he proudly announced the results. "The great County Down election terminated this day at 4 o'clock. The returns to the High Sheriff in Downpatrick from all the booths were as follows: Hill 4676, Ker 4138, and Crawford 3165 leaving the two Conservatives elected, with a majority for Hill of 1511, and Ker 973. The official returns announced by the High Sheriff were slightly different, but the results were the same. Lord E. Hill – 5654, Mr. Ker 4117. Both men returned."

§

George was so pleased with the defeat of Crawford that he quickly moved on from the election defeat in Newry. But there was one unusual loose end he pursued, the story that a Presbyterian elector had violated his pledge to support Hallewell. Hallewell supporters claimed that a local Presbyterian elder had promised to vote for him, and instead voted for Kirk. His name was Henry Hawkins, the owner of a small business in Newry. In his letter, which George published, Hawkins claimed that he had never told Hallewell he would support him. When the election process began, Hallewell was the only candidate. So when Hallewell did his canvass, Hawkins told him that he leaned in his direction, nothing more positive than that. Then when Kirk became a candidate, he leaned to a fellow Presbyterian. He maintained that support despite pressure from Hallewell's supporters.

George claimed in response that he had gotten his information from a good source. A few days later, there was another letter, possibly from George's "good source." One of Hallewell's staunchest supporters, Samuel Fraser, rebutted Hawkins's statements. He challenged Hawkins to come forth with proof of his claim to refute his contrary evidence. Then he went on to charge Hawkins with being a poorly educated man who was incapable of writing the letter that had appeared in the *Telegraph*. Hawkins made no response. So the issue soon faded from the news. After all, Mr. Hawkin's vote made no difference to either candidate.

With the election results published and digested by winners and losers alike, local residents focused their attention on the upcoming execution of Francis Berry, a rare event in the area. Francis was to be hanged on August 7th at the Armagh gaol. These events were public spectacles and followed a well-established formula. A Roman Catholic priest who was charged with ensuring that Francis was prepared to die accompanied him on the day of his execution. Francis had a last visit from his distraught mother and his sisters. He had a last meal, though Francis was unwilling to eat much of it.

In the early afternoon, he was required to change into prison clothes, was bound, and taken outside to the scaffold. Francis appeared to be quite stoic and at peace, claiming to the end that he was innocent. There was a sizeable crowd on hand for the execution, but his mother wasn't one of them. Officials feared that she would disrupt the decorum of the event. So they managed to lock her into the superintendent's office until after the hangman had executed her only son.

The hangman was hooded to ensure that he couldn't be identified. Francis walked to the hangman who placed a hood over his head, and then the noose. People stretched to get a good view of the drop to death about to take place. The hangman opened the trapdoor, and Francis fell into the void, dying instantly. He remained motionless, dangling at the end of the rope for almost an hour. Then his stiffening body was cut down and turned over to his family for the sad funeral procession. Only a month had passed between his sentencing and his execution. In Ireland in 1852, justice was swift.

Chapter 4

Reunions

1852 – 1854

On August 3, 1852, James received a newspaper from New York City. This wasn't an unusual occurrence, as Willy often sent along newspapers from New York City to keep his family informed about his new life in America. But there was something distinctly unusual about this particular paper. James noticed that it wasn't addressed to him or some other member of the family. It was addressed to Willy himself. James rustled through the pages and found an announcement of intense interest: Willy had sailed for Ireland. This was great news that he was anxious to share with the family.

That same day, George provided some distressing local news. He mentioned that there was some blight damage appearing already in the potato crop in the area. This could be financially disastrous for yet another year, since James had risked planting a number of fields with that crop. George also reported that tar barrels had been blazing in the night on the hills of Loughorne and Ringbane to celebrate the election victories of Hill and Ker.

James was up about 6 a.m. to make the most of a fine summer day. After breakfast, he walked up the lane to the Brirey Brae. He soon heard thumping footsteps behind him as though someone were rushing to overtake him. James turned to see who was chasing him. And there was Willy. Father and son hurried to close the remaining distance. The reunion hug brought James such great joy that he had difficulty describing his feelings in words. He simply wrote that he "saluted" his son. Together they retraced James's steps to take Willy home to Ringbane.

A whirlwind of visiting began. James left Sarah making tea for Willy and walked up the Ardkeragh Road to share the grand news with daughter Mary Douglas. Soon Mary arrived to greet her younger brother. James Martin came down the hill from Loughorne to see his cousin. It was a grand reunion gathering.

There could be no great lingering over such wonderful moments. James had the all-important flax harvest to attend to, work that couldn't be delayed. Flax had to be cut at the right time, bundled and put into the flax ponds to rot the tough outer covering. Not even a visiting son could interfere, as too much income depended on a successful harvest. With his father back at work, Willy set about visiting old friends and favorite places.

On his first Sunday since his return, Willy joined the family at services in the meetinghouse. Rev. Patrick White preached the sermon and returned with the family for a dinner celebration. Also present were Willy's sisters Jane and Mary, Mary's husband Alexander Douglas, James Martin, John's brother, and several other close friends.

The flax harvest continued to require a lot of James's time, but on August 19th, he had important business in Newry. He was happy to have Willy accompany him on this errand. After James had concluded his business, they stopped to visit Willy's Martin cousin Elizabeth Todd for dinner. They arrived home just before dark.

Willy made a trip to Kilbroney to visit more of his Martin cousins, Robert and David. He had to make the most of the limited time he had in Ireland, as he intended to return soon again to America. So every day was precious on one hand and sad on the other as each new day brought everyone closer to the day when the family would be separated again.

That day occurred in early September. James was still occupied with farm work. But he recorded Willy's departure in his journal. "Willy left about ten for Belfast, Glascow, and Newyork." He was accompanied by his cousin, James Martin, and his brothers, Robert Hugh, Andrew, and Samuel. The party stopped along the way to visit the graves in the churchyard. It must have occurred to Willy that if he returned again to Ireland, he might find his parents buried there as well.

The party enjoyed a few final minutes with sister Jane and her husband Archy Marshall. They left them in the Fourtowns around 2 p.m. for nearby Poyntzpass to catch the train to Belfast. Willy left Belfast on the steamer to Glasgow at 7 p.m. Ireland soon faded from view in the growing dusk. As bittersweet as this moment was in one way, he knew that there were happy times ahead for him in America. Willy had found love and intended to marry very soon.

There were still some chores remaining to divert James from his sad thoughts. James completed the harvest three days after Willy left. According to Irish tradition, each harvest was celebrated by "cutting the churn." One last sheath had been left for one of the workers to cut with his scythe to symbolize that the harvest was complete. Following that, the landlord fed all the workers and their families who had brought the harvest to a successful conclusion. As James described this ceremony, "John played the fiddle and the sheerers danced." Only the potatoes remained to be dug. And despite early fears, they came from the ground without a sign of the blight.

A month after Willy departed, James got word that he had arrived safely in New York after a trip of twelve days and some hours. Two days later, James, or rather his son John, had another very much appreciated letter, this one from John Martin. He also enclosed a letter for Willy, which would now need to be redirected to America.

§

In mid-October, James mentioned a minor event that George soon covered extensively. "John [Harshaw] in Newry at the Rainey trial before the Magistrates." Tommy Rainey had worked for him in Loughorne, but sometimes crossed Ringbane Road to do some work for James as well. The issue wasn't resolved at this first meeting, as John returned a week later to deal with Tommy's issue yet again.

With this second entry, the issue of the Raineys disappeared from James's journal. But the saga of Tommy Rainey would continue for months. It was a case that George followed closely. His articles provided a clear explanation for John's two trips to Newry. Tommy's case was heard on Oct. 21st. He was charged with having an unlicensed gun in a proclaimed district. Apparently, Tommy possessed a gun that wasn't even legal. Tommy's defense was that he was just repairing the gun for his brother-in-law. This defense didn't seem convincing to the Magistrates, partly because Tommy also had a powder horn and ammunition in his possession. John Harshaw testified about Tommy's good character. He also stated that he hadn't known that Loughorne was in a proclaimed area either. Despite John's positive testimony, Tommy was found guilty and sentenced to four days in jail.

The police had discovered the illegal gun as a result of a search of Tommy's cottage following an earlier confrontation with the law. Tommy and his brother William had gone to Newry to visit Irvine's Pub on Water Street for a few drinks According to testimony at the trial that followed, both men had been drinking heavily. They were sufficiently drunk that they began to join other Protestant drinkers with loud laughter and the usual Protestant taunts directed at Catholics, "To hell with the Pope," and "No surrender," a motto of the Orange Order.

This tumult attracted a number of local Catholics who were passing by. Some of them lingered outside the pub, waiting for the drunken men to leave. Tommy and William were unaware that there was a dangerous mob growing outside in the dark. A night watchman named Francis Hart was patrolling in the area near 10 p.m. and observed what was going on. He stood beside the crowd and urged them to wait for the shouters to come outside, when they could be dealt with.

Tommy came out first. He was immediately set upon by the crowd and then grabbed by Hart. When William came out, he saw his brother being manhandled and immediately grabbed at Hart in an effort to free his brother. Hart hit William back causing a black eye.

With a riot going on around him, Hart blew his whistle to attract the attention of a nearby watchman, Michael Burns. Burns was quickly able to subdue William and arrest him. The watchmen proceeded to drag the Raineys toward the watch house. They made no effort to disperse the crowd or keep them away from their captives. By the time the procession reached the watch yard, the Raineys had been severely beaten across their backs and legs.

The next morning, Tommy could barely walk. When he was called by the police, the effects of the beating were clearly visible. He had cuts on his nose and on his cheek. The Raineys were such a sorry sight that they were offered the services of a doctor, but declined, saying that they could get help themselves. Having sobered up, they were later sent home, but their legal problems weren't yet over.

Two trials stemming from the pub fight were held at the same Quarter Sessions that heard Tommy's gun charge. William Rainey was charged in the first trial for hitting Hart. Several witnesses testified that Hart had urged the crowd to wait until the Raineys came out, and then they could have at them. The judge said the case was simple and that William should be acquitted. The jury was sent out to deliberate. Disregarding the judge's directions, the jury found William guilty of hitting Hart. But in view of the severe beating that William had suffered, they settled for a fine of 6d. William paid it and was discharged. Tommy went to jail on his gun conviction.

The second issue was a counter-suit by William charging Hart, David O'Hagan and Patrick Toman with assault for the beating the Raineys had endured. In this case, Tommy was a witness. He stated that he had been in the pub about half an hour. When he left the pub to go home to Loughorne, he was attacked by Hart. Both he and his brother were set upon by a vicious mob after they had been taken into custody. He was severely beaten all the way to the watch house. He wasn't sure who had been hitting him, but he was sure that he had had no assistance from the watchmen.

Several of the same witnesses who had testified at William's trial repeated their previous testimony. However, there was additional testimony that seemed very odd. A new witness asserted that he had witnessed the entire episode from a vantage point just across the street and maintained that no one had hit the Raineys. That testimony was verified by Elizabeth McNaughton.

The judge rejected this new testimony, as it conflicted with known facts, instead presenting clear evidence of perjury. This perjury alone represented sufficient proof of guilt "beyond a reasonable doubt" to warrant a conviction. Again the jury rejected the judge's directions. They found O'Hagan and Toman innocent. However, they did convict Hart, who was immediately sentenced to three months in Downpatrick jail.

This wasn't the end of the case. The Town Commissioners who oversaw the night watchmen had to decide whether or not to fire Hart from his job because of his conviction. They met in early November to discuss what to do. Rowan McNaughton stated that Hart was the best watchman in Newry and shouldn't be fired. Two other members, James Henderson, George's brother, and George Scott felt strongly that Hart had participated in a sectarian incident and should be fired. They made a motion to that effect. This motion was amended by McNaughton to state that no decision should be made until Hart had finished serving his sentence. McNaughton's amendment passed by three votes.

McNaughton wasn't yet finished with his support of Hart. At a Commission meeting in the middle of November, McNaughton brought up the issue again. He claimed that the Raineys were running up and down the street shouting their taunts at a growing crowd. Nothing Hart could have done would have prevented the crowd from attacking them. In fact had not Hart taken them into custody, they would certainly have been killed. So Hart was in fact a hero for saving the lives of both Raineys.

Then McNaughton continued with a claim that the jury had voted seven to five to acquit all three men. After the judge sent them back to deliberate again, they came up with a compromise verdict. They acquitted O'Hagan and Thoman and convicted only Hart, thinking that he would get a very light sentence. When they saw how harshly Hart had been treated, the jury members were very upset. To make matters worse, the unjust verdict had left Hart's family destitute.

This case continued to be a problem for the Commissioners into the next year. When Hart's sentence had been served, the issue of whether or not to return him to his job or not flared again. Henderson and Scott tried to offer a motion to terminate his employment, but the presiding officer declined to accept it. Henderson was furious, and offering his resignation, stormed out of the meeting. After another long hearing on the subject during which the Commissioners heard additional testimony as to what a good watchman Hart had always been, he was allowed to return to his job.

§

Long before the Hart situation was resolved, James had another problem to deal with. On November 23rd, Samuel Jardine disappeared. Jardine held the property up the hill next to James's house in Ringbane. On that day, Jardine had taken a load of turnips into Newry to sell. He was seen heading toward Rathfriland Road in Newry late in the day, as though he was heading home. Some hours later his horse and cart were spotted about three miles farther on along the road. When no one came to pick up the horse, his friends were notified and a search for him began.

For several days, no sign of Jardine appeared. So James took some of his workers into Newry to drag the canal and basin for his body. He reported "men all (5) away on sarch for the body of Sam Jordine. – did not get him."

The disappearance of Jardine wasn't the only tragedy to befall the Jardines. Just three days after the great search for Jardine's body, James reported visiting Jardine's wife. He visited daily for several days before announcing that Mrs. Jardine had died. He attended the funeral the next day and arranged with Jonathan Jardine to take custody of all Jardines's possessions until arrangements could be made by the heirs.

Shortly after Sam's disappearance, presumably somewhere into the murky waters of the Newry Canal, another drowning took place. This time the victim was a young man who was seen stumbling drunkenly around Newry streets by one of the night watchmen. As this was happening, a resident appeared and stated that he would see that the young man made it safely home. The watchman released the drunk to the custody of this volunteer. Unfortunately, there would be no "safe home" for this man either. He too fell into the canal and drowned. Having two drownings in short order caught the attention of the Newry Commissioners. They seemed more concerned about the role of the night watch in dealing with drunks than in the danger the canal and basin held for them.

On December 20th, James was working on his farm about 1 p.m. when he was visited by Samuel Jardine of Shinn and a policeman. They reported to James that Jardine's body had been found in the basin about 9 a.m. that morning. James immediately went to the graveyard and put John Kinney and Sam Boyd to work digging a grave. Then James went to Sheepbridge to join the funeral. Sam was buried before 8 p.m.

The body had been in the water so long that quick interment was necessary. The inquest was held after the burial. There was concern that Sam might have been murdered. This stemmed from the fact that his horse was found wandering some three miles along the Rathfriland Road, by a man named Fagan who knew Jardine and recognized his horse. Testimony at the inquest gave great credit to the efforts that James and his friends had taken to find the body, the canal having been dragged below and above the town at James's expense.

The body had been found by a crewman on a lighter anchored in the basin. He reported being alerted by the barking of his dog. When he released the dog, it jumped into the water of basin and swam around the boat. When Smith went around the boat to follow the dog, he saw the dog was resting his nose upon Jardine's head. Eerily, Jardine appeared to be standing upright in the dark water.

Elizabeth Smith testified that she had seen Sam on the evening that he disappeared. At that time, he was headed for Rathfriland Road. He might have had a couple of whiskeys, but he wasn't staggering at all. The medical examiner reported that there was no sign of trauma on the body, and that death seemed to have been caused by drowning.

That same day, the Newry Commissioners met to discuss the problem. They supported establishing new rules for the watch. Any drunk the watchmen encountered should be taken to the watch yard and reported to the superintendent. They should be held there until they were sober, or someone came who would guarantee to get them safely home. There was no discussion of the dangers posed by the canal flowing through the center of town, unlit and unprotected.

§

As 1852 neared an end, John was doing something decidedly un-Irish in Van Diemen's Land. Hunting was a popular sport in Ireland, birds and foxes and other small animals being the favorite targets. John and Mitchel went on a hunt for a decidedly different prey, a kangaroo. According to local tradition, hunts used only a couple dogs. Neither man owned a dog, or had any great interest in hunting, but they had been invited to participate in a hunt by a good local friend, Mr, Reid, who did have two dogs available. One was a type of greyhound, the other a larger kangaroo dog.

For the hunt, they headed west from Bothwell in the direction of the Blue Hills. This was a very densely wooded area, crisscrossed with gullies and fallen trees. This made fast riding impossible and keeping a sense of direction difficult. The dogs kept close, until they suddenly flushed a kangaroo out from behind a fallen log. The dogs were instantly on the trail and out of sight.

The hunters remained on the spot, for the dogs would return to them when they had either killed the fleeing kangaroo or it had escaped them. They could tell as soon as the dogs came into view whether or not the kangaroo had been killed by observing the dogs' behavior. If they had succeeded, they would come bounding back with heads and tails held high. They wouldn't quite reach the hunters but would turn aside to guide them back to where the kangaroo lay dead, his throat cut or back broken.

The first time, the dogs returned panting with heads and tails low and threw themselves at the horses' feet, clear signs of failure. This kangaroo had escaped. So the riders continued the hunt. But soon they flushed another kangaroo and the dogs were off again. This time there was a lot of barking as though the kangaroo was cornered. This triumphant barking was soon succeeded by terrible yelping. The three riders could do nothing but wait. When the dogs came bounding into view, they could see that one had suffered a bad cut from ear to muzzle from the sharp claws of the cornered kangaroo. But tails and heads were held high, clearly telling the hunters that they had taken down their prey.

John and his companions charged forward with the dogs keeping close beside them. Suddenly, they flushed another kangaroo. The older, and now injured dog, took only a few steps and stopped. But Dart, the younger dog, dashed off after the new target. After some minutes of silence, he returned with a look of triumph. Now they had two kangaroos taken, but in different directions. Only the dogs could get them to their prey.

Dart led them off moving confidently in the direction from which he had just come. After some minutes of riding through the daunting terrain, they came to the body of the kangaroo that they had just flushed. They tied the kangaroo body across a saddle. Then Reid directed the other dog to find their first kill. It started off confidently though the hunters weren't at the spot where the first attack was launched. Again they were led straight to the first kill. There they found that this was a mother with young joey still in her pouch. Again they tied the bodies over their saddles, this time heading home.

This had been a good hunt. Despite the increasing scarcity of kangaroos, they had taken three of them. Kangaroo meat tasted rather like rabbit, and the skins made very fine leather once they had been properly cured. So in Van Diemen's Land, such hunts were held not just for the sport of it, but because their prey would be very useful to the settlers in this remote high plateau.

§

About two weeks after the kangaroo hunt, Mitchel took a trip to Hobart. When he returned he wasn't alone. Patrick J. Smyth was with him. Smyth had been a fellow member of the Young Irelanders. When the revolt failed, he escaped to New York City. His sudden appearance so far from New York was a total surprise. In America, he had been active in Irish affairs. He explained to John that the Irish in New York had raised a large amount of money to assist the remaining Young Irelanders to escape from Van Diemen's Land. He told John about Meagher's new life in New York City. He had been warmly welcomed by the Irish community there and was happily living in a hotel on Broadway, a far cry from his former home at Lake Sorrell.

Smyth had been instructed to help O'Brien and Mitchel escape. However, O'Brien had refused to consider the idea when it had been presented to him. So the focus had turned to Mitchel should he wish to make the attempt. John was part of the discussion along with Jennie Mitchel. Though she would have a difficult time moving again, she supported the idea. Since the escape would have to take place from Bothwell, it seemed practical for John to attempt the escape with his friend.

With that much settled, Smyth decided to go to Melbourne to make arrangements for a ship to transport Mitchel and Martin to freedom once they had made the initial escape. In order to preserve their honor, they would have to present themselves at the Bothwell Police station, and there renounce their tickets-of-leave. As soon as they had announced that action to police, they would be subject to arrest. But honor didn't obligate them to wait for the arrest to take place. They were free to try to evade re-arrest and escape.

Days of waiting followed, before Smyth sent coded word that he had hired a ship and arranged a meeting place where John and Mitchel could board the ship and sail off to America. However, on the day that the escape was to take place, a friendly neighbor hurried to the Nant Cottage, and in hushed tones, warned them that the whole plan had been known for days by local authorities. So the plan had to be discarded.

Unfortunately, Smyth was arrested on the assumption that he was actually Mitchel attempting to escape without turning in his ticket. He was transferred back to Hobart in an open car in winter weather and became quite ill. This required more delay. So it was June, the beginning of winter, before the next attempt was made. This time, John decided not to make an escape attempt. He feared that wandering through rough terrain in cold weather would cause health problems that would make him easy to apprehend. Because of his physical abnormalities, deformed rib cage and curved back, it would be also difficult to successfully disguise himself.

By the time that the escape was made on June 9th, it was clear that John's concerns were well founded. The ship they had planned to take had been forced to leave without them. A prolonged period on the run across the island was now inevitable. But Mitchel remained determined to make the attempt. He said goodbye to his family and rode into Bothwell with Smyth. John hurried along the Clyde to reach Bothwell to witness the escape. Mitchel and Smyth went into the police carrying a letter from Mitchel renouncing his ticket-of-leave. There was confusion in the police office, allowing the two men to hurry off without an arrest attempt. The two men mounted waiting horses and rode away to the applause of many residents of Bothwell who understood the importance of what they were witnessing. The police ran after them. but too late to prevent Mitchel's escape. John stood among his friends in Bothwell and watched his best friend disappear from sight. Long years would pass before they would meet again.

§

Parliament had authorized a commission to study complaints from Irish farmers about the fairness of market practices that seemed to greatly favor the mainly English buyers of Irish goods. Early in 1853, the Commissioners came to Newry. James reported this unusual opportunity in his journal. "Market commission in Newry." This Commission had been appointed by the Lord Lieutenant and was comprised of Captain G. Robinson and J. Macbeth. The hearing took place in the Court House in Newry, with both merchants and farmers testifying. They seemed to generally agree that there should be improvements in the Newry markets. There should be one market where all the produce of the area farms would be sold. There should be regular hours for opening and closing. All goods should be weighed at cranes with carefully calibrated and standardized weights. No deductions would be allowed.

This wasn't the way the Newry markets, held under the authority of Lord Kilmorey, were currently conducted. Market days were held three days a week, Tuesday, Thursday and Saturday. Fair days were the first Monday of the month. Most products were sold on the streets, only butter and flax being sold in a closed market. Items such as poultry, fish and eggs were sold by people wandering around the streets. There was a separate market area where potatoes could be weighed and sold. Grains were weighed and sold in merchants' stores. Much of the corn was brought to town in carts, which clustered near the courthouse. But buyers also staked out the roads leading to Newry to buy cartloads of corn before they even reached Newry. The buyers would give the farmers a ticket stating the number of bags and the price. They would then be taken to the buyers' shops to be weighed and paid for. Farmers had many complaints about the accuracy of the weighing of their goods. So there were many practices that needed repair.

Joseph Luptin, a corn trader, was one of the local men who shared his experiences with the Commissioners. He testified that grains were bought by the hundred-weight, deductions made for the weight of the sacks. Most farmers weighed their own produce before coming to market to help reduce fraud. Pigs sold were required to weigh 120 pounds to count as a hundred-weight. This meant that farmers lost between eight and 12 pounds of weight from the sale of each pig.

Another of the witnesses was John's brother James Martin. He thought that it would be a great help to have regular market hours. The opening could be signaled by the ringing of a bell. He supported having uniform weights and abolishing all deductions. Merchants at the time took 16¼ of every stone of products the farmers produced. Martin thought this should be reduced to 14 pounds. Some merchants even added an extra charge for what they claimed was storage. He also knew of cases where farmers delivered flax to merchants who had agreed to pay a set price, who then on delivery refused to complete the deal without an additional reduction of six shillings per stone. Martin agreed that the improvements to the market system that farmers proposed would have a cost, but he believed farmers would be willing to pay a small fee in support of a well-regulated market. Sadly for the farmers, nothing concrete resulted from this commission

§

Though the campaign for tenant rights began to sputter due to lack of progress and defections of some of its leaders, local religious tensions remained at a high level in the spring of 1853. The Rainey confrontation of the previous year wasn't an isolated incident. In March, another situation involving one of John's tenants took place on the Rathfriland Road near Sheepbridge. Robert Andrews was on his way home in the evening with a friend David Clegg. When they reached Sheepbridge, they were accosted by a man named Thomas McKenna who was accompanied by two friends. The three angry men demanded to know if Andrews had taunted a passersby with the claim he could beat any "Papist in the County." Andrews denied that he had ever said any such thing. Despite his denials, Andrews and Clegg were immediately severely battered by clubs wielded by McKenna and his friends.

A hearing on the attack was held five days later at the Newry Police Station. McKenna was charged with the attack along with Peter Murphy and John Reavy. Testimony at the hearing showed that McKenna and Andrews had met earlier in the evening, but nothing hostile was said during the conversation. So Andrews was unprepared for what appeared to be an unprovoked attack. Though Andrews was carrying a spade, he dropped it attempting to block the blows with his arms. After the attack, the spade disappeared and hadn't been recovered. The hat that was knocked from his head was later found and returned.

Another witness said she had seen Andrews that night and he was bleeding badly from his wounds. Clegg's testimony was similar to Andrews's. He recognized McKenna, but couldn't identify the other two as he had been knocked into the dirt when the attack began.

Bernard Hurley testified that he was on his way home from Newry earlier in the evening when he heard that Andrews would be attacked somewhere along the road that night. Hurley hurried along the road in an effort to catch up with Andrews and warn him. When he got to Sheepbridge, he discovered he was too late. Andrews was already dripping with blood when he caught up. Before he had reached Andrews, he did see McKenna lurking behind a pillar.

At that point in the hearing, McKenna attempted to say something. But he was warned by Captain Warburton that anything he said could be used against him. At that warning, McKenna stopped talking, and the hearing was adjourned. Andrews commented that this was the first time in his life he had ever been involved in a police hearing.

When the hearing began on the cases of Murphy and Reavy, conflicting statements were read into the record. Their employer, Mary Thompson. testified that they were out of the house during the attack. But this was contradicted by the testimony of Thompson's maid who claimed the two men were only out of the house for a few minutes. Another witness described meeting the three men who were apparently heading to Newry. McKenna claimed that Andrews had hit him with a spade, so the men turned back toward Sheepbridge to accost Andrews. The two men were described as wearing white jackets, the same description that Andrews had provided to the police. After more testimony, the men were released on bail.

When the trial was held, the testimony was quite similar to that at the original hearings. The jury found McKenna guilty and the other two men innocent. McKenna was sentenced to six months in prison.

George seemed to throw fuel on the sectarian hostiles with his frequent attacks on the efforts that were underway to centralize control of the Catholic Church in Rome. In one of his leaders, he called these efforts by Archbishop Cullen and Pope Pius IX a "hideous, merciless monster that must be strangled for the sake of civilization."

Since religious tensions were unlikely to be eased by such words, more violence wasn't surprising. And indeed there were more local problems before the end of the summer. During the night of July 30th, an attack was made on the home of James's friend, Hugh Todd. According to an account in the *Telegraph,* the household was alerted in the dead of night by the barking of a dog. Mrs. Todd directed one of their workers to investigate. When he refused, she did the inspecting herself.

Finding nothing amiss, she returned to the house. She had just closed the door when multiple slugs were fired through it, hitting the furniture on opposite side of the room, and barely missing Mrs. Todd. At that point, daughter Ellen Todd, described in the paper as "an interesting young woman" took the family gun to a window and fired in the direction of the door. A shout was heard just beyond the door and the attackers turned tail and ran.

Apparently that was the third attack on the Todds. Previously, Todd's plow and several of his other farm implements had been destroyed. There was hope locally that the perpetrators would be promptly apprehended.

James mentioned this attack in his journal a few days later. He traveled into Newry to meet town leaders, Captain Warburton, Irvine, Corry and others about the attack on the Todds. This meeting wasn't apparently part of any public meeting as George didn't refer to it in the paper. This was the last mention of the subject, so in all likelihood, no one was ever caught and charged for the attacks on the Todd family.

§

George was very well attuned to these local events and gave space in his paper to share with all readers news of what was going on in the Newry area. But there was one subject occurring that summer to which George gave only passing notice. The major impact of this legislation would become clear years later.

The Conservative government had introduced a new package of taxes in an effort to raise revenue and equalize Irish taxes with those paid in England. If the bill passed, the Irish would for the first time have to pay a tax on income. When the issue had been raised before, it was determined that Ireland was so poor that the cost of collecting the tax was greater than the revenue that could be raised. Despite the fact that Ireland was still suffering from the effects of the famine, the new Conservative government was determined to levy the tax this time. At first, the tax would be relatively moderate, but it would gradually be increased until the Irish paid the same income tax as the English.

Logically, George could have been expected to fight fiercely against this new tax. But that wasn't at all what happened. He mentioned the legislation only three times as it swiftly passed through Parliament with little opposition. As it was introduced, a single effort was made to delay the law though the creation of a commission authorized to see if any new taxation would maintain the financial balance required by the Act of Union. The vote on the amendment showed clearly that resistance was futile. And that was the position George took on the subject, only mentioning the completion of each major step toward passage. Final passage occurred at the end of June. Taxes on Irish farmers would rise again.

§

With Mitchel hiding somewhere on the island, John was responsible for getting Jennie and the children safely on their way to America. He booked passage for them on the Emma, which was leaving Hobart in July. Jennie wanted to hire a servant girl to assist her with the children on the long trip to America. This was especially important as she had given birth to her final child Isabelle during their stay in Australia. John wasn't successful in finding anyone in the local area who was willing to assist. But O'Dogherty was able to find a young girl in Hobart who met Jennie's demanding standards. One particular concern was that this new servant should be a good sailor. She would be of little help if she suffered from seasickness for much of the trip.

But there were other considerations to attend to as well that John couldn't help Jennie with. Ships offered different amenities, so it was important for the Mitchels to determine whether or not the ship supplied such items as mattresses and bedding. As many of the local ladies were helping her with the sewing and other preparations for the long trip, Jennie was in a position to supply them for herself if needed.

Besides the household preparations, all the furniture and household goods had to be disposed of. The new tenant of Nant Cottage had agreed to take them all at a fair evaluation. The sheep and cattle had been sold at a good price, and they were still hoping to sell the horses at a good price as well.

There were some final visits to make. Miss Connell and one of her sisters were hoping to make trip down from the Sugar Loaf to bid them goodbye. A meeting of the friends was set up for the following week, just before the Mitchel family left Bothwell. The Connell sisters would be accompanied by their brother John who had participated in Mitchel's escape.

The Emma sailed from Hobart on July 18th with all the family and Smyth on board as well. There was unexpected passenger on the ship, a Catholic Priest, who came on board the ship after it had left the harbor and cleared its final police inspection. In reality, the priest was Mitchel himself in disguise. So the entire Mitchel family left Van Diemen's Land together. Since Patrick

O'Donohue had escaped previously, only three of the convicted Young Irelanders remained in exile, John, O'Brien and O'Dogherty.

News of the escape reached Newry in early October. George immediately passed the information on to his readers by reprinting a somewhat garbled account from the *Nation* that included information that John had escaped as well. All were safely heading to America. O'Donohue had already made his way safely as far as Tahiti.

George added his own comments to this news story. He had by then gotten confirmation that John was still in his allotted district in Van Diemen's Land. The news of John's whereabouts pleased him. "This report affords us great pleasure as it confirms our belief in the honour of an estimable and valued friend, characteristically as high-minded as he was kind-hearted."

The reward for Mitchel's capture had been set at just two pounds. George was sure that this would be very humiliating to Mitchel. He went on to find fault with the local authorities who certainly made escaping easy. That aside, although George had opposed the Revolt of '48, he hoped that the remaining men in exile would soon be pardoned and allowed to leave Van Diemen's Land and to freely travel anywhere except Ireland or England.

Now that the Mitchels had left Bothwell, John had lost not only his dear friends but also his employment and place to live. Since most of the Young Irelanders had escaped, local officials relaxed the restrictions placed on the remaining prisoners. Now that he was free to live wherever he chose on the island, he had other options. So he decided to find a place to live that was closer to his two remaining Young Irelander friends. O'Dogherty recommended that he try the town of Broadmarsh in the Brighton District thinking it might suit his needs.

On August 18th, John passed along to O'Dogherty news of his whereabouts. He had hired a room in the Broadmarsh Inn, a place where Terrance McManus had once stayed. John's accommodations were very much to his liking. He had a private room that opened onto a garden. This made it possible for him to come and go without going into the inn.

Relocating had not been completed without complications. Somehow, all his luggage had been lost, so he arrived at the Inn without a change of clothes. Fortunately, his new landlord was willing to loan him a fresh shirt and trousers. As he was settling in, a coachman delivered a message for John that a letter was waiting for him in Brighton that contained some much-needed money. This was a problem as Brighton was eight miles away, and John had no horse.

On Sunday, John decided he would climb Mount Dromedary to get a good view of Storm Bay, and New Norfolk on his way to retrieve the much-needed money. This decision soon put John's life at risk. By the time he neared the summit, the weather had turned bad. Light rain had turned to snow, and the summit was soon covered with clouds. John couldn't see more that twenty yards in any direction. So he decided to wait for a few minutes in hopes that the clouds would blow away.

When that didn't happen, John decided to head back down the mountain in what he hoped was the right direction. This was just a guess as there was no indication as to which direction the sun was shining. The climb down over steep slopes was very difficult. Often he found himself slipping on wet rocks and plunging awkwardly down slopes. After hours of such dangerous hiking, he finally emerged from the clouds and could see the world below them. Unfortunately, he had selected the wrong direction, and was looking down on New Norfolk. This wasn't where he was supposed to be. There was nothing to be done, but to climb back up the mountain.

John had always loved climbing. But his adventure on Dromedary Mountain was the hardest climbing he had ever experienced. Dogwood and boxwood intertwined making a passage through them very difficult. He was plagued by termites he disturbed as he passed over the dead trees they inhabited. This experience convinced him that he wouldn't make a "Tasmen bushman."

Nine dangerous hours passed before John made his way safely back to the Broadmarsh. When he arrived, he was a terrible sight. His borrowed clothes were wet and torn. His new landlord and one of the waiters immediately came to his rescue. They supplied him with fresh and dry clothes, and food and drink for the inner man. Under the kind care of his new friends, he began to feel human once again.

Money was always a problem for John. His family in Ireland sent him money, but it arrived irregularly. Finding a paying job in Van Diemen's Land was difficult. O'Dogherty, with his medical background, had found a job in a hospital in Hobart. O'Brien came from a wealthy family, so money was no issue for him. So not too long after John's adventure in Broadmarsh, he moved to Ross, where he had been offered a job tutoring two young boys.

This was a tedious job for him, but he had no better option. The best part of the job was that after lessons on Friday, he would climb over the mountain that separated Ross and Sugar Loaf where the Connells lived. He enjoyed spending every weekend there. This special family reminded John of what Irish families were like before Ireland was devastated by famine and emigration.

John spent Christmas of 1853 there as well. These were very special days for John. He enjoyed the company of the Connell children, especially Julia, the eldest daughter. She shared many of his interests and treated him as an equal, though he was twenty years older than Julia. Since John's parents were very different in age, his father being sixty-one and his mother twenty-three when they married, a relationship between a man and woman of different ages, didn't seem daunting to him.

However, John soon retreated from any thought that he and Julia might marry. She was a Catholic. While a marriage between Protestant and Catholic might be accepted in Van Diemen's land, it most certainly wouldn't be accepted by many friends at home in Ireland. Should the two marry, John would have to remain in Van Diemen's Land for the rest of his life. This was a step that John could never take. So John rejected his romantic impulse and returned to Ross when the holiday was over.

Some months later, as winter set in John sent the Connells a small gift and an accompanying note

"My dear Mrs. Connell,

I shall never forget the true Irish heartiness of the hospitality with which you, Mr. C. your daughters and your son received my "rebel' comrades and myself that moonlight night when we cantered over the marshes to visit the Irish family at the foot of the Sugarloaf. It was both very sad and very delightful to me to find in a forest in the Antipodes the warm Irish feeling and the grace and intelligence natural to the Irish character and to think that it is fast being extirpated at home. Many a dozen times, since I last visited you and your good family have I wished and even proposed to visit you again. But I fear now I shan't be able to enjoy that pleasure until the winter is past.

The book which accompanies this note I beg you to accept as a keepsake to remind you of one who would gladly dare and endure far greater penalties than any he has yet endoured, in order to see poor old Ireland inhabited by families like yours. Alas! 'tis a slave population there now, and one fast degenerating into all the vices of slavery. When Miss Julia, Miss Margaret or Miss Ellen plays or sings some of the 'rebel' Irish songs of this volume, let her and all of you kindly think that a more determined rebel Irishman does not breathe than your grateful and attached friend and countryman, John Martin."

As John moved back to the highlands, George diverted from tenant rights to national education. He argued that new schools should be run just as the Protestant schools had always been run, with school books being the same approved religious texts schools always used, including the Protestant version of the Bible. Protestants expected Catholics to support their education plans, so children of all denominations could attend the same schools.

Catholic leaders insisted on the right to use their version of the Bible, which differed from the Protestant version on important issues like the Reformation. They expected this religious education to be incorporated into all subject areas. In addition they wanted all textbooks no matter the subject, to be submitted to Catholic authorities for approval. With such conflicting goals held by competing denominations, the government was struggling to find an acceptable compromise.

George believed that the Commission of Education was abandoning traditional education to please the "Papists." He objected to a move by the Commission of Education seeming to support denominational schools, schools paid for by the government with students segregated according to religion and receiving quite different educations.

In the middle of September, a large meeting on this topic took place in the Savings Bank meeting room. Most of the people attending were members of the Church of Ireland and were of the same mind as George. They wanted nothing less than the establishment of good traditional scriptural schools for the children of Newry. This wasn't an issue that could be resolved in one meeting, but would fester for months.

Education wasn't the only problem facing the citizens of Newry. Residents and visitors alike were plagued by the appearance and stench of Newry streets. What could be solved by strong arms working a shovel got tied up in a bureaucratic struggle. Parliament was slowly passing laws for Ireland that would bring more effective government to the towns of Ireland. Newry had no mayor or council yet. Instead they had two organizations that seemed to consider their own remits more important than cooperation. The Town Commissioners had jurisdiction over the town watchmen and citizen complaints. The Board of Guardians managed the workhouse, health and hospitals. They didn't always work cooperatively.

Conflicts between the two bodies presented a critical problem when cholera broke out in England. Cholera epidemics had swept across Ireland a number of times before, and now that bad sanitary conditions had been linked to the outbreaks, Newry officials became anxious to clean up the contributing problems in Newry. When the Newry Town Commissioners met on a Monday in mid-September, they drafted a letter of concern to the Guardians who had charge of health issues. When the Guardians met the following Saturday, the official letter from the Commissioners was read. It reported that "The poor areas of Newry are loathsome." The Guardians complimented the Commissioners on their excellent letter and moved on.

A week later, the first case of cholera was reported in Belfast. Clearly, action in Newry was needed and quickly. However a month passed during which the two bodies argued about who was responsible for the cleaning and therefore who would pay for it. The position of the Commissioners was that the Guardians were responsible, as only they had the power to raise the money. But the Commissioners did promise that they would see that the streets remained clean once the Guardians had paid to clean them.

Finally a compromise was worked out, prompted in part by an increase in the number of cholera cases in Belfast. The Guardians formed a Sanitary Committee under the leadership of Isaac Corry. Committee members were to inspect the town and record the locations of the worst offenders. The owners of the buildings would then receive notices to clean their premises. Then a member of the Commissioners would be assigned to each area of town to make sure that the cleaning was actually done. If the landowner failed to complete the cleaning required, he would be summoned to appear before the Commissioners.

§

The year of 1854 began in a very unusual way that both James and George wrote about. A great snowstorm began in Newry and Donaghmore on New Year's day. James reported this event in his journal of that day. The next day, James reported that the ground was covered with snow. More snow fell the next day as well.

As the snow cover grew ever higher, George noted that the snow had been accompanied by frost and extreme cold. He saw no signs that the weather would soon change. He also urged the police to take notice of a problem the large piles of snow had created. Children happily converted the random snow hills into slides. Too often they would sweep down the snow hill and collide with unwary pedestrians. George wanted the practice stopped immediately.

James tried to maintain his normal schedule as the snow kept falling. On the 4th day of steady snow, he was able to climb over the snow drifts to reach the Four Mile House for a meeting of the Dispensary Committee. But the next day, additional snow fell making even that limited activity impossible. "Deep snow. Roads all blocked up by it. No work can be done. The mail stopped. Snow falls through the day." And the next day, he reported that "Deep snow lies on the ground. No post at the fourmile house this day either."

After a week of snow, George updated the situation in Newry. Three feet of snow had fallen, and in some places, nothing could move along the roads. Mail deliveries stopped, and so did the trains. The road from Belfast to Dublin was impassible. Newry had become a snowbound island. Finally, on January 8th James reported that "it thaws." Though more snow fell a couple of days later, the worst was over. Two days later, James was able to get into Newry to sell oats and meet with Hill Irvine.

By the middle of February, the last dirty heaps of the snow had melted away, and spring work was well underway. George had discovered a small item in a Liverpool paper to the effect that the British government was going to pardon O'Brien, as long as he promised not to participate in politics again. George was hoping that this report might indicate that freedom for John was a possibility also.

Others noticed this article as well. An MP rose in Parliament to ask Lord Palmerston if this report was true. Palmerston confirmed that this report was indeed true. The reason for this change in policy, since O'Brien had been sentenced to life in exile, was the fact that he had honourably kept his word while others had violated theirs and fled. The Government felt it was fair to grant O'Brien the same degree of liberty that the others had dishonorably seized. When this was announced in Parliament, there was loud and prolonged cheering from both sides of the aisle.

At the next session of the Commons, Isaac Butt rose to express gratitude at the conditional pardon granted to O'Brien. But he pointed out that there were two other prisoners still serving their sentences in Van Diemen's Land. He was referring, of course, to John Martin and Kevin O'Dogherty. He pointed out that these men had been convicted of a far lesser crime than O'Brien. They hadn't actually taken up arms against the British government as O'Brien had. They had only been convicted for what they printed in their papers. And for that far lesser crime, they had already served a longer punishment.

Two days after Butt's speech, George wrote an editorial on the subject. He was glad that Mr. Butt had raised the issue of the other two prisoners also still confined to Van Diemen's Land. "We need to scarcely state that it is for

John Martin that we are <u>specially</u> concerned." He repeated Butt's statement that John's crime was less severe than O'Brien's. "On the principle of even-handed justice, therefore, clemency must reach John Martin of whose exemption from the doom of a felon we shall hear with heartfelt pleasure."

George reported in the next edition that the government had decided to officially pardon O'Brien, but had still taken no action on John and O'Dogherty. And he offered a warning. "The Executive should not provoke Ulstermen to raise the contrary dealings of our rulers with political offenders of different sects." Then he reminded the government that Lalor, who wrote most of the offending articles for the *Felon* for which John had been convicted, had been released on a plea of ill-health. Lalor was a Catholic. When a similar plea was made for John, it was refused. Certainly there was favoritism at play.

Soon, George was able to report to his readers that his hope for John's release had been well founded. The British government had decided to grant a Queen's pardon to both John and Kevin. They would be free to leave their penal colony, and travel anywhere they wished to go, except England or Ireland. O'Dogherty was expected to join his family who were already living in France. John had already served more than half of his ten-year sentence and had therefore effectively served the longest sentence of any of the Young Irelanders. But clemency only went so far for George. He certainly hoped that there would be no discussion of granting a pardon to the other Young Irelanders who had violated the terms of their ticket-of-leave and escaped.

§

The news of the John's conditional pardon was common knowledge in Newry weeks before John learned the news. James was delighted even though he understood that it didn't mean that John could return home and resume his management of Loughorne. He mentioned the good news in his entry for March 9th. "Saw a free pardon mentioned in the Times." He would also have noticed that Mr. Whiteside who had been O'Brien's lawyer in his trial and was now a member of Parliament, asked permission to introduce a law that would make the treason laws of Ireland match those of England. Had that been the case at trial, neither O'Brien nor John would have been convicted. Permission was granted, so legislation could proceed even though it wasn't likely to pass.

There was much other work for James to attend to. On the same day that he learned about John's pardon, he visited the Bank of Ireland. James held leases on large amounts of land. Increasing taxes and lower crop prices thrust him into a financial box from which he struggled to escape. So he had begun to take out mortgages on the value of his leases, hoping that better times would allow him to repay the loans before they came due.

March was the time for new elections to the Board of Guardians. This time, James's son John was elected the Guardian for Donaghmore. His nephew James Martin was elected Guardian for Ouley. So two members of the family would participate in setting the Poor Rates that had such a negative effect on his bottom line.

Just before the new Guardians were to take office on April 1st, James performed one of the most odious of landlord's jobs. He had a tenant named John Moffit who leased a farm at the Cashe. He had been unable to pay his rent for some time. But despite his need for money, James did not have his goods seized as many richer landlords would have done. Moffit died on March 28th. It was a cold and windy day when James set out for the churchyard with Sam Lyons and his son to pick out a site and dig a grave for John. He attended the funeral in the afternoon.

When the funeral had ended, James went back to the home to have tea and punch with Moffit's friends. Then he directed Lyons to seize all Moffit's assets as partial payment for the overdue rent. Lyons "arrested" two cows and a calf, manure, the contents of the single room in the cottage, and all the tools in the yard. The value amounted to 1£ 10s.

While James attended to this sad duty, Queen Victoria announced the beginning of the Crimean War with Britain allied with Turkey and France against Russia. James then mentioned the fighting for the first time. "The newspapers of this day report the Defeat of the Rushians by the Turks with the loss of 15000 men."

With the fighting now officially classified as a war, Queen Victoria designated April 26th as a day of prayer and fasting, imploring God to bless the British with a quick victory. James recorded the event in his journal. "Government fast day. Publick worship in towns and some of the country meetinghouses." The government had created special prayers for each of the churches to use in their services.

Newry essentially closed down for the day. Businesses were shuttered. The Custom House shut down as well as town offices and banks. Even the military unit that was stationed in Newry was given the order to stand down. Only the mail trains were running. All the churches were open as though it was the Sabbath, so they could focus on prayer for England and its armed forces.

The war didn't begin well. The first troops were sent off with great pomp and fanfare, including a personal visit from Queen Victoria. However, when they arrived in Gallipoli, they found that the French and Turks had occupied the best camping sites. British supply had failed to provide basic weapons and food. Parliament erupted in anger searching for someone to account for this poorly planned expedition. Ironically the man in charge of supplies was Charles Trevelyan, the very same man who had mismanaged famine relief in Ireland.

§

On the other side of the world, John was unaware of the war or his pardon. The first word of the pardon didn't arrive in Van Diemen's Land until May. The notice was delivered on May 18th by William Carter the Mayor of Hobart. But there had been no official instructions from England, so nothing happened, and John and his companions remained tethered to Van Diemen's Land.

Three days later on May 21st, John wrote to the Connells that he intended to head to Ross in a couple of days, perhaps to take up his tutoring again until official directions arrived for their release. All the prisoners had received letters from home telling them they had been pardoned. However they weren't yet clear as to whether or not the pardon was conditional or full. At any rate, John promised the Connells he would be visiting there in a few days. It would give him a chance to say a proper farewell to his best friends in exile.

It was actually July before the felons were finally officially free to leave and head away. John and O'Brien both intended to travel to France, O'Brien to rejoin his family and John to move to Paris. O'Dogherty intended to try his fortune in the gold fields of Australia. On July 4th, a salute to the departing prisoners was held in Hobart with O'Brien as the special guest. While John was mentioned during the celebration, it didn't appear he was actually present. The leading citizens were there to give O'Brien a proper send off. There was another interesting visitor attending. P. J. Smyth had returned to Hobart after successfully delivering the Mitchel family to New York City. While he had been in Hobart previously, he had met and fallen in love with a local girl and had returned to marry her. It was Smyth who offered a salute to John. The two men would interact throughout the rest of John's life. Following the formalities, the group gathered for a champagne lunch.

The three newly freed felons left Hobart for a stop and change of ships in Sydney. There a grand banquet had been planned on July 24th by the immigrant Irish community as a salute to the highly respected Irish patriots. There were the usual toasts and responses. O'Brien was presented with a goblet made of gold from the Australian gold fields. John and O'Dogherty each received a gift of £200. John hated the necessity of accepting this money. But he desperately needed some financial help to fund the trip to Paris. So he accepted the money with the promise to donate an equal amount to a charity of the sponsor's choosing, as soon as he gained access to his own assets.

The next day John and O'Brien headed west toward Melbourne on the Norma on the next leg of their journey to Ceylon. The ship was supposed to hold only first-class passengers, but the standards were more those of second class. The crewmembers were mostly from Malaysia, and the servants were mainly Chinese. Their standards were well below those that would be expected in a British ship. John shared a bunkroom with twelve other men. The ship was very crowded with passengers, many of them women who were accompanied by children. Wine and food was of poor quality despite the steep fare of £10 to Malta. Still John reported that they "got on well enough."

The Norma faced strong waves and head winds on the trip from Melbourne to Adelaide. The weather was so severe, the ship had to wait outside the harbor for a full day, before the waves calmed enough to make an entrance attempt safe. In Adelaide they would lay over for over 24 hours while the Norma took on coal for the long sea leg to Ceylon. So John had some time to explore. The port town of Albany was about the size of Bothwell. The inhabitants were mainly officials or paroled convicts from Swan Lake. Surrounding the port were high and barren hills.

As John set out to climb the hills, he noticed that the shrubs that did manage to grow in such a dry place produced many very colorful flowers that would have attracted great attention in any London flower show. The hills were high enough to afford a good view of the surrounding area. Though he could see a distance of almost ninety miles, there was not a single large tree in sight. He could however get a good view of some of the local aboriginal settlers. At first, John found them repulsive looking. But after observing their actions for a while, he was able to discern signs of their humanity and character.

After refueling was completed, the Norma headed northwest for Ceylon. Even for a steam-ship, the crossing took several weeks. John had a project to keep him busy. He had purchased a book with blank pages that he planned to fill with his favorite poems. Some he wrote in English, others in Greek, German and French. This was a gift he intended to present to Smith O'Brien when they separated in Ceylon.

John was happy to arrive in Ceylon where he had a week to await the ship that would take him to Suez. He greatly enjoyed exploring the new places he visited and observing the local populations. The description that John wrote to friends shows just how carefully he observed this country, so very different from any of the others he had previously visited.

The trip to Suez was sufficiently uneventful that John didn't write about it. But he found his voyage up the Red Sea riveting. There before his eyes lay the Sinai Desert and some of the mountains he had read about in the Bible. From Suez he traveled overland to Cairo in a covered vehicle drawn by four horses. He commented that he might have enjoyed making the trip bouncing along on a camel. The track across the desert was bordered by parallel piles of sand. Every fifteen miles or so, there was a rest area where familiar beer and English cheeses were available.

Along this road, John saw many camel bones bleaching in the sun, and for the first time, the strange phenomenon of a mirage dancing along the horizon. John enjoyed comparing reality with the mental images he had created when he first learned about Egypt during his days at the Glebe School in Donaghmore. The Egyptian people were friendly and apparently happy. He was impressed by the green world created by the annual flooding of the Nile. Cairo was like a city from the Arabian nights, so John found much to delight him in this ancient place. While he was there, he climbed the great pyramid of Giza. From Egypt, he sailed across the Mediterranean Sea to Marseilles, and from there by train to his new home in Paris.

John arrived there in early October. Within a few days, he was celebrating happy reunions with visits from some of his family. He gladly embraced his brother David who made the first trip. His sister Mary and her husband Maxwell Simpson came soon after. He also learned that his youngest sister Anna would soon be married to a British mathematician named Thomas Hirst. They would be settling in Paris after the wedding. So the long years of his separation from family were behind him. Still, he longed for a day when he could again return to his much-loved home country.

Chapter 5

Finally Home
1854 -1856

John arrived in Paris as winter was setting in. So different was this city from Ireland or the highlands of Van Diemen's Land, there was nothing that hinted of home for him there. But he couldn't allow himself to indulge in the discomfort of being a stranger in a strange place. Since he could speak French well, he could talk to people he encountered in his explorations of his new home. Urgent tasks to be done provided another diversion. First, he needed to move from temporary accommodations to something more permanent. He settled on an old pensione at 26 Lacipide, described by John O'Leary as "a queer old boarding house", which would later be occupied by other Irish nationalists. His 4th floor flat provided sufficient space for a single man, but there was nothing of comfort or style to his room. Many of his fellow residents were elderly single men and women. Though John had little in common with most of these neighbors, he set about becoming their friends.

Once he had settled in, John could extend his walks around this ancient city. Much of the historic heart of Paris was being demolished as Louis Napoleon Bonaparte, recently made Emperor Napoleon III, had grand plans for his capital. He wished to make Paris a more modern city of wide avenues, parks, fountains and restored water and sewer systems that would make Paris a proper symbol of his power. The first step in his great plan was the creation of a wide street running north and south, right through the heart of medieval Paris. This major project was underway when John arrived there.

A number of Irish had moved to Paris before John, some of them Young Irelanders who had fled Ireland with the failure of the revolt of 1848. Once he had made contact, John could reminisce about the homeland that he missed so much. Many of them became lifelong friends. Two of these were George Mahon and Miles Byrne. Mahon had been a student at Trinity college at the same time John had been studying there. He was a member of the Church of Ireland, so the two friends had different perspectives, as they talked about political issues in Ireland.

Byrne had lived through two major revolutions in Ireland. He was a leader in the Revolution of 1798 in Wicklow. When that revolt was lost to superior British forces, he escaped to Dublin. From his hiding place there, he participated in the uprising of 1803. After that second failed attempt at independence, Byrne escaped to France. There he became the head of Napoleon's Irish Brigade, his valor in battles bringing fame and respect. Certainly the two men shared eyewitness accounts of their three different struggles for Irish independence.

§

John had lost his access to the *Telegraph* when he left Bothwell, so his knowledge of what was happening in Newry was spotty and out of date. He did know something of the family in Donaghmore, that two of his cousins, Willie and James, had emigrated to America, that cousin John was managing Loughorne at his request, and that Andrew was working with his uncle Harshaw at Ringbane. While he knew that cousin Robert Hugh was studying for the ministry, he didn't know that he had successfully completed his studies and would soon be ordained a Presbyterian Minister, or that Samuel had begun a banking career. His awareness of life in Newry would be a void until he arrived in Paris.

And there was much going on in Newry that John would have found interesting. When James's term as Guardian ended, his son John was elected to succeed him as Guardian for Donaghmore. A couple of months into John's term, he encountered a problem of special interest for the citizens of Donaghmore. Dr. Saunderson, who was the doctor in charge of the newly combined Dispensaries in Donaghmore and Poyntzpass had suddenly disappeared, leaving both areas without a doctor to attend to the local poor or authorize admission to the poorhouse or fever hospital in Newry.

John missed the meeting when the problem was explained to the Guardians. Apparently, Dr. Saunderson had left the area without notifying the dispensary committees or the Guardians or leaving a proper substitute. Guardians decided to ask the Newry Commissioners if they had the authority to appoint a substitute and dock Dr. Saunderson for his absences.

Dr. Saunderson soon heard of the Guardians' question and wrote a letter which George published in the *Telegraph* a few days later. Dr. Saunderson claimed that he had left a properly qualified substitute to take his place.

The Guardians took up the issue again at their next meeting with John Harshaw present and an active participant. John began by complaining that no one at the previous meeting had any first-hand information about the situation in Donaghmore. He informed the Guardians that Dr. Saunderson actually had left a qualified person to see patients in the Donaghmore Dispensary. This point of view was very different from that of the Poyntzpass officials. They claimed that Dr. Saunderson told them that he was free to leave whenever he wished to.

John asked questions. "Where will you draw the line of demarcation? Has he a right to go out of his district at all?"

The Chairman put an end to the conversation by saying that the town Commissioners had taken on the issue and the Guardians could only await a decision. With no further action in the foreseeable future, John met with Dr. Saunderson and other local leaders a few days later to discuss the issue. This seemed to be the end of the issue as the Commissioners didn't render an opinion.

Indeed, several weeks passed without further action. It was September when the dispensary committees of Donaghmore and Poyntzpass acted on their own, organizing a joint meeting. James reported what happened in his journal.

Tuesday, September 5th was a fine dry day. Workers continued the flax harvest. But James left with John after getting work organized and underway, heading to the meeting in Poyntzpass. Along the way, they stopped to pick up Samuel Boyd Marshall, who was his daughter Jane's father-in-law. Their destination was the courthouse in Poyntzpass where a meeting of the dispensary committees of both towns was scheduled to take place

Dr. Saunderson was on hand to explain and offer his apologies. The committee members seemed satisfied that no additional "absence without leave" would occur again. They voted to request the Newry Commissioners to allow the charges to "fall into oblivion."

When the Commissioners met in Newry, they heard the report of the Poyntzpass meeting. They seemed willing to agree with the dispensary committees. It was also suggested that the dispensary groups of the two towns should be separated, due to the problem of getting members to meet. They forwarded this information to the Guardians. A week later this was also agreed to. The Donaghmore dispensary would be separated from Poyntzpass and united with the Glen. John objected to a proposal that the salaries of the two districts should be different. A vote to have the salaries uniform passed unanimously.

These changes would have to be approved by the Poor Law Commissioners. So the issue dragged on until October. The reorganization of the dispensaries was approved, and Dr. Saunderson permitted to continue as the doctor for both dispensaries. The Commissioners would return to the issue of Dr. Saunderson's performance again in six months.

This was a busy summer for the Guardians. At this same meeting that addressed the missing doctor, the Guardians faced another issue that was a frequent source of irritation, the dumping of people from English poorhouses in places in Ireland with which they had little or no connection. That morning a new inmate and her illegitimate child had appeared at the poorhouse seeking entrance. She was called before the Board and asked to explain her circumstances. She identified herself as Sarah McMahon. For the last eight years, she had lived in Liverpool. About thirteen months before, she had been forced to enter the poorhouse there. Three months later she had given birth to her child.

The previous Monday, she had been summoned with some other inmates to visit the nurse. The nurse first directed her to put on her own clothes. When she complied, she was taken to the door, pushed onto a waiting cart with her infant and a small bundle containing all her possessions, and driven to the dock where a steamer was waiting. She was placed on board and taken to Warrenpoint. She had made her way to the Newry poorhouse on her own. After considerable grumbling, the Guardians allowed her admission.

A third issue was whether or not to put the school of the workhouse under the control of the National Education Board. Doing that would have the advantage of providing the Guardians with additional money, but they would have to give up the freedom to establish their own rules about how religion should be taught in the workhouse school. James reported the results in his journal. "The motion to put the schools of the Newry Union under the National board lost by 12 to 21." John voted with the minority.

This was a sectarian issue and therefore not a calm discussion. Differences of opinion were strongly held and angrily proclaimed. Rowan McNaughton, one of the Catholic Guardians strongly supported putting the workhouse schools under national control. He expressed his opinions in words that other members found highly offensive. This was an issue that didn't end with the adjournment of the meeting.

At the next meeting of the Guardians, Isaac Corry offered a motion of censure against McNaughton. Not surprisingly, McNaughton erupted again. He attributed the entire episode to the Orange members from Rathfriland and Dolly's Brae. With that, he stormed out of the meeting. Minus the subject of the vote of censure, the vote was quickly taken. John Harshaw was the only Guardian to vote against censure.

§

This was a busy summer for James as well. A good friend of his, Rev. Hugh Todd, had been appointed minister of a church in nearby Bessbrook. The Presbytery had refused to allow the appointment on the grounds that Rev. Todd wasn't a qualified minister. This decision was quickly appealed ensuring that the subject would be discussed at the summer meeting of the Presbyterian General Assembly in Belfast. James was appointed to represent Donaghmore.

James left Ringbane at 6:30 on July 5th with his son Andrew. They headed first to the Fourtowns where they had breakfast with daughter Jane and son-in-law Archy Marshall. From there, they walked the short distance to Poyntzpass to catch the train for Belfast. They arrived in Belfast before noon where his son Samuel was waiting. After attending an early session of the Assembly and doing some shopping. Andrew headed home to Ringbane. James stayed overnight with Samuel.

The Todd case, in which James had such an intense personal interest, was heard the next day. The opposition was led by Dr. Henry Cooke and the Banbridge Presbytery. This must have been personally painful to James, as Dr. Cooke had been a mentor for his son Robert Hugh. Dr. Cooke acted as prosecutor, claiming that there was an important principle at play in this case. According to Dr. Cooke, Todd had appeared before the Banbridge Presbytery and had been informed that he needed another year of training. Instead of following that advice, he had gone to Scotland where he got an undergraduate degree. Then he joined the Free Church of Scotland. For two years, he had done no studying or appearing at trials during which his sermons could be evaluated. Nevertheless, Hugh Todd was then given a license by Dr. Alexander of the Free Presbyterian Church of Scotland of which Todd was then a member.

On his return to Ireland, he rejoined the Presbyterian Church of Ireland, and attempted to obtain permission to preach freely there. This history was too different from the customary path to ordination to be accepted by Cooke and other ministers who supported his view. Todd had his supporters as well, so when the testimony ended, the subject was turned over to a commission to make the final decision. When Dr. Cooke was placed on the Commission, James must have known that Todd would lose, and indeed that was what happened.

Before July ended, James had another civic duty to fulfill. He was called to jury duty on July 21st. James left his men cutting turf and headed toward Downpatrick. Again, he got an early 6 a.m. start, getting to Rathfriland an hour later. There he stopped with Mrs. John Todd for breakfast. Then he met Mr. McClanaghan who had "kindly" offered to drive James to his destination. The two men left Rathfriland around 10 a.m. and arrived in Downpatrick about four hours later.

His first stop was the Downpatrick Court House located above the town on the hillside near where St. Patrick's grave was located. He was there in time to witness the grand entrance of the presiding official, Judge Crampton. He stayed to watch the rest of the day's court proceedings. Then he went to have tea with Rev. William White, who was a brother of Donaghmore's Rev. Patrick White. James spent the night in the manse.

Saturday was a cold and wet day, but James was up early. After he shaved, he went to the Downpatrick reading room to read the newspapers until time for the court to open. The court session for the day began at 10 a.m. James watched as several appeals were heard. Then Judge Crampton heard the case that James was interested in, McClelland vs. McBlain.

This was a case of great interest to farmers. McBlain was an attorney for Joseph Martin, who had brought the case. Efforts to resolve the issue through arbitration had failed, thus making a trial necessary. Martin had purchased a lot of grass seed from Mrs. McClelland. When he went to pick up his seed, he found that some of it was inferior, so he took only the satisfactory seed and left the rest. He refused to pay for the unsatisfactory seed, but Mrs. McClelland wanted full payment. After hearing the case, the judge ordered Mr. Martin to pay £30 pounds for all the seed he had contracted to buy.

The following day, James spent at various services with his host. The first one was at the Downpatrick poorhouse. The next was a noon service in Rev. White's church. At 2 p.m., Rev. White held a service in Downpatrick jail. There was one last service at Rev. White's church at 7 p.m. James couldn't be charged with neglecting his religious obligations during his jury service.

On Monday morning, James had breakfast with his host and headed to the courthouse again. James had been summoned to appear at the Record Court that morning at 9 a.m. However, he wasn't selected to serve on the jury. So he was free to head home around 11 a.m. with Mr. Clougher. The two men arrived in Rathfriland around 5 p.m. James paused again to have tea with Mrs. John

Todd, and then headed home, arriving back at Ringbane after one of his longest absences from home.

The day after the September Commissioners meeting, the Four Mile House, owned by David Woods, was robbed, a very unusual event in Donaghmore. Late on Sunday evening, several men forced their way into the shop that Mr. Woods ran as part of his inn. The thieves stole a 55-pound chest of tea, four shillings, and five flannel shirts.

Local farmers reported to the police that they had seen two suspicious men in the area. And thanks to that help, police arrested James Breen the next morning, and William Conn, Michael Hagan and James Connolly the same afternoon. All of the men appeared in the Newry Petit Court the following Saturday. After hearing evidence, the men were held for trial at the next Quarter Sessions.

The trial began in Newry in the third week of October. There was much local interest, though James didn't mention it in his journal. The first witness was Robert Woods, the son of the owner. He explained that the family ran a grocery store and general business, which sold clothing. They had six lamb-wool shirts in stock, one of which had already been sold. When he came downstairs on that Monday morning at 5:00 a.m., he discovered the shirts were missing and called the police. At this point, one of the shirts was offered in evidence.

Inspector Madders testified that he had solved the case quickly, as the men were found wearing the missing shirts. They also had braces that had been stolen at the same time. Apparently Conn and Hagen were rather well-known robbers from Armagh. With that in mind, after listening to testimony, the judge charged against them. The jury quickly returned guilty verdicts against Conn and Hagen, but Breen and Connolly were released. As repeat offenders, the guilty parties were sentenced to four years penal servitude.

§

Though the struggles of the Young Irelanders to free Ireland from English control had occurred more than six years before, George remembered. He took a special interest in reporting on the two Newry men who had played such important roles in the rebellion.

By this time, John was nearing his new home in Paris, and Mitchel had already been in Brooklyn for over a year. In September 1854, news from New York prompted George to mention them in his newspaper. Mitchel and his friend Meagher were now publishing a new newspaper, the *Citizen,* which was strongly anti-Catholic and he had already stirred up a conflict with Rev. Hughes, the Catholic Archbishop of New York. Rev. Hughes well understood the problems of Ireland as he had grown up in County Tyrone. Archbishop Hughes angrily denounced the Mitchel attacks on the secular actions of the church and claims that Catholics in the Vatican had a right to change their government if they wished.

Mitchel fired back, blaming the Catholic Church for the failure of the Young Irelander revolt. "If that insurrection failed and ended without so much as a blow being struck, the failure is due, not to the cowardice or faithlessness on the part of those you call the 'Young Irelanders' but to the treachery and meanness of the Roman Catholic Priests."

Mitchel concluded his attack on the Archbishop and his Church with a diatribe that George might well have agreed with. "If half the nations of the earth must be held in civil bondage, for ever, if democratic freedom is to be openly denounced in the old world and undermined and sneered at in the new, if American republicans and Roman Catholic Irish are to be set against each other in deadly strife, and all because the Pope rules, and rules badly, a petty Principality in Italy, be assured that the Irish here will begin to curse the Pope, and his tiara, and inquisitions, congregations, conclaves, colleges and the rest of the Clerical apparatus."

This battle with the Archbishop was one about which Mitchel was obviously passionate, and one he expected to win. So he was surprised when numbers of his faithful readers began to desert him. Since the paper was the source of income for him and his family, this was an unhappy situation.

Shortly after this word from America, George was happy to include a small notice in his newspaper. "We have the gratification of hearing that John Martin, permitted to leave Van Diemen's Land in pursuance of a recent act of Royal clemency, arrived in Paris…having reached the French Capitol by way of Marseilles…We hope we may anticipate Mr. Martin's return to Loughorne, where the philanthropist will be heartily welcomed even by those who repudiated the political views with which he unhappily associated himself." George certainly counted himself among those who would be happy to see John once again.

Meanwhile, the Crimean War was going badly. The army had lost many men, and badly needed replacements. When members of Parliament returned to London in November, they moved quickly to solve their manpower problem. First, they authorized the formation of militias in Ireland to keep order while English troops stationed there were diverted to the front lines. The target for Ireland was 27,000 men. The Royal South Down Regiment of Militia was quickly organized with the Marquis of Downshire as their colonel. This risky move made clear just how serious the manpower shortage was, for the last thing the British would want was for Irish farmers to have the skills needed to become Irish soldiers.

Secondly, Parliament took another important, but most unusual action, to authorize the government to hire mercenaries from Germany to fill the depleted English ranks. One English newspaper explained the need for such actions. "'As for the Irish, troublesome at all times, they are gone, that is, the surplus is gone, gone with a vengeance.'"

George was furious that any English paper would print such a horrid point of view. "Surely Englishmen will have little difficulty in connecting the nefarious scheme of hiring foreign mercenaries with the natural and inevitable consequences of the awful national crime into which they were betrayed in 1847 and 1848. Listen to the words of one of the best men in Ireland, when writing of his own prospects of raising men for the too-late embodied militia. 'The Whig massacre of the Irish in 1846 and subsequent years has left but few recruits, for in 1846 children who would now serve as recruits died in numbers, and though the population may be diminished only by 2,000,000, we are now but a nation of old women and cripples.' Well gentlemen of England, how like you the consequences? As the *Times* tells you, you will have the 'placid blue-eyed German,' instead of the 'troublesome Irish.' We fancy, however that even the Guards, glorious fellows as they are, would rather have the 88th regiment by their side, however 'troublesome,' than any German corps, even were they as stout men at arms as the 'lanzknochta' of old, which they never will be."

In the first edition of the paper for 1855, George provided his readers with his analysis of the former year, and prospects for the new one. The last year had begun ominously with the threat of war. Despite efforts of the government to avoid war, it had come upon them anyway. But in Ireland, there was peace. This was clearly the result of the exit of "Old Ireland and New."

George explained his thinking this way. "Old Ireland having undergone the process of natural decay, while Young Ireland had undergone the process of premature decrepitude, has died the death of faction, and shrouded in shame, has been consigned to the tomb of political oblivion." The opponents of both Irish groups had risen greatly in the esteem of the world with the glorious victories on the battlefields of Crimea.

Local residents were being called on to support the war efforts. Some responded by enlisting in the British Army. But other Newry residents did choose to join the South Down Militia. In the beginning, recruitment was slow. But George was confident that there would be strong local support, that there are hundreds of "strong men and true" who will come forth to serve. And indeed recruiting numbers improved. The first local recruiting drive had produced 125 volunteers This was seen as a positive result by local leaders, but George was sure that more would soon be enlisting.

In early spring, Newry and the rest of Ireland were called upon by the Queen to participate in another day of National Humiliation to pray for victory. George hoped all churches of all denominations would again participate. While the day of prayer that had been held the previous year was deemed a great local success, George made clear to his readers how events of the past year had changed the situation. "Anguish unutterable, sorrows and misery beyond all reckoning, hearts crushed and broken, lives most dear and precious sacrificed, brightest hopes darkened, hearths laid bare and desolate, widows and orphans' tears falling bitterly–all these, and far more than these, have been in the train of the last few months of the rule of blood and carnage. A Nation may well dress itself in sackcloth at this sight." "The right thinking of the community will have assured faith that the humble and devout prayer of a suppliant people shall not be in vain."

As March 21st arrived, the day of prayer, George reported that in Newry, even the Catholic churches, were going to participate. James and the people of Donaghmore participated as well. As he reported in his journal, the family participated despite the sad news that one of his family members had died. "Dry cold air from the East—general fast—was at meeten, Hugh & Absalom [Samuel] there also. Mr. R R Todds son 'William Kirk' died aged about 3 years."

§

In the year 1855, James Harshaw was a man in his prime, fully able to manage his property and participate actively in the endless hard work needed to bring in a good harvest every year. With the Crimean War continuing, food production in Ireland was very important to the war effort. James had his men in the fields as long as daylight allowed, preparing fields for planting and ensuring that the seeds he would need were ready. Some he bought from the shops in Newry and some were seeds that he had saved from previous crops.

However, he always found time for his charitable projects. He regularly attended the meetings of the Donaghmore Dispensary Committee. But he added a new civic project. He was a strong advocate of education, both for the children of church families, but also for all the residents of the Donaghmore area. Most local residents also felt the need for a local school to replace the Annagbane School that closed when Mr. Irvine moved away. So one day he left his farm work and walked over to Tullymurry. There he walked over the fields with some of his neighbors to explore a possible site for the new school. He also contributed financially to the effort.

There was much activity among James's large family. Robert was busy every weekend filling in for other ministers in their churches. But there was no sign that he would be able to get a church of his own. Still though he didn't yet have secure employment, he went off to Belfast to marry Jane McKee whom he had met while studying in Belfast.

Soon after, there was another wedding. Son John married Ellen Todd, whom James called the Spartan Queen. She was the only child of his friend Hugh Todd of Ringclare. The couple went to Newry where the ceremony was performed on January 25th. There seemed to be no celebrating attached to either of these weddings. James himself didn't attend. John and Ellen settled into Loughorne House where John Martin had lived before his arrest in Dublin.

Samuel, James's youngest son was now working in a bank in Portadown. With his remaining sons following professions that James greatly hoped would provide a good income and keep them home in Ireland, he at least had the satisfaction of knowing that he had done his best to achieve this goal.

§

Soon, John found his new life depressing. He had brought materials with him that would allow him to write a book on the Irish famine. However, he couldn't muster the energy or initiative to undertake that major task. He was then forty-two years old without any major accomplishments, and no profession. He didn't want to return to his farming life, and he feared that the time when he could serve his country had already passed by. His only pleasure was meeting with his new friends for conversations in the evenings, smoking his clay pipe while they chatted. He passed the days by writing letters to friends and newspapers.

John had just reached Paris when he wrote his first letter, this one to Dr. Gray who was the editor of the *Freeman*, published in Dublin. He had two objectives in writing the letter. First, he wanted to make clear that none of the Young Irelanders were required to sign any declarations or promises to obtain their freedom. "Of course, none of us had solicited the 'pardon' directly or indirectly."

However, he did very much want to publicly thank those who had supported him. "For myself, I wish to hereby offer my thanks to such of my countrymen as may have shown a kindly interest in my fate, either by desiring my liberation or any other way."

But the main object of this letter was "to remind the people of Ireland and the generous portion of the British people that there are still eight Irish prisoners in Van Diemen's Land besides four in Bermuda or some other British penal station. After naming each of the prisoners, he reminded Dr. Gray and his readers of the extraordinary situation that existed in Ireland at the time these men were arrested, tried and sentenced. "The conspiracy was entered into at the time when the Irish people were disarmed, their country occupied by a…large British army and police force, and their ports threatened by British ships of war—the Habeas Corpus Act suspended, and the Crime and Ordinance Act the law; when men whose national sentiments were those of ¾ of the Irish population were, for the sake of those national sentiments, under sentence of death or transportation, and the British governor imprisoned Irish men and women at his discretion; where the hundreds of poorhouses were crammed and reeking with half-starved, plague-stricken wretches, once Irish farmers or laborers, when the youth, strength, spirit of Ireland thronged the seaports, flying in despair any-whither from the desolation of their country; in short during the worst time of the IRISH FAMINE. If partial sympathy, or respect for our motives, or generous pity, has induced any person in Ireland or in Great Britain, to desire the liberation of O'Brien and his comrades, surely there are the same and stronger considerations for desiring the 'pardon' of those Irishmen who are yet suffering all the penalties of their patriotism."

A few weeks later, he wrote a letter back to Van Diemen's Land to the Connells. He apologized for not getting the letter written in time to catch the first mail to Australia. He thought that the delay would allow him to collect interesting material to entertain them with. But he also delayed because he thought he would be able to write in "a more cool and decorous state. The remembrance of you and some other friends of my exile was still such as to make my heart throb in a disorderly manner and to agitate the pen so that it might write queer disorderly things."

His expectation of calmness was unsuccessful. "But I feel not a whit more decorously inclined now. And I suppose it will be the same after years, as it is after months. Memory carries me back to the dear old Sugar-Loaf; I see the white house, the object to which my steps are bent in many a pilgrimage. From among the flowers and fruit-trees it seems to beckon me on as if to say. 'Here poor exile is welcome and cead mil Failta [sic], here are those who love Ireland and feel for Irelands miseries like you; here is rest and peace!'—Ah, and it was to one rest and peace for all within its walls! May peace and love reign there among father, mother, sons, daughters and all, Amen!"

How strange it was that what was essentially a prison could so capture John's affections. Just how intensely he felt about his friends became clear as he continued. "Yes, there I was among the generous, faithful friends the companions with whom my heart would not wear disguises. And there too, I had many a frolic, and sometimes felt in danger of something more serious than politics with all my bashfulness and gravity and the rest of it, I am a confounded old fool, and I am ready to cry and to laugh this minute as there is nobody by to see—Well; God bless the Sugar Loaf, at any rate! May its fields give rich harvests and its flocks and herds be many and thriving, and may industry, health, honour and happiness abide there, and O'Connells own and enjoy it for generations!"

While letters to Dr. Gray and the Connells were infrequent events, John had one friend with whom he corresponded regularly. George Mahon and John had enjoyed each other's company in Paris for a time before George did what John could not and returned to Ireland. In their letters that followed over the years, John discussed many of the issues that were of great importance to George Henderson. In a letter to Mahon, John responded to Mahon's questions on tenant rights and religion.

John didn't concern himself too much with tenant rights, as he didn't think that it could be solved to benefit Irish farmers until Ireland ended "the foreign domination and gained the country for its own citizens." "What I really want, is simply that our country should belong to its own citizens, to own it, rule it, use or abuse it, as their own wisdom or folly may think fit. I hold it for an axiom that the worst native rule is better for a nation than the best foreign rule."

It was clear to John that religion was dividing the Irish and making them weak before the power of England. "I hold that there is one right and effectual way to settle the religious question, and that is simply to obey the dictates of equity and common sense. Let the state immediately on becoming its own master declare all religions free and all sects equal, by the constitution and before the laws. If once perfect religious equality were established in Ireland, I think there would not arise any serious danger of its being overthrown…Let us suppose that all the churches are left to support their own forms of worship out of their own monies; and that none of them is compelled to pay for supporting the worship of others."

John went on to discuss the religious persecution of churches and the potential domination of Ireland by the Catholic Church, which was a great fear of George's. He concluded the letter with a summary. "To sum up: I think that religious equality would surely be established immediately upon the Irish people attaining their national independence. I trust the Protestants would have the grace to give their ready and cheerful assent to such a just & wise settlement, & would willingly sacrifice their present unfair advantages." George Henderson believed something very different. Should John's wish for Irish independence and subsequent religious equality be achieved, George believed that Ireland would erupt into civil war.

Despite the care John took in framing his opinions, he wasn't able to convince Mahon that he was right, Mahon wrote an immediate response, rejecting John's arguments. "Better to be ruled by the devil we know than by the devil we don't know."

§

George Henderson wrote an interesting leader for the *Telegraph* as John was beginning his correspondence with Mahon. Apparently, members of Parliament were considering a total pardon for O'Brien. This rumor resulted from a letter leaders of both parties from all over England had written asking Prime Minister Palmerston to set O'Brien totally free.

George had John in mind. "But gross injustice were involved should the amnesty have merely an individual reach. We put in a claim on behalf of a friend, once a neighbor, whose crime reached not the altitude of Smith O'Brien's who has been subjected to a like measure of retribution, who had equally respected his parole of honor, and who is not only as high minded an Irish Gentleman, but as amiable and good a man as his fellow-exile. If an act of Royal Clemency restore Smith O'Brien to his native land, let the Representatives of Ulster, see to it that even-handed justice have full scope, so that the amnesty may include John Martin."

In a few weeks, George published another update on John Mitchel. George was happy to report that Mitchel was going to Russia, Britain's foe in the Crimean War. He thought that Mitchel would really enjoy throwing bombs at the British. However, in the next edition of the paper he was obliged to offer a correction. Members of the Mitchel family who still lived in the area had notified him that he was mistaken. Instead Mitchel and his family were moving south to Tennessee where Mitchel intended to take up farming. "The friends and his family, as well as his own personal well-wishers, in the North of Ireland, will be gratified by this announcement." George was clearly not among Mitchel's well-wishers.

The British Parliament had for some time been discussing how to better structure Irish government. They finally passed a Town Improvement Act that authorized towns to adopt a new governmental structure. Local approval was required before the new law could be activated.

The Commissioners, who had powers too limited to meet the needs of the growing town, would benefit from new powers the legislation authorized. They had discussed this issue on several occasions, but they had been unable to reach any agreement. Finally the Lord Lieutenant of Ireland stepped into the impasse and directed the people of Newry to make the decision. So a meeting was called requesting all voting citizens of Newry to assemble in the Court House on September 3rd to decide whether or not to accept the new structure.

This legislation allowed for the appointment of new commissioners. They would have expanded authority to install water pipes, pave the town streets, and require adequate street lighting. Naturally, taxes could be increased as much as a shilling to pay for the new improvements. This new taxing power would be placed under the authority of the new commissioners along with the obligation to manage the town improvements.

There was one special exemption for Newry. Since the town already had a water system, Newry would be excluded from this obligation. The new requirements to manage cleaning, paving and lighting the town came with needed powers. Commissioners could now appoint a health officer to ensure that the town was able to avoid any major outbreak of contagious diseases. The health officer would also ensure that food wasn't adulterated. New commissioners were empowered to take land for sewers, regulate the location of houses, and ensure proper flow of the sewers from any of these houses. They could also ensure that there were party walls between connected houses to contain fires.

Commissioners would also manage a new consolidated rate to pay half the cost of more police. Citizens whose property was valued at less than five pounds at present paid no rates. Under the new legislation they would be required to pay their share of taxes. The town would be divided into wards. Each ward would elect a Commissioner to represent its interests. Anyone having property worth four pounds or more would be allowed to vote on these important changes to Newry.

The town improvements drew a lot of support. Newry residents had long complained about the bumpy and filthy streets, and poor lighting. However, the discussion of the benefits soon veered into a focus on the costs attached to the legislation. When the vote was finally taken, the new governmental structures allowed by the Town Improvement Act were soundly defeated.

§

While James and his laborers worked hard to bring in a large crop of flax because of the demand for linen to make the uniforms needed for the expanded British army, John continued writing letters, frequently to Mahon. In a new letter, John began by explaining that he hoped to convince Mahon that "the policy for which I offered my fortune and my liberty is just, wise and needful." John saw English rule as the main obstacle in achieving sensible solutions for any Irish problems. It was what made each side seek to benefit its own interests no matter the cost to the other side. If British rule ended, interests could more easily be balanced and reconciled to benefit everyone. Centuries of experience provided a sound basis on which to begin this work.

Unfortunately, the question of "priestly influence" was a different matter. There was no understanding of any kind. "We are away in cloud-land, dream-land, misty regions of speculation as vague, as metaphysical as religious controversy. There is no firmer footing to be found."

Then, John dove into the "cloud land." He told Mahon that the church establishment would end when British control ended. When that was done, Ireland would be left with a policy of "religious equality and liberty." John believed that this was "the only just and wise settlement of the religious question." While Mahon and John were united this far in the debate, Mahon believed that John's desired settlement would be prevented by the urge of the Catholic church to dominate Ireland, to meet the demands of Rome. Mahon offered three rebuttal arguments. The first was that in a free Ireland, Catholics would have a majority of representatives, and could establish "priestly rule." Second that priests were agents of a foreign power. Finally, that rule from Rome was the most unprincipled as they "trade in religion." These were the same sentiments that George Henderson held strongly and frequently provided to his readers.

John provided a general comment before he responded to Mahon's points. "I say, the influence of the priests is only such as every free man is entitled to exercise, such as you and I would contend for to the last—that of reason and advice. Every man has a right to give such advice and every man has a right to take it or refuse it." Perhaps the moral standing and education of priests might give them extra influence, but "For the Nation to assail their moral influence with coercive laws would be as unjust and as vain as a similar method for the prevention of the influence of women over men, of wise men over foolish, of old men over young." All men, even Catholic priests, were subject to the laws of Ireland. It they committed a crime, they would be face the same penalties as the least educated peasant.

Then John turned to Mahon's points. First, Catholics already sent more members to Parliament than any other religion. This was because of the religious situation in Ireland. If that were to be ended, "they and their flocks, as citizens would have no oppression to combat, no wrongs to redress, no interests apart from those of the non-Catholic citizens. If the Catholics happened to form the numerical majority of our people, there would be more votes given by Catholics; but I see no reason why those voles should not be as honest, wise and patriotic as mine or yours."

When it came to influence from outside Ireland, John saw a big difference between Rome and England. Rome's influence was "moral and voluntary." Citizens could still exercise their free judgment as to their best interests. However, English control was very different. They occupied "us by force of arms; the material appropriation of our land and its resources, against our will and for foreign purposes, the ruin of our national interest, the enslavement of every Irishman, the cause of internecine discord between classes, sects, races; the depth of degradation and the depth of misery to our people. It operates and by force of arms, not spiritual merely, upon the lives, liberty, property and honour of Irishmen…The Roman Catholic ideas might be very distasteful to you and me as men, but as citizens we have no business to seek laws against them."

John didn't quite understand what Mahon meant about "trading in religion." He surmised that Mahon meant using spiritual authority for "worldly purposes. Perhaps that is so; but that is not our affair. "Catholics submitted of their own free will. In this, the Catholics didn't differ at all from the actions of the established Church of Ireland.

Mahon had summed up his arguments "Better the devil you know than the devil you don't." John concluded his remarks on the religious issues of Ireland, by responding to Mahon's reference to "devils." John advised Mahon to tell his friends "that now they have both the devils; then they would have neither."

At this point, John ended his comments on the religious problems of Ireland and concluded his letter with his ideas on solving the landlord and tenant problems. First, all current property owners who pledged allegiance to Ireland should be confirmed in their tenures. Others could sell land to Irishmen or buyers who were willing to become Irish citizens. "I would recommend that no subject of a foreign land should be permitted to own land in Ireland." Primogeniture, and entail should be ended allowing for distribution of land in different and fairer ways.

As to how the landowners related to their tenants, John wouldn't interfere with the arrangements the two parties made as to rent. He objected strongly to "summary evictions" of tenants. He also favored allowing farmers to apply their rent to acquire ownership of their farms. Farmers should have the right to the value of all the improvements they had made to their leased farms. He would give certainty of continuous occupation of their leased lands to the greatest extent that was possible while considering the interests of others. "In short, I would desire to make both labourers and tenants proprietors."

Mahon responded quickly to John's discourse on Catholics in Ireland. Mahon still felt that if Ireland were to become independent, they would follow Rome and degrade the Protestant position in Ireland. Since John hadn't been convincing in his previous letter, John took a different tack this time. He asked if Mahon had ever tried to picture Ireland from the point of view of the Catholics of Ireland. Then he proceeded to do that himself.

"Born to an inheritance of degradation, your substance torn from you to support in insulting wealth the Church of the Foreigner, forced to pay for having your own worship called 'damnable idolatry' and your own Church the 'Mother of Abominations.'–I am not constitutionally fierce or vindictive; but I know I would not feel amiably towards the men who aided the Foreigner to treat me so & shared the spoil with him."

§

Newry was a quiet place in the fall of 1855. George focused on the continuing war with Russia. However, negotiations were underway, and there was optimism that the war might soon be ending. Despite his war worries, he was still greatly concerned about the status of religious education in the National schools. He wrote a leader advising Protestants to work hard to transform the schools to match their religious views. First, they should petition the Board of Education to add Bible study to regular classes, instead of the current practice of using it in separate classes. This effort would surely allow national policy to accommodate the wishes of the people.

The Newry Canal claimed yet another victim. James reported the tragedy in his journal. In late November, James reported "Alex'r Heslip of Curley drawn out of the Canal in Newry." George supplied additional detail. Heslip lived near Rathfiland and had come to Newry on business. While in town, he drank in abundance. As a result, he fell into the Albert Basin. Two sailors, stationed on boats there, heard the splash, but were unable to offer help in time. The coroner found the cause of death to be due to accidental drowning.

On the day of Heslip's funeral, much of the family went to Newry. James's daughters Jane, and Sarah Anne, alias Wee Child, and daughter-in-law Ellen went shopping. Ellen bought tea, ¼ stone of sugar, ¼ stone of white soap and ¼ stone of brown soap. Joe Duff was trusted to sell a pig for which he got 54s per cwt. James went by himself to the Heslip funeral at the church yard.

James was busy as usual with the harvest. He reported that his potato crop was very extensive and free from blight. However, the markets in Newry were still a problem. He took oats to town to sell but couldn't find a buyer that would offer a fair price. Son Robert was busy every Sunday filling in for other ministers. Once he even preached in Donaghmore, much to James's delight. Son James Jr. had opened new grocery store in Milwaukee which seemed successful. Many family gatherings took place in the old Ringbane house. All in all, times were good in Ringbane.

On Christmas Eve, James held a party in the upper house. This space was attached to the main Ringbane house and was large enough to hold parties and sometimes even church services. Robert and Samuel arrived from Belfast to join the dancing party which included Rev. Reid, and Rev. and Mrs. McClelland. Several groups of neighbors were there as well as James's married daughters and their husbands. Son John played the fiddle for the dancing.

§

The New Year leader for 1856 that George wrote for the *Telegraph* was quite similar to the one he had written for the previous year. He was very happy to report that the patriotic spirit was still prevalent in Ireland. He greatly hoped that this year the negotiations to end the Crimean war would bear fruit and peace would be finally achieved.

Still George had local concerns indirectly connected with the war effort. Since Sugar Island was near the barracks where the militia members were now stationed, militia members liked to congregate there by the canal. So did young women, whom George called "the women of the street." So he was pleased that the issue was raised at the first meeting of the Newry Commissioners for the new year. He reported that there was much discussion, but no actions were taken.

The Board of Guardians met early in the year as well. There were two important issues to discuss, both of which would cost money. In the cold weather of the season, there were concerns raised that the inmates had too little heat or warm clothing. Reports were presented that two of the children had died as a result. The Guardians directed that more coal should be provided and that the tailor should be directed to make clothes warmer.

Next they discussed a significant change in the arrangements for the important position of relieving officer. At the moment, Guardians hired a single officer for the local Poor Law District, A new proposal would divide the existing area into four smaller sections, each having its own relieving officer to be paid £20 per year. Donaghmore would be in a district with Ouley, Poyntzpass, Mount Norris, Tullyhappy and the Glen. The prevailing opinion seemed to be that one Relieving Officer worked quite well. More officers would surely result in having more people admitted to the workhouse. The result of this divisive discussion was an indefinite postponement. Finally when the Guardians discussed the subject of relieving officers again, they decided to keep the old arrangement. A new officer was hired, though some members still thought one officer wasn't enough. John Harshaw didn't comment on the subject

At the meeting where the new relieving officer was hired, another personnel issue was raised that festered from time to time during much of the year. Dr. Davis of the Workhouse was supposed to have a salary of £100 a year. However, his salary had been docked by £25, because Davis had refused to make two visits a day to the workhouse, maintaining that he was only obligated to make a single visit to earn his full salary. After considerable discussion, a compromise was reached. The doctor would get his full salary if he agreed to make a second visit if a pauper had been admitted and needed to be seen. This seemed satisfactory to all, so the full salary was restored.

George found himself appearing in the Newry Quarter Sessions. George had brought charges against a neighbor, Dr. David Waddell. According to testimony, Dr. Waddell had flushed a rabbit during a hunt with two greyhounds and a pointer and chased it onto George's property at Emyville. This case was an appeal of a previous hearing as Dr. Waddell maintained he had a right to hunt anywhere he wished. This was a claim George considered worth fighting.

A compromise to Dr. Waddell's claim was reached. George would agree not to pursue damages, if Dr. Waddell would agree not to hunt in Emyville again. To ensure that this agreement remained in force, the Court continued Dr. Waddell's conviction.

§

The new year at Ringbane began with very good news for James and the family. John and Ellen Todd became parents for the first time. "The Dandy, at Johns—about twelve oclock at night the Sparten had a 'Daughter.' She was attended by Dr. Johnston."

There was another interesting event, which in other times might have caused James or his son-in-law problems with the law. "Mr. Speers returned home from A Douglass where he had (on the 9th) found a gun that had been hid in A Douglass garden since the year 98, viz 58 years." With Ireland relatively tranquil, both James and his son-in-law Alexander Douglas, escaped prosecution for having an unregistered gun.

While George thought that sectarian tensions had declined during the war, apparently that wasn't wholly the situation in Donaghmore. Attacks that were typically sectarian had occurred there in the new year. A mill belonging to Andrew and John Marshall of Aughnacavan had been damaged by intruders. This was the second recent attack in the area. A sheep had been slaughtered on a nearby farm and part of it carried off. The police thought they knew who the vandal was but hadn't been able to collect enough information to bring charges.

There was other news in Donaghmore that saddened James and his neighbors. Long time resident John Johnston of Traymont was leaving the area for Kings County. So a farewell dinner was held on Feb. 12th at the Four Mile House. John's brother Robert Martin was in the chair. A few days later, James visited Johnston, having stopped on the way to watch stoves being installed in the meetinghouse for the first time.

Mr. Johnston had generous gifts for James, "six laurel shrubs—four of the portugeese—3 yew trees, ten Turkey oaks, gooseberrie cuttings, &c &c." The next day James reported that "Hugh, & men tore up scarlet willows from the top of the Bee garden and planted two commen & four potuguese Laurels in their place, Hugh also set three yew trees before the windows, and Turkey oaks in the hay garden."

Every spring, as James prepared his fields for planting, the better weather of the spring made the ocean passage safer for the emigration of friends and neighbors. This year it was Rev. Andrew Marshall who was leaving. Andrew was a brother of his daughter Jane's husband. As usual, there were events to help families prepare for what was often a final celebration. James followed Andrew's departure closely, as one of the reasons for Andrew to emigrate was the difficulty for young Presbyterian ministers to get a permanent church. This was a constant worry for James as well.

On March 7th James reported, "dined with Jane & Archy, a farewell dinner &c to Rev Andrew Marshall; in compney of Mr. Boyd Marshall, the Dandy, [Sarah] A Douglass, John & Hugh. [Robert]." Boyd Marshall, actually Samuel Boyd Marshall of the Four Towns, was Andrew's father. Two days later, Rev. Marshall "preached his farewell sermon in Donaghmore." Three days later, Robert went with his fellow ministers to Warrenpoint to watch Andrew board a ship for New Brunswick, Canada.

Rev. Marshall was still making his way across the Atlantic when James made a long awaited announcement. "'Treaty of peace' with Russia signed in Paris." For James this news was a mixed blessing, as he well understood that the prices for his products would quickly fall, making it difficult to pay the taxes that had been increased to fund the war.

For George, there was no such concern. He headed his leader with a banner headline. "Peace Proclaimed." He began his leader with a quote from the Bible. "Blessed are the peacemakers!" Then he let readers know just how he felt. "From many a full heart to many a tremulous lip, such a grateful utterance will impulsively spring, as the ear heard the grateful tidings have been flashed from the electric wire on Sunday afternoon, and thundered forth by the mighty voice of the cannon."

George went on to describe the way that the glorious event had been celebrated in Paris. The first sign of peace was the "thundering cannons of the place invalide." John would have certainly heard the joyful cannonade from his pensione. The sound of 102 thundering cannons would have carried across the city. The next night, Paris was ablaze with lights, as citizens created their own illuminations. Quickly placards announcing peace covered every available wall.

With the war over, the British government was anxious to dispense with the militias they had created in Ireland. They had a clear memory of the problems that were created by the Irish militia when England had removed all its mainline troops from Ireland to fight the American revolutionaries. The South Down Militia was ordered to disband within a few weeks. However, there were problems. Each person who enlisted had been promised a £6 bonus. Now that the need for militias had ended, the government was reluctant to pay the bonus. Instead, they would ensure a quick release to take advantage of plentiful jobs

Early in May, George announced a beneficial result of the end of the war. Queen Victoria, as a gesture of gratitude, issued a full pardon to all the Young Irelanders who had faithfully served their sentences. However, he did observe that "we trust all the exiles may return to their native country in a wiser mood, their minds wholly free of the taint of disaffection." Surely George knew John well enough to suspect that John's "taint of disaffection" would remain intact.

James got the same good news from his son Samuel. It had been almost eight years since James and John had shared a farewell cup of tea in Loughorne. On that sad occasion, James had little expectation that he would ever see his cherished nephew again. And now soon a reunion would take place. Certainly John would hurry home to Ireland. But the fact that John had to wait for official paperwork documenting the pardon before he could return to Ireland delayed his return. He had been sentenced to ten years transportation, leaving two years yet to be served before he was free without a pardon.

§

Shortly before the official pardon reached John in Paris, he wrote another letter to Mahon. He passed on to Mahon news of John Mitchel's move to Tennessee where he had bought a primitive farm in the wilderness area in the eastern part of the state, an event that George had already printed in the

Telegraph. Then he described for Mahon, what he was experiencing in Paris. The garden at the pensione was beautiful at this time of year, a pleasant place to sit and read, or walk about when it was sunny.

There were new residents since Mahon had lived there. But some would have been familiar, one a Mr. Comerford. He had once studied for two years in the Irish College. That seemed to make him an authority on the subject of the Catholic Church and its doctrines. But he also had opinions on many issues that pertained to Catholics in Ireland, which John found worth listening to and reflecting upon.

Before John concluded the letter, he returned to the topic of tenant rights, this time from a personal perspective. Farmers always wanted full compensation for improvements they had made, money landowners were reluctant to pay. In the area of Loughorne and Donaghmore, farmers had a right to sell their leases at a public auction. The price buyers were willing to pay at auction determined how much farmers would receive for their improvements. Sometimes land sold for more than farmers had invested. Sometimes farmers had invested more than they could recover. John himself had purchased two farms when the tenants emigrated. He had offered the highest price for the property during the auction. If this practice became common, disputes between land owners and tenants about the value of property improvements would diminish.

In his next letter, John discussed the structures of government and which forms might be preferable. "You know how anti-dogmatic is the disposition of my mind. In the matter of government, I should say (if compelled to pronounce) that the best in theory is pure republicanism and that despotism is better than oligarchy or than any of the forms called 'Constitution' which exclude from political power, any class of people. It seems to me that the exclusion of a class or classes of the population from the franchise is a priori argument that that class or those classes will be wronged by the portion of the citizens in the enjoyment of the franchise...When all the citizens share in the rights and responsibilities of government the interests of all have a fair prospect of being served. When only a portion of the citizens whether minority or majority of the population has exclusive possession of the ruling powers, the probability is that the interests of the portion excluded from political rights will be injured."

He continued to press his case. Different kinds of governments had existed at different times since human organization began. They might well have suited the conditions at the moment but been totally unsatisfactory at others. A common threat to individuals was the issue of class. One such class that was familiar and problematic to the people of Ireland was the landlord class. "But for the modern landlord, whom custom and public opinion expects only to make as much money as he can legally take out of the lands occupied by his tenants—for him to have extensive power [to determine land values or eject at will] over his tenants would seem hardly safe for the latter."

Soon after writing this letter, John received the pardon documents he had been waiting for. But instead of going directly to Ireland, he went first to Hampshire England. There was a pressing reason for this seemingly strange decision. There he greeted his youngest sister Anna and her husband Thomas Hirst. Anna had just gotten the devastating news that she had tuberculosis. Her condition was sufficiently dire that Hirst had been forced to retire from his position as professor of mathematics at the local university to care for her. When John reached Anna in England, he was shocked to see just how sick she really was. Great care would be needed to keep her alive.

Since John could provide some medical assistance, if needed, it was deemed safe for Anna to travel. John had originally planned to take Anna and Hirst to visit their sister Mary Simpson. However, Mary's children had developed measles. So plans were changed. Instead, the party would travel to Newry to stay with sister Elizabeth Todd on Downshire Road.

They took passage on a steamer in Liverpool making a scheduled trip to Warrenpoint. John must have been gratified at the first sight of Ireland rising above the edge of the Irish sea. He must have gloried in the sight of the two mountain ranges, the Mournes on the right, the Carlingfords on the left as they neared the entrance to the Lough, remembering as they grew more distinct the many times he had climbed them both.

Once in the calmer waters of the Lough, familiar sights he had never expected to see again, appeared, first at a distance, then clearer and more distinct as the steamer came closer to the dock in Warrenpoint. The Martin family home at Kilbroney was clearly visible as the ship passed beside the Mournes. It was a moment to savor.

John described what he had seen in Newry in his next letter to Mahon. "We arrived on Saturday morning. I have seen my brothers and several friends. Newry town is not a whit changed in the 8 years since I left it, except that it may be a little duller. For the first time since I had been removed from Ireland, I have seen men in ragged clothes. Poor Ireland!"

On June 3rd, George reported on John's arrival in Newry. "John Martin reached Newry on Friday evening, and of the hands that have grasped his, in the warmth of friendship, sure we are that not the least heartily have been pressed by him have been those of the many who were known to him to have repudiated 'Young Ireland' principles the more earnestly just because that to the infatuation which such principles engendered were ascribable the perversion of a generous-hearted Country Gentleman into an erring Politician." Surely George was one of those people happy to "grasp" John's hand once again.

A full week passed before John returned home to Loughorne. As his carriage turned down the lane to Loughorne, he saw that his friends and tenants had lined both sides. They waved and cheered lustily as he passed by. They walked beside him as John neared Loughorne House, and clustered about as he climbed down. James was working on the Ramper meadow when he was called home. "Found John Martin in the parlour; I saluted him & spent the day—from 4 oclock—with him in Loughorne—dined with James & drunk tea with John & Sparten." The words that James wrote were simple, but his great joy at seeing John again was obvious.

In the ensuing week, James was able to see John again several times, often over dinner when there was time to catch up on the eight years that had separated two men who had previously seen each other almost every day. Anna and Tom came to visit as well. This was the first time that James and Tom had met. Anna was still the Young Queen to James, so he was pleased to meet her new husband but very saddened to see her so ill.

§

While John was enjoying his time back home in Ireland, George's attention turned to some apparent problems in Donaghmore. In the June 24th edition of the *Telegraph*, George made a somewhat cryptic comment on sectarian marches that had taken place in Donaghmore. He also pointed out that since such marches were illegal, constables were looking into these reports.

In the next edition, George returned to the unrest in Donaghmore. He hoped that the Orange Order would obey the laws in place against marching even if the Ribbonmen didn't. Instead, George advised the Order to let the authorities handle the illegal marches.

And George's hopes were quickly fulfilled. The first hearing on the Donaghmore marches took place in the Petit Sessions in Newry two days later. The constables had indeed been busy. Twenty-six men had been arrested and charged with illegal marching, on two different occasions, apparently as a reaction to rumors of an earlier Orange march in Glascar. Constable Madden handed the prosecutions and Mr. Brown the defense. Before any witnesses were called, Mr. Brown asked that the charges be dismissed if the accused agreed not to march again. Mr. Madden objected on the grounds that the people of Donaghmore were sufficiently distressed to ask for a local police station be created, even though they would have to bear the expense. So the court case continued.

The march went from the Donaghmore Meetinghouse to St. Bartholomew's Church. That took the marchers through Aughnacavan. where John Porter lived. He provided the first testimony. He had been in his garden there on June 16th around 8 p.m. when he heard the sound of drums. There had been about 100 men marching along the road, heading toward the church. As they got near, he heard a shot. There were no flags, and he didn't recognize the songs. Since everyone knew that Mr. Porter was a Protestant, everyone also knew that for him not to know the songs was a clear identification that the marchers were Catholics.

Other witnesses followed who testified that there were two drums, one white and one green, also some men playing fifes. Mr. Madden seemed most interested in getting witnesses to identify the marchers with special interest in those who seemed to be carrying guns. When the marchers reached the church, they marched back and forth a few times, and then headed off in the direction of the Glen. None of the men who testified seemed in anyway offended by the marching. The Court hearing ended with sixteen men being released on a bail of £10 and £5 sureties to guarantee their appearance at the Quarter Sessions.

The men charged with illegal marching didn't have to wait long, as the Newry Quarter Sessions took place in early July. Testimony was similar to the original hearing. Seventeen men, many with well-known local names, were all found guilty and sentenced to two months in jail.

This march had been triggered by an earlier Protestant one that had taken place in Glascar previously. Seven men faced charges similar to the participants in the Catholic march, for illegally marching and carrying guns. Again locals testified that they weren't bothered by this Orange march. But these Protestant marchers were also sentenced to two months in jail.

These sentences would have substantial impacts on family members, as they would be in jail still when they would be needed to work on the harvest. So before the month had ended, George published a leader requesting that all the convicted farmers should be released from the rest of their sentences. In the *Telegraph* of August 2nd, George was happy to report that the Lord Lieutenant had pardoned all the men in prison for marching law violations. They would be restored to their families a month early to participate in the harvest.

§

After this first visit to Loughorne and Ringbane, John left to visit other family members, but returned several more times to Loughorne. On his next trip, John found his uncle Harshaw in the Bogpark. Together they walked back to Ringbane House for tea. The next morning, James joined John for breakfast at Loughorne. Afterwards, they walked to the Bower, and to the top of the Leckey and saw the garden. On the final day of this visit, John, James and Samuel went to services at the Meetinghouse. After church, they gathered at Ringbane House with the Rev. White, James Martin, son Samuel, and daughter Mary.

Near the middle of September, James mentioned John's next visit. On a "fine dry day," James went to Newry to do some banking business, possibly to mortgage more of his property to allow him to pay his taxes and maintain his workers and his property. On the way home, he went to Ballymackratty where he met Samuel returning home from his bank job in Portadown. Next day, John came over the fields from Loughorne to join James as he gathered with friends and family. Later James went up the Meetinghouse Path to Loughorne House to have tea with John Martin and sister Mary Simpson, John Harshaw and his wife Ellen.

The rounds of visits with friends continued for several days. On September 15th, James explained the reason behind the gatherings. "Dry with some clouds—Absalom marked the young Ash tree at the wall in the street to be called 'Absaloms tree' and the young yewtree in the Bee garden to be 'Absalom's yew tree,' my youngest son the 'Beautyfull Absalom,' left thus, about ten oclock accompanied by John, Chiefton, and Mr. Riddle. He dined with Jane & Archy and left by the half past four train for <u>Belfast</u> and <u>Glascow</u> on his way to New York. I kissed his brow, & said to him, '<u>Go</u> and the <u>Lord</u> be with you.'" Now James would suffer the pain of yet another family loss. Three of his sons would now live far away in America.

Samuel and his brothers reached Greenock at 4:30 a.m. on the Stag and took a train to Glasgow where they had breakfast, Then Samuel boarded the Glasgow which sailed at 1:30. John stayed with his brother until the ship pulled away. He arrived back in Glasgow as Samuel's ship approached. The brothers waved their caps in farewell as the ship passed. John returned to Belfast by the night mail ship, the same route he had taken to get to Scotland. He hurried to Ringbane to tell James about Samuel's departure.

§

As Samuel was preparing to depart, John wrote to Mitchel from his brother Robert's home in Rostrevor. He was upset that a letter he had written to a Dublin paper hadn't been published. John had wanted to explain to a wide audience that he hadn't done anything wrong that should have placed him in a position for a pardon. "I have never done anything to forfeit my just right to live in Ireland enjoying the protection of my country's laws as an honest and inoffensive citizen. So as it was an outrage for the English Government to banish me, it is an insolence for them to treat me as a pardoned criminal whom they graciously permitted to return."

Then John went on to describe his return to Ireland to his old friend. "I have been in Ireland for two months. My hand has been grasped by many a kindly neighbor and friend of old times, and my eyes have looked upon many a dearly-loved scene that I had hardly hoped ever to visit again except in dreams. I am congratulated on all sides upon the present 'prosperity' of Ireland. And to those who witnessed the years of famine, the present condition of the country may well seem prosperity. There is no longer starvation, and the laboring people are able to procure enough of tolerable food and the number of paupers supported by rates is greatly diminished, and beggary & rags are far less remarkable then for many years past. Industry has to a great extent recovered from the effects of the famine and the desolation that was then brought upon property of rich and poor that was Irish is nearly at an end. But I am afraid that it is mainly to the recovery of the potato crop that we owe this happy change. For some years past the potato disease has been gradually wearing out, and the farmers and labourers have been profiting by the return of this most valuable of Irish corps. Yet, delightful as it is to see this comparative prosperity in Ireland, I cannot help remarking that of all peoples that I have seen or read of the Irish enjoy the least share of their own country's produce. My nation—alas that I should have to say!—is the shabbiest nation in the civilized world."

Just before John left Ireland, he wrote another letter to Mahon. He reported that his sister wasn't doing well in the part of France where she had gone, so she and her husband were going to move to the mountains of Pau. John was going to her there as soon as he left Ireland. He was hoping that

Anna's health would stabilize. If that happened, he was planning to make a trip to America to visit Mitchel in Tennessee. Then he would go to Ontario to visit his sister and her family in Canada.

This was a trip John never took.

Residences

Harshaw home at Ringbane

Robert Martin home at Kilbroney

Henderson home -- Emyvale

Chapter 6

Angels of Death

1856 - 1858

The days were growing shorter when John left Ireland and returned to France, which he then considered to be his home. But he didn't return to Paris, going instead to Pau to be with his sister Anna and her husband. He hoped that his medical training and the healthful climate would help Anna live longer. Pau was in the southwest of France in the Pyrenees. Winters there were milder and damper than in Paris, factors that might help Anna's tuberculosis.

Initial reports seemed hopeful. Anna improved in this different climate. Her doctor in Pau spoke hopefully of recovery. Unfortunately, the climate wasn't so beneficial for John. For the first time in nine years, he began to suffer symptoms of asthma, though much less severely than when he was young.

Unfortunately, Anna contracted a severe chest infection. Though she was able to recover, the setback clouded her overall prospects for recovery. Still she remained hopeful and cheerful. But John had observed her symptoms and no longer believed that she would be able to survive this killer disease. However, he would continue to ensure his sister lived the rest of her life in comfort and peace.

§

James finished the harvest of 1856, selling his produce in Newry, despite the lack of action by Parliament to remedy the unfairness of the system of weights and measures. Free trade had also pushed the prices of farm produce downward as well. These commercial practices substantially reduced James's income. Combined with higher taxes, James found himself growing poorer by the year. George shared James's distress over the heavy tax burdens placed on Ireland. The new taxes that had been levied to pay for the Crimean War had yet to be removed as promised. Heavy import duties were still levied on products most consumed in Ireland, such as tea and imported malt. James in particular and Ireland in general seemed to be sinking into a dark new pit of poverty.

James was waiting anxiously to hear from Samuel [Absalom] that he had arrived safely in New York. While the days dragged on, he noted in his journal every Sabbath how many weeks had passed since he had seen Samuel. It was the middle of October before the anxiously anticipated letter from Samuel arrived, including a letter from Willy. Absalom would live in New York City with Willy and his family, which now included a son William and a daughter Emma.

This word arrived just after James and George both commented on an unusual astronomical event. There was an almost total eclipse of the moon. George alerted his readers to the event, which would start shortly after 8 p.m. on October 13th and last until just after midnight. James described how the eclipse looked as he watched it. "Fine night the moon rolling thrugh clouds, as the eclipse came on."

Despite James's financial worries, he remained busy. Between the eclipse and the end of the year, James attended eight funerals of friends and neighbors. He still had unsold crops and livestock to manage. He slaughtered a cow and sold the fat and skin in Newry. He bought a new sow and a ram from Rostrevor. These were ordinary actions for an improving Ulster farmer. But he had some less ordinary activities to attend to as well.

James had five workers digging potatoes on November 19th, when he made a cryptic comment. "Mr. Guy enquired about Mr. Todds Registry." He offered no additional explanation. However, less than a week later, Guy's name appeared in another entry. "Mr. Guy & Crawford got a copy of Connaways marriage, out of Mr. Todds Registry." Again, there was no explanation as to what was so important about Rev. Todd's registry.

Four days later it became clear from another entry that the registry was evidence in some sort of court case. "Mr. Guy[,] Bridwell keeper, of Newry came here & drove me to Newry where I was examined by Mr. Frank JP about the late Mr. Todd of Croan marriage Registry, which Registry I left with Mr. Frank to be returned after the Assizes."

The trial that had unexpectedly involved James began on a Thursday morning March 12, 1857. The weather was frosty but clear as James started out on foot about 10 a.m. He walked to the Newry Road near Derryleckey to wait for Guy who had promised to drive James to Downpatrick. They arrived there between 6 and 7 p.m. Both men took lodgings with William Gibson in Sauls Street.

When James rose the next morning about 7 a.m., the weather had decidedly turned stormy with a cold wind blowing off the Irish Sea. James had to wait until midafternoon before he was examined by Sir Edwin Hill before the grand jury. When he was dismissed, he went to the newspaper reading room to follow the latest news. He had a daguerreotype of Samuel on the table beside him. Again, he slept at Gibsons.

Saturday's weather hadn't improved. James had breakfast about 9 a.m. and then returned to the reading room for a while. Then he climbed up the hill to the Court House to wait to be summoned. But no summons came. So James stopped by the home of Rev. William White, before heading back to Gibsons.

Since James had to be in court again on Monday, there wasn't time for him to make the trip home. The weather had improved on the Sunday, the 26th Sabbath since Samuel had left Ireland. So James rose early and climbed the Downpatrick hills. The wind came in sharp from the southwest and bringing snow to the summits.

James returned from his walk in time to attend services at Rev. White's church. Fortunately, he had already reached the church when the area was struck by a terrific snow squall, which lasted until about 3 p.m. Still he and Rev. White tramped up the hill to the Downpatrick Jail for services there. The third service of the day was in Rev. White's meeting house about 7 p.m., following which James had dinner and tea with Rev. White and his family.

Finally, on Monday morning, James was called to testify. James described the experience, "was examined before the judge & jury on David Carnaways Bigamy case respecting Mr. Todd of Croans marriage Registry."

George covered the trial as well. The case involved a man named David Carnnaway. Carnnaway had married Martha Clarke in Rev. Todd's parlor on Jan. 2, 1834. Both of the participants were members of the Presbyterian Church, making the marriage legal under prevailing law. Testimony from the Clarke family at trial verified the church records, which James had produced.

James was finally called to testify. He stated that he had known the Rev. Todd for six or seven years. After Rev. Todd had died, his son had given the minister's records to James. It was these records that James had produced to give documentary evidence of the time and place of the wedding ceremony.

Some years after this ceremony, Carnnaway had apparently deserted his wife and changed his name to David McCracken. Under that name he married again. The jurors were confused as to whether McCracken and Carnnaway were the same person. So, the jury acquitted Carnnaway of the changes.

§

John remained in Pau. Besides providing constant medical care for Anna, he had time to consider the issues of the day and his failure to impact them in any positive way. He shared these personal thoughts in letters to Mahon. This correspondence became a lifeline for John. In one letter, Mahon expressed surprise at John's stated support of landlords. In turn, John found Mahon's surprise surprising. "Was not I myself an employer, a landlord (in a small way to be sure) all the time of my political action in Ireland? And ever since my transportation as a felon, have I not been drawing rents out of Ireland for my support? My interests are altogether those of a landlord and of an employer of Irish labor."

John's life had been planned for him by his father and his Martin uncles to meet the need to manage the family's townland of Loughorne, while younger brothers David and Robert managed the family mills in Rostrevor. He would be a resident landlord for life. It was only the scenes of the famine, "so horrible for the sufferings of the people, so ruinous to industry and property, so destructive of morality, so sinful and intolerable in its causes and character" that propelled him to political action.

The education he had received as a child walking the fields of Loughorne with his father had instilled in him support for the existing structure of land ownership. As a result, he had no worries that gaining Irish independence would bring any great change in or damage to the interest of Irish landlords. Any disruption in landlord and tenant relationships would be minor and temporary, representing a much smaller risk than the horrors of the famine, that "intolerable" famine. On the other hand, he would have made any sacrifice for freedom from England up to and including confiscation of his land. If other landlords shared his beliefs, they would join with the peasants to lead the revolution and ensure stability in an independent Ireland. "My ideas of social policy are very conservative, and they grow more and more of that character— perhaps on account of my age. Any sort of social order to which people have got accustomed has something good in it, something that makes it far preferable to anarchy."

If a different social system were instituted in independent Ireland, it would have to be a better system. One such improvement John envisioned was for Irish farmers, but not farm laborers, to become owners of the land. There was no reason for such a change to be anything but peaceful once the Irish were in charge of their own decisions, as long as "all sects and classes…consider and respect the feelings, the interests, the rights, the force of others." Everyone would benefit from being part of an independent nation.

"Even as things are I am satisfied that it would be best for a proprietor to deal as much as possible on the principle of permanence with the people he employs. Yet he must not submit to their roguery, he must maintain his authority and liberty of actions."

John concluded with an explanation for his depressed spirits, aside from the sickness of his sister. He reported that he did "no work either of brain or limbs."

When John next reported to Mahon, he was back in Paris at his old pensione at 26 Rue Lacipide living directly under the rooms in which Mahon had lived when they met. Sadly, Anna's long feared death was drawing very near. The small party had returned from Pau the end of May. Despite her precarious health, Anna tolerated the trip well enough. She had taken up residence in an apartment 65 Marbauf, Champs Elysees with Tom and a servant she was very fond of. Sister Mary Simpson, husband Maxwell and their children had taken an apartment in the same building.

In his next letter, John confirmed that last sad prediction. John walked the streets of Paris under the hot summer sun to see Anna every day. She remained cheerful and hopeful till the end, considering it her duty to continue to struggle for life until the last minute. So it was that she rose and dressed on her final day. Hirst carried her to the living room where she ate breakfast and dinner. Then he assisted her into their carriage for a ride around Paris. They shared happy conversations. However, by the time they returned to their apartment it was obvious that death was near. She was barely able to "rise from her chair." When she realized that her moment had come, she told her family with her final breaths, "I'm not afraid to die." She was buried in Paris, far from the green fields of Loughorne.

§

As 1857 began, George knew nothing about Anna's struggle for life. In his greeting to his readers, he raised two new concerns, one reflecting his philosophical thinking, the second very practical advice. "The one is, the terrible havoc, made in society, and in the bosoms of the numerous happy families by the modern insatiable desire for accumulating wealth." He went on to justify this belief, citing the rise of a powerful class of manufacturers, the frantic search for gold in the ground and in the expanding system of banks, insurance, and railroads. "This malady has too much infected all classes." He warned those with the money lest they become the victims of their own greed, since such acquisitiveness was contrary to Biblical wisdom.

Now that the Crimean War had ended, the people of Newry were still waiting for the promised end of the income tax that had been levied on the Irish supposedly to finance the war. At the time of passage, Parliament members trolling for votes, promised that the tax would be ended once the war ended. As the new year began, this promise hadn't been kept. However, George remained hopeful that the tax would soon be ended.

The first weeks of the new session of Parliament passed without any action to reduce the Irish tax burdens. The outrage over the issue that George hoped to trigger in Newry had yet to happen. George attributed this to local divisions and the ineptness of their member, William Kirk. Even worse, from George's perspective, was that Parliament also broke another promise. Besides using a tax on income to fund the war, they had raised tariffs on products that were very important to the Irish, one of them being tea. These tariffs too were to end with the end of the war. And again, that didn't happen. Instead, Parliament voted a small reduction in the tariffs with the promise to gradually phase them out. George urged groups in Ireland to flood Parliament with petitions to show local opposition.

While George followed the actions of Parliament closely, printing large portions of the actual debates for his readers' enlightenment, he also followed events unfolding in the United States. He had expected that civil war would break out with the election of Buchanan. So far that hadn't happened. But that didn't diminish his certainty that a horrid civil war was inevitable. He frequently printed news of efforts to spread slavery as the country expanded. And sometimes he reprinted stories of the nature of slavery he found in other papers.

One such account appeared in the *Telegraph* in early February. The episode occurred in Carter County in Kentucky and was witnessed by a reporter for a New York paper. A man named William McMinnis held a large amount of land there. Someone warned him that there was a slave revolt being planned on his farm. The slaves who were supposedly involved were arrested and tried. But there was no evidence that any revolt was being discussed. So McMinnis selected one slave to be threatened with torture in order to produce the desired evidence. When he denied any knowledge of an uprising, he was stripped and lashed 200 times while he screamed that he didn't know anything.

When the whipping didn't produce the desired information, the bleeding body was tied to a stake, and wood was placed around his feet. At this point, the reporter could watch no more and left. But he learned afterwards, that a fire had indeed been lit, causing major burns before the victim was finally released. He died the next morning. Mr. McMinnis had lost a slave worth several hundred dollars and learned nothing, all because of a vague rumor.

The issues of taxes and slavery faded from George's attention in March when there was a stunning surprise. Parliament was dissolved, and a new election was called. This news must have wearied Newry electors, but George was delighted at the opportunity to defeat William Kirk who had announced that he would stand again for his seat in Parliament. George expected that the Conservatives would find a good candidate to run against him and recapture the seat. Within a few days George reported that a local businessman and activist named Dickinson would run to replace Kirk. There were rumors that others would enter the competition as well. As it turned out, Dickinson decided not to run. But that brief disappointment turned to delight when George learned that a local friend, Major Henry Waring, was going to contest the election for the Conservatives.

James and his family were focused on the County Down elections. They would again assist in the campaign of sitting MP David Ker, whom they had worked hard to elect in the previous campaign. George had supported Ker then, but he wasn't satisfied with his actions in Parliament. He was greatly pleased when a new candidate appeared to contest for the Down seats. Lt. Col. W. B. Forde announced that he was going to run as a team with the other current member, Lord Edwin Hill, in hopes of defeating Ker. George advised the voters in County Down to vote for this new team as both men were both staunch conservatives. However, if voters chose Ker as one of their members, his liberal views would cancel Hill's conservative ones, essentially leaving the electors of Down without any effective representation.

Mr. Kirk came back to Newry before the end of the session to begin his canvass and announce his platform. He supported free trade, seeing it as a benefit to Newry. He wanted educational opportunities extended to older children in order to prepare them for the competitive examinations for college. He still supported a permanent settlement of the conflicts between landlords and their tenants.

When it came to George's favorite topics of taxes, and tariffs, Kirk agreed with him that tariffs on raw materials and necessities such as tea should be reduced in order to increase consumption. He had voted to keep the income tax for three more years until 1860 in exchange for Parliament cancelling all the outstanding Irish debts incurred by building the poorhouses and giving supportive loans during the famine. Finally, he was in favor of religious equality. Most Newry residents supported religious equality, including George. But the interpretations of what that actually meant and would produce in practice differed widely. Kirk's idea was that all religions in Ireland would be equal under the law. That goal could only be achieved by ending the power of the Established Church. As for strictly local issues, Kirk had always supported improvements in the navigation of the Lough, and all the local efforts to build new railway lines in the area.

All Major Waring offered to justify his candidacy was that he was from Newry and that everyone there knew him. However, when George wrote his leader on the election, he felt that Kirk was the candidate who hadn't properly revealed the principles he supported.

Kirk met his voters on March 28th. He was still supported by John's brother-in-law Robert Ross Todd, and Hill Irvine, owner of the Donaghmore estate. Following Kirk's meeting, George wrote another leader making clear to readers his objections to re-electing Kirk. He didn't believe that Kirk had done anything to augment the efforts of Newry leaders to get the Lough designated a safe harbor. He disagreed with Kirk's vote on the income tax, claiming that the debt forgiveness mainly benefited the south, as Ulster had little debt left to pay. Contrary to George's beliefs, Kirk had supported removing the Bible as a major text in government schools. The idea of intermediate schools might be beneficial, but it served as a distraction from the faults of the Board of Education.

There was one last issue on which George and Kirk disagreed. Kirk believed that until there was a secret ballot, there would be no settlement of landlord and tenant issues or other issues of great importance in Ireland. He pointed out that the secret ballot had been tried in France and had worked well there. George claimed that landlords had a right to tell their workers how to vote. With the current ballot system, votes were cast in the open and could be easily checked to determine whether or not they had voted according to instructions.

The meeting to formally select the two candidates took place in the Newry Court House. Most of the speakers supporting Major Waring spent more of their time attacking Kirk than explaining why Waring would be a good candidate. When Waring came forward to accept the nomination and speak, he was roundly booed by the Kirk supporters. George didn't approve of this conduct and didn't think most of the disrupters were actual electors.

When the vote was called, the presiding Seneschal declared that Kirk had won. The Waring supporters demanded a vote.

James recorded the election in his journal. "nomination of Messers W. Kirk and H. Waring in Newry." George urged the Waring voters to vote early. He blamed the partisan divisions on the Kirk supporters.

James recorded the results of the election on April 1st. "Gray morning, & fine dry day—ploughed on the Round hill, men thrashed &c. drove the Dandy, & Mary to see Jane & Archy, dined & drunk tea there—Mr. Kirk elected for the town of Newry by a majority of fifteen over Mr. Waring."

In the same journal entry, James reported that the family were again supporting Ker's campaign. "John canvising for Mr. Ker in Balnaskeagh, & Balnagrass."

George wasn't a bit pleased with the results of the election. He made that plain to all his readers as the election results were made official. Voters did come early, when the booths opened at 8 a.m. By 10 a.m., two thirds of the voters had already appeared. Waring had an early lead. By noon, Waring led by 4 votes. But then the Kirk supporters turned out every voter on their lists, the infirm being carried in chairs and the mentally ill led in to vote. By 4:30, Kirk led by 14 votes. Kirk supporters accompanied him to the hotel where he addressed his jubilant supporters. George attributed Waring's loss to Conservative electors who hadn't voted.

George was still grumbling about the election when the next paper came out. He didn't see how Newry residents could have voted for Kirk as he had not done a good job for Newry. Then he moved on to the underlying issue that George had raised during the previous election. Kirk was a Presbyterian in a seat that had always been held by a member of the Established Church of Ireland. In order to win, Kirk and his Presbyterian supporters had to unite with Catholic voters. George called the Catholic religion a "fearful and soul destroying error." As Presbyterians and Catholics had united to fight for tenant rights, now they had united yet again to oppose the wise governance of the Church of Ireland. George saw this cooperation as a terrible threat to Irish stability. Robert Ross Todd had checked the poll books and confirmed George's fears. All except one of the Catholic electors had supported Kirk.

But there was another election battle to fight, which George hoped would have a better outcome, the County Down contest. The Harshaws were working to thwart George's hopes. On April 5th, James wrote, "met Mr. Todd, Mr. Ker & Mr. McColla in Johns, Mr. Conorey was there—dry day." The actual nomination of the three candidates took place the next day in Downpatrick.

The nominations of Ker, Forde and Hill were very contentious. The courtroom was largely filled with Ker supporters. They were very loud, and some appeared actually threatening. Much of what candidates and their nominators said was impossible to hear. Ker claimed he was the candidate who represented all classes and religions. While he was running as a Conservative, he was considered by important people like George to hold beliefs matching the most liberal parts of the party. Forde was running to give the voters of Down two truly Conservative representatives. When the vote was taken by a show of hands, Ker and Hill were declared the winners. Forde immediately called for a ballot vote. That was scheduled to take place on Thursday and Saturday. This date gave George more time to campaign against Ker. He told his readers that Ker was "unreliable," while Hill and Forde were "men of steel."

When the first day of voting arrived, James and his family were up early. "Dark soft morning—left about seven oclock with A. Douglass, & Chiefton for Newry to County Election, voted for <u>Ker</u> & <u>Hill</u>." James's jaunting cars were used to collect other voters from Donaghmore and drive them into town to vote. This effort didn't seem to be enough as James added to his entry "poll of the country against Mr. Ker."

On the second day of voting, the Harshaws were again at work. Andrew [Chiefton] went into Newry early on Saturday morning. He acted as "clerk in booth no 6." George was happy to report that the Harshaw's efforts to support Ker had failed. While Ker did well in other parts of the county, he did very poorly in Newry. The results confirmed George's belief that Down wouldn't support democracy and popery over Conservative Protestantism. The Down results helped heal his disappointment at the election of Kirk in Newry, though the Whig government of Prime Minister Palmerston had increased its majority in Parliament.

§

This year 1857 was to be a year during which there were many changes for James, his family and neighborhood. He well knew that his niece, Anna Hirst, would probably die before the end of the year. But the first death of the year occurred much closer to home. On January 28, he recorded the death of his neighbor and friend John McKelvy of Ringolish. He died unexpectedly around eight in the morning. James quickly walked over to the McKelvy's cottage to offer condolences. Two days later, he attended the funeral and took tea with the family afterwards.

There was a much happier event in the cycle of life a month later. James recorded that "Samuel James came here about ten oclock at night, & took the Dandy away with him." He noted at the time, that it was a "fine cleer night." Samuel James Marshall was James's first grandchild. Though he was only a child, he could be entrusted with important errands. The reason for this late-night visit became clear as his entry continued. "Jane had a young Daughter about eleven or twelve oclock."

The next day James visited the new baby. He left about one o'clock with daughter Mary, and spent a pleasant evening with the family, including the other new grandfather, Samuel Boyd Marshall.

Local deaths continued during the spring months. Some of dead were poor, like Mary Jane Duff, the daughter of James's servant and close friend Joe Duff. Others like Mr. Parker of Mountkerny were well-born members of the upper class. James and other members of the family attended the funeral at Parker's home near Newry.

The word that the family had been dreading arrived on July 1st. "A Telegraphic despatch arrived in Newry before ten oclock from John Martin announcing that the 'young Queen'—Mrs Hirst had died about two oclock this morning in the 'City of Paris,' we had the 'dispatch' in Loughorne and here by one oclock—visited James Martin in the evening."

§

A day before the Harshaws and Martins received the telegram with the news of Anna's death, George reported a horrendous event that had taken place in India. First dispatches reported that the 50,000 English residents and troops in India were in grave danger. A group of sepoys in Mereete had revolted against their English officers, killing many of them before riding for the capital to attack the cantonments and slaughter many English men, women and children.

India was one example of a country where a small minority controlled a much larger majority, members of the Hindu and Muslim religions being controlled by English Protestants. There were enough similarities to Ireland to make George and many other members of the Church of Ireland wary when religious tensions broke into violence. The fact that the Protestant marching season was at hand made the situation even more tense.

Not surprisingly George was paying particular attention during the early days of July. The first report from Newry was promising. Peace had prevailed. Local members of the Orange Order assembled in their headquarters on Downshire Road. Then, with Bibles in hand, they marched to St. Patrick's Church for a commemorative service. The processions were entirely peaceful. Then members assembled in their lodge for dinner and speeches.

However, trouble erupted on the evening of July 13th. It started with groups of young boys throwing rocks at each other at the intersection of Church and Stream St. The stones were accompanied by religious taunts. Soon older people joined in to support both sides, and a general riot occurred. Constables Madders and Hamilton hurried to the scene of the confrontation and attempted to separate the two sides. When they were unsuccessful, they called for reinforcements from Jonesboro to assist them. By that time, some of the mob produced guns and began firing indiscriminately into the windows of surrounding buildings. Even St. Patrick's Church had some of its windows broken. When order was finally restored, the arrests began. Most of those arrested were younger Catholic boys. At their arraignment the following morning, those who had been charged were ordered to jail in Downpatrick. As the procession of police and prisoners passed the fever hospital, a crowd was waiting, and more trouble broke out.

During the fighting, a man named Mahood was stabbed, resulting in a number of additional arrests. Those accused men were brought before the Court in Newry. Patrick McAteer was found guilty of the attack and sentenced to a month in jail, no more severe penalty being inflicted as the condition of Mr. Mahood was unknown. The others received lesser sentences.

As for the boys involved in the Newry fighting, their lawyers arrived at an agreement. In exchange for pleading guilty, they would be released without further penalty, as long as they continued to demonstrate good behavior. The presiding judge agreed to this arrangement as the boys involved were only 13 and 14 years old. But he also delivered a stern lecture: these boys were all neighbors and should be friends who lived in peace with one another.

Confrontations between Catholics and Protestants typically died down after the July 12th marches. But this year, there was another contentious issue that caused riots in Belfast. Protestant ministers had begun preaching outside on Sunday afternoons in an attempt to convert Catholics who passed by. The Catholics resented what they considered an encroachment on their right to practice their own religion. Not surprisingly, religiously based rioting followed, and Belfast was proclaimed. George thought that Protestants were fully within their rights and fulfilling their obligations to their own religion. This was especially true since Protestants followed the true religion, while Catholics' religion was evil. Outdoor preaching continued to be a flash point between Catholics and Protestants.

James and his family went into mourning for Anna, the women in the family going into Newry to buy some new black clothes for the mourning period. Anna's death was soon followed by another death, this one a prominent local minister, Rev. Marshall Mee, for many years the vicar of the Church of Ireland Church in Donaghmore. His funeral was held at the church on July 23rd. Despite the fact that James attended a Presbyterian church, he was asked to be a pall bearer, a task he readily accepted. He was part of the solemn procession that carried the much-loved minister up the walk and into the church, past the place where the body would be interred. A few days later he signed an address to Rev. John Campbell Quinn on his appointment to succeed Rev. Mee.

There was an important event in the Meetinghouse as well. The Newry Presbytery announced they would make an inspection to ensure that the congregation was in good order. On the first Sabbath of August, Rev. Robert Lindsay of Drumbanagher exchanged pulpits with Rev. White. Following the service, a meeting of the congregation was led to make arrangements for the visitation. Members chose Samuel Boyd Marshall and Thomas Greer to represent them. The elders chose Archy Murdock and James to represent them.

The inspection took place on August 11th. It was a dark and rainy day at dawn, but the weather soon cleared resulting in a fine dry day. James and Archy Murdock were questioned by Rev. Moran, the head of the Newry Presbytery, assisted by Rev. Lindsay, the Clerk. Then the same two men questioned the representatives of the congregation. James summed up the meeting, "the visitation passed off quietly, and well."

After the formalities were over, the visitors and members of the congregation met for "a well lade out lunch of bread, beef and ham, with porter & whiskey in the classroom where we were well attended by James Martin, William Young, Robert Jeffrey and Hugh, but Absalom [Samuel] was not there."

Two of James's sons had been in America for eight years. But his youngest son had left more recently, the sense of loss more raw. The entry in James's journal for September 13th marked the anniversary of Absalom's departure. "The 52nd Sabbath since Absalom left me on this Sabbath last year. I had Absalom with me in meeting and here, but not since, only I have had him in my pocket to look at, every day since he left me—the twisting strings of ardent hearts combined, when rent asunder how they bleed. How hard to be resigned."

John Martin had been almost like a son to James, though he was actually his nephew. So John's conviction and long separation had been yet another pain for James to endure. As he anticipated the painful anniversary of Absalom's departure, James was greatly cheered by a visit from John, almost a year after his previous visit home. John came with his sister Elizabeth Todd, the Queen, to visit his uncle.

It was a most pleasant day. James went with John and Elizabeth of Loughorne to visit their brother James. Then together they all went to

Loughorne House to visit with James's son John and his wife Ellen who lived there. James's daughters Mary and Sarah Anne joined the party also.

John certainly enjoyed his day with his family, but as he explained to Mahon, he didn't find the rest of his trip to the Newry area much to his liking. By the end of September, John had traveled to Dublin. He wrote Mahon from the Imperial Hotel, where he was staying. There were few people whom he met in the north that seemed to have any "strong political feeling of any sort except the hatred some of them bear to popery & its adherents. Perhaps, had I not shunned all intercourse with others beyond a shake of the hand & exchange of friendly greetings with old neighbours, I might have found some Irish feeling–Protestant or Catholic–among the Northerns. But if such exists it hides its light under a thick-bottomed bushel."

He continued, "I assure you I grew quite sick at heart, so that I would stick in some quiet corner of my sister's house or my brother's house & consume the time with reading some Dickens or Thackeray…instead of rambling among the well-remembered, dearly-loved haunts of my former life." When he did attempt to express his opinions in Newry or Rostrevor, he was met with "surprise and fright."

After some days in Dublin, John traveled to Cahirmoyle to spend some time with O'Brien. During his pleasant stay, the two old friends could freely discuss the political situation in Iceland…While he was in the South, he had time to explore conditions there. He was surprised to find how bad conditions still were. Peasants there lived in "miserable hovels of mud or peat." "humans…squalid, ill-fed, look dirty, ragged & comfortless in their dress." Even more depressing than what he had actually witnessed was the information that the Catholics of the south no longer looked to Protestants to fight for their freedom as they had at the time of the '48 uprising.

§

The Indian Mutiny transfixed the people of Great Britain. The reports that began flowing from the battles there filled newspapers including the *Newry Telegraph*. George printed long reports of the fighting and wrote many leaders on the subject. Queen Victoria ordered a day of humiliation. George urged the people of Newry to be truly humble, as they had much to repent for. Christians had been far too accepting of local religions, when they should have been spreading Christianity and ending the Hindu and Muslim religions. "England had ignored the truth that Christianity is essentially an aggressive religion." In fact, George believed that was its essential characteristic. There was no other religion that was equal. As George saw it, that included the Catholic religion. It was no more a Christian religion than the Muslim religion.

The mutiny diverted George from many of the subjects he usually found interesting to himself and to his readers. He was pleased that once again the Irish militias were being reactivated, as they had been during the Crimean War. However, his hope that the South Down Militia would be stationed in Newry wasn't realized. It was dispatched to occupy Hillsboro, while the North Antrim Rifles were assigned to the barracks in Newry.

Another item that George deemed interesting for his readers was from a Young Irelander who was far away. George reprinted a letter that Terrance McManus had written to Thomas Meagher in response to rumors that were spreading in the United States that Britain was considering a pardon for the two of them plus John Mitchel. McManus was then living on his ranch in San Jose, California. He had become an American citizen and had no intention of accepting a pardon or going back to Ireland. In his comments on the letter, George indicated that he favored pardoning some "outlaws," but never these three.

There was another mention of the Young Irelanders much closer to home. O'Brien had come north to Newry. John Martin met his train at the station. Though George didn't mention where the two friends went from there, most likely they went to the family home at Kilbroney. This visit was in return for one that John had recently made to O'Brien's home.

George hadn't forgotten his interest in having Newry designated a safe harbor. So when a governmental surveyor reported that he had found a wide and deep channel through the Carlingford Bar, that would allow larger ships to enter the lough without dredging the sandbar, George happily reported that. He also kept his readers informed as to any progress in reforming the honest functioning of the Newry market.

Two new issues broke through the reports from India. One was an outgrowth of the rioting in Belfast. The government was planning to ask all future candidates for the Magistracy whether or not they were members of the Orange Order. Those that affirmed their membership would be denied appointment to that important legal position. In response, George praised the Orange Order, "So real, so strong, so vital, so breathing a system, is not to be cancelled by the stroke of a pen."

This act, George believed, was another act of Catholic appeasement. After all, the government had allowed Catholics to become magistrates; and gave money to Maynooth to educate Catholic priests; Catholics controlled public education; and they were getting preferential treatment for public positions. With resentment building against the Catholics, George challenged the government to dismiss any member of the Orange Order who was currently a Magistrate. He also began referring to Catholics as "Irish sepoys," the Indian soldiers who began the revolt in India.

As the year 1857 neared an end, a financial panic swept across Great Britain. George explained to his readers that the panic began in the United States. He attributed the problem to the greed of American banks, large corporations and creation of large commercial farms. This led to a large and rapid increase in interest rates, and a panic. In many parts of England, runs on banks began. But George assured his readers that the banks in Ulster were sound. There was no need to be concerned, but interest rates continued to rise.

To solve the problem of rising interest rates, the government allowed banks to print more money. This currency would soon be backed by a shipment of gold that was in route from Australia. They hoped that this measure would stem any run on the banks, or manufacturing reductions causing short hours for employees.

This emergency action seemed to slow the rise of interest rates, and then to reverse them. Just before Christmas, James wrote that "Bank of England lowered their rate of discount to 8 per cent (from ten)." In the last edition of the paper for the year, George announced that the crisis was over.

§

Sectarian tensions continued to rise following the Belfast riots and the resulting decision of the Whig Lord Lieutenant to refuse to appoint members of the Orange Order to the Magistracy. A case where these tensions erupted in violence was heard at the Newry Quarter Session in mid-January. The incident occurred in Kilkeel in November. A man named John McCollough was on his way home from town, when he was attacked by three men, John Donnan, John Magee and Patrick Donnelly. Donnan was the participant who was on trial. The attack took place after dark, making it difficult for McCollough to identify the people who had beaten him so badly that he had yet to recover. While the attack was taking place, Donnan shouted, "D-n him, kick the Orange soul out of him!"

Donnan was represented by a Mr. John Rea, a well-known Belfast lawyer. His questioning of McCollough was very aggressive. He asked McCollough if he was an Orangeman. McCollough testified that he had been a member for eight or nine years. He said that he was a member of a lodge that met at Moses Hill's Public House and was led by a Mr. Lee.

In response to objections from opposing counsel, Rea "submitted that he had a right to put such questions, on the ground that the Orange Society was an illegal one, and the fact that the witness was a member of it would go to impeach his credibility."

Rea's probe of the Orange Order continued. He got McCollough to say that oaths were no longer required though he had taken one when he joined. He also admitted that they had secret signs and passwords. The existence of such practices were the reasons that the government had declared the organization to be an illegal one. When the Order was reorganized in 1845, the practice of oaths and secret passwords was expressly forbidden.

While answers on the operation of the organization provided important information, seldom admitted to in public and under oath, it didn't help Donnan to escape punishment. The jury found him guilty and sentenced him to four months in Downpatrick jail, and a fine of 6d.

George had warned that there would come a day when the prohibition of magistrates belonging to the Orange Order would be tested. That day came just a few days after the Donnan trial and occurred in County Down. The current magistrate was a man named William Price. He was forced to retire due to poor health. According to tradition, he was free to appoint his successor. Thus no one was surprised that he appointed his brother J. C. Price to assume the appointment. He was the resident landlord of the Saintfield Estate. But rather than assume the position, J. C. claimed the right to appoint someone else to assume the position.

His choice for the position was his estate agent, Walter Hore. Price wrote to Lord Londonderry requesting him to make the appointment. Lord Londonderry replied that he would be happy to comply with Price's request. However, Hore would have to stipulate that he wasn't a member of the Orange Order per the instructions of the Lord Chancellor. But since Hore was indeed an Orangeman and had no intention of leaving the organization, he did not become a Magistrate. George was not pleased.

However, George's mood would soon brighten. On February 18th, a delegation supporting the Orange Order, and strongly opposing the actions of the Irish Chancellor Brady appeared before Lord Palmerston. The Prime Minister began the audience by restating the history of the Orange Order from a governmental perspective. The Order had been properly disbanded. Though it had reconstituted itself, there was little reason to expect that the new version would be different than the previous one. The reason for the current policy relative to Irish magistrates didn't stem from any fault of the upper classes of Ireland who held these positions. Rather their concerns rested solely on the perceptions held of the Order by many Irish citizens.

Lord Palmerston was sorry that the situation in Ireland had led to the ban that his petitioners were protesting. He emphasized again that he had no evidence of magistrates exercising their powers for political gain, which might have justified this action.

However, when Palmerston mentioned that Orangemen often paraded while armed, which he did find concerning, the Earl of Enniskillen protested," No, my Lord."

Palmerston seemed surprised. "Ah, they have dropped that, have they?"

Enniskillen responded, "Yes, my Lord, there is now nothing of the kind."

Sir George Grey interjected. "You mean that there have been no armed processions since the reorganization of the association?" Mr. Whiteside affirmed the validity of this statement.

Palmerston asked if the organization wasn't a relic of the past, not needed in the present circumstances, when the rights of all citizens could and would be protected by the government. So he could see no purpose for the organization in this modern time.

Lord Enniskillen said that the purpose of the Order now was defense. Palmerston regarded that as an attack on the efficiency of the government. Enniskillen proclaimed that his statement was sadly correct.

The audience ended with a statement by Lord Palmerston. "I do think that the protection of individuals should be left to the law of the land, and that the foundation of private association for the purpose of supplying defects in the law is not a system suitable to the spirit of the times in which we live."

Within a few days of this audience, after losing a vote in Parliament, Lord Palmerston had gone to the Queen to submit his resignation. Queen Victoria invited the leader of the Conservatives to form a new government. Within a week this had been accomplished. George was delighted to have the Conservatives back in power.

On March 15th, the new Parliament met. Lord Derby, the new Prime Minister, made clear that he had no intention of honoring the restrictions that Palmerston had placed on the Orange Order. However, he did say that "on the whole, that the organization of the Orange Society is rather calculated to do injury than serve in the present state of Ireland."

§

While the new Conservative administration was taking power in England, James was devoting some of his limited time to help a neighbor and friend. On the first of April, James had a visitor late in the evening, after he had already gone to bed. It was Joseph Robinson of Gransha, asking for James to help his brother prepare his will. Once James had sent his workers to the fields to plant oats the next morning, James went to Gransha, where he met Rev. White and Hugh McKee. John Robinson dictated the items he wanted included in his will. James took the draft home with him to revise.

A second meeting was held the next week. There James had a long conversation with John Robinson, who gave him some general directions as to what he wanted for a wake and funeral. James finished the will while he was there. Robinson signed the will with McKee, Rev. White, along with James and his son Andrew…When James got home, he had great news from son Joseph [James Jr.]. He planned to be home again in May for his first visit in almost ten years. Sadly, he was unable to come as promised.

John Robinson lived until May. James described their last meeting. "Visited John Robenson of Granshaw, found him very weak and low. Prayed with, and took fearwell of him believing that I would not see him again." James's prediction was correct, as he recorded the next day. "John Robenson of Granshaw died about ten this evening, much regretted by his numerous friends and neighbours."

James was quickly notified. "was awoke about five oclock this morning by the rap of a man with a horse, & note from Joseph Robenson anounceing the death of John Robenson about ten oclock last night. Rode the horse to Granshaw. Breckfasted with Mrs. Clotworthy, Mr. McKee also, after which Joseph Borenson drove Mr. Mr. Kee & me to Donaghmore to point out a grave, then to Newry where we prepared for his, John Robensons funeral."

The wake was held the next day. James was there from 5 to about 9 p.m. He noted that it was a fine spring day as he went home.

The funeral was held on Saturday May 8th. It was another fine sunny day. James went early enough to have breakfast with Mrs. Clotworthy. James helped her receive visitors upstairs, while Hugh McKee and James's son Andrew "received the funeral people below." The sad procession left Gransha about noon. James walked behind the hearse to the Donaghmore cemetery where John was buried.

After the service, James returned to Gransha with Robinson's sister, Mrs. Clotworthy, nephew Mr. Frazer, and wife, McKee and Andrew Harshaw.

There the party had dinner. And after tea, James read the will to the group. The next Friday, James returned to Gransha along with Hugh McKee, Thomas Greer, and Joseph Reid to take an inventory of the possessions of the deceased. Following that important step toward resolving Robinson's affairs, he had tea with Mrs. Clotworthy and a number of other guests.

Despite the many hours James had devoted to helping his friend, James didn't fulfill his obligations to John Robinson until after the churn was cut in September. On Friday the 17th, James went back to Gransha to have tea yet again with Mrs. Clotworthy, Mr. McKee and Joseph Robinson to finalize plans for an auction of John's property. They agreed on a date of October 1st.

A few days later, James met Joseph Robinson and Hugh McKee at Miss Malcomson's where they all drove to Newry to the *Herald* office to arrange to publicize the Robinson auction. He made some preliminary sales as well, selling Robinson's two mares to Joseph for twenty-nine pounds, a field of wheat for twenty-eight pounds, a two-year-old heifer for six pounds and the oats of Grahams farm for two shillings a stook.

On the day of the auction, the weather was cloudy but not rainy. James was able to get good prices for the oats, wheat, and hay that were up for auction. Andrew served as the clerk at the auction. The sale brought over fifty-five pounds. James had certainly been a good friend. As James headed back to Ringbane, the rain began.

§

John Martin left Ireland to return to Paris on December 9, 1857. Once there, he settled in for long damp winter, the gloom leading to a renewed depression. Not only did he feel he had lost his purpose in life, but he was growing ever more concerned about his financial situation. As he explained to Mahon, he had been unaware of the extent of his financial problems, information his family had kept from him while he was in exile. Now that he had returned, he had discovered that the inheritance, which had seemed so generous when he was young, now was insufficient to maintain him. And he could see no way that he could earn a living.

To afford himself some relief, he distracted himself by imagining what an independent Ireland would be like. John trusted that it would not be an acquisitive country, but a sharing, caring one. "Such competition–such competition as that which England has now made the condition and sole means of her existence as an empire at least, if not as a nation–such competition I loathe. I hate it for itself, because the source is in greed and malignity. I hate it for the evil it brings upon the people that practice it and upon the people that are impoverished and debased by it. I hate it for the cant and tyranny and injustice which are needed to support it. I hate it because above all other things has tended to ruin us. It makes our condition as subjects of England far worse than it could be if we were subjects of Austria or Prussia or France."

On June 4, 1858, John wrote a letter of a different sort. He had heard that Dr. Hyde Salter was writing a book on asthma. As part of his work, he was searching for stories from asthma sufferers. John felt that his long experience with the disease, and his medical training would be of help. So, he invested many hours writing a many-page letter describing his medical history. His attacks returned for the first time in years in a different form during his stay in Pau. Asthma attacks had become a symptom that occurred during attacks of a severe form of bronchitis. While his earlier asthma attacks had disappeared after a day or two, outbreaks of bronchitis with asthma overtones lasted as long as six weeks. During that time, he would resort to an old tactic to relieve his labored breathing by sitting up all night, resting his head on a pillow. During that extended time, he needed the constant care of an attendant to supply his other needs. He also limited the time he spent in Loughorne where his health seemed always at its worst.

John sent off this letter in two parts to Dr. Salter, and then returned to his correspondence with Mahon. In one letter, John frankly confessed that he had been unable to totally conquer his low spirits. But he had been able to rise above his lethargy to continue writing. John shared some of the ideas he had generated as he thought his way out of depression. He made clear that his ideas on Irish independence hadn't changed. He had little confidence that any conversation he might have would change any minds on the subject. "I feel more and more every year that the time is past and is not again to come for me to do any work. It is sad and humiliating; but I fear it is so." "I have had health, leisure, convenient circumstances, and have done nothing. Habits of idleness are grown so immoderate and thinking upon the subject of Ireland only brings on a gnashing of my teeth and a sense of impotence."

John concluded this letter with three sad words. "I do nothing." As he posted the letter in Paris, he had no inkling that his life was about to turn dramatically. On October 3rd, John got a letter from his brother Robert bearing sad news. Robert's wife Millicent was dangerously ill. A few days earlier, she had safely delivered her 7th child, a daughter. Unfortunately, within a few days, she had contracted scarlatina. This was usually a very mild disease, easy for victims to survive. However, it seemed to be much more dangerous for new mothers.

Immediately John began making plans to answer Robert's call for help. He relayed the bad news to Maxwell Simpson, who was living in Paris at the time. But both men decided not to tell Mary Simpson who was about to have a baby herself. With Maxwell forced to stay in Paris, John was happy to have a traveling companion, John O'Hagan...In fact O'Hagan, made all the arrangements while John attended to his packing. The two friends managed to book passage from Paris the same day. They left by railroad just after 7 p.m., traveling by Calais, and Dover to London. They completed the trip in twelve hours. After a quick change of railroad stations, the travelers left for Liverpool. There the men separated, O'Hagan taking a ship to Dublin, John taking one to Warrenpoint.

John's ship left Liverpool just twenty-four hours after he had left Paris. Unfortunately, the steamer encountered strong storm winds from the west, so it was too late to catch the tide to carry the ship safely cross the bar into the

Carlingford Lough. The ship had to wait outside the bar to catch a favorable tide. The trip from Liverpool had taken almost twenty-four hours by the time the ship tied up at the dock in Warrenpoint. John hurried to get his luggage into a hired car for the drive to Kilbroney.

The trip was an anxious one for John. He had traveled halfway to Kilbroney before he dared ask the driver for news. It was the car driver who told John that Millicent had died. The seven children had been removed from Kilbroney for their safety. But Robert himself had become ill. To make matters even worse, brother David had just left for New York. John would have to manage the crisis alone.

As the car rattled down the avenue to Kilbroney, John was stopped by a servant and his brother James who came running toward him to prevent him going further. Apparently, any slight noise such as the car wheels agitated Robert. Quietly, John entered the house. As he described the scene, "I found Elizabeth [Martin Ross Todd] in a miserable house."

John hurried up the stairs to Robert's room. He found Robert very feverish and a bit delirious and restless. He didn't speak much of Millicent's death. Fortunately, Elizabeth had hurried over from Newry at the first word of Millicent's illness and had taken charge of the new baby. The newborn had been given over to the care of the monthly nurse. However, Elizabeth, who had a four-month-old daughter herself, was nursing the baby until someone could be found to help permanently. The baby's cries seemed to greatly agitate Robert.

Millicent's mother and sister had come from Carrickfergus and stayed until Millie had died. Then they insisted that they were going home despite Robert's pleas that they should stay. But they were too frightened by the contagious nature of the disease to stay on to help.

Millicent's funeral was held the day after John's return. Robert was too ill to attend, so John stayed home to help care for Robert while the burial took place. So strong was the fear of the disease that none of the people who attended the funeral would come to the house, and few came even close to it. James and some of his family did come. "Chiefton [Andrew] drove John Bradford, John Harshaw and me to Newry from which we went by train to Warrenpoint, and from that by cars to Kilbroney, and attended Robert Martins wifes funeral to Rostrevor Church and churchyard, Dined in the Hotel and returned by Newry. Robert Martin very ill. Saw and spoke to John Martin." The sad day ended with a steady rain.

Robert's condition continued to be very alarming. He tried violently to get up and get dressed to go outside and take a walk. His doctors gave him a mixture of tartar emetic and laudanum in hopes that he would be able to sleep. Late on the day of Millicent's funeral, he did fall asleep for several hours. Hopes for his recovery began to rise, thinking that sleep indicated that the crisis had passed. However, when John checked Robert's pulse later in the evening he found it very thready.

The doctors were alarmed enough to suggest that Robert should have a will made, hopefully just as a precaution. Since Robert Ross Todd had gone back to Newry, John took over the task. John did his best to fulfill what he thought would be Robert's wishes. The eldest son Bobby was entitled by entail [right of the eldest son to inherit] to the land that Robert had gotten from his uncles Robert and John. The land that Robert himself had acquired was to go to his second son Jack. The five daughters were to get amounts of eight hundred pounds each.

John then read the results of his efforts to Robert, sentence by sentence. Robert seemed to rouse himself to the task. He objected to giving his daughters that large a sum of money at first, but John was able to persuade him of the fairness of the bequest. When Todd arrived, he read over John's efforts and with a small change or two, put it all into proper legal form. By the time that work was completed, Robert needed help to sign the document. "I'm a dead weight on the paper," Robert noted. Despite efforts to increase his strength with brandy, wine and meat soup, he continued to weaken. He didn't seem to be suffering much anymore, rather just dozing somewhat fitfully.

Robert died at 5 a.m. on Saturday morning without a struggle. John talked about how much Robert had liked farming, more than the linen business. "Business concerns seemed generally oppressive upon his spirits, while farming, dealing in stock and managing tenants and labourers, seems always to give him pleasing interest."

James recorded the funeral in his journal. "Robert Martin of Kilbroney died about five oclock this morning very much regretted by all classes. John Harshaw at Kilbroney on a visit to John Martin, and the Queen, and to know of Roberts funeral. Wrote to Hugh [Robert] boath morning and evening about Robert Martin. Chiefton reported Roberts funeral to be on Monday."

When Monday came, James wrote, that the family "left about seven oclock for Robert Martins funeral. William Camble drove John and me with James Martins horse & car by Doraylacky to Rostrevor. From that we walked up to Kilbroney where people was collecting for the funeral. Chiefton [Andrew] drove A Douglas, John Bradford, & Ralph Todd by Newry, and the trean to Warrenpoint, who joined us at Kilbroney where we got gloves and walked behind the hearse to Rostrevor Church-yard. The coffin was lowered on the north side of Mrs. Martins, his wife's, coffin. Mr. Morgan read the 90th Psalm and Doctor Morgan prayed, and the grave was filled up. John Martin attended the funeral."

George wrote a thoughtful obituary for the *Telegraph*. He commented on the great sorrow that Robert's death had occasioned throughout the area. He spoke of how this young family had seemed so full of life a few days earlier. Robert was only forty-four years old and Millicent was ten years younger. And yet in one short week both parents had died, leaving seven young children without parents. "Mr. Martin was senior of a firm representing a name long and honorably associated with the linen-trade of Ulster. By all who had the pleasure of knowing him, he was most worthily held in high estimation, as a man of unswerving rectitude; and in the relations of private life, he was characterized by a kindly sprit and warm heart, prompting him to that considerate beneficence, in regard alike to his tenants and workpeople, which had won for him the grateful respect of all his dependants."

John had never married, but now he found himself with seven young children to raise. His days in exile in Paris had to end. He would now move home to Ireland, to Kilbroney to raise his brother's children. He would live in Ireland for the rest of his life. And he would discover that his days of service to the cause of Irish independence were far from over.

Leaders: Orange Order and Fenian

Orange Leaders

Lord Roden was the head of the Orange Order when Dueling Dragons begins.

William Johnston organized the big Orange Order parade in 1867 for which he was jailed, but then elected MP for Belfast.

Lord Roden

William Johnston

Fenian Leaders

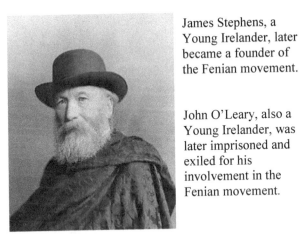

James Stephens, a Young Irelander, later became a founder of the Fenian movement.

John O'Leary, also a Young Irelander, was later imprisoned and exiled for his involvement in the Fenian movement.

James Stephens

John O'Leary

Chapter 7

Revival

1858 - 1859

The funeral of Robert Martin ended, and the guests finished their tea and left. Since the children were being cared for elsewhere, Kilbroney House was quiet. John walked through the house alone, trying to digest the shocking twist his life had taken. He was now responsible for raising seven orphaned children, the youngest a newborn, the oldest ten years old. He resolved to do his best to raise the children as Millicent and Robert would have wished.

A week after the funeral, James visited to offer John his support. He started out on a dark and windy morning for Kilbroney. James Martin drove his uncle into Newry. From there, they took the train into Warrenpoint. Goodwin, one of the Martin servants, met them at the station and drove them into Rostrevor, and from there, the two men walked the rest of the way to Kilbroney. John and four of the Martin daughters were there, and the party gathered for dinner.

Afterward, John joined his brother and uncle as they retraced their travels into Newry. They stopped there to have tea with sister Elizabeth and her husband. The new-born girl had been taken there to live, so plans for her care must have been part of their conversations. By the time that James and James Martin headed home around 10 p.m., the day had cleared and the moon shone brightly.

Early in November, yet another death occurred at Kilbroney. Jenny Cully died. She had been a servant of the Martin family for a number of years, and her services to the family had been invaluable. She had been working for John's brother David for a number of years but had returned to work at Kilbroney as soon as the Martins had died. She had survived scarlatina, only to die of an unrelated cause; Jenny's death was a great loss, as John had surely counted on her for support in fulfilling his new responsibilities. James sent his son John to represent him at the funeral.

Finally there was some good news for the stricken family. David Martin returned to Newry from New York. Two days of family meetings at the Elizabeth's house in Newry followed. John would soon return to Paris, to close out his affairs there. He would return to live in Kilbroney and supervise the children. David would manage the family property and linen business.

§

In early December, James received news he had longed to hear. Son Robert Hugh had been called to be an assistant minister of a congregation in Mullingar. His days of being an itinerant substitute had finally ended along with the danger that he too might emigrate to America. James's son John represented the family at the installation ceremony.

This event warranted a comment from George. He pointed out that Robert had been licensed by the Presbytery of Newry. But his new post was within the Presbytery of Athlone. The installation was led by other ministers of the Presbytery who offered sermons and prayers. Then they posed theological questions to ensure Robert was ready to assume his new responsibilities. The ceremonies concluded with a laying on of hands by local ministers and a charge for both Robert and the congregation. Though James wasn't present, the events of the service were very familiar to him, helping him visualize the events that John recounted when he returned.

In the same edition of the paper, George made sure that his readers were informed on an action from the new Lord Lieutenant Lord Eglinton. Though he had just taken the job, Lord Eglinton had been informed about an ominous increase in attacks by illegal groups. He promised a reward of £100 for any information on the Ribbon Society. George greatly approved of this active approach. He blamed Catholic priests for this increase in activity, reasoning that if the Catholic Church really disapproved of such actions, they could easily excommunicate participants. Since none had taken that step, their protestations of innocence had no value. Like most Protestants in Ireland, George had no idea that something more dangerous than the Ribbonmen was lurking unseen and growing. Fenian secret cells were already sprouting across Ireland.

Sectarian attacks on property in the Newry area were also increasing. The British government had acted to help farmers who had been harmed by such activities. They had established a system of low-level courts called Special Presentment sessions at which farmers could appeal for monetary compensation for damages caused by sectarian vandalism. These sessions were presided over by local magistrates, supported by local representatives of the cess payers. These sessions were frequently contentious as they pitted the injured parties against the cess payers.

One such session took place not long after the Lord Lieutenant issued his appeal for information. James mentioned this meeting in his journal entry on Wednesday, December 8th, 1858. There was rain and a cold wind, as James set off for the Four Mile House for the meeting. "Attended the road sessions in the four-mile-house. Sat with the Majestrats. John McKelvy was awarded damages for three malicious burnings, David Ferris for one."

George provided a great deal more information in his report in the *Telegraph*. John T. Reilly presided over the meeting, which was held in the large meeting room on the second floor of a barn behind the inn. There was such great interest in this court hearing, that the courtyard filled with carts and horses. Many local farmers climbed the stone steps to find a vantage point from which to watch the proceedings, filling the large room to overflowing. At one point, there was ominous cracking from the wooden floor provoking fear that it would collapse. Wind rattled the windows and swept the room with a damp chill. Only the magistrates sitting next to a roaring fire in the fireplace were warm. There were eight magistrates present, one of whom was Hill

Irvine, the owner of Donaghmore Estates. There were six men chosen to represent the cess payers, including Dr. Saunderson and James Harshaw.

Among the attendees whom George identified were Thomas Greer and James Martin, and local ministers, Rev. Quinn and Rev. White. Several constables were on hand to maintain order. There were seventy-two applications for compensation which would cost cess payers £3,180 if all requests were granted.

A few road issues were attended to first, and then the compensation cases began. The first case involved the malicious burning of an unoccupied house. The previous occupant had been ejected. The owner had found another occupant, but before he could move in, the cottage was almost completely destroyed in a fire set by the stepson of the previous occupant. The magistrates and cess payers voted unanimously to provide the requested compensation.

The next case was brought by John McKelvey of Ballylough for malicious destruction of some of his farm products. Apparently, McKelvey wasn't popular with his neighbors as each mention of his name prompted loud hisses and shouts. He testified that he was a tenant of Mr. Innis. In the middle of August, he awakened to find that a haystack had burned. He hadn't detected the fire earlier as the stack was on the far side of a barn and not visible from the house. A neighbor David Ferris helped him watch over his crops, but Ferris soon had his haystack burned as well.

McKelvey was asked about an encounter in Mr. Innis's hall that might have precipitated the burnings. McKelvey had gone to the Innis estate at Dromantine to visit the estate steward on business. He was directed to the hall to wait a few moments. A coachman was in the hall at the time, reading a report about the atrocities of the sepoys in India. McKelvey offered his opinion that there was an Irish version of sepoys threatening Protestants supporting English rule in Ireland. He had seen two hundred Ribbonmen, alias Irish Sepoys, marching in the area. Immediately after that chance meeting, McKelvey began to receive threats, one of them from a neighbor named Murtagh. While Murtagh hadn't said anything directly to him, he had spoken to some of McKelvey's servants. There were certainly hard feelings in the area.

Some of his neighbors had spread the rumor that McKelvey himself had set fire to his own hay, a charge McKelvey vehemently denied. He did testify to one particular fact that seemed to give substance to the local gossip. He had three dogs that roamed freely outside his house that barked loudly at any intruder. But strangely, on the morning of the fire, they failed to provide any warning. This arson attack on his property was only one of five that had taken place on his property. His losses amounted to the equivalent of a year's rent. When asked by John Rea, lawyer for the cess payers, in cross-examination if he were a member of a secret society, he denied he was. "I am a True Blue, [i.e. Protestant] and I need not be afraid to say so, I do not know anything about Ribbon Societies." He went on to say he might have seen Ribbonmen on the road, but he wouldn't know how to identify them. He closed his testimony by stating that he lived off the road from Poyntzpass to Sheepbridge. The stack in question was close enough to the road that anyone passing by would be able to see what was going on. However, since the fire erupted at an early hour on a Sunday morning, there weren't many people passing along the road.

Mrs. McKelvey was also called to testify. She stated that the couple had gone to bed about nine p.m. the previous evening. Since they slept in the same bed, she would have been aware if he had gotten up. She claimed he had not done so. Contrary to what McKelvey had testified, she had been awakened by the barking of one of their dogs and went out thinking a cow might have been calving. It was then she saw the smoke over the barn. When she got to the fire, David Ferris, and others were already there, trying to put it out.

Next to testify was David Ferris. He confirmed McKelvey's account, then claimed helping McKelvey had resulted in personal threats followed by a fire in his own oats.

Mary Boyle, a servant of the McKelveys testified that she slept at the foot of the McKelveys' bed. McKelvey couldn't have gotten up without her knowing it. She said that she knew Murtagh. After a previous court case, he had told her she was wrong to help the McKelveys. Another servant of the McKelvey's testified that he had heard Mrs. Murtagh threatening McKelvey's life.

Rea told the magistrates that farmers were using the law as a substitute for insuring their crops, passing a personal expense to the cess payers. In this case, he wanted to observe that "So long as there were Orange Societies, there would be Ribbon Societies, and that wherever the members of an Orange Lodge assembled, a Ribbon Lodge should sit beside it." This statement caused some consternation in the hall. When the noise subsided, Rea reiterated that charging cess payers for McKelvey's property losses was unjust.

However the magistrates and cess payer representatives did vote that the damage was malicious and McKelvey was therefore entitled receive a fair compensation for all his ruined crops. James voted with the winning majority. Dark had fallen long before the meeting adjourned about 8 p.m.

George found the events presented at the Four Mile House sessions most disturbing. He made his anger the subject of a major leader. "It should be known that there is a Protestant and a Romanist Ireland. Within the limits of the former, none of those crimes are to be found which have made Irishmen infamous in the eyes of the civilized world. Those crimes are exclusively confined to Romanist Ireland. It is absurd to say that they are natural consequences of race."

Then George pointed out that the same kinds of attacks occurred in other Catholic countries. So it was clear to him that the evil qualities weren't natural to the Irish, but natural to areas controlled by Catholic leaders and teachings. An Irishman "with all his quick feelings and tender emotions is transformed into the fierce and furious monster. A Romish branch has been grafted upon the Irish stock, whereby it has been poisoned and polluted."

Between actions by the government that made religious practices difficult for Irish Protestants, they were further harmed when they were prevented from studying the true Bible. "The Priests do not, they cannot, instruct their flocks in those precious promises, glorious truths, and holy precepts, of the Bible which improve, and cultivate, and comfort." He called Catholic religious services a "pantomimic show, mere sensualism. There is nothing to stimulate the intellect, excite deep thought or awaken elevating emotions. When we add to this the positive evil that is inculcated, we need not wonder that such a people sit in places of darkness and are children of cruelty." Instead, Catholic sermons were full of attacks on Protestants and their efforts at conversion, on government actions, and even on the rare efforts of Catholics to rebel against the actions of priests. "Thus the bitterest feelings are engendered, and the fiercest passions roused. Nothing can be expected from such teaching and training but sensuality and devilishness."

Having set out for his readers, the problem as he saw it, George made clear that he didn't hold followers of the Catholic religion harmless either. They willingly submitted to the dictates of the Catholic church though they lived in a country where they were free to follow a more Godly religion. The only solution for the Irish religious problems would be for Catholics to free themselves from the dictates of Rome. Members must cease to regard their priests as religious people. Until those changes occurred, "we must always expect that the calm of to-day will be succeeded by the hurricane of to-morrow, laying waste and destroying, in proportion to its force, whatever improvement time may have effected in our hapless country."

James ended the year with a small Christmas celebration. A soft Irish rain fell most of the day. He enjoyed having his grandchildren with him. James's little dark-haired granddaughter, the child of John and Ellen was on hand along with Samuel James. James Martin came by for breakfast and Mary and Alexander Douglas came by in the evening. However pleasant that gathering might have been, James couldn't resist mentioning the family members who weren't there. "Neither Absalom [Samuel] or Hugh [Robert] was here personally, but they were present in mind."

§

When George published his New Year's letter for 1859, he didn't mention the sectarian problems that had so concerned him a few weeks earlier. Instead he focused on the glorious achievements of the British army in quelling the Indian mutiny as the main reason for celebrating the preceding year. He again mentioned the financial problems that began in America and were the center of his previous New Year's letter. Then he had believed that the financial crisis had already ended, but now he realized that the effects were being felt almost a year later. Underlying the financial problems was a great greed that was sweeping across Great Britain.

"We have seemed as a nation, to be surrounded by an atmosphere of commercial immorality, dulling and confusing our perceptions of right or wrong." He went on to enumerate what has happened. Good businesses have been corrupted into "commercial gamesters." Good businesses have degenerated into corrupt ones."

On the political front, George liked the accession to power of the Conservative Derby administration. England now had a "manly administration," worthy of such a great country. As a result of this change, peace in Ireland would spread. Conservatives would squelch any attempts from secret societies to cause trouble.

During the winter lull in farming, James kept busy. He began by helping another of his neighbors. Isaac Bradford had encountered financial problems, which James attempted to resolve, through legal advice from Todd and forgiveness of overdue rents by Irvine. He made a number of trips to Newry to conduct negotiations and convert the oral compromise into words on paper. Bradford would be allowed to transfer his rights to his property to his sons William and John, so they could sell the leases to resolve his debts. The final resolution took an entire month.

On his way home from one of the early meetings, James happened upon William Parker sitting in a daze on the side of the road. He had fallen from his gig. James helped Parker into his car and drove him home to Mountkerney. After helping him into his home, James summoned the family doctor.

Son John had been chosen to be a juror at the Newry Quarter Sessions. He sat on a case of a young woman named Jane Templeton who had been charged with shoplifting fourteen yards of ribbon from the store of James McGovern. Miss Templeton had come into the shop and asked to see some ribbon. McGovern produced several rolls from his ribbon drawer and put them on his counter. When his attention was briefly distracted, Jane grabbed a handful of them and stuffed them under her cloak and hurried toward the door.

McGovern apparently found Templeton somewhat suspicions, so when he again focused on the potential sale, he scanned the ribbons still on the counter and realized that some ribbon was missing. By that time, Templeton was disappearing through the door of the shop. McGovern rushed after her and immediately shouted for help. Fortunately, a constable was nearby and quickly responded. He grabbed Templeton before she could scurry away, and holding her tightly, marched her back into the shop. Being propelled by the constable, Templeton was unable to secure the stolen ribbon, and some fell to the ground in plain sight. The constable retrieved the ribbon, and McGovern informed him that the ribbons had indeed come from his shop. Since Templeton had been convicted of shoplifting before, John Harshaw and his fellow jurors sentenced her to a year in jail at hard labor.

On Monday, January 29th, James experienced a joy that few Irish families would ever know. The weather that day started out dry, but by midmorning the early good weather had given way to a storm and strong winds. Only a little farm work took place as the storm worsened. So James had time to enjoy a visit to Ringbane from John Martin and his brother David. Then accompanied by John Harshaw, they all plowed through the storm to have dinner with brother James Martin at Loughorne cottage. After the pleasant visit James hurried home through the rain to Ringbane. He was warming himself by the fire, reading the *Banner of Ulster* around 6 o'clock when suddenly, the door behind him burst open letting in a gust of wind. James rose and turned around to see who had come in. There stood his son James, dripping wet from his hike through the rain. James described his joy. "I was rejoiced to see him, got him in my arms and kissed & kissed his brow." Nine and a half years had passed since James sadly watched his sons James Jr. and Willy ride away from Ringbane. Since then James Jr. had established a successful grocery business in Milwaukee, Wisconsin, leaving James with little hope of seeing him again. However, a creditor had called in an essential business loan, though James Jr. was not behind in his payments. This brought financial ruin to James Jr. and his partner. Finding that the American dream had eluded him, James had come home to Ireland to stay.

The family gathered in great joy. A dancing party was held in the upper house. Robert came home from Mullingar to see his brother and preach a sermon in Donaghmore. Robert was about to have more good news of his own. Though he had only been in Mullingar for a few months, he had received a call to become the lead minister in a growing congregation in the town of Mountmellick.

George wrote a fine column about the installation there, which James Jr. attended to represent the family. He reported that Robert came to Mountmellick "bearing a high character, and it is confidently anticipated that the Ministry will be greatly blessed in promoting the cause of vital godliness in this locality." And indeed Robert proved so vital a locus of the Presbyterian Church in a mostly Catholic area that the Dublin Presbytery would never approve of a transfer when he was called to other churches.

With a happy heart, James turned his attention to another of his projects. Finally a school for Donaghmore was moving from dream to reality. In mid-February, James, James Martin, Mr. Greer, and William Young met at the site at the Lane-ends to lay out the school foundation. A few days later, James sent his horses to pull four loads of sand to the new school. Then in the afternoon, he set about raising money to pay for the school construction. He called on James Malcomson, Alex Douglas, John Bradford and Wilson for contributions. Before the end of the month, James attended a funeral at the Meetinghouse and took the occasion to ask the congregation to make contributions to the new school.

As the school building began to rise, the managing committee met in the church classroom to make an important decision about the future of their school. The committee voted to continue to build the school with local resources only. They chose to pass up the financial assistance that would result from placing the Donaghmore school under the authority of the National Board of Education, preferring the freedom of independence instead of money.

The day after Robert's installation to his own church, James was enjoying the pleasure this long-awaited event evoked. Robert would stay permanently in Ireland. But his joy was soon interrupted with some worrying news. On Wednesday March 23rd, James wrote in his journal, "Mary becam ill this evening. Her Mama and the Sparten went to her after six oclock and Dr. Waddell is sent for about nine oclock."

James was up early the next morning to hurry up the Ardkeragh road to Mary's cottage for the latest news. He arrived there about 5 o'clock. "She is stil ill. Dr. Morrison is sent for, who arrives at about eleven oclock and laves about <u>one</u>." Mary was in fact in labor. During her forty years of life, she had endured several pregnancies that ended with the loss of her child and danger to her own life. This time, she had carried a child to term.

After his visit, James returned to his farm work for a while. He was at work when James Jr. returned from Hugh's installation in Mountmellick. Father and son walked back to Ardkeragh for the latest word on Mary's condition. She had by now been in labor for nearly twenty-four hours, but the baby had yet to be born. Other members of the family visited as well; Jane had come to assist her sister early in the morning. It was a long and difficult day for the family. James made five trips altogether to get the latest news. Finally he reported that Mary "had a son about <u>one</u> this morning. Mother and son were doing well."

This was incredibly wonderful news for the entire family. James Jr. had been pacing about outside Mary's cottage when he heard the baby cry, so he was the one who hurried back to Ringbane with the happy news around 3 a.m. A couple of hours later, James was in Ardkeragh to see Mary and meet his new-born grandson. He couldn't linger as there was work to be done. But after the work of the day was over, James returned to share the joy of the moment with other neighbors and family members.

The next day, James returned to his usual work. However, on Sunday, the news from Mary became somber. She had fallen ill in the morning, and before the day had ended Doctors Waddell and Morrison had been called again to see her. They confirmed what the family most feared; she was ill with scarlatina. It seemed impossible to grasp that a replay of what happened to Millicent Martin a few months earlier was happening yet again to the family. The situation was sufficiently alarming that James Jr. wrote to Robert and requested him to return home.

Still there was hope that Mary would be better the next morning, the usual result of this generally mild disease. Alarmingly, when James visited again early the next morning, he found that Mary's condition had worsened. "I could not refrain tears when I saw her, as I believed she was in the 'valley of the shadow of death.'" James could not bear to stay, but his wife and daughter Jane remained with Mary despite the danger that they too might catch the very contagious disease.

James returned about noon "when she was dying. I joined in very earnest prayer at the bedside, and she died or rather entered into her <u>rest</u> about ten minutes after twelve oclock at noon. She was hospitable, generous, and kind."

Despite how deeply the shock and grief of Mary's death had wounded the family, there were things that had to be done. Since Mary died of a very contagious disease, it was important that a coffin be obtained quickly. John

Harshaw and a friend named Hanna left shortly after Mary died to go to Newry to buy the coffin. "Brought home a coffin, large, & black at £4 price, and my Dear Marys remains was committed to it about ten oclock and it hermetically sealed."

The next day, James visited Mary's cottage several times, enduring a great shower of hail on one visit. James Jr. made the trip to Goragh station in the evening to meet Hugh, who had hurried from his new responsibilities in order to attend Mary's funeral on the following day.

During the night, there was a great "shower of snow early." After a restless night, James was up early. He went immediately to Mary's house to see how Alexander Douglas was doing. He seemed well, with no signs of the disease. After breakfast at Ringbane, he joined sons Hugh, James Jr., John and Andrew along with a "large company in a funeral procession. The coffin was put into the Hearse about half past ten oclock, and we proceeded up the big hill, down the Ardkeragh road, along the race and up the mill road to the church-yard. Mary was buried in our burial ground…in the grave that was dug for the 1st Samuel Alexander in March 1835, and again dug for the remains of Elizabeth Martin in May 1842. Mr. White had worship in A Douglas before the funeral left it and gave an impressive address when her remains was laid in the grave. A Douglass and I carried Mary from the bed on which she died to the Hearse, and John, Joseph [James Jr.], Archy and Andrew carried her from the church gate to the grave on their shoulders. I wish that Willy and Absalom [Samuel] had been here, and then it might be said that Mary had died in the presence of all her Brethren."

Those who had visited with Mary and cared for her as she lay dying had risked their lives to do so. James watched anxiously for signs that someone else had been infected. One of those most at risk was Mary's new son. With the threat of an early death looming over him, the new baby needed to be quickly baptized. That ceremony took place in the early evening at Ringbane on March 31st, less than a week after his birth. "Mary's son Baptized about six oclock this evening in presence of John, and all her Brothers, Archy, Weechile, John Bradford & James Martin. Mr. White introduced the Baptismal service, by reading the 6th Chapter of Ephesians and gave an address, after which Hugh prayed, and Baptized. The child was called 'James-Alexander-Harshaw." The Grandmother lade the child in A Douglass arms while it was sprinkled, and Mr. White concluded the service with prayer and Apostolic Benediction."

Fortunately, the new baby escaped the infection that killed his mother. However his aunt Jane was infected. Dr. Saunderson came over to Ringbane to take care of her. Within a day, James could report that Jane was recovering from the disease that had killed her sister. This good news was a small glow in the darkness.

Filling his time with responsibilities and projects that interested him helped James normalize his life. On April 9th, James reported that there had been a great thunderstorm and heavy hail. It was fortunate that crops were still being planted. The storm didn't keep him from keeping an appointment at the new school. He met Greer, and Young at the site. The three men decided to hire Mr. McQuarter to do the carpentry work on the new school. And he continued to raise money to pay for the work. By mid-May he reported donations of a pound each from Thomas Malcomson, and Alex Douglas, and 10s. from John Bradford.

There was one last obligation left before his responsibilities as executor of John Robinson's ended, a trip to Belfast to register the will. He started out early on an April Tuesday. Joseph Robinson came by Ringbane to drive James and Mr. McKee to Poyntzpass. There they purchased round trip tickets on the Belfast train. James carefully recorded his expenses. The 2nd class tickets cost 13s 6d. The two men walked directly to the Registry Office where John Robinson's will was officially recorded. Then James and Hugh had a dinner of pork chops which cost £¾. James also did some shopping, He bought a mourning gown for his wife, and a bonnet for his daughter Sarah Anne. There was another great storm of rain and hail on their way home.

James had not once mentioned the baby that had cost Mary her life, since the day young James was baptized. Caring for the newborn was a duty for the women of the family. The first major problem to surmount was to find a suitable person to serve as a wet nurse. James decided to follow his wife's recommendation and hire a young Catholic woman, Catherine O'Hare, who lived nearby. She had recently borne a child out of wedlock that quickly died.

Almost two months passed before James mentioned the baby and his nurse. "Weechile, nurse, & the 'Wee <u>Baby</u>' visited A Douglass." This was the first hint from James that baby James had begun to brighten his grandfather's life.

§

The Derby administration voted to call for a new election in order to strengthen its power in Parliament. George was very happy that the resulting Newry election had returned a Conservative member to Parliament. However the Derby government didn't gain enough support to survive a quick loss in Parliament. Lord Derby thereupon submitted his resignation to the Queen.

Despite George's interest in the election and change in government, he did notice something different happening in Ireland. A spirit of revival had reached the hearts of a few young men who met in a small cottage in Kells in County Antrim. They struggled to open their hearts to allow the spirit of God to turn them from pro forma religious practices to actions dedicated to holy submission to God's will. Soon their efforts attracted the attention of Rev. Samuel Moore in nearby Ballymena, the former pastor of the Donaghmore Presbyterian Church.

A few days later, George returned to the subject with additional detail provided by the *Belfast News-letter*. The revival had already spread from Ballymena to Belfast. "'Evangelical Protestants of all denominations, Roman Catholics, and Unitarians have all been reached by it, and have yielded to its sway, have become penitent, and in many cases have professed conversion.'"

Catholics who joined this new route to salvation did so over the intense objections of their priests.

These revival meetings were soon the subject of some controversy and questioning. George published a letter from Rev. Henry Cooke, whose opinions on the issue would influence many Presbyterians. The source of the revival was without doubt a group of young people in Rev. Moore's church. They had been meeting for some time, before anyone noticed. But now revival meetings were spreading. During these meetings, the emotional pitch reached the point where some participants were overtaken by a sort of insanity, throwing themselves about and wailing. Dr. Cooke said that some of these outbreaks seemed to be followed by genuine changes, like drunkards giving up drink. But in other cases, there seemed to be no great change in conduct to indicate genuine repentance for sins. He had yet to make a judgment on the benefits of the rapidly spreading revivals.

Given Rev. Moore's ministry in Donaghmore, he could be expected to quickly share the movement with his former parishioners. Still, James didn't mention the subject until June 26th. In the evening service, Rev. White gave a lecture on the new movement, mentioning large meetings in Carrickfergus and Belfast. On July 2nd, George had a report of his own on a great meeting that had taken place in the Botanic Garden in Belfast. The crowd was immense, somewhere between ten and fifteen thousand people. Rev. Moore was one of the leaders. He explained to the large crowd how the movement had started and then sang several hymns for the audience.

Many people were too far away from the stage to hear the speakers, so smaller groups conducted their own services around the edges. Many people were impressed, or overcome, by the services. Those people were escorted to ministers waiting beyond the crowd.

On Sunday, July 3rd, the whirlwind arrived in Donaghmore. James described the events this way. "Mr. White prayed and entroduced Mr. Beaty of Ballymena to the congregation, who gave an address on religious revivals and prayed. Mr. Beatty spoke with power. Mr. White was greatly effected." While this service was underway in Donaghmore, Rev. Moore had traveled to Newry to preach. George described this meeting for his readers. "The services were unusually impressive, and such was the feeling produced as warranted the calling of a congregational prayer-meeting on yesterday evening at eight o'clock." The revival had arrived in Newry.

However, as this new force spread around the countryside, it coincided with the usual marches of July 12th, always an anxious time in Ulster. The new restrictions prohibiting sectarian flags, symbols and music that Parliament had passed made the event even more worrying. To calm the situation, William Beers, the Grand Master of the Orange Order in Down, wrote a letter to his fellow members urging marchers to obey all laws. George printed the entire letter in his paper.

Beers began by reminding his members of the importance of what the occasion celebrated. "To commemorate events in which Truth and Liberty triumphed over falsehood and tyranny, events by which all classes of the people were benefitted, and peace, happiness, and prosperity were secured for the people of these kingdoms."

The work of the Orange Order was the work of their much-loved Queen as well. "Although it may be fashionable to deride the principles on which the Orange Institution has been founded, it should be borne in mind that these are precisely the same as those which our present Gracious Queen is pledged to uphold. Her Majesty has solemnly 'sworn' to maintain the laws of God, the true profession of the Gospel, and the Protestant reformed religions established by law." Mr. Beers also agreed with the Queen that "the leading doctrines of the Romish Church are 'superstitious and idolatrous.'"

Mr. Beers made clear that he understood the difficulties the members of the Orange Order faced. "Brethren, the times are dark and gloomy. Popery is still fostered by the State, Priestcraft is still a governing power in this country, and to be an outspoken, earnest Protestant is to be, as heretofore, exposed to insult and injury." Despite these undeserved provocations, the Grand Master urged his members to celebrate the glorious anniversary in strict accordance with existing law, and in total peace. George was happy to report that Marching Day did indeed pass in the area in "total peace."

§

The revival had taken a powerful hold in Donaghmore. Just a week after the first appearance, meetings were taking place almost every night. On Sunday, July 10th, James recorded that "Mr. White preached & gave a detaled account of how he had passed the last week, and in the evening also."

There was an unusual Monday meeting the next day. "Attended a prayer meeting in the meetinghouse. Mr. P. White opened the meeting and Mr. V. White gave an Excellent address from the 9th of 'Acts' Pauls conversion. A good maney lingered in the meetinghouse with Mr. White after the meeting had closed."

Tuesday was a fine day for another meeting. First James worked with Mr. Speers and Alick Rainey thrashing hay. "Then we all went to the meetinghouse, where I joined with Thomas Ward, and from the Elders bench read the 1st nine verses of the 84th Psalm. After it was sung, Mr. P. White, Mr. Moore and Mr. Verner White addressed the largest congregation I have seen in the meetinghouse since the day of Mr. Verner Whites ordination in October 1840. Several persons was impressed including Miss A J McCollough." Rev. White, now Doctor White, preached again the next night to another large audience.

These events in Donaghmore were so unusual that George noticed and commented on what had occurred. "Immense congregations have met in the Presbyterian Church, we understand, night after night, during the past week. Such an amount of religious earnestness was certainly never witnessed in this parish before, nor did any of the people believe that it could possibly have been produced. Many even of those who witness it are unable to believe the testimony of their own senses. If this great movement be judged of by the moral influence which it produces, there is no question but that this and other parishes will stand forth to declare that it suppresses sin in every shape and form and promotes the highest interests of religion and morality."

There were some important religious leaders beside Dr. Cooke who weren't sure that what was happening was authentic. Rev. Daniel Baggot, the very Rev. Dean of Down, made his doubts an element in a sermon he gave on the prodigal son. He mentioned these doubts at the beginning of his sermon. "Is this movement of man or of God?"

Rev. Baggot viewed the parable as the definitive example of what God viewed as the true example of penitence and forgiveness. "We have a sure criterion to detect spurious pretences to conversion and to eliminate from what is real and genuine the cunningly-devised fables of those who would 'make a gain of godliness,' and the deluded though sincerely entertained fancies of the visionary and the enthusiast."

Religious people must adhere to the "unerring word of the living God. To the law and to the testimony, be ever our appeal, on the Rock of God's eternal Truth be our faith ever fixed, firm and immovable, unshaken by every passing wind of doctrine, uninfluenced by any traditions of men, by the voice of the multitude, as by the madness of the people."

In this long sermon, Rev. Baggot continued to explain his thinking that the current revival was without a connection to the real route toward religious conversion. Practices like physical collapse, wailing, and revealing before a large crowd sins that should remain private were not proof of genuine repentance. "Remember that the larger the crowd of those who profess sudden conversion, just in that proportion does the probability decrease that it is a genuine work of God, and the likelihood increased that it is an ebullition of epidemic enthusiasm, a phenomenence as well known and yet as unaccountable as the contagion of the pestilence that walks in darkness."

Rev. Baggot believed that the only way to know whether the revival was an appeal to human hysteria or the work of God was to wait long enough to determine whether or not the supposed conversions resulted in changed conduct. He concluded, "I desire not to oppose, and I desire as distinctly to keep aloof from any approbation of, or participation...what I do not feel that there is evidence sufficient to pronounce decidedly a work of God."

A few days later George published an angry response to Rev. Baggot's sermon from James's pastor, Rev. White. Rev. White didn't mince his words. "It is truly melancholy to see a man, whom God has endowed with great mental powers, and placed in a prominent position in one of the most important sections of His Son's Church, using these gifts, and the influence of his station, to misrepresent and obstruct a work upon which the Head of the Church has stamped so marked evidences of His approval. The Dean is evidently as faulty in his knowledge of the movement as he is unsound in his theology. He speaks as if 'prostration of strength, spasm, and hysterics were our evidences of the conversion of souls to God. These do often accompany the inward wrestlings of the soul in its striving to enter the kingdom of heaven. But we adopt the

Bible rule, 'By their fruits ye shall know them' and we thank God these fruits are most abundant."

After this scorching rebuke of character and theology, he charged the Dean with lack of Christian Charity and ignorance of the reality of the effects of the revival. "Truly it is a strange specimen to be presented in a Church of Christ, in fact, I do not know that I ever saw more heresy upon a cardinal doctrine of Christianity condensed in a single column of a newspaper."

Rev. White offered numerous examples from other portions of the Bible that he claimed disproved Rev. Baggot's perception that the theatrics of revival meetings proved that no real conversions were actually taking place. Because the Bible also provided evidence that real conversions could take place in large events, Rev. Baggot's philosophy was also faulty. Then Rev. White questioned the truths that came from the Church of Ireland. Current practices of the church brought it ever closer to the abominable Catholic Church.

"I dare not express an opinion, but say, to be consistent in opposing and denouncing the Revival movement, he should have warned his people, with all fidelity and earnestness, against the abominations of Popery."

Having published the different analysis of the revival movement by the Dean of Dromore and the minister of Donaghmore, George wrote a leader expressing his opinion of the religious revival. He titled the leader "Moral influences of the Movement." First, he stated that he would no longer provide reports of specific events in specific places, since the movement was too wide-spread to report any level of detail.

Then he told his readers that he sided with Rev. White. George didn't get his endorsement from any theological argument. His judgment that the hand of God was at work came from viewing the results. "It is generally conceded that drunkenness is the prevailing vice of the age, scattering broadcast over society beggary, irreligion, and vice, in every form, but, wherever the Revival comes drunkenness disappears." One proof of the correctness of this view was that public houses were closing down in areas where the revival was strong.

Another observable effect was the decline of rioting and crime. "The bridewells are empty, and districts once noted for party brawls and drunken riots are now as remarkable for peace and godliness." A local minister reported that for miles around, every family was now engaged in Bible reading and prayer. George affirmed this with an observation of his own. The Presbyterian meeting houses in the entire area from Rathfriland to Armagh were filled to overflowing. Meetings were held in fields and schoolhouses as well. These ceremonies were held in the most quiet and religious way.

So George's conclusion was that "a great religious earnestness is pervading the people, and that there is as little of the human and erroneous mixed up with it as we could possibly expect in a great popular movement." This analysis was printed less than a month after the local beginning of the movement. The question remained just how permanent these beneficial effects would be.

As July turned to August, the revival was still keeping James very busy. There were almost daily services for prayer, Bible readings, and sermons. These commitments consumed large amounts of time that would be hard to find as the harvest began. However, James was present whenever a meeting was held.

James began to offer more detail about the meetings. His journal entries gave a personal account of events that George reported with a more distant viewpoint. A meeting was held on Tuesday, Aug. 2. "Attended evening service in the meetinghouse. Showers." But the next day, James took personal action to bring the Revival to his employees. "Had a meeting with the men…in the parlor."

At this time, Rev. White left on a missionary trip to England, "Mr. White preached, and gave a fearwell address, being about to <u>lave</u> for Liverpool." Though the harvest began the next day, James attended a service at the meetinghouse. Two days later, on Friday Aug. 17th, there was a service despite Rev. White's absence. "Attended evening service in the meetinghouse. Mr Dickie addressed the meeting, and Mr. Hall of Athy concluded with prayer & singing the 23rd Psalm."

On "Sunday, the services were conducted by a supply minister, a Rev. Boil." Despite Rev. White's continuing absence, there was another event in the meetinghouse the next day as well. "Opened a prayer meeting specially convened on behalf of Mr. White, & Mr. Beaty gone to Liverpool, on a mission, in the meetinghouse, after <u>seven oclock</u>."

The third meeting of the week was held on Thursday. "Attended a missionary meeting in the meetinghouse of the congregations of <u>Donaghmore</u> and <u>Ryan</u>. Heard Mr. Hall of Athy & Mr. Patterson of <u>Dundalk</u>, Elder, address the meeting which was large. Mr. McAlester of <u>Ryan</u> and Mr. Lindsay of <u>Drumbanagher</u> prayed. One impression." This was the first time that James mentioned the manifestation that had sparked controversy.

Before August ended, Rev. White had returned from Liverpool. "Mr. White preached, the gerl <u>Sloan</u> <u>impressed</u>. Was very ill & made a piteous noise. The congregation seemed alarmed and requested Mr. White to pray. He was about the middle of his sermon. We all went to prayer. Mr. White preached again at six oclock, and Mr. Bane, a Scotch minister who came into the meetinghouse during Mr. Whites service, preached about <u>eight</u> on the ten 'to be virgins."

As George had mentioned in his leader on the effects of the Revival, many had given up drinking. At the end of August, the Donaghmore church held a special meeting to support this most positive result of the Revival. "Attended a temperance meeting in the meetinghouse and heard a very excellent address on the subject from Mr. Benson, a <u>colloured</u> Gentleman from Belfast. I moved a vote of thanks to him for it."

One important issue in Ireland hadn't gained any prominent attention in the *Telegraph.* Would the revival change the Protestant versus Catholic divide? In early September, George reprinted an article from the *Morning Post* published in London. This article made clear its position in the opening sentence. "'One of the chief causes of the semi-barbarian and backwardness of a people so shrewd, apprehensive, and intelligent as the Irish, is that there has never prevailed in the sister country that religious respect and reverence for the law which has ever obtained in England.'" This was an important signal that however the revival might change the character of the Presbyterians, the awakening of their Christianity would not require them to extend their new respect for the Golden Rule to their Catholic neighbors.

By the middle of September, Rev. Baggot seemed to have come to believe that the Revival was indeed the work of God. After the service in Donaghmore on September 11, James wrote, "Heard Mr. Bagot preach on Joseph Robinsons field in Grandshaw. (Chiefton [Andrew] drove A Douglass & me to it). Drunk tea with Mrs. Clotworthy, Fine dry day and evening also. Mr. Bagot said he thought there was 3500 people at it. I think there was 1000."

The revival movement had occupied a lot of James's time and energy. But it also increased demands on the time of those who were newly called to religion as a result of the meetings. Many of these people were farm laborers, whose days from dawn to dark were already filled with work. Only a really strong commitment to include active religion in their lives would keep up the level of participation. There were thirteen events in the Donaghmore meetinghouse in August, fourteen in September like the one in Robinson's field. By October, the number of events had dropped to ten. And finally in November, there were no extra revival meetings in Donaghmore, just the regularly scheduled church activities. However, these services still fostered the revival spirit, and impressions and conversions still took place.

§

Rev. White had shown great leadership in the movement, devoting extraordinary time and energy to reach the population, even beyond Donaghmore. So it wasn't surprising that a grateful congregation wanted to show their appreciation. James explained what took place on October 11th in his journal. The weather was fine for October as James set off to visit Rev. White in his home. After having tea with John and the Sparten in Loughorne, he "accompanied a Deputation to Mr. Whites on Buskhill, consisting of Messers Thomas Greer, James Martin, John McMaster, James Smith & Ralph Thompson. We had Mrs Greer, Nancy & Lisabath McGaffin, Misses Kildere, Boyd, Andrews, Fargeson & Lindon. We met in Mr. Greers about six oclock and got to Buskhill about seven where Mr White and his father, Mr & Mrs Hannah with their son & Daughter and Miss White greeted us. I moved that Mr. Greer should take the chair which he did, and asked James Martin to read the address we had prepared for Mr. White. He, Mr Martin, read it after which Mr White read his reply under strong feelings. James Martin then handed Mr White a purse containing forty sovereigns. Mr White assured the Deputation that he valued the address, more than the purse, and asked his father to pray which he did. Tea was served round, and we spent a plasant evening singing hymns & Psalms. Supper was entroduced about ten oclock and we all left about eleven oclock. A fine mild moon-light night."

George published both the testimonial and the response. "You have, dear Sir, proved yourself an able and faithful Minister of Jesus Christ, and your unwearied, almost superhuman, exertions in the cause of religion in this neighborhood call forth our lively admiration and sincere gratitude." They referred to his work with the children and young people of the area for special commendation "Your own warm and loving disposition, but, above all, your sincere and unaffected piety, had endeared you not only to the members of the congregation, but has secured for you the esteem and kind regards of many not connected with us." This salute was signed by Thomas Greer, Chairman; James Martin, Secretary; Robert Jeffrey, Treasurer; and James Harshaw, Ruling Elder.

Rev White responded first to the specific areas to which the testimonial had referred, the work he had done with the young people of the church and the close connections he had established in the wider community. He affirmed the pleasure he felt in working with the young of the congregation, saying that his happiest hours were spent with children in their religious classes. He was pleased that his work had earned the esteem of the wider community. "I trust I can say, if I know my own heart, that these feelings are heartily reciprocated by me towards all my Christian friends of every communion, devoid of sectarian prejudice."

Only in his concluding remarks did he mention the revival. "To be a Minister of Jesus Christ was among my earliest aspirations; yet, with deep humility, I must acknowledge that for years I have very unworthily and imperfectly discharged the duties pertaining to that holy calling, but, 'by the grace of God,' in this season of blessed awakening to our Church, I have been brought to see myself in a new light, and impressed with the grave responsibility impending my sacred office, the true value of immortal souls and a just consideration of my own mortality, have determined to 'work while it is called to-day,' and live for Christ."

George not only published the address and response, he also added a comment of his own. "It gives us pleasure to record this and similar instances of kindly feeling subsisting between Pastor and people. It is highly creditable to both, and, in the present case, at least, gives indubitable proof that the *spirit* of 'Revivalism' is at work in Donaghmore."

§

As the months had passed since Mary's death, James gradually became a doting grandfather. Once the newborn had been baptized and a nurse had been hired to care for the baby, James stopped even mentioning his grandson in his journal. However, by September, as young James neared six months of age, James began to mention the baby frequently, with obvious pride and affection. In the middle of September James mentioned an outing. "The mistress, the 'weebaby' & nurse gerl spent this afternoon with <u>Mrs William</u>

Young & other friends <u>there</u>. The "weebaby" was visiting his grandmother Harshaw's sister.

A week later, James mentioned another outing, "Dined with the Dandy, Joseph, the 'wee baby' & nurse in A. Douglas. The baby and his entourage had traveled down Ardkeragh Road to visit his father.

In between these two visits, James went visiting without the baby. "Joseph drove his mama, Jane & me to Newry and to Rostrever, where we breakfasted with Dr. Simpson (Mary being poorly) [pregnant], John Martin then took Jane & me to the great stone on the mounten. From that we went down to Kilbroney, where we met Dr. Simpson & David, dined & drunk tea there, & got home at <u>twelve oclock</u>."

A few days later, James met John again. It must have been a great pleasure for James to have John living an easy distance away again. Over ten years had passed since James and John had enjoyed such opportunities for time together. On this occasion, John came to visit his old home base. "Spent the evening with John Martin & eight children he had with him in <u>James Martins</u>."

When Mary's son had reached the age of six months, the family made a difficult and frightening decision. Young James was old enough to be vaccinated against small pox. Though immunization had been discovered years before, there was still apprehension about its safety. The Harshaws, along with father Alex decided to take the risk. "Dr. Saunderson, Jane & Archy dined here after three. He, Dr. Saunderson, vaccinated 'James Alexander' on the sholder of <u>its</u> right arm about five oclock in the parlor. Jane had <u>it</u>, the 'wee Baby' on her knee, and Joseph done what he could to amuse it while the vaccination was going on."

"Wee baby" wasn't the only infant in the family. Mary Simpson, who had been unable to attend the last family gathering at Kilbroney, had delivered a daughter. So the family gathered again for that baptism in early November. It was a nice day for an outing. "Joseph drove Hugh [Robert] & me to Newry where we took the trean to Warrnepoint and walked to Dr. Simpsons house at Rostrevor Quay, where we dined with <u>Mary</u> & her family about <u>three</u> oclock. <u>We</u> then went up to Kibroney house, and saluted John, and David Martin, and the children. Joined with them at dinner and returned to <u>Mary</u> with <u>John</u>, <u>David</u> & <u>Baby</u> about seven oclock, and Hugh [Robert] Baptized <u>Mary's</u> child '<u>Anna Millicent</u>." Drunk tea there & left after <u>eight</u> & got home about eleven oclock."

At this point, James began to mention each milestone in 'wee Baby's" life. "The wee <u>Baby danced</u> on the table." "The 'wee Baby' first cryed after A. Douglass, viz to get gowing <u>with</u> <u>him</u> when about to be parted from <u>him</u> on the race." "The Baby has the cold and coughs." "James A D gets the 2nd <u>tooth</u>."

§

The power of the revival failed to eliminate sectarian confrontations. James mentioned the latest local violence on Thursday, November 24th. "Mick Turly beat at <u>Cowans Corner</u> on his way home from Newry."

George supplied a full account of what happened to Michael Torley, a local farmer. On the day of the attack, Mick had been in Newry on business.

He completed his business at half seven in the evening and headed home down the dark Rathfriland Road. He had gotten within fifty feet of the entrance gate to Emyville where George lived, when he was jumped by three or four men. The first blow was a sharp hit by a blunt instrument to his forehead. This blow rendered Torley insensible, and unable to remember anything else that happened.

A farmer named Robert Cowan, who lived nearby, was alerted that something was happening outside by the barking of his dogs. Thinking that they were greeting Cowan's son returning from the Newry market, he went out to the road. Instead of greeting his son, he discovered Torley's body lying near his gate. There seemed to be no one around, and when Cowan's son arrived he told his father he had seen no one along the road but a patrol of constables.

The two men carried Torley into their cottage and summoned a doctor who reported the grim news that a blow had shattered Torley's skull and lacerated his brain. His benefactors helped move him home where he was attended by Dr. McConville and Surgeon Taylor. They agreed there was no hope for recovery.

Because Torley was a Catholic, neighbors quickly concluded that the attack was a "party affair" carried out by a local Protestant. George reached a different conclusion. He claimed the attack happened as a result of a conflict Torley had had with a Catholic neighbor over a bog. When Torley regained consciousness, police asked about this theory. Torley wouldn't answer, saying he "did not wish to get people into trouble."

James recorded the final outcome in his first December entry. "Mick Turley who was beat coming out of Newry on the 24th ult. Died <u>this</u> morning."

George covered the inquest that took place in Newry two days later. The coroner, Dr. Tyrell, was the first person to testify. He claimed there was nothing of a "party nature" in the attack except for one fact. Torley had refused to give any information about the people who attacked him. This was typical when party was the motive behind an attack. "If Catholics testified against Protestants, survivors would possibly be at risk at the hands of the killers."

The jury next heard evidence that Torley had been seen buying groceries in a shop in Newry, before heading home to the townland of Carnecally. Even if he had had a bit of whiskey, he didn't consume enough to make him drunk. There was no evidence that he had been followed out of Newry.

Then Robert Cowan was called to testify. Cowan knew Torley enough to recognize him even in the dark. When he looked about, he saw no one. He tried to talk to Torley but couldn't make out what Torley was telling him. Cowan thought he must be drunk.

Cowan stood by Torley for several minutes trying to decide what to do next. When his son arrived from Newry, the two men decided to get a lantern to improve visibility. When Cowan held the lantern close to Torley's face, he could see Torley was bleeding. At that point, the Cowans brought Torley into their house and summoned Torley's family. They came and took Torley home.

Dr. McConville was the next witness. He had examined Torley and found wounds consistent with an attack with sticks and stones which Torley had described. But Torley steadfastly refused to tell the doctor who his attackers were.

For the next several days. Dr. McConville had continued to care for Torley. Dr. McConville told the jury about a curious conversation between Torley and his brother Phelomy. Torley was quite agitated that Phelomy couldn't remember seeing a man look at him "wickedly" when they had been together in Newry a few days before the attack. This was the man whom Torley said had attacked him.

After Torley died, Dr. McConville discovered four more injuries on the back of Torley's head suggesting either more than one attacker or that the beating had continued when Torley was on the ground. There were four separate skull fractures, which were the direct cause of death.

At this point, the inquest was adjourned, because the investigating constables had been unable to find witnesses willing to testify. The hearing resumed, when one new witness came forward to support the prevailing wisdom that the attack had been sectarian. Henry Hazlett from Finard testified that while the murder was on the minds of local people, he had met a man who told him that Torley would habitually walk along Rathfriland Road uttering party slogans whenever he had had a bit too much whiskey. But Hazlett testified that he couldn't remember the name of the person who had passed on this information.

At the point, the inquest ended. The jurors rendered a verdict of death by "person or persons unknown." The inquest would resume if new information warranted. In fact, this was the end of the affair. No one was ever charged with Torley's murder.

Chapter 8

War and Disunion

1859 - 1861

A year after the death of his brother Robert, John had organized life in Kilbroney, hiring cooks, housekeepers, groundskeepers, and a governess for the children. He was then free to travel around Ireland. In October of 1859, he took a very special trip to Paris. When he left the train, he saw a very familiar person, rushing toward him, a person he had last seen riding away in Bothwell. John Mitchel had come to Paris from Washington DC to write for a couple of newspapers, one based in Paris, one in Dublin. Six years had passed between the two events, so the two friends had much to talk about. Mitchel could tease John for his bald head and luxuriant beard. John could point out in return that his friend's hair was turning gray.

Both men were curious about the other's families and eager to understand events in their different countries. Mitchel had been living in Washington, DC, and could discuss governmental leaders from personal knowledge, and the possibility of civil war. Mitchel's family had remained there expecting that Mitchel would return in a few months. John talked of old friends in Ireland, and possible political initiatives.

These happy weeks passed quickly, but before John returned home, he attended a breakfast meeting Mitchel had arranged with two other Irish visitors. John O'Mahony had traveled from New York to Paris to meet Mitchel. John O'Leary had come to the meeting from Ireland. Both men were working with James Stephens to create a new movement for Irish independence. They were interested in recruiting some of the Young Irelanders to join in their new effort in order to give legitimacy to their cause. Neither John nor Mitchel was willing to endorse any organization headed by Stephens, since they both saw him as unpleasant and shifty, not the kind of person to be successful in achieving Irish independence.

George knew nothing of the Paris meeting or the secret movement discussed there. Therefore, he was optimistic when he wrote his leader for the year 1860. He was delighted that the Indian Mutiny had been crushed, and peace had returned to the British Empire, a peace that extended to Ireland. Perhaps in part due to the Great Revival, Irish citizens increasingly appreciated the benefits of the union of the two countries. Food was cheap, and sectarian conflict wasn't of great concern. He predicted happy days ahead, despite one small cloud on the horizon.

This cloud was the impending civil war in America, a war George had expected to break out some years earlier. John Brown's raid on Harpers Ferry the previous fall seemed to ensure that the outbreak of a terrible civil war was imminent. Not only was America polluted by the institution of slavery, but their republican form of government was far inferior to the English monarchy. He conceded republican governance allowed greater freedom, freedom with a negative impact as well. He viewed republicanism as "The very form of government under which the ruffian is licensed to enjoy himself."

To illustrate how easy it was to unleash ungoverned mobs, George reprinted a circular from the south. The circular urged the Irish living in the north to commit themselves to a campaign of arson against abolitionists in the places like New York and Boston. If they needed to escape capture, the people of the south would help with money and sanctuary.

This plot hit home for George, as his leader made clear. "Such a system of terrorism and secret criminality as is recommended, must necessarily shatter and overturn the very fabric of society. The Ribbonism in our own country, with its silent and murderous ravages, would be more than matched in the desperate wickedness by the dastardly yet deadly plotting of American Slaveholders."

Though not a call to war, this scheme made clear the depths of the rupture between states promoting expansion of slavery and those fighting to prevent it. George believed that America couldn't long continue under the strain of these two different beliefs. He predicted that oppression would lose out to freedom. But he did have some reservations. "True it is that John Mitchel, the ranting patriot and licentious and loud-tongued freeman when in this land, became in America the bitterest foe of the down-trodden slaves and the coarse and blustering apologist of the deeds of the cruel dealers in human flesh and blood."

Certainly, the Irish in America wouldn't follow Mitchel's path. But then George quoted another Irish immigrant who seemed to echo Mitchel's beliefs. "We white men, as a nation, made our laws, vesting political rights in the white American People. We left the Negro in the condition of a bondsman. To that condition the Negro is assigned by Nature. That Nature gave him a master, to coerce his will, and that will make him a useful and valuable servant, capable of living for himself *and for the Master who governs him.*"

§

While George was writing about Mitchel's support for slavery, Mitchel had written a letter on January 1st to the Dublin based newspaper the *Irishman* for which he worked. In the letter he attacked the treatment of Ireland by the English, claiming "that the prosperity and power of the British Empire requires England to have and hold the entire use and enjoyment of all Irish produce and wealth, except only so much as will subsist in a certain beastly manner, the minimum of Irish human stock needed to labor. No race of white men, or even brown men, will submit to be stripped so bare, themselves and their little ones, if they have it [guns] in their hands: - for when a strong man armed, keepeth his palace – or his cabin – his goods are in peace."

Mitchel wasn't endorsing guns for slaves, but rather guns for the Irish. One of the critiques of Mitchel's role in promoting the Young Irelander revolt was his failure to consider that few Irishmen owned guns. Now he was making clear that widespread possession of guns would be required for any successful revolt. The editor of the *Irishman* followed Mitchel's views with a quote from Thomas Davis, who had been a leader of the Young Irelanders, and a man John Martin greatly loved and admired.

"*'To carry arms is the first right of man for arms are the guardians of property, honour and life.* God gave weapons, as well as clothing to the lion and the eagle; but to man he gave skill to furnish himself with all bodily comforts and with weapons to defend them and all his rights *against every assailant, be he the beast of the forest or the tyrant of society.*

TO *carry arms* is the ultimate guarantee of life, property and freedom. *To be without their* POWER *of resisting oppression is to be a* SLAVE. What matter that with delusive words, your rulers *say* he will not rifle your altars, or pollute your hearths – what matter that your ruler boasts his power to 'protect' you, and flourishes his weapon before your cell! ARMS AND LIBERTY ARE SYNONIMOUS. *If you are* [see] *an unarmed and an armed man together you instantly conclude that one is a prisoner and the other a guard.* ARMS ARE THE BADGES OF FREEMEN. *He who is* UNARMED *will soon be* IN CHAINS.'"

§

The peace that George had felt during the darkness of winter was threatened as spring drew closer by new legislation making its way through Parliament. It was the first attempt of members to change voting laws, converting the open voting to a secret ballot. The idea was discussed and soundly defeated. Years would pass before voting became a private affair. George believed strongly that secret ballots would "degrade and demoralize the people of this country and turn the electors into law breakers or hypocrites."

Defeated along with the secret ballot were two other innovations. One was a proposal that would increase the number of Irish voters, another innovation George rejected. If there were more voters, Ireland would have rule by mob. He thought America again provided a good example of that bad idea. Demagogues could easily take over a mob. Disenfranchisement was a better idea than expansion. The other new proposal would require only authorized electors to vote, another idea George rejected. Instead to better protect voters, he believed parliament should impose more stringent controls over voters and voting.

George finally commented on Mitchel's presence in Paris, though by that time he had returned to his family in America. Claiming that his time in Paris made him an expert on European affairs, Mitchel had written a speech on the subject, which he was delivering in several cities. George saw this as a swindle. However, he no longer viewed Mitchel as the threat he had been when he lived in Ireland. To George's mind, Mitchel should have been hanged or at the very least have shown great gratitude for the kind treatment he had received from the British government.

John read George's attack on Mitchel with shock and immediately wrote a response. John couldn't believe that George had actually written the letter and urged him to disavow comments he knew to be untrue.

"I know pretty well the intolerance of political enmity, and the odium that attached to failure among both friends and enemies. Mr. Mitchel, like myself, was transported as a felon in 1848 for advocating the national independence of Ireland and neither of us has repented of his political conduct since. There are individuals in Ireland who think or pretend to think, that whoever entertains such a political sentiment as that of Irish independence, must be a base miscreant, unworthy of all respect. But for my obscurity and unimportance they would write of me also as a base miscreant. That strangers who know nothing of Mr. Mitchel and me, except that we are Irish nationalists, should see no impropriety of that kind of argument for dealing with his case or mine, is, perhaps not astonishing. But it is astonishing–aye disgusting–to see anyone in Newry trying to treat Mr. Mitchel's character with disrespect, and that while he is still in exile."

George did print John's letter in the paper, but added a comment defending his editorial, claiming that his remarks were "fully justified."

§

James began the year still attempting to live beyond the pain of losing his daughter Mary. In his first journal entry, he tabulated the number of weeks that had passed since major family events occurred, two sad and one very gratifying…The 162nd Sabbath since Absalom [Samuel] left me, the 49th since Josephs [James Jr.] return, and the 40th since Mary entered into her rest. 'There remaineth therefore a rest to the people of God."

Most of his days were spent in routine church and farming duties. But he made sure to record the progress of his grandson. James no longer referred to him as "WeeBaby," instead using his given name James Alexander, the name frequently underlined in the journal. In early January, James recorded a family prayer service in the living room when James Alexander was brought into the room. James reported that the baby "appeared puzzled to know what we were doing."

On another winter day, James went to Newry to attend to a court case. While he was there, he bought his grandson some boots. James Alexander would soon need those boots, as James reported that James Alexander was walking with some assistance before his first birthday. By the end of June, James reported that "'James Alexander' first walked alone. I saw it roam about in the meadow of Moffits Hill."

Once James Alexander reached his first birthday and had been weaned, there was no need for Catherine O'Hare, "nurse girl" as James referred to her, to remain. So on May 15th, the family paid her for her care of the baby. She had already been paid £4 pounds for her services during the year she had lived with the Harshaw family. James paid her an additional £4.4s. Alex also gave her a "hand note" detailing the great care she had taken on his son. "She seemed very sorry at parting with the child, and the family." But around 6 p.m. she walked away.

However, two days later Catherine returned, and handed back the money she had been paid. She clearly couldn't bear to leave the family and the baby. James and the entire family were happy to welcome her back.

James didn't seem to be as active in the Dispensary Committee as he had been in previous years. But he certainly continued his interest in church and other civil activities, particularly his support of the Donaghmore School. There was always a need for infusions of money to help support the school. So on March 11th, a special collection was held on both Sabbath services. James reported that they collected £17.5s.4d. A new meeting was held during which a committee was chosen to assist Thomas Greer, the school supervisor. James was one of the members selected. When the school committee elected a new schoolmaster, James was in the chair. They selected Robert Sloane to teach in the school at Tullymurry.

There was another project very important to James as well. He had participated in efforts to build a manse for the Donaghmore minister several times over the years. Despite the previous disappointing efforts, James was ready to try again. Again the project began with fund raising. Despite growing financial problems of his own, James pledged £10. When pledges were totaled up, £106 was promised. Another round of fund raising produced £51, which was enough for plans to move forward.

John Martin came over from Kilbroney to meet with his brother James Martin, James and John Harshaw to discuss where to locate the new manse. John promised to donate a section of his property on which to build the home to offer their ministers. A happy celebration followed. This commitment was realized by the end of May. The committee in charge met and picked out a desirable site on land that James Martin was currently farming. It was on the side of a hill with a nice view across the valley to the Mournes. It was just a short trip down the road, later called Manse Hill Road, to the meetinghouse.

John Martin met often with his family members either in Loughorne or Kilbroney. One such meeting took place in late June for a rather different purpose. John came up from Kilbroney to participate in a conversation between himself, James Martin and Uncle Harshaw about James Martin's plan to marry. He was a middle-aged man, who had never shown great interest in marriage. But now he wanted to marry a young woman Rebecca Andrews who also lived in Loughorne. Her father was of a lower class than the Martins, so Rebecca wasn't considered a suitable wife. On this evening, the three men held a long conversation on the subject.

The next day, there was another family gathering, Chiefton [Andrew] drove James and Alex Douglas to Newry, where James bought a couple of frocks for James Alexander. Then the men took the train to Warrenpoint, where David Martin met them with his car. During dinner and tea, the subject of the possible marriage must have been part of the conversation. On the way home, they stopped at Elizabeth's in Newry to share what had happened. Despite family objections, James Martin did indeed marry Rebecca Andrews.

Just before the annual Orange marches, James had a busy day planned, He took a trip to visit a sick friend. On the way home through Rathfriland, he left some fabric with Robert McAnuff and ordered a suit. So he didn't arrive home until after 10 p.m. When he got inside he reported. "I found <u>Absalom</u>, [Samuel] Jane and Archy in the parlor. I had not heard of Absaloms return from New York, but I knew him at first sight, saluted him as my 'youngest son' and kissed him." One hundred and eighty-nine weeks of separation had ended.

§

Samuel [Absalom] had returned to Ireland just before the Orange Order celebrations. While these events weren't of great interest to James and his family, they were to George. He paid close attention to local demonstrations. This year, he was very pleased with events in Newry. Members of the Orange Order celebrated with a dinner in their lodge. Newry Commissioners assured citizens that there were extra constables on duty to prevent any Catholic misconduct. Happily, they were not needed.

However, there was a major sectarian confrontation in a townland called Derrymacash, located on the far side of Lurgan. George didn't mention it, at least not at first. He was more interested in a debate that had taken place in Parliament about education. Isaac Butt, who had been John's lawyer in his 1848 felony trial, had moved that all money given by Parliament for Irish education could only be spent in schools without religious education. George was pleased that the resolution got only six votes. George quoted one speech opposing the resolution: "with Popery, the object in view is undoubtedly, not to enlighten, but to degrade the mind, not to strengthen its powers, but to degrade them." In his view, concessions made to the Catholics already had set Irish education back a generation.

But within a few days, George pivoted to the rioting in Derrymacash, prompted by a discussion on the subject in Parliament. There had been a large Orange gathering in Lurgan to celebrate the July 12th anniversary. Authorities were so concerned that violence might break out that they had sent police there from as far away as Dublin. While the day passed in total peace, trouble started as members of the Orange Order left in groups heading home.

One group lived beyond the Catholic townland of Derrymacash, located near Lough Neagh. They had to march through town to return home. While the march through the town in the early morning had been peaceful, the trip home in the evening was decidedly not. The Orange marchers claimed that they were met by a barrage of stones. Catholics claimed the stones were defenses against Orangemen armed with guns. Though the beginning of the fight was murky, the ending was not. The battle was brief. Sixteen Catholics were shot, two of them critically injured. Police hurried to the scene to take testimony from the dying. It was the largest sectarian battle since Dolly's Brae over ten years earlier.

George applauded quick action by the Lord Lieutenant in proclaiming the area around Derrymacash, which authorized them to send more troops to start collecting guns. The taxpayers would pay all expenses for the extra protection. George believed that the government actions should be impartial, and both groups condemned equally for their actions. But he believed the Protestants were being judged more harshly because Protestants had guns and Catholics had stones. He lamented that there was something in the Irish people that periodically gave up civilization's limits and acted like a country with only the outside appearance of civilization that "resists discipline and culture."

Parliament acted quickly. Less than a month after the fighting, legislation had passed through the Lords and become law. It gave the government power to treat any display of party colors or music as a misdemeanor. Authorities had a right to enter any building displaying sectarian colors and seize them or any musical instruments or guns that they found inside. This legislation took direct aim at the Protestant custom of flying Orange flags from church steeples every July. George wasn't pleased with the new law. It was clearly an invasion of privacy and proof of sectarian bias. But he wouldn't oppose any law that might prevent more events like that in Derrymacash.

But he warned the government to remember that when passing legislation for Ireland, the contest was "not in this country between Whigs and Conservatives as such, but between the loyal and disloyal, the friends of England and its enemies, a religion that is the nurse of freedom, and one that is hostile to freedom in the highest degree."

§

The surviving Young Irelanders were scattered now, their hopes for a free and independent Ireland a depressing memory of failure. John and O'Brien were the only main players in the movement again living in Ireland, but both were politically inactive, though both occasionally wrote letters to newspapers on topics of interest. Meagher lived in New York City, and McManus across the American continent in California. Both men had renounced their Irish citizenship to become American citizens, and Mitchel was soon to become a citizen as well.

In November, John wrote a letter, not to a newspaper, but to Mitchel. He was again living in Paris, this time with his family, minus the two older sons. Mitchel wrote a public response to John's private letter in the November 17th edition of the *Irishman*. In his letter, John had made clear his concerns about the new nationalist movement he had learned about in Paris, plans to establish a new organization in Ireland, secret, armed and illegal.

One of the difficulties that John had seen in the plans being formulated was the problem of putting together an efficient organization without corruption, especially difficult in an organization led by Stephens. One of the ways to create a worthy organization would to establish some basic obligations for members, such as members "should never vote for members of Parliament nor attend Tenant-rights meetings, nor break bread at independent opposition dinners."

Mitchel began by making clear he didn't agree with John's assessment. "I do not approve at all of what you say about a National Organization; and I am sorry to think that your remarks may tell against the efforts which seem about to be made for the institution of a Repeal Association or something of the kind." If Ireland were to gain its independence, some sort of organization would be required.

Mitchel didn't agree that there should be any preconditions put on members of any organization. To this idea, he responded, "Ought it not be enough for you and me to do and to avoid such things as we think right or wrong, wise or foolish, in the National Cause and to state our own views and argue frankly in favor of them, without denouncing and prosecuting any body who does not adapt our ideas? I say every man in Ireland ought to be free, and welcome to join in a National organization and to hold his own ideas of policy, and to have the tolerance and respect of his countrymen."

Mitchel then repeated some of the problems that any national organization would face, that John had written about in his previous letter. England was strong and at peace. Since the Young Irelander's revolt, reforms in the police and detective systems made both more threatening. Now Irish railroads could quickly transport soldiers and troops to the places they were needed while the telegraph made the dissemination of warnings almost instantaneous. These changes were certain to make any successful revolt much more difficult.

Mitchel didn't dispute John's concerns about conditions. But there were actions that Irish patriots could take to promote the national cause. There would certainly be difficulties in forming the necessary military organization, which must be formed in secrecy. But this time Irish patriots could fight with guns not pikes or pitchforks. Prominent nationalists could legally buy guns for themselves and their poorer neighbors. They could sign the national petition for Irish independence that had been created earlier in the year at a meeting of nationalists in Dublin. It was now circulating around the country and had already been signed by 200,000 Irishmen. This time, priests and ministers like Father Kenyon were promoting the cause. Finally, the new movement had time for careful organization and intense recruitment, unlike in 1848.

A week later, the *Irishman* printed John's response. John didn't think that public discussions would be helpful. However, "so objectionable do some of Mr. Mitchel's arguments appear to me, that I request a place in the Irishman for a few sentences, to explain and define my own views."

John believed that the form of the nationalist organization was secondary. "More depends upon the virtue of the people than upon the form in which they protest against foreign rule. Nor am I able to pronounce whether it is practicable at the present to form an Irish National Organization worthy of the name." However, should any attempt be made, John argued that it must be a public one, and so must operate under terms that the British government would accept as legal. That condition also meant that the organization would have to be peaceful.

"I know Ireland lies under peculiar disadvantages; our nobles and gentry, the natural leaders of our people, are educated in English ideas, and our people are divided by the sectarian enmities which English rule has created and maintains. The attempt to revive a national association might have results as unsatisfactory as is our state of political anarchy."

The actions that he and his friends had taken in 1848 seemed to achieve the most with the least risk. Perhaps, a new effort could actually bring about independence. If the movement was led by the most moral and ethical men of Ireland, their efforts might convince the nobles and leading landlords to think of themselves as Irish lords and Irish gentry. We could be organized into a country. "Ever since I first took part in politics, my own object has been my country's independence – independence at any risk, at any cost." Though he had his own preferences, he would accept and support any form of government in Ireland that a majority of the citizens supported.

"I don't admire the British constitution and I don't profess to do so, but vast numbers of my countrymen do admire it, and therefore, they may honorably say so." "Though I preferred the Republican theory of government, I would give my loyal allegiance to the Queen, Lords and Commons of Ireland."

John concluded his letter with a bit of a cover for what he knew already. "All this I write not as bearing upon any actual movement in Ireland. The country is not yet sufficiently recovered from the effects of the defeat of 1848, though I see some hopeful signs. But I fear that Mr. Mitchel's remarks might lead to misapprehensions, injurious to our cause."

Mitchel wrote one more letter. He discussed the possible results of an impending war between England and France should France successfully invade England. France would leave England once it had won, but he didn't believe that it would leave Ireland. So any action by France wouldn't be helpful for Ireland.

There was a great defect in what John would propose for a legal struggle. No matter how legal the struggle was, "The British Government can at any moment treat it as *illegal,* and layup its leaders in jail. For the present state of Ireland nothing is really legal, nothing truly illegal, there is no law in the land."

"Mr. Martin too generously judging his countrymen by his own large heart and tolerant spirit, desires a national organization." Mitchel was more skeptical, believing any such effort would cause trouble. If it was a non-religious effort, it would be shunned, and any leader "denounced as an atheist." If it were a Catholic organization, it would antagonize the leaders who were English loyalists. "I know Mr. Martin himself would eagerly aid any national movement, even though it had a Catholic character, or a Mohamedan or Pagan character, or an Orange or a Kentish-fire character, so that it promised only to rid us of the English, but there are unhappily few Irishmen of any sect like Mr. Martin."

This conversation by way of letters in a newspaper attracted the attention of the editor Denis Holland. "For my part I look upon the fact that these two men, John Mitchel and John Martin, can differ and strongly and publically differ, and yet love one another all the same, is the most noble and needed lesson that has been presented to us for many a long day. The words of Swift that we have religion enough to make us hate, but not enough to make us love one another, have been too long true, of our Patriotism also. Here, then, is an example for us to follow. There is a sermon in this controversy between John Mitchel and his bosom friend, greater and grander than what they preached from the dock."

John wrote these letters from Kilbroney, watching over the children, strolling about his garden, and contemplating what, if anything, he would do next to serve the cause of Ireland.

In early December, he decided to accept an invitation to attend a gala gathering in the Rotunda in Dublin, so very familiar to him from the Young Irelander days. Daniel O'Donoghue, the O'Donoghue, was hosting an event celebrating the conclusion of the national petition campaign. It was a grand event. Sackville Street was crowded an hour before the meeting was to begin, as men and women hurried to find a seat in the hall. Many were disappointed as the room was soon filled to capacity. It had been more than a decade since John had shared a stage with so many important people. Denis Holland of the *Irishman* and A. M. Sullivan of the *Nation* were there. Rev. Patrick Lavelle, an old friend, and William O'Neil Daunt who would become a close new friend were also on the stage. The O'Donoghue was in the chair.

Over the stage on which the speakers sat was a huge banner of green silk with gold lettering. In the center of the banner was a large harp surrounded by a glory, with the motto. "aid yourself and God will aid you."

After T. D. Sullivan gave a report on the progress of the petition, the O'Donoghue strode to the lectern and gave a history of the efforts of many generations to obtain Irish independence. Daunt offered the first resolution, asking for an Irish legislature.

Then it was John's turn. As he stood up and walked to the podium, he was greeted by great and continuous applause. When the crowd quieted, John began by telling the audience, "It is after a good deal of hesitation that I am come to attend this meeting." While he approved of new moves toward independence, he didn't believe that he was the right person for any leadership position. "All the political reputation I can have arises from the part I took in the movement which ended in the sad failure of 1848. And I have neither the social position nor talents to enable me to do good service to our movement." That is how John always viewed his situation, and the insufficiencies that made his service challenging.

However, he very much hoped that someone on that stage would come forward and take on the great project that he and his companions had been unable to fulfill a decade before. He had only come to make his feelings on independence clear to a new audience. "I for one Irishman am not content with the subjection of my country to England–that I desire the national independence of Ireland and will be content with nothing less.' At this point in his remarks, John was interrupted again by extended cheering.

"I desire that the people of Ireland of all races, creeds, classes and conditions should have possession of our own country and rule it as best we may." There was more loud cheering. What he wanted for Ireland, he wanted for all countries as well. Then he shifted to talking about the price that Ireland had paid for her unwilling connection to England.

"General poverty, occasional starvation, is bad enough in a land like ours, flowing with milk and honey. But more than that, the foreign rule sets sect against sect, and class against class, and causes anarchy and hatred where order and kindliness should also prevail...And then – O' merciful God! Grant me to see that blessed day when the long torture of my country is ended, and independence will be here to heal the wounds of our state, and give us peace, honor, and prosperity."

John concluded his speech by encouraging potential new leaders to act for Irish independence. "I do not believe that the national spirit is dead in Ireland. I will not believe that it can die. I may not be worthy to assist at the triumph of our just cause, but it will triumph as sure as there is a God of Justice." With that, John returned to his seat to the great applause of a crowd happy to see John again.

This event got great coverage in many newspapers, but George did not mention it in the *Telegraph.*

§

As 1861 began, George returned to the threatening situation in America that he had mentioned in his New Year's letter the year before. He warned his readers that America was disintegrating. "Old empires have no worse disease than slavery, which the United States inherited from Europe and Asia. There is a bitterness in every human cup, and the United States with all its juvenile vigor and hopefulness, has to taste of it, as well as other Kingdoms and Empires, that have gone before them. The events of 1860 have given the Federation a severer shock than it has ever yet experienced: and proved, even to the Americans themselves, that Republics, governed by the will of the people, are just as likely to go wrong as Monarchies and Despotisms."

George believed that English commerce would quickly be damaged. And that the areas of England and Ireland that made cloth from southern cotton would suffer greatly. "The ill feeling in the United States will not be allayed for many years to come, and the operations of agriculture be the first to suffer."

This prediction would all too quickly come true. Before the month of January had ended, the British government had recognized the danger George saw and began to take action. They were attempting to ensure that other supplies of cotton would be found to protect the manufacturers of Manchester. There seemed to be less concern about the smaller cotton manufacturing businesses in Ireland. On the bright side, the government didn't believe that there would be any interruption of supply from the American south. But in any case, they would have alternate sources available.

A leader in the *Irishman* explained that the connection between Ireland and America went far beyond commercial interests, and why the Irish were so fixated on war in another country. "Peculiarly in Ireland the subject bears great interest, for we are bound up to the American people by many a tie of memory and affection. So long ago as their days of struggle, her interest was linked to their destiny and their hopes, and it has become intensified in the years that have gone by since. The hand of Ireland was there. Lifted in stern assertion of American rights, the blood of Ireland was poured forth for their maintenance, and crimsoned every battle field with its tide of love...Is it not her children who have gone into the forest, into the wilderness, into the swamps, and have conquered and civilized nature, until she grew fair, and rich and populous, under the reign of man?"

George found it difficult to understand why the southern states would do something so harmful to their interests. They didn't seem to have thought through the "disruptions of war," how much it would cost, how difficult it would be to maintain a position nearly as strong as an independent country as they enjoyed in the Union. But in the end, "cool-headedness" wasn't a characteristic of southerners.

Abhorrence of slavery, the heart of George's perspective on the American Civil War, wasn't the only point of view. The editor of the paper for which Mitchel wrote had a very different position. "The slave is not generally a discontented being. It is one of the conditions of slavery as prevails in America to sink its victims to a depth below the power of knowing or feeling their own degradation. Moreover, in five out of six southern families, the slaves are as animals, kindly treated and would, it is averred, be much more likely in their ignorant and dog-like attachment, to fight for their masters not against them."

§

In March George began to cover a very different subject with a local twist that transfixed his readers in Newry and readers across Ireland. This was another bigamy case that incorporated the issue of mixed marriages. The two people involved were William Yelverton, a Protestant from a noble Irish family, and Theresa Longworth, an English Catholic.

This couple had met years earlier and Yelverton was immediately attracted to the beautiful young woman. After a brief period of time together during the Crimean War, they went separate ways. However, Yelverton continued to pursue Theresa through letters and occasional personal meetings. He came from a prominent family, and as much as he wanted a relationship with Theresa, it wasn't marriage that he had in mind. He recognized that Theresa would be unacceptable to his family. But that wasn't information he intended to share with Theresa.

Yelverton came up with a solution. The couple could marry and keep the marriage a secret. Theresa wouldn't consent to such an arrangement. On one occasion, when the couple was together in Scotland, Yelverton proposed that a Scotch marriage could be perfumed and be legal. So the couple recited the marriage vows without witnesses, fulfilling the conditions of the Scotch marriage custom. Still Theresa would not agree that this was sufficiently valid that she would agree to consummate it. While Yelverton was pursuing Theresa, he attended Catholic services, and claimed he too was a Catholic. When none of his tactics worked, William came up with a new approach. The two of them would go to Ireland where it would be easier to marry.

And so, they came to Newry. However, the first priest they contacted refused to perform the ceremony. After a brief stay there, they moved on to Rostrevor. There they were able to get a dispensation from the Bishop, allowing them to marry immediately. The marriage finally took place on August 15, 1857. William and Theresa lived together in a hotel there, before heading back to England. Still he insisted that the marriage must remain secret.

The newlyweds made several trips together, as a married couple. Then Theresa became pregnant, a pregnancy that made her very ill. At that point, Yelverton left her and traveled again to Scotland. And while Theresa was ill, Yelverton married a woman acceptable to his family in Scotland. When Theresa learned what Yelverton had done, she demanded a divorce, something that Yelverton rejected, as he greatly feared having Theresa testify. Under English law, a divorce tried in court would have allowed Theresa to testify against her husband.

But Theresa wasn't one to be trifled with. She found a way around the problem. She went to live with a friend. When the friend asked Yelverton to pay to support his wife, Yelverton refused. So Theresa's friend took Yelverton to court for the costs of supporting his wife. In this situation, Theresa was eligible to testify. The trial took place in Dublin. Theresa's appearance on the witness stand was followed word for word in the *Telegraph*. Her conduct was greatly admired, her appearance very positive.

When Yelverton took the stand to testify, he was greeted with great hostility. He claimed that he and Theresa slept together while they were in Newry, and that it was Theresa who had pursued him. Strangely while he was on the witness stand, he seemed unable to remember important details.

The people of Ireland were greatly pleased when the verdict supported Theresa. However, Yelverton won by a single vote when his appeal was heard in the House of Lords. His marriage to Theresa was declared void and his second marriage legal.

§

James was involved in a different romance, one that he actively supported. Though Catherine O'Hare was seen as a sinner by the Catholic Church for having a child without a marriage, she had been a great help to the Harshaw family, providing tender care for James Alexander. She came to be seen as a member of the family.

On November 9, 1860, just 2 weeks before Samuel left to return to America, James had gone into Newry to the first hiring fair in search of a laborer. He selected a young man named Pat Kelly to come to live at Ringbane, and work until the first Thursday in May 1861. For his work, James would pay

Kelly £3.15s.0d. Upon reaching the deal, James paid Pat a single shilling. By nightfall, Kelly had made his way to Ringbane.

It was apparent from the time Kelly arrived that James had made a good choice. Kelly proved to be a hard-working employee. He seemed particularly adept at handling horses, so James soon entrusted him with one of the most critical farm chores, plowing the fields. But he also sent him to Newry to buy items that James needed. One day James sent Kelly to a cooper's shop. There he ordered a number of basic items, including a churn and a bucket. When the items had been constructed, Kelly returned to pick them up and pay for them.

Life at Ringbane was not all work though. Kelly certainly noticed Catherine as he worked. Soon James and his family noticed that Catherine and Pat were interested in each other. A month before his time in Ringbane came to an end, Kelly went to Newry to visit his priest to obtain special dispensation for Catherine to allow a proper Catholic marriage. Clearly marriage was on Kelly's mind.

James recorded the marriage in his journal on Thursday, April 25. "Nurse gerl & Pat married by the priest (Mr. McDonnell). Miss McAravey & Mr. Speers with them to the Glen Chapel." Clearly, the priest in Newry had refused to perform the wedding, so another option had to be found. Father McDonnell was a well-liked priest at a small chapel nearby. After the ceremony was completed, the newlyweds returned to Ringbane and slept in the sheep house which had been converted to sleeping quarters for James's boarding workers.

The following Monday, James settled his accounts with Catherine and Pat. James paid £1.5s.0d. to Kelly to pay the priest to perform the marriage rites, plus another £1 to the priest so he would consent to allow Catherine to marry in the church. In addition, Kelly still was due another £2.15s.9d. as his final payment. James also paid Catherine £4. Thus he sent the young couple on their way to their new life with a sizeable nest egg, enough to start a new life in a new country. After hugs for James Alexander and the family, Catherine and Pat left Ringbane for the last time. James was confident that he had done everything he could to make their dream of a happy life come true.

§

Once the extensive coverage of the Yelverton trial ended, George had space in the *Telegraph* to return to the crisis in America. making clear his continued support for the north in the war. One leader was prompted by President Lincoln's inauguration, which was attended by 30,000 people. While the speech had gotten mixed reviews in America, George reported that it was just the kind of speech he expected, that Lincoln wouldn't agree that states had a right to leave the union once they had joined it. However, George noted that Lincoln had promised that he would take no action against the south, as long as they didn't attack first. Lincoln pointed out that the president had limited powers. "In your hands, dissatisfied fellow-countrymen and not mine, is the momentous question of civil war."

George concluded his leader with Lincoln's words, which he much admired. "We are not enemies, but friends. We must not be enemies. Though passion may have strained, it must not break our bonds of affection. The mystic cords of memory, stretching from every battlefield and patriot's grave, to every living heart and hearthstone, over this broad land, yet will swell the chorus of Union, when again touched, as surely they will be, by the better angels of our nature."

While no actual battles had yet taken place, the South was very active in promoting its cause. They sent a delegation to England in an effort to get England to recognize their new nation. George didn't think that England could ever accept the independence of the Confederacy because of their support for slavery. To promote his opinion, George quoted from a speech by the Confederate Vice President Stephens. He said that America was founded on the principle that slavery was wrong. "Our new government is on exactly the opposite side, its foundations are laid, *its cornerstone rests upon the great truth that the negro is not equal to the white man, that slavery, subordination to the superior race, is his natural and moral condition.* Thus, our new government, is the first in the history of the world based on this great physical and moral truth." George added the italics to make clear what he saw as the fatal flaw of the Confederacy.

Like much of England, Ireland, and Europe, George was watching and waiting anxiously for each news dispatch. Before the month was out, the fighting actually began with the firing by the Charlestown guns on Fort Sumter located in Charlestown Harbor. This first battle was one in which Mitchel's oldest son John participated. The younger Mitchel was charged with the targeting of the cannons. His skill helped produce significant damage to the fort.

This would be a time of great challenge for the new president, as George saw the situation. There were two ways for Lincoln to move forward. Either he could appeal to Congress for legislation that would give him "extraordinary powers," or he would have to assert that he already possessed the powers that he needed.

Though the potential fighting was thousands of miles away, there were dangers much closer. England claimed total control of the oceans through the power of their extensive fleet. But the Confederates had authorized any ship that they possessed to be part of a southern fleet, and to act as a privateer, attacking any ship it came upon. George saw this challenge to British authority as a danger that might lead England into a war against the south.

Not only was the South becoming aggressive on the sea, they had formed armies that were now on the march heading toward Washington. Saboteurs in Maryland had cut telegraph wires in an effort to help. George had some sense of what a civil war would be like, as Ireland had had a number of small-scale battles and a population separated, not by race, but by religion.

However, George saw hopes for something positive to come from the war. "Mankind, like water, becomes putrid by stagnation. The nature of man not being pure enough for undisturbed repose, it requires tempests and hurricanes to cleanse it thoroughly." "The mask of hypocracy is torn off a whole nation or race, or community, and in one moment is revealed to a whole people what its morality, what its piety, is worth."

Whether or not benefits would flow from the war in America would not be known until the damage could be balanced against this positive potential. In the meantime, England was taking actions of its own to protect itself against any accidental entrapment into America's civil war. No British citizen could sign up to join the fighting on either side. British ships were directed to take no action against any ship at sea, be it from the north or from the south. This action followed Lincoln's dispatch of Union ships to blockade the southern coasts.

George started the month of June with another leader on the war. He continued his strong support for President Lincoln. It was clear to George that he was a man suited to the dangerous times of the country. "Impetuosity is evidence of anything but thoughtful forecast. President Lincoln has not been either supine or rash, but has been, on the contrary, equally vigilant, cool and calculating."

News of the first major battle of the war arrived in Newry in time for George to write a leader on the news in his paper of August 6th. He had no spin on the results to offer. He called the battle a total rout of the north. They had dropped much equipment before running away from the fighting. England looked at the results of the events in America and saw the American system failing. While Americans proudly proclaimed a high status among nations, the action of their troops at Bull Run should teach them that "modesty is required." When compared to the British army and their record of historic victories on many battlefields, the United States "cuts a very sorry figure."

George had been confident early on that slavery was at the heart of American disintegration. But by harvest time, he wasn't quite so sure. The English government had begun to make claims that the war was an effort to regain the government facilities in states that were now part of the Confederacy rather than a struggle to end slavery. England had rejected slavery but had managed to end it in its Caribbean colonies without going to war over the issue. They had bought the slaves from their owners, like buying any other form of property. Then they established that the newly freed Negroes would be apprenticed to their former owners long enough to learn a trade and provide a good transition. To the English, this approach was much preferable to fighting a war.

§

John followed George's reports on the war closely. But he was also carefully watching the growth of the Fenians, the revolutionary society Stephens and O'Mahony were building on both sides of the Atlantic. These Fenian groups had grown quietly in the major cities of America. Though Stephens was much disliked by many Irish yearning for independence, he had made sufficient progress to stage a grand event to display their power and claim control of Irish nationalism, pushing the Young Irelander remnants into the dustbin of history.

This growing threat still seemed to pass George undetected. He didn't even mention the death of Terrance McManus in California, though he might well have seen the leader in the *Irishman:* "There is a bright spot – one, only one, in the gloomy night of disgrace that has closed o're our country for the last 16 years – the time when Ireland gathered that gifted and gallant band of sons around her glowing with hope and throbbing for the hour when they fondly hoped the stars of her sad destiny would set forever…One by one are fading away the members of the gifted band of 'whose failure only the more endeared them to Ireland'…Is it the fault of Ireland that too many of our patriots are neglected and forgotten?"

McManus had died in abject poverty in San Francisco and been buried in a cemetery for paupers. Local Fenians knew of McManus's dire situation, as they had occasionally given him food and a place to stay when they saw him begging on the street. In one of their meetings, they discussed a wild notion that the dead body of McManus could provide the opportunity the Fenians had been waiting for. They communicated with the leaders in New York their idea to disinter McManus's body and return it to Dublin for burial in Glasnevin Cemetery with Daniel O'Connell and other Irish patriots. At each step along the way, there could be large demonstrations that would publicize the Fenians and display their strength.

What the Californian Fenians were suggesting was essentially kidnapping the corpse of one Young Irelander, as a way to claim the Fenians as the logical successors to the Young Irelanders. The Fenians would carefully control the entire affair, since they would control the body. Out of respect for their fallen comrade, John Martin, Father Kenyon, O'Brien and others would be compelled to submit to everything the Fenians planned.

O'Mahony and the other national leaders were delighted with the suggestion. The San Francisco branch was well funded and anxious to put their plan into action. Once they had obtained permission from McManus's sister to their plan, they moved quickly to implement it. In a few short months, the Fenians would be known in Ireland and England, and become the most dangerous revolutionaries in Ireland.

The plan was enacted smoothly. A delegation from San Francisco Fenians supervised the disinterment They prepared a large and extravagant coffin in which the body was laid. Then the first formal service was held in San Francisco. It was a huge success.

Most of the journey across the country, over the mountains and across the prairies, covered places that McManus had never seen while he was alive. Finally, the body arrived in New York City. There it was welcomed by Archbishop Hughes for a grand send-off in St Patrick's Cathedral on 5th Avenue. Then the body and traveling escort went aboard ship for the trip across the Atlantic.

John was following the events in America as closely as he could. On the first of October, he wrote a letter to the *Freeman,* which was widely copied in papers around Ireland. He had received confirmation of the disinterment and the plan to rebury McManus in Dublin. Therefore, it was "the duty of his friends in Ireland to take measures for receiving the remains and conducting the funeral in a manner worthy of the man, and of the entire cause for which he was devoted. He was an honest, brave, generous man – a passionate lover of his country, faithful to the death to his friends and his cause. He died in banishment, and the cause he offered his life to serve, though undying in truth and light, has not yet recovered from the defeat of '48, and the famine."

Then he offered a warning to the Fenians as to how he felt the funeral should be conducted. "It is not the vain pageantry of the undertaking, nor hollow political displays that can fittingly honor his memory and serve the interests of his holy cause. It is the multitude of sorrowing men that will follow his hearse, and their orderly, sober and reverential behavior in the solemn procession." Apparently, John was not yet aware that the Fenians had no interest in what John thought was appropriate.

John donated £5 toward the expenses of the funeral, which were being collected by James Plunkett, a man James knew. "The committee, of which you are treasurer, I believe to be animated by a sincere desire to conduct the funeral as I feel it ought to be conducted with order and decency and solemnity." By making his feelings public, he hoped to move the Fenians to follow his vision.

The *Freeman* in an editorial, supported John's perspective, and reminded the Fenians of the Processions Act. "Let him be buried in peace. Do not let his dust be made the occasion for a gathering of the clubs of 1848 to deplore their dead leader, and to revive, if possible, the course to which he was devoted." The editor correctly suspected that something of this sort was just what was planned. The Fenians had gone to much effort and expense to create an action, using the McManus funeral, to engineer a great triumph that would suppress any remnants of influence of the Young Irelanders and proclaim themselves the new leaders of Irish nationalism.

Though John and editors of the newspapers in Ireland skirted around the edge of Fenian intentions, they understood that one of the major elements of the plan was to humiliate the '48 men, "despised and vituperated as they were." In addition, John would certainly be at the event thus providing cover for the Fenian leaders. They knew that men like John would be under intense scrutiny from the British government, which was ready to swoop in to arrest him if he did anything suspicious.

McManus's body arrived in Queenstown on Wednesday evening, October 30th and was immediately moved to the Catholic Church. There were numerous officials from America accompanying the body, including a group from the San Francisco Fenians on hand to enjoy the culmination of their plans. Flags on the ship flew at half-staff as the body came ashore. Also on hand were former Young Irelanders, now Fenian converts Michael Doheney and Francis Maguire. Miss McManus had come back to Ireland with her brother. The Fenian group in Philadelphia had selected John T. Mahony to represent them at the funeral. He was happy to be back in Ireland. "You send me to our brothers in Ireland and desire me to say to them that neither time nor space, sorrow or joy, can efface from your memory the green hills and valleys of lovely Erin."

The transfer of the body to the church in Cork was very carefully planned. The hearse was very ornate, and drawn by matched black horses, their heads bearing white and black plumes. The hearse was accompanied by the Cork Temperance Band, playing the Dead March. Great crowds assembled to watch the procession pass by. There was a special carriage for Miss McManus, who was accompanied by Mrs. Doheny. The official deputations all wore black scarves over their shoulders, on each was printed in white letters the name of the town they represented. It was a grand procession. The Fenians were certainly proud of the results of their careful planning.

From there the body was placed on a train and transported to Dublin. Crowds were waiting along the tracks to show respect as the funeral train passed through their small villages. Though the train came through Limerick about midnight, there were several hundred people waiting to view the train as it passed.

It was 4:30 a.m. when the train pulled into the terminus at Kingsbridge. The weather was bad, but more people were waiting in the rain for the train to arrive. The Fenians had hoped that the body could be taken to St. Patrick's Church, but Archbishop Cullen had refused to allow the body near his church, which greatly pleased George. So the Fenians had arranged to take the body to the theater room of Mechanic's Hall by the river Liffey.

A procession of eighty men marched two by two, carrying torches to light the way. In the Hall, a catafalque had been erected, six feet tall, and eight feet by five feet. This structure was surrounded by white plaster pedestals, four on either side, two on each end. There were other pedestals that held urns in which incense was burning. The catafalque was covered with a black cloth. On each corner were satin rosettes with bunches of shamrocks. At the sides were crosses of white satin, from which were hung girales with silk tassels. At the head of the coffin was a cross of bog oak, three feet by six feet. There was also a flag from the California Fenians. The stage was decorated with black panels on which were pictured in white John Mitchel, O'Brien, Meagher. There was a large crowd on hand to view the body.

A meeting was held the night before the funeral to make final plans for the actual burial. It was at this meeting that a major confrontation took place between the Young Irelanders and the Fenians. John Martin, Father Kenyon and the O'Donoghue were among those present. Since John was the closest friend of McManus attending the funeral, everyone had assumed that he would be among the speakers. The Fenian leaders made clear at this meeting that they had no intention of allowing that to happen. The Young Irelanders put up a vigorous fight. Angry words came close to becoming physical battles.

Exact descriptions of the events were few, but Stephens described the scene later in a letter to O'Mahony. "An infamous attempt was made on Saturday night to make the burial the next day a failure and this attempt was the work of Father Kenyon (the leader), John Martin and such carrion as Cantwell, etc. and the O'Donoghue who had later disassociated himself from the miserable clique, who were all utterly crushed by the wise and manful action of the committee. Kenyon lost his wits all but – he insulted every member of the committee." As a last resort the Young Irelanders appealed to Miss McManus, but she refused to intervene to support them. The funeral of the Young Irelander would be a purely Fenian event.

John O'Leary wrote about that meeting as well. O'Leary agreed that this was a Fenian demonstration. The immediate cause of the argument at the meeting was over who would be the chairman of the event. The Young Irelanders wanted the O'Donoghue, the Fenians wanted a different O'Donoghue, Maurice, to be the chairman. This struggle represented the wish of the Young Irelanders to have the event extol the past while the Fenians wanted it to show that they were the new extension of the earlier effort. In addition Father Kenyon wanted to speak at the cemetery. But Stephens didn't like what he wanted to say, and so refused.

Later when the Fenians had established their own newspaper, O'Leary explained the Fenian views behind the funeral and the confrontation with McManus's friends in the Young Irelander movement. "A providential necessity we now call it, though at the time we regretted the backwardness of those who had been leaders of the people in accepting the position that was tendered to them–nay that they were implored to accept. But these leaders wavered and hesitated. For a long time they could not be persuaded that the proposal to carry the dead patriot's remains over two oceans and a continent, was anything but Irish-American 'bunkham,' and of course they could not allow their names to be mixed up in a sham. These men had no faith in the people, they never had, they have not now."

The weather on the day of the funeral was the worst that November in Ireland could provide. It was dark and cold, and a heavy rain was falling throughout the event. Still the people of Dublin turned out in impressive numbers in the rain, their feet sinking into the muddy streets, as the procession moved from Mechanic's Hall along Sachville Street toward Glasnevin. It left about half twelve and moved slowly among the waiting crowds. Many carriages accompanied the hearse as the procession moved toward its destination. John rode in a carriage with Miss McManus, Mrs. Doheny and Father Kenyon. This was all the participation they were allowed.

Father Lavelle gave the funeral oration. "McManus is the key to the future. We will not be oppressed forever. The iron hoof of the intruder, the stranger, the spoliator, and the tyrant, will not forever tread upon our necks." At this point, Miss McManus and the others in her carriage left the other speakers to linger in the rain.

The event was sufficiently impressive to impel editorial comment. The *Nation* issued a stern warning. The editor felt that it was time for new leaders to step forward. If that didn't happen problems would arise. "Earnest but inexperienced men will join them, seeing nothing better to be had; violent men will dominate them, the rudest-mannered will set up for being the best patriot; men who do not approve of this order of things will either retire in disgust or be expelled; internal and external quarrels will soon develop themselves, the societies will alarm orders and interests that should be conciliated and that are naturally friendly to Ireland, the Government will know all about their doings; it will not interfere while damage so great is being done to the Irish cause, but when the worst in that way has been accomplished, then it will pounce on them; a jail or two will be filled with the bones of young men who meant patriotism but did not act it wisely and the progress of Irish nationality will receive a check from which it will take years to recover.

"These things, will, we think, come to pass if men whose positions, abilities, and services constitute them to be national leaders of the Irish people do not speedily place themselves in the van of the national force, and organize the struggle for Ireland's independence. The time is growing critical."

George printed accounts of the McManus funeral in a couple of different editions of his paper. But he made no editorial comment. However, his nephew who edited the *Belfast News Letter* wrote several leaders on the topic. In the first one, he described the processions and then he offered his opinion. "The peaceful Sunday was desecrated, and the streets of Dublin were blackened by a procession, the significance of which was in all respects hostile to the Government of England. A party procession in the worst sense of the word, and a procession eminently offensive in all its characteristics, both from the circumstances under which it was organized and the time at which it was carried out." If this sort of procession was allowed, the Orange Order must be allowed to march next summer.

In the edition of the following day, James Henderson returned to the topic. "We were never disposed to regard the affair as one worthy of serious notice for we did fancy the common sense of the Irish Roman Catholics would guide them in forming a just estimate on the subject. We thought that a few hundred young fools might be found to follow the coffin and the whole business would end in Dublin as absurdly as it began on the shores of the Pacific. It is useless to disguise the truth, that we have been disappointed in this. If from 20-30,000 men, including respectable tradesmen and mechanics swelled the procession that disturbed the Metropolis on Sunday, the significance of the fact is not to be laughed away."

George certainly expected England to quickly quell this dangerous new group.

Irish Religious Leaders

Paul Cullen was appointed Archbishop of Armagh in 1849 and was made Cardinal in 1866. He was a forceful leader, who worked to reinforce the position and authority of the Catholic Church in Ireland, with a particular focus on education. His "ultramontane" positions were strongly opposed by Protestants. He opposed both the Young Irelanders and the Fenians.

Rev. Robert Lindsay was active in the Protestant revival movement of 1859. He tried to have Protestants unify against the threat of the Catholic Church led by Cardinal Cullen. Sympathetic to the Orange Order, he pushed for a new minister for the Donaghmore Presbyterian Church who would support his positions.

After a prolonged and bitter dispute over candidates, Rev. John Elliott became the eventual compromise choice for the Donaghmore Presbyterian Church. He was the first minister to live in the manse which was promoted by John Martin and James Harshaw.

Chapter 9

Divisions

1861-1862

The McManus funeral attracted a lot of newspaper attention. However, that wasn't the case with George. He wrote no leader warning readers of the rise of a new group bent on rebellion. He only published a small article, containing the barest details, mentioning that many residents of Dublin participated in this illegal march and were accompanied by bands at the front and back. But what seemed most worthy of note to George was that the march took place in total silence followed by speeches that were both noisy and rebellious.

Rather than focus on a rising threat of rebellion in Ireland, George was more attentive to the rebellion raging 3,000 miles away. He was particularly interested in one incident, the Trent Affair, which threatened to entangle England in the war. A Northern ship, enforcing the Union blockade of the Confederacy, had stopped a mail boat, the Trent, which flew the British flag. On it, they found two men who were emissaries from the Confederacy on their way to England and France to plead for recognition of the South by both countries.

Instead of enjoying a safe passage, the two men, Slidell and Mason, found themselves seized at gunpoint and taken off the Trent. The English government was outraged. They immediately dispatched an ultimatum to President Lincoln, demanding an apology, reparations, immediate release of the diplomats, and their transportation to England at American expense. The Union faced a self-inflicted danger that their armies might soon be fighting the British and the Confederacy at the same time.

Days passed without any response from President Lincoln. George suspected that President Lincoln would offer an apology to the British government but would not release the prisoners. This response might well lead to war. A few days later, George provided his readers with another theory. President Lincoln would release the prisoners, an act that would so enrage his Northern supporters that they would force him to resign.

The British government wasn't content to wait for a response to its ultimatum. They began to transport troops to Canada to provide a military force ready for action near the northern border. The British regiment currently stationed in Newry was among the troops sent to Canada. England assumed a war footing.

Only on the last day of the year did the British learn the reason for Lincoln's silence. The ship carrying the ultimatum had been delayed during the Atlantic crossing and had only recently reached Washington. George wrote in his New Year's leader that word of war was expected momentarily.

In the next edition of the *Telegraph* George was relieved to report that President Lincoln intended to resolve the issue peacefully, that Mason and Slidell had been released and would soon reach England. So it was time for a bit of crowing. He called the American government and President Lincoln "vaporing beggars," who had 'gone down on their knees.' Then he called their actions, which George had demanded of them, a "craven-spirited surrender" at the last minute before the "giant strength of Old England."

§

George had had a lot to say about the Trent Affair, but nothing to say about the actions that followed the McManus funeral. Nationalist leaders held a large meeting in the Rotunda in Dublin to capitalize on the passions energized by the Fenian funeral, the goal being to create a new nationalist organization that the Fenians wouldn't control.

However, the meeting didn't go exactly as planned. After the O'Donoghue took the chair, the speeches putting forth resolutions were read as they had been written, seconded and approved. Before the final prepared resolution setting up the new organization had been offered, a Mr. Kavanagh rose to speak. Strangely the O'Donoghue allowed him to speak out of order. Kavanagh offered a different organizational structure with twenty-one people on the executive committee. There would be a chairman, two secretaries, and twenty-one members who included the O'Donoghue and P. J. Smyth, plus a number of Fenian supporters. This Fenian resolution was surprisingly adopted, and the meeting adjourned.

This unsettling result propelled John into additional political action. The first meeting of the new committee was held the next day in Dublin. John hurried to Dublin to attend and make clear his concerns. After thinking over his actions for a couple of days, he sat down in Kilbroney and wrote a letter to the editor of the *Nation*.

Before printing the letter John wrote on December 11th, the editor offered an introduction. "Anything emanating from Mr. Martin upon it [affairs of the country] is entitled to the gravest consideration of our countrymen."

John was clearly unhappy about the events of the Rotunda meeting and the deviation from the plans he had participated in creating. "The subject of National organization is become of such pressing importance that I feel bound to offer my views concerning it to the consideration of my fellow-countrymen…They will remember that I have adhered to the national cause with unswerving fidelity. They will listen to me, as to a patriot, whose sincerity, whose fortitude have been tried by sufficient tests and have not been found wanting."

John then explained why he had attended the committee meeting held the day after the Rotunda meeting. "I was chagrined at the report of that extraordinary proceeding, which the great public meeting of the preceding night had been surprised into formally accepting a list of twenty-one names for a National Council. It seemed to me that the meeting was not aware of the real character of the proceedings which it was called upon to sanction, and I could not believe that the country would sanction it. I soon learned that the committee which had convened the meeting of the Rotunda and prepared the resolutions, had no part in that proceeding, but, on the contrary, entirely disapproved of it; and that the names of several gentlemen had been put in the list of twenty-one without their consent, and that the only reason why the contested resolution had been allowed to be put to the meeting without open opposition was the anxiety of the chairman and committee to avoid a scene of clamour. I therefore went to the meeting of the committee on Friday in order to show that I approved of the course its members were taking in promptly disavowing all participation in that affair or the list of twenty-one.

"I listened attentively to the remarks of the various speakers in the committee meeting about the difficulties which beset the national cause for the want of some authoritative general organization. I agree with them in thinking that the rising spirit of the people, the serious aspect of foreign affrays, the actual condition of Ireland, makes the duty of all Irish patriots, at once to take such measures as will enable them to consult and act in one united body for the common good."

John then offered his own ideas for a national organization. At the beginning, the governing council should have twelve members "qualified by their own experience and honorable character and by public confidence" to lead the new council. O'Brien was the proper person to name the members. This council could attract other organizations and the 430,000 people who had signed the national petition. "Such a Central council may prove able, by careful and judicious selection, swell the number into a Council of Three Hundred *worthy of the place of an Irish parliament."*

With this letter, John returned to political action, the depressing years of exile and feelings of uselessness forever behind him.

John had reached the age of fifty, an age when most of his friends had well established families. From time to time, he did indeed think of marrying and "extending his existence." However, he feared having children in the poor conditions existing in Ireland. He worried that his children might not agree with his political opinions and turn out to be quite content to live in occupied Ireland. But had he chosen to go to America, he would most certainly have married and had children of his own. As it was, the Mitchel sons were most like his own, and now their lives were endangered by the devastating Civil War.

While the war dragged on, and the Fenians continued their efforts to establish a new national movement, John continued to parent his brother's orphaned children. He found the experience somewhat depressing. The children seemed quite able in their studies but showed little interest or excitement about learning. They seemed to lack the curiosity so exhibited by the children of his sister Elizabeth in Newry. They were too compliant for John's taste. Sunday after Sunday, John provided them with a proper religious education to which they didn't make the slightest objections. The older of the two boys, Robert, was a dour and obstinate thirteen-year-old. He learned what was of interest to him. If it wasn't, he learned nothing. This was the child who would control his late father's property when he became an adult.

§

The first day of the new year of 1862 seemed very ordinary when James described it in his journal. Fog shrouded the frosty fields. James attended a dispensary meeting in the Four Mile House while he sent son Andrew and some of the men to the marsh and Betty's field to spread dung in preparation for planting. He also reported that James Alexander was unwell. The illness didn't seem alarming, though a week passed before James wrote that the little boy was better.

On January 15th, an unexpected event occurred that would challenge James in ways he could not have imagined. This Tuesday was another frosty day. James walked across the fields of Loughorne to attend a prayer meeting in the schoolroom of the church. Part way through the service, the door burst open and a young messenger hurried in to bring bad news to Rev. White. His father, Rev. Patrick White, pastor of the Corglass Church located close to Ballieboro in County Cavan, was ill. Rev. White was being called home to his bedside. Hastily closing the service, Rev. White hurried away, leaving the congregation behind, waiting anxiously for news.

When no word had come by Friday morning, it became obvious to James that Rev. White wouldn't be back in time to preside at the Sunday services. James was responsible for finding a replacement. So he sent James Jr. into Newry to arrange for Rev. Hutchison to fill in. Before the day ended, word had come from Cavan that the Rev. White, Sr. had indeed died. He had been a prominent preacher and teacher in this rural area of Cavan for about fifty years. He was well known as an "evangelical preacher." He provided a sound education for many prominent young men of his area, some of whom became ministers themselves. He had six sons, all of them would be Presbyterian ministers once the two youngest sons completed their training. Two of them, Rev. Verner White and now Rev. Patrick, had been ministers of the Donaghmore church already. Rev. William White was the minister in the Downpatrick Presbyterian church whom James visited when summoned to court there. The link between the two churches, Corglass and Donaghmore, was longstanding and strong.

James conducted the Tuesday service himself. First, he sang the 90th Psalm, and read the 11th Chapter of Hebrews. He followed the scriptural offerings with a prayer. Before the meeting adjoined, James read for the worshipers the obituary that George had reprinted from the *Banner of Ulster*. An event like the death of an elderly minister shouldn't have shaken James, but the death of this man James knew only slightly would soon do just that.

Robert hurried home from his church in Mountmellick to help James cover for Rev. White. It was soon clear that his absence would be somewhat protracted. Word came a week after Rev. White's death, that his wife was ill as well. In fact, she died the same day the message was received in

Donaghmore. The Corglass church immediately issued a call to Rev. White to succeed his father. Rev. White accepted the call.

For two weeks. Robert became the de-facto minister of the Donaghmore church. Robert preached before a large crowd, twice on Sunday January 26th. He baptized two children in Loughorne on Tuesday. Then he and James walked together to the classroom for the usual Tuesday evening service. James described what happened. "Hugh [Robert] gave a feeling address on Mark 5." The next day, James drove Robert to Jane and Archy's house in the Four Towns. Then everyone moved on to Samuel Boyd Marshall's house for dinner before listening to Robert deliver a lecture on Lots wife in the Four Towns school house.

Following this event, Robert had to return to his duties in Mountmellick. Despite the circumstances, this was a happy and proud time for James, his dream that Robert would someday become the minister at Donaghmore seemed about to come true. He as yet had no idea that this dream would be caught up in conflicting currents that were about to divide the congregation.

Many Ulster Protestants were more alarmed than usual by the Fenian stirrings because the nationalists might all too soon have an army well trained on the battlefields of America to support their political actions. Also upsetting was a belief that the British government had adopted a program of appeasement of Irish Catholics. Certainly Catholics were marching at will despite the Processions Act, which made such marches by both Catholics and Protestants illegal. The Protestants in Ulster viewed the McManus funeral march and the procession to the site of the New Catholic University in Dublin to lay a cornerstone as proof that flagrant violations of law were permitted when Catholics marched.

George believed that total Protestant unity in Ireland was required to ensure British support and favorable laws from Parliament. However, he saw danger signs that the unity between the Church of Ireland and the Presbyterian Church was alarmingly fragile. Presbyterians had united with Catholics to support the Tenant Rights League. Local Presbyterians had joined Catholics in Newry to defeat a Church of Ireland candidate for Parliament. Such disunity could no longer be tolerated.

Other local Protestants had observed the same problem. In quiet conversations, local leaders had created a strategy to mitigate their concerns. Leaders who were members of the Orange Order and supporters of church establishment must control the ministers and sessions of local churches. Vacancies in the ministries of Presbyterian churches were an ideal time to achieve this goal. Should Donaghmore become a target for this movement, Robert's candidacy would be endangered. James's views on Catholics were well known. He hired and paid Catholic workers in cash. He attended Catholic funeral services. He had even paid a priest to marry Catherine and Patrick.

Still, the path forward for Robert's election in Donaghmore seemed on track as the formalities of the departure of Rev. White proceeded during the month of February. The Newry Presbytery met with James present to accept the resignation of Rev. White, during which local ministers and laity spoke glowingly of his successful ministry, particularly during the time of the great revival. Steps were taken to supply ministers to fill the void until a new minister could be chosen. Rev. White sold the lease for his farm at Buskhill for an unheard-of price per acre. It was purchased by a man from Antrim for £65 per acre. Rev. White settled in at Corglass while James waited anxiously for the election in Donaghmore.

§

Suspicions about James's political views were reinforced by some of John's actions as well. John wrote a letter to the officials of the new Catholic University, which included a donation of one pound for the building fund. He apologized that it couldn't be larger, but his finances were still suffering the effects of the famine. "The Irish Catholic University deserves the sympathy of all generous minds, because it has been founded and is maintained by the offerings of the patriotic and religious zeal of the poorest people of Europe…No Christian people have been subjected to such debasing oppression as the Irish Catholics; and yet no people can point to more honourable testimonies of the national character."

John concluded the letter, "But an Irish protestant, who desires civil and religious liberty and equality, may feel proud in being permitted to assist his Catholic fellow countrymen, while they be under such unjust disadvantages." Many Ulster Protestants would say that they also wanted "religious liberty and equality," but they would vehemently disagree with John's interpretation of the words' meaning.

Next John participated in the St. Patrick's Day celebration in Dublin sponsored by the Brotherhood of St. Patrick. This was an organization established to sponsor a grand St. Patrick's Day celebration every March 17th. However, there were growing suspicions that it was being infiltrated by elements of the Irish Republican Brotherhood, which was increasingly affiliated with the Fenians. John participated in hopes that he could prevent this organization from falling under control of the Fenians. The room was extensively decorated with laurel boughs, a green flag was adorned with an Irish Harp in gold letters. Behind the head table were flags of France and America. Along the balconies were banners bearing the names of many of the Young Irelanders, including John's. The room was filled as John rose to speak. His assigned topic was "the honoured dead."

John's remarks began on a somber note. He realized that few would ever truly recognize or remember any "acts of a subject people like us." "They lie obscure and unrelished under the malignant shadow of England."

With hard times sweeping across the farms of Ireland, another famine seemed increasingly possible. Poor and frightened people made ready recruits. "It is not a secret society. My friends, we have no secrets here. We invite all our countrymen to listen to us, while we declare that we desire the independence of Ireland. We desire Ireland for the Irish. We desire that our country should get rid of the English dominion. Such is our object, our only object and we make no secret of it." Here John was interrupted with shouts of "here, here."

John was under no illusion that independence would prevent Irish poverty. "Some poor would always be found among us. But those would be God's poor – some maimed, and blind, and helpless...citizens dependent upon holy charity which blesses him that gives and him that takes."

Then John described the effects of the famine in his own neighborhood. "My poor neighbors whom I had known till then as hard-working inoffensive, God fearing people, earning their bread in the sweat of their brows, and anxious to live in the good repute of their neighborhoods. I saw very many of them, under the pressure of want, lose spirit and self respect and decent shame and care for good repute and fear of God. And most of them went into the poorhouse, became liars and thieves and regardless of right or wrong and outcasts from all that is good. And girls that but for English rule, might be wives and mothers of honest people, became lost – lost to God and good. It is horrible to talk of this. But we know we are at the beginning of another famine and as we care for the souls of the people, let us devote ourselves to the removal of that plague that ruins so many souls in Ireland, the plague of English rule." The audience broke into loud cheers.

Before he concluded his remarks, John mentioned some of the people that he had known and worked with for Irish independence who had died. He had special mention for Terrance McManus and Myles Byrnes who had recently died in France. "Both of them love, loved their native land with all their hearts, and their highest ambitions, their only ambition was to fight in the cause. Both would have been prime and honoured citizens of a free nation and both died in exile because they were faithful to the cause of Ireland. But here the parallel ends. For the one found a soldier's career and died full of honours, while the other sank broken-hearted to the grave at the age of 38 after wearing away the best years of his manhood vainly longing for the day when he might bear the sword of this country, or at least against his country's oppressors. Both died in exile for the cause of Ireland."

George noted the proceedings in Dublin. He explained to his readers that nothing that was led by a grocer and a publican had any value. To make matters worse in George's eyes, the people attending were equally undistinguished. He didn't mention that John was one of the "undistinguished" participants. Since there was religious peace in Ireland at the moment, any new organization was unneeded. The speakers clearly hoped to renew sectarian violence and "plunge Ireland into misery again." But the government should be watching as "they spouted sedition, hinted treason."

Despite his increasingly busy schedule, John took time to go to France for a last visit with Mitchel, who was about to leave his wife and daughters behind in France to return to America to support the Confederacy from Richmond. John described the walking trip he had taken around France with Mitchel and his son Willy in a letter to O'Dogherty's wife Eva.

"While I was in France I was very pleasantly engaged, most of the time as one of a walking party making a tour of Dauphine, Savoie and from the lake of Neufchatel in Switzerland across the Lura mountains into Bourgogne. John and William Mitchel were my comrades. You know how I have always benefitted in health from bodily exertion and fatigue especially in pleasant company; and one could hardly be pleased if company of John and William Mitchel did not please him. Then our attention was drawn to new and changing scenes and people and incidents of all kinds that befell travelers and particularly travelers on foot; and so the dreary hopeless, bitter contemplation of the shame and squalid misery of Ireland was intermitted for a while and we feasted our eyes and hearts on spectacles of beauty, grandeur, happiness; all human governments are imperfect, even the poor Popes...

"I incline to think that the system of government of France is about the best in the world. And perhaps of all the provinces of France, Dauphine is the one where there is most of that kind of prosperity that I like best. There the rural population vastly outnumbers that of the towns; and almost every peasant family owns the land on which it resides. There is nowhere any appearance of want or of severe poverty, or indeed any poverty (in our Irish sense) at all. The people are well grown, good figures, handsome in features, frank, polite, kindly, cheerful – like a people that have always plenty of good food and means for defending themselves from the weather, and that had no oppressive labour, and that own their own country. The cultivation of the fertile valleys is very careful and neat. The mulberry trees, orchards, vines, walnut trees, planted over all the country amidst the crops of corn and clover and harriots, give the appearance of an endless succession of gardens. There are among the mountains just tracks of pasture land with tinkling herds of cattle, and substantial villages raising their spires here or there. Forests of beech and pine clothe the higher steeps except where long lines of lime-stone bluffs stand out bare and awful.

"The snow-covered tops of the Alps of Dauphine met our eyes first as we began to descend to Grenoble. A most magnificent country! – Everywhere, everywhere, might be seen signs of the all-watchful care of the government and the public spirit and taste as well as wealth of the people in the public works and edifices and monuments of all kinds and in the race for building and embellishment in the towns. Lyon seems quite as much rebuilt as Paris and in some respects is a finer city. Paris, Lyons, Roen are the three most beautiful cities I have ever seen, each for its size."

§

John believed that England was the obstacle that prevented Ireland from being as beautiful and well run as France. But for many of the men of Ulster, England was their shield against Catholic domination. Some Presbyterians were determined that people with perspectives like John's should be marginalized and silenced. One such man was Rev. Robert Lindsay, who was a minister in the Drumbanagher church near Donaghmore, and, for many years, clerk of the Newry Presbytery. Both James and John had known Rev.

Lindsay for many years. After the success of the great revival of 1859, he joined an effort to minimize Presbyterian independence and forge a permanent political union with the Church of Ireland and the Orange Order. Ministers and elders would be targets of the new effort.

This position was exposed in a letter another Newry minister, Rev. Judson, wrote to the *Telegraph*. He excoriated "timid, trimming, time serving Protestants. They are an offense to the Constitution." "I declaim all fellowship with such Protestants."

A few weeks later, Judson made his position even clearer in a presentation to the Newry members of the Orange Order. "The specimen I have seen lately of half-and-half Protestantism naturally tends to disgust me with such for the rest of my life." "I now understand Orangeism and Protestantism as convertible terms. Orangeism…is not the narrow, exclusive affair which I once thought it to be. It is not the affair of this Church or that Church; it is an earnest union and combination of all who hold hard and fast to the great and glorious principles of the Reformation. If ever there was a time when it was incumbent upon the clergy of all the reformed Churches to renew the old, original protest against the doings of Papal Rome that time is the present." Before he concluded, he repeated loudly and publicly the quiet whisperings that Rev. Lindsay had heard and taken to heart. "I am prepared to make every concession to bring about a better state of Protestant unity, and I do not know, brother Protestants, how to express my indignation at the conduct of some who call themselves Protestant and are the first to traduce the Orangemen of Ulster."

Meanwhile, the usual business of selecting a new minister was underway in Donaghmore. James recorded the event. "Attended at the meetinghouse, and assisted to make out a poll list, on which there was about 158 names." This was very normal.

On April 1st, Archy Marshall, James's son-in-law, attended a meeting of the Newry Presbytery. The commission appointed by the Presbytery to supervise the Donaghmore election placed before the Presbytery the results of their work, the poll list of voters, and two nominations for minister. One nominee was James's son Robert Hugh, the other was a younger brother of Rev. White, the Rev. Tommy White. However a complaint was brought to the Presbytery that the nominations hadn't been properly read to the congregation. The Presbytery voted to delay the ministerial election.

Then several members of the congregation raised objections to the poll list that had been prepared. Considerable discussion took place on what the issue was. Rev. Lindsay was on hand to participate and support the dissidents. Finally Rev. John Elliott made a motion that the commission's work had been accurate based on the materials that had been presented. However, as a result of the complaints, another commission was chosen to take a new poll. An amendment was quickly offered that the original poll list be approved. This amendment was defeated by a single vote. So a new commission comprised of Dr. Strain, Rev. Black, and Rev. Elliott was appointed. Archy stopped by Ringbane to report on the unusual events of the meeting. He gave James the names of the people who had opposed the poll list and nominations. Hearing the names of people whom he knew and counted as friends becoming enemies was certainly painful.

The following Sunday, Rev. Elliott preached in Donaghmore and read a message from the Presbytery. The next day, the commission met to redo the poll list. James described what happened, "A good many names were added to the new list." People whose connection with the church were tenuous would now be allowed to vote for the new minister. These new marginal members would have an equal say in the selection of the new minister as members who had most devotedly supported the church for years.

The Presbytery met again the next day to hear the report of the commission. Some of the names on the list and some who weren't on it were discussed and debated. The Presbytery made the decisions. The final list was accepted, and a date set for the election of the new minister. James would have to wait anxiously until Wednesday April 23rd.

James recognized that this unusual event represented opposition to the selection of Robert as the next minister. And he knew that it was being led by members of the Presbytery colluding with members of the congregation who disliked James. The tensions made James ill, suffering as he did from high blood pressure.

Finally, the day of the meeting arrived. James watched anxiously as the names of certified voters were called. Many of the new members supported Rev. White. Despite that, Robert received a substantial majority of the votes. Customarily, a spokesman for the losing side would offer a motion to make the vote unanimous. But this time, that didn't happen. Supporters of Rev. White refused to cast the unifying vote for Robert. He would not become the new minister of Donaghmore. James was devastated. Two other names were put into nomination, Rev. Elliott and Rev. Commie. Neither of them received a sufficient number of votes to be elected either.

For James to write his short explanation of what happened was undoubtedly extremely painful. "Attended at the meeting house at 2 oclock where a poll was taken for Robert and Tommy White. Robert had the majority but not sufficient."

George included a fuller description of the events at the meeting in the *Telegraph* three days later. "A good deal of warm feeling has occasionally been exhibited," in the past. However, this meeting proceeded in an orderly way. "We understand Mr. Harshaw had a considerable but not a synodical majority." The other names offered failed to win sufficient approval. "The vacancy in consequence threatens to be somewhat protracted."

The failure to elect Robert to be minister in Donaghmore was a crushing disappointment for James. But he had suffered losses before in his life and was strong enough to move on. However, the goal of his opponents to firmly link Presbyterian churches to the Church of Ireland and the Orange Order had not yet been achieved. Enthused by their early victories, they were determined to press on.

Rev. Lindsay continued to be a major presence in the Donaghmore church. When a new communion was held in Donaghmore later in May, Rev. Lindsay administered the Sacrament. According to James's report, it was a very successful service. "About 316 <u>communicated</u>." Rev. Lindsay returned the next day, with Rev. Dodd of Newry attempting to mediate between factions of the divided congregation. This was James's report on the meeting. "Had a long discussion with Messers Lindsay, & Dodd in the session-room, and then again in the meetinghouse."

That James would not consent to accept Rev. Lindsay's views was made clear by the events that followed. In June, the congregation met to discuss a memorial to be sent to the Newry Presbytery on behalf of a number of parishioners. It requested the Presbytery to approve younger candidates to be permitted to preach in Donaghmore. This was a routine request. However, James's opposition took the opportunity to present another memorial, which also passed. "Opposition memorial passed by Messers Todd, Murdoch, & Ward."

The first memorial was quickly permitted. Three young ministers, Rev. Herbison, Rev. Todd Martin, and Rev. McGaw were assigned to preach in Donaghmore in upcoming weeks. The second memorial produced considerable discussion. Two members of the session had come forth to take their seats in the session after long absences during which they refused to participate in the affairs of the church. They were strongly supported by Rev. Lindsay's followers. Current elders, including James, refused to allow them to participate. One of the men had been inactive for seventeen years, one for eleven. James and other members of the session had met with them years before in an effort to persuade them to attend to their obligations. Both had firmly refused. As James analyzed the situation, coming forward at this time was "to serve a purpose."

Members of the Presbytery expressed concern over such dereliction of duty, and suggested having them return now, in times of dissention, was problematic. However, there seemed to be no rule to prevent their return to the session, since the congregation had failed to sanction them for their neglect of duty at any time. So the Presbytery decided to allow the two men to return. One of the absent elders was Thomas Marshall of Tullymurry House. The other was Samuel Boyd Marshall, father of James's son-in-law, Archy Marshall, and James's long-time friend, sharing as they did two grandchildren.

James and his supporters had no intention of surrendering without a fight. They created a new memorial for the next meeting of the Presbytery against seating the two absentee elders. James didn't attend the meeting.

Rev. Elliott was the moderator for the proceedings. He announced that he had received a memorial from the church stating the objections other elders had against seating the two men. They hadn't participated in more than a decade, and they hadn't attended church regularly. With this in mind, they had decided to ask guidance from the Presbytery.

Again, this wasn't the only memorial presented for consideration. Again, the opposition was ready with their own memorial signed by one of the elders and several members of the congregation. It claimed that the two men involved were men of "unimpeached and unimpeachable character." It was necessary for them to come forward and take their places in the session "to prevent the congregation being tyrannized over by the acting members, one of whom induced three of the others to follow him in anything he proposed."

This memorial created great excitement among the members of the Presbytery, as everyone well knew James and his character and recognized that he was the elder being called a "tyrant." After much agitated conversation and discussion, the Presbytery essentially repeated their previous advice. If the church had "good grounds" for indicting these men, the memorialists should put their concerns into written form to bring to the Presbytery for action. The memorialists should meet to decide whether or not to proceed as directed.

Rev. Elliott then asked Ward, who was there as the representative of the session, if he had any distinct charges to bring forward. He responded that the memorial was not just from him but from the session. He was sure they could prove the charges stated in their memorial. But he would wait to say anything further until he had consulted with the rest of the session.

With Rev. Lindsay present, it was unlikely that Rev. Elliott would take any action against the two absentees. But he did attempt to soften some of the division in the congregation by saying to the members of the session that he would immediately entertain any additional charges. He told the Marshalls' supporters that the Presbytery wasn't intentionally shielding the men in question. "They were only anxious to keep order and proper form and render justice to all parties."

No one left the meeting without a full awareness of the deep division that had suddenly opened in what had been an active and united congregation. Rev. Lindsay and his supporters could now claim three important victories, adding new supporters to the poll list, preventing James's son from becoming minister, and adding two supporters of their cause to the Donaghmore session. The two men acted quickly following the decision in the Presbytery meeting. James reported on June 22nd. "Messers Thomas and Boyd Marshall appeared, & sat for a little while in the session room."

James was still fighting at the service the following Sunday. He reported. "Protest against Mr. Boyd Marshall taking a seat in the sessions read to him in the session room by Mr. Thomas Ward at which Mr. Marshall seemed highly displeased." This was the displeasing message. "We, Hugh Todd, Thomas Ward and James Harshaw, members of the Session of Donaghmore, Protest against you, Mr. Samuel Boyd Marshall, taking a seat in this Session at present, as you have declined to act with us for about the last 17 years, and because when a friendly deputation from this session waited upon you about six years ago and invited you to resume your seat amongst us, you declared you would not, in such a manner that your doing so at any time seems strange and at this time to be more for a political object than for the Glory of God."

Marshall was indeed not pleased. He sent a response in July. "Mr. Thomas Ward, Sir, - I hereby require you on or before the 10th instant to furnish me with a true and exact copy of the paper you read in the Session room on Sunday, the 29th June last, containing three allegations against me which are not true, as I am determined going to my solicitor and taking whatever action he may direct. Therein fail not as you shall answer the contrary at your peril." Boyd Marshall dropped his threat following a new vote allowing him to take his seat in the session.

Rev. Lindsay and his supporters weren't content to savor their victories. They still needed to elect a supportive minister. Since James was a widely known and respected church leader, Rev. Lindsay recognized that James would still be an obstacle to their plans. Clearly it would be helpful to their cause to diminish James's reputation and subsequently his influence.

Lindsay saw an opportunity in early in July. James performed a routine task, signing the financial reports as clerk of the session during a prayer meeting that Rev. Lindsay attended. Almost immediately after this meeting, Lindsay supporters began to whisper rumors that James had been mishandling the finances of the church. Most of the rumormongers were well aware that they were spreading lies but their political desires took precedence over honor and decency.

The divisions in Donaghmore dragged on for months. In late July, the congregation tried to unite enough to choose a replacement for Rev. White. The name of a minister from Belfast, Rev. J. Thoburn McGaw, one of the young ministers the Presbytery had assigned to Donaghmore, was placed in nomination by James's son John. Following this "neat speech" as James saw it, the nomination was seconded by William McClelland.

But, there was another name put into nomination after "some – much hesitation" by James's nephew, James Martin He nominated a person who would greatly please the opposition forces, Rev. John Elliott of Clarksbridge. His nomination was seconded by Archy Murdoch. At this point in the meeting, Archy Marshall, James's son-in-law, gave what James described as "the speech of the evening." Archy argued that it was improper to put Rev. Elliott's name in nomination at all, because he had been nominated and defeated before. When the voting ended, Rev. McGaw had 72 votes, and Rev. Elliott 60. So again, there was a majority too small to result in nomination. However, unlike when Robert led Rev. White by many more votes than the small margin by which the Rev. McGaw led Rev. Elliott, the opposition surrendered, and voted to make a unanimous call to Rev. McGaw.

The pleasure over the final resolution of months of dissension was short lived. Rev. McGaw received another call at the same time to another church. And it was this church's call that Rev. McGaw decided to accept. Certainly the split in the congregation didn't make it an attractive placement. So the parishioners of Donaghmore continued to have itinerant ministers preaching while the divided session attempted to lead the church.

§

Despite the conflict in the Donaghmore as well as a similar problem in the Sandy Street church in Newry, George devoted much space to the American Civil War during the spring. His leaders showed that his perspectives on the war were changing as the news reports continued to arrive in his press room from America.

The northern strategy for winning the war seemed incomprehensible to the military strategists of Britain, a position that George supported. The war office of the Union seemed to move troops around in an effort to catch up with the movements of the Southern armies. As a result, Northern troops weren't where they were needed the most. The South seemed to have so well managed their movements that George came to believe that the Union troops were outnumbered in any battle they fought.

It was clear to George that if Lincoln wanted the North to win, they would need to free the slaves. In fact, Lincoln did make a small move in this direction, declaring that the government would begin buying the freedom of slaves in the border states. That seemed to George more like a calculation to keep the border states from supporting the South than any full-throated determination to end slavery.

The first great battle of the iron-clads Monitor and Merrimac in March 1862 was a stunning event in England. So much of their imperial power flowed from their powerful navy roaming every ocean. Now clearly this new technology would have to be quickly adopted by the British government to ensure that their sea-power could continue its dominance.

As month after month went by with news of one inconclusive battle after another reaching Newry, George began to believe that the South might actually be able to gain its independence. He could see no other outcome than permanent separation. He hoped that this result would happen soon in part to end the suffering of the cotton weavers in England and Ireland.

§

To make clear his support of the Orange Order and Protestant unity, George wrote a leader on Marching Day, July 12th. He claimed that the Orange Order was a totally legal body and should be allowed to march freely without interference from the Lord Lieutenant in Dublin. The government had decided to send a substantial number of constables north to maintain order at this year's celebrations. With George's usual caustic wit, he wrote that he didn't care if the government wanted to send constables north on a paid vacation. But he didn't think that the local cess payers should have to pay for such an influx of security that they had no need of.

George felt confident the celebration would pass peacefully. After all, this was the anniversary of the day that the Protestants of England and Ireland "won freedom for themselves and their countrymen of other denominations." This noble act showed the power of a distinguishing feature of Christianity, "Good will to men." The marchers didn't intend to offend their Catholic neighbours. Except for Catholic actions, Marching Day would always be a day of peaceful demonstrations.

This year, with Protestant activity increasing, the celebrations of July 12th did not end the activities of the year. A month later, George reported about a hugely successful meeting of the Orange Order and its supporters in the Ulster Hall in Belfast. The room was packed to overflowing with four thousand people. The meeting and speeches were totally peaceful. There was nothing said or done that would promote the slightest bit of worry to any Catholic. Instead, they attempted to convince Irish Protestants that the Orange Order was an organization that all of them should join, just the kind of effort that Rev. Lindsay was leading in the Newry area.

But the Orange Order, strengthened by increased support and control of all elements of the Protestant community in Ulster, had an agenda they intended to pursue. And indeed, they planned to hold similar large gatherings all over Ulster to promote the first two actions they wanted to accomplish. They wanted an end to the recently enacted Emblems Act, and an end to the Maynooth grant, which supported the education of Catholic priests.

George returned to the same topic in his next edition. The Maynooth grant was always controversial. It was designed to placate Catholics who along with Presbyterians were still forced to support the costs of the Established churches. The regium donum payments to support Presbyterian ministers served the same function.

This might seem sensible to many Irishmen, but George saw a flaw in the logic behind the grant. George didn't mind the government supporting religions, but he did mind paying for a religion that was bad. He saw no point in educating priests who didn't like the country that was supporting them. Like many other Protestants, George saw this as a form of favoritism to Catholics.

But this government "favoritism" had had a beneficial effect on the Protestant community as a whole. Loathing of this gift united what might otherwise be a divided community. The government had turned the "most lukewarm Protestants into supporters of the loyal Orange Institution." Still this was the time to end Catholic privilege. Protestants should rise to the occasion and take back their rights and demand religious equality.

Planning for a second gathering of Protestants in Belfast soon followed the meeting in the Ulster Hall. This time it would be held in the open air in Balmoral Park to accommodate more of the Protestants of Ulster. This was an event that George strongly supported and publicized in his paper in early September. The goal of this meeting was to demonstrate to the British government that they wanted the laws to be enforced equally for Protestants and Catholics or not enforced at all. They felt deeply aggrieved that the Catholics seemed to be able to march with impunity as they had at the funeral of McManus and the laying of the corner stone at the new Catholic University. On the other hand a boy in Belfast had been prosecuted for wearing an orange lily pinned to his jacket. Certainly this increased Protestant activity would produce positive results if only Protestants persisted long enough.

The Balmoral gathering was a great success. The crowd was generally estimated to be 70,000 people, with some estimates reporting a crowd size of nearly 100,000. George declared that the people who attended represented the best of Ulster. They bore no resemblance to the rag-tag laborers who gathered in huge numbers to listen to Daniel O'Connell during the year of the Monster Meetings. Rev. Henry Cooke was one of the featured speakers. As in previous years, he offered the support of Presbyterians for this grand cause. He reminded the crowd they didn't wish to crush anyone under their feet, but he wouldn't support anyone crushing the united Protestants of Ireland either. The unity that Rev. Lindsay supported seemed to be succeeding.

The huge crowd left the meeting peacefully and in great spirits. However, after they had safely returned to their homes, many Catholics living in the Pound area of Belfast came out into the streets. Despite efforts of local priests to keep the situation calm, they were unsuccessful. Mobs roamed the streets breaking windows as they moved through the neighborhoods, some of which they were able to occupy. Protestants refrained from joining the riot for two days. Unfortunately, George's hope that, despite Catholic hostilities, Protestants would remain peaceful was dashed after Catholic rioters threw stones at the windows of Protestant churches. A Protestant mob joined the battle. Rioting continued for several days before order was restored. Sectarian divisions had spread far beyond the Presbyterian church in Donaghmore.

§

During the summer of 1862, George had hinted that he was changing his mind about the American Civil War. As summer ended, he told his readers that he had indeed changed his opinion and explained why. He now believed the time had come for the British and French governments to recognize the independence of the South.

The people of the South had already proven themselves to be very brave and skilled fighters, thus fulfilling one of the major international principles for recognition as a nation. They had proven that they could defend themselves against the better-equipped Northern forces. George also felt that Britain had been badly treated by the north. They had barred British ships from waters that they had always sailed freely. They had boarded British ships, requiring captains to sign documents that guaranteed that the goods they were carrying wouldn't fall into Southern hands. Also painful were increased tariffs designed to keep British products out of America.

George was sure that the only reason that Britain refused to recognize the South as an independent country was the issue of slavery. George now argued that this issue shouldn't prevent recognition of the Confederacy. He believed blacks in the North were little better off than when they had been slaves in the South. President Lincoln himself showed little sympathy for the black slaves, supporting the deportation of freed blacks. And he clearly wasn't willing to free the slaves held in the South.

Now George found a rather unusual argument to complete the case he was making. If supporters of the Union were really concerned about slavery, they should accept an independent Confederacy now. Slavery would most likely end under an independent south. Planters would gradually come to see that they would be more successful having free labor grow their cotton than slaves. One by one, they would free their own slaves. Slaves would be better off if the war ended now with the south relatively undamaged than if they were forced by a prolonged war to live with their former masters in a southern wasteland.

In another editorial, George enjoyed taking on Irish fighters in America. He was amused that Thomas Meagher had been made a general commanding the Irish Brigade. He and other Irish military leaders weren't of sufficient quality to merit such positions. George pointed out how unsuccessful General Meagher had been in his new career. He also suspected that Irish casualties had been very high because they had been put in the most dangerous locations in the fighting.

Though acknowledging that the Irish were naturally "a brave people," George believed they hadn't succeeded in Ireland because they were too lazy to work and "too vicious" to be accepted by the British. Irish men would fight in an American war because "they like excitement," and dreamed of returning to Ireland to the fight for independence.

George had one last reminder of something he had mentioned to his readers in an earlier editorial. The Lincoln who was executing the terrible war was quite different from the leader that most people had admired when he was elected and gave his first major speech. It had turned out that President Lincoln had become an "absolute Monarch." Fewer and fewer recruits were willing to fight for such a person and such a failing cause. They had begun to accept the fact that the Confederacy was going to win. "A free people whose territory is invaded, whose liberties are threatened, whose honor is outraged, and whose houses are desolated, can never lay down their arms." The North was fighting for empire, not freedom. Given these faults, George believed that the conflict should be quickly ended through foreign intervention.

Shortly after George expressed his new views on the war, the great battle of Antietam took place followed quickly by the Emancipation Proclamation to free the slaves. Though George had been writing about this option for some months, he was less than impressed when it happened. He didn't think Antietam was a very large battle and hadn't changed the situation enough to provide justification for Lincoln's actions. At this point in the war, the Proclamation didn't mean anything. George wasn't convinced that Lincoln wouldn't consent to a continuation of slavery, despite the Proclamation, if the South would rejoin the Union. He didn't think the British government would find it of value either. With the South essentially independent, his words would have no effect there, beyond giving the South even more incentive to fight on.

At any rate, the English should take immediate action to end the war. The winter was approaching and thousands upon thousands of Lancashire weavers were facing death by starvation. To prevent this local calamity, the government needed to intervene and mediate an end to the war.

Without waiting for the war to end, the people of Ireland acted to help prevent starvation in Lancashire. As the months of either reduced pay or no pay at all dragged on, weavers had used up any savings. Local English guardians had agreed to pay them a small stipend, but not enough to prevent starvation. Now charitable minded Irishmen began to help raise money to provide additional financial support.

The citizens of Newry had always come forward to promote charitable causes. So a meeting was called in early November by the town commissioners. There was much to do as there were two hundred thousand people in need of help. Unfortunately, the attendance at the meeting was smaller than had been expected and hoped for. However, those who attended set to work, setting up a subscriptions list. This money would be managed by a council of twenty-seven local citizens. A month later George reported that the people of Newry and Down had raised forty thousand pounds to help English weavers.

§

More than a month passed during which the spurious charges against James continued to spread around Donaghmore and Newry. But James had supporters of his own, anxious to rise to his defense. At a Sunday meeting at the end of August, Archy Marshall read a memorial to the congregation that he intended to bring to the next meeting of the Presbytery. Following the approval of the memorial, John Harshaw and Robert Megaw went to Newry to present it to the meeting. Archy Marshall presented his memorial requesting the Presbytery to "force the collectors, Robert Jeffery, Copland, and John Cowan to publish their accounts from May – 61 to May – 62." The memorial asked about "the mode in which the names of the members of the congregation had been printed in the financial statement and requesting the Presbytery to enjoin the stipend collectors to attend before the committee and have their lists examined." Charges from these men were the basis of the rumor that James was mishandling church funds. Unfortunately, the Presbytery was dealing with the still contentious problem of replacing the minister at the Sandys Street Church and didn't have time to discuss the issue from Donaghmore.

Less than a week later, James noted more activity by the conspirators in his journal. "Mr. Lindsay passed up the race, & Mr. Allison also." Four days later, James wrote another entry of interest. "Visited Thomas Marshall at his request." Clearly this was a peace overture from one of Lindsay's activists.

James recorded something even more remarkable on September 21st. Perhaps since division had been spread in what was a religious institution in order to render it a political body, it wasn't unexpected. "A row in the classroom between Archy & Cowan, and Robert Young & Robert Jeffry outside."

When the Presbytery met next, they dealt with the Donaghmore Church on "their internal affairs." The memorial to force the publication of the church finances was finally heard. The Presbytery voted to create a commission to investigate the issues behind the request. Members of the commission were Rev. Dodd, Rev. Black, Rev. Lindsay and Mr. Patterson an elder. They were charged to investigate, take what steps they considered necessary and report back to the Presbytery. The report of the commission was never discussed or made public.

However, when the commission went to Donaghmore to meet with church members, Rev. John Dodd presided over a very different discussion. Another effort was made to elect Rev. Elliott minister. Rev. Elliott had strong political opinions that pleased Rev. Lindsay, but he separated his political beliefs from his ministry enough to placate James and his supporters. The congregation voted to violate tradition and place in nomination a minister who had previously been rejected. George reported that this was a "cordial and unanimous call." Rev. Elliott would face the daunting task of unifying a very divided congregation.

The next step in the process was to determine if Rev. Elliott wished to accept the call. He clearly understood the divisions that had erupted in the congregation would provide an unusual challenge. On December 9th, the Presbytery met again to receive his answer.

Rev. Elliott, who had been the chairman of the Presbytery meeting stepped down to give his response. He seemed to be somewhat surprised at what had happened. He said the call was "totally unexpected." He knew that he had been considered earlier in the process but felt that the moment he was being considered had long past. When he heard of the result of the vote, he felt sure that the hand of God was a work in the call. Therefore, he had given the opportunity some serious thought.

While that was going on, he had received many messages of encouragement. Rev. Patrick White had written to assure him that "there are few congregations like Donaghmore, that I will find the warmest friends among many whom I may be disposed to think opposed to me."

The next supporter Rev. Elliott mentioned was a most unlikely one. This support explained why James and his supporters had voted to call a person they felt was closely affiliated with Rev. Lindsay and possibly supportive of his efforts. "My college companion and friend, Mr. Harshaw, of Mountmellick, has written me many very kind letters expressing his delight at the settlement in Donaghmore. I feel that even if I had been disposed to refuse this call it would be great hardihood in me to set up my individual judgment in opposition to that of many wiser and more competent to judge." Given that, he asked the Presbytery to free him from his ministry of the Clarksbridge congregation so that he might transfer to Donaghmore.

After kind words about his current congregation and all the support he had received from the congregation and the resident landlord, he returned to his seat, so the meeting could continue with a response from the Clarksbridge congregation, which was presented by Samuel Lockhart. This church would put no roadblocks in Rev. Elliott's transition to Donaghmore. They too believed that the hand of God was at work. Certainly Donaghmore needed "his well-tried abilities as a Gospel minister, his careful and laborious pastorate, and the unfailing interest with which he has watched over our spiritual and temporal welfare.' Mr. Lockhart also referred to his ability to expand church facilities and support the "religious and secular education of the rising generation."

Rev. Dodd made the formal motion to support the call of Donaghmore to Rev. Elliott. He was greatly pleased with the presentation of Rev. Elliott and Mr. Lockhart. Most pressing in the decision of the Presbytery was that Donaghmore had issued a unanimous call. "He had a great deal to do with that congregation since their vacancy and in truth he did not expect that they would ever have come to such unanimity as had, by the blessing of God, been arrived at."

There was a special blessing in this move for the Presbytery. They would not be losing the fellowship of a well-admired minister, both churches being part of the Newry Presbytery. Summing up all the elements of this decision, Rev. Dodd believed that this change "would result in the greatest spiritual advantages to one of the oldest and most respectable congregations in this Presbytery," as well as to the Presbytery and the Presbyterian church in Ireland. With that said, Rev. Dodd offered a motion to support the transfer of Rev. Elliott to Donaghmore.

This motion was seconded by Rev. Cromie and unanimously passed. The installation in Donaghmore was set for December 29th. With that action, the meeting adjourned. James recorded that son John attended and reported to his father that "Mr Elliott accepted the call to Donaghmore."

With this result which was pleasing to the anti-James faction of the church, it might have been expected that Rev. Lindsay would have savored a gratifying result and moved on. However, this wasn't what happened. Less than a week after the Presbytery meeting James recorded what happened the following Sunday.

Rev. Dodd was on hand to preach and present the vote of the Presbytery. James recorded this in his journal. Then he added a cryptic comment. "Talk in the session room about the mission collection." Clearly Rev. Lindsay and his supporters were still on the attack. James made his feelings on the subject clear in a letter he sent to Rev. Lindsay the next day.

While the meeting of the Presbytery was going on the previous week, Rev. Lindsay was busy telling members of the Presbytery that James had failed to make any mission collections in Donaghmore for the past year. "Now Sir that statement – if made – was not correct." James said that though no mission collections had been asked for, the Donaghmore church had certainly made a number of them. He had made four collections in all over the last few months. And he had turned the money over to Mr. Speers who managed such collections. He had receipts for each donation.

Having explained his evidence, James went on the attack. "Now, sir, I can suppose you had no design or wish to make me a Scape-Goat in the case where you made the statement; yet as I am an older man than you, I may just say that you should have been more cautious than to hurl or throw out any insinuations before my few, very few enemies, who has been trying to make political capital out of your statement to my disadvantage, viz that collections was taken up here – that I took charge of them and that you informed the Presbytery and them that they had not been forwarded up to the present, if you never made the statement then you are to be pitied as well as myself, but if you inadvertently led the people to whom I have already alluded to believe what some of them report, how are you to counteract the slander – you know the party who raised the sneer when you made whatever statement you made, and I leave the antidote to your hands for the present." If Rev. Lindsay responded to James's letter, there remains no evidence. But following James's strong response, the charges against James fell into oblivion.

James made no additional comment on the dissension in the church. The day before his installation, Rev. Elliott preached both sermons with James in attendance.

The installation of Rev. Elliott to be the 7th pastor of the Donaghmore Church began at noon before a full church. Among the guests, were a number of ministers. The ceremony began with devotions. The Rev. Mr. Martin, new pastor of the Sandys Street church, read from the Scriptures, 1st Epistle of Peter, 1st Chapter, and 23rd verse. Then Rev. Martin preached an elegant and impressive sermon.

Rev. Lindsay then came up to the pulpit to explain ordination. As Rev. Lindsay rose, so did James. He got up from his seat near the pulpit, walked down the aisle and out the door, leaving the stunned congregation behind him.

James described his act of defiance this way. "Was at meeting and left after Mr. Martin preached. Archy convayed me up the Longhorn road"

British Government

Queen Victoria with Prince Albert and her 9 children.

Whigs/Liberals	Tories/Conservatives

Prime
Ministers

Lord Palmerston

Lord Derby

William Gladstone

Benjamin Disraeli

Chapter 10

John Martin and the Fenians

1863

When the year 1863 began, John was in Dublin to give a speech, another step in his increasing political activity. His speech was sponsored by the Brotherhood of St. Patrick to raise funds to erect a statue to Daniel O'Connell near the river Liffey. It was held at the Mechanic's Institute across the river from the proposed site of the statue. Appropriately, John chose to give his speech on the life of the great Irish leader. He covered O'Connell's achievements, as well as his refusal to accept that an actual revolution might be necessary to achieve independence. John made clear that he had a different perspective. He would accept revolution to free Ireland from foreign domination no matter the price.

The reviews of the speech depended on the reviewer. The *Daily Express* claimed that the attendance was sparse and lacking in respectable people. The report in the *Irishman* was more positive. It was a "Noble address" "Calm, impartial, just – it was incomparably the ablest commentary on O'Connell's life that has ever come under our notice." "For who is John Martin? Not an emancipated Catholic, not a believer in the doctrine that 'no political amelioration is worth the shedding of a drop of blood.' But a man professing the faith of the ORRS AND TONES, a patriot proved and tried, who in opposition to O'Connell, risked his life and fortune for that which he believed to be his country's cause."

§

Neither a speech on O'Connell nor the affairs of the Donaghmore Church merited George's attention in his New Year leader. Instead he focused on ominous signs of poverty in Newry. The number of inmates in the workhouse had increased. Poor farm laborers around Newry were struggling to remain independent, often surviving on small amounts of outdoor relief. As the winter dragged on, George put his continuing concerns into another leader.

Ulster might well have been used to thinking that poverty was an issue for the south and west. George wanted his readers to know that this wasn't the case now. "The poor we have with us always, and in our own town the pallid face" and scrawny, poorly clothed beggars "meet us at every turn." He applauded the people of Newry for generously helping the Lancashire weavers, severely impacted by the shortage of cotton resulting from the American Civil War. But that donation shouldn't mean that local people would forget their local poor "cowering round our own doors."

Winters were always hard for the Irish poor. "The present Winter has exceeded, in duration, intensity, and unhealthiness, that of any of its predecessors for some years past. Disease follows close in the footsteps of cold and hunger." This situation forced many to take the last extreme steps and enter the poorhouse. While George admired the work of the people who managed the poorhouse, many regarded "it as a last resort, and entering it a degradation. There are hundreds now in Newry who are suffering the most severe pinching of want sooner than degrade themselves or their families by seeking either in or out-door relief from the workhouse." To George, these were "the truly deserving poor." "With a moral heroism deserving our highest admiration, crime is not resorted to, and it is only on particular inquiry that the true state of affairs in laid bare."

These people must be helped. "It is the bounden duty of the humanely disposed among the wealthier classes to be up and doing." Clergymen of all denominations had to be involved in the work as well. "An effort should at once be made, and speedy relief given to those who now suffer the bitter pangs of hunger in silence, and without the least murmur of complaint."

The power of George's appeal soon achieved results. Within a week, the Chairman of the Town Commissioners had called a meeting and advertised in it the *Telegraph*. The meeting was held a few days later in the Courthouse on Trevor Hill.

After the meeting, George published a long account and offered his opinion on the results in another leader on the subject. There seemed to be little disagreement with George over the current state of affairs, and the imperative to promptly give additional help to the poor. He explained that the problem had started on local farms. Several seasons of wet weather, and repeated "bad harvests" had led to lack of money in the countryside. That problem rippled into Newry. "All seemed to plunge the working classes, who manfully struggled against penury, deeper in misery and want." The committee, including Hill Irvine, agreed that a central place should be set up in Newry to which the poor could come for help, administered by a committee to detect any fraudulent attempt to gain undeserved help.

This committee was quickly appointed. Denis Maguire was the Chairman. Prominent men of Newry were appointed to assist him, along with two doctors, and clergymen of all faiths. Fund raising began on the spot with £60 pledged by the members.

§

Despite, the local hardships, and a growing sense of foreboding over increased signs of a nationalist resurgence, George continued to watch for each new dispatch from the battlefields in America and read them with great care when they came across his desk. He was struggling to sort out in his own mind what the purpose of the war truly was.

Near the end of February, he explained his evolving thoughts to his readers. The Irish point of view had begun with a hatred of slavery and a love of liberty. However, the Confederates argued that they were just waging a war for independence, a cause the Irish could understand and support. While most Irish continued to oppose slavery, George was beginning to believe that slavery wasn't an important factor in secession despite having published a statement from the Vice President of the Confederate States Stephens that the South was fighting to establish a nation based on the principle of black slavery.

The Northern position seemed increasingly muddled as well. The world would support the Union if it were fighting to free the slaves. However, it was unclear if that was the issue at the core of their actions. Many Northerners supported slavery as strongly as the southern planters, but they had been silenced by the belligerence of the abolitionists. Though Lincoln had issued the Emancipation Proclamation, he seemed to indicate that he would accept the existence of slavery in the South, if the southern states would agree to return to the Union. So George had come to believe that the North was actually fighting for supremacy and the South for independence.

One issue remained to be resolved, the right of a state to leave the country once citizens had voted to join the Union. Even if they didn't, George wondered why the North would wish to keep the South as part of a country they rejected? The North would have to keep fighting to force them to rejoin the Union. That could mean years of war and terrible death and desolation followed by an occupation of the south as conquerors for many years.

George no longer believed that such a high cost in money and lives would produce any result worth the sacrifice. Certainly, the North would soon see the "folly" of continuing the war and agree to end it. The Irish would be very happy to see the two sections of America go their separate ways. There was sufficient territory on the continent to accommodate two separate countries. Finally, George had concluded that the slaves wouldn't suffer too much by continuing to be slaves. Just let the war end. John would heartily agree with George on this issue and support his new thinking

Soon after George wrote this leader, his brother James suddenly died. From that point on, the *Telegraph* was published by James's son, Henry George, who had already participated in the paper's management. George would still be the editor. So though there wouldn't be any major changes in the paper, there were some smaller changes that readers would immediately notice. The paper would be published in the evening on Monday, Wednesday and Friday. It would then be available to readers earlier in the morning. The pages were also rearranged. The advertisements that had previously occupied the front page of the paper were moved to the third page. That way, readers could immediately begin reading the news. The basic principles that governed its content would remain the same. While the arrangement of news and advertisements was changed, it would continue to support Conservative principles, Protestant unity and "evangelical truth."

§

Once Rev. Elliott had assumed his new responsibilities as minister of the Donaghmore, James would set aside his disappointment and personal attacks and work diligently to ensure that Rev. Elliott's ministry would be a success.

Robert came north from Mountmellick to support his friend and assist James in mending the divisions. James often accompanied Rev. Elliott as he visited the members of his new parish. He continued to attend all the church activities as well. When Thomas Marshall, one of the elders who supported the dissidents died, James attended the funeral.

However, the painful experience had changed him. James never mentioned Rev. Lindsay again. He reduced his charitable activities, sending son John to take his place at the dispensary meetings. Most of his journal entries were confined to farm news and church activities. More personally distressing, James was unable to heal the breach in the family. Archy Marshall [husband of James's daughter Jane] had sided with James during the dispute instead of his father Samuel Boyd Marshall, an unusual action that complicated any reconciliation. James never mentioned Marshall again, indicating that the break was permanent.

Apparently, the Presbytery made no effort to punish Rev. Lindsay for his attempts to politicize local churches or the slanderous charges he had made against James. But soon they took an action that indicated they didn't believe Rev. Lindsay and wanted to show support for James. Certainly the Newry Presbytery appreciated what James was doing to heal his divided church. The problems stirred in the Sandy Street Church by the actions of Rev. Lindsay weren't so easily overcome as they had been in Donaghmore. Some members of the church refused to accept the pastorate of Rev. Ross Martin whom Rev. Lindsay had supported. The efforts of the Presbytery didn't help either, as Rev. Lindsay was still the clerk there. So the Presbytery reached out to a neutral body, the Synod of Dublin, to act as an intermediary.

In May, James was appointed a member of the commission from Dublin. "John drove me to Newry, where I attended a commission of the Synod of Dublin in the session room of the 1st Congregation of Newry to settle differences between the members of that congregation, but the endeavors of that commission failed."

This was an event that George covered as well. The opponents of the new minister refused to accept his presence in the church. They felt that their concerns should have been given the greatest weight since they comprised all the Session members and the members who most generously supported the church. When this mediation effort failed, they requested permission to form a new church, the third Presbyterian church in Newry. The Presbytery agreed, and a new church was created. So this division became permanent.

But the greatest joy in James's life continued to be the young grandchild growing up in his house. James recorded the steps in the four-year old's life. In February, James wrote, "The sonny first stated his name to be 'James Alexander.'"

James Alexander was a farm boy. So it wasn't surprising that he was introduced early to farm jobs. Just after his 4th birthday, James noted that James Alexander helped his uncle James drive a cow to a neighbor's farm.

In early June, James, his son James Jr., and James Alexander went down the Ardkeragh Road to take tea with his father. James reported that while they were there, "James run down a young <u>peeweep</u>." [Likely a "pipit."]

§

During the spring of 1863, the Civil War seemed no closer to resolution. John was greatly worried about Mitchel and his three sons, now all in harm's way. In the fall of the previous year, Mitchel had ended his second stay in Paris, and along with his youngest son Billy, had returned to America. After a harrowing trip across the Potomac, barely evading capture by ships enforcing the Union blockade, father and son had returned safely to Richmond. Billy immediately joined his brother James in the Army of Northern Virginia. With John in Charleston, all the Mitchel boys were serving in the Confederate army.

Meanwhile, Jenny had returned to Ireland with daughter Minnie. The oldest daughter Henrietta had joined a convent in Paris, and the youngest child, Isabelle, the daughter of the Mitchel's Australian exile, had elected to stay with Henrietta and attend the convent school. For the first time in ten years, John enjoyed the pleasure of having Jennie and her daughter nearby.

John watched the war unfold through the numerous articles and leaders that George wrote in the *Telegraph*. Federal gunboats attacked the forts that guarded Charleston with a new gun that was capable of penetrating the fortifications of Sumter where John Mitchel Jr., was stationed. The Army of Northern Virginia beat the invading Army at Chancellorsville in May. Following the battle Stonewall Jackson was wounded by one of his own Confederate troops.

In a sad irony, it wasn't one of the Mitchel sons who was the first to die. Daughter Henrietta seemed safe in the cloistered walls of Sacre Coeur in Paris. However, in late April, she had contacted brain fever. The sisters notified the family in Newry, but indicated that there seemed to be no danger. When the illness suddenly worsened, Jenny was quite ill herself, so ill that the family didn't dare tell her of her daughter's peril. Instead Mitchel's sister Henrietta, who was in London at the time, was notified of the situation and urged to go at once to Paris. Sadly by the time she arrived, her namesake was already dead. She could only provide comfort for Isabelle and represent the family at the funeral and burial in Mount Parnesse.

John wrote to O'Brien with the unexpected news. In the same letter, he also explained to his good friend, another stress he was enduring. He was trying to start a new nationalist organization, that he had been "provoked into starting." The purpose of the new organization was to unify Irish factions into a nationalist organization strong enough to impress the British. So supporters of peaceful resistance and Fenian revolution were both welcome. "But I shall probably make a conspicuous failure for want of money and public cooperation from Nationalists of some influence. If the thing could be respectably started, I think it could carry the country. I am very sorry that your personal views forbid you to connect yourself again in a public organization.

It strikes me as foolish presumption in me to go forward as a leader while you are alive."

But John did persist, despite his qualms about the likelihood of success. The plan that had been devised by his political friends who had convinced John to take on the task of getting the organization established and functioning with promises of involvement and funding. This new national organization would be called the Irish National League. It would be totally legal to minimize personal risks. The head of the organization would be the O'Donoghue. John's role would be limited to taking the basic steps to establish the organization, mainly through a series of letters. This he could do from the family home in Kilbroney. These long letters were printed in a number of newspapers across Ireland. Not surprisingly, the *Newry Telegraph* wasn't one of them.

In his first letter, John took advantage of a letter his friend John Dillon had written to the British government complaining about the over-taxation of Ireland and supporting his charge by comparing the financial obligations established by the Act of Union in 1801 with subsequent British actions. John totally agreed with Dillon's careful work and used it to bolster his belief that only independence would remove unfair Irish burdens.

Complicating English and Irish relations was the political system in England. The two parties, Conservative and Whig, had different visions of English obligations toward Ireland. As power shifted from one party to another, laws for Ireland often changed profoundly. The Conservatives did only what was needed to keep the Irish subjugated. However, John believed that had the Conservatives remained in power during the famine, many Irish lives would have been saved. This belief was shared by many Ulster Protestants, who thought the opposition Whigs maintained their power by giving Catholics positions of importance that historically had belonged to the Protestants.

John concluded his first letter, by making clear his position that the Protestants were most to blame for religious differences. "And I may fairly add, that the want of patriotism in our Protestant fellow-countrymen, is in great measure, caused by their sectarian prejudices, which keep them ignorant of Irish affairs."

This first letter got a positive response from Andrew Bradley, clearly one of John's supporters. "Who has not heard of John Martin? Who fails to remember his acts, his sacrifices, his suffering? All noble disinterested! The writings of such a man, at least by our heroically aspersious youth who yearn for liberty and love manhood could not be displaced! They would hold out an undying confidence to the peoples hopes, as well as an assurance that however baffled, their chivalrous efforts could not be finally overcome. His sentiments would be readily endorsed, his experience, openness and plan of action, during any emergency, would be of enviable advantage to the general struggle in which all should be engaged."

"Let Mr. Martin, therefore, think of the hint here thrown out to him and from a conviction of capacity, he will not, probably, shrink from the task. A lover of his country in the truest sense of the word, he will be proud of the opportunity to serve her.'"

John was certainly pleased by the support of people like Bradley, and he continued to write letters to explain his ideas for the new organization and attract new adherents to the national cause. John spent much of his second letter arguing that the first action of Irish nationalists had to be obtaining freedom from England's control, their actions causing thousands of young Irish men and women to flee Ireland. "Who shall estimate the torture of body and soul, the moral and material ruin attendant upon the depopulation that we have seen in Ireland? Who shall count the famine graves of Ireland, the Irish bones that strew the bottom of the Atlantic, the indignant sights of the best of our youths and maidens as they look their last upon their native land? Who shall shudder and tell of the pauper system, whose operation is to make thieves and prostitutes of those whom foreign rule has made poor?"

Then John pointed out to his readers other effects of English rule. "It is foreign rule that enables a foreign sect to rob and insult Ireland as the church Establishment; it is foreign rule that drains away the wealth of Ireland, banishes manufacturing industry, reduces our people to poverty, evicts, depopulates, pauperizes, enfeebles, demoralizes, debases a people as finely and nobly endowed as ever born in God's image and likeness. It is foreign rule, that has lessoned our population by 3 millions within the last 17 years, and intends to lessen it by 2 million more within the next 10 years. England wants to make Ireland a 'pasture farm.'"

John concluded his letter with a plea to those who had yet to become active in the cause. "The great mass of the people of Ireland desire self government. The majority of the middle classes that raise their minds to Irish politics at all, desire it. There is not an anti-Repealer in Ireland, except through ignorance, prejudice, selfish greed, sectarianism, hatred, cowardice, corruption, or some other mean and wicked motives."

The next letter explored the justification for establishing a new national organization. It was addressed to the Irish people who weren't in favor of repeal. Many of them, "the nobles, the clergy of all the churches, the professional classes, the learned, the wealthy, the men to whom their social position gives power and responsibility in Irish affairs, the natural leaders of the people of Ireland that they are neglecting their duty as citizens, as Christians, as men." These people would ordinarily have been the leaders of a free Ireland but were doing little to help Ireland to become free. The new organization could provide another option for national action to compete with the growing power of the Fenian movement.

Then John explained why he had remained in Paris. When he had received amnesty, he had had to decide whether or not to remain in exile or return to Ireland. "My patriotic sentiments, for the sake of which the English had made of me a transported convict, and classed me with their swindlers and murders, were unchanged—or rather, long years of reflection and the personal observations I had made in foreign countries had intensified my hatred for the

English yoke, under which my country still suffered injuries and miseries unparalleled in the civilized world."

Several years after his decision to remain in exile "family circumstances" required him to return permanently to live in Ireland. The circumstances in Ireland had changed from 1848. The potato blight had finally diminished, Crops had been good for several years, and prices were higher due to the Crimean War. Anyone desiring work was able to find it. This seemed like prosperity to the remaining Irish population. The nationalist leaders of the 1840s had fled to other countries following the sad failure of the revolt of 1848. Even those who supported the idea of independence seemed resigned to the idea that the time for such actions had passed, at least under current circumstances.

Given the apparent unwillingness of the majority of Irish citizens to support any kind of Irish nationalism, John wanted to remind them he was an unwilling subject of England "which had inflicted so great an outrage upon myself." Though he clearly recognized that he was flying against the wind, his hopes for an independent Ireland impelled him to at least try again.

There had been small changes since his return that might hint at hope. Hard times had returned to Ireland with the end of the Crimean War, resulting from falling prices and the continuation of the high war taxes. The declining economic situation led to an increasing boldness among the Irish who desired to ultimately attain independence. "Many Nationalists have called upon me, both publicly and privately, to take part in the organization of such a movement, I dare not refuse my humble services in any and every capacity in which the national cause may seem to demand them. For a leading position I am unfitted by want of rank, wealth, ability and ambition; as well as by political reputation, which is one of failure." However, he believed that in the early stages of a new nationalist movement, he might be of service. The more natural leaders had promised him that once he had launched the organization, they would take prominent positions of leadership.

Then John moved on to argue against the actions of England that had proved so disastrous to Ireland, which would only be ended by Irish independence. Under the Union, Ireland had very little power, as their representation in Parliament was only a "mockery and fraud." The actions that England took that were so damaging in Ireland were beneficial to England. As long as this situation prevailed, Ireland would continue to suffer.

His idea for national action was simple. It would follow the pattern of O'Connell's Repeal Association, and the Young Irelander's Irish Confederation. All across Ireland, patriots should rally to support this organization that had only one objective: "obtaining of self-government, consisting of all Irishmen who say that they desire self-government." To achieve this goal, the Irish National League would reach out to the governments of other countries with clear explanations of Irish issues in order to gain international support. Finally, it would prepare Ireland to act when action for independence might be successful.

John had no illusions about the difficult task he was undertaking. The negative effects of British actions on the Irish population had created a major obstacle for united action. "The rule of England has divided, demoralized, and enfeebled our community to an extent unknown in any other subject country of Europe."

But the effort must be made. "To turn the public mind towards the grand object of National Independence is the only means by which the moral tone of the country can be raised from its present baseness."

There were positive factors that could flow from a widely supported organization. English imperial positions would weaken in the face of an Irish demand for independence. Other nations subject to the Empire would be inspired to demand their own freedom. Ireland already enjoyed international sympathy in America and France. The international outreach of the new group would enhance international awareness of English mistreatment of Ireland. Finally, Ireland would have a trained army formed from the ranks of thousands of Irishmen who had become skilled fighters during the American Civil War. "And if our freedom be yet far distant and but dimly visible to the eye of hope, let us, at least, turn towards it."

John sat down in Kilbroney on July 1st to write another in his series of letters, this one laying out his position on the problems of tenant and landlord relations which had defied any solution the English Parliament was willing to support. The current land system had been created to help England and was enforced by the British Army. Any tenant could be ejected from the land he leased with six months' notice. Around five thousand families suffered violent ejection from their cottages every year.

It was these often unjust acts that led to assassinations. As atrocious as these murders often were, they had some positive results. Many landlords hesitated to eject tenants lest the tenants rise against them. United actions by local tenants and laborers often reduced any financial gains to landlords through ejectments by threatening any prospective replacement tenants. Assassination or the threat of it toward landlords or replacement tenants is the "only protection which English rule has left to the vast mass of our population against exile or pauperism – a horrible protection!" The Ulster Custom that supposedly provided protections against such ejections, as well as fair rent and fair returns for the hard work of Ulster farmers was too often ignored by powerful landlords.

"I am an Irish landlord myself. My rent-roll indeed is small, but it forms the entire of my income and means of life." John noted that much land was owned by absentee owners who would have little interest in keeping holdings in Ireland once it became free. This land could then be sold to the farmers who leased it. Thus independence was the best solution to the land disputes that so greatly plagued Ireland.

§

While John was struggling to create a new national movement through his letter writing campaign, George continued to focus his editorials on the

American Civil War. He believed that the on-going battle for Vicksburg would be critical for the hopes of the Confederacy. But he recognized that the movement of Lee's Army north might well provoke a second critical battle somewhere in Maryland or Pennsylvania.

When General Stonewall Jackson died of his wounds, George wrote a glowing tribute. Everyone in England, Scotland and Ireland would be greatly saddened to hear of his death. Most people had been following his exploits with great interest. Gen. Jackson was a Presbyterian, a true Christian. He had become the greatest general in the war. There was no Union general that could approach his talents. He had fought valiantly for the independence of the Confederate States, not for slavery. since he owned no slaves himself.

George maintained that he was keeping an even-handed approach in his coverage of the war. But at the same time, he reminded his readers that the South had given him more reasons to support them than the North had. The South treated England with great respect, while the North didn't. The South had generals like Stonewall Jackson. The North had generals like Gen. Butler, notorious for defaming the women of New Orleans when he was the general commanding there, after the North had recaptured the city earlier in the war. Southern leaders controlled the passions of their citizens while the Northerners formed into violent mobs.

Given that, George was sure that the South, so valiantly defending Vicksburg, would prevail in the on-going siege. But he did concede that if the North should take the city, it would command the entire Mississippi River, and essentially divide the South. This would be a bitter blow, but it wouldn't greatly alter the Southern will to fight on.

George couldn't end the leader without making another attack on President Lincoln. Lincoln was an insincere man who could not be trusted. After all, he was continuing to spread "barefaced falsehoods" about Union successes on the battlefields.

Lincoln soon took an action that George could applaud. Captain Wilkes who had started the Trent affair by boarding an English ship, had been promoted to admiral by the president, and assigned to patrol the British West Indian waters. His presence, and the threat seen to English shipping and its general interests there, seemed like a deliberate provocation to the English government. Finally, Lincoln had removed Wilkes from that assignment. George saw this as an act of some courage by President Lincoln. Admiral Wilkes was greatly admired by American "rabble." This low part of American society was "all powerful." They carried American presidential elections "by numbers or by force and actually appoint the President." George hoped that having taken this step Lincoln would take additional steps to appease the English.

As July began, George awaited word on the great battle, he believed might be underway in America. He had no idea what the goal of Lee's army might be, but he hoped that he wouldn't waste the strength of his army in a vain attempt to take Washington.

Clearly, with more bloodshed at hand, it was time for the English and French governments to send negotiators to America to arrange an end to the fighting. The evils of slavery had ceased to be an element in the continued fighting. The only issue of importance remaining was getting the horrid war to end. The end result of any negotiations was already clear. It was time to recognize the independence of the Confederacy. If the Northern reason for fighting the war was reunification of the country, they had already lost. There would no longer be one country on the American continent. Their army could never capture Richmond, as they were too weak and incompetent to cross the Rappahannock. And they would never take Vicksburg. So they had no reason to fight on.

The first reports on the great battle in Gettysburg arrived in Newry on Friday, July 17th. Early optimistic dispatches reported that Lee and his army were sweeping into the northern territory unopposed by any Union opposition. This belief colored the first reports of an actual resistance to Lee's advance by any Federal troops. It was too early to establish the winner, but it was clear that Lee's advance had indeed been engaged despite George's confidence that no Union army could be found to fight him.

However, George must have been concerned that his optimism might not be justified when more information arrived. Before the battle began, he had believed this fighting would teach Lincoln and his "fellow-idiots" a lesson they would not forget. The President's conduct is "such as one would expect from an egotistical and fanatical person, who understands as much about the duties and responsibilities of his position as the insect does of the laws of nature which regulate its periodic changes."

Three days later, George grimly reported that he had been wrong. Vicksburg had indeed fallen, and on the same day the Union forces had defeated Lee at Gettysburg. He couldn't understand why General Lee would order a charge over an open field and up sloping ground at the top of which waited a well-fortified and armed army. Why Lee had forgotten the lessons of the battle of Fredericksburg puzzled him greatly.

However, unexpected news from New York lifted his spirits. The Draft riots in the city convinced George that the North was too divided to win the war, despite Southern reverses. George described the extensive damage to many buildings, and the general fighting that occurred in major parts of the city. More clarifying for George was the news that the mobs had hunted down any Negroes they could find and killed them. It confirmed for him that Negroes were unwelcome in the North and freeing them from slavery wasn't the real cause of the war. He hoped that the South could muster some quick victories and regain the initiative, as, by the following spring, the Union Army would be replenished by the new draftees.

By August, George had to report that General Meade, the victor at Gettysburg, had achieved the unthinkable. He had moved his army across the Potomac and was now operating in Confederate territory. The summer military actions had made any intervention by England and France unlikely. The war and the slaughter of soldiers of both armies, many of them sons of Ireland, would likely continue, the ending beyond view.

§

George had devoted so much of his editorial space to the Civil War that he began to get questions about why the people of Newry should be interested in a war being fought over 3000 miles away. George responded to those complaints in another leader. This war gave the English military leaders an opportunity to observe evolving tactics and leadership without any loses or costs to themselves. New weapons developed by American designers must be studied and the best ones quickly adopted on this side of the ocean.

There were two new inventions of particular interest to England. The Union industrialists had developed a high-powered cannon that had a longer range and enough power to destroy masonry fortifications. Both sides had produced iron-clad warships. Following some mysterious negotiations in 1862, the English government had agreed to build two of these new ships in the Mersey. The buyer remained a mystery but was suspected to be an emissary from the Confederacy. Technicians appeared to share the American designs and teach English shipbuilders how to build the new kind of warship. This deal apparently violated English neutrality, but this was a small matter compared to the need to have the British navy at the forefront of nautical innovation. When the iron-clads were finished, the British government took possession of them.

The second reason for Irish interest was the large number of Irish families that had sons or brothers at risk whenever the two armies faced each other. The wait for this news from America often seemed endless. When one of the armies yielded the battlefield to their opponents, they were usually unable to confirm identities of the injured or dead. The Mitchels were one such family. They knew that William was in Pickett's division when it made the hopeless charge against the Union lines. They also knew that there had been no word of him since that day.

As the waiting became unbearable, Jenny decided to return to Richmond herself with her two surviving daughters. John decided to make the trip to Washington with them to ensure their safety. However, just before they were due to sail, John learned that there was no way, no legal way, to get from Washington to Richmond, so the trip was cancelled. Mitchel had written that the only way to get to Richmond was to run the blockade, and he requested that Jenny and the two girls remain safely in Ireland, advice they shelved in favor of a daring run through the Northern blockade. Though it nearly cost them their lives, they did make it safely to Richmond.

Their reunion was darkened by news of Billy. Mitchel finally confirmed for the family that Billy had died during Pickett's hopeless charge. John explained what happened to a friend. "The gallant boy was killed on the field. I think I told you before of the manner of his death – how the color Sgt beside him was shot down in the dreadful last charge upon the Yankee positions and how Billy snatched up the banner from the falling hand and bore it in the death storm of shot and shell till he in turn was struck down. A noble death and like the boy and his blood."

§

Certainly grief over Billy's death influenced John's feelings about the war when he engaged in a controversial exchange of letters in the *Irishman* with his friends Thomas Meagher, who was then a Union general, and former commander of the famous Irish brigade, and O'Brien in Ireland. Denis Holland had sold the newspaper to P. J. Smyth on April 1st. Under his leadership, his good friends from the Young Irelanders were sure to have any letters they wrote given a prominent place in the paper and published without omissions or edits. The American Civil War had divided these old friends as it had friends and families in America. In October, Gen. Meagher wrote a letter to the *Irishman,* detailing his opinions on the war. He viewed the war as an attempt by the United States to put down a rebellion of the slave owning aristocrats of the South. The situation there was very different from the relations between Ireland and England. The South had suffered no injustices comparable to those endured in Ireland. The North had always observed the "special rights of the South." "The plain truth of the matter is fidelity to the South was a more vehement passion with the North than love of gain, love of adventure, love of liberty itself." Secession was an "insolent pretension, lawless ambition and lust for power" Meagher ended his letter by arguing that if creating the country was noble, then fighting to preserve it was equally noble.

O'Brien responded first. He viewed Meagher's letter as an effort to entice young Irishmen to emigrate to America and join the fight, rather than an attempt to explain the reasons for the war. Two years earlier, he had given a speech urging the American government to accept arbitration. Congress had refused. He lamented the loss of Irish lives that had occurred in small skirmishes and major battles during the two years since. Had these men died for Ireland, they would have been honored as heroes. But instead they had died as "mere mercenaries" of the North. O'Brien could not resist pointing out how many of these Irish soldiers under Meagher's command had died during the hopeless charge at the battle of Fredericksburg.

Like John, O'Brien believed that the war was not about slavery but about preserving the Union. Blacks were treated better in the South than in the North, just as the Irish immigrants had been. Lincoln could have freed all the slaves, but he had not done so. In fact, O'Brien believed that if Meagher had inherited slaves himself, he would never grant them freedom either. Meagher approved of the Lincoln's suspension of habeas corpus and the draft, thus proving he was a phony "champion of freedom."

John responded to these letters in early November. "For my own part, I fear that I could not write with such temper upon that subject. I am, heart and soul, a partizen of the Confederates in this war. And to me it is misery to think of the hundreds of thousands of my countrymen who had taken up arms to kill the men of the South and insult their women and lay waste their homes in order to force them to submit to a yoke they reject."

New publisher of the paper, P. J. Smyth, added a note to John's letter when he published it. "It is the first time such a charge (attacking women) has been brought against Irish troops and must surely have escaped in the haste of composition."

As the letters to the paper showed, each of the men involved had different opinions on the war. General Meagher wanted the Irish to join the Union army and help end the fighting sooner, not to oppress the South but to restore the Union. The O'Donoghue joined the conversation with strong support of the newspaper's position that the South might have had a right to secede, but the North had a right to fight to prevent that. "Separation could not fail to be disastrous to the Southern, as well as to the whole of the country." John certainly had a very different point of view which he pursued in his letters.

On November 21st, John wrote, "If all people of Ireland were of one mind upon the question of the *justice* of the war which the United States are waging against the Confederate States, it might be needless to discuss before them the policy of that war and its bearings upon the national interests of Ireland." If this war were unjust, as John believed it was, it would be wrong to support it just because it would have a positive result for Ireland. So John was puzzled as to why his friends would think that is was proper to force a union that the South didn't want.

"I desire the separation because the people of the Confederate States think proper to separate; because the restoration of the Union is impossible, except by means utterly destructive of the freedom of America; because the subjugation of the South and the maintenance of federal authority over the conquered provinces would be ruinous to the prosperity and the power of all America; and bad for Ireland."

John found the O'Donoghue's argument foolish. If the South become a conquered country at the end of the war, they would have a right to revolt that they didn't have when secession occurred. Instead, John believed that the Union government had mismanaged the separation by initiating hostilities. Had the North been patient, the South might well have consented to rejoin the union, as there was substantial support for the Union in the mountainous areas of the South where many Irish had settled. They were subsistence farmers, most of whom worked their farms without the use of slaves.

Now the situation had changed greatly. The only way the North could win was by killing Confederate soldiers and laying waste to their cities and homes. John concluded with a grim thought. "If they *succeed,* farewell to freedom in America! It will be a lamentable victory."

Smyth added his own opinion to those of the letter writers. They all agreed on the subject of Ireland, but not on the war in America. He believed "The Southern Confederacy has not the remotest chance of success." But he agreed with O'Brien that it was time for the war to end. "But peace to be lasting must be based, not upon disunion, lawlessness and slavery, but upon union, law, and freedom."

In his next letter, John turned to the issue of foreign intervention. England refused to enter into any negotiations with France to end the fighting. John lamented that France had not acted alone. "Had the French Government a year ago recognized the independence of the Confederacy and opened the blockade, it seems to me that the northerns must have given up their attempt to conquer the south as thenceforth impractical and hapless. They would have withdrawn their invading armies and ceased to rob and kill their former fellow-citizens, who only asked to be left alone. The constitution that till the outbreak of this war prevailed in all the states would have been restored to the North and could now be guarding the rights and adorning the prosperity of two nations, where there had been but one." "[W]hat insane lust for power is it that says territories twice as large as the rest of Europe without Russia must in America belong to one government only?" And if Canada should join the North and Mexico the South, there would still be two very large countries.

The O'Donoghue responded to this letter. He called the Civil War the most important issue of the times. Ireland should support the Union to keep America strong enough to face up to England. And he repeated his argument that the South had fared well under the Union and participated fully in the unified government.

Smyth commented as well. "There is much in this portion of Mr. Martin's letter with which we agree...Mr. Martin, as yet, has not ever attended to slavery though he must be aware that the object of secession was to establish an empire whose corner-stone would be slavery and that if it were not for slavery there would have been no secessions. To attempt to discuss the American question without referring to slavery, is to enact the play of Hamlet with the part of Hamlet left out."

John tried to discuss the issue one last time in early December. "I am conscious that my arguments can have no influence whatever upon the war and none upon the circumstance which makes Ireland a great recruiting-ground for the Washington government." He agreed that the Constitution favored "human freedom, dignity and prosperity." He also conceded that there would be negatives if the Union remained divided. But it was the Union that had suspended the freedoms of the Constitution to fight the war, not the South.

"The war is for subjugation or for revenge, but certainly not for the Union." If the North succeeded it would harm Irish interests. Every soldier in the Union Army would be needed to hold the South. There would be none free to fulfill the dream of many Irish nationalists that when the war ended, a trained army would be ready to fight for Irish freedom.

He restated his argument that a peaceful separation would have been the best solution. Had that happened, "all the wondrous resources of America would have remained intact, and in their full vigour. Each part would have become equal to the original."

In his postscript, John ended his participation in the chain of letters. He deeply lamented "this frenzy of destruction and massacre that decimates a people whom kinship and interest make so dear to Ireland, those horrible, but most heroic suffering of another people whom we are equally bound to love, and whom every noble heart must honour."

For the first time, John also mentioned the topic of slavery, denying that slavery had any part in secession. "'Cato' in the *Irishman* challenges me to discuss the question of negro-slavery as a portion of the question of the war. It is not a portion of the question of the war. All the world knows that the war is not made for the object of freeing the slaves, but solely to establish the government over all the states."

§

Though John worried greatly about the Civil War, he continued to struggle to create the Irish National League. Unfortunately, the effort wasn't going well. In a late August letter, he announced that the time frame for beginning the new organization had slipped from what had been originally planned. "Most of the parties desirous of establishing such an association, look to me for the introductory steps in the movement, yet I have received no mandate nor authority from the country, beyond by my nomination as one of the secretaries by the private meeting [at which time the officers had also been selected] of nationals held in Dublin some months ago. And residing so far away from Dublin, and having been absent from Ireland some weeks lately, I have not bestowed so much personal care and activity upon the matter as was, perhaps, expected from me" He pledged to his readers to be more active in the future.

"I am but a humble volunteer in this cause. But the cause is the highest and dearest that an Irishman can try to serve. I may fail in my puny effort. But let my friends believe that I will do my best to deserve success. Let them consider my efforts with indulgence, let them wait patiently for the results, believing that I shall faithfully labour to serve our country."

John continued to write more letters in the next few weeks. The first was a very long letter, detailing the history of Ireland under the Union. Often, he included statistics that would certainly attract attention. One such statistic concerned taxation in which John had a particular interest. The average income in England was £13 a head. They were taxed at a rate of four shillings per pound on that income. In Ireland, the average income was £3.15s. a person who then had to pay a tax of five shillings.

Voting was another issue. Irish landlords moved to deny leases to the people who worked their estates. Those without leases weren't allowed to vote. In 1849, well into the famine years, 72,216 people in Ireland were entitled to vote. With the decrease in the number of leases, the number of voters had dropped to about 35,000. At this point, even England realized that they must take some action to increase the number of voters.

John believed that just stating such statistics would convince the Irish that they had to be a part of a new struggle for independence. Only independence could right the wrongs that the Irish had experienced since the Union. Though he didn't yet see any signs of success, he intended to continue his efforts to stir the nationalists to peaceful and legal action.

A couple of weeks later, John wrote a final letter, recapping the history of the last attempt to attain independence. He concluded his arguments this way. "It is hoped that the national cause may thus obtain confidence and support in Ireland and respectful sympathy abroad and may be placed in a situation to profit by the opportunities which the Divine grace vouchsafes to a people who righteously endeavour to help themselves."

Smyth had published all John's letters in the *Irishman*, something George seemed unwilling to do. So it wasn't surprising that it was Smyth who announced that the letters would be published in a pamphlet form. He added a personal endorsement. "All true Irishmen have carefully perused these letters. Mr. Martin does not require that all should agree with him in matters of detail. He places his views before the country and expects that all who agree with him in the principle, firstly that all our wrongs spring from foreign rule, and secondly that organization is necessary to give effect to the unanimous desire of the Irish people for self-government—should aid him in the great work he has undertaken. How most efficiently to cooperate with John Martin is the question, which above all others, should now engage the attention of every earnest, thoughtful, practical Irish patriot."

George was certainly paying attention to the new moves of Irish nationalists. What John was doing was public and well known, but George must have been aware of increased secret activity. In early September, he wrote one of his scathing leaders that so pleased his loyalist readers. He titled the leader "The Last Monster Meeting." "The empire has survived the shock—England is still in the land of the living! Dublin Castle still remains in possession of the Earl of Carlisle and his inferiors, and the Saxons have not been exterminated. On Sunday last—the Day of Rest—a crowd of juveniles, on pleasure bent, nobly responded to the call of the leaders, and assembled in one of the wildest spots that the wildest county in Ireland can produce, the obtainment for 'Ireland' of the blessings of self-government has such a charm for the children of Tipperary that they forsook their various pales of worship, forsook their dwellings, and left their overflowing farms to the mercy of the elements on Sunday last; for what?

"Let Father Lavelle answer; let The O'Donoghue answer; let even John Martin answer. 'If they thought their presence, would render the meeting any more effective,' they would have attended. But, to add up this unkind cut, they gravely add that, although they do not think it worthwhile to visit Tipperary, the movement has their best wishes! No doubt. Yet it looks strange to see the Reverend Patrick Lavelle, PP., The Donoghue, MP., John Martin, Esquire, Nationalist, and a host of other worthies quietly declining to attend and leaving the scum of the movement—the Gills and Kickhams—to expose their figures, and bare their breasts to the drenching rains of Tipperary." This gathering had been arranged by the Fenians, not by John and his supporters. If George was aware of the disagreements between the groups, he didn't make that clear.

John still read his friend's paper regularly. This leader brought a quick response from him, which George published in the *Telegraph*. Since George had mentioned his name in a previous paper, "and that in anything but a courteous manner," John hoped that George would publish his response. George happily did so.

"You are probably aware that I have been for many years an advocate of Irish Legislative independence—that I regard the 'Union' of this country with England as a usurpation of our national rights by the English, and one which produces most disastrous effect upon our country, and that I earnestly desire to see our fellow countrymen of all sects, ranks, and conditions united for an effort to repeal the Union and restore self-government to Ireland. This being the most serious political question that Irishmen can have to consider, I readily admit that those who conscientiously differ upon it, may be excused for employing vehement language in debating it; and if the Newry Telegraph really *debated* the question, I for one would not care nicely to distinguish whether its language was scurrilous, rather than manfully vehement. But, though a constant reader of your paper, the only way in which I have learned that your opinions are hostile to Irish legislative independence is by occasionally seeing articles like the one in your last number, in which you apply foul language to those persons who declare that they desire Irish legislative independence. Permit me to say that if in heart and conscience you are opposed to a Repeal of the Union, you ought, as a public journalist whose readers are deeply interested in that question, to state the reasons which have led you to form your own opinion concerning it.

"I believe that at this moment the vast majority of those Irishmen who consider Irish politics at all are Repealers. If you think that we are wrong in the conviction at which we have arrived, show us how we are wrong, let us hear your arguments; deal respectfully—or at least courteously—with our sincere delusions; convince us that we are wrong. If you have no arguments to produce, devote your leading columns to some other subject than the national cause of your unhappy country. Ribaldry upon such a subject will in the end disgust all your readers."

George was happy to respond to John's letter. However, it was far more a personal attack on John than a careful exposition for his support of the union between England and Ireland. His defense of his position was a single sentence. If the Act of Union were to be repealed, "Ireland would suffer to such an extent, religiously and politically, that it would require many years of toil and trouble, and perhaps internal bloodshed to compensate it for the loss."

John may have still considered George a friend, but in the first sentence of his own response, George made clear that he felt limits to the obligations of friendship. "Mr. John Martin, of Kilbroney, Rostrevor, feels the indignation of a fiery National Legislator at the references we have made from time to time to the proceedings of the so-called Nationalists in Tipperary. This is not surprising; for, on the contrary, we were astonished beyond measure to find that he–for reasons known only to himself–refrained so long from thrusting himself forward in print, or in person, to defend the cause which he has espoused, but which he has not supported by climbing to the aid of his friends...Mr. Martin has considered it judicious to remain in the background of late, leaving the active service to be discharged by Messrs. Gill and Kickham, and others of a similar stamp; but, forsooth, we are not 'courteous,' we are 'scurrilous,' and are 'disgusting all our readers,' because we venture to take the name of John Martin in vain. We are not aware of the exact grounds on which our correspondent has once more taken his stand from which to fire his volleys of indignant wrath."

George continued his own "volleys." "Mr. John Martin, in his letter to us to-day has the hardihood to ask for 'arguments.' The 'reasons' demanded by our correspondent are known to everyone—Roman Catholic and Protestant alike—and if silly people persist in allowing the delusions of a misguided career, and the visions of an excited fancy to interfere with realities, no one is to blame save their monitors and themselves."

John understood George's message to mean that he had no intention of debating the issue of independence, that he would only continue to disparage John and any idea of Irish independence. So John wrote no more.

§

However, George wasn't the only supposed friend of John's on the attack. In late November the Fenians began publishing a newspaper, the *Irish People,* to spread the Fenian version of Irish Nationalism. The editor of the paper was John O'Leary. A young member of the Young Irelanders, he had successfully fled to France while John was seized and punished. When John returned from exile to live in Paris, they resumed their friendship.

O'Leary seemed considerably less friendly in his new position for his new organization. In the second edition of the *Irish People,* O'Leary explained the importance of the McManus funeral. "The night before the procession, the supremacy of the people was first vindicated in Ireland." That referred to the confrontation between the Fenians and John Martin and Father Kenyon over plans for the funeral. He called John's repeal actions "political humbug' and its members a "hideous brood."

Just before Christmas, O'Leary turned all his fire power on John. Though he never actually referred to John by name, no one with any ties to the Irish independence movement would mistake whom O'Leary was writing about. He accused him of working with the elites of Ireland. "Since O'Connell didn't succeed, the amiable gentleman in question must succeed. The amiable gentleman apparently does not in the least take into account the fact that the members of the ruling-class are not even an Irish aristocracy; that they are, for the most part, English in race, and in feeling more English than the English themselves; that they are a foreign garrison, whose existence is an obstacle to our prosperity, second only to that of British rule itself; in short, that any attempt to make Irish nationalists of them at this time of day, would be as rational and practicable as an attempt to induce hyenas to play the part of lap-dogs."

In the early part of this leader, O'Leary had discussed political issues. But next he mixed the political issue with a very personal attack. "But the amiable gentleman we refer to will drearily persist in his efforts to convert them. His boundless toleration views their shortcomings as mere trifles, his charity would have mercy in store even for fiends. Besides, he thinks obedience to our superiors in rank a duty, incumbent on all good and proper folk. He has above all, a special horror of presumptuous men, who emerge from obscurity to dream of leadership. People should dread to meddle with existing authority. He drivels interminable lectures and letters to this effect. This meek and amiable gentleman, apparently has no belief in the celebrated maxim 'the career opens to all talents' or in that other 'the tools to him who can wield them.' *Reverence the nobility* would seem to be, in his eyes, equal to any one of the 10 commandments. We fear, however hardened the confession may cause us to appear, that we shall never go over to the views of the 'amiable gentleman' however, in return to his advice to the people, we shall presume to offer him a little advice. It is thus agreeing with him in one opinion at least (which his exquisite modesty never lets him slip and opportunity of putting before the world – namely, that he is both an indifferent speaker and writer) we would suggest to him the propriety of devoting himself henceforth to that retirement, for which his amiability so benefits him; in a word, he would write and speak no more."

O'Leary ended his leader with this. "Let us each and all put trust in the might, the majesty and the glory of the people, and the revival of true national aspirations and action in our country shall, be MANIFEST TO THE WORLD!"

John Martin was not a man to be deterred by the attacks from his erstwhile friends. There was much more steel in him than was apparent from his "amiable," kind, and generous exterior.

Chapter 11

Two Paths to Independence

1863 – 1864

The negative aftermath of the attacks and disappointments that James had endured the previous year became quickly obvious. He wrote briefer entries in his journal, many days including only reports on the weather and farm activities. But he still kept track of the deaths in Donaghmore, and the progress James Alexander was making. He stopped referring to his wife as the "Dandy" and began referring to her as "grandma." Still, there was no mention of any health problems in any entry or a descent into despair.

On the day before Christmas of 1862, James, acting on behalf of the Donaghmore Session, described an event that was a major step forward in his long dream to have a manse for the minister of his church. "Joseph drove A Douglas, & me to Newry—fine dry day—where I signed a Lease of three acres &c of the lands of Loughorne for the purpose of building a manse for the minister of Donaghmore, on it."

A family reunion occurred just after Christmas. "A fine day—met John Martin and Lizze Frazer, at your Aunts about two oclock. John Harshaw came out of Newry on the car with them, John, & me brought her over <u>here</u> where we had tea. She gave me a book containing the likeness of <u>Absalom</u>, & <u>Willy</u>, his wife & <u>three children</u>—two boys & a girl. Miss Lizze John and Joseph left immediately after tea & fell back on your Aunts, & Joseph showed her the bower, & the old Lake shore &c &c."

Lizze was James's grand niece, the daughter of Jane Martin and Robert Frazer, who had emigrated to Canada two decades earlier. She had traveled to Ireland from her home in Ontario Canada to visit her parents' homeland for the first time. So there were many places that her mother had told her about that she wanted to see, one of them the bower. This was a ruined cottage surrounded by briars. The Harshaw and Martin children had found a pathway under and around the prickly barricade, which they kept secret. They often gathered there when they had time to play and wanted a place to escape the commands of their parents. James's son Willy wrote a poem about it, which certainly had been sent to the family in Canada. James had included a copy of the poem in his journal.

James had never met any of his niece's many children. However, the advent of faster ships made the trip across the Atlantic less daunting. The fact that she brought with her such a special present showed how close the ties between the families in America and Canada remained.

A month later, word of John's donation of land for the manse was reported in the *Telegraph*. This time George set aside his attacks on John, writing a very complimentary report. John had increased the amount of land he donated to five acres of prime Loughorne property. "It is only in keeping with the generosity of Mr. Martin's character to make such a grant as this, but the value of the gift is enhanced in the present instance by the fact that, notwithstanding the high value of land in "Donaghmore, no purchase money has been asked, whilst the yearly rent is fixed at a very moderate sum."

With land for the manse ensured, the manse committee moved on to planning the construction of the new building. James attended one meeting at the church classroom. There the contract to supervise the work was given to James Lyons. The carpenter work was given to Calvin & Coughran. These men would follow the plan designed by a well-known architect, Mr. Barre, who formerly lived in Newry but had moved to Belfast. The building would be a two-story brick building with a grand view of the Mourne Mountains.

Both James in his diary and George in his paper described the ceremony to lay the cornerstone on June 8th. James and his son Robert walked over to the property where the ceremony was to take place. The weather was not cooperative. Rather than enjoying warm sunshine, members attending the ceremony huddled under umbrellas for some protection from a heavy downpour. The rain started as Rev. Elliott began to speak and continued while John gave his remarks. Still the stone was laid, and a long-held dream had become concrete.

George published his own account of the event. Despite the bad weather, a large crowd of neighbors as well as members attended. Many dignitaries also attended. Beside John and Rev. Elliott, the minister of the local Church of Ireland, Rev. J. Campbell Quinn, came to offer support. Hill Irvine who owned several of the townlands of Donaghmore had come out from Newry. George also acknowledged the presence of several ministers, including Rev. Robert Harshaw. Rev. Lindsay was not one of them.

After singing and prayer, Rev. Elliott offered remarks based on a passage from Nehemiah. He thanked the people of the area for the financial sacrifices and persistence needed to make this day possible. He gave special thanks to John for his generous donation of the five-acre site without a purchase price. Besides the donation of land, John had donated additional funds for the construction of the manse.

John was pleased that the manse was to be built in Loughorne, the townland in which he had been born. It was a central place for the minister to live. Ever modest, John maintained he deserved no more thanks than any other donor.

John's brief remarks were followed by a measurement of the site by Thomas Greer who was the treasurer of the congregation. Thomas himself donated £50 toward the construction. Then the cornerstone was set in the proper place and John fixed it in place with the assistance of James McWatty who was another large donor for the cause.

Rev. Quinn then ended the ceremony with a closing prayer for the men who would build the manse and Rev. Elliott who would be the first minister to live there. The rain had stopped, the cornerstone properly laid, and a long-held dream had come true.

§

John was pleased that the manse construction was proceeding well, taking advantage of the long summer days. But nothing deterred him from his efforts to establish the Irish National League. John was such a well-known man in Ireland, and so deeply respected by friend and foe alike that he was seen as a threat to the growth of the Fenians who intended to foment a revolution in Ireland. They had little interest in the peaceful agitation that John supported. So the attacks by John O'Leary in the *Irish People* which had begun in the first editions of the new paper continued.

In early January, O'Leary wrote a leader on the subject of John's letter on Irish land issues. He explained how he was putting aside his personal feelings toward John to fulfill his perceived obligations to the Fenian cause. "It is painful to us to be obliged to speak harshly of so well-meant a politician as Mr. Martin, but an imperative sense of duty compels us to pronounce it, for all practical purposes, utterly useless." The only thing that John had said that O'Leary agreed with was that John lacked "that force of character which fits a man for a leading position in times of trouble."

The Fenians intended to ensure the failure of the movement John was laboring to build. "We shudder at the prospect." However, he didn't think John could succeed, so there was no impelling reason for the Fenians to launch a full-scale attack on John. O'Leary and the Fenians believed the majority of Irish nationalists would prefer the Fenians approach than that of the Irish National League. He was certain that 90% of Irish nationalists believed that independence could only be achieved by revolution. O'Leary ended his leader with these words. "The present writer cannot bring this notice to a close without expressing his very high respect for Mr. Martin's moral character; but it is not because he feels strongly the private worth of the man that he should neglect to point out the public faults of the teacher."

Despite the attacks from the Fenians, John persisted in his efforts. He wrote a letter from Kilbroney on January 18th, which was published in many newspapers across Ireland, announcing the first meetings of the Irish National League. He began by condemning the Act of Union. It was supposed to allow Ireland to be governed as a free people, "in accordance with our own interests and wishes." As John had watched the results of sixty years of the Union, he believed that the results were greatly different. The Union had, in reality, "made England our masters, and given them absolute control over our liberties, our land, our industry, our revenue, and all that is ours." England had grown rich over the years, while Ireland had become poor. All Irish classes had suffered greatly from the arrangement.

The Irish National League was founded as an outlet for the frustration of all classes who had been damaged by the Union. Most importantly, they hoped to be a voice for Ireland's wrongs, not only in England with the British government, but across Europe as well. The organizing committee was hoping that enough people would join in this legal movement to impress England with the need to listen to the Irish pleas and free their country. The British government had given independence to Canada and Australia, so clearly the wishes of the Irish weren't revolutionary. This was the time for the Irish to follow the path of those two countries and achieve Irish self-government.

At the end of January, O'Leary reported progress in the formation of the Irish National League. The group now had an official leadership. Daniel O'Donoghue was the President, J. F. Maguire the Vice President and Peter Gill the Secretary. O'Leary was pleased John was not an officer. "We regret exceedingly that so well-meaning a man as Mr. Martin should have set such an infernal machine as this in operation, but it will be some elation to us for this League, if for the future we can leave Mr. Martin alone and deal only with co-Leaguers. It is unpleasant to us to have to speak in terms of condemnation of Mr. Martin or his proceedings. But, of course, about your O'Donoghue and people of that kind, we need have no such compunctious visitings."

The Irish National League and the Fenians could have cooperated on various issues, but they did not. One such issue was a plan to place a statue of the late Prince Albert in College Green on a site where nationalists had dreamed of erecting a statue of Henry Grattan. A protest meeting was scheduled at the Round Room of the Rotunda for Monday, February 22nd. The crowd attempting to get into the room was estimated to be at more than twenty thousand. The O'Donoghue was to take the chair but was caught in the massive crowd and had great trouble making his way to the stage.

Between the crowd that overwhelmed the capacity of the room, and a suspicious looking group of shabbily dressed men who had come early to occupy prime spots in the front of the stage, organizers should have anticipated trouble. John was on the stage as A. M. Sullivan took the chair. Sullivan's appearance was greeted with catcalls and hisses from the audience. Much as he struggled to be heard, his words were buried under the noise. The O'Donoghue finally gained the stage, but before he could offer the first resolution, the ruffians who were near the front managed to rush the stage, overturning chairs to use as clubs, scattering the speakers and sending most of them fleeing in panic from the stage. The invaders grabbed the green covers from the tables and waved them about over their heads like victory banners. Even the efforts of priests couldn't gain enough order for anyone to speak. With that kind of tumult continuing unchecked, the panicked audience fled for safety into the dark night.

John quickly returned to his sister's house in Dublin, and wrote a letter of support for his friend, A. M. Sullivan, who had been the target of much of the anger at the meeting. "There were some rowdy Irishmen there, who took means to prevent the citizens of Dublin from publicly saying their mind upon the proposed desecration of College Green." John referred to the rioters as "flunkeys of the Corporation and the government." "They can *do* nothing for Ireland themselves, but they can *obstruct* the efforts of others."

"I wish we had real loyalty in Ireland–the honourable submission, the proud obedience of free citizens to their own National Government and laws– the chivalrous fealty of free citizens to the Constitution and throne which their own country has freely adopted."

John believed that the disruption was caused by loyalists supporting the planned honor for Prince Albert. However, the true source of the attack was soon made clear in the *Irish People*. O'Leary claimed that the "people had gained a great moral victory." Though the Fenians also disapproved of the Albert statue, they were more disturbed by the idea that A. M. Sullivan would be part of the meeting. They believed Sullivan had been implicated in the arrest of some of the early Fenians, by publishing a piece about them in his paper. So to them, Sullivan was only "pretending to be a patriot."

O'Leary claimed that they hadn't paid anyone to disrupt the meeting, though they believed that someone had. The Fenians in the audience had happily joined in the rioting to oppose the leaders of the meeting.

John and the ad-hoc committee that had organized the ill-fated meeting met again to plan their next steps. Many suggestions were made, one being that Sullivan should disappear from the meeting in an effort to attract Fenian supporters. That suggestion was soundly rejected. The committee instead proceeded with plans for a second meeting to carry out the thwarted plans of the first meeting. This time they would plan more carefully.

Many people volunteered to help secure the meeting. Tickets were restyled and handed out to carefully vetted supporters. The stage was fitted with fencing that prevented anyone from charging the stage. Only the space occupied by the speakers would be open to the audience. Additional policemen were stationed outside ready to arrest any rowdies. Still, the Fenians were able to obtain a ticket and print counterfeit ones to dole out to Fenian supporters. Fortunately, news of this scheme reached the planners in time for them to print new ones.

Crowds gathered several hours before the start of the meeting. Stewards with long poles were stationed just inside the doors to keep them in order while they waited. Fenians tried very hard to break through the guards to enter the hall. But they proved unable to breach the barricades. The balconies were soon filled to capacity, as the floor capacity was reduced in part to allow a space between attendees and the stage. All the precautions seemed to work. The O'Donoghue was the main speaker, and his remarks received thunderous applause. While there was occasional shouting, there was no rioting. This time John didn't attend.

Strangely, the fact that the meeting proceeded without interruption was seen as yet another Fenian victory. "The ruin of Mr. Sullivan and his party as politicians is truly overwhelming. No human shell arrayed against them could have ruined all their prospects so irretrievably as they have contrived to do themselves." He ended his leader by claiming that "the revival of agitation is an impossibility. The anti-agitation party is stronger now than ever. No agitation monger dare meet the people face to face!" O'Leary was mistaken in his prediction. John had the Irish National League up and running.

George noted this in a leader in early March. He chose a title that he knew would attract readers, "New Irish Dodge." "We had thought that the ridiculous retreat of the O'Donoghue and his coadjutors at a meeting of nationalists in the Rotunda, would have deterred them for the next ten years at least. The triumph of the coal porters was so complete, and the defeat of the leaders so ignominious that, except in Ireland, the days of sham patriotism were ended."

An editorial in the *Nation,* currently edited by T. D. Sullivan, A. M.'s older brother, had stirred George to action. Sullivan's article gave George a great opportunity to employ his skill at writing and the power of his sarcasm. The *Nation* had published the principles of the Irish National League, which John had put into action. The committee had voted unanimously to proceed with what George considered the next in line of failed attempts to separate Ireland from England. The Irish National League put the goal this way, "'the restoration of a separate and independent Irish legislature.'" George saw that statement as it was intended, broad enough to attract everyone with similar wishes, "a small number, we should hope."

George informed his Newry readers about the Irish National League that most of them would have been unaware of. This group, George reported, hoped to attract members who differed "'in religion, in politics, in tastes, in everything except in the one principle of loyal resolve to restore the legislative independence of their country.'" George saw treason when the League spoke of "means." They pledge to pursue their goal of "'self-government by any and every means which it may deem righteous, honorable, prudent, and expedient.'" In order to support the expenses of the group, there would be annual dues of 1 shilling or more. This fact allowed George to make his case that groups such as this had a "characteristic itch in the palm…for the money of the starving peasantry."

Then George made an unusual argument against the basic concept of independence. He claimed that "the independence of our island is a myth. It never had what could properly be called independent Government." He described the scene at the meeting in Dublin as proof that Ireland wasn't capable of governing itself. "[O]f all nations in the world we should be the most ridiculous; for if there never were a loyal Protestant party in Ireland, the Nationalists, and the Fenians would deluge the land with blood." If there were enough members of the group to attempt to enact their plans, "there is a loyal element amongst us sufficiently powerful to baffle their plans, while England coming to the aid of this element would leave the country a desert."

The final argument that George offered his readers was a restatement of the promises of the Act of Union, which Nationalists believed hadn't materialized. "Our prosperity is irrevocably dependent on Great Britain, and our true policy is to cultivate her friendship, to imitate her industry, and to share the rewards of her energy. This we cannot do by pursuing every phantom of the imagination of which the O'Donoghue or Mr. John Martin may approve. We have had too much of national nonsense, and this latest effort to reproduce it will be a signal and contemptible failure."

The Fenians joined George in his strong critique of John's efforts with another attack of their own. O'Leary, in a leader of March 12th, began by contrasting Ireland in the days of O'Connell and the present. At that earlier time, Ireland had had a population of eight million. They should have been able to attain independence. "The blame has been laid at the door of the Young Ireland party, who broke up the great national confederacy created by O'Connell. The truth is that the great national confederacy was a great national delusion."

The charges leveled against the Young Irelanders, that they were "enemies of religion, the enemies of their country, incapable of effecting any good themselves, and only potent to obstruct the efforts of others," were baseless. "Who could serve Ireland manfully and truly must be prepared for misrepresentation and calumny, not only from the enemy and the enemy's hirelings, but from men professing to love Ireland–nay from men who perhaps do love Ireland."

More had changed since those days than just numbers. Now the majority of Irish citizens were determined to be free. "The misty longing for liberty has given place to a manly determination to work for it." This determination was real even though outside observers might see no signs of action yet. "But those who know the people, see in their silence the surest symptom of life."

Then O'Leary turned to the recent events in Dublin, giving his perspective as to their meaning. He told his readers that the demonstration against John and his friends was "a growl to warn all whom it might concern that they were no longer to be trifled with. Let us hope that the warning has been understood, and that there will be no necessity for repeating it."

Having set the stage, O'Leary launched a full-scale attack on John and his supporters. No true Irishmen would allow themselves to be tempted to work for independence through legal and constitutional means. "Nor will they permit bad men or even weak men to appear as the recognized representatives of their principles under any circumstances whatsoever."

O'Leary then asked his readers what he believed was the crucial question, "How can the people have faith in the National cause if men whom they distrust play the part of National Leaders?" O'Leary answered his own question with a perspective on John's deficits. "The conduct of Mr. Martin and the O'Donoghue is utterly inexplicable. They have done their best to place a weapon in a hand which has aimed many a treacherous blow against men whom the Nationalists of Ireland regard with trust and love, and gratitude. Mr. Martin's tactics are, to say the least, peculiar." O'Leary was confident that most Irish patriots had already discovered that John wasn't a leader worthy of respect or support.

As O'Leary wrote those words, he knew that John would never be deterred by this warning and personal attacks. But as he closed the article,

O'Leary urged his readers to just laugh at John and his fake patriots and drive them "off the stage" with humor.

§

George certainly followed events in Dublin closely, but he seldom wrote about them. He had several other overriding interests, one being the war still raging on across the Atlantic. In March Lincoln changed his military assignments: Grant to be in overall command and immediate command of the Army of the Potomac and Sherman to command the forces in the west. Beginning in May, Grant drove towards Richmond, Virginia, the Confederate capitol, while Sherman drove towards Atlanta, Georgia, carrying the war to a new area of the Confederacy and ultimately threatening to divide it further. Through the summer, the battles were bloody and progress of Northern armies slow. After Stedman captured Atlanta in September, his army on their march to the sea cut loose from its supply lines, and lived off the land, destroying railroads, seizing food, and destroying plantations in their path. Grant's army had invested Richmond and Petersburg by mid-June, and his campaign evolved into trench warfare with unsuccessful attempts to break Lee's lines. George didn't approve of the tactics of either general. He found them totally unlike "dignified warfare."

Despite the Northern army's invasion of Confederate territory, George still supported independence for the South. He believed that the South had organized its armies more skillfully, and its troops had showed greater valor. However, they didn't have the reserves of soldiers that the North could deploy on any battlefield. Many of these new Northern recruits were refugees from Ireland.

When George next returned to the subject in May, he believed that little had changed. He still held fast to his belief that the North could never win. It hadn't gotten the number of new soldiers that they expected from the draft and had begun to offer a signing bonus of $350. In despair, George mused that it might be time to let the two sides, "cut their own throats."

As the weather warmed, and planting was underway in Ireland, George clung to his hopes for a quick end to the American war. After a three-day battle in Virginia resulted in the loss of 40,000 men with no important visible results, George repeated his recommendation that negotiations should begin without more delay. Since it was obvious that the North couldn't win, mediation was the only way to end the carnage.

No country stepped forward to offer to conduct mediation meetings by the first anniversary of the battle of Gettysburg. So the fighting continued. But other significant things had happened. Congress repealed the Fugitive Slave law, though that action left George unimpressed. He still believed that most Northerners had no more interest in freeing the slaves than the plantation owners of the South. George did still hold his strong views on the evils of slavery. He would be well pleased if the war actually resulted in freedom for the slaves. That would certainly happen no matter which side won. "Slavery is doomed."

A week later, George wrote another long leader on the war. He reported that the war wasn't going well for the North on any front. Grant's moves toward Richmond were still resulting in many casualties. Sherman seemed to be motionless around Atlanta. Finally, a move that George had long predicted seemed to be taking place in the North, a growing demand for an end of the war no matter what the terms of settlement were. Increasing numbers of Northern citizens seemed to realize that the Union had ended when Lincoln issued the Emancipation Proclamation and freed the slaves. Surely no Southern supporter would assent to rejoin the Union when his property had been stolen away from him. Now was the time for the North to admit the truth and end the fighting. Though George didn't admit it in writing, his theories were influenced by his fear that a civil war could be in Ireland's future, with even more difficult problems. In America, the armies came from two different sections of the country. If civil war broke out in Ireland, the fighting would pit neighbor against neighbor.

§

One of the other events that attracted George's attention was the death in early June of William Smith O'Brien. George acknowledged O'Brien's ancient Irish lineage, going back to Brian Buru who drove the Vikings from Dublin at the battle of Clontarf. Therefore, "he would have had a distinguished position in society if he had taken his inspiration from reason instead of imagination and regulated his conduct by argument rather than impulse." He was the son of a baronet, a brother of a lord, and an elected member of Parliament at the age of twenty-three. A great life had stretched before him.

When O'Brien took an interest in the "foolish agitation for the Repeal of the Union, he bartered everything except honour. Still, he gave up a proud and productive future on a strange view of patriotism." "Patriotism is a nice thing, but it does not necessarily involve a revolt against the constitutional authorities–a rebellion which would have deluged the land with our blood, and left England still more than ever the mistress of this country. Patriotism in Ireland is to teach the people to observe the law; to rival England in her cultivation of the arts of peace; to grow better crops and induce capitalists to come and open up means of employment; to spread quietness and industry in society, and comfort and contentment in domestic life."

Instead, of following the true path that George so clearly saw, O'Brien had followed a different path, seeking to obtain Irish independence. "Simple-minded men invariably become the victims of the agitation in which they engage." George saw O'Brien's efforts toward independence as pathetic and humorous, ending his efforts in a remote mountain cabbage patch in 1848. He was soon arrested, tried, and sentenced to death. Only his high station in life allowed him to escape death dangling from a noose, and instead receiving the very lenient sentence of a life in exile. Even that generous sentence was remitted by further leniency allowing him to return to Ireland, a free man again. His later speeches and writings showed that he had not repented from his faulty notion of the true meaning of patriotism.

And so another of the Young Irelanders had died. His character was pure, but he put his faith in people who were duplicitous and venal. "But his views were erroneous, and the mode he employed to accomplish them the most extravagantly absurd that could have been attempted. Rebellion against England. It has been repeatedly tried, and always ended disastrously. We have no fleet to challenge their authority on the sea, where she is all-powerful; no standing army to meet her on the land, where she is almost equally invincible. Furthermore, we are not united amongst ourselves as to the propriety of self-government. One-third of the population, and that including a monopoly of the wealth and intelligence, not only do not seek any such change, but would risk life and property in opposing it."

This opinion was one that John recognized and made actual revolution impossible at the moment. That was precisely why his Irish National League promoted Nationalist unity legally and peacefully. Should the divisions in Ireland be overcome, John was convinced that England would grant Ireland her independence. But he would distinctly disagree with George's conclusion. "We are united to England for weal or woe, and we are bound to make the best we can of the bargain."

John was somewhat sanguine about O'Brien's death. He recognized that O'Brien had been very unhappy after his wife's death and very concerned about problems with the family estate. He was also distressed by the apathy of Irish nationalists and the actions of the Fenian branch of Irish nationalists. "So he wished to die and be at rest, and he is at rest."

On the other hand, John felt differently about life, as he explained in a letter to his friend Eva, a prominent nationalist poet, who had married fellow exile Kevin O'Dogherty. There was something in his nature that "causes me to eat and drink and laugh lightly and enjoy life as much now that I am descending the vale of my years leaving friend after friend buried behind me, and fast approaching my goal with nothing affected of all I most desired to do as ever I did when my fellows were full of youthful blood and hopes, dreams were the brightest. Or it is partly the bountiful cheerfulness of heart that nature bestowed upon me and partly the indifference to life—not God knows that I do not love things beautiful and enjoy the exercise in myself and others of all the power of life in innocence—but the indifference of dying soon or late has grown upon me for several years past."

There were two other issues reported in the *Telegraph* that attracted but small attention at the time. They were not burning issues in Parliament either. Only later would the status quo be challenged. The first was possible legislation to repeal the special status of the Church of Ireland as the official church established by law and to be supported by law forever. There were rumblings of change coming, as choosing one religion to stand superior to all others violated the growing realization that old practices of government were undemocratic. But as yet there seemed no sign of any action that would unleash this potential crisis.

The second issue was a growing idea that the current voting system in Ireland was an obstacle to democracy. George supported the status quo, maintaining that voting was a "solemn trust." That meant that everyone was entitled to see how every voter handled that trust. The fact that sometimes voters were bullied or beaten when their votes offended someone else was no problem for George. Public voting meant that only people who had voted badly were subject to such treatment. If Ireland had a secret ballot, innocent voters might be subject to the same treatment, though they had voted as directed. The secret ballot produced "sneaking." The better solution would be to increase the voting requirements thus disenfranchising irresponsible voters.

§

John's positive attitude toward life had made it possible for him to remain optimistic in the early months of 1864. The Irish National League had occupied much of his time and attention during a year of planning and organizing. But months after its launch at the end of January, the League wasn't flourishing as he had hoped it would. Still, month after month, he traveled to Dublin to hold meetings on the first Tuesday of each month in the rooms that he had leased at 24 D'Olier Street. When the friends who had offered support failed to honor their commitments, John recognized that he would have to keep the League functioning alone. The O'Donoghue, the president of the League never attended a single meeting, despite frequent promises to do so.

John soon wrote a letter reaching out to the Irish people explaining the new organization and inviting them to join. He stated that its primary goal was to restore an Irish Parliament to lead the country. The British government had promised the Irish people they would greatly benefit from the Act of Union despite the dissolution of the existing Irish Parliament. However, something very different had resulted. It had "made the English our masters and given them absolute control over our liberties, our land, our industry and all that is ours. The 'union' is a fraudulent political partnership, maintained by force against the consent of the Irish people, in order to enable the English to appropriate our wealth, and rule our country for their selfish purposes, its effects are manifest in Ireland's miserable poverty, her decay and decline in industry, and commerce, art, science, and literature, public spirit and national considerations." Only England had benefited from the Union.

Naturally, the British would hold tightly to the arrangement that had been so advantageous to them. With concentrated power existing on the other side of the Irish sea, a feeling of helplessness had settled over Ireland, resulting in "political division and weakness." But John clung to the belief that most Irishmen hated the current situation and were willing to act to free Ireland, perhaps in greater numbers at that moment than at any time since the revolt of 1848.

The aristocracy of Ireland remained one of the great obstacles to any independence movement. They were educated in England and adopted English ways, forgetting about their obligations to Ireland. "Our middle classes are afraid of the effects of English displeasure upon their business or professional interests. Our peasantry and the mass of our population, profoundly disaffected against the rule who see oppression weigh heavier upon them begin to despair of obtaining protection either through patriotic action of their national leaders or from the mercy of England and to sigh for foreign intervention as their only chance of relief."

The Irish National League would seek to unify the different classes of Irish society, "to gain the union of all races, creeds, classes and parties to work in honorable ways to get an independent legislature in Ireland."

While John might have felt that he was alone, he learned that he did have support across Ireland when responses to his letter produced editorial support in many papers, and some personal letters of support as well. The *Nation* had a major leader on the subject, although the editor did have some doubts about whether even John could "bring fractured nationalists together." Certainly the Fenians had made it clear already that they had no intention of helping John. Still A. M. Sullivan, the editor wrote, "It is not bluster or threat, or lamentation that is wanted from the new society, its business is not to wander among the tombs, uttering rhapsodies or vowing vengeance. It is rather to bring a number of patriotic Irishmen into concrete political association, consolidating their strength and making it a power which can really…be employed by the Irish nation in her resistance to a hateful bondage, and for the assertion of her national rights."

A letter of personal support arrived from William O'Neill Daunt who had been an Irish activist since he first joined O'Connell's Repeal Association two decades before. "John Martin of Kilbroney, the great Presbyterian repealer" had written "asking permission to insert my name in the list of provincial committees of repealers. Although I see no ground for expecting proximate triumph yet, I comply with readiness. The Union is a most chimera and horrible outrage on Ireland, and it is the duty of every Irish nationalist to say so, time and place fitting."

John had completed the basic steps that were traditional to create any new organization. He had established a support committee and created a set of rules to explain how the organization would work. Finally he had issued an invitation for all Nationalists in Ireland to join him in the work of achieving Irish independence. Now it was time for the League to actually do something to help the cause.

§

Some months before, John Dillon, an old friend from the days of the Young Irelanders, had written a carefully researched letter to Parliament making the surprising accusation that for over a decade the British government had been overtaxing the Irish people. Parliament had responded by creating a commission to study the issue. The committee was holding hearings to collect information on which to base their report. This was a cause that John wanted to support. So he asked his new friend Daunt to write a report from the League to assist Dillon's effort.

Daunt was willing to honor John's request, but asked John to provide some information that he could use in his letter. John was happy to help. On April 28th, he wrote a long letter to Daunt laying out his beliefs. He told Daunt that he didn't think that anyone could actually prove in a court of law what most Irishmen believed, but it was important to raise the issue. John explained his view of the general financial situation of Ireland since the Union. One after another, Irish industries had left for England, and so now merchandise which used to be made in Ireland had to be imported with loss of jobs on one hand and increased costs on the other.

"Before the potato famine that whereas the great part of the poorer peoples food and clothing was produced by their own home industry, now nearly all of it is bought with money from English and foreign markets." The only industry left in Ireland was the linen industry which was making some mill owners rich. However, the people of Ulster were no more able to afford clothing made of linen than the citizens of the rest of Ireland.

Farms were suffering as well. Fields across Ireland that were once carefully cared for and very productive, that supported many large Irish families, were now going into "desert wastes." The farms along the west coast which previously supplied great quantities of food to England were now producing nothing "except fly-fishing and deer stalking."

"We see the decay of our country in EVERYTHING by which other countries judge of their own prosperity—everything, both moral and material. I see the steady demoralization—the steady civilization BACKWARDS—of our people, that is in progress." He saw the Catholic Church more interested in expanding their facilities than in easing the fears of their people. This perceived neglect was causing Catholics to move away from their church.

At this point in his letter, John acknowledged that he hadn't yet touched on the issue of taxation, which was after all the purpose of the letter. John again expressed his worry that the reality the Irish faced would be very hard to prove to English satisfaction. Over-taxation was a matter of opinion. "Certainly the English will not admit that they rob us, that they snatch the food from our hungry lips, the tools from our hands, the clothes from our backs—will not admit that they do us any wrong, or that any misery we suffer is in the remotest degree chargeable upon them."

But John saw a glimmer of hope. There might be people well versed enough in financial affairs to provide the critical link between cause and effect. Statistics should offer the required proof. But John still didn't think that England would accept even statistical evidence. Without providing great help to Daunt, John turned to reporting that the League wasn't doing well. He was still getting little assistance from the very people who had urged him to action with promises to help. To make matters worse, the Fenians seemed to enjoy disrupting League meetings.

Letters from the League and Dillon's analysis became part of the official record of the Parliamentary commission. In July, the Commission released its report. They reported that their assignment was impossible. They were attempting to cover the sixty-five years the Union had existed and would need much more time for proper study and deliberation. Thus they just requested that the work of the committee be continued during the next session.

Some members, including four Irish members produced their own addendum to the official report. Their assessment of the situation in Ireland was rather stark, according to the testimony that they had heard. They supported a reduction of taxes, and efforts to support farmers who made permanent improvements. Farmers should be able to fund any improvements through reductions in their taxes. Extending manufacturing could also help the Irish economy. What inequalities that existed in the tax code between Ireland and England should be repealed.

George wrote a long leader explaining the results to his readers. There wasn't time before the end of the session to process the great amount of personal testimony they had heard. "But there is one disadvantage in this plethora of information. No art can make the several parts consistent with one another. Ireland, we are told, has suffered from a severe attack of acts of British Parliament, and also from a repeal of former acts, the Union has increased her debt say some, and, according to others, it alone preserved her from destruction, the failure of the potato crops, the emigration, the subsequent bad harvests, the want of capital, skill and energy, over-taxation, the absence of dockyards and manufactures, the moist climate, the spongy soil, absenteeism, and in general her 'barbarous' character are some of the causes that have been assigned for her poverty and wretchedness."

Unfortunately, the value of land had declined, so much of it had gone out of cultivation. Cereal crops had lost much of their value as had cattle. But once this testimony had been offered and seemingly had convinced the committee of their validity, another group of witnesses appeared with a different view. They maintained that the complaint was "imaginary." Ireland was about to become very prosperous if political "quacks" could be silenced.

George didn't approve of the cures that had been suggested by the Irish members. "We want no more than to be treated fairly. That officious over-kindness which is always insisting on doing us with new medicines and making us the subjects of every experiment in the art of legislation is not less injurious to our welfare than the restrictions which in former years, cramped our commerce and destroyed our manufactures. Let us determine to help ourselves instead of parading every petty cause of complaint before the world, and in a short time the population of the country, though less numerous than it was twenty years ago, will be far more prosperous and happy than even in the golden age when native kings ruled over naked warriors."

§

The commitment prominent leaders had made to John remained unfulfilled as the months passed. Foremost of those friends was the O'Donoghue, the man who was the supposed head of the organization. John had "consented to found the League because the O'Donoghue entreated me to do so. Unfortunately, he is both lazy and unambitious though possessed of all the material of character for a good and respectable Irish leader."

Still, John pushed on with a second action. In July, John created a Declaration of Irish Grievances, thirteen separate issues that were publicized across Ireland. He began by pointing out the ultimate grievance. In 1782, England had signed an agreement with Ireland to establish a Parliament in Ireland. The agreement stated that it was to be a permanent law that couldn't be overturned by any later Parliamentary action. Clearly the Act of Union which did away with the Irish Parliament after years of existence violated this agreement.

This violation had led to all of Irish grievances. "That the decay of public spirit of genius, of literature, of art, of industry has here as elsewhere resulted from the loss of independence. And in addition to this, the foreign rule under which we suffer is the source of abuses and of suffering such as are found nowhere but in Ireland."

The Irish population had dropped by three million people in the same time that the English population had grown by four million. Ireland could feed all its population, even a much larger one than they had at present, while England was unable to do the same. So they needed to take Irish food. Also unfair were English actions that prevented Irish participation in the growing industrialization occurring in many countries around the world. The British government wanted no competition so close to home.

The Irish farmers who produced so much food for England were under the total control of the landlords many of whom were English. They kept farmers working under yearly leases, which meant that they could be ejected from their holdings without cause. Farmers were left with only three options, "leave, starve or beg."

Then John turned to specific acts of the British Parliament that treated Ireland differently than the rest of England. The first was the Establishment of a religion to which only a small number of Irish belonged, and which required followers of the majority faith to support this minority church. "The religious feuds thus perpetrated between Protestants and Catholics embitter all the relations of life in Ireland and keep Irishmen from combining for the common interest and honour of their country." These feuds made English control in Ireland much easier.

To ensure that the Irish voice in Parliament was weak and easy to ignore, the Union allotted Ireland 105 seats out of a total of 658. This was far short of the membership in Parliament to which the size of the Irish population entitled them. When seats were reapportioned some years later, Irish gained a mere three seats.

Some sections of the Act of Union were strictly observed. Others weren't. Ireland was to have gained equality with the rest of England under law. But as the years passed, the laws for Ireland differed greatly from those enacted for the rest of Great Britain, including Scotland and Wales. Ireland wasn't allowed to form voluntary militias; they had only a limited right to guns and no right to a fair trial, all rights provided to the rest of Great Britain.

Next on his list of grievances was the issue of fair taxation, which was currently being investigated in England. Though Ireland was the poorer country, its citizens had to pay almost exactly the same taxes as rich England. When it came to the income tax, England paid 4s 3/4d to the pound. Ireland paid 6s 3 3/4d. Certainly that was strong evidence of unfair taxation, even though the Taxation Commission failed to see that fact as definitive. In addition, Ireland had to pay three million pounds annually to the British treasury. Most of the five million pounds paid in annually in rentals to the landlords passed on to England for use there. The Irish population was left starved for cash as well as food.

Emigration to other countries to escape these problems did provide some help for Ireland. Those living elsewhere sent home to Ireland more than a million pounds a year to help their remaining relatives and the Catholic Church. But with the young and strong leaving in huge numbers, more than a hundred thousand a year, there was another problem. These refugees were the healthy young people who were needed to work in Ireland. The people who couldn't leave were the elderly, blind, and mentally ill. They were fast becoming a large enough percentage of the population to further strain Irish resources.

John ended his List of Grievances with a reminder of the disdain shown the Irish people by Queen Victoria, at the direction of the government. A petition circulated around Ireland asking for independence had been signed by four hundred eighty thousand citizens. But the Queen made no acknowledgement of its existence, and violating custom, never produced a response.

Item 13 concluded the list. "A people, who, disarmed, disorganized and in effect disfranchised, suffer under irresistible force, will have sympathy from all who love freedom and hate injustice."

John intended this document to be read across Europe. To achieve this goal, he began by translating his list into French, intending to provide translations for other countries of Europe. With that in view, he commissioned two thousand copies to be published to send to France. He hoped to raise sympathy for Irish wrongs among England's neighbors, who would hear Irish cries and quickly act to remediate the situation.

George noted John's creation, but he didn't publish it. He focused mainly on the issue of the petition. He admitted that the nationalists had collected an impressive number of signatures. But he disputed that this number would be matched if the issue of independence actually came to a vote. The Protestants of Ireland would uniformly vote against Irish independence. Furthermore, George offered a novel argument. If Irish separation should come to a vote, all the citizens of Great Britain, not just the Irish, should have a vote on the issue. Separation itself would be a grievance to many in Ireland, a grievance created not by England but by themselves.

§

Despite special events like the laying of the cornerstone of the Donaghmore Manse, spring of 1864 was difficult for James. On two occasions, he complained of "feeling poorly." His handwriting was increasingly shaky. To make matters worse, Robert's son James became suddenly ill and quickly died.

However, with warmer weather at hand, James seemed in better spirits, returning to his more newsy entries. On July 26th, James was working in the fields with his men, "who was taking off hayseed, on pennyspark," when he noticed someone walking across the field toward them. James rushed forward to embrace his son Willy. It had been eleven years since Willy's previous visit.

The next days were filled with family activities to make the most of Willy's time. He kept Willy as close as he could, though haying season was in full swing. James and Willy went with James Jr. on a trip to Newry. When the haying work on another day was done, James went visiting again with Willy, first to see Mr. McGaw, and then to see James Todd. On the next evening, Willy went with his father, his sister Sarah Anne and James Alexander to have dinner with Alex Douglas up the Ardkeragh Road. They lingered late in the day, having tea before they headed back down the road to Ringbane.

The weather for much of Willy's visit home was wonderful. Days were warm and sunny, the best kind of weather for getting crops harvested. James couldn't neglect this work even though he would have preferred to spend all his time with Willy.

They did make a special trip together. Willy drove James to Kilbroney to see John and his brother David. When they first got to Kilbroney, neither John nor David was there. While waiting for them to return, James and Willy walked around the lovely gardens, and enjoyed the view across Carlingford Lough to the Carlingford Mountains beyond. However, both John and David soon drove down the long driveway for the happy reunion. They sat together till midnight talking politics.

The weather the next day continued fine. So John, Willy and James climbed the mountain to see the Cloughmore Stone. The view from that high perspective was lovely, the lough, the mountains, and beyond the Irish Sea making the rather steep climb worth the effort. They returned to Kilbroney around 4 p.m. and had dinner before returning home.

James's enjoyment of his son's visit was interrupted by the death of a relative, which James noted in his diary for Aug. 17th. "Mrs. Corbett died this morning at 2 clock." Mrs. Corbett was born Elizabeth Harshaw and was one of James's cousins. She had married John Corbett, the prominent owner of the Glascar Mill. They lived in a comfortable country home, Lisnacreevy House. John Corbett had previously died, so with the death of Elizabeth, the property would pass on to their son Robert Swan Corbett. James attended the funeral at Ballyroney Church. A few days later James and Willy went to visit more Harshaw relatives in nearby Ballynafern.

As Willy's visit neared an end, father and son had one last quiet time together. Willy drove the cart as the two men went to Dromantine for a ride through the grand estate of Colonel Close. Then they drove out the back exit and clopped along the narrow road to Poyntzpass before heading home to Ringbane. Two days later, James recorded that Willy had gone to Robert in Mountmellick. Willy would leave for America without returning home to Ringbane. The parting was too painful to James for him to record his feelings in his journal. Certainly both men knew that they would likely never meet again.

Not only did James have to again mourn the departure of his son, but he had to face a mountain of financial difficulties. For years, James had been putting mortgages on his fine lands to enable him to pay his workers and meet other expenses while farm prices declined, and taxes increased.

This problem led to two trips to Dublin before 1864 ended. On November 25, James rose earlier than usual. He was at the Newry Station by 7 a.m. to take the train to Dublin. There he hired a car to take him to Ross Todd to discuss his problems. After dinner with Ross Todd, James met John, who walked with him to the station. John often urged James to sell the leases on one or two of his farms, which would relieve him of his financial worries. But James wanted to keep all his property, so he would have something to leave to each of his sons. When he returned to Newry, he stopped to visit with his niece in Newry, before heading home the next morning. James returned to Dublin in mid-December for a quick one-day trip. In his journal, he offered no explanation for the trip, or what he had done in the hours he was in Dublin.

§

While James was enjoying Willy's visit and working on his harvest, a sectarian eruption occurred over what seemed at first a relatively simple activity. A group of leaders from Dublin had decided to build a statue commemorating the life and work of Daniel O'Connell. The fund-raising campaign had been underway since the beginning of the year. A site at the head of Sackville Street had been approved. John wasn't a member of the committee, but many of his friends were, including Smyth.

On July 20th, John wrote a letter to the committee enclosing £5 for the monument fund. This fund would support not only the statue for O'Connell, but also one for O'Brien. John stated his belief that one way for Irish patriots to show their respect for the great leaders of Irish history would be to continue to keep "striving for independence." These two great statues one for O'Connell, and one for O'Brien would "serve to tell the world what the heart of Ireland loves, what it burns for."

Smyth then made a motion that John's generous donation should promote a vote making him a member of the committee. Other members told Smyth that this donation would automatically do that very thing. That was within the rules, but another member suggested that they should bring the resolution to a vote as a "special compliment" to John for his devotion to the cause of Irish independence. That motion was quickly passed.

George was well aware of the plans for the laying of the cornerstone early in August. He saw this activity as another way to divide the country by continuing the efforts to free Ireland from England. "Self-government in this island would mean self destruction." He went on to explain why. "We have neither harmony of race, or political or religious feeling." Even worse, they had no foundation on which to build a unified country, or any resources to defend it should one be created.

The cornerstone was laid on Monday August 8th. The day dawned with showers and dark skies. But by the time the first units of tradesmen left St. Stephen's Green at 10 a.m., the skies had cleared, and the sun was shining. Each of the trade unions marched as groups, each group decorated with emblems suitable to their trade, and each one featuring the color green. They marched to Merrion Square to salute O'Connell's home there, before heading toward the Liffey. They were led by sixty horsemen each wearing a green scarf. One witness said the procession looked like a "moving forest."

Catholic school children, lodges, and clergy also rode to the site of the statue. They passed by ships anchored along the bridge and decorated for the event as well. Near the site of the statue on Sackville Street, a very large platform that could accommodate many special guests had been erected. It stretched from the site of the statue to the corner of Abbey Street. There were bleachers on three sides, and on the fourth an area for the dignitaries. There was a green carpet under foot and a canopy overhead. O'Connell was represented in the form of a bust, flanked by statues of two eagles.

It was 4 p.m. before the Lord Mayor of Dublin opened the formal ceremony. After several speeches, the head of the construction team performed the actual laying of the cornerstone, a large stone that had been partially carved out. In this space, a small ceramic bust of O'Connell was placed along with some coins and O'Connell medals. Another stone was laid on top, the cement to hold them in place spread with a special silver commemorative trowel. That being accomplished the crowd began to disperse, the guilds and spectators going home, and the dignitaries going to a grand banquet at the Round Room of the Rotunda.

The laying of the cornerstone might have been seen by many as a great outpouring of affection for a much-loved historical leader. George saw it quite differently. He devoted a leader to the subject three days later. Every Irishman should recognize, as he did, that O'Connell was a total fraud. He had no interest in Irish independence at all, despite his speeches proclaiming this to be his goal. Actually, he was attempting to wrest additional rights from the English government for the Catholics of Ireland. To George, this was a ridiculous concept in the first place. He believed that the Catholics already had equal rights with the Irish Protestants. In fact, he was prepared to argue that Catholics had greater rights than Protestants. They were in fact, "ascendant."

Had O'Connell actually been seeking independence, that too was foolish dreaming. "Repeal of the Union is impossible. The Protestants of Ireland would oppose it to the death." How could anyone who cared for the Irish people support such activities. After all, O'Connell was a "religious bigot, a political mountebank, and a convicted felon."

After two days of reflection on the events in Dublin, George returned to the topic. He maintained that the ceremony was a provocation requiring action from the British government. It was a violation of the Processions Act, which went unreprimanded, never mind unpunished, by the authorities, proving how unfair the government had been in enforcing Irish laws. When the statue was completed, it would remain a threat to the English. George suggested that the Protestants of Ulster should create a counter statue in Belfast.

The Fenians weren't impressed with the event either. O'Leary offered his own review. "We cannot for one moment believe that the working men of Dublin who but two short years ago followed McManus to his grave have since forgotten the creed of manhood." It was a misplaced reverence for O'Connell, that brought them out in such numbers that Monday morning. "He loved his country well, if he went the wrong way about serving her." O'Leary wouldn't use the harsh words that George did, but the critique was no less forceful. O'Connell didn't deserve credit for the emancipation of Irish Catholics in 1829. And this was the achievement for which he was given universal acclaim, even by those who found fault with his later work.

The Protestants of Ulster had ideas of their own in mind to show how displeased they were that Catholics were allowed to have such a large sectarian event without punishment. They created a rather clumsy effigy of O'Connell and then lit it on fire on the Boyne Bridge where it could be widely seen around Belfast. The next day, they found a coffin in which they supposedly put the ashes of the effigy and set it on fire in the same way.

For a couple of days, the police in Belfast were able to keep the Protestant rowdies from Sandy Row separate from their Catholic counterparts from the Pound. But then the rioting began. When the young men of the Pound burned an effigy of King William, the intensity escalated, and the fighting became more widespread. Roving bands armed with rocks and sticks, and some guns rampaged through the area, smashing the windows of churches of the opposing sides and houses in enemy territory.

This fighting ebbed and flowed for several days. Many people were injured, and one person was killed before the fighting finally ended. George had no trouble identifying the people responsible. It was all the fault of the Catholics. Had they not carried out their illegal procession in Dublin, nothing would have happened in Belfast.

Soon the violence spread to Newry. The local situation was made worse by the burning of another effigy of King William in nearby Dundalk. A group of quay porters and butchers began a march through Newry. Rumors flowed around town that they planned to attack the Orange Hall or burn another effigy of William at the Corry Monument. However, whatever plans the mob actually had were thwarted by a phalanx of police drawn up at the Sugar Island Bridge to intercept them. To prevent more such threats, police reinforcements soon arrived. George was confident that "Ulster will nip treason in the bud." But he warned that there would only be peace if the Catholics gave up the idea of independence.

Exhaustion finally set in after days of rioting and many arrests, and quiet if not peace returned to Belfast. While George blamed the Catholics, he also blamed the Palmerston government...He allowed that Prime Minister Palmerston had done well for England, though he had done little for Ireland. He seemed to want the majority of good jobs to go to Catholics because they were the majority in Ireland. As a result, Ireland was on the verge of rebellion. Catholics can only be peaceful if they are granted special treatment, and no amount of favors would satisfy them. "One religion was loyal, the other not." The Catholic people believe that Ireland belongs to them and will one day return to their ownership. "The demon of discord is everywhere rampant, and conciliation so far from appeasing it, has increased its fury."

§

Despite the rioting and the divisions in Ireland, George still kept space for coverage of the Civil War in America. John followed the war as well since it involved the Mitchels even more intensely. In July, he got word that Mitchel's oldest son John had died on the ramparts of Fort Sumter. The death of this young man, so much like the son John might have had, was particularly devastating. While John mourned, George seemed more hopeful that a negotiated settlement would soon end the war. The Confederates had already reached out to President Lincoln for terms. Lincoln would only accept return to the Union and freedom for the slaves. George worried that any opportunity for peace, if wasted, might not return again. "It has turned up once more, perhaps for the last time, and Mr. Lincoln is too stupid or too stubborn to embrace it."

George once again declared that he wasn't in favor of slavery. "But we cannot see that we would be justified in employing force to accomplish our desire, or, that to set a negro free to enslave the white man could be regarded as an improvement." He continued, "With all our enmity to slavery, we must not forget that the white man could not do the duty assigned to the negro, and while he would be glad to elevate him, we should be sorry to put in his hands, a power which he might abuse."

In another leader, he assigned to the South the determination that he always ascribed to the Protestants of Ulster. "The south will perish before submitting, and the question for Humanity will be is the price not too high for conquest on one hand and independence on the other."

John was not only a faithful reader of the *Newry Telegraph,* but also of the *Irishman,* which was then edited by P. J. Smyth. This paper had had the same great interest in the Civil War that George's paper did. It strongly supported the Northern cause. So from time to time, John wrote letters to Smyth explaining his contrary support of the Southern cause.

In early September, John wrote a response to comments that Smyth had made in a previous edition of the paper, suggesting that the Confederacy was allied with England, and that the North was allied with Ireland. This was an idea with which John strongly disagreed. The actions of the South were very noble in John's eyes. How could anyone think otherwise? "Let who will insinuate that the cause…in whose defense, two noble sons of John Mitchel have given their young lives, the cause in which John Mitchel himself and his remaining son will fight and endure till the last, is a cause unworthy of the sympathy of honourable men and patriotic Irish men." And even should there be an informal alliance between the Confederacy and England, he would still support southern independence.

John was also puzzled about any connections between the North and Ireland. What the Irish should be doing was throwing their full support behind an immediate end of the war by agreeing to the secession of the South. "If the North succeed in its attempt to subjugate the people of the Confederate States it will employ whatever means it deems sure and most convenient for holding its conquest. Penal laws as to religion won't be resorted to, but wholesale confiscation will. Garrisons of American Orangemen with plenty of laws to make and keep the Southern people disarmed, disfranchised, disorganized, unmanned, helpless and safe!" To John, this made the North just like England.

This prediction wasn't the only uncharacteristically harsh comment that John made in his letter. He launched a savage attack on the people of New England, unlike anything he had put in writing before. "I say that the English and New Englanders are the two people likest to each other in all the world. They have similar virtues and similar vices–similar characters–similar objects in life. In fact they are the same blood and race and they differ only in *age* and in circumstances. To make money, to make it for the sake of making it, to enjoy it mainly in displaying the possession of it, or in feeling the consciousness of possessing it, is the *summon bonum* of the New Englander, just as it is of the Englishman. To admire grand principles of morality, and fine sensibilities, but not to suffer them to interfere with their own interest, or pride, or ambition. To be draconian judges of the crimes of others and commit the very same crimes themselves. To love and vindicate freedom for themselves, but not to allow freedom to their neighbors, if they can help it. To hate their rivals, scorn their inferiors, trample on those who are down. To have clamourous sympathy for the questionable wrongs of negroes–other people negroes, any wrongs, the righting of which will cost them nothing. That is English character and New England Character."

Despite his vastly different view of the war in America, John indicated that he hoped his strong feelings wouldn't harm his long friendship with Smyth. "Meantime, however, we differ in our sentiments regarding war, believe me ever your sincere friend."

Smyth found John's letter so stunning that he delayed his response, giving himself time to fully study the letter. John had offered strongly stated beliefs. The North would confiscate Southern property, seize their guns, and remove the right to vote. The only justification that John offered for his opinion was his belief that Northerners were just like the English. His experience with English control in Ireland justified his conclusions.

This flaw in John's thinking was noted by Smyth at the beginning of his answer. "Never did a bad cause enlist in its support a better name than yours, and never was a protest so destitute of foundation in reason, in truths, in argument and in fact." "I search in vain for proof, authority, reason or patriotism."

This letter of John's was written in a convulsion of grief, which Smyth couldn't have understood. Word of the death of John Mitchel Jr. had only recently reached Ireland. To John it was an additional bitter blow following the death of Willy Mitchel the previous summer at Gettysburg. He was still devastated by the loss of a second Mitchel son. Only such an intense personal sorrow would explain his harsh attack on the character of the Northerners, many of whom were Irish, some friends and former neighbours, some members of his family.

Smyth noticed the intensity of John's words, though he didn't recognize the reason behind them. What he saw was a total allegiance to the Confederate States that defied reason. After all, success of the Northern army with its large number of trained Irish fighters, might well be brought later to the aid of the Irish struggle for independence John was working so hard to achieve. Smyth put his confusion this way. "The course of the south is, in your estimation, so supremely noble that rather than it should fail you welcome chains and slavery perpetual for your own country."

Smyth continued to make his disagreement with John very clear. This southern part of America had no justifiable reason to revolt. Countries across Europe had revolted because they were being held in subjugation by other countries. This wasn't the case with the South. "It is not even pretended that it is. Is it that of a people in legitimate revolt against their government because of the manifold wrongs inflicted by the government against them? So far from that, the leaders of the South avowed that the government against which they rose was the 'most beneficent that ever existed on earth.' Every state in the South, as every state in the north, enjoyed under the constitution of the United States plenary powers of self-government. Each regulated uncontrolled its domestic affairs, and each was protected against foreign aggression or violence by the all-embracing arm of the Union." Not only was freedom guaranteed to all parts of the country, the South had special benefits bestowed by the Constitution. Voters in the South had a proportionately greater influence in Congress than the North. So. "throughout that whole period, Southern influence was supreme in the councils of the National Government."

It was the Vice President of the Confederacy, Mr. Stephens, who made clear that slavery was the "*sole cause*" for secession. The Southern states had participated freely in the election of 1860. So they had "guaranteed that it would abide by that election. Had its own candidate been returned all would have been well—there would have been no secession, no war. It had not been denied but that Mr. Lincoln was constitutionally elected, yet the South made his election the pretext for revolt, thus striking at the root of all free governments—which is that the minority shall bow to the constitutionally declared rule of the majority. Mr. Lincoln's election was the pretext, but the object was the erection upon the ruins of the Republic of Washington of an empire whose 'corner-stone would be slavery'…The ruling power in America is the ballot box. And the character of the administration is determined by popular vote, not of east nor west, but the whole nation."

Then Smyth moved on to strong support for the people of New England. "The North East have shown how tyranny may be resisted, freedom won, the foundations of national prosperity laid, and the flag of civilization advanced to the furthest confines of the desert. Brand them as criminals if you choose, but rest assured that the people who have given to liberty and humanity a BENJAMIN FRANKLIN, to poetry a LONGFELLOW, to eloquence a DANIEL WEBSTER—a people who can count among their monuments a Bunker Hill, rest assured that such a people will survive the assaults even of an Irish patriot. But what is their great crime? To have clamorous sympathies for the *questionable* wrongs of negroes, *other peoples negroes!"*

Finally, Smyth took John to task for supporting slavery. "Here then, at last, you openly identify yourself with slavery—slavery in the abstract and in the concrete! It were impossible for you to avoid it, for you are too honest a man to shrink from all or any of the logical conclusions which a support of the Southern Confederacy involves. The man who supports the Southern cause and pretends, at the same time to condemn slavery is a knave, a hypocrite, and an imposter. You, like a truthful man, as you are, while upholding the south shrink not from upholding the institution in the interests of which the South rebelled."

"Questionable wrongs of negroes! They admit of no question. They are written in characters of blood. They may be traced in the fair skin and handsome features of the quadroon as plainly as in the mutilated members, the branded back and brow, and arm of the full-blooded African. The Virginia wilderness, the New Orleans auction block, all testify against the atrocity of the institution which has degraded the black man below the level of brute and caused the white man to become a rebel when he ceased to be a ruler."

"This letter has caused me much pain. Your devoted friend I shall ever be, but on this subject there is a gulf between us, which I fear, can never be bridged."

Before John responded to Smyth, he responded to a letter he had gotten on the subject of his support of slavery from Isaac Varian, a friend from the time of the Young Irelanders. "If negro slavery was the damning blot you describe it to have been, it seems to me that *separation* was the very measure that the states opposite to negro slavery ought to have adopted. That would end fugitive slave laws, which the North should hate. North would no longer be morally responsible for condition of negroes."

John used this argument to refute the idea that slavery played any role in secession. He viewed the two parts of the country as partners. Certainly, partners had a right to dissolve their partnership, if either one of them chose. He seemed puzzled that anyone would view slavery to be the reason for the horrid war. If the right to secede from the Union was the cause of the war, there was no reason to discuss slavery, so he had avoided doing that.

But in this letter, he addressed the issue for the first time. "But I was also glad that I could properly avoid handling such a burning issue as that of negro slavery. I have not been able to make up my mind upon this question, although I have earnestly labored to do so; while the bulk of my fellow country-men, without knowing the facts and without taking any trouble to learn have had no trouble."

John believed that in learning about the South from Mitchel he was getting the real facts. Everything that Mitchel said was "entitled to respectful consideration for those capable of discerning and appreciating grandeur of intellect and nobility of character. If John Mitchel errs, it won't be from intellectual poverty, or from moral cowardice, or from want of love for truth, beauty and right. I have no doubt there are imperfections in the institution of negro-slavery and 'foul blots,' and 'damning stains.'" However, he didn't believe that what was bad in the South was any worse than what was going on for Negroes in the North.

"We cannot have perfection in human institutions." That said, John thought that American institutions could be altered to provide a better balance of the needs of Negroes and their white masters. In neither segment of the country, did Negroes have any say in how the institutions of the country should be run. Both sections had different ideas about black capabilities. Southerners believed that the inferiority of negroes was a proven fact and that they must be managed by whites. The North believed that any evidence of inferiority was accidental and temporary.

Summing up his beliefs, John declared that he wouldn't consider slavery an evil until convinced by his own eyes.

A flood of letters arrived following John's published support of slavery, disagreeing with his ideas. One letter commented that John's views on slavery meant that he was lost to Ireland. Another letter said, "I read Mr. Martin's letter with pain, because better should have been expected for one pledged to upset English rule in Ireland." Thadeous O'Malley wrote, "What a pity so pure a man shall be linked to so foul a cause."

John also responded to Smyth. In this letter, his opinion on slavery seemed more conflicted. "For my own part, I don't *condemn* negro slavery. Neither do I advocate for it." He had studied the issue thoroughly for a long time. "The weight of the argument seems to be upon the side of those who advocated slavery, but my instincts are still upon the side of abolition."

This was the last time John mentioned slavery publicly.

Residences—Seaview and Dromalane

Dromalane House was owned by Hill Irvine, husband of John Mitchel's sister. It was where both Mitchel and Martin died.

The Martins lived in Seaview after moving from Kilbroney when Robert Martin Jr. became an adult.

Chapter 12

Irish National League

1864 - 1865

John's optimism that his Irish National League might succeed had begun to waver by the autumn of 1864. He had read the letters in popular publications that claimed his views on slavery made him unfit for any leadership position in the independence movement. He could not know how greatly this furor damaged the League. However, he could easily observe that it was far from achieving its goal of unifying Irish nationalists. Still he persisted in his efforts. Even as he was debating slavery with Smyth in the *Irishman,* he gave a major speech about the poetry of the founder of Young Ireland, Thomas Davis, in Dundalk. In his response to the address of thanks, John spoke to the audience about respect and unity. George recorded his remarks in the *Telegraph.*

"Mr. Martin, in replying, said he heartily rejoiced that there were many of his own neighbors thus kindly felt towards him. Whatever his political opinions had been, no one could deny that he had stood to them firmly. (Applause.) Whatever principles may have guided his conduct he had acted conscientiously else he would not have been subject to insult and calumny. He would never force his opinions on any man, no matter how firmly he believed them; and with regard to his opinions (he was going to call them peculiar) he might remark that in any other country in the world…the man whose political opinions lead him to stand up for the rights of his own country—those which appear to him to be just and adequate, will obtain a recognition of the right of his country. Any Englishman, Scotchman, Frenchman or any other man but an Irishman that held such opinions would not be obliged to apologise for them to his own neighbors. (Applause.)"

Then George moved to directly quote John's words. "Nor do I apologise–(great cheering)–but I recognize my neighbor's right to differ. I respect his opinions and demand that he shall respect mine. And this much I think I may say in praise of myself–I have not been a bad neighbor nor a bad landlord, nor a bad tenant; nor, as far as anything you know, a bad brother or a bad son; nor have I been a bad husband (laughter)–for I was never married. But what I wanted to say, Mr. Chairman, is that I think (I say it because I would desire that it should be known through the Press) I say that it is not only hard, but it is unfair and intolerable, that a man living in his own neighborhood, and known there as an inoffensive and honorable man should be held up to obloquy in that neighborhood on account of his opinions. (Applause.)"

John concluded with this comment that was received with great applause. "Believe me that every neighbor of the English faction or of the national opinions—Tory, Whig, Protestant, Catholic–no matter what his creed–no matter what his political opinions, I desire not to do him wrong nor to give him offence, but I would befriend him so far as I conscientiously can."

Unfortunately, unity was something beyond John's ability to achieve. The Fenians had no intention of unifying with any national group they didn't control. John recognized this reality but hoped against hope he might by word or deed divert them from actions he believed were doomed to fail. But he wasn't surprised that as the days shortened and the harvest was stacked or stored in barns across Ireland, the Fenians continued to carp away at his Irish National League. "We had faint hopes that Mr. Martin would come to see the error of his ways, but we fear he is fact-proof." In fact, O'Leary showed no respect for John at all. He called the League and John's efforts "ludicrous."

However, George, along with John, was thinking about divisions in Ireland. A few months later, he commented about the results of the religious divisions that had led to the Belfast riots the previous summer. These confrontations resulted in "impoverishment of land, neglected resources, and unemployment." "How could it be otherwise when men will not only not agree to differ, but differing will try to destroy each other."

To make the future of Irish nationalism even darker, before the year was out, another national group was formed in Dublin with the support of Archbishop Cullen, called the National Association of Ireland. While a number of Catholic priests had supported the League, they joined the new organization as well. This group, which had more limited goals than the League, was led by activists in the Catholic laity, one of whom was John's friend John Dillon. Dillon had urged John to create the League with a promise of participation but had defaulted on his commitment. The National Association planned to lobby England and its Parliament for three goals: better laws regulating tenant and landlord relations, disestablishment of the Church of Ireland, and sectarian schools funded by government taxation.

George thought this organization would falter as the Irish National League had, once members discovered that Parliament would ignore their pressure. The Association's intention to supersede the League and the Fenians would be equally unsuccessful. Though they claimed to be another legal organization, the goals relative to education and the religious establishment were clearly treasonous.

Reviews of the new nationalist group were mostly as negative as the one George had offered. Still John offered his support at the first League meeting of 1865. John declared to the attending members that he was "delighted at the foundation of the new Association." He applauded their basic concept of attempting to obtain positive actions to benefit Ireland. The selection of issues to pursue seemed wise to him as well. Should Irish farmers gain an improved right to retain their land, they would be able to vote. Increased Irish voting would have a positive impact for Ireland.

However, John paid his greatest attention to the issue of disestablishment. "The religion was sent over from England. The people to teach it were sent over from England, and the forces by which the teaching were to be enforced were sent over from England, and the forces by which it has been maintained to that day were of course paid out of the pockets of Irishmen."

John reminded his League members that he was a Presbyterian. "The Presbyterians were very nearly as numerous as Episcopalians in Ireland, but they were content to be the slaves of the English power against their own countrymen; for though they were nearly equal to Episcopalians, they received about 1/6 of the public plunder that the Episcopalians had."

Then Daunt spoke, explaining why he had also joined the new group. He thought that the agenda of the Association would advance the efforts of the League. He wanted the League to push for independence even though that wasn't part of the agenda of the new group.

Before the meeting ended, John expressed his position on a contentious issue, what role Irish MPs should play when elected to seats in Parliament. If he personally were ever elected to Parliament "He would consider that his sole business in the English parliament was to take all proper occasions of letting that Parliament, and through it the world, know that his constituents sent him there to let it be clearly understood that they desired to get out of that Parliament."

Smyth commented in his paper on the increasing number of nationalist groups. He apologized to John for not giving more support to the League as he had been among the most ardent advocates for such an organization and John's leadership of it. Given the proliferation of nationalist groups, he now believed that all would fail.

O'Leary made clear the Fenian position. They did not support the other organizations. "Old Ireland and Young Ireland, Grattan and O'Connell, hide your diminished heads. Your ways were ways of foolishness, and the job was botched in your hands." He mocked the leaders of the Association, a minor group of little stature, though Archbishop Cullen was leading it. "It is more than folly—this new agitation inaugurated at the Rotunda the other day. It is criminal and places the leaders in a degraded light before the moral sense of the nation." "It is now generally admitted that the Rotunda meeting of the 29th of December was one of the driest, dullest and most driftless meetings ever held in Dublin. The speeches were utterances of the most deplorable feeble-mindedness and the resolutions were the offspring of timidity."

Before he concluded the leader, O'Leary seemed to be in agreement with George about the different treatment of Ulster Protestants and nationalists. "The Genius which presided at Dublin Castle, and visits with pains and penalties the loyal men of Ulster for the display of their loyalty is powerless or indifferent when an aggregate meeting is held to do honor to the memory of a rebel, or to inaugurate a new agitation striking at the rights of property and the authority of the Crown. No wonder that mob rule is triumphant, and that the country is ever on the verge of revolutions; that our people fly to other lands; and we are left to mourn our undeveloped resources and an impoverished society."

§

George found the new nationalist organization appealing, as it further splintered Irish nationalists at the time the League was failing. Nationalist disunity lessened his fear of a civil war erupting across Ireland. But since the continuing American Civil War offered a possible exemplar of what could happen if actual fighting erupted between Protestant and Catholic citizens began in Ireland, he continued to closely follow events and then write about them in the *Telegraph*.

Meanwhile a critical presidential election was taking place in America. News of the outcome reached Newry on November 22, 1864. George had hoped that Gen. McClellan would defeat the sitting president and bring the terrible carnage in America to an end. He wrote a leader on the subject four days later in which he had critiques for both Lincoln and Davis. To George, Lincoln was a "vain old man." In his election speech, Lincoln had reaffirmed his intention to reunify the country. Though there were problems facing the Southern armies, Davis refused to acknowledge reality. He would not free the slaves. And he would fight on until the South was either destroyed or free.

This stance disappointed George. He had hoped that Davis would see the light. Southerners had suffered so much "for their own freedom while denying freedom to the negro." Davis should recognize that no matter how the war ended, slavery in America was at an end. The sooner Davis recognized that fact, the better.

But a few days later, George was impressed by a speech that Davis had made, laying out the case for the Confederacy. Davis declared that they didn't want to go to war, but they had to stand up for the heritage of freedom, which they had been left by the valor of their ancestors.

The issue of slavery that bedeviled John was still an obstacle in George's thinking. The legacy of freedom that Southerners had inherited also included the heritage of slavery. Slavery was not compatible with modern "enlightened opinions." It was a "great blot on their fame."

Then George repeated his belief that the Union and its Constitution had only one purpose, to establish a military force for the individual states. But the states were in all other respects independent countries. Therefore, the Southern states had a total right to leave the Union. They were insulted by Northern aggression. So they had exercised "a right consecrated in the great charter of American liberty—the right of a free people when a government proves destructive of the ends for which it was established, to recur to the original principles and to institute new guards to their security." The time had come then for Lincoln to submit to the Southern viewpoint.

Next, George reported on efforts from the Southern government to have representation in England. This gave him an opportunity to again criticize Lincoln's policies. If General McClellan had been elected, the war would be over. Lincoln was the only Northern leader who wanted to continue the fighting. Other Northerners had no interest in ending slavery, as they too have found slavery profitable, some New England towns even participating in the slave trade. "The South has nothing to fear. She has sufficient resources to carry on the contest." Other countries like England needed these resources, like their extensive cotton crops, and would happily loan money to the South to continue the fight. There was just one obstacle. "She has only to relieve the slave, and the world will sympathize with her, and cheer her on to speedy and complete victory."

George read the speech Lincoln gave to Congress in December and found it most disappointing. The President had said that he wouldn't negotiate an end to the war on any terms but return to the Union. There were no words of conciliation that George had hoped for. "Instead we have a fiendish glee at the prospect of more blood, characteristic of a mind with 'such indifferent reference to the carnage of the past.'" The war had been very costly both in lives and in money. This position only made sense if the war was nearing an end, but it wasn't.

In his next report on the war, George stated that despite the fact that Sherman had taken Savannah, the situation in the South overall was little changed from the previous year. The Southern government had six hundred thousand fighting men in its army. All they needed to win was the help of its Negro slaves. They had proven to be good fighters during their service in the Northern army. They could be deployed to prevent guerilla fighting that had broken out in some remote parts of the South between southerners who supported the Confederacy and those supporting the Union. George hated this style of fighting, perhaps because he feared that someday that kind of fighting would break out in Ulster. It wasn't a tactic that "was becoming to the South."

George always urged that a negotiated settlement should be undertaken to end the war. So he was pleased to read that such a meeting had actually taken place. However, four hours after it began, it ended. There wasn't a solution that both sides would accept. So the South began recruiting Negroes to serve the Army in support roles. They could dig fortifications, down trees, etc., but they would not be taught to be soldiers, or allowed to possess guns. George changed course and finally began to concede that the best outcome would be for the North to win. "Slavery caused the sword to be drawn; slavery terminated the conference; and slavery must be abolished before peace can be announced."

In a later leader, George conceded that Lincoln had offered concessions, but the South had refused to budge. After this meeting, George reverted to his original analysis. "It is pretty clear that the maintenance of slavery is the motive of the Confederacy." But he believed that the Union was always fragile. "There never was a feeling in common between the peoples. The Union was a rope of sand." The differences were not only racial, but also structural and political differences between the aristocratic South and the democratic North.

John wrote one last letter on March 18th about the Civil War, which was published in the *Nation* three days later. He stated that he had seen nothing in the situation in America to change his mind about the war, since his discussion of slavery. He had never believed that England would intervene to stop the war, but he had always held hopes that the French government would. "Such friendly intervention would have saved the citizens of the South from becoming subjects and the citizens of the North from becoming oppressors; would have secured their homes and their freedom to all the citizens of the states; would have preserved to them and told the world that glorious free constitution, of which only the dead form will remain if the armies and fleets of the North accomplish the subjugation of the Southern people...As to England, I never dreamed of her lifting a finger to save the blood of American citizens, or doing anything in the quarrel, except to make money out of it."

John had grown very depressed about the outcome of the conflict. "The Northern invaders have yet many thousands more of brave men to kill before they can take quick possession. And when at length the country of the confederacy becomes a conquered province—if such be the will of God! If the widows and orphans of its gallant defenders lie helpless at the feet of the conquerors, history will have to tell of another national struggle against subjugation which for patriotic union of all classes and for heroes deeds, and sufferings of men and women, and boys, has never been surpassed, and has scarcely ever been equaled."

John then returned to his beginning statement, that nothing had happened to change his view of the war. "Nothing has been alleged which justifies the attempt of the northern to replace the old free union with a union of force— the union of hearts by a union of chains. Of all that I have written on the quarrel I have nothing to retract. I have written always as a friend of both northern and southern. And if I were the friends of only one party—if an Irishman, who knows that the exiles of his race had received hospitable welcome and permission to thrive equally from both parties of America, could feel the enemy of neither, still God forbid, that an Irishman should wish to do wrong to his enemies, or should encourage his friends in wickedness."

John concluded the letter with a final judgment. "If the northerns accomplish the conquest of the South, they will have committed, in my judgment a great national crime, and also a great national folly. Certainly, they may become a grand and terrible nation of conquerors, and may plant their Eagle with their stripes and stars in triumph over many a desolated county, over the bones of myriads of slaughtered patriots. But is that *good?* No; by the conquest of the south, they will merely gain territory and subjects, and will be obliged henceforth to employ the means of which subjects are kept in obedience, and subject countries debased and plundered."

Certainly John was greatly worried by the dangers that he knew the Mitchels were experiencing in Richmond. Had he actually known what was happening, he would have been even more alarmed. Grant and Lee's armies had engaged in a costly trench war around Petersburg south of Richmond for months. So the fighting was alarmingly close. Union forces finally broke through the Confederate lines on April 2 forcing the evacuation of Richmond. As Confederate troops fled the city, they set fire to tobacco warehouses and military supplies, a fire that spread through much of the city endangering the civilian population remaining in the city. John Mitchel and son James fled south with the departing troops. Union forces entered the city the next day.

Jenny and her two daughters were left alone to face the rape and villainy John expected from the northern troops. Fortunately for the Mitchel family, John was wrong. The occupying force was led by Major General Weitzel. When his forces marched into the city, much of the city had already been destroyed by the fleeing Confederates. All the windows in Jenny's house were blown out, but the fire that raged across the city stopped miraculously across the street, leaving them a house to live in.

Most Southerners shared John's expectation that a horrid rampage would be inflicted on the fallen capital by the conquering soldiers. Such views weren't surprising as these were the common results whenever a triumphant army entered a defeated city. But that wasn't at all what happened in Richmond. The occupying troops maintained total discipline. They immediately spread out over the city to maintain order. Any looting that took place was the work of Richmond residents.

Jenny took the safely of her family into her own hands and made a trip to Union Headquarters to ask that guards be placed at her house. This was agreed to. When Mitchel and his son finally made their way back to Richmond, they found the house and the family safe, with two guards standing duty outside the house. The Mitchels had survived the end of the Southern Confederacy. John was greatly relieved when he received this news.

Finally George announced the meeting of Generals Lee and Grant at the small brick house at Appomattox Courthouse during which General Lee surrendered his army. The Civil War was over. But John had incorrectly predicted what would happen next. The defeated Confederate soldiers were allowed to keep their guns and swords and return peacefully to their homes. They marched away between lines of Union soldiers standing at attention and saluting their opponents. Less than a week later, telegraphs brought the stunning news to the *Telegraph* office that President Lincoln had been assassinated.

George wrote an obituary for the murdered leader. He felt that the murder was especially sad, coming so soon after he had achieved victory in the war. George now referred to the man that he had once called a "tyrant" and an "idiot" in a different, somewhat less harsh light. The late President was not a man of "brilliant genius." He had no claim to "literary fame." Still "History will record to his merit that he guided the helm with sagacity, and rode out the storm more successfully than many wise men amongst us had imagined—he guided it with great sacrifice of human life, and at great costs to the owner of the vessel, still he guided it so far safely, and the haven for which he sailed was in sight, when a coward arrested his progress to increased fame."

Now the question for the Mitchel family was what to do next. Mitchel needed employment, and the likelihood of a writing position was greater in New York City than in Richmond. So Mitchel left Jenny in the house in

Richmond and moved north. There he got a writing job from a friend at the *New York Daily News.*

In July, George reported on the surprising event that happened to Mitchel one day at work on June 18th. Union troops invaded the newspaper office and placed Mitchel under arrest for his work for the Confederacy. Without a chance to collect any possessions, he was placed aboard a ship in New York Harbor and transported to Fortress Monroe in Virginia. His treatment seemed like a replay of his 1848 treatment in Ireland. He was confined there for several months in harsh conditions and without charges.

However, the American branch of the Fenians quickly began an intense campaign to free him. After negotiations with military officials, they were able to obtain his release on condition that he leave the country. The Fenians offered him a position is Paris as the manager of their European funds. Mitchel left Jenny behind again and headed to Europe after taking an oath of citizenship to the newly united country.

§

Early in the year 1865. James recorded in his journal that his friend James Todd was ill. His first mention of his friend's illness was on February 6th. James noted that "my friend James Todd worse." The next day was "a fine spring day—spent most of this day in my friend James Todds. I found him stil living." Later in the day James Jr. made the trip to Ringclare and reported to his father that James Todd was still living.

On the 10th, James wrote, "My friend James Todd very ill." The next day, he was "very low." During the night, James's dear friend died. James wasn't the kind of neighbor who stopped helping when the funeral was over. One day he had planned to visit the Todd family, but was hindered by a snowstorm. Despite a continuation of severe and cold weather, James slogged over the hills to Ringclare. However, when he had almost made it safely home, he fell on the road and cut his lip severely enough that he missed the next church service.

Other than his sad loss, the year followed the expected patterns of his life. He continued his work in church, and in the fields. In May, James recorded the acquisition of a new communion service, "two flagons, three plates and five cups." He was also chosen to represent the congregation at the July meeting of the General Assembly in Belfast. He spent two days at the sessions, helping to choose professors for the new college in Derry. After the sessions on the second day, he visited the Belfast Cattle Show before taking the train home.

Two weeks later, James recorded a very special event. "'Fine dry day— men mowing—when at dinner my youngest son, Absalom [Samuel], came walking into the wee parlor." This visit lasted for two happy months, during which James enjoyed a number of family gatherings while he continued to harvest the year's crops.

Robert and his wife came north from Mountmellick despite the recent death of their daughter Elizabeth. On the last day of July, Hugh and Jane went with Samuel and James to Kilbroney. Certainly John was happy to see his cousin. They headed off together to climb the mountain to the Great Stone.

But because of increasingly bad weather, they had to turn back. James and Mary Martin Simpson went across the road to visit Leacain House, which David Martin had built for his growing family. David Martin had been away on a trip to Belfast, but they encountered him in Warrenpoint on their way home.

Finally, the dreaded day arrived when Samuel would return to America. James recorded this last farewell with his favorite son. "Dry day—Absalom [Samuel] & I walked down the lonen together after a somewhat early diner, talking about his prospects in New York. I kissed his brow, at the fall-gate, & we parted." They would not meet again.

Before the year ended, James experienced another disappointment. While Samuel was still visiting, Robert had preached one Sunday at a church in nearby Newtownhamilton. In September, the congregation invited Robert to be their new minister. This would relocate him within short distance of the rest of the family. Unfortunately, the Dublin Presbytery had heeded the pleas of the Mountmellick congregation and refused to release him from his duties in Mountmellick, so the call was refused.

There was another reason for the refusal to honor Robert's request to leave Mountmellick. Robert had become a very important Presbyterian presence in the center of Ireland. He was well respected by members of all faiths. His presence there was thus too important a bastion for the Presbyterian Church to allow him to leave.

§

Just before Samuel had returned to Ireland, yet another election for Parliament was held. If James or members of his family participated, he did not mention it in his journal, but it was of great interest to George. In early July, he reported that local Conservatives were looking for a proper candidate to support for Newry. Local Conservative electors decided that they should approach Arthur Charles Innes of Dromantine to ask him to run for the Newry seat. The young man agreed. As a member of Irish nobility, he could count on general support without mounting a significant campaign. In fact, his only statement was a pledge to work for the interests of Newry.

The Whig party seemed at first intent on re-nominating Presbyterian William Kirk who had previously been Newry's representative in Parliament. He could expect support from both Catholic and Presbyterian electors. This would be another contested election that George would closely cover. George scoffed at the notion of a Whig representative for Newry, telling his readers that Conservatives were the "true friends of Ireland." He summed up the stakes in the election. "Remember the issue is between Constitutional progress and democratic revolution."

George's confidence was well placed. Mr. Innes did indeed win the seat. "Glorious triumph over an unholy, unnatural and incongruous alliance!" The final vote was 267 to 235. But it was the vote breakdown that made George happiest. Most of the Catholics in Newry voted for Mr. Kirk, but only 26 Presbyterian electors did the same.

Despite the positive results for the Conservatives in Newry, they did not obtain control of Parliament. George attributed this loss to a failure of Conservatives to organize properly to defeat Whigs who were "emboldened and very active." The more ignorant voters believed that Conservatives would end moves toward free trade, resulting in higher prices and lower wages. No party could stand still. They must either move forward or fall behind. "We have a great and wealthy nation and we want to have it managed by educated men, neither aristocrats nor democrats; but sensible men, whose stake is so large that they will be all the more cautious of not driving us to ruin."

Enjoying the victory, George made a comment that wouldn't be helpful to Protestant unity, which was so critical during the time when nationalists were on the move. Protestants were divided into two groups, "blue and better blue." The "better blue" were the members of the Church of Ireland. It was much wiser to vote for the "better blue" than for "blue" Presbyterians, who might make common cause with Catholics.

This political position of the *Telegraph* was strongly attacked in an opposing leader written by the editor of the *Louth Examiner*. George responded with a leader of his own. The *Telegraph* had supported the Conservative party since the paper's founding fifty years before. "We regard it as a truism–as truth intensified, accepting the responsibility of ameliorating, improving and preserving the social framework in harmony." The paper wasn't a foil for Toryism or Orangeism. He denied the charge that he was willing for these organizations to infringe on the rights of others.

The Conservative party was very much opposed to disestablishment, and he believed that most of the citizens of Ireland, no matter their faith, would agree. This party "never was more popular or more vigorous, because time has attested its adoptability to the true interests of the population, preserving us alike from the wild fury of democracy, of which we have had a melancholy spectacle on the continent of America; and the tyranny of military despotism, of which the examples are so numerous on the Continent of Europe."

When a Londonderry newspaper made the case for religious union that George feared, he wrote a response that reinforced his hopes for Presbyterian action. "The Presbyterian laity unlike the laity of the Romish Church, will not be driven by their ministers like sheep. Especially, they will not tolerate their ministers presuming to force them into an unholy alliance with the disloyal Ultramontainists of this country. We hope their ministers will make no such attempt. Let them rather incite their people to make all efforts, religious and political, for the overthrow of Romanism in the land." The political portion of this exhortation was just what James had hoped to prevent during the crisis at the Donaghmore Church.

§

Not long after the election, George and John began an extraordinary conversation carried out in the pages of the *Telegraph,* the kind of conversation the two men might have had if John had dropped by the *Telegraph* office or George had stopped for tea at Kilbroney. The opening salvo from George was a critique of John precipitated by a newspaper account of the August meeting of the League. "We know he is patriotic; but, unfortunately, he has got into the wrong place for patriotism." George intended to warn John that his erroneous perspectives on Irish and British relations was leading him down a dangerous path. His mocking approach was likely to attract John's attention, but less likely to lead to common ground.

In his remarks at the League meeting, John had used the word "bosh," a synonym for the common word "balderdash." George proceeded to use it in that way in his critique of the meeting. George declared it was "bosh" to work for Irish self-government. That would only lead to control of Ireland by the Catholic Church and its mobs. To achieve his goal, John would have to end the Establishment that Parliament would never end without consulting the Protestants. "The Protestants of Ireland "would accept a civil war sooner than a price of a very uncivil robbery."

George declared that the Established Church, the Church of Ireland, wasn't the English church Catholics and Presbyterians believed it to be. It had been the official church in Ireland for many centuries. Its dominant rights had been established by conquest and through the sale of any claims to it by a Catholic Pope, a claim that resulted from an interpretation of an agreement (since lost) between the Pope and King of England, Henry II, many centuries before.

John had stated in his remarks at the meeting that he was willing to give his life for self-government. George believed that was a sincere statement but hoped that John would renounce that idea as his death wouldn't in anyway improve the position of his ideas. "The moment there was the slightest chance of England being so thoroughly demented…we would take the most effectual means to oppose it ourselves." George concluded with the flat statement that John's dream of self-government was a delusion. Two million Protestant Irishmen and the entire population of England would oppose such action. Ireland could never achieve self-government by "force of arms," as the English Empire was overwhelmingly strong. "We could sincerely wish his kindly feelings were turned into some channel which would practically serve our country."

John sat down at his desk in Kilbroney to respond. The main purpose of the letter was to clarify for George the difference in the Association and the League. His Irish National League hoped to unify all nationalists to struggle peacefully for Irish independence. The Irish Association, sponsored by the Catholic Church, planned to achieve the passage of three laws supported by the church leadership.

Before he ended his letter, John issued an invitation to his friend. "If at any time you should feel disposed to argue the question of Repeal, it would give me pleasure to assist you in a debate so vitally important to all the interests and honour of all Irishmen. The opinions which I hold upon the subject are well weighed in my own mind; but I am willing and anxious to hear and consider whatever serious objections may be offered against these by you or any of your correspondents."

George added a postscript to this letter when he printed it in the paper. He told John that he would be happy to enter into such a dialogue as soon as John assured him that his aim wasn't "the destruction of the rights of property, nor of the Protestant institutions and Protestant character of the Constitution, settled by the Revolution of 1690."

The discussion of Irish independence between John and George was underway.

§

John's speedy response skirted George's preconditions. Instead, he outlined his vision of the sequence of results that would follow independence. The most pressing first step would be to establish a new Irish government. John pictured this form of this government as a duplicate of the existing government in London. It would consist of a House of Commons and Lords under the authority of Queen Victoria. This Irish Parliament would have the right to create the laws for Ireland. "You and I, after Repeal, would have simply the same political rights with all other Irish citizens and no more; and I don't think a loyal Irishman should desire anymore."

John explained to George that the first issue they should discuss was how a new government would change existing practices, it being a question raised by potential supporters and opponents alike. The other important "branch" of this issue was how responsive an Irish Parliament would be to the needs and wishes of the people.

How would a new Irish Parliament act? John believed the first current practice to be addressed would be the Establishment. "I think it would immediately abolish the imperial establishment of a Protestant Church and would substitute entire religious equality upon the voluntary principle. [members of each church paying their own costs] As a Protestant, I desire that change with all my heart. I don't believe that any Christian religions benefited by robbery and I consider that it is simply as robbers that Anglicans of Ireland enjoy their establishment, and the Presbyterians (my own church) their dirty donum. Besides the anti-Christian character of our system of supporting the Protestant Churches of Ireland, it has the disgraceful distinction of being one that could not exist in our country but for foreign force."

Another concern that George had expressed was that there would be an extensive confiscation of property to avenge the seizure of property from the Catholic population in 1689. John began his answer by repeating his previously stated opinion that Repeal or a form of Home Rule wouldn't disturb the current ownership of land. As an extra bonus, the excessive amounts of money that Ireland was compelled to deposit in the English Treasury would be available to the Irish for Irish use. John estimated that this would amount to "twenty million pounds a year."

George printed John's letter along with his lengthy response. He began his letter by writing, "it is plain that we could never agree on the terms of the bargain; for his friends would disturb the Settlement of 1690—to procure which cost us one revolution, and to preserve which we would risk another. Under those circumstances, there would be no basis for negotiating; and every one will admit that nothing could be more absurd than to discuss a conclusion on whose preliminaries we are not agreed. Like Mr. Martin, we have given the matter serious attention; but unlike him, we never could discover in Ireland the materials out of which to construct an independent kingdom."

Then George explained the reasons he believed that Ireland lacked the "materials" for independence. Certainly he agreed that Ireland had many resources that could and should be put to better use. However, Ireland lacked some important resources such as coal and iron, items that they currently imported from England. If Ireland achieved separation, England would view Ireland as an enemy and make importing these necessities more expensive.

Furthermore, Ireland lacked another essential ingredient of an independent country, "a united people." George regarded this division as resulting not from religious differences alone, but from the fact that the Irish population came from two different races. "We Anglo-Celts could never amalgamate with the offspring of the aboriginal Celts; we should be found armed against each other, instead of co-operating together; and that, not because on our part we have any enmity to our fellow subjects; but on the principle stated by Mr. Martin that the Celts would break through an arrangement on which our highest hopes depend."

George then turned John's words into an affirmation and intensification of the determination of the Anglo-Celts to resist any attempt to remove the Establishment. After all, John had confirmed that this would be the first act of an independent Ireland. "We cling to the Union, because we hate revolution, and nothing could avert it the moment Mr. Martin and his party began to rob those who are flippantly called 'robbers.'"

Then, George wrote a history of how the Anglo-Celts came to Ireland about seven hundred years earlier. It was a result of a purchase of Ireland from the Pope, and then by conquest by Henry II and submission by the Irish chieftains. Since then, Ireland had belonged to England. "We have established our right whenever it was rebelled against, we have rescued the land from barrenness and the people from barbarism, and are we still to be described as 'robbers?' Are we 'robbers' because we took what the Pope gave, and what the Irish kings and Irish prelates confirmed by their submission?"

Since John had mentioned the regium donum, which the British government paid to Presbyterian ministers, George discussed that situation as well. This payment had begun with the invasion of King William. Presbyterian ministers had helped him as he came through County Down on his way to the Battle of the Boyne. In gratitude, King William had paid them a stipend to support each minister's salary. George wouldn't object if the Presbyterians wanted to end that long-standing payment, but he didn't agree with any such action.

George closed out his response by dealing with John's belief that additional money would accrue to Ireland from independence. He didn't argue with John about the validity of the amount of money, but he felt it wouldn't equal the sacrifice. "Our wealth increased; and our faith destroyed. Our provincialism to the Vatican secured; and our union with St. James severed. Mr. Martin promises to enrich us by an additional twenty millions a year but Mr. Martin's friends would take away that which would leave us poor indeed."

§

John certainly read this leader, but he didn't respond. He was in Dublin for the September meeting of the League. This was a very routine meeting. John began the meeting with comments on cattle raising in Ireland. English beef had been badly infected with cattle plague. Fortunately, that deadly decease hadn't infected Irish cattle. This made increasing the number of cattle raised in Ireland a financial benefit to both the English consumers and the Irish farmers. While the British could now get grain from other sources, they needed Ireland to supply the beef so essential for English dinners.

There was a downside to raising cattle in Ireland. John noted that cattle grazing was hard on Irish land, as the animals consumed vegetation needed to enrich Irish soil. Overgrazing in Ireland would all too soon result in beef shortages across England and ruined farmland in Ireland.

The only other topic of the meeting was the reading of a letter from Daunt. He reiterated that the League denounced all efforts to obtain independence through insurrections. This caused some hoots and whistles from the Fenian members. Daunt also reported to members what he had learned from his study of the financial problems between England and Ireland. With that, the meeting adjourned.

Nothing that occurred during this meeting would seem to warrant any space in the *Telegraph*. But George wrote a long leader on the subject, thereby continuing his correspondence with John. "The National League is not defunct, but it is evidently in an advanced stage of consumption." Still George considered it important to take issue with some of the items that were discussed. He disputed the idea that English legislation since the Union had been detrimental to Ireland, using as an example recently rejected legislation that would have prevented the importation of Irish beef. "Do what she may, England cannot please Mr. John Martin and his friends." England had rejected a law that would have prohibited the importation of beef from Ireland. According to the League the demand [from the Irish] just made and acceded to was one that was not injurious but beneficial to England, and that was why it had been granted. "Such argument is really contemptible." George didn't mention how odd it was for Parliament to even consider that moving beef from one part of a single country to another was importation. After all, the promise of the Act of Union was that Ireland and England had become one country.

George took exception to another of the ideas John offered at the meeting. He had suggested that the population of countries grew until they reached the limit of their food supplies. George believed that the amount of food increased at a faster rate than populations. So there would always, under Divine arrangements, be more food than needed for populations. "The resources of Ireland, properly developed, have been calculated as adequate to the support of twenty millions of a population…and that is the number which Mr. Martin would crowd into this island, to perish by plague, pestilence or famine under some of those mysterious visitations to which all peoples and countries are liable and especially…this variable climate of ours." "We are astonished that Mr. Martin's enmity to England would carry him so far as to prefer seeing our country one vast charnel-house rather than have it part and parcel of the greatest kingdom in the world."

The idea that John favored keeping Irish produce at home for Irish use seemed preposterous to George. If Ireland ended farm trade with England, Ireland would lose a great amount of money. "Mr. Martin's experience ought to have convinced him before now that this is not a grain growing country, and if we can make some money honestly by cattle we are not only justified, but are bound to do so. England is a ready market for anything we can produce and it is our interest to keep her so." "For our own part we do not doubt the sincerity of his motives; but we have no faith whatever in the sagacity of the means he would employ. He might be useful if he separated himself from such connexions; but at present, he is obstructing the progress of our country by keeping false hopes and inspiring men's minds with notions which can never be realized, not even with the aid that can be commanded from the rooms in D'Olier Street."

This time, John responded to George's leader. He was happy that George seemed to finally be willing to carefully examine the relationship that existed between England and Ireland. Now George might be willing to admit to the validity of the arguments that nationalists put forth to support the need for independence. "And I am persuaded that any Irishman of average intellect who fully examines the question will convince himself that, under the Union, the laws which bind us, and the authority which administers them, are English, and not Irish; that the purpose of those laws, and the business of that Government, is to employ Ireland and all that belongs to Ireland, for English uses and not Irish, that England, in consequence, grows continually richer, more populous, more flourishing in industry, commerce, and the arts, while Ireland, in consequence, grows continually poorer, less populous, and more miserable." When Irishmen become convinced by the evidence that what John said was true, they would have to take action to end the exploitation.

John turned next to George's analysis that he was "impelled by my 'enmity to England.'" John made clear to George what he really thought. "Certainly I do entertain a vehement antipathy to English rule in my country, and also to the prevalent English ideas in nearly all matters of national and of social economy. But God forbid that I should wish to exclude England from the benefit of the Christian law, or that I should wish to do wrong to any Englishman. My 'enmity' could not impel me to wish to do unto the English otherwise than I would that that they should do to us."

Despite the apparent progress in creating a helpful dialogue, John wasn't yet convinced that they could achieve any movement toward a consensus. "If you are determined to be merely an advocate of the English interest, and not to consider the Irish question judicially, and as an Irishman, then it were idle for me to controvert your arguments."

§

The response that George published seemed to be a retreat from his previous more responsive approach. In fact, George was in full attack mode, using his writing skills to belittle John and his work. First he interpreted John's response as angry. He said of the Irish National League, "The only thing characteristically national about it being its folly." "Their natural tendency is bad and dangerous and transportation or the gallows is at the end of the way. It was so in '48 and it is turning out so in '65."

Next George mocked the esteem with which John was held in Ireland. "Now, is it not a shame to say the least, that men who have pretensions like Mr. Martin to 'length of day,' and matured knowledge, and great experience, to not turn those privileges to better account for that Ireland and those Irishmen of which they are so very fond?" "These are the tribunes of the people, the tongues of the common mouth, and we will not complete the sentiment by saying we despise them, our feeling assuming the aspect of pity that they are not themselves better advised, and do not give better advice to others."

There were very practical reasons that would make John's hopes for independence a demented delusion. "Would it not strike the intellect of any man, even a young man, that if Irishmen were all united against England they could not wrest this island from the United Kingdom? Our countrymen are brave, but with all their bravery how could a population of six millions conquer one of twenty millions; how could a people with no army, no fleet, and too poor to employ foreign mercenaries, defend themselves against a people who have a powerful army, a more powerful fleet, and money to any amount to hire foreign legions to garrison our country and destroy us? Even if we could raise the army, and get the fleet, and hire the foreign soldiers, or be aided by the American Fenians (after they had landed), Ireland would be the battle-field and the conflict would terminate in seeing it a wild waste."

George did acknowledge that the Irish National League was the kind of national organization that should succeed. After all, it was being led by "Mr. John Martin, a gentleman of enlarged experience, admitted integrity, ripened judgment and whose age attests 'how many years a mortal man may live' while 'in his years are seen a youthful vigour and autumnal green.'" But that wasn't what was happening. The League was "in a deep decline," having been damaged by supposed friends. It had become a "poor, weak, and sickly thing."

To prove his point, George then published the letter of resignation from Edward Power who was one of the members of the governing committee of the League. While Power conceded that in former times, the League might well have succeeded, it had been looked over by the people for some months now, and they had turned away. Power hoped that John would listen to the people and put his talents to their use.

Two days later, John wrote another letter, but not in direct response to George's dismissal of the League. "The only question which I have shown any disposition to discuss with you is that of self-government." "You and I are Irishmen, both acknowledge the same Christian morality, the same general principles of honour and duty for our guidance both in private and public affairs—do we find the 'Union' good or bad?" "The English hold our country for their property; the English use and abuse us as things in their hands; they serve their own purposes with our revenue, and rents and produce, and labour, and intellect; their country grows richer with our money; more industrious by the ruin of our industry; more populous, while ours (alone of all the countries in Europe) decreases in population, more distinguished in literature and the arts, while literature and the arts are disappearing from Ireland; England fattens upon the decay of our country: do you and I like that?"

Then John turned to the issue of the future of the Irish National League that George had disparaged. He would be very happy to see it succeed, to have its goals and the honorable way it was being run, generally approved. "I would be charmed to receive your adhesion as a member, if on proper consideration you should become a convert to the political doctrine of the League...But whether the League prove a success or a failure as a political society, whether John Martin be deserving of your editorial pity for his silliness and his absurdities, whether six millions of Irishmen could conquer twenty millions of Englishmen, are the questions of no moment for your readers. The question is whether Ireland ought to seek for self-government and whether she can obtain it–whether the union is ruinous to the interests of our country, and whether we can get it repealed? Will you take that question into your consideration?"

John concluded his letter by offering his own analysis for the likely failure of the League. Not surprisingly, he differed from George. John argued that the majority of the Irish population did want Irish independence, but they had given up hope "for justice to be obtained by peaceable means." This was the alarming reason behind the increasing strength of the Fenian movement.

Even with the help of trained Irish soldiers from America, this revolution while England was at peace "seems to me a mad project. If it has ever been entertained, I trust my countrymen will consider and acknowledge how mad it is, and will give it no countenance; and I trust that the upper and middle classes of our countrymen will also consider the whole subject of Fenianism and will be roused from their shameful and wicked apathy to some sense of their duties as Irishmen." On the analysis of the Fenian plans, George and John agreed.

§

Again George wrote a lengthy response in the same edition of the paper. "We desire it to be distinctly understood that we have no personal quarrel with this gentleman, no wish to employ harsh language towards the political opinions he entertains. We believe him to be sincere, and therefore the more liable to be duped by those who are insincere, and we should be very glad if we could rescue him and every other Protestant gentleman similarly infatuated from a position as false as it is dangerous."

He continued with an homage to Ireland that was rare in his writings. "There is a charm to us in her lofty mountains, and pleasant valleys, in her noble rivers and beautiful lakes, in her old grey hills and green pastures, in her healthy climate and grateful soil. We love her for what she did in the far back past, when she gave the first written characters to England and religion to Europe–for her saints and her soldiers, her poets and her scholars. A Tory can be an Irishman and a lover of Ireland."

The two men agreed on their love of Ireland and opposition to the Fenians, but this was where their agreements ended, as George made clear. "Perhaps it is that we are too suspicious, or that he is not suspicious enough. Perhaps our reading has been different, as our conclusions differ." As for his response to John's question about independence, George sailed on, still convinced that Ireland shouldn't even try for independence, and should she try, she would certainly fail.

George then went on to repeat his reading of the history of Ireland, which made it the property of the Anglo-Celts. He then repeated that definitive argument against his desire for independence which John himself had provided. "Mr. Martin candidly stated in one of his letters, that he would not guarantee our religious endowments; that he would not guarantee the Settlement of the Revolution; and we could have no stronger motives for opposing a Repeal of the Union."

But George felt the most important reason for his opposition to the cause of independence was that it would be impossible to achieve. Even if Protestants received guarantees that there would be no Catholic ascendency, "no degradation of Protestants–no repetition of massacres, and no form of physical force applied to expel us from our country," there would be no similar assurance that their "resources would be better developed, and our industry better requited, that we grew richer and greater among the nations and happier at home."

"Think on it seriously, Mr. Martin. Is it wise to keep pursuing what we can never catch; seeking what we can never find; agitating the popular mind on an object which can never be accomplished? The independence of Ireland is gone for ever. And it is just as well." Should Ireland gain its independence, England would become an aggressive enemy, closing its borders and those of the rest of the world to anything that Ireland might manufacture, and stifling industry and making Irish land less valuable.

George issued a warning. "But look at it in another light, Mr. Martin, we Protestants of Ireland are one third of the population, and it is only when our throats shall have been cut, and we cannot speak, that we shall cease to cry 'No Repeal.'"

George ended with personal advice for John. "You have made sacrifices for Ireland, and you have suffered for Ireland, and we wish your sacrifices and your suffering had been in a better cause." "Look at your own reward. The

League is a failure in every way–a few…stay with you from respect to yourself; but where are the people? They have no confidence in any Protestant gentleman, and they would just use you to abuse you! Come out from among them; for they will pervert your patriotism; they have perverted it; and when your neck had been doomed to the halter, they would laugh at your simplicity. It is no use to seek self-government for Ireland. We cannot obtain it, we could not make good use of it, nor turn it to any advantage. It is according to the natural condition of things that the weaker must eventually succumb to the stronger power."

In John's quick response, he began by applauding the outreach of George's leader. "I feel bound to admit that there is a generous boldness to the declaration you make in your paper of the 26th inst., that you have no personal quarrel with me, that you believe me to be sincere, and that you do not wish to employ harsh language against the opinions I entertain. The tactics of Irish papers in the English interest are generally either to suppress and pretend to ignore Irish national aspiration, or else to stigmatise any Irishmen who avows their desire for self-government, as disreputable persons whose sentiments are unworthy of consideration. Such policy is certainly convenient for bad excuses and unscrupulous advocates. But you have no fear of weighing your cause in the scales of justice, and of exposing its lineaments to the light of truth. So much the better for both of us. We are to fight fair. It is hardly necessary for me to say that I entertain no personal animosity against you, and that I should scorn to treat you unfairly, even if I did hate you. We are two Irishmen disputing the question of Irish self-government."

At this point in his letter, John declared that people who opposed his country's rights had the greater burden of proof in any discussion. Then John framed the debate in Ireland as comparable to a similar situation existing between England and France, at the time of the Norman Conquest. How would the English have felt if the English capital been moved from London to Paris and England become a minor appendage to France? Would George then have believed that reality was acceptable? John clearly believed that English leaders subjected to control by France would feel the same way as Irish patriots felt about their subjugation to England.

"I am afraid you will think I write bitterly; and so I do. And it is because you seem to be a sincere advocate of the 'Union.' Because some prejudices, factious hatreds, selfish creeds that assert their claims in the name of Christ at utter variance with His commandments, are enough to make an honest and intelligent Irishman favour the wronging, the robbery, the debasement, the torture of his own people."

Then John tried again to explain what he meant by self-government. It meant the rule of Ireland by leaders in Ireland, a return to what the Protestant Volunteers of 1782 had achieved. Then all citizens were free and equal under law, Irish wealth would again be used for Irish purposes. The Irish would be their own masters, that the "English shall have no heavy foot upon our neck, no greedy hand in our pockets."

George had claimed that independence would mean a displacement of the Queen and the Parliamentary form of government in favor of a republican form. Perhaps all the Saxons would be expelled from Ireland. John conceded that this might happen. However, he didn't think this would be a likely result if independence were achieved by peaceful means. Ownership of the land and the social order wouldn't likely be disturbed. There wasn't a single sentence that indicated any interest on the part of the nationalists in expelling the Saxons from Ireland or confiscating their holdings. "Tis time that such stupid calumnies were stopped."

As to justification for his belief that England would "let us go in peace," John asked permission to discuss in another letter his reasons for that conviction. "But I must acknowledge that many men of national sentiments think like you in this matter–that England estimates so highly the advantages she derives from our subjection that she would fight to the death to maintain her rule over us."

In his response to John's letter, George claimed that John had failed to respond to his concern that Ireland would not be able to continue to be free with a hostile and well-armed country beside them. John had made assertions without proof, seemingly not recognizing that he was making predictions about what would happen after independence as well. The two men had very different expectations of English actions. Only the future would reveal whose assertions were correct. "Mr. Martin can never induce England to concede, because it knows it would be suicide for herself–which we, the Protestants of Ireland, would not allow her to commit, if she were ever so willing."

John's English/France analogy didn't dent George's judgment of the situation. George took the illustration as a comparison between what had actually happened in England and what had happened in Ireland. In so doing, he repeated his reasoning behind the assertion that church property in Ireland had never been Catholic property.

Then George provided his ultimate argument that independence for Ireland could never be achieved. "The English and Scotch settlers were literally coaxed to occupy a territory, then reduced to barrenness, and inhabited by a people sunk in barbarism. It is plain, therefore that this country whether won by the sword, or by the submission of the chiefs, we Anglo-Celts are the owners of Ireland, and we must be consulted before any change occurs in the government of the kingdom."

"We Protestants have the faith of the primitive Irish; and we have thus a double right to what we enjoy…We are the equal of one of the greatest countries in the world…We have the fullest measures of civil and religious liberty–that for which every right-minded man would fight…and as the country is ours and the choice is ours, we will never consent to a Repeal of the Union."

John did not reply again.

Chapter 13

Endings

1865 – 1867

While John and George were engaged in their newspaper dialogue on national independence, the government in Ireland acted against the *Irish People* newspaper. About 9 p.m. on September 14th, policemen stormed into the paper's offices. O'Donovan Rossa was the first arrested as he came into the office and Thomas Luby soon after. Four police were sent to the home of John O'Leary and arrested him. However, before taking him away, they allowed him to finish smoking his pipe and to drink a whiskey and water. After being charged with high treason, the newspapermen were taken to Richmond prison. This was the same place that John had been held for almost a year.

John referred to O'Leary in a letter to Eva, the wife of his fellow felon, Kevin O'Dogherty. "For some considerable time–indeed until quite recently– the Fenian newspaper here never mentioned me but for the purpose of lowering me in popular esteem; not, I am persuaded from any personal dislike of the men who conduct it towards me but as carrying out their policy of destroying the reputation of all politicians not of their action. And, strangely enough, John O'Leary was principle editor of the last year and half or 2 years. He and I never met nor had any correspondence since we parted in Paris till quite recently. Quite recently he wrote to me urgently requesting an interview in Dublin. I replied saying I would be in Dublin about 10 days after for a League meeting and would gladly receive him. He wrote in the old friendly spirit of our Paris intercourse. Accordingly, he did call and we had a long chat in which I gave him my settled opinion in general grounds of the utter folly of the scheme attributed to the Fenians. I expected that he would offer to submit to me private information, but he offered nothing of the kind and asked for nothing. I was glad and sorry to see him again. He and I are friends still, though diverging farther and farther in politics."

Not surprisingly, George had a very different reaction. He was greatly pleased that the government had finally taken some action against the Fenians. The trials that he was sure would take place very soon would dampen the enthusiasm for such activities in the future. Despite his pleasure at the arrests, he found fault with the British actions overall, which he felt had led to this unfortunate situation. "England's great fault is that she will not discriminate between the loyal and the rebellious, and that she punished the one and pets the other." This failure was what had permitted the Fenians to thrive.

Another reason for the Fenians' existence was the reaction to the Young Irelanders revolt. "The rebels of '48 were advanced to the dignity of heroes, when they ought to have been allowed to make a last speech and dying declaration on the gallows. The Fenians of '65, if their conduct be proved treasonable, must be dealt with differently, if we are to have peace in our country." "We want the snake killed, not merely scotched, for the sake of our country which the scheming demagogues have ruined."

George continued on the same vein in a leader a few weeks later. "Orangemen never did the country harm. On the contrary, they have materially served it by their intelligence, property and industry, and by their very presence which keeps treason in check, and by overthrowing it when it is openly displayed. Fenianism, on the other hand, agitated the minds of the people, sent them in pursuit of what they never could obtain so long as Orangeism is faithful to itself, and intended to massacre all who were on the side of law and order."

Next George mentioned some of the important contributions of the Orangemen to Ireland. "Their ancestors founded the present dynasty, and they will maintain it. What men buy dearly, they prize highly. And history shows us the value we ought to place on the privileges we obtained. Orangemen want no monopolies. Give them fair play and they are sure to win wherever you plant the two elements of loyalty and disloyalty."

The Fenian arrests had taken place in Dublin. But George was concerned that Fenian supporters were increasingly dangerous in Newry as well. There was an alarming rumor circulating around Newry that the Fenians were running guns into Newry. He asked questions of local officials to which he demanded answers. Had five hundred guns come into Newry and then been dispersed? Had customs officials found more guns hidden in a cask? And had they then ordered that the cask and guns should be delivered as addressed? Why was a request from an Armagh landlord to import guns to arm his tenants refused? Apparently, no one answered the questions as he repeated them in the next edition of the paper.

By the end of November, trials of the arrested Fenians were underway in the Green Street Court House. The leaders of the *Irish People* were charged with felony treason, the same law that had been created in 1848 to convict John. Luby was tried first, and O'Leary second. They were defended by Isaac Butt, as had John been over a decade before.

Both men were convicted mainly on the strength of letters they had written and testimony from Pierce Nagle, a British spy. Both men were immediately taken to Mountjoy Prison. O'Leary was forced to endure having his long hair and beard shaved before he was locked into his cell, sentenced to twenty years at hard labor.

While the trials were underway, George wrote another angry leader condemning the government laxity toward the Fenians. George believed that the Fenians should have been arrested and tried at the time of the McManus funeral for the speeches that had been given at Glasnevin Cemetery. But the government had failed to take any action. As a result, the Fenians had become much stronger during the ensuing four years. Even worse, British officials running Richmond Prison had allowed one of the former members of the

Pope's Brigade to serve in the police force guarding it. This one stupid mistake had allowed James Stephens, the Fenian leader, to escape, thereby endangering the safety of Ireland.

George worried that the Dublin trials weren't putting an end to Fenians, Surely, there were others who were active in the Newry area and were now possibly armed with something more deadly than pikes and scythes. And soon enough, a local man was arrested and charged with being a Fenian. Timothy McArdle was a stonemason who was working on the Riverside Church, which was under construction near the Canal. A man from Antrim claimed that McArdle had administered a Fenian oath to him. McArdle vehemently proclaimed his innocence. Still the word of one man was enough to get him arrested. When his home was searched, nothing at all that would substantiate the charges against him was found, but he was sent to Antrim where he would face trial at the Antrim Assizes. Perhaps he was able to convince police there that he was innocent, as he never appeared in court.

Shortly after Christmas, George was pleased by the news O'Leary and Luby had been taken from Mountjoy Prison early on Christmas morning, and shipped across the Irish Sea to Dartmoor Prison. There they would have the extra punishment of having all the orders they were compelled to obey delivered by "a Saxon voice." They would understand that they have been conquered and would be working hard in harsh conditions. "The rest of their lives will be miserable." Had they been allowed to stay in Ireland, they might still have dreamed of escaping. In England, that hope had been yanked away. A new law in England had assured the prisoners that though they had been convicted of treason, they would not suffer the death penalty as long as no one had died as a result of their actions. George dissented, as he was a strong supporter of capital punishment and would have preferred they hang.

As was his custom, George began the year with his usual New Year leader. He had some reflections on life that he wanted to share with his readers. "Happy he who can live while he lives, and takes the world as it is, ascribing everything to a beneficent cause, whose mysteries are specially reserved for the study of the future." "We go on, and hope on, and enjoy on, as if the years were never to end, and time exempt from the common doom."

He had less to say about the Fenians than his readers might have expected. He ended with a challenge to the Protestants of Ireland. If they stayed true to their principles and history, the year 1866 would be a good year.

§

James Harshaw was nearly 70 when the year 1866 began. This was a good age for an Irish farmer who performed such hard physical work. Since the controversy in the Donaghmore Presbyterian Church, James had lived a quieter life. Still there were many stresses on Irish farmers that he couldn't avoid. Weather was always an unknown factor that greatly affected the quality and quantity of each harvest. He also understood that each year his income would be squeezed between lower prices for the things he grew and the taxes he had to pay.

On the first Sabbath of the new year, the results of stress and age caught up with James. He recorded the event in his journal entry for January 7th. "was awoke about 5 oclock by my nose began Blooding." James made no mention of any activities that day.

His entry for the next day was much more alarming. This time, he was awakened earlier with another nose bleed. This time, no amount of packing or pinching could stop the flow of blood. It flowed down his chin, and onto his shirt and sheets. This hemorrhage continued until dawn when son John arrived from Loughorne. Very alarmed, John and then Andrew struggled unsuccessfully to contain the hemorrhage. In desperation, they held their father upside down over the end of the bedstead. Finally, the bleeding stopped.

Unfortunately, he had lost so much blood that he was unable to function as usual. So as soon as his wife and the servant girls had cleared away the blood, and changed the bed sheets, he returned to bed for the rest of the day, and the next day as well.

Word of his poor health spread around the neighborhood, and friends came by to enquire for him. Son Robert hurried north from Mountmellick, concerned for James's health. On the third day, James got up, dressed and walked about the farm, attending to business. And he wrote in his journal as always. He recorded Robert's return to Mountmellick, and the birth of a new granddaughter born to his youngest daughter Sarah Anne.

One of Ireland's folk sayings was that cocks crowing at night was a sign of bad luck or death. This must have been in James's mind when he wrote this in his journal at the end of January. "The cocks crowed, in the foul house about ten at night."

As the weeks passed, it became clear to everyone, that James wasn't going to recover his usual good health. He walked about the farm, now with a shawl or cape around his shoulders to keep him warmer. His journal made clear that he had been greatly affected by his excessive bleeding. He seldom wrote about any subject except the weather and the tasks he had assigned to his workers each day. And on the Sabbath, he would record the number of weeks that had passed since he had last seen his missing loved ones.

On April 1st, he recorded the count one last time. "The 28th Sabbath since Absalom [Samuel] left me, and the 363rd since I parted with Mary, & the 78th since I parted with Willy." On April 6th, James wrote his last entry. "very dry – Grubbing and harrowing."

§

Despite George's concern, there had been little overt Fenian action in the Newry area. Aside from the arrest of Timothy McArdle, no accusation of Fenianism had been reported. However, George did note many reports from the rural areas around Newry of small groups of men, assembling in the dark of night. While there were no reports as to what they were doing, clearly their actions were attributed to the Fenians.

So it was somewhat of a surprise, when early in February, the Lord Lieutenant notified local magistrates that Newry had been proclaimed, and its restrictions were to begin on the next Monday. It would apply not only to the town itself, but also to the nearby areas, some in Armagh, some in Down. Among the proclaimed townlands was Loughorne, and the ones around Warrenpoint.

George informed his readers what this would mean to them. The Lord Lieutenant had sent in additional constables. The cost of this additional law enforcement would be levied against the rate payers. These constables would be charged with making sure that no one brought guns, or other contraband outside their dwellings. The penalty for this crime was two years in prison. Police had the right to detain anyone they deemed suspicious, to search them and to confiscate anything they judged to be contraband. Any civilian could detain any neighbor he saw with one of the forbidden items. Everyone would be required to turn in their weapons at designated collection points. Military and police would be exempted along with those who were allowed to hunt. And police were permitted to burst into any home at any time of day or night without a warrant.

George strongly supported the government actions. However, he felt that one more location should have been proclaimed, the parish of Killeavy, south of Newry. The exemption of this area seemed strange, as a manufactory of pikes was suspected to be hidden somewhere on the mountain side.

A month passed before there was any action within the proclaimed areas. Police converged early on a March morning on the home of Michael Grant on Rathfriland Road, near Crown Bridge. The police found considerable incriminating evidence: a flask of powder, blank cartridges, bullet moulds, seditious songbooks, and two copies of a Dublin newspaper. Michael's son Patrick was also arrested and remanded in custody for a week.

Police returned to make additional searches of the nursery which Michael Grant owned. As the search was about to end, one policeman noticed disturbed soil on the floor of a hothouse. A bit of digging uncovered a military style gun buried there. Michael was immediately arrested, but later released on heavy bail. Patrick was sent to Downpatrick jail to await trial. However there was no record that Patrick ever stood trial.

The arrests put the Fenian movement under great stress in early 1866, but their troubles didn't help the League. It was in such great financial difficulties that at the February meeting, John announced that they would cease having monthly meetings and give up their offices to save money. The meeting went peacefully enough, though John felt that over half of the people attending were Fenians. Afterward, John let his friend Daunt know what he thought of the Fenians. "I declared my conviction that the Fenian scheme was impracticable without the help of a first-rate power, and that our scheme of peaceful public repeal association was practicable & was the only safe and effectual means of relief and regeneration for Ireland. REPEAL can be obtained in no way other than a peaceful one."

John had held this position from the moment that he first joined the Repeal Association after O'Connell had been convicted for conspiracy. As he had told George in their correspondence on the subject, John was sure that independence would be given to Ireland if the Irish nationalists unified to demand it. He had always been a moral force repealer even when O'Connell charged the Young Irelanders with supporting armed revolution.

However, should the Fenian approach, "destruction of English rule by military force" be strong enough to be successful, he would consider that preferable to continued English rule. "But I see no means of a military expulsion of the English power." The idea that Ireland would be liberated by an invading army of trained Irish soldiers from America seemed a delusion. If England remained at peace, it "would be sure to prove a miserable failure. And all the bloodshed & confusion it would cause would be in vain and worse than in vain. I HATE revolution. I LOVE order, authority and peace." "I AM A REPEALER. But my hopes of repeal are not rising but falling."

There was one additional reason that John thought that the Fenians would never succeed. He seldom mentioned this, as he preferred to argue the issue on his belief that the existing situation between Ireland and England would make a successful armed revolt impossible. And he hated attacking any nationalist leader. Only in a private letter, did he make his feelings about James Stephens, the Fenian Head Center, clear. "Mr. Stephens is (in my own judgment & I know the man well) a very unsafe man for a leader, & among his other faults he is fanatically republican, socialist, and all that sort of thing. He is also vain, egotistic, ambitious, unscrupulous, to a very high degree."

George wrote his epitaph for the Irish National League in the middle of April. This followed the League meeting in April at which John announced that they hadn't received enough money from member dues, or enough new members, to continue in the present manner. He proposed that the advisory committee should continue to exist to call occasional meetings or make public statements. George saw this as a tactic to fade away without any sign of public failure and mocked them for hiding their failure behind the activism of the other two groups, the National Association and the Fenians. George thought they should have admitted that "their object is unattainable, or the means insufficient, or that the people have grown tired of such agitations."

George found the entire idea to be "folly." England would never "consent to a repeal of the Union." Most important, people in Ireland loathed the idea. Such a crazy notion "could only reside in the Brain of a 'nationalist,' whose enthusiasm had blinded him to the circumstances of the times."

The fact that England had already granted to Canada and Australia what John wanted for Ireland seemed to provide a significant basis for John's hope for peaceful resolution. George was ready to dispense with this idea as well. "The union with Ireland is necessary to her [England's] safety, and even to her existence as a great Power."

Furthermore, George said that self-governing arrangements such as those in Canada and Australia would be impossible as Ireland and England were geographically close. In this different situation, there must be "an entire separation of the two countries, and this latter event England never can permit to happen. Mr. Martin perhaps would say no such consequences would follow from repeal, but they are, as we believe, both natural and necessary. The true remedy for us is to imitate the wisdom of the Scotch, forgetting the dreams of national 'independence,' and endeavouring by peaceful organisations to help forward our country in the path of prosperity. The utter failure of the League is gratifying, because it shows that one bubble has finally burst, and that the people have one sham the less to distract their attentions from their true interests."

Nothing in George's comments were either a surprise or a reason for despair. However, John suffered intensely from the results of his failure. In July, he wrote of his feelings to his close friend, Father Kenyon. "I am sinking heavily too, and this is also a shame, though it may be no pity. We are only in our 54th year each and both of us had constitutions of body and mind to live well till the 74th at least. It is Ireland no doubt, Ireland that dings and crushes us down." "It is Ireland that does it all. I know and feel that. It almost seems as its fate won't permit anybody to save Ireland."

John's words turned even more gloomy as the letter continued. "I suppose we will all die – rot into our graves and you among the first...It is becoming a dreary business for me in spite of my wonderful gift of cheerfulness, to live at all. Everything that concerns me goes wrong more or less. No brightness, all gloom."

The Irish National League had certainly failed, despite John's best efforts. However, there were still actions that needed to be taken to terminate its existence. So in August, John went to Dublin to handle these official duties with one last meeting in D'Olier Street, and to clear out their offices there.

When John walked into the League rooms, he was surprised to see a large crowd in attendance. Still, he began the meeting as planned, by explaining the decisions that the he and the advisory committee had made. He talked about the actions that the British government had taken and the danger that resulted for everyone. At this remark, there was loud applause.

John responded, "I find that there are friends of the Fenians here." More cheers. He hoped that "any Fenian that came to attend its (the League) meeting–any Fenians that do us the honour of being our guests will behave like gentlemen."

But as John continued, it became clear that civility wasn't on the Fenian agenda. "It is fact that on many occasions the meetings of the Irish National League have been disturbed in a rowdy manner by those that purported to be Fenians." This time the Fenians responded by shouting, "No, no."

"I have been told on unexceptionable authority, that on more than one occasion the leader of the rowdy...disturbances which were unworthy of any patriotic Irishmen was Mr. Nagle, Fenian and government spy." As John made that charge, the Fenians responded with hisses.

But John was not to be intimidated. "I think you will consider I am entitled to say I have never yet endeavoured to bully anyone, but I have never permitted anybody or any number of men to bully me, and I never will." These defiant words were interrupted three times by shouts of "hear, hear," from the Fenians.

"I understand, and I suppose orders have been given by some of those who direct the Fenians in Ireland by any means, by rowdyism, to prevent John Martin and those who think with him speaking their sentiments out before the country."

At this point, Fenian members of the audience began to interrupt John and take over the meeting. John challenged one particularly loud Fenian to come forward, give his name and make any remarks on Ireland that wouldn't take him to prison. This his interrupter was unwilling to do. "Please proceed," another of the Fenians told John.

So John did just that. "I have stated that monthly meetings were interrupted owing to the suspension of habeas corpus act, and to the fact that certain persons purporting to be Fenians came here and attempted to prevent the proceedings by uproar. I will add another one, that though I myself have always been treated with more respect and consideration than I consider myself entitled to as a politician, the country does not seem disposed to join with me and with other gentlemen to assist in the League. From these 3 reasons…the course of our monthly meetings has been interrupted."

John then turned to an affirmation of the reasons that Ireland was getting ever weaker and poorer. "Emigration continues to go on exhausting the strength of the country." And the Irish citizens who were leaving were the young people that Ireland needed most. They were leaving because of the high taxes and the poor relations with the people who owned the land they farmed. "So far as to the material condition of the country, it is not more heartening than the constitutional condition, for we have actually no national rights and no constitutional liberty at present."

A Fenian responded, 'Begorra, and we'll fight for them." The Fenians applauded lustily

"The liberty of every man in Ireland is enjoyed by merely the caprice of the police in Ireland or those who order them."

"You mean the G division?" [plain clothes detectives of the Dublin police] Great laughter followed from fellow Fenians.

At this point, one of the Fenians got up and left the room. A remark he made on the way out seemed to cause increased agitation among the Fenians. John declared then that he would make no more attempts to speak and just close up the meeting.

Despite that announcement, John had one more thing he wanted to say, and he hoped the Fenians would listen quietly. "I do not expect them to respect me, but I ask them to respect themselves. I do not ask their approval, but I ask them to seek the approval of their own consciences. I understand pretty well their reasons for acting as they do. I understand the secret authorities, whom they blindly obey." John was interrupted with loud hissing and some renewed shouting.

Still John persisted. "These men do not come before the public as I do, and do not make themselves responsible as I do for whatever I say and do. I do not pretend to speak about the system they adopt, but I only ask that I may be free to speak my own sentiments." A mixture of applause and hisses. "I do not pretend to criticize the leaders of the Fenians, as I am not in a position to do so."

One of the Fenians responded. "it is a d''d good job for them." The Fenians erupted in loud laughter.

John had the last word. "But I will say this, that I do not believe any scheme will succeed in the end which endeavours to prevail by rowdyism and conduct unbecoming the character of any good Irishman, or any man whatever." The Fenians hissed their displeasure at John's critique.

"I now dissolve the meeting." John then went into the crowd and began to speak to some of them, but the Fenian uproar was so loud that he couldn't be heard. That effort to communicate with the Fenians having failed, John headed toward the door. At that moment, the Fenians unleashed a barrage of rotten eggs. One hit the wall, just behind John and spattered its rotten yellow contents over his jacket. Reporters and other League members were also pelted as they hustled from the room.

Not surprisingly, George treated his readers to his comments on the episode in Dublin. "In the whole history of human folly it would be difficult to find anything more ludicrous than the proceedings at the last meeting of this body. The fading glories of Mr. John Martin, once a star of the first magnitude, were completely eclipsed on this occasion. It would appear that this gentleman is not sufficiently national, or rather revolutionary for his crowd of rowdies who formed the principal part of the audience. Since he is not foolhardy enough to get himself deposited in gaol, they refused to listen to his oratory, which was cut short by a volley of disreputable eggs. Mr. Martin ought, by this time, to understand the nature of the materials with which he has to deal, and if he persists in his efforts to revive agitation, few will pity him when he is driven to the laundry to remove the pungent odor to which he has just been treated. How the mighty are fallen! Mr. Martin pelted with rotten eggs! This is the last phase of Irish martyrdom, and truly it is hard to have to endure the indignity."

§

Though James had stopped writing his daily entries in his journal, he did continue as best he could to attend to the harvest. There was great concern about the hay crop as the weather had been bad. When the harvest concluded, James had more time to relax.

However, on October 25th, the normal rhythms at Ringbane House ended. Sarah had risen early, as Irish wives were expected to do, getting tea and breakfast for the men of the house before they headed off to their full day of work. On this day, Sarah noted that James hadn't come downstairs for his breakfast. So she went up to their room to see what was amiss.

James was sitting on the edge of the bed with a sock in his hand, shivering with cold. He had been preparing to put his sock on when he was struck by a massive stroke. Sarah summoned one of the servants, and together they were able to get James dressed, and assist him down the stairs to his chair by the fire. He complained of a pain in his head and was unable to keep from vomiting up his tea. He seemed alarmingly weak to the women.

Still he requested to be taken outside. Son James got on one side of his father, and with one of the servant girls, Jenny Bradford, on the other, they were able to get James to his feet. Together, they helped him out the back door, around the south side of the house, and through the big door. From that spot, James could look across the fields of Loughorne. Together James and Jenny were able to get James back into the house by the fire.

Sarah and the servants kept the fire high during the day to keep James warm. He sat there until after sunset. Around 7 p.m., the Harshaw sons assembled to help get James back up the stairs to his room and settled into bed. The blood clots in his brain had caused additional damage during the day. James was no longer able to move his legs at all, and the stairs from the kitchen had a bend partway up that made the move even more difficult. However, sons John, James Jr. and Andrew working together were finally able to carry James up the stairs and lower him into his bed. He would spend the rest of his life in his bedroom.

Naturally, this stroke was very concerning to the family. One of the children wrote to Robert in Mountmellick and asked him to travel home at once. Medical help was also called. Dr. Saunderson was nearby and quickly visited. John Martin was in Kilbroney and came to see his favorite uncle as well. The news from both men was grim. There was no hope that James would recover. He might linger on for days or months in his current state. But he would not improve.

Despite the hopelessness of James's situation, John Martin came often to see James, to offer medicine that would keep him comfortable. And since James could still talk, the two men could recapture some of the wonderful conversations they had had before John became politically active. Though James had become incontinent, Sarah and the servants worked very hard to keep him dry and comfortable. Every day, he would be assisted to the chair beside the fire to talk with friends and family.

In the first days after James was stricken, one or more of the family sat up with him through the night. After the first shock had passed, Andrew slept with James, keeping faithful watch over his father, and providing some relief to Sarah. Joe Duff came in every day to shave James who preferred to be clean-shaven. Robert returned to his church, and a sort of new normal settled over Ringbane.

This situation lasted exactly three months when James caught a cold. The racking cough which accompanied the cold clearly represented a major turn for the worse. This new illness seemed to cause him considerable discomfort on the second day. Again word was sent to Mountmellick for Robert to come home. It was soon clear to everyone that James would not live much longer. Again the sons sat up with their father, first James Jr. and then the next night, both James Jr. and Andrew. John came over from Loughorne and read some of James's favorite parts of the Bible to please him and provide comfort. This condition continued for four days. By Tuesday, January 29th, James could barely speak. Late in that afternoon, John asked his father if he could hear him reading the Bible and Robert praying. James replied, "I do." Those were the last words he ever spoke.

James's poor condition on Tuesday deteriorated further during the night... "He was weaker and less conscious." About 9 a.m., he was lifted into his chair so clean sheets could be put on his bed and a dry shirt put on to replace the wet one. In order to make this change, James had to be held in the chair. So he was quickly put back to bed.

The hours of painful waiting dragged by. Around noon, it became obvious that the end was near. Local family members were called home and stood weeping by the bed, while John and Robert read from the Bible and prayed. James Jr. held his father's hand, and kept the family informed as to the "fitful motions" of James's heart.

The day had been damp and cloudy. Around 4 p.m., the sun came out of the clouds. It "shone brightly and just kissed his noble brow and at 4 minutes past 4 o'clock his pure noble generous saintly spirit winged its flight to glory to bask forever in the realms of the Sun of the Redeemer."

James had slipped quietly away without "a groan or a struggle – in peace." Most of his local family were with him as he left. James had died exactly one year to the day after he heard the "cocks crow in the foul house."

There was much to be done. Ellen, son John's wife, James's much-loved Spartan Queen, hurried over from Loughorne to take charge. With the help of Nancy Bagnel and Joe Duff, she carried James downstairs from his room to the low closet off the living room. After some discussion, the funeral was set for the following Saturday.

Joe and some of the other workers came in and sat all night in the kitchen. Son James Jr., daughter Sarah Anne, Nancy and some of the other women were up all night preparing food that would be needed the next few days. Early the next morning, James Jr. and Alex Douglas went into Newry to get the expected items needed for the wake. They brought two wagons with them expecting to bring home the coffin. But it had to be made special and wouldn't be ready until the next day.

Neighbors who heard the sad news came in during the day to visit for a while, as James had so often done for others. By 4 p.m., the parlor was full. Ellen served them all tea. Afterward, most people went home, so a sort of quiet settled over the house.

On Friday, the long coffin arrived from Newry and James's body was placed in it by Joe Duff, Nancy, James Jr. and Ellen. The house was filled with mourners for the wake. Again Ellen served tea to the entire crowd. Many of them stayed all night, some in the parlor, some in the kitchen.

The weather on Saturday was cold but sunny. Some neighbors came in early to stay with the family. Relatives began to arrive around 9 a.m. They received the traditional crape to tie around their arms, as well as black gloves. "All his neighbors and friends and acquaintances came to show their last sad respect by attending his funeral." Three of the Martin family came, John, David, and their sister Mary. Robert Corbett came over from Lisnacreevy, along with other Harshaw relatives from Ballynafern. Many local ministers attended as well. Notably, Rev. Lindsay wasn't among them.

The ceremony began at 11 a.m. in Ringbane when Rev. Elliott gave a brief address based on 1 Thess. IV 13 – 18. Rev. Rogers offered a prayer. Then the boys removed their father from the low closet to the hearse that was waiting outside. About noon, the procession left Ringbane, and headed down Ardkeragh Road toward the Glascar Church.

The hearse stopped at the gate, and James's sons raised the coffin to their shoulders, and carried it to the gravesite. James was buried with his children, the first Samuel Alexander, Elizabeth Martin, and Mary Douglas who had died before him. Since Glascar Church had been built on high ground, there was a lovely view of the valleys and mountains of southern Down for anyone visiting the site to enjoy. Unfortunately, there was no money to pay for a proper headstone. His grave would remain unmarked for over a century.

Chapter 14

Turning the Other Cheek
1867 - 1868

The death of James Harshaw was a sad blow to his family and friends, but his long decline had given them a chance to prepare for the inevitable ending. While James lay dying, George had become increasingly concerned about Fenian activities. He devoted several leaders to the subject, making sure that the people of Ulster realized they were in danger. "In a word, Fenianism is a deadly and devastating curse, and until we have heard the last of it, Ireland cannot advance with the other nations of the world."

The government shared George's concerns and acted quickly by imposing new restrictions on gun possession. Equally pleasing to George were the special watches established in port towns like Newry to intercept any American man who stepped foot on Irish soil. With these preparations in place, any Fenian attempt to revolt would be impossible. "The invasion bubble has burst, and the wonder now is that it continued to float so long in empty air, dazzling the eyes of dupes, while they lavishly contributed to fill the 'military chest' of the Head Center [James Stephens] and his redoubted companions." "Ireland will advance to a foremost place among the nations of the earth, prosperous because loyal and industrious, and honoured because it shall have fulfilled the requirements inseparable from material and moral greatness."

But as soon as George had written his bold claim that "the bubble had burst," there was news of arrests in Belfast. The suspects had weapons and equipment needed to make bullets. With this new information, George returned to the topic in the very next edition of the paper. He asked any Fenians who might see his paper what they thought they were going to gain even if they should achieve Irish independence. "We live under the best constitution in the world, where the utmost freedom is given to every man, rich or poor, high or low, except the freedom of doing evil without restraint. We heartily wish that the would-be rebels who live among us, would compare the position of every honest or good citizen in this land with the citizens in other countries, and not be deluded anymore by the foolery of those Fenian leaders."

From nearby Kilbroney, John was following the unfolding events as carefully as George was. Soon after George's message to the Fenians appeared in the paper, John wrote a letter to his friend Mahon about his continued support for independence and firm belief that it would be achieved without violence. He lamented that he hadn't been able to make more of a success of the League, in part because of the Fenian's intense obstruction. "And Fenianism has carried off nearly all of the lower class. Of course I could keep up appearances of a respectable Repeal party still. But I don't choose that sort of proceeding. Meantime the country is going to the devil."

At the end of his letter, John told Mahon that the Fenians wouldn't have progressed as an institution without the help of his friend John Mitchel. Stephens had traveled to Tennessee as he was beginning to form the Fenians to ask Mitchel to become the American leader. Mitchel had refused. But after the Civil War ended, and Mitchel was freed from prison with Fenian help, he did go to Paris to act as a treasurer to disperse Fenian funds as directed. "Mitchel seems fated ever to fail. And in all the world, and in all history, there is no braver nor truer man."

As January ended, and the days began to grow longer, George again reassured his readers that the Fenian actions had been suppressed. He even applauded efforts by Catholic priests to separate their parishioners from the Fenians. However, neither their efforts nor George's leaders actually suppressed the Fenians. In mid-February, fighting began.

For the first time, George used the words "Fenian Uprising." The main fighting had occurred in the south, but arrests were being made across Ireland. They came as close to Newry as Dundalk to the south, and Banbridge which was just a few miles north of Newry There a man named John Murray was arrested under suspicion that he was the Head Center in Belfast. Police reported that when they searched his home, they found substantial incriminating evidence. He was brought to the Newry bridewell before being sent north to Belfast.

Newry officials were also on high alert. Any stranger in town was immediately stopped and questioned. Four men were detained on suspicion that they had participated in a Fenian uprising in Chester, England. However they were released from prison a few days later. Armed patrols across the town were increased along with closer inspections of the local pubs. Despite the visible police presence, residents of Newry were on edge. When they saw fires burning on the mountains around town, many believed them to be signal fires set by the Fenians. George calmed the panic. These were the usual fires local farmers set in late winter to burn off the whin [gorse] from the hillsides.

As Saint Patrick's Day neared, nerves became even more raw. The day before the holiday, police arrested a stranger in Newry. He caught their attention because he had a military walk, and apparently knew no one in Newry. The suspect told police that he was on his way to Belfast where he worked. This aroused suspicions as he was walking in the opposite direction when stopped. Police believed that he was a Fenian drill master. His name was Michael Roller of Carlow. He claimed to have been working locally on a farm, but his hands weren't marked by farm work. He was held for a week, but then released without charges. Worries that there would be problems on St. Patrick's Day proved unfounded.

John wrote a letter to the *Nation* a few days afterward, expressing his opinion that the Fenian uprising had ended in inevitable failure, that it had been a "disaster." The British had already established special Commission Courts to try the Fenians who had been arrested. John believed that these trials were all that was left of the Fenian uprising. "We submit to superior force, but we do not consent the destruction of our independent Parliament and government, the people of Ireland have never sanctioned the usurpation of 1800, nor do I believe they ever will. It is that false position that is the sole cause of all the political troubles of Ireland, of the embittered feeling between the two people and the danger which now assuredly begins to threaten the English Empire."

A few days later, John wrote another letter to the *Nation*. After some explanation of his position, John advised readers that nationalists must adjust to living under the law as it existed, until Ireland could be free to make laws for its own benefit. Then he returned to his critique of the Fenians. "The late Fenian uprising was imprudent, was mischievous, was insane; but it was not a crime against natural law, or a sin against God."

§

Though St. Patrick's Day in Newry had been totally peaceful, the day after was not. Hugh Wallace owned a small grocery store and "spirit shop" in Loughbrickland. On March 18th two men, Murnaghan, and a blind man named Hawthorn, got into a minor dispute, more of a wrestling match on the floor than a fistfight. Still, Wallace was anxious to clear out any drinkers who might cause trouble. He separated the two combatants and threw Murnaghan out along with another patron named McClory.

These two were both Catholics, and Wallace was an Orangeman. In fact, his small business was the very place that the local lodge held its meetings. As Wallace was none too anxious to risk having the men return, some of his Orange patrons held the door closed. They were still holding the door closed when constables arrived and burst open the door, sending the men holding it flying to the side. The first constable to enter was a young man named Peter Breen. Wallace claimed that Breen had drawn his sword and held it to his throat and threatened "to let your guts out." More constables rushed inside, and calm quickly returned. All in all, it had been a minor affair.

However, a few days later, Hugh Wallace learned that he had been charged with assaulting Peter Murnaghan. He filled a counter charge against Constable Breen for threatening his life. This was the charge that was heard a month later in the Newry Quarter Sessions. The men on the jury trying the case against Breen were local men. Two of them were well known to James, one a neighbor Ralph Todd, the other his son-in-law Alex Douglas.

Wallace retold his account of events, and others supported his claim that Breen was drunk, in fact having bought his liquor in Wallace's shop. He told the jury that at no time did the constables identify themselves in order to gain entry. The constables made contrary claims. They had indeed announced their presence and still the door was held against them. They were responding to a breathless Murnaghan that there was a beating going on in Wallace's establishment. Other constables testified that Murnaghan was suffering cuts when he arrived at the station, though the witnesses in the pub supported Wallace's testimony that Murnaghan was uninjured when he was thrown out.

When the judge charged the jury, he informed them that it was lamentable that the issue of religion had come up during the testimony. He instructed them to make their judgment on the reasonableness of Wallace's testimony. Apparently, Wallace wasn't convincing, as the jury returned a verdict of innocent. Breen was released and left the court happily escorted by his fellow constables.

While the trial of Peter Breen had been pending, George reported that far more consequential trials had begun. The first sittings of the Special Commission trying the Fenian leaders began in the Green Street Court House in Dublin. Judge Whiteside, who had defended William Smith O'Brien in the trials of the Young Irelanders nineteen years before, was now the Lord Chief Justice of Ireland and would preside. Isaac Butt, who had defended John during his trial, would be one of the defense attorneys.

The most important Fenian caught and the first to stand trial was Thomas Burke. He was alleged to be the leader of a futile rising in Tipperary. He had been born in Ireland but had emigrated with his family to the United States. He had military experience from the Civil War where he served in the Confederate Army. He had been severely injured at the battle of Gettysburg and was captured. As a result, he walked with a limp and required a cane. After his indictment, the trial was postponed until April 24th.

On that same day, John wrote a letter to the *Weekly News* about the Fenian trials. To facilitate the suppression of the Fenians, the British government had suspended the right of habeas corpus. John pointed out that Parliament had never inflicted the loss of freedom on English citizens. England was resorting to despotism to control the Irish. "For our country is in the sad situation of being forbidden to have her own will and voice respected in law." So for Ireland, there was no freedom. "Far be it for me to undervalue constitutional liberty; but it is the real liberty I value; and by so much as I love and cherish real liberty, by so much I loathe its mocking, lying counterfeit."

He pleaded with the Catholic leadership to join in the struggle for independence. "The price we have to pay for our subjection to England is becoming so heavy that even the greatest worshipper among us of English civilization will be ruined by aping it much longer…If the Catholic Bishops and other clergy would seriously reflect upon the ruinous influences brought to bear upon religious faith, upon conjugal fidelity, upon female purity, upon manly spirit, upon all that is good or Godlike in human nature by the political subjection to which our people are placed, surely they would endeavor to Repeal the Union."

The evidence against Burke at trial was supplied mainly by two men who had been well-connected Fenians before turning informer. In his edition of May 4th, George was happy to inform the people of Newry that Burke had been convicted of high treason and sentenced to die for his crimes against the Queen. The hanging was to take place before the end of the month. Burke was returned to Kilmainham prison to spend the last hours of his life. This man and his companions had come to Ireland to kill law-abiding supporters of the

Queen. They deserved no sympathy or mercy. So Burke's execution by hanging, having his head cut off, and his body quartered would deliver a warning message to Fenians who had not yet been captured. They would certainly be appropriately terrorized by this public execution. The American soldiers who had spread across Ireland despite government precautions would quickly flee home to America.

Reaction to the verdict was immediate in other circles as well. A petition signed by thirteen Irish members was submitted to Parliament asking for leniency for Burke and the other Fenians. The petition argued that British law had created so many problems in Ireland that the Irish had no choice but to take actions that they otherwise would never have considered.

George found this excuse most objectionable. After all, there was no misgoverning in Ireland. "The Roman Catholic population have the fullest civil rights and liberties. They have had for years the sunny side of Government favor and patronage. They have been petted and pampered. All recent legislation has been in their favor. They groan under no oppression, no tyranny. They enjoy the blessings of living under the best and freest government in the world." They just hated the English, and the complaints they raised about the establishment, education or land laws were fabricated.

As the date for Burke's execution drew near, George returned to the issue. He was alarmed that other convicted Fenians had been not been sentenced to death, but to prison at hard labor for terms ranging from a few years to life. While the government had certainly done well to quash the revolt with the minimum loss of life, the danger hadn't yet ended. Many Fenians were still roaming free and able to do more damage. There were also alarming rumors that Fenians were planning to help those leaders in prison to escape, just as they had managed to free James Stephens from Richmond prison in November. If Burke wasn't executed, the remaining Fenians would hold the British law in contempt, and new members recruited to the cause.

The Special Commission ended its work and the trials in Dublin ceased just before Burke was scheduled to die. George thought they had done the work efficiently, and the juries had shown great courage throughout the sitting. But efforts to save Burke continued. The remaining committee members of the Irish National League met in Dublin to request clemency. John apparently did not attend.

A very angry George had hoped his leader of May 30th would have described the death of Colonel Burke. Instead he had to report that Burke's sentence had been commuted to life in prison by the Queen. Prime Minister Derby and his ministers had decided to take this step and sent a telegraph message requesting Queen Victoria to issue the official order to save Burke. "We continue of the same mind on this issue. Burke and the others convicted of High Treason deserved to die, and they ought to have suffered accordingly. They were murderers in intent. They came to Ireland to plunge the country in all the miseries of civil war." The commutation of their sentences would "provide comfort" to those like them. "The disloyal in the country will be stimulated in their dark work of treason."

After venting his distress, George reported that when the pardon documents had been delivered to the officials of Kilmainham Prison, they immediately carried out the orders. The number of guards surrounding the prison were increased, and some served as escorts for the prison van that transported Burke to Mountjoy Prison. There, Burke was required to put on a prison uniform. His hair and long moustache were cut. He wasn't immediately put to hard labor as his health was poor, his war injuries making heavy labor almost impossible.

Not surprisingly, John differed from George on the commutation. Once the news was received, John wrote a long letter to the *Nation*. Since the end of the Irish National League, John had expressed his opinions in letters to various Irish newspapers. The one he wrote on June 1st was particularly long.

He began by discussing the breaking news about the Fenian prisoners. The British Cabinet had convinced Lord Derby that his desire to execute Burke would place England in a diminished position in Europe. After all, Burke's efforts had been feeble, and no one had died as a result. "Europe is hardly aware that the English make the laws which determine what words of ours shall be sedition or treason felony, what acts of ours shall be high treason, what conduct of ours shall be any denomination of crime they fancy; that the English also determine what kind and amount of testimony shall be sufficient to convict us of the crime alleged, and that they select the judges who shall interpret the laws and the jurors who shall try the testimony."

John then repeated his strongly held belief that these problems dated from the Act of Union in 1800, an act that was passed through "fraud and violence." What was sold as an elevation of Ireland to equality with England was actually designed to place Ireland in subjugation to England, to be used for English purposes. "It is easy for the English to make a law or 100 laws (as they are called) declaring any particular expression of that general Irish disaffection to be a crime, and a crime of whatever degree they may think proper. Thus, in 1848, I myself was tried and convicted of treason-felony and I was indicted, tried and convicted not only in due legal form, but in a sumptuous extravagance of legal forms." "In legal and constitutional form my country was made solemnly to declare a man [was] moved and instigated by the devil to hold and express such sentiments." Charges of evil against John Martin were so opposite his true character as to be more a measure of the government than of John himself.

John then repeated ideas similar to those he had expressed when he spoke from the dock in the Green Street Court House almost twenty years before. "From inquiries into the condition of other subject countries, both in modern and ancient times, I have come to the opinion that in all the world, and in all history there is no case of any one people suffering so cruelly from the rule of another as the Irish people have suffered, and continue to suffer from the rule of the English. I ardently long for the restoration of my country's self-government."

Then John made clear that he didn't agree with the Fenian idea of a military revolution. "I would anxiously avert revolutionary changes in Ireland, both because I love order and because I think that revolutionary anarchy would be particularly disastrous in Ireland." He lamented that no national organization including the natural leaders of Ireland existed devoted to a "peaceful restoration of self-government by way of Repeal of the Union."

He warned the Fenians not to expect their revolution to succeed. "All secret conspiracies in Ireland, all schemes of invasion by the unaided strength of the Irish in America are mischievous and foolish." Instead, he had a very different prescription for future actions. "The Irish people ought to submit peacefully to the overwhelming material force by which England holds the country...but on the contrary, continue to protest peacefully against its injustice." This was the route that John clearly intended to take himself. He would follow this path "with a clear sense of my responsibilities as in Irishman and a patriot. I am reluctant to say one word which may tend to confirm the leaning of the mass of the Irish people towards a revolutionary method of national redress. My conviction in favour of the peaceful arrangement of Repeal are drawn not merely from constitutional dislike of violence and anarchy, but also from careful consideration of the qualities and character of the different races, classes and sects that (under English influence) live in hatred of each other upon Irish soil."

§

Soon after John wrote this long letter, he wrote a shorter one to his friend Daunt. He told Daunt he would be away for a month, as he was soon leaving for a trip to Paris and Germany. While he still had many friends in Paris, he wouldn't be able to see the Mitchel family as they had returned to America to live again in Brooklyn. Though the letter was short, John took time to lament the unexpected death of Thomas Meagher who had been appointed governor of the Montana territory after the Civil War. "You will be grieved for the sad and sudden end of Tom Meagher! A very brilliant genius was he. He was full of life animal and spiritual. I wish he had lived...for a few years longer. I hoped to see him burst out from under the cloud that has obscured his career for a time and shine again with all brightness and purity of his old flame of the days of the Confederation & Association."

The tensions between the sects that lived "in hatred of each other," that had so concerned John erupted close to Newry before John left for the continent. George found the events alarming and gave the local events considerable play in the *Telegraph*. On June 25th, a group of Catholics had gathered in the townland of Tormore [Turmore] to celebrate the coming of summer. This townland was close to Lisserboy, the townland where the Donaghmore Presbyterian Church was located.

At the time, English law forbade any sectarian group from marching with banners, symbols or musical instruments. But the Catholics did apparently have drums with them as they marched along the narrow roads and climbed Traymont Hill. There they collected large piles of fallen branches, and any other flammable items they could find, and set them afire. Local estimates claimed that a thousand Catholics were whooping and dancing on the top of the hill. Local people paid them little attention, but the police were on hand carefully watching the proceedings.

As the fire died down, the Catholic group marched back along the road the way they had come. However, a few of the members broke away from the march to attack the cottage of a local Protestant, Robert Gamble. Using whatever rocks were handy, they hurled them at the windows and broke most of them. The rest of the marchers passed on without participating in the violence. When local Protestants heard about the attack, they hurried to the Gambles to provide protection. Some of them diverted to protect the Orange Hall, which was being built in nearby Sheepbridge. When the Protestants appeared, the Catholics dispersed.

The trouble was quickly reported to the local constables. Robert Gamble's daughter Catherine gave them the names of the people she could identify. Before dawn the next morning, a squad of constables arrived in the area to arrest the people who had been identified for them. Their arrival was so unexpected that all but one of the accused had been arrested before 5 a.m. Neighbors in the area were unaware that the raid had taken place, so efficiently was it carried out. Most of the accused were sons of local farmers. When they were brought into court, they were released on a bail of £40 along with additional sureties. All of the accused were able to make bail.

George wrote a leader on the affair. He maintained that it showed clearly the hatred Catholics felt toward Protestants. Had Protestants behaved this way, the entire Catholic establishment would be outraged. Police conduct on the Traymont Hill also displeased him. He did understand that they wanted to contain the situation rather than make the situation more dangerous. However, he felt they could easily have taken the names of those participating and would then be able to arrest them later. Before he ended his column, he promised his readers that he would continue to follow this event. "It was fiendish in the extreme."

The court hearing on the Tormore marches was held as scheduled on July 12th at the Newry Petty Sessions. There was so much interest in the trial that many were unable to get into the courthouse and were left standing in the street outside. Several new people were added to the number of people who had been originally charged. And a startling new issue appeared, one not mentioned during the original hearing. There were new reports that shots had been fired on the hill while the bonfire was burning. Patrick Connell of Lisserboy testified that there were many shots fired in the direction of Donaghmore, but he had seen no damage resulting from the shooting. Other testimony reported that the gunfire was coming from Marshall's hill, and directed towards the Catholics. Officials were unable to establish that there had been any gunfire at all.

Catherine Gamble repeated the testimony she had given previously. However, she now remembered the names of two others who had participated in the attack. There didn't seem to be any conclusive testimony that the Catholic party had marched to the beat of drums. While it was clearly illegal to attack anyone's private property, it wasn't against the law to hold a bonfire. Still most of the men that Catherine had identified were held for the Downpatrick Assizes, which were to be held later in the summer.

In view of the trouble at Tormore, George was concerned that the Protestants might respond in kind during their celebrations of July 12th. So he was happy to report that the Newry Orangemen held a peaceful dinner in the lodge building in Newry. There were many other celebrations in the area, including marches with flags and music, which violated the Party Processions Act. They were also totally peaceful.

The final action connected to the trouble at Tormore took place at the Downpatrick Assizes on July 26th. Constable Fitzpatrick testified that the whole event was peaceful when he was around. But then he stated that he thought any shots must have come from the Catholics at their bonfire despite his further testimony there was no shooting while he was there. The Gambles testified that they didn't understand the attack, as they had always been on good terms with their neighbors. Some witnesses felt this was a dangerous situation, and that "the leaders were cowardly, savage ruffians."

George was happy to declare that the reason behind the attack on the Gambles was that they were Protestants. He wasn't pleased when only three of the men were convicted and sentenced to serve time in Downpatrick Jail. Fagan, who was the most clearly identified as one of the attackers, was sentenced to only three months incarceration there. The other two men, Rourke and O'Neill, would serve just one month. None of them were sentenced to hard labor. This was greatly offensive to George. He attributed the very lenient sentences to the fact the presiding judge Justice O'Hagan was a Catholic.

Another event took place on Marching Day that didn't attract comment from George at the time. There was a large Orange March in Bangor, held as an act of defiance against the current Party Processions Act, led by William Johnston of Belfast and William Beers. Members of the Orange Order who marched in large numbers carried the usual Orange banners and were accompanied by several fife and drum bands. Both banners and music were illegal under the current version of the Processions Act. Still the march proceeded without police interference and ended without violence.

So it was shocking that the British authorities decided to take action against the march leaders more than a month later. George quickly responded to rumors that action would be taken against Beers and Johnston. He fired off a quick warning to authorities that any action against the two men would "rouse the whole of Ulster." He proclaimed himself to be a Conservative who believed strongly in the rule of law. But this was an instance when the law was being unjustly applied. He pointed out that the government took no action against the march that occurred when the cornerstone for the O'Connell monument was laid. George's pain was intensified because a Conservative administration had taken the unjust action.

But it became clear within a week that if the government had read about George's warning, they didn't intend to heed it. William Johnston had indeed been referred to court for a hearing on his actions on July 12th at the Bangor Petit Sessions on September 12th. George worried that this outrageous action would nurture hostility toward the Conservative government. Still, his support for the government remained strong even when it took actions that George didn't like. He had objected strongly to the appointment of a Catholic to the important position of Irish Attorney General. He didn't like legislation that allowed the Lord Chancellor, who was charged to appoint magistrates, to appoint Catholics to this important position. But his support of the government didn't waver.

The government did indeed proceed against Johnston though the trial was delayed until the next year. With the outcome of Johnston's trial in doubt, anxiety among the Protestants remained high. But before that trial, there would be Fenian unrest for the government to deal with.

§

The day before Johnston made his first appearance in court, an event took place in Manchester, England that diverted George from his coverage of the unjust treatment of Johnston. Early on September 11th, between three and four in the morning, several constables were on patrol on Swan Street in that city when they noticed four neatly dressed men acting oddly. For a time, they followed the men, noting additional suspicious activities as they crept along behind them. The constables suspected the men were about to rob one of the nearby shops. After a whispered conference, they decided to end the pursuit and arrest of all of them.

During the ensuing confrontation, two of the men managed to escape into the predawn darkness. The other two were arrested after violent resistance. They seemed to be struggling to get their hands into their pockets. When they were searched in the police station, authorities discovered each of them had a fully loaded revolver. One of the men was identified as Colonel Timothy Kelly, a wounded Civil War veteran, who was reputed to be the Chief Organizer of the Fenian Military Department, which had planned the ill-fated Fenian rebellion in Ireland. The other captive was identified later as Timothy Deasy. Not much was known about him, but he had been under surveillance by authorities in Liverpool for associating with known Fenians.

At their first court appearance, they identified themselves with false names of John Wright and Martin Williams. However, warrants were produced under their correct names with orders to transport them to London. They were put in cells to await the arrival of a prison van to make the transfer to the capital.

The van arrived near 8 p.m. But by that time, word of the arrests had been spread in whispered conversations across the large Irish community in

Manchester, and a large crowd had assembled in the narrow street outside the police station. To ensure that the captives couldn't escape, police formed up two lines between which the handcuffed prisoners were forced to walk to the van.

The Fenian prisoners weren't the only ones in the van. It was divided into sections to keep prisoners separate. However, the van was already uncomfortably crowded with other prisoners, several young women of the street and some young boys. Nonetheless, Kelly and Deasy were hustled into the van. When all was secure, the van pulled away accompanied by eleven police plus the driver. Seven of the police rode on the van, four others rode in a cab behind. One, Sergeant Brett, rode inside the middle section of the van. He had a cutlass, but the rest of the police in the escort were unarmed except for their usual truncheons.

The van then moved through Manchester streets on its way to London. All proceeded easily until the procession approached the railroad arch. There they spotted a crowd of perhaps fifty or sixty men. Most of them were armed with revolvers, leaving the police at a huge disadvantage. The delay at the police station had allowed local Fenians to plan a rescue attempt. The driver whipped the horses in an attempt to drive the van through the Fenians. However, the Fenians shot both horses, bringing the van to a total stop. The mob then turned their guns on the police sitting exposed on the top of the van. Knowing that to stay was to risk death, all seven jumped from the van and fled into the dark. None were seriously injured as they escaped. The policemen in the cab fled as well.

About twenty of the Fenians surrounded the van, forming a barricade, and shooting at anyone who dared come close. Several times, the police with volunteer reinforcements attempted to rush the van but were driven back by heavy fire. The apparent leader of the effort was William Allen, a man well known to be a Fenian. He directed other Fenians to gain entrance to the van by use of large stones, hatchets and hammers.

After some furious efforts, the attackers had greatly damaged the roof and appeared about to break through. However, Allen was anxious to complete the mission and escape. Inside, the prisoners were being guarded by Sergeant Brett who held the key the Fenians needed. Certainly it would be quicker to shoot the lock off the door. Allen fired one shot through the keyhole of the van, unaware that just at that moment, Sergeant Brett had his eye at the keyhole. Brett fell dead on the floor. One of the other prisoners took the keys from the dead man and pushed them through a ventilating slit in the side of the van. The Fenians opened the door and released Kelly and Deasy. Rescuers and rescued scattered in different directions and raced to safety across the nearby fields. By chance, a policeman was near the escape route, and helped take two prisoners. Allen and a young man named Michael Larkin were captured and taken to Fairfield Street Station. Kelly and Deasy escaped and were not recaptured.

Not surprisingly, early testimony about the chaotic scene had changed by the time the inquest was held. Police Constable Shaw testified that the door was still locked when Allen fired into it, countering the rumor that had been widely circulated claiming Brett had been shot after the door was open. So there was no evidence presented in court that Allen had deliberately executed Brett to get the keys to the cells.

Manchester residents with rumored connections to the Fenians were rounded up, twenty-eight men in total. All were guarded by members of the 57th Foot, well-armed with bayonets fixed. The accused Fenians were forced to stand in two lines while witnesses filed into the room to make identifications. The pistols with which the men were armed during the rescue were of considerable interest as well. They were all breech loaders made in America. Witnesses identified most of the men arrested as participants. All but one was charged with riot and murder.

A second viewing was held. But his time, each prisoner was identified by name and number. When a witness made an identification, he reported that to a police clerk who took down the identifying information. George reported every detail of the arrests, and preliminary investigations for his Newry readers. However, when the trials began, George provided his readers with only brief summaries.

The first trial began in Manchester before a Special Commission Court on Friday November 1st. Those charged in this first trial were Allen, Michael Larkin, Michael O'Brien, Thomas Maguire and Edward O'Meagher Condon…The evidence presented against each man was limited to identification by witnesses. The jury took only an hour and twenty-three minutes to return a verdict of murder against all the men. When they spoke, Larkin and Allen both expressed regret over the death of Sergeant Brett. Maguire claimed that he was innocent, as did Condon. They all claimed that the charges, trial and verdict were the result of unfair prejudice against the Irish. O'Brien ended his comments at his sentencing with "God Save Ireland."

The trial of the next six men began just a day later. This time the jury deadlocked. These men, plus all the others charged were freed, though seven were charged with assaulting the police. These men were sentenced to five years of penal servitude. All the trials were finished by the middle of November. The only act remaining was to hang the five men convicted of murder.

As soon as the trials ended, there was a push, supported by many Englishmen, for the prisoners to be spared. Maguire was indeed spared because the evidence identifying him seemed weak. Condon was freed as he was an American citizen. But the death penalty still hovered over the other three men. The British government intended to ensure that their deaths would be witnessed, and the reports of the execution would be widely distributed to serve as a warning to all other Irish revolutionaries, just as George wished.

So they built the scaffold on top of the prison wall, where it could be seen by anyone standing outside without risking security inside the prison. The execution took place at 8 a.m. A large crowd indeed clustered around the wall and peered from adjacent windows. Unfortunately, the hangman was inept. When the three men dropped, only Allen suffered the broken neck that was to cause death in hangings. Both Larkin and O'Brien survived the fall, instead writhing about as they began to slowly strangle. The hangman hurried under the scaffold to grab Larkin's legs and, by violently yanking them, managed to complete the execution. But the Catholic priest on the scene refused to allow the same treatment for O'Brien. As a consequence, O'Brien took three quarters of an hour to die. Then the men were taken down and buried unceremoniously in the prison yard.

When the executions had been completed, George felt free to comment on the proceedings in a leader titled, "The Executions at Manchester." George commented first that Allen and O'Brien had died well, but Larkin seemed "totally prostrated." But he turned much of his attention to the crowds of people who had appeared in London to support clemency for "the wretched criminals." He claimed that they were Catholics, Republicans, actual Fenians and Fenian sympathizers. George believed these demonstrations had actually strengthened the government in their determination to execute the three men.

George concluded his leader with his usual passion. "For the sake of the peace and prosperity of the empire Fenianism must be struck down with an iron hand. There must be no mercy extended to Fenian assassins and rebels. These miscreants are the worst enemies of Ireland. They are men of violence and blood. Had they the power they would plunge this country in all the horrors of insurrection, and would massacre every loyalist in the land."

§

Not surprisingly, John saw the executions quite differently. "The three Irishmen, Allen, Larken and O'Brien—whom the English government with the sanction of the English Legislature and the English nation, hanged last Sunday at Manchester, I regard as martyrs to the holy cause of Irish nationalism. They have done nothing to make any virtuous Irishman blush for his country. On the contrary, the motives which actuated the rescue of the Fenian officers were of the purest and loftiest kind that human nature can boast of. It was for love and duty to mother land, for loyal faithfulness to those whom they believed to be devoted to the vindication of Irish rights, for self-sacrificing protest against national wrong." It was in the noblest spirit that the men "acted, and it was in hatred and scorn of those very motives *when stirring the hearts of Irishmen,* that the English Government and nation hanged my three noble-souled fellow countrymen."

Then John challenged the legal issues of the case. "Not one of the three had any purpose of killing an English constable or anyone in charge of the Fenian prisoners. The death of Brett was an unlucky event, but at last, so far as it concerned Allen, Larkin, and O'Brien, an accident only. To call it a murder, even by legal construction, seems almost too absurd. If such really be English law, as the two judges pronounced, the sooner the English legislature may change it, the better it will be for English reputation." John claimed that the government itself didn't find the evidence presented at trial as satisfactory. "It is then a *legal murder* that the English authorities have committed upon those 3 Irishmen—a national murder which England commits against my country."

John concluded his letter by expressing his worries about the effects the executions would have in Ireland. "I am sorry of the political effect which anticipates from this horrible demonstration of English spite and rage. It will render more difficult any peaceful solution to our national questions. Already a large proportion of our most virtuous young men are drawn into sympathy, more or less active, with Fenian conspiracy. The faults of the founders and leaders tended to warn our population from attaching themselves to the organization. But, on the other hand, the wrongs, the noble bearing, the high intelligence, the unflinching spirit of all sacrifice, the unquenchable love of dear old Ireland exhibited by almost every man of the vast number of Fenians that have been tried and convicted by the law-courts, have given Fenians a great and terrible moral strength."

John's viewpoint on the Fenians was remarkable. He had spent much time, effort and money in an attempt to create a path for Irish independence different from the secret revolution that the Fenians supported. He had argued strongly against the Fenian path to independence, continuously forecasting its failure. He had endured mocking attacks on his character from men who had once been his friends. He had suffered a barrage of rotten eggs thrown at him by a Fenian mob. And yet, despite this personal history, he looked beyond his interactions to a greater principle, his belief in justice for everyone, friend or foe. He saw clearly that any verdict that used the same evidence to find some men guilty and others innocent was not an example of justice for all.

Sentiments like those John held were quite common in the Irish press. George found them highly offensive, as he made clear in another editorial. "The articles in some of the Romish journals on the subject of the execution of the Fenian murderers at Manchester are diabolical. They are calculated to inflame the ignorant and deluded masses of the Roman Catholic population, and to intensify their hatred to the English Government."

One editorial in the *Freeman* was particularly galling to George. "That paper published on Monday an atrocious editorial on the subject of the Manchester executions. Allen and his wretched companions are represented as martyrs. The *Freeman* shrieks wildly over their doom. That paper, which is ever assailing the loyal Orangemen of Ireland, thus writes of the Fenian rebels and the murderers of poor Sergeant Brett."

The editor of the *Freeman* stated that to gain Irish independence many other Irishmen would welcome the same fate as the three men in Manchester. Further, he claimed that had Englishmen been accused of the same crime, they would have been convicted of manslaughter and sentenced to penal servitude. "'But the Manchester rioters were Irishmen. They were Fenians, too, and with such a combination they had no chance. They had few friends in England except the London working classes, who exhibited a generous sympathy for their fate and made exertions not always prudent, to save them. They must die and die they did bravely, piously and silently... They died a firm resigned and edifying death.'"

These words were contrary to everything George believed about England and its treatment of Irish Catholics. "Such are the terms in which the leading Romish journal speaks of men who righteously die on the scaffold. They were great criminals. Their hands were red with the blood of a fellow-creature. Moreover, they were guilty of murder in carrying out their treasonable and infamous project. And if they could they would have had England running red with the blood of the Queen's loyal subjects."

From the time of the executions, George and John had been confining their actions to words in newspapers. But John had an active agenda as well. Since the three men had been buried without a proper burial service and interment in sacred ground, supporters in Ireland began planning to at least hold a symbolic funeral and a simulated burial in a consecrated grave yard. John went to Dublin to organize the event.

While plans for funerals for the three men executed in Manchester were underway, the Prime Minister, Lord Derby, issued directives from London. A funeral procession wouldn't be illegal. However, the color green was a party emblem, and would be illegal. The "wearing of the green" by participants should make that funeral illegal. If it didn't under current law, the law should be changed.

With word from the British government that the funeral processions planned in several Irish towns were legal, John proceeded with arrangements for the big funeral in Dublin. Just before the day arrived, he issued a final instruction. "Peace, Order and Regularity are to be the order of the Day. GOD SAVE IRELAND, by order of the Committee, John Martin, chairman."

As part of the preparations for the march, John had written to prominent Irish leaders inviting them to attend. The O'Donoghue was one who turned down the invitation. "I heartily sympathise with the demonstration, believing it to be a necessary patriotic demonstration. I wish it every success, and I beg you to believe that though absent in person I am with you in spirit." Given the O'Donoghue's failure to fulfill his promises to John at the founding of the Irish National League, this refusal couldn't have been a surprise.

The funeral procession was scheduled for Sunday, December 8, 1867. Government officials in Dublin Castle were disturbed by John's skillful planning. They met until late Saturday evening to formulate plans for the event. They decided to put all the British troops stationed in Dublin on full alert for all of Sunday.

Unfortunately, John had no power to control the weather. A heavy, cold rain fell for much of Sunday. Despite weather that should have kept most Dubliners at home by their fires, a huge crowd came out into the streets well before the time the procession was to begin. Many were the working people of Dublin who gathered with their families to watch as events unfolded. Members of different trades mustered together, each in a different street, planning to join in as units as the parade passed by. They wore insignia to show their support for the Manchester Martyrs, many defiantly choosing something green.

As planned by John and the committee, the procession began promptly at noon, led by three men on horseback. They had a hard time making their way along the street, due to the size of the crowd pushing forward into the muddy street. They were directly followed by two hundred men marching slowly and in good order twelve across to the beat of a band playing muffled drums marching just behind them. Then came young boys, wearing green rosettes, marching twelve across also in good order. The parade was following the plans that John and his committee laid out.

When the first band reached Middle Abbey Street, they began playing "The Dead March" from Handel's "Saul." The next band played "Adeste Fidelis". There were seven bands in all. Some had flutes and brass in addition to drums. Whenever one of them passed a church, they stopped the music and passed by in respectful silence.

The hearse designated for Allen came first. John Martin and some of the other leaders followed behind in carriages, fulfilling their role as chief mourners. The other two hearses followed. When they reached O'Connell's statue, the marchers broke into enthusiastic cheers. As many as forty thousand people marched in the procession. All was perfectly peaceful.

When they reached Glasnevin Cemetery, John appeared on a balcony overlooking the throngs below to deliver a memorial speech. "Fellow countrymen. This is a strange kind of funeral procession in which we are engaged today. We are here, a vast multitude of men, women and children, in a very inclement season of the year under rain and through mud. We are here escorting three empty hearses to the consecrated last resting place of those who die in the Lord. The three bodies that we would bear tenderly to the church-yard and would bury in consecrated ground with all the solemn rites of religion are not here. They are away in a foreign and hostile land, where they have been thrown into unconsecrated ground, branded by our enemies as the vile remains of murderers. These three men whose memories we are here today to honor…were not murderers. These men were pious men—virtuous men who feared God and loved their country. They sorrowed for the sorrows of the dear old native land of their love. They wished…to save her and for that love and for that wish they were doomed to an ignominious death at the hands of the British hangman. It was as Irish patriots that these men were doomed to death. And it was as Irish patriots that they met their death…Now it has come to pass as a consequence of the malignant policy preserved for so many long years—it has come to pass that the great body of the Irish people despair of obtaining peaceful restitution of our national rights. And it has also come to pass that vast numbers, Irishmen whom the oppression of English rule forbades to live by honest industry in their own country, have in America learned to become soldiers. And those Irish soldiers seem resolved to make war against England and England is in a panic of rage and fear in consequence of this…and being in a panic about Fenians, she hopes to strike terror into her Irish nationalists by a legal murder…Many a wicked statute she has framed—many a jury she has packed in order to dispose of her Irish political offenders, but in the case of Allen, O'Brien and Larkin, she has committed such an outrage on justice and decency as to make even many Englishmen stand aghast…this demonstration [is] mainly one of mourning for the fate of these three good Irishmen…but fellow countrymen and women, boys and girls, it is also one of protest and indignation against the conduct of our rulers. Your attendance here today is a sufficient protest. Your conduct has been admirable for patriotism,…for fine spirit, for solemn sense of that good duty, you were resolved to do. You will return home in the same good order and inoffensiveness. You will join with me here—in speaking the prayer of the three martyrs whom we mourn. "God save Ireland."

As the crowd began to disperse, John took a walk about the cemetery, doubtless stopping at the last resting place of a distressing number of his good friends, Terrance McManus, John Dillon, James Magnon [Irish poet who supported the Young Irelanders] and Daniel O'Connell among them.

§

George was furious over the Dublin procession as he made eminently clear in the *Telegraph*. He couldn't understand why the government had yet to take action against those who praised men whose hands were red with the blood of an officer of the Queen. Then he turned to John. "Mr. John Martin of this neighbourhood was the leading man of the demonstrations. His speech was execrable. He calls himself a Protestant, yet he blasphemously offered in the graveyard prayers for the executed murderers. Nothing could be viler than these utterances of this misguided gentleman." Next he reprinted John's speech, so his readers could see how horrible it was.

Then he returned to a critique of John himself. "Mr. Martin was transported as a felon in 1848. The Government generously reduced the period of his sentence, but his enmity to British rule has not abated. Traitors and murderers like Allen, Larkin, and O'Brien he extols as 'pious' men who 'feared God!' His notions of piety must be singular. He proclaimed in the hearing of the wild and thoughtless masses around him that 'the Irish patriots,' whose virtues and death they had met to commemorate were 'legally *murdered.*' Whatever may be Mr. John Martin's personal merits his public appearance last Sunday was very disgraceful, and the language employed by him could not be spoken by any loyal subject of the Queen."

George closed his leader with a challenge to the government. "How long will the Government remain quiescent? These seditious processions, sanctioned by the priesthood, are spreading Fenianism in all parts of the country. In no other land would they be tolerated. If the Party Emblems Act fails to bring them under its powers, it should be abolished or amended. For the present, it is simply of use to crush loyalty in the North of Ireland."

As though it had been reading George's leader, the British government did take action, and quickly enough that George could report it in the next edition of the paper. "The Government has at length issued a proclamation against the disloyal and dangerous Fenian funeral demonstrations. The movement of the Government is late, but all classes of Her Majesty's loyal subjects will rejoice that an end is now put to the seditions Sunday processions. They had done an immensity of mischief. They had been instrumental in giving a great impetus to the spread of Fenianism. They will give to other countries the idea that the whole country is ready to revolt against the British Government." He did hope that more arrests would be made, including the editors and writers of many papers who were extolling the funeral march.

"The extraordinary outburst of disloyalty in the South and West should gravely warn the Government in regard to the impolicy of proceeding with their prosecution of the Orangemen of the North. The Party Emblems Act has failed to bring under its provisions the public processions of the Fenians. Why should it be employed to crush the most devoted and loyal subjects of the Queen in Ulster?"

John was quite pleased with how the demonstrations had gone, recognizing that it "was a very delicate affair to manage and a doubtful measure as to the safety both as regards the English Government and as regards the Fenian conspiracy." He was concerned that the Fenians would assume from the event that the Repealers had joined them. "Happily, it proved a complete and marvelous success. And it was the intense connection of the people's sentiment and their moral instinct of organization upon great occasions hereon their hearts were touched, and perhaps in some measure also their flattering confidence in me, that made it such a marvelous demonstration."

Before he finished this letter to Daunt, he had picked up the morning edition of the *Freeman*. In it he learned that the Government intended to take legal action against him. "Well, this is one consequence of the great importance which the demonstration attained. And as to me, the thing will certainly be very inconvenient, and annoying personally, but I must grin and bear it. Upon the whole I see no reason to anticipate evil to the national cause from either the processions or the persecutions. At all events Ireland was bound to make her indignant protest against that legal murder and to utter her sympathy for the fine character developed by these poor fellows. It would be a burning shame... if the protest had not in some way been made. It is made now, thank goodness!"

Another Fenian outrage occurred in England, just as the effects of the Manchester attack were beginning to diminish. This was an attempt to rescue Burke from Clerkenwell prison. The plan had been to attempt to blast their way through the outer wall of the prison while Burke was in the yard getting his two hours of exercise. However, the plan had been leaked to the police. So Burke was exercised in a different yard earlier in the morning. The blast however was very powerful, leaving twelve people dead and more injured. But Burke remained in prison.

In the same edition of the paper, George inserted a small notice under the title "Disappearance of Mr. John Martin. It is stated and very generally believed, that Mr. John Martin has left this country to evade service of the summons against him for taking part in the Dublin funeral proceedings. On Saturday (14th) a detective from Dublin arrived at Kilbroney, Mr. Martin's residence to make inquiries respecting him. But we have not heard with what success."

George published a correction in the next edition of the paper. "In our last publication we find we were in error in stating the Mr. Martin had absconded in order to evade service of the summons upon him for taking part in the Dublin funeral procession. He was served with the summons at his residence at Kilbroney on Friday last, and, as our readers will perceive from our report of the proceedings at the Dublin Head Police Office, attended there on the following Monday to answer the charge preferred against him."

John had indeed made the trip to Dublin and appeared at the Head Police Office with two other leaders of the funeral procession. Officiating magistrates Dix and Aiken called the hearing to order, at 1 p.m.

John announced, "I am appearing on behalf of myself."

Mr. Murphy represented the government. John promised to be as helpful to him as he could be. He listened as the government started laying out its case. Richard Wolf testified that he had seen a placard that John signed. Superintendent John Haw testified that he had seen green ribbons and men with white wands keeping order.

John interrupted the proceedings. "It would save a great deal of time if you would examine me. (laughter)."

Magistrate Dix responded. "We could not examine a person accused."

"Cannot you caution me not to say anything that would incriminate myself?" John asked.

Dix answered John's question. "Oh no, I'm afraid that would be contrary to law."

John wasn't pleased. "This is very tedious."

So the hearing lumbered on. More police testified as to what they saw, and a shorthand writer reported that he had taken down John's words.

John again attempted to expedite the hearing. He was willing to admit he was at the procession and to take all responsibility for it, believing it to be both legal and moral. He did admit that he had delivered remarks, but he denied that they were seditious or inflammatory.

"The mere fact that a prosecution is commenced against me for that act and for those words is the expression of an opinion on my part that this country does not at present enjoy real constitutional institutions, guaranteeing a free trial—guaranteeing that a man accused shall be really put upon his country." John protested that there was no right in a Commission trial to challenge jurors. That had been the case in his first trial, and the same jury selection method would ensure his opponents would again try him.

People across Ireland began raising funds for the trials. One donor wrote, "I presume the people of Ireland will not allow the noble-hearted and pure-minded patriot, John Martin, to bear the expense of defending himself from a prosecution instituted by a powerful government."

John's friends rallied to his defense as well. John Mitchel commented in his new New York newspaper. "John Martin, no Fenian but a good and honest Irishman, is now we believe in prison awaiting his 'trial' as they call that murderous business in Ireland. He has faced their packed jury of Orangemen before, and can face it again. No doubt, they can work their will on him—they can glut their vengeance upon his poor feeble frame once more. Whatever life has been in him since his first penal servitude, they can now grind it out of him for he will continue to speak the truth, until he is chained up, and yet by all this they will only be raising up against themselves more and fiercer enemies."

His good friend George Mahon wrote a letter to John's brother-in-law Maxwell Simpson. Mahon found it difficult to believe that the British would again try John. They surely knew that he wasn't a supporter of Fenian ideas or tactics. He promised to donate £100 pounds to help pay for John's court expenses. But since John hadn't hired lawyers to defend him, he had little need for any donations.

§

John had no intention of sitting idly about while he waited for his trial date in February. Instead he had a very different project that occupied his time. George mentioned it as the new year began. "Our estimable but sorely misguided neighour, Mr. John Martin, has vainly appealed to 'the country' to subscribe funds for the families of the executed Fenians. He has been sadly galled thereby, and had written in his indignation to the editor of the *Irishman,* a letter which George reprinted. The plan was simple: reaching out to Catholic parishes, asking for a collection of one penny from each parishioner to be taken up to benefit the martyrs surviving families. "I hoped that in most of the towns and parishes of Ireland volunteers would come forward, with permission of the clergy, to collect the peoples pennies at the church doors, it seems now that I was mistaken in this hope. The fault is altogether my own."

Johns failure made George very gleeful. "Poor, deceived, honest, John Martin! It appears that the whole amount received in the course of a week for "the national fund to defend himself amounted to one shilling and sixpence! Mr. Martin's patriotic friends have scant purses, or, what is more likely, scant gratitude. It is clear that the Fenians are the very off-scouring of the population—reckless miscreants who would gloat in riot, revolutions and bloodshed."

It was clear from what George wrote that he had been confused about the purpose of the penny campaign, so John dispatched a response. "My appeal has not proved successful in the sense I intended. The collection had not been universal, nor great nor made in even a score of parishes in all Ireland. But the fault is mine, and not the people's. I am satisfied that the people everywhere are well disposed to give their pennies, and shillings for the purposes of the collection; but I have taken no measures whatever to provide in any of the parishes of Ireland for making the collection. I have left each parish, undirected, and unsolicited, except by my original note of general invitation to act or rest quiet as it might. And my error has been in greatly underestimating the power of the political and social terrorism which prevails in Ireland, and which has prevented volunteers from coming forward to act...as collectors except in merely a score of parishes. The unsuccess of the collection, however, is not such as you have been misled into supposing. You speak of 1s 6d obtained in a week, but you will be surprised to learn from me that over £30-0 has been received already for the collection."

"There is no collection for my defence. There are, I think, few politicians in Ireland except yourself, who could suppose that I would demand or accept any money for my own defence, as long at least as I possess any property of my own.

"Let me assure your readers that I am neither 'galled' nor 'indignant' at the small success of my scheme of the National Penny collection. I am only sorry and a little ashamed that when I dared to make the appeal, I did not also bend myself to take the proper and usual measures for organizing the success of it. It was my first experiment in begging, and I have bungled. But the experience only adds to my love and gratitude to the Irish people."

George maintained that he didn't misunderstand the purpose of the National Penny Fund. "The true explanation of the matter is this, that our countrymen who have any money to spare are not disposed to squander it in an exhibition of their sympathy with Fenian revolutionists and assassins. The class who look to Mr. Martin as a kind of leader are the scum of the population."

Then George gave his justification for his claim that a defense fund for John existed. He quoted from the *Times* to excuse his mistaken report that the most unsuccessful fund existed to support his defense.

"Everybody knows that Mr. Martin is a rabid Repealer; and unhappily for himself he has taken the most public opportunity of demonstrating his hostile feelings toward the British Government, that generously remitted his penal sentence, what kind of a Parliament would assemble in College Green, having members who would feel and speak in this way." George then reprinted some of the comments John made at Glasnevin.

"Mr. Martin is to answer at the bar of justice for those sentiments; and, therefore, we shall not characterize them as otherwise we would do. But we cannot avoid asking if men of such principles and speech prevailed in "the national Parliament,' what would be the nature of its allegiance to the British Crown.

"We pity Mr. Martin. Poor man, he is grievously misguided and misled. He is the victim of delusions. The Union has been the source of incalculable good to Ireland. Its dissolution would lead to civil war. The loyal men of Ulster will never permit such an event. They have overwhelming power. They are able to crush any revolution &c, &c"

With the Penny Campaign behind him, John spent the remaining time before his trial, carrying out his usual responsibilities in Kilbroney, writing friends and planning his speech to the jury at his trial. He responded to his friend Mahon's kind offer of financial aid at his trial. "The only thing I shall say about it is that my occasional quarrellousness of manner has deceived you into fearing that my cheerfulness & solidness of spirit and also my bodily vigor was in much worse case than they really are. For my spirits, I am more given than formerly to moan and grunt and rage—especially to rage—at the perversity of our politics here. I think the ignorance, meanness, pharisism and cruelty that characterizes the Irish Protestant political practices vex me the most of all. But though it grieves me sore to see that Irish Protestant political perversity is likely to bring my country into civil war, anarchy, bloody revolution & Fenian conquest, with new confiscations, expulsions &&— though it grieves me to contemplate as now most likely to happen the loss to Ireland of the very classes that would be most valuable for national defense against England and against the world, classes of men with great and useful qualities both as individual men and as citizens."

John continued to reassure Mahon as to his situation. "I may challenge any one of my age in Ireland to run down a mountain with me. I play whist every night except Sundays. I enjoy human society (when the people are human). I enjoy all nations animate and inanimate with much zest and comfort. And suppose if I be convicted at my approaching trial, I shall bear the imprisonment, even if it be under Mr. Price [head of Kilmainham Jail] quite as bravely and well as another. To confess the truth I am afraid the Government intend to convict me and also the representatives of the repeal papers. And of course (barring accidents) they can convict us, if they resolve it. It can't be helped. It will be very inconvenient for me but…many a better Irishman has been hanged for no greater love to Ireland than mine. I can't help it. I have said nor done anything different from what I have been saying & doing these three or four and twenty years past. I can't unsay a sentence. Thank God! My conscience is not bad, so bad as my countrymen are concerned & the duties of a citizen and subject…My intention is to employ no counsel nor attorney. Probably I shall speak in my own vindication. But perhaps I shall not say a word but leave myself perfectly passive in their hands."

In a letter to Daunt, John expressed similar thoughts. "If they obtain a conviction it must be by very flagrant packing & which will increase the odium against them: if they fail it will be a blow against their prestige. For me the worst will be a year or two of imprisonment—an incomparably smaller pain than to retract or pretend to deny or to modify my real sentiments as an Irishman and at their bidding or in fear of them. I shan't employ either counsel or attorney & so shall save all that heavy expense. I am confident that my chance of acquittal & of a divided jury will be quite as good without, as with professional defense. I could not bear to receive a shilling from the country for any personal purpose of my own. And (to confess to you the whole truth) I want to offer the country my example to prove the idleness and wastefulness of the system of paying attorneys and counselors to defend politically accused in Ireland, and to misrepresent or suppress the genuine & virtuous sentiments and aspirations of the said accused, more or less."

Just before the trial began, John informed a friend about his feeling toward his expected conviction and time in prison, this time under harsh conditions and hard labor. "I don't intend to die in jail. I don't intend nor fear to lose my cheerfulness. I shall eventually come out of jail not much the worse in any respect and perhaps much abler than before to serve my country." However, now gentlemen convicted of political crimes were sentenced to the same harsh labor as common criminals, so any sentence would be greatly different than John's previous year behind bars. His advancing age and increasingly poor health would make surviving any sentence problematic.

So on Friday, February 21st, John was back in the Green Street Court House facing trial. Almost twenty years had passed since he had stood in the same dock. Yet again he was looking up at judges, this time Justice Fitzgerald and Mr. Baron Dessy, in their grand robes, men who were there to obtain a conviction. Below them sat the jury that had been selected to obtain the desired conviction. But this time, John wasn't going to sit passively by while lawyers argued points of law. This time he would stand in the dock and defend himself.

The northern accent with which John spoke seemed a bit foreign to the courtroom full of Dubliners. But he spoke in a clear, firm voice that everyone could understand. He began by making clear that he believed that the proceedings were unjust. "Gentlemen, I regard you as twelve of my fellow countrymen, known or believed by my prosecutors to be my political opponents and selected for that reason for the purpose of obtaining a conviction against me in form of law...This is a political trial, and in this country political trials are all conducted in this way. It is considered by the crown prosecutors to be their duty to exclude from the jury box every juror known or suspected to hold or agree with the accused in political sentiment...as a loyal citizen I am willing and desirous to be put upon my country and fairly tried before any twelve of my countrymen no matter what may happen to be the political sentiments of any of them. But I am sorry and indignant that this is not such a trial."

At this point, John turned to an explanation as to why he had chosen not to hire legal representatives, feeling that dwelling on the niceties of law in a political situation was a mistake...Then he addressed the prosecutors. He didn't want to harm them because their opinions differed from his. "Gentlemen, this prosecution against me...is part of a scheme of the ministers of the crown for suppressing all voices of protest against the Union, for suppressing all public complaint against the deadly results of the Union, and all advocacy by act, speech, or writing for Repeal of the Union...I consider it to be my duty, as a patriotic and loyal citizen, to endeavor by all honorable means to procure Repeal of the Act of Union, and the restoration of the independent Irish government of which my country was by fraud and force and against the will of the vast majority of its people of every race, creed and class, though under false form of law, deprived 67 years ago, ever since this country was thereby rendered the subject instead of the sister of England."

This bad situation had deteriorated in the last twenty years. During that time, the Government had only appointed people to the most important positions in Ireland, people who "would submit whether by parole or by understanding, to suppress all public utterance of their desire for Repeal of the Union." "It is a hard trial of men's patriotism to be debarred from all career of profitable and honorable distinction in the public service of their own country."

One charge against John was violating the Party Processions Act. The judge had stated that to be found guilty, John must be convicted of violating one of seven conditions, which determined the legality of a march. John repeated them: the procession was designed for an unlawful purpose, was a threat to public peace; the procession alarmed peaceful citizens, created disaffection, incited hatred against England, attacked the administration of justice, and intended to "bring the administration of justice into disrepute."

John rebutted each one in order. The purpose of the procession was to express opinions peacefully. There was no danger to the public, as the procession included women and children, and no one carried guns. No harm was attempted or inflicted. There was no panic as a result of the event. Since they adopted a peaceful avenue for expressing public opinions, they actually lessened any chance of public disaffection. There was no incitement against the English. It gave leaders an opportunity to speak of issues that needed to be aired. If unaddressed, the danger of rising hatred would simmer and actually increase. The same benefits would flow from discussing the limits of the current system of justice. Finally, nothing was done which would impair the functions of justice.

Next, John turned to the subject of the Manchester Martyrs whose executions were the reason for the procession. "The constitutional way for good citizens to act in striving to keep the administration of justice pure and above suspicion of unfairness is by such open and peaceable protests. Thus and thus only may the functions of justice be saved from being impaired. In this case, wrong has been done. Five men have been tried together on the same evidence, and while one of the 5 [Maguire] was acknowledged by the crown to be innocent, the whole conviction was thus acknowledged to be wrong and invalid, 3 of the 5 men were hanged upon that wrong conviction...I say the persons responsible for that transaction are fairly liable to the charge of acting so as to bring the administration of justice into contempt, unless gentlemen, you hold those persons to be infallible and hold that they can do no wrong. But, gentlemen, the constitution does not say that the servants of the crown can do no wrong. According to the constitution, the Sovereign can do no wrong, but her servants may."

Given this point of view, this court proceeding couldn't "right that wrong" by putting any of those charged in this court into prison. Even if the court believed that John was wrong in his opinions, it had no right to convict him for peacefully expressing his opinion. And if they decided his actions were a penal offence, there were thousands of others who committed the same offense. Justice would demand that all of the participants be charged and convicted as well. To fail to do that would be a dereliction of duty. Not to prosecute them all puts the law into "disrepute." "Equal justice is what the constitution demands."

In concluding his speech, John returned to the Party Processions Act as he viewed its restrictions. He maintained that for an action to fall under the law, the marchers had to be armed and to carry political symbols. This march had neither. With these words, John ended his defense. "To prohibit or punish peaceful, inoffensive, orderly and perfectly innocent processions upon a pretence that they were constructively unlawful, is unconstitutional tyranny. I would not have held the procession had I not understood that it was permitted...In this country, it is not the law that must rule a loyal citizen's conduct, but the caprice of the English ministers. For myself I acknowledge that I submit to such a system of government unwillingly and with compliant hope for a restoration of the reign of law, but I do submit."

With these words, John sat down. The courtroom erupted in loud applause, and officials had considerable difficulty restoring order. Since John had offered no defense beyond his speech, the trial quickly moved to jury deliberations. They retired from court around 2 p.m. Less than an hour later, they returned with a question. The foreman asked the court if they considered John's speech seditious, did that make the parade illegal?

Mr. Justice Fitzgerald replied that it did not. Many of those who participated in the march were unaware that John even intended to give a speech, so they could not be held accountable for the words he said. With that instruction, the jury retired again for more deliberations. At 5 p.m., they reported that they were unable to reach a verdict. Judge Fitzgerald dismissed them, and immediately announced that the government did not intend to retry the case. John walked out of the courthouse this time a free man. The sidewalk around the Court was crowded with people who gave John rousing cheers as he left.

George was predictably angry. With Orange trials taking place in Belfast [Johnson, Beers] to act as a contrast, George saw the law wasn't enforced fairly. John had been acquitted while he expected William Johnston and the others on trial would most likely be convicted. It was clear to George that the march in Dublin fell under the Party Processions act. The marchers there all wore green. "Green in the North is regarded as much a party color as orange is in the South. A procession with green scarves and banners in Belfast would involve the town in riot and bloodshed. Such a procession as that in which Mr. John Martin took part, if taking place in Belfast, would be the cause of instant tumult and violence."

Besides the use of symbols George found offensive, he claimed the procession was disloyal. It was calculated to rouse the Catholic populations against the government. "It was a most daring seditious display. He noted that another newspaper had declared it was a "'roar of defiance.'" He concluded his leader, "We entreat the Government not to proceed against Mr. Johnston and his companions. Ulster will be convulsed if they are to be convicted while Mr. John Martin and his fellows go scot free."

John made clear his feelings regarding the outcome of his trial soon after. "It is something gained to have met their packed jury fairly and frankly and to have outflanked it and be able to pursue my march onward. I am confident that, BUT FOR THE LAWYERS this infernal system by which public opinion is stifled in Ireland might be overthrown in the law-courts." But I assure you I am very desirous to keep out of jail and highly delighted to be healthy in the delicious air of Kilbroney valley and looking out upon the Cloughmore and the Bay & Finn Mc Columkil's granite face as he lies upon Carlingford mountain and playing my sociable game of whist …instead of tenanting a separate solitary cube in Mr. Prices's model jail."

When John read George's leader lamenting the outcome of his trial, he felt entitled to respond. John totally agreed with George that William Johnston and all his fellow Orangemen who faced trial should be immediately released. "I always regarded that statute as an unconstitutional and unwise measure—as an arbitrary and intolerant piece of makeshift legislation worthy of those Parisaical patrons of free institutions—the Whigs. The Orangemen ought to be perfectly free to celebrate publically any sieges, any battles, any triumphs they care to celebrate. So long as they refrain from breaking the common law, they have a constitutional right peaceably to employ whatsoever symbols they think proper for their celebration—colours, music, even arms peacefully handled, fireworks—anything which they do not use of the purpose of injuring their neighbours and breaking the peace." The wisdom of the activities might be questioned. "But the law has no right to punish men for bad taste."

John ended the letter to George in a very uncharacteristic way. "Mr. Editor, you call me a 'seditionist,' 'disloyal' and other ugly names. But, in fact, I consider you a disloyal subject, a seditious writer, a mischievous citizen; and I put it to you whether, so long as the law declines to pronounce me seditious, disloyal and so forth, you have any right in propriety to speak so of me ex cathedra of your editorial chair. But our most important difference is, that I could not bring myself to wish you put in gaol, or legally punished in any way, for publishing your opinions upon public questions, while you seem rather disappointed at my escape from the Green Street jury. I shall trouble you no further at present, but subscribe myself, your obedient servant. John Martin."

Chapter 15

Disestablishment

1867 – 1868

In the spring of 1867 while the Fenian trials were underway in Dublin, George was watching an attempt underway in Parliament to sever the crucial connection between the Church of Ireland and the government in England, thus ending that denomination's position as the official church of Ireland. Sir John Gray who was a bitter opponent of the church establishment had introduced a resolution. His first action had been to strongly condemn the Orange Order. George rushed to their defense, "It came well for the man of Young Ireland antecedents to assail the body of the most loyal men in the kingdom, and to pour on them the slime of his abuse."

George warned his readers that he had begun to believe there was increasing danger that this legislation might actually pass. The people of England are "heartily sick of Irish politics." So they are growing more comfortable with the idea. But they didn't realize that they were really overthrowing Irish Protestantism. George claimed disestablishment wasn't an issue that the ordinary Catholics cared deeply about given their increasingly positive response to Protestant missionaries working in the southern and western parts of the island. This threat to Catholic leaders' positions and income would ensure that Catholic members of Parliament would offer their strong support to this legislation.

Gladstone explained the justification behind his new intentions. Establishment supporters often claimed ministers of the favored church were engaged in good works across Ireland that benefited citizens of all religions. Gladstone found this justification unconvincing. In order for there to be any substance to such an argument, the favored church had to be the church supported by the "vast majority" of the population, the government and the poor. The favored denomination was supported by less than a quarter of the population. Gladstone also argued that the English government had officially recognized the Catholic church through its Maynooth grant, a concept George strongly objected to. George urged the Protestant clergy of Ulster to go in large numbers to Parliament to make sure the members understood the truth about the situation in Ireland.

As the government supported the Catholic church with its grant to Maynooth, they also supported the Presbyterian church with the Regium Donum. In July, a discussion took place in Parliament on this topic. The members from Ulster stoutly defended this support by the state for Presbyterian ministers. They even argued that the fund should be increased. The contribution had begun under King James and continued when William defeated King James in battle. "Presbyterian ministers have a claim to it. Their work has kept Ulster the best part of Ireland, the people pious, industrious. They preach rule of law and adherence to the Queen. The Catholics fill the workhouses and jails, not the Presbyterians."

One of the arguments offered against continuing the Regium Donum was that the Presbyterians could afford to support their own ministers. George argued that this might be true in Scotland, but the situation in Ireland was different. "The Presbyterians of Ulster are generally poor. Their small means do not enable them to contribute in any extent for the support of religion."

George then argued that the stipend given to Presbyterian ministers should be increased. Presently, six hundred ministers were given a stipend of just £100 a year. Since the cost of living had doubled in the last twenty years, the stipend should be doubled as well, so a minister's family could live comfortably. But presently they could no longer maintain a fitting standard of living with what the state provided.

In the fall, George returned to the subject. He was alarmed that the Catholic Church had been strongly promoting disestablishment. Priests claimed that the interconnection between church and state was at the heart of the problems Ireland had with the English. George feared that this sentiment was taking hold in England. In both England and in Scotland, there were many people who believed in the voluntary principle. They believed that churches should be supported by their members and not by the government. However, Parliament adjourned without passing any legislation on the issue. George hoped that the danger had passed and turned to savoring the failure of the Fenians.

§

The idea of disconnecting the Church of Ireland from its position as the official church of the government had been discussed across Ireland, and the back rooms of Parliament for decades. During 1867, the notion took more concrete form, with actual discussions on the topic taking place in formal Parliamentary sessions. As 1868 began, so did a new session of Parliament, and a renewed threat to the established church. George was not content to sit passively on the sidelines wringing his hands and writing cutting editorials. He set about rousing Newry citizens to oppose any revival of the noxious idea. He used the *Telegraph* to spread the good news that his effort to generate organized opposition to any new attempt to overthrow the Establishment had born fruit.

By early February, a new organization, the Protestant Defence Association, was unveiled in Newry. The initial meeting was held in the meeting room of the Savings Bank on Hill Street. "We were glad to see all denominations of Protestants uniting heart and hand to face a common foe, and to uphold the claims of the Protestant Churches of these lands to those endowments which the Ultramontane party are endeavouring, in their onward reach to power, to destroy. Episcopalians, Presbyterians, and Methodists—all were united last evening, and when so unanimous, what power in the state can withstand them! Long may be it so! Though divided on minor points–and perhaps uniformity of thought and sentiment on every point is not desirable–yet, in heart, when a common danger calls them, they know they are really one."

Then George explained to his readers that this new organization didn't claim that the current state of the establishment was perfect. Indeed they pledged strong and united efforts to make whatever changes were needed to "aid in its power; but it does aim at defending the principle and existence of Protestant Establishment, a principle which was equally dear to the hearts of previous leaders." "Reformation is one thing, destruction another."

He concluded, "We have every reason to congratulate our Protestant townsmen on the prompt and ready manner with which they came forward to give their assistance to preventing the proposed spoliation of the Church in these realms."

Within a week, this unity between George and local Presbyterian ministers had vanished. Some members of the Newry Presbytery opposed George's support of an increase in the Regium Donum currently providing income support to every Presbyterian minister. They noted that Presbyterian churches in Scotland were fully funded by their members and believed a similar system would enhance religious freedom in Ireland as well.

George forcefully argued against their position. "The Rev. John Dodd and those who agree with him would have the Irish Presbyterian ministers to cast away the Royal Bounty, and rely altogether on the support of Voluntaryism. We have again and again asserted that the laity in this country could not raise anything like an adequate income for their clergy. In towns, no doubt, a sufficient stipend might be raised, but what would become of the great bulk of the rural congregations? Their ministers would be starved from them."

He restated his position a few days later. "Voluntaryism never will do in Ireland. It has failed in America, in England, and in Scotland. The Presbyterian Church of this country is entitled to the Royal Bounty. The only pity is that the Royal Grant is so small."

Lord John Russell wrote a letter to the former Irish Chief Secretary, which George decided to comment on. "Lord Russell comes forth against our National establishment as one of its most determined enemies. He adopts the silly and most unfounded allegation, that the Irish Church is the chief of Irish 'grievances'; that the Romish clergy and laity are alike disaffected because of it. He maintains that the Establishment can no longer be tolerated. It must go down. That is Lord Russell's first remedy for the good of our country! One of the most glorious results of the Protestant Reformation is thus to be destroyed. The Revolution of 1688 saved the Irish Church, but in 1868 Whig and Radical statesmen are combined to destroy what the illustrious William of Orange and our heroic forefathers so nobly preserved."

For the first time, George informed his readers about the financial implications of disestablishment, at least as viewed by Lord Russell. The required tithes or rent charges that the Irish people paid to support the Established church financially would continue. But the great bulk of the funds would now go to the Catholic Church since they represented the religious affiliation of that vast majority of Irish citizens. This would mean about three fourths of the funds would go to the Catholic Church, one eighth to the Church of Ireland, and a little less than one eighth to the Presbyterian Church.

Much as George loathed this idea, he thought it was a benefit that the idea had been floated so early in the battle. "It is well that the Protestants of Ireland and of the empire generally should know that Whig statesmen are resolved to restore Romanism to its old status in the nation. It is well that Protestants of all denominations should see the necessity for merging all their minor differences, and rallying a combined mighty host, for resisting this infamous attempt for the overturning of the whole work of the Reformation, and the virtual re-establishment of the Roman Catholic Church. Is there a Protestant in Ireland, worth the name, whose soul is not filled with indignation at this impious and odious policy of Lord Russell? By all classes of Protestantism in the kingdom it will be execrated."

As George began his efforts to defeat the idea of disestablishment in whatever form Parliament decided to adopt, John made clear that he didn't agree with George yet again. "My very soul revolts at the mere greed, expediency, factiousness, selfishness, which form the ground whereon the bulk of the noble lords, holy bishops and clergy and lay adventurers support the Establishment and the dirty Donum."

In March, George was greatly surprised as Conservative leaders warned their members that if the Liberal forces in Parliament united against the government to push for repeal of the Establishment, they would likely win. The government had already decided that should that happen, they would dissolve Parliament and request a new election. "It is well that the Conservatives should be forewarned on the subject. In every borough there should be preparations…for an election within two months from this date." This action seemed especially odd given that in just one year, a new election was mandated by the new reform voting laws. "But it is evident Mr. Gladstone must be in dread of the results of the enlarged franchise. It is generally believed that the new and greatly enlarged constituencies in England will return generally, representatives of Conservative principles."

Then George laid out for his readers the immensely important principles at stake in the next election. "It is whether or not shall Romanism have the ascendency in Ireland. The overthrow of the Established Church and the spoliation of the Presbyterian Church of its Regium Donum, would be disastrous to the cause of Protestantism in the land. Voluntaryism would utterly fail to preserve hundreds of congregations from going down. Their faithful ministers would be unable to remain with them. And the young students of both the Churches would be driven to other pursuits, since as clergymen they could have no prospect of obtaining an adequate support."

The Catholic Church wouldn't endure similar poverty. There was plenty of money to support their chapels. "The essence of the Papal system is to make money." All the services provided for the laity had to be paid for. "They believe that their salvation would be imperiled if they did not liberally pay their 'dues.'"

This leader ended with a call to arms. "A few days will reveal how soon the trumpets of battle will be sounded. The warfare is now not a political one. It concerns the stability of Protestantism or its downfall, and the commencement of the dire ascendancy of Romanism in the nation."

However, before George turned his total attention to Disestablishment, he criticized the revised Party Processions Act that had just become law. He claimed that the measure had been passed in great haste and only operated to suppress the "loyal Orangemen of Ulster," while in other parts of the country it appeared to be totally useless. In Ulster, William Johnston was convicted and John Martin was freed. In John's trial Judge Fitzgerald had described the conditions necessary to prove an illegal march. One of them was wearing party symbols. But there was no general understanding of what constituted a party symbol. "Everybody knows green is a party colour, and yet Sir Robert Peel, when Chief Secretary for Ireland, declared in the House of Commons that green was not a party colour in Ireland; and the then Law Officers of the Crown, Messrs. Lawson and Sullivan endorsed that doctrine."

The problem could be easily remedied. The bill just needed a single amendment. It should henceforth proclaim that any procession involving the color green or orange and purple would automatically be illegal processions.

§

The first step toward disestablishing the Church of Ireland as the official government church took place in late March. Gladstone introduced three resolutions into the House of Commons. The first resolution stated that it was "necessary" that the Church of Ireland should cease to be the Established Church. The second stated that while this process was underway only "immediate necessity" should lead to any changes in the current situation in Ireland. The final resolution asked the Queen to authorize Parliament to make decisions on the status of religious leaders and their benefices in Ireland.

In the same edition of the *Telegraph,* George wrote a fiery leader, which he titled "The Political Crisis–The Irish Church." The vote on Gladstone's resolutions could come as early as the next week. If approved, profound changes in the religious practices in Ireland would become inevitable. "If the Church be plundered of her revenues, of course the Regium Donum of the Presbyterian Church will cease. All the Presbyterian chaplaincies will be abolished, and it is well for the Roman Catholics to remember that the Maynooth Grant must of necessity come to an end, together with all Roman Catholic chaplaincies."

Gladstone believed that this would solve many of the problems that had plagued Ireland for centuries. "Vain delusion! Why, we will be plunged into religious warfare that will…convulse the country, and that in the end may lead to all the horrors of civil war. The Liberal party are madly playing into the hands of the Ultramontanists, whose object is the annihilation of Protestantism in Ireland. They are driving us into a tremendous struggle that may lead to the most fearful results. If Mr. Gladstone succeeds in his movement against our National Church then the flames of sectarian discord and deadly contention shall blaze over all the land."

"The battle cry for all the Protestants of the empire is evident. It is no surrender to Ultramontanism! Again and again we say, let every loyalist of the land be alive to the importance of the great political crisis." If the Gladstone forces should succeed in their plans, Mr. Disraeli would call for a new election. "The battle for religious endowments will thus be fought at the hustings. Shame on those Protestants who will not rally eagerly round the standard of Conservatism! Let it be borne in mind that the final issue will not be the preservation or fall of the Irish Church, but the upholding of Protestantism in the British empire."

George also had a message for the Protestants of Newry. "Let our Protestant friends in Newry wake up from what seems a lethargy when all the country is astir, and prove that even persecution by those who should be friends cannot extinguish the flame of their devotedness for their much loved Church…It is not worthy of us, Protestant inhabitants of this prosperous commercial town, to sit quietly by and receive the benefits which others may win for us. We therefore hope that our influential landed gentry–that class of men whose voice should be heard--with the clergy of every Protestant denomination, will rouse themselves to action, and prove that we are worthy of the position we have hitherto held as part of the Protestant community of Ulster."

George was hopeful that the Conservatives in Parliament could repulse the attack on the Established Church. He informed the people of Newry the steps the party was taking. Lord Stanley had risen in Parliament to offer an amendment. "That this House, while admitting that considerable modification in the temporalities of the United Church in Ireland may, after pending inquiry, appear to be expedient, is of opinion that any proposition tending to the disestablishment or the disendowment of that Church ought to be reserved for the decision of the new Parliament." If approved, this amendment would delay the decision until the next election.

The struggle taking place in London was vitally important for Ireland. "The Irish Church question is the greatest that has been before the Legislature we might say for centuries. What is proposed by Mr. Gladstone is to a very great extent the reversal of the policy of the State since the glorious Revolution of 1688. It implies the renunciation of the State to protect and support the Protestant religion in Ireland. It would be a concession of the vastest magnitude to the Church of Rome. It would be an aggression on a gigantic scale on the rights of property hitherto held most sacred."

Next, George warned his readers that they were watching the first stages of a revolution. And it was a characteristic of revolutions, that once started, even those who lit the match, had no idea where the revolution would lead. Would this action undo the rights of property generally? Would it lead to fixity of tenure? Perhaps even general land confiscation might follow.

Then George broadened his warnings to include all the Protestants of Ireland. "In addition to all this there is another consideration of weighty importance to be remembered. The proposed destruction of the Irish Establishment is in opposition to the Protestant people of this country, to all those who are the representatives of the property, the wealth, the industry, and the loyalty of the nation. All who have made Ulster what it is must indignantly protest against this intended act of confiscation. Why should an expiring Parliament perpetrate such an outrage on the loyalists of Ireland? Why exasperate and drive them into the conviction that the British Legislature is resolved to consign this country to the supreme domination of the Pope and his emissaries?"

George concluded with a personal attack on Gladstone's character. "Mr. Gladstone is an intolerant bigot." He once visited the Queen in Scotland and refused to attend Presbyterian services with her. He would have no Methodist tenants on his property. And yet, he had attended Catholic services. "His feelings are with Rome."

"We appeal to Protestants of all denominations to be aroused to their duty. Let them combine and cooperate. Petitions from all towns and parishes should flow into the House of Commons. No time is to be lost. No energies should be spared to preserve, not the Irish Church merely, but Irish Protestantism."

And the local Protestants of Newry didn't waste any time in gathering together to make their opposition to the actions in Parliament very clear. Another meeting of the Newry Branch of the Ulster Protestant Defence Association took place in the Scriptural School on Downshire Road. George couldn't have been more pleased with the results. Attendance was large and included members of the local artisan community who weren't believed to be much interested in the subject, along with members of all Protestant religions who were there to support the members of the Established Church. Archibald Erskine, Esq., MD, ran the meeting.

Dr. Erskine spoke to the crowd before the resolutions were introduced. This organization wasn't an offensive one, he explained to the audience, but rather one assembled to act defensively. This was a group brought together to "defend the castle." He intended to raise a couple of issues: was it politic to endow a church, and what would justify doing that? Then he put forward his answers to these questions. Religion and state had been connected a long time before. So "the voice of antiquity was in favour of it." Early Irish settlers saw the benefits of having religion as part of the laws they created.

For centuries, it was the Church of Ireland that had been thus connected with the state. This ancient tradition had been continued to the present. In fact, this connection had had very positive benefits in elevating the character and conduct of the Irish people. So it made great sense that breaking this connection would have a very negative result. Certainly, improvements could be made to improve the functioning of this connection, but it should never "be taken down."

The prominent Doctor continued by refuting the allegation that the early members of the Established Church had taken land that belonged to the Catholic Church. There was no truth to that complaint, according to Dr. Erskine. The land on which the churches were built was land that had been abandoned by Catholic farmers not by the church itself. So it was clear that the land issue couldn't be a source of dissention for Catholics. Furthermore, if the Established Church hadn't taken the land, the nobles would have, perhaps leaving the Catholic population in a worse condition.

Having offered convincing arguments that the clergymen of the Established Church had been a force for good in their communities, he then explained the principles on which a church could be made the official religion. One was a numerical majority. That precept would apply only if the religion of the majority was acceptable to the government. Clearly the Catholic religion, being just as defective as that of the "Mohanmedons," would not meet that requirement. It was in fact the duty of the state to select a religion that would teach the Word of God according to the scriptures. Clearly that was what the British government had done. And he didn't believe that the Irish people objected to that decision.

At that point, Dr. Erskine focused on the three resolutions that had been prepared for voting. One pledged support to the Queen in these dangerous times. This was a time for ties of iron between Ireland and England. The second attacked disestablishment as a violation of previous legislation and a weakening of the Act of Union. The final resolution opposed the idea that the Catholic Church would have immense influence over education in Ireland, to the point of having universities run by the Catholic Church.

Rev. G. T. Stokes supported the second resolution. "They (Catholics) wanted all, and if they got it, they would crush the life out of the people, and there would be the end of Protestants...It was also said the Roman Catholics were in a majority in the nation. This he denied. England, Ireland, and Scotland were all one nation, and Protestants being in a majority, and having a Protestant Government, they were entitled to remain the Established Church."

All resolutions passed unanimously.

Despite George's support, and local efforts to enhance his voice, Lord Stanley's amendment failed. George was decidedly gloomy in his leader on the subject. "It is assumed that the vote of Friday night has settled the fate of the Irish Church. All over the country its enemies are frantically shrieking in triumph. It is gone, they exclaim—it has received its death blow—the Establishment will no longer be tolerated in the land."

But George still refused to agree that the situation was hopeless, continuing to rally hope in the hearts of the Protestants of Ulster. They could actually still save the Established Church. "We fancy they may yet find they are mistaken. They have begun to rave and shout over the ruins of the Church before it has fallen. The truth is, the battle has only begun. A majority of the House of Commons has rejected Lord Stanley's amendment. It has yet to be decided what will be done with Mr. Gladstone's resolutions. Even suppose they are carried by a majority, that will not be the final issue. The country will be appealed to. The Protestant people of England and Scotland and of this country, in the general election of next year, will settle conclusively the matter. With them–not with Mr. Gladstone and his out-of-office confreres–will rest the grand issue."

Not only would the Irish voters play an important part in the final outcome of the issue, but they were gaining many important allies to their cause. The people of England were rallying in support of the Irish Church. "They now know that such an event would result in fearful damage to the stability, progress, and prospects of our faith; and there is another truth they have learned–namely, that the fall of the Irish Establishment will precede and secure the ruin of their own Establishment…Public meetings are being held on the subject that are attended by enthusiastic audiences. The 'No Popery' cry will thoroughly arouse the English nation. That question will become the great question of the day. The moral force of Protestantism in England is overwhelming, and its irresistible influence will be felt next spring on every husting in England. We believe confidently that the newly enfranchised classes, who in many boroughs will decide the issue of the elections will be found staunch supporters of Protestantism and of our national Protestant Establishments."

George concluded his leader with a pep talk. "Let the friends of the Irish Church not be disheartened. 'All is not lost that is in danger.' We believe that no living man will see our glorious National Church driven from its high position in the land, and plundered of its temporalities. There will be reform, there will be desirable modifications, there will be more justice done than hitherto has been done to the faithful, hard-working devoted clergy, but the wild predictions of the Romanists and Voluntaries will never be fulfilled."

"Let us impress upon the Protestant public the fact that the agitation against the Irish Church and the Regium Donum, as carried on by Protestants, is a crafty political moment. It is designed to promote Liberalism. It is hoped by it to break up the Conservative party, and to crush its power in Parliament and in the country. By this agitation in the North of Ireland it is sought to alienate the Presbyterians and the Methodists from their Episcopalian brethren…The good work of defending our national religious institution will be advanced in this town despite all opposition, whether of Romanists or Voluntaries. We have a faithful zealous, true-hearted band in our community, who will not be driven from their duty by abuse and bravado. The cause they maintain is dearer to them than life, and at all hazards they will maintain it."

Rev. Henry Henderson, a Presbyterian minister, and George's brother, gave a local speech to offer the kind of strong support for the existing Establishment that Rev. Henry Cooke had traditionally provided. "This was a period when sectarian differences and alienations should end, when the sections of all Protestant Churches should range themselves under on common banner–the banner of Christ–in maintenance of those great principles which were dear, or ought to be dear, to all their hearts."

After these introductory remarks, Rev. Henderson extolled the Orangemen and the important part they played, proclaiming that they could maintain order in Ulster, even if there wasn't a single British soldier or policeman there. Even though many of its members were Presbyterians, they would support their Church of Ireland brothers in the Protestant religion. Together they would maintain the union of Ireland and England.

Being a Presbyterian minister, he disputed the common belief that Presbyterians had been abusively treated by members of the Established Church. While some Presbyterians believed that disestablishment would reduce "discord," he used a proverb to show the folly of such an idea. "'Never do evil that good may come.' If they surrendered their principles–if they bartered the principles of truth that they might have peace–the blessing of God could not attend them." Certainly the Catholic Church would never be satisfied with disestablishment. The grand principle of Rome was universal supremacy over the world; and Protestants were aiming for the overthrow of Popery in Ireland, until which there would never be peace." But he hoped no one would think that he had anything against local Catholics, friends and neighbors he actually loved.

In the second part of his speech, Rev. Henderson attempted to convince the audience that repealing the Establishment was actually a sin. "It was the duty of the State to support, maintain and protect the Church of Jesus." Voluntarianism was "opposed to God's truth. Its principles were that the State as a State should have nothing to do with religion. It should have to do with civil affairs–with art, education, literature, &c.–but as a State it should have no religion at all. Was that not infidelity?" The State must endow Protestant religions, but not the Catholic one. Finally, he echoed the argument that doing away with the Established Church would also end the Union.

As summer neared, other local meetings on the issue took place in Newry. George covered all of them. One focused on the issue of Voluntarianism. The idea that local congregations should and could support their own churches, a core pillar of Disestablishment, prompted a quick response. "We warn the Conservative Presbyterians of Newry not to be imposed upon. These lectures to which they are treated are intended to spread Voluntaryism. They are calculated to set one class of Protestants against another. They are most hostile to the Established Church, as they have a political aim–namely, to break up the Conservative party of this town."

After some reflection on this critical concept, George returned to the subject in a leader he titled "Protestant Union." He believed Protestant unity to be a religious duty to thwart Gladstone's intentions to "grant extraordinary concessions to the Romish Church in this country. To please them the Irish

Establishment is to be abolished. The national Church is to be disestablished and plundered of its temporalities."

So what were Gladstone's plans for disbursing all the funds that would be taken from the Established Church? George asserted that instead of the Regium Donum, a grant of about one million pounds would be given to the General Assembly, a little more than one million would go to the Irish Church. The remaining would go to the Catholic Church to support Catholic education, monasteries and nunneries. The Romanists were to be thus endowed. "We defy anyone to refute that assertion."

George then offered a heartfelt message to the Presbyterians of Newry. "Now, we appeal to the Presbyterian laity on this subject. They are stanch Protestants. They would shed their blood for the principles their forefathers maintained to the death. They know that Romanism is the bane of Ireland. They know it is the foe of civil and religious liberty. They know it is the deadly enemy of God's Word. We ask them will they be influenced by Radical emissaries to stand coldly by while the Protestant national Church of this country is plundered of its property in order that the property may be handed over to the papal hierarchy?"

§

George was almost totally preoccupied with the issue of disestablishment and wrote leader after leader on the subject. Still, there were other local events that were of interest to his readers on which he reported.

One such issue was the ongoing dispute over the Party Procession Act and what the local residents saw as unequal enforcement. William Johnston who had led the large Orange March in Bangor the previous summer had been convicted of participating in an illegal march and had been sentenced to serve a month in prison. Events to protest his treatment took place in many of the towns in County Down. This treatment of Orangemen stood in stark contrast to the treatment of those who participated in the mock funerals. While they were supposedly designed to protest the execution of the Manchester Martyrs, George believed they were really designed to spread revolution. No one was put in prison "although the Processions Act was trampled under the feet of Mr. John Martin and his followers."

George continued. "Surely, under such circumstances, it was short-sighted and unfair policy to prosecute Mr. Johnston and his companions. The Executive made a deplorable blunder in doing so, and the best and truest friends and advocates of the Government acknowledge that fact. Mr. Johnston has had the victory. His popularity has been vastly increased. The loyalists of Ulster are more attached to him than ever."

This edition of the paper had scarcely been bundled and placed in the hands of the paper boys when word arrived in Newry that William Johnston had been released after serving only two weeks of his sentence. Celebrations broke out immediately. In the townlands of Sheeptown and Desert, Orangemen gathered and built huge bonfires which were kept burning through most of the night. They also marched about to the music of fife and drum. No party tunes were played, and all was peaceful.

A larger demonstration took place in Rathfriland. Orangemen assembled in the town square. The crowd was first serenaded by thirty-six drums and double that number of fifes. Again no party tunes were played. Then the Orangemen marched off to the home of William Beers, who had been arrested with Johnston. Mr. Beers appeared and spoke to the crowd of his delight at the freedom of Mr. Johnston. Later in the evening tar barrels were lit on surrounding hills. All passed off peacefully.

A similar if smaller scale celebration took place in Loughbrickland. Orangemen from the surrounding farms marched into town, accompanied by fife and drum bands. They played songs popular among loyalists, but none of the Orange music. Along the main street were placards with the words, "Johnston is free." The large crowd moved to a nearby hill where they too created a large bonfire. There the participants danced about the fire and engaged in sports. The surrounding hills were ablaze with fires as far as the eye could see.

§

John Martin was not an active participant in the struggle over disestablishment, though his support of disestablishment was well known. Instead, with one exception, he remained quietly in Kilbroney during the spring. He came into Newry to give a non-political speech before the Newry Young Men's Society, a Catholic organization, in the large meeting hall at the Savings Bank on April 20th. His topic was the "Literature of Ireland." There was a large crowd on hand to hear John's presentation. The front seats were filled with widely respected Newry traders, but the back was filled with men of "the humbler classes."

When John appeared escorted by the Rev. Bernard O'Hagan of Newry, there was a large burst of applause. The men at the back of the room stood on the chairs and waved their hats. The applause and cheering continued for several minutes. Rev. O'Hagan acted as chairman of the evening's events. "It was his duty or rather his privilege to introduce to them that night not an unknown stranger, but an old, true, tried, and trusted friend–(great applause)– one of the best of Ireland's sons–(renewed applause)—a man who was not his own property, but his nation's property–(applause)–a man who, whether they found him in the simplicity of his quiet homestead or in the dungeon of the felon–whether they discovered him breathing the sweet air of his own native mountains or banished far away in the land of the strangers–he ever clung with unchanging tenacity to the cause of poor old Ireland–(great applause)–a man who placed under his feet the trammels of sectarianism–a man who had raised his voice proclaiming the glorious doctrines of civil and religious liberty. (Applause) Such was the man whom he begged to introduce to them that night–a man whose heart rebounded as he found justice, however, scanty, meted out in his country–who hoped–and he (the Chairman) hoped with him– to see the sunburst of freedom tinge the glorious soil of their native country.

(Tremendous cheering) he would now introduce to them John Martin of Kilbroney. (Renewed applause)"

"Mr. Martin, on rising, received a perfect ovation, and was not allowed to speak for several minutes." However, the reporter covering the meeting felt the need to cast cold water on the warmth of the reception. "As we have already, however insinuated, the applause for the greater part came from the distant end of the room, few of the respectable persons in front joining in it."

John, however, was greatly moved by the ovation, and diverted from his planned remarks to thank the audience for their greeting. "He thanked them from his heart for the kindness shown towards him. During the whole of his political life, he had remarked the trustfulness with which his countrymen had treated him in all parts of Ireland. This gratified him very much, because he had never gone out of his way–and he said it proudly–he had never violated or suppressed his own real sentiments in order to obtain popularity. Therefore, when popularity came, it was all the more welcome, because it could be the more heartily enjoyed. But if he enjoyed popularity in Dublin, Cork and Limerick, how much more did he enjoy it in his own native place in Newry. (Applause.) He did not intend to make a speech on this subject, and he had only to repeat that he heartily thanked them for their kind reception."

With those opening remarks, John turned to the subject of the evening, Irish literature…The theme of the speech was that literature was an "index" of the times in which the writing took place. It was a great loss that no one yet had done a history of Ireland from that point of view. Some efforts had been made, but they were incomplete. He believed that this was a good time for this deficit to be ended. He then read from several existing works to prove his point. He believed that the skill of Irish poets ranked Ireland with "as great literary endowments as even that shown in the plays of Shakespeare."

"The conclusion he intended to arrive at was, that the Irish people were able to take a position with the greatest people in the world, or the greatest people that had ever been in it, in literature, science, art, and philosophy; and to enable them to do so, they only wanted their national independence. (Applause.) He thanked the audience for the attention which they had given him and resumed his seat amid great applause."

Rev. Mr. O'Neill, of Rostrevor was among those participating in the ritual resolutions of thanks. He expressed "a hope that the day might soon come when the country would be free from a foreign supremacy, and that his audience could endeavour to cultivate that spirit with which Mr. Martin had endeavoured to infuse in the blood of the youth of IRELAND."

Then John responded to end the evenings events, echoing Rev. O'Neill's comments. "After thanking the meeting for the honour they had paid him, because as he took it they believed him an honest man, he wished that they all would live–and he, too, might live–to see the day when Ireland would be an independent nation, free to render thanks to her countrymen. (Great Applause.)"

Other than the speech in Newry, John remained in Kilbroney, thinking about whether or not to take a major step in a very different direction, running for a seat in Parliament. He could foresee problems resulting from such a decision, the main one being that his strongly held beliefs might differ from those of his constituents. If a constituency should request him to run, there was still the problem of getting elected due to his refusal to resort to the usual corrupt practices that dominated most Irish elections. So he remained undecided.

He made his current political thinking public in a letter to the *Nation* near the end of June. Besides revealing his interest in running for a seat in Parliament, he also made clear how he intended to act as a Member of Parliament. He would not speak on or vote on any issue that related to England alone. To do so would only enhance the myth that Ireland and England were equals in Parliament. His goal would be different. "But I should use my position and my representative character for the purpose of divulging the truth of clearing away the delusions which prevail among very many English, as well as among some Irish of plainly setting forth before England how it is that England stands over Ireland and that Ireland lies under her sister's foul feet...I must be elected <u>free</u> to act when and as I think proper."

How an election took place was equally important to John and vastly different from what was customary. "Concerning the manner of my election...I will not become a candidate for any place except where the constituency is, in my opinion, decidedly and loyally in my favor. I will not pay a single shilling directly or indirectly for my election...I shall be very proud of the dignity of a real freely-elected representative of the Irish people."

At about the time that John was informing his Irish supporters about his new political direction, he was stricken by another severe attack of bronchitis that lasted for weeks. During much of the duration of the attack, he was unable to breathe lying down. As usual, he was forced to sit in a chair, propped up with pillows, his feet resting on another chair that created an improvised chaise.

This time, John had been ill for four weeks before he was able to begin any kind of normal activity. He had caught a cold during a chilly, and "too long" trip on a jaunting car. Before he had recovered fully, he set out to go to Lisdoonvarna in County Clare to visit Father Kenyon, John Mitchel's brother William and youngest sister Henrietta, both of whom lived in London. This trip required John to spend eight more hours in yet another jaunting car in the dark and cold of night. He was hoping that the spa waters there would restore his health. Instead he suffered a relapse. Henrietta's care gradually produced some improvement. John had known Henrietta since she was born, but their paths had diverged since his exile. She had always been involved in political activity, supporting the actions of her brother John. Over her adult years, she had become a wise, and courageous woman. John greatly enjoyed her company as his breathing began to improve.

§

As John attempted to recover his health in County Clare, George turned his attention to what he recognized was the most critical battleground where the future of Ireland would be resolved, the local elections. He was pleased that Newry was currently being represented by a superior young man, Mr. Innes of Dromantine, who would keep his Conservatives in local control.

Though the election was anticipated, no date had been established. Still George was watching all local preparations. Rumors were circulating around town that Mr. Innes could no longer count on impressive Conservative support. George attempted to squash any such rumor. "Newry will triumphantly return Mr. Innes as its faithful and worthy representative. He eminently merits that honourable position."

George then added his own endorsement. "Mr. Innes is one of our best and most popular resident landlords. He has gained the respect and esteem of all parties in this town because of his courtesy, his good will manifested towards his constituents of every sect, and on account of the deep and active interest he has taken in all matters affecting the prosperity of Newry. We put it to the good sense of the electors if it would be wise to reject Mr. Innes for the sake of any stranger?"

Those locals who might vote against Mr. Innes were opposed to him because he was a Conservative. George then provided his readers with a list of Conservative accomplishments. Most impressive to George were changes to voting rights. This had been a major part of the Liberal agenda, but they had never been able to enact any legislation to accomplish this goal. It was the Conservatives that had enabled many more men to vote across the United Kingdom. Newry now had increased voter rolls for this election. "Mr. Innes has taken his part in procuring for the working classes of our country their just rights in regard to Parliamentary representation, and it would be disgraceful to the working men of Newry if they did not enthusiastically support him at the next election."

However, Innes stunned George by announcing he didn't intend to stand for reelection to Parliament due to the illness of a family member. Fortunately for George and his fellow Newry Conservatives, Viscount Newry had agreed to be the Conservative candidate from Newry. "His lordship is the natural representative of this town, and is a young nobleman highly esteemed in his own social circle, much thought of in the metropolis of the kingdom, and possessing qualities which will render him very popular. As a landlord he holds an important position and we are confident he would give his undivided attention and support to everything having a tendency to advance the interest of the town and port of Newry."

On the other hand, the "Radicals" had indicated that they would put William Kirk forward as their candidate. George hoped that Kirk would withdraw in order to save the town the expense of an election. Now that Viscount Newry had come forward, Kirk's "chance of success would be at the best very doubtful." Apparently, Kirk didn't listen to George's advice. There would indeed be a local contest

George reminded his readers of the enormous stakes of this election. Should Kirk and the Radicals win the election, dire consequences would ensue. The unwritten British constitution would be "violated," its Protestant character destroyed, its institutions overthrown, and the power of the Crown weakened.

All of these dangers boiled down to one issue, "whether the Queen or the Pope shall govern in Ireland, and whether Protestantism or Romanism shall be the religion of the State. When they consider these issues we have no doubt as to the course which will be pursued by the manly Conservatives in the ancient and important borough of Newry."

Despite George's apparent confidence as to the outcome of the election, he continued to attempt to persuade Kirk not to run. He informed Kirk that Viscount Newry was rapidly gaining support among the electors. Even members of the Liberal party were joining in the efforts to elect the Conservative candidate. When Lord Newry actually began his canvass, former opponents were likely to flock to his support. "We therefore think it would a most graceful act, and one which would likely prove very popular amongst the constituency if Mr. W. Kirk would leave the field in favour of his lordship, and thus save us from all that bad feeling which a contested election invariably gives rise to."

Early in August, the Viscount in his address to the electors said he would be ready to give "general support" to the current government, not blindly, but consistently. After that rather confusing statement, he ended with words that George ardently hoped to hear, he would devote time and energy to serving the people of Newry, and strongly support the current Conservative government.

After this announcement, George turned again to attack Kirk. He claimed to hold Kirk in "the highest regard." His objection to his candidacy was that he was a member of the Liberal party. "Mr. Kirk may madly contest this town, but he is certain to be defeated. Viscount Newry had overwhelming claims on the suffrages of the electors, and he will be triumphantly returned as our representative."

Notwithstanding George's opposition to his candidacy, Kirk published a letter to his supporters in the *Telegraph*. Kirk made clear that he was running as a Presbyterian. Kirk wrote that as a result of a meeting he had recently held with local Catholics, "it was agreed to support me as a candidate for the representation of the borough *on certain easy conditions* which I have been able to comply with!" George declared that this statement was sufficient proof that Kirk realized he couldn't trust the Presbyterian electors, necessity thus requiring him to make common cause with local Catholics.

Kirk must have realized his statement would prompt George to demand voters should be told what the "easy conditions" were. George was certain Kirk had committed to do the will of the Catholic Church. Their foremost goal was to end the religious establishment of Ireland and the Regium Donum which was so important to the ministers of Kirk's own church. But what position had he taken relative to the Maynooth Grant? What was his position on National Education? Would he support Catholic demands that the government supported schools should be denominational as opposed to the current nondenominational education? When it came to landlord and tenant issues did he join in support of fixity of tenure, leases for tenants, and opposition to the Conservative plans to solve this seemingly endless problem?

Despite this secret agreement with local Catholics, George didn't believe that he would gain the support of most local Catholics. "They will not vote against their future landlord. They will not vote against the son of the lamented and universally esteemed Viscount Newry, who so long most worthily represented this town in Parliament. They will not elect a merchant from Keady in preference to a young nobleman of promise and great influence, whose interests are all bound up with the interests of Newry."

George ended his leader with the strongest condemnation of Kirk that his writing skills could create. "Mr. Kirk shows in his letter that he dreads he will not have Protestant support. How could he? The members of the National Church will not vote for one of its avowed enemies, who gloats at the prospect of its despoilment. The intelligent and highly respectable Presbyterian community are staunch and true Conservatives, and they will deal with Mr. Kirk's pretensions in the future as they dealt with them in the past. He will not have a dozen Presbyterian votes.

"We cannot conclude without expressing our deep regret at the depths to which Mr. Kirk appears to have sunk as a politician. Years ago he was almost a Conservative. Now he avows his full approval of the anti-constitutional and revolutionary policy of Messrs. Gladstone, Beales, and Bright. Such a man cannot be the representative of Newry."

Kirk was undaunted, proceeding to publish his address to voters. He made clear just what he intended to do if elected, fulfilling George's expectations. He would indeed support disestablishment. He saw it as an obstacle to religious equality, which he supported. He didn't believe that the current landlord tenant bill was the solution, but he would hope to support an actual solution to this most important issue. On the great social issues of the day, he supported the liberal position. He strongly supported the expansion of railroads and the port of Newry, as well as any other subject that might arise during his term to benefit Newry. Since he was newly retired from business, he would have ample time to serve Newry well.

An editorial that was published in the *Northern Whig* so irritated George that he wrote a sharp response, even though it gave additional publicity to a paper he very much disliked. The *Whig* praised the candidacy of William Kirk for Parliament in Newry, stating that Kirk would be an active representative of the Presbyterian church, "not a mere handmaiden and bondswoman of the proud and haughty Establishment."

George blasted a response. "Let us reply to this that the Protestant electors of this town will never elect any mere sectarian representative. They will have nothing to do with the stupid, stunted bigotry of sectarianism. What we want, and what we shall have in the person of Lord Newry, is a representative, not of sectarianism, but of Protestantism." "There is not a borough or county in the North where the great mass of the Presbyterian voters would not oppose Mr. Kirk to the utmost."

Though the date for the election had yet to be established, both Viscount Newry and Kirk had completed their canvasses of the electors. So there was a good idea already of how the election would turn out. "Mr. Kirk's local friends have grown wonderfully silent on the subject, and they have much reason to stop their vain boasting. Mr. Kirk has not the slightest chance in the contest. He will be thoroughly beaten."

Not only did George confidently predict Mr. Kirk's embarrassing defeat, he most positively supported Viscount Newry. "His lordship's election is secure. We publish that as an unquestionable fact. The Conservatives stand together in unbroken rank." Even more heartening was the movement of many prominent Newry Catholics to support Lord Newry. They had come to understand that their own interests would be better served by Lord Newry and maintenance of the existing establishment.

George then moved to one of the underlying controversies resulting from establishment. He quoted extensively from a letter on the subject written by Lord Elcho in support of the continuation of the establishment. Lord Elcho resolved the issue for himself this way. "In 1688 civil and religious liberty were founded on the principle of religious inequality."

George agreed with Lord Elcho and warned his readers that they should think long and hard about this new doctrine of religious equality. More was at stake than just the establishment. Under law, the Lord Lieutenant had to be a Protestant. The Sovereign must also be Protestant. If religious equality become a fundamental principle in Ireland both positions must be open to Catholics. This was the position that Kirk supported. "Mr. Kirk is pledged to his Roman Catholic allies to do their work in overturning the great results of the glorious Revolution of 1688. How any Protestant can vote for him under these circumstances we know not, unless it be that for the sake of party they ignore their Protestantism?"

As the expected election drew closer day by day, George returned to the issue in almost every edition of the paper, generally expressing similar ideas. But in the middle of September, he added a new issue to his discussions, the nature of the revised voting lists. He accused Kirk and his supporters of falsifying the results of the newest revisions as turning strongly in favor of the Liberals. "It is well known in Newry that the electoral lists as they now stand show a triumphant Conservative majority. As we stated in our last publication, the contest for the representation of the borough is virtually settled. Lord Newry's return is certain. Mr. Kirk may remain in Keady. Here he has no chances. If he ventures to go to the poll–if his injudicious friends recklessly force him into that position–he will be ignominiously defeated. There is nothing before him but a disastrous failure."

George concluded this leader by repeating his challenge to Kirk to answer a series of questions on his positions on such things as the Maynooth grant and education. "We know these questions never will be answered by Mr. Kirk. And why? Because he is prepared to be an out and out supporter of the Gladstone pro-Papal and revolutionary policy. On that account he is unfit and unworthy to be the representative of Newry; and he will never be so. Even his friends know that well. In their hearts they feel–bitterly feel–that Lord Newry's election is past all doubt. His answers will float gloriously in the hustings."

§

The election which had seemed imminent in September still hadn't occurred by October. But George remained ever vigilant for events that might negatively impact the certain victory of Lord Newry. One such event occurred at the monthly October meeting of the Newry Presbytery. On October 6th, Rev. Elliott requested that the Presbytery discuss the issue of Presbyterian representation at their November meeting. Rev. Elliott was still the minister of the Donaghmore Church.

George was quick to respond, as soon as he learned that Rev. Elliott had sent a resolution to the Presbytery on the subject he intended to raise at their November meeting. Rev. Elliott pointed out that important issues "connected to religious endowments in Ireland are likely to come before the next session of Parliament." Though Presbyterians represented half of the Protestant population of Ireland, there was not a single Presbyterian member of Parliament "to look after their interests whilst the other religious denominations are largely represented by members of their own communion." He asked that the Presbytery discuss steps that could be taken to "secure the return of Presbyterian members to the next Parliament."

George viewed this action as a threat to Protestant unity at a critical moment, and fired off a leader titled, "Is the Newry Presbytery to become a Political Club?" attacking Rev. Elliott's proposal. Rev. Elliott did not see this discussion as a political issue. George found that concept ludicrous. "What does Mr. Elliott mean by such an outrageous assertion?" "Does he fancy that any person will be blinded to the fact that this dabbling of the Presbytery into matters which, as a Presbytery, it ought to have nothing whatever to do with, is a covert scheme for furthering the interests of Mr. Wm. Kirk in this borough? Mr. Elliott is not a Conservative."

Certainly, Rev. Elliott had a right to his own political point of view. But "it is a different matter when he asks the Newry Presbytery to turn itself into a kind of political central club. This is a new and most dangerous movement. It is a novel one moreover. We say deliberately it must be put down, and promptly put down. The laity must at once bestir themselves and prevent their Presbytery and Congregational Sessions becoming political clubs."

The Presbyterian church had always confined itself to religious affairs, George claimed. And he intended to ensure that that tradition would remain in force. Apparently, he had forgotten the efforts to turn the Presbyterian Church into an arm of the Orange Order that had caused such pain to James Harshaw and resulted in the election of the same Rev. John Elliott as minister of the Donaghmore Church instead of Rev. Robert Harshaw. Then politics seemed a proper concern of the church.

George did admit that Presbyterians had a valid point about representation. "It is only reasonable that Presbyterians should desire to have members of their own Church in Parliament...But we object to gentlemen being elected just because they bear the name of being Presbyterians."

Rev. Elliott had also mentioned the endowments that Presbyterians enjoyed. He believed they had a right to them. So why would he support Kirk who would abolish them? "Lord Newry, on the other hand, although an Episcopalian, would resist with all his ability the robbery of the Presbyterian Church by the Puseyite Gladstone and his revolutionary associates and fellow-conspirators."

Before closing his leader, George offered a way forward for Rev. Elliott. "We strongly advise Mr. Elliott to find it convenient to let his resolution fall to the ground. It is with regret that we have been forced to refer to him in this movement. We hold him personally in much esteem as a worthy and estimable clergyman. We suspect he is the unconscious tool of other parties, more crafty, who are for the present in the back ground. It is rumoured in Newry that a somewhat similar motion may be brought before other Presbyteries–the Newry Presbytery apparently setting the example. It is a bad and dangerous movement, and Mr. Elliott, for his own sake and the peace of his church should 'wash his hands of it.'"

To emphasize his point that Rev. Elliott had stepped outside the bounds of proper Presbyterian thinking, George quoted a letter that Rev. Henry Cooke had written on the duty of Presbyterians. It proved to be his last action as one of the most prominent of Presbyterian leaders, a man who had been a mentor to James Harshaw's son Robert. Rev. Cooke wrote, "'I lament the abuses and errors which have crept into the Church of England; but I bless God that I have always been able to overlook the minor and essential points on which we differ and to recognise in her noble branch of the great Protestant tree planted by the hands of the Reformers. I have been able to hear in the living voice of her teachers the testimony of that glorious company of martyrs and confessors by whom a free Bible and Liberty of conscience were secured to my country. For THESE REASONS I stand by her.'"

Rev. Cooke concluded this final letter with a personal appeal to his supporters. "'Fellow Protestants, be faithful to your country, to your religion and to your God. Be watchful against the insidious advances of Popish error and despotism; be united in defense of liberty, and truth; and He who ruleth King of Nations will bless and prosper your cause. Farewell! H. Cooke.'"

George expected that these words of a man so universally esteemed by Presbyterians would have a substantial impact on his Presbyterian readers. But he wanted to add an exclamation point of his own. "Presbyterians of Newry, we appeal to you. Study and ponder carefully this solemn dying testimony of

Dr. Cooke. Look upon it as the last expression of the deepest conviction of him who has been the greatest champion and ornament of your Church. Do as he does. Regard as of primary importance the interest of Protestantism, and scorn to support, as Henry Cooke would, every man who tries to trade upon his nominal Presbyterianism to induce you to surrender the welfare of Protestantism and of truth."

George's efforts appeared to bear fruit. The Newry Presbytery was to hold its November meeting at the Sandys Street Church. On the last day of October, officials of the church met and voted not to allow the Presbytery to hold its upcoming meeting in their church. George was quick to exploit the surprising news. The governing committee of the church had met and passed a formal resolution to also deny the use of their school-room for the upcoming controversial meeting. However, two days later a minority of the governors met and rescinded the resolution. "We know not as yet to whom such disgraceful conduct is attributable but disgraceful it certainly was."

George then returned to his attack on Rev. Elliott. "Mr. Elliott stated when he gave notice of his motion that it was not of a political character. Well, here it is, and let the public judge: 'That this Presbytery hold a conference in Newry at their meeting on the first Tuesday of November next to consider what steps can be taken *to secure the return of Presbyterian members to the next Parliament.'* What Mr. Elliott asserted he believed as to the non-political character of his motion we shall not venture to say he did not believe. We do not question his truthfulness, but we are bound to say his statement is one of the most amazing we have ever had under our notice. What kind of delusion is he under? There in not a man in Newry who does not believe that the subject directly involved in the motion is purely political. Nay, more, there is not a man in the town who does not believe that the introduction of the motion into the Presbytery was designed to further the hitherto hopeless prospects of Mr. Kirk. The Conservative Presbyterian laity feel insulted by this effort to degrade one of their Church Courts into a partisan political spouting club, and the Sandys Street Committee most properly decided that the doors of their sanctuary should be closed in the face of the Rev. John Elliott and his helpers."

George wasn't through yet. "[I]it is an outrageous act on the part of the Rev. John Elliott to endeavour to make the Newry Presbytery the scene of political discussions. Church Courts are spiritual courts, and they should be sacredly guarded from the intrusion of all party politics. Fancy, the Presbytery becoming an electioneering general committee for Mr. William Kirk, and Sandys Street and Donaghmore, and all the other congregational sessions, becoming sub-committees to promote the return of that gentleman! Every congregation in the Newry Presbytery would be convulsed by electioneering contests, and spirituality, piety, and peace would suffer. The Presbyterian laity will not suffer their Church Courts to become political clubs for promoting the election of any parliamentary candidate. Ministers trying their hands at such a movement as the Rev. John Elliott has proposed to begin may find their pulpits indignantly closed against them."

The controversial meeting did indeed take place as originally scheduled on Tuesday Nov. 5th, in the schoolroom rather than the Sanctuary. Rev. Elliott's motion was the second item on the agenda. From the beginning it didn't go as planned. Rev. Cromie, who had been one of James Harshaw's attackers, had prepared a motion stating that the subject Rev. Elliott had proposed discussing was not a proper subject for discussion.

Rev. Elliott said that it was his understanding that there was to be a series of conferences, one on the topic he had introduced, another on public baptism, and a third on temperance. That plan was what he was attempting to carry out. Rev. Cromie had more support than Rev. Elliott. Some of those who spoke against Rev. Elliott echoed the arguments that George had raised in his paper.

The meeting then moved to conflicting matters of process and priority of motions, the nature of a conference, whether or not it should be held in public or private. This back and forth was interspersed with comments by the moderator and clerk. Finally, it was agreed that Rev. Elliott could raise his issues and raise them in public.

Rev. Elliott began his presentation with the explanation for the motion he had made. It was clear that the next session of Parliament would be making decisions that greatly affected the Presbyterian Church in Ireland. At that moment, they didn't have a single member of Parliament to speak to their interests. They were the only religious denomination in this situation. So his motion had been merely to discuss this situation at the next meeting to see what if any steps the group wanted to take on this issue. He had come to the conclusion that with such great changes pending, he needed to take action.

Despite the furor his motion had unleashed, he still felt it was an important conversation to have in the Presbytery, an action his conscience had prompted him to take. And what were the facts at issue? "I believe there is not now a shadow of doubt but that the Established Church in this country will be disestablished and disendowed, and the Regium Donum, which our Church has received for centuries in lieu of the tithes of which we were unjustly deprived, will also cease. Who, in the adjustment of these revenues, is to look after our interests? We are left in the humiliating, degrading position of not having a single Irish Presbyterian to lift his voice in the House of Commons on our behalf. We are half the Protestants of Ireland–surely not less respectable or prosperous or loyal than our brethren–and yet while they have more than seventy we have not one. We have been taught the effects of this non-representation…Who is to protect our vested interests next session when that question comes to be dealt with?"

This was why Rev. Elliott had brought up the topic. He was sure that most fair-minded people would be as concerned about this inequality as he was. As to the issue of it being political, he had an argument to put forward as well. "Surely because we are ministers of the Gospel we are not to neglect our duty in things civil and temporal. We ought to know the history of the past, at least as well as others, and we ought to be able to take at least as intelligent a view of the great questions of the present day as other men, and I think it is our Church's duty to let it be known that God has greatly blessed us, that we have weathered the storm, and in the face of bitter opposition have come to be a great power for good in the land. In the days of our weakness we had to depend on others, but we have passed over childhood, and we are now able to select from among ourselves those who will be able to stand up for us, and tell where we live and what our fathers did, and what manner of persons we ourselves are."

Rev. Elliott's final concern resulted from a speech from the Prime Minister. Disraeli asserted that "The religious liberty which all her Majesty's subjects now happily enjoy is owing to the Christian Church in this country having accepted the principles of the Reformation and '*recognised the supremacy of the Sovereign as the representative of the state, not only in matters temporal but in matters ecclesiastical. This is the stronghold of our spiritual freedom.*' These are the words of the supreme director of the Queen's conscience, of the man who is to guide her in the exercise of her Royal prerogative. The supremacy of the Sovereign not only in matters temporal but in matters spiritual is the stronghold of our spiritual freedom."

Before he concluded his remarks, he reminded his fellow ministers of what Presbyterians had suffered as a result of this assertion. "This was the cause of all the persecutions of our forefathers in Scotland. They would not submit to the supremacy of the King in things ecclesiastical, and the scaffold flowed with the blood of the noble Argyle, whose hands had put the crown on the monarch's head, and of James Guthrie, the most loyal of men, and of thousands of others whose terrible sufferings have invested with a sacred interest almost every glen in Scotland. Is this a political question? Would we be true to the King and Head of the Church if we met to-day and separated without conferring on such a subject as this? Would it not be a grand result of this day's conference, if we stirred up some true-hearted Irish Presbyterian gentleman to push his way into the British House of Commons, and there lift up his voice for the Crown rights of Emmanuel? In what spirit has this most just and reasonable resolution of mine been met? Our endowments are doomed, our vested interests may be utterly disregarded, and when I venture to suggest that it might be well for us to try to have some Presbyterian representatives to see that justice is done to us, it is at once admitted that the thing is reasonable and just; but because I dared to mention it very hard things are written about me. This is the way we are always met."

Only two ministers disagreed. Rev. Cromie stated that as bad as the Established Church had been, they had maintained the religious freedom of Presbyterians. Certainly a reformed version of the Establishment which had been promised would be even more helpful for Presbyterians, and they would have no need of engaging in politics. With that, the meeting ended.

Rev. Elliott had the last word on the issue. He wrote a letter to George's paper, taking issue with the interpretation of his statement discussed at the Presbytery meeting. The reporter for the *Telegraph* raised issues that weren't raised either directly or indirectly during the meeting, or by anything he said.

"Two important facts are put forward by me. The principles for which our fathers were persecuted, and which we hold as firmly as they did, are called in question. We want some Irish Presbyterians to lift their voices in the House of Commons for these principles. We are about to be deprived of our endowments, which our Church has enjoyed for more than two hundred years. We want some of our own denomination to look after our interests–these endowments. The Episcopalians have hundreds of members in the House of Commons. The Roman Catholics have a powerful party to fight their battle. We have not a single member of our Church.

"I shall be grateful to anyone who will show me anything objectionable in this demand or in anything I said. I am your faithfully. John Elliott"

A week after the contentious Presbytery meeting, the Sheriff notified Newry electors that the nomination of candidates for Parliament would take place during the next week on Wednesday, and that the actual voting would begin two days later on Friday. There wasn't much time for George to instruct Conservatives how to prepare for and insure their impending victory.

But he was quickly in action with a leader he titled "The Work To Be Done and How to Do It." He began by making sure that his readers understood the importance of what was about to take place. "The electors of Newry have this week to do a great work. The eyes of the country are upon them, and we believe they will not disgrace themselves and prove unworthy of the privileges and blessings of our matchless but endangered Constitution. On the contrary, we have no doubt or fears as to Lord Newry's success."

Having bolstered any failing Conservative spirits, George made sure they understood how bad the alternative, Kirk, would be. This was evident in the kind of campaign he and his supporters were mounting. They had boasted of victory to attract any wavering voters. They had slandered the Kilmorey family and their manager Mr. Henry. They had stressed Kirk's Presbyterianism but hidden his subservience to local Catholics. Even efforts of some local ministers to support his cause had only resulted in intense opposition from most Presbyterians. Given the unattractive nature of the Liberal candidate, victory for the Conservatives was assured.

But George didn't want his Conservative readers to be overconfident, so he included a warning at the end of his leader. "Lord Newry's victory is certain if his friends are vigilant and vigorous. *Every Conservative should now be working.* Every one should feel that on his individual exertions ultimate success depends. We entreat the friends of the Constitution to be on the alert by day and night. The principles and interests at stake are of incalculable importance. For them every Protestant should be prepared not only to toil and suffer, but to die. We know that the loyal men of Newry will set a proud example to all other constituencies."

"And there is no doubt NEWRY IS SAFE! To the poll, loyal men of Newry! Be early there, be all there, bring all you can with you there. Vote for your future landlord, support our patriotic Government, rally for our imperiled Protestant institutions!"

Despite the brief amount of time between the announcement and the actual election, official preparations were completed in time for George to publish them before the nominations were scheduled to begin. Military reinforcements were sent from Dundalk and Dublin to ensure that there was no violence. The nominations would take place in the Court House on Trevor Hill on November 18th at 10:30 a.m. Polling booths would be set up in the yard of the Court House. The Conservative tally rooms were also on Trevor Hill, while the Radicals would have theirs on Kildare Street.

George reported that chaos had prevailed in the Court House as the nominations took place. The room was filled early with many Kirk supporters whose raucous jeering and whistling disrupted the proceedings. When the nominator and seconder for Lord Newry tried to speak, they were drowned out by shouts from all around the hall. George did credit Kirk with attempting to obtain silence so the Conservatives could be heard. Still George compared the two sides. "On the one side was scurrility, bad temper, intolerance, and mob violence. On the other side was gentlemanly conduct, politeness, fairness, and toleration. It can be easily decided which side have done themselves most credit."

Strangely enough, the main topic of discussion at the nomination wasn't the fate of disestablishment. Instead it focused on education. George maintained that the Catholic Church was against civil and religious freedom for the Catholic laity. They wanted Catholics educated in Catholic schools, denominational education funded by the government, but free of any supervision from the government. And Kirk supported them in this idea, while Lord Newry was in favor of integrated schools. "There would be no freedom of education in the land so far as the Roman Catholic children are concerned. They would be reared completely alienated from Protestant youth. They would be trained not merely to be bigots but to be the undying enemies of the British Government. Loyalty in their schools would be a forbidden thing. They would be taught to regard as their rightful Sovereign not Queen Victoria but the Pope of Rome. From their earliest years they would be reared Fenians. What else could they be?"

George emphasized this argument in his close. "Whoever votes for Mr. Kirk votes for the enslavement of the Roman Catholic children of the nation. Whoever votes for him votes as an enemy to the great and glorious Revolution of 1688. Whoever votes for him votes against the cause of Protestantism. Whoever votes for him is a traitor to the British Constitution."

Election day didn't unfold as George had anticipated. Polling booths opened at 8 a.m. and remained open until 5 p.m. Both candidates arrived at the scene early in the day to encourage their supporters. Kirk's polling station was filled early, with many of those attending armed with bludgeons. The non-voting tenants of Lord Newry on the other hand convened at the Edward St. Railroad Station where any potential weapons were removed. Later they were sent back to the estate without be allowed near the voting area. Nothing comparable was done to the Kirk supporters.

As the day progressed, there were additional reports of groups of Kirk supporters roaming the town, threatening Lord Newry's supporters. One gentleman who came into town to vote for Lord Newry reported that he had been taken by a mob to Kirk headquarters where he was offered drinks, and attempts were made to force him to vote for Kirk. He refused the offer of drinks as they were often drugged to prevent voting. Eventually he was released and made his way to the polling booth and successfully voted for Lord Newry.

Throughout the day, the tallies remained close. Both sides tried their best to get every supporter into Newry to vote. Conservatives reported that several people who had indicated an interest in voting for Lord Newry decided instead not to vote at all. When the polls were closed, the preliminary vote count showed Kirk winning by five votes. When the Sheriff read the official tally the next morning, Kirk had won by eight votes.

George was stunned by the outcome, but not deterred. "Mob violence of the most savage and outrageous description, clerical intimidation of the worst character, and the lavish use of money, have achieved a slight but most temporary success for the radical parry in Newry. Mr. Kirk for the next month or so may style himself MP for Newry. His tenure, however, of that title is but short: for, thanks to the wise and able legislation of Mr. Disraeli, the unseating of a member for the commission of such practices as those of Mr. Kirk's friends is very easy and inexpensive."

Then George discussed some of the base conduct of Kirk supporters that had been brought to his attention. He promised his readers that he would be relentless in pursuing legal action against the perpetrators. "For the present we end by congratulating the Protestants on the manner in which they stood together. All the good and honourable and real Protestants among them voted as they should. They did their duty and they have their reward."

George wasn't so kind to the winners. "The Radical party have no reason to rejoice at the temporary triumph over Lord Newry. His lordship will yet be the representative of this town. Of that there is no doubt. He, above all men, ought to be our representative. His great talents and immense influence would all be devoted to the advancement of Newry. This is a Conservative borough, and Lord Newry is a sterling Conservative."

When the voting throughout the kingdom concluded, the result that George most feared had taken place. The Liberals had 366 members, the Conservatives 243. Gladstone would become Prime Minister, and the religious establishment in Ireland would end.

§

George was still digesting the stunning defeat of the Conservative party in the election, when John did something totally unexpected. Instead of adding his voice to the issues during the campaign, he had remained silent. He was instead very involved in planning a life-changing event. About the time the election took place, John went to London. On the 25th of November, John married Henrietta Mitchel, called Hentie by her family and friends. At the time of his marriage, John was fifty-six years old, a supposedly set-in-his-ways bachelor.

The romance that led to this marriage more than likely began the previous June when Hentie helped John recover from bronchitis. It was a rather natural union. Hentie had spent her life in and about politicians and political events. She could be very helpful in encouraging John to make the most of his political efforts. Perhaps it was she who convinced John to consider running for Parliament, as it was soon after the time they spent together with Rev. Kenyon in Clare that he first began to mention an interest in the subject.

John had not informed his friends of his plans before the wedding took place. He explained the event afterwards." I got married on the 25th November to Miss Henrietta Mitchel, youngest sister of my friends John and William…I was 56 years old the 8th Sept. last, and I must admit to myself within these last 2 years there have now and then appeared signs of the wear and tear of age upon my constitution. On the other hand, I am surprisingly youthful in spirits and temperament, and though short-winded at the least ascent, I can run down a mountain with anybody my age—aye and give him 3 or 4 years. At all events, my wife has known me since she was born. She is only 16 years my junior, and she has taken me with all my years upon my head. It was at London we were married, where my wife's brother and sister are residing. After the marriage we went to Eastbourne on the Sussex Coast, where we had exceptionally mild and pleasant weather a great part of our stay. We came back to Kilbroney in time for Christmas."

The years they were together were some of the most productive and important of John's life. And Hentie's care when John was ill, certainly extended his life.

Home Rulers

William J. O'Neill Daunt, a close friend of John Martin, was a Catholic convert. He advised the Catholic hierarchy on strategy during the fight over disestablishment of the Church of Ireland and then became a leader in the Home Rule League.

Isaac Butt was an attorney who defended Young Irelanders and Fenians. He organized and led the Home Government Association and Home Rule League. He was MP for Youghal (1852-65) and MP for Limerick (1871-79).

Prof. J. A. Galbraith was a prominent scientist, writing several leading textbooks on science. He often worked with Professor Samuel Haughton on the books. Galbraith and Haughton were prominent members of the Home Rule League.

Charles Parnell was the charismatic successor to John Martin as MP for Meath and eventually the successor to Butt as leader of the Home Rule movement in 1880.

Chapter 16

Trip to America
1868 – 1870

John returned to Ireland in December with his new wife, settling happily into Kilbroney. As John showed her around her new home, Hentie certainly spotted deficits that needed addressing in management of the house and the children. The oldest Robert, who was ten when his parents died, was already nineteen. When he became twenty-one, John would turn Kilbroney and the rest of the family property over to him. Then he and Hentie would find a home of their own. In the meantime, he was delighted to have Hentie assume most of his parenting burden.

George had experienced great changes in his personal life as well. Though George was a skilled and powerful writer, and an ardent advocate of all things that benefited the Protestant Ascendency, he was a very private man. In 1868, he left his position as editor of the *Newry Telegraph*, and without a mention in the paper, without a grand farewell banquet, moved his family to Dublin. While he would no longer manage the paper, he would continue to write his popular leaders.

So it was in Dublin that George suffered yet another devastating personal loss. On February 25, 1869, his youngest child Emily Catherine died. Losing his last surviving daughter must have seemed like a burden too heavy to bear. Her death was only the most recent of many personal sorrows. He and his first wife Isabella Barclay Williamson had had four children. None of them survived to become adults. His wife died while still a young woman.

George married a second time, Catherine Ward, who again bore him four children, three sons, George William, James Ward, Alexander and his daughter Emily. Alexander died in infancy. However, William and James continued to thrive. But now he had lost Emily. Despite his grief, George continued to write his leaders for the *Telegraph*. Less than a week later, George produced a leader opposing the possible early release of Fenian prisoners. He continued to rant about the election of the liberals and Gladstone. He hated the new administration's solutions for the lingering issues of disestablishment, education, and tenant/landlord relationships. George intended to be the forceful Conservative voice in Newry even though he now lived in Dublin.

First he needed to vent. "Lord Newry must feel that the Presbyterian electors nobly did their duty. The small faction who voted with the Romanists have reason to be ashamed of themselves. They are not worthy to be called Protestants. They are a disgrace to the church of Knox and Chalmers, and Cooke. They are traitors to Protestantism. They voted against a young nobleman who would faithfully in Parliament have upheld the cause of our holy religion, who would have earnestly supported–both by his voice and vote–our imperiled Protestant institutions. These unprincipled Presbyterians, in their alliance with Romanism, form a modern band of 'United Irishmen.' We warn them not to forget '98 and its disaster. They are advancing to the brink of a precipice. Let them turn back in time. If they go forward with their Papal allies in their anti-Protestant and anti-Constitutional course, they may find themselves involved in all the perils and miseries of a tremendous revolution. The Newry 'Lundies,' [treacherous cowards] clerical and lay, should tremble as to the future."

In a later leader, he wrote, "We live in strange times. The great battle now being waged in Ireland is a religious more than a political one. Is Romanism to triumph? Are all our Protestant institutions to be overthrown? Is our unhappy country to be flung back into the hands of the Pope of Rome? Are our civil and religious liberties and privileges as Protestants to be wrested from us?" George would fight to prevent that from happening.

As the days passed, George felt little better. In his last leader of 1868, he laid out the obligation of every Conservative. "Romanism has now attained to tremendous power in this nation. Cardinal Cullen is our virtual ruler. Dublin Castle, in many respects, might as well be the seat of government of his Holiness at Rome. What we thus write our Liberal Protestants of course will scoff at. They are still blinded by their party politics. But we think with humiliation and burning indignation of the treacherous betrayal of Irish Protestantism by the Radicals of England and Scotland. They have fastened on our country the iron fetters of ultramontanism. They have done all they could to retard the social and religious advancement of Ireland. The Conservative representatives of Ulster will have a grand struggle to maintain in the new parliament. They will do their duty faithfully; and their constituents have the fullest confidence in them."

George suggested a new strategy that Conservatives might mount against the Gladstone administration. Conservative leaders in Parliament should challenge Gladstone and his government to reveal their plans to solve Ireland's most contentious issues all at once. That tactic would split government supporters, all of whom were needed to push disestablishment through Parliament. "The trick of the Government is to conceal their intentions as to the appropriation of the revenues of the Irish Church, and also to keep to the background what they purpose doing for the settlement of the Education and Tenant Right questions. Their hope is to keep all the discordant parties together in their support who have been drawn together into alliance against the Irish Church. When they get the Church in ruins, then the Gladstone Cabinet will have some other concessions to propose to propitiate the Romanists. Concession will be the order of the day, and every concession will be a deadly blow at Protestantism.

"Well, we shall soon see some of the effects of this policy. Meantime let all Protestants be vigilant, combined, and ready for any emergency."

There was no serious effort to goad the government to swallow George's bait and disclose their entire legislative agenda. But he had another idea that was more successful. "Are the friends and supporters of our Protestant religious Establishments asleep in this town? Have they been paralysed by the late election? Let us see some manifestations of life. There ought at once to be held in Newry a meeting such as has never before been convened in this town. Every Protestant gentleman of the neighbourhood should be present, and all worthy the name of Protestant should, for the occasion, unite in making a solemn public protest against the robbery of the Irish Church and the abolition of the Regium Donum. Who will put their hands and hearts to accomplish such an assemblage?"

Before anyone acted on George's plea, he told his readers in Newry that Gladstone had yet to clinch victory. There were "almost insurmountable obstacles in his path." When Parliament actually opened its new session, Conservatives might discover that success of disestablishment legislation was less likely than it appeared. After all, any legislation had to pass through the House of Lords who would certainly stand their ground. They understood that it was their duty to "resist to the last." "We know no crime more dreadful than for a nation who has professed the truth of Christianity, and maintained and defended it, ceasing to do so, and becoming wholly separate and alienated from religion. A nation without religious faith is an infidel nation. That, in reality, is what our nation will become if Mr. Gladstone's policy is carried out; and there will be this aggravation of our national guilt, that the State ceased to profess and uphold the Protestant religion to satisfy the demands of the Church of Rome." "Traitors yield, patriots struggle to the last."

Soon George saw positive results from his almost incessant pleas for action. Local members of the Established Church appealed to the vicar and church-wardens to call a meeting to allow local members to speak forcefully during this time of crisis. This request was signed by some of Newry's most important and influential businessmen, magistrates and merchants. Notices were posted on the walls of local churches announcing that this important meeting of the local Vestry of Newry parish would be held on Monday February 22nd at twelve o'clock at the parish church. It was signed by Rev. Bagot, Vicar, and church-wardens H. W. Wallace and T. Wheatley.

George was delighted and reported the results. There were two major lines of thought expressed. "First, an admission of great abuses and anomalies in the distribution of revenue, and an earnest wish to correct them. Secondly, a firm determination not to suffer one single link of State connection to remain if the church is to be deprived of her present position." Hopefully the first admission would reduce the possibility of the second.

§

Naturally, the issue of disestablishment was among the plans Gladstone inserted in the Queen's opening speech. "I am persuaded that in the prosecution of the work you will bear a careful regard to every legitimate question which may be governed by a constant aim to promote the welfare of religion through the principles of equal justice, to secure the undivided feelings and opinions of Ireland on the side of loyalty and law, to efface the memory of former contentions and to cherish the sympathy of an affectionate people."

Money was an important issue for the opponents of the Gladstone bill. What would be done with the money that was currently devoted to the established church? They feared that most of it would be given to the Catholic Church to help fund facilities like hospitals and nunneries. "They may depend upon it that under the latter part of the bill of the Government lies a deep dark scheme for the endowment of Papal charitable institutions on a scale of frightful magnitude. Will our Voluntary advocates, who pretended to have such a horror of the endowment of Romanism, keep silent now?" On the Presbyterian side, the cutback of money available for young Presbyterian ministers would result in fewer young men being willing to become ministers.

Once George had read the entire text of the disestablishment legislation, he provided his readers with his most passionate defense of the concept that had led the state to establish the supremacy of one religion over all others. Even the Protestant religions that had not been chosen to be the official church had an obligation to prevent the government from severing the connection between government and religion. "And besides that they have common interest, they also have a common duty to discharge in maintaining the principle that it is the duty of the State to maintain, uphold, and defend the Protestant religion. Surely they should with all their power defend and support the great Scriptural principle that it is the duty of all Christian nations to recognise and support the religion of the Reformation."

Certainly George recognized that some Protestants opposed the idea that the Church and State should remain connected. "They see no national evil nor national criminality in the State repudiating the claims of religion. They are not prepared to contend against the divorce of religion from the state. For our part, we believe that this is in reality the worst, the most flagrant evil of the Government scheme. It is a practical denial of the claims of the Supreme and Divine Ruler of the Nations. The State thereby becomes practically an infidel state; and nothing but the most awful results can be anticipated from such national turpitude and unbelief."

§

Disestablishment legislation was inching its way through Parliament. However another divisive issue, the Party Processions Act, was raised by William Johnston who had been convicted the previous year of violating that law during an 1867 march in Bangor. Johnston had parlayed Protestant anger following his arrest, conviction and two weeks in prison to a seat in Parliament during the autumn election. For George, this new revision of "that most obnoxious law" was one he strongly supported. Johnston, in his speech in Parliament, argued that the Orangemen should have the same rights to march as the Fenians.

Though George strongly supported the legislation, he didn't agree with some of Johnston's remarks. George didn't believe that the Fenians had any right to march, as "their system is an illegal, disloyal, treasonable one. We hope the day will never arrive when those traitors shall be permitted to parade our streets and highways with banners bearing such inscriptions as these— 'Hurrah, for the Irish Republic!;' 'Ireland for the Irish!; 'Repeal forever!' The Fenians are the avowed enemies of the British Crown, and they are striving to overturn the Queen's Government in this country. To allow them to make public displays of their numbers and their symbols would be ruinous policy." Then George warned his readers of the fear that was ever in his mind. "Such toleration would soon involve the nation in all the horrors of civil war."

The loyal Orangemen had been harshly and unfairly treated, though they were united in support of the Union through their displays honoring the victory of King William. On the other hand, the funeral that John had organized in Dublin was clearly a violation of the act in question, and yet they had suffered no penalty. Johnston supported repeal of The Party Processions Act rather than patching together any reforms.

Strangely, one of the men who seconded Mr. Johnston's resolution was the O'Donoghue, who supposedly was John's partner in the Irish National League. He seemed to agree with Mr. Johnston that this might be a start of union of interests between Catholic and Protestants.

This was another idea that George abhorred. "For such union and amity Mr. Johnston is anxious; but neither he nor the loyal men of this country will ever join with Romish agitators, who gloat in national disaffection, in seeking to further the principles and projects of Radicals and revolutionary Ultramontanists. Between these parties and the Orangemen there can be no political union and co-operation."

Despite the flourish with which the legislation was introduced, and George's editorial support, Gladstone stifled the legislation. No discussion or vote ever took place.

§

John understood George's perspectives on the major issue of disestablishment and lesser ones such as the repeal of the Party Processions Act. John often offered his own opinions, usually so different from those that George expressed. Some of the letters he wrote for Irish newspapers were reprinted in the *Irish Citizen,* Mitchel's latest publishing effort in New York City. There John's articles informed many émigrés who yearned for a chance to help free Ireland from the English about issues and opinions in Ireland.

While John was very much in favor of disestablishment, he wasn't totally pleased with the solution that the government was crafting for Ireland. Half of the funds that would result from the ending of the establishment would remain in the custody of the Anglican Church and not offered to the use of the Catholic Church. This was a pot of money worth fighting for, as it amounted to nearly one million pounds. Some would go to England to reduce its Irish obligations. Other funds would recompense the Presbyterians for the loss of the Regium Donum. "I described this re-endowment of the Anglican Church with about half its present revenues as a hocus pocus measure I meant that it would affect incorrectly what the mass of the Irish people desire to abolish."

The opposing opinions of George and John had no impact on the legislation. But Irish Protestants hoped that a giant meeting of the Presbyterians of Belfast would. They filled the Ulster Hall with about ten thousand protesters who made clear their contempt for the legislation and their loving brotherhood with their fellow Protestants of the Church of Ireland. Surely such numbers would send a resounding message to Parliament.

But just to make sure, another meeting was at once planned, this time a gathering of the united Protestant community. It was held outside in Botanic Gardens in Belfast near the end of May. Indeed this was a much larger meeting than the previous one. Nearly one hundred thousand Protestants filled the gardens. Most people attending the meeting were too far from the platform to hear what was being said. So small sub-meetings with spontaneous speakers took place around the edges.

George proclaimed the meeting a great success. "Ulster has now spoken out in a way that must tell upon the Legislature. The destructive Church bill will receive its merited doom in the House of Lords. The loyal Protestants of Ireland are not to be trodden down, and their most valued institutions be laid in ruins, at the instance of Cardinal Cullen and the Roman agitators who are his henchmen."

Not surprisingly, John didn't see the great Belfast gathering in the same light as George did. He saw it as a giant meeting of the Orange Order. He did agree that the gathering had been impressive as far as attendance was concerned. However, he called out the Orange Order for "religious bigotry, ignorant prejudice, and insolent bearing and malevolent disposition towards their Catholic countrymen produced by the bigotry and prejudice." But he didn't believe that this problem resulted from the character of the Orangemen, but rather from the harmful actions of the British Government.

John always strove to find the best in others, even those who disagreed with him and regularly attacked him personally. "And no matter how serious and how lasting the religious differences in the Ulster population may prove— no matter how vehemently the Orangemen may continue to dislike the Catholic religion—I am of opinion that the great bulk of the Orangemen...sincerely desire, both as Orangemen and as men, to carry out the principles of Bible Christianity, and are willing to concede to Catholics the rights they claim for themselves, and desire only freedom for the Protestant people."

Though a supporter of disestablishment, John recognized when the legislation passed, as he was sure it would, the Orangemen of Ulster would be very angry at such a fundamental change and their reaction might lead to violence. There was another potential problem if supporters of disestablishment misinterpreted what the government was doing. "But what I do contemplate with sadness and apprehension is the attitude taken, since the announcement of the new English policy of redress of Irish wrongs, by Irish patriotic leaders and the press which speaks for the Catholic bishops and the wealthier class of Catholics. The 699 years of English greed, insolence, cruelty and fraud practiced against Ireland by every English government, of every sect and party of statesmen, are all to be forgotten, because for 1 year past an English statesman has declared himself in favor of redress of some flagrant Irish wrongs and for 6 months past, he has been Prime Minister. We are to trust implicitly to this great Englishman's benevolence and wisdom. We are to suppress every truth that may be unpalatable to him. We are to treat it as a crime—aye as a sin—if any Irish do a rash act or say a rash word, lest it may irritate English opinion against his merciful intentions toward us. We are to behave so that England's pride may be soothed at the spectacle of our abject submission to English will, and that it may appear to the world as if English magnanimity and justice were the origins of the promised redress and not English fear and policy."

John felt that this change in English policy resulted from the Fenian rising, and the potential danger that an invading force of trained soldiers might be sent to free Ireland totally from English control. He was distressed that many Irish leaders were crediting the legislation to a change in the core beliefs of England. "And if the whole people of Ireland or that majority of them, adopted such a policy, in my poor opinion there would be no chance of Irish independence or merciful English rule."

Both John and George worried that the Orangemen could erupt during their July marches to protest disestablishment. Leaders on all sides appealed for peaceful celebrations. And that was indeed what happened. George observed something surprising, Orangemen and Catholics interacting peacefully during the marches, and was moved to write one his most unusual leaders.

"Why should not all Irishmen live together in peace and amity? Their religious differences should not cause them to be inimical, hating one another. As conscientious men they are all bound to endeavor to advance the interests of their respective creeds, but surely that is no reason why they should regard one another, as in the past, with deadly animosity. Around the sacred symbol of their faith which all profess to revere–around the hallowed Cross–there should be no hatred, no uncharitableness, no act of violence. The day has departed, we trust for ever, when Protestants–rather we should say so-called Protestants–fancied that they were maintaining the cause of Protestantism by casting in the teeth of their Roman Catholic neighours irritating and insulting expressions about them and their faith. Our religion is a religion of love, of good-will to all, of universal charity; and from every platform in Ulster last Monday these sentiments were ably enunciated and earnestly commended. We are grateful to the Roman Catholic laity for the position they have maintained during the whole controversy as to the Irish Church. We do not believe they wished our Protestant Churches to be despoiled and robbed. The Protestant clergy have been their kind friends and neighbours, and in days of adversity many in poverty and great straits have experienced how ready these clergy were to extend to their sympathy and aid."

One evening John had a pleasant visit from a friend from Trinity College who offered a contrary perspective. "'We Protestants' (said he) 'were employed in Ireland to do England's work in keeping down the Catholic population, the bulk of the Irish people. We bargained for certain advantages in return for that service. We have manfully trampled down the fellows near two hundred years in fulfillment of our bargain, And now the English think they may do better without us they have gained much of what they sought...Well: we are not afraid of our Catholic countrymen. If they wish to hurt us, we are able to hold our own. Barring religion we sympathise with them far more than with the English. Our material interests are the same with theirs, as Irishmen. I hate the English. They are most arrogant, most insolent, some greedy, most hypocritical, most stuffed. Let us have an independent Ireland & have done with England.'"

John wrote a letter in the same vein as the disestablishment bill neared final passage. "I recognize the fact that no nation rules another except for the first nations profit and the second nation's loss. I know England rules us for the purpose of robbing us. I know that England's rule here is necessarily destructive to our peace, to our industry and wealth, to our rights and honor, to every good interest of ours, moral and material...The only law which in my opinion, it is possible for the English Parliament to make for us would be one to give up once, and forever the attempt to make any laws for us."

When final passage occurred, John wrote a rather muted critique. "I think, notwithstanding its many and serious shortcomings and vices, I may congratulate you on the passing of the Church bill. We may call it something pleasing, though certainly not anything satisfactory. The moral effect, I think, will be good."

George's first comments were also surprisingly moderate. "We have already expressed our sentiments as to the final settlement in regard to the Church Robbery Bill of the Government. We have no hesitation in saying that no greater blow could be inflicted on Irish Protestantism, except, indeed, its complete proscription. Perhaps in time even that event may take place."

After Parliament adjourned, George returned to defiance. "The parliamentary session has ended. It will ever be regarded as one of the most disastrous to this country in the whole history of the British Legislature. The future historians of the empire will point to its records as indicating the black period when Britain began as a nation to cast off the faith of the glorious Reformation, and to assume the position of ruling its people without any regard to the principles of religion. Of course this infidel mode of Government will ere long be fully carried out. The Established Churches of England and of Scotland are sure to be overturned, and then our State's apostasy from the truth will be complete. It is a deplorable future for Great Britain. National apostasy from God will–if all history be true–lead to national judgments.

"Meantime, however, Mr. Gladstone has done Rome's work thoroughly. He and his tyrant majority have smitten the cause of Irish Protestantism with heavy hand. They have laid our National Church in ruins beneath the feet of Cardinal Cullen, and they have inflicted the most grievous wrong on the Presbyterian Church. While they have afforded an immense triumph to the enemies of the British Crown, they have exasperated beyond expression all the loyalists of the country.

"Nor is it to be forgotten that England and Scotland acted basely toward our cause. If the avowed enemies of our Protestant Churches had not been elected by the English and Scotch to support the revolutionary policy of Messrs. Gladstone and Bright, the Church Plunder Bill would not have been passed. When the Union took place between Great Britain and this country it was supposed that one of its fundamental articles, guaranteeing the preservation of the Established Church 'forever,' would bind the people of the sister kingdoms to maintain that Establishment in the full enjoyment of all its rights, privileges, and property. In the session of Parliament, however, now ended, all that solemn guarantee has been treated as so much waste paper. We refrain from adverting to the solemn subject of the Queen's oath taken by Her majesty at her coronation, wherein she vowed before God to uphold the National Church. The Legislature decided that the Queen was not bound to abide by her sacred oath, and accordingly she signed the sacrilegious Church Bill. It is now the law of the land. The whole time of the session was wasted in the passing of this infamous Act."

The termination of the special status of the Church of Ireland didn't have the results that George had so vehemently predicted. Though a supposedly essential pillar of the connection between England had been torn away, no civil war broke out. Instead the Protestant denominations focused on a critical new decision, how to disperse the funds that had been made available to them. A substantial sum of money had been given to each of the major denominations. Each denomination could decide how to distribute these new funds. Presbyterians had two options. They could use their funds to support their existing ministers for the rest of their lives, when the funding would end. The second option was to give the funds to each congregation to augment the voluntary contributions of members. In that instance, the funding would be permanent. Rev. Elliott decided to release his grant to the Donaghmore Elders. This important decision formed the focus of interest after the bill passed. While many meetings were held, there was none of the violence George had prophesied.

§

As Parliament was ending their most consequential session, John was turning his attention to plans to travel with Hentie to America. Thirty years had passed since John had last visited America. During that time, many of his friends had left Ireland to settle there. His cousins, Willy and Samuel Harshaw, lived near New York City in Paterson, New Jersey. In addition, his sister with her grown family still lived in Ontario Canada, and Hentie's brother and

John's great friend, John Mitchel lived in Brooklyn. The months they planned to spend in America would be busy and happy ones.

Before leaving Ireland, John wrote a letter to Mitchel's paper under the pseudonym of Bignan hoping to arouse some nationalist fervor in the Irish in America. "I have also told you how I am persuaded that the political force of the united Irish nationalists at home and abroad would prove so great a power as to induce the English to yield to it...And, much as I hate or dread revolution, from the conservative character of my own mind and from my conviction that it would be injurious to many of the best qualities of the Irish people, I would welcome revolution—the bloodiest revolution—if that could make my country Independent, and if there were no other means available...I am not able to report any general turning of the popular mind in the direction which to me seems the right one. I am hopeful of seeing, before very long, such a movement."

John and Hentie left for America on the Inman lines newest ship "The City of Paris" the end of September. It was the first ship using a screw propeller to equal the crossing time of the older side wheelers. While the ship lived up to its reputation for quick passage across the ocean, this trip wasn't very pleasant for the passengers, as the sea was rough and stormy. As John described it, "the vessel rolling and shaking in a torturing fashion during the stormy weather. I myself had no seasickness, but Mrs. Martin and almost everybody else of my fellow passengers were in a state of extreme discomfort all the time of the storms, which was all the time of the voyage except 2 ½ days."

Hentie must have been happy to step off the ship in New York City. She was familiar with the city having lived there with her mother and brother some years earlier. John observed many changes as their carriage took them across Manhattan. The squalid tenements, teaming streets of the Lower East Side were now home to crowds of Irish immigrants escaping that famine. As the couple crossed the East River, they followed the route that would soon be disrupted by construction of the great pillars that would support the Brooklyn Bridge.

Both travelers were happy to pull up to the Mitchel house at 161 Carleton St in Brooklyn. The house was located a block away from Prospect Park, where walking would provide needed exercise for Hentie's wobbly sea legs. It was a bit of country designed by Frederick Law Olmsted who would later create the much larger Central Park. The city had spread out greatly since John had explored it on his previous trip, expansion made essential by a population which now exceeded one million.

When John and Hentie arrived in Brooklyn, they were stunned to see how ill Mitchel was. He had been forced to stay in bed for some weeks before the couple arrived and appeared "seriously delicate," and made John "feel anxious." John had told Jennie previously that there didn't seem to be any hope that he would be able to defeat tuberculosis. But there was every hope that with care and attention that he would live for a number of years longer.

After a few days of rest, John and Hentie planned to leave on an extended visit with his sister Jane in Upper Canada [Ontario]. Then they would return to New York for the rest of their visit. Other than a few short trips to Philadelphia, Washington, and of course, Framingham Massachusetts where Mahon and his family now lived, they would stay with the Mitchels in Brooklyn.

These plans would go forward despite the fact that John wasn't in the best health either. "I have never quite recovered my strength since the bad times I had last spring in Dublin, but I am pretty well for my age (57) and bodily constitution. My wife is right well and a kind master enough."

He explained his plans to Mahon. "My wife is, from former acquaintanceships, a great friend of the NE people. I am you know of vehement conservative or anti-liberal sentiment (or instincts) and so antipathetic to your NE neighbors. But then I like variety in opinions etc. as in all nature; and I am glad to think these Puritan-Liberals have free scope and opportunity to develop their liberalism and let the world see what comes of it. My only quarrel with them—which quarrel is only in my private mind—is that they shew a disposition to take means that seem to me unfair to prevent other people—Catholics and Irish for example—from having free scope, or any scope at all."

John and Hentie realized soon after their arrival that they would have a scheduling problem. Mitchel was planning to give a speech to raise money for the widow of one of the Manchester Martyrs during the time they were to be in Canada. This was a speech both Hentie and John wanted to attend. They decided to shorten their visit in Canada, returning to Brooklyn for the speech. This change upset his sister Jane. To calm the situation, John promised they would extend their stay until the end of January, so they could follow this short visit with a longer one later on.

So both Hentie and John were on hand to hear Mitchel's speech. It was held in the large meeting room of the Cooper Union. The speech was a fundraiser for the widow of Manchester Martyr Michael Larkin. Mitchel spoke on the subject of Grattan and O'Brien. John was on the stage during the lecture along with the Mayor of New York City. Despite his intention to confine his visit to private affairs, he responded when he was called on to speak. He rose to great cheering.

John made clear how overwhelmed he was at this unexpected and warm welcome. "But I have no such distinction, nor any gifts of genius nor accomplishments whatever. Yet I know well why it is so many Irishmen all over the world feel so kindly toward me. It is for the sake of something which they esteem beyond price even when it appears unadorned by genius and unblessed by success. And this something is loyalty to Ireland (Much cheering.) Ladies and gentlemen you kindly regard me as a man, who, through a pretty long political life—which I trust is not yet ended—(cheers) has, in his humble way, and not without some personal sacrifice and danger, steadily upheld the faith of Irish nationality. (much cheering.)"

Then, he talked about his friendship with Mitchel. He had a mixed reception when he stated that he believed that independence would be achieved without overthrowing "constitutional forms." He recognized that opinions differed as to how to achieve the dream of independence. As John saw the issue, those who supported achieving independence by peaceful means and those who "advocated...war and violent revolution" must avoid divisions.

"I hope confidently to see before I die though I may have but a few years longer to live, all the good men and women of the Irish race in Ireland, here and all over the world, united for a national movement to seek and to obtain a peaceful settlement of our quarrel with England...I respect the opinion of those who differ from me. (hear, hear). The only very serious difference that has ever existed between my friend Mr. Mitchel and myself is this very one...That difference is a serious one, and it causes my friend and me to take different roads in seeking to reach the same end. But it does not cause either of us to pretend to doubt the other's honor or patriotism. It does not set us against each other as hostile factions to thwart each other in trying to serve Ireland, each in his own way. (hear, hear.)"

Then John turned to talk about the reason for the meeting. "I am glad to have this new opportunity of denouncing that atrocious and scandalous crime which the English union committed in hatred of my nation. (hisses for England). The memory of these three men whom England then murdered for their love to their native land, will live as the memory of martyrs and heroes, in the grateful hearts of the Irish race generation after generation, forever. (more cheering) And that base deed of England will live in history too and future generations of Englishmen will recognize it for a stain upon their national honor and will regret it as an unprofitable crime. (Renewed cheering)."

In his concluding remarks, John returned to the theme of unity. "There is no material difference, I say, between good Irishmen as to what that end is. It is, that England shall cease to make laws for Ireland, to appoint the officials for Ireland, to spend the revenues of Ireland, to exercise no control whatever over Irish affairs. (Cheers) That Ireland shall make her own laws, own her own land, spend her own money and have absolute sovereign control over all Irish affairs. (Cheers)...I hope all who now hear me will live to rejoice in the national independence of Ireland. (Prolonged cheering)"

Once John had appeared in public, his planned private visit became much more public, as invitations began to flood into the Mitchel home. The first invitation John accepted was an engagement to speak before the Celtic Association of Philadelphia on Dec. 12th. Dr. Shelton Mackenzie was the chairman of the event. The dining room where John spoke was nicely decorated with American flags, and green flags containing the names of each of the four Irish provinces. Above the chairman's head was a banner with the words "Cead Mille Failte."

John responded to the toast of the chairman. "Mr. President and Gentlemen of the Celtic Association—I thank you from my heart for the kind hospitality with which you have received me, and I feel proud of the honour that you do me by toasting my health. It is particularly gratifying to me to receive this kindness from you, because the one single object that I have followed all through my life, the restoration of Irish National Independence, though it is not identical with the object of this Association, is yet very closely allied and kindred to it. I do not intend on this festive occasion to bore you and tire you, and to occupy your time, which may be much more pleasantly engaged with hearing the songs of such artists as I have had the pleasure to listen to to-night, and of the many eloquent gentlemen that I am sure are here…I shall say only a very few words to you about the cause that I have at heart, and that I believe that you have at heart, at least as much as I have—the cause of Ireland. (Applause). This Association, gentlemen, as I understand, is founded for the purpose of investigating Celtic history, of preserving Celtic literature, of studying the manners, the arts, the laws, the institutions, that have prevailed in Celtic communities when Celtic communities were free—free to develop the Celtic genius, free to exhibit their energies and their character in their institutions; and there is one Celtic people in whose history and whose fortunes all of you, as well as myself, take a paramount interest—I mean the Celtic people of Ireland—of our own dear old native Ireland. (Applause and 3 cheers for John Martin)."

§

Meanwhile in Ireland the Liberal MP for Longford, Greville-Nugent had been elevated to the House of Lords and a movement to nominate John to run against his son for the vacancy was underway. His great friend O'Neill Daunt reported this in the *Irish Citizen*. "To elect John Martin will show that this constituency participates in this principle held by the vast mass of their countrymen; the principle of self-rule for Ireland. To elect him in his absence, and without his solicitation, will show their well-placed confidence in one of the purest and noblest of our patriots. Such a choice will demonstrate that the electors of Longford can appreciate the qualities of stainless honor, great ability, copious information on the present and past politics, and a pure devotion to the legislative independence of his native land…John Martin is a Presbyterian. I confess that I consider it peculiarly fortunate that an Irish electoral body, principally Catholic and of national principles, should have an opportunity of showing their warm regard for their noble countryman is not in the smallest degree diminished by the differences of religious belief. The best interests of Ireland imperatively require that all sectarian feelings should be banished forever from the region of national politics."

John had previously authorized constituencies in Ireland to place his name in nomination for election to a seat in Parliament. However, he made clear that if a constituency should decide to nominate him, he had no intention of participating in the usual campaign customs. He would not appear to campaign. He would not put up any of his money to secure election. Should any constituency be willing to abide by his conditions, he would agree to serve if elected. With John thousands of miles away at the time of the election, participation would be impossible should he have desired to campaign actively. Instead, he continued his visit in Brooklyn awaiting results.

In the Christmas edition of the *Irish Citizen,* Mitchel made some comments on the Longford election. They represented a strange sort of endorsement of John's candidacy. "Isolated as he will be there—for no <u>Liberal</u> member will dare to take his part—those ruffians will overbear him, will wear him out, will reduce him to silence or else provoke him to some rash and futile act of self-assertion; in short, they will break his heart. He will soon understand that the proper place to make protest against British domination is not in the British Parliament…John O'Leary in his cell would be a still better representative for Longford than Mr. Martin, yet Mr. Martin would be innately better than the Hon. Greville-Nugent. The Longford men will do themselves honor by electing the Irish Felon of '48; and he will do them credit in return, though it may not be precisely in the very way he now anticipates."

Mitchel recognized as John certainly did the great difficulties he faced in this election, one being that he was an outsider running against a local landlord. Mitchel concluded his article further explaining the difficulties that John faced. "We trust then, that John Martin will be elected. But it will be a difficult contest for not only will money be lavished by the Government partisans to prevent this second defeat, but Longford will be occupied by troops and armed police under the false pretence of guarding voters from intimidation, and with the real purpose of intimidating the people or provoking a riot and making a salutary slaughter. If in the face of all this, the County of Longford deliberately carry to the head of the poll, a man known to be obnoxious to the British government and known to hold that government in such holy hatred, the triumph will be grand indeed."

Supporters of John sprang into action to assist him in winning the seat. A. M. Sullivan in the *Nation* urged readers to support him. One of the people to respond to his appeal was the Marchioness of Queensberry. She wrote a letter of support.

" 'Dear Mr. Sullivan.—In your paper to-day there is a request to 'men and women, boys and girls' to work for Mr. Martin, of Kilbroney; but what can I do at this distance excepting to enclose £10 towards the fund which will be required for necessary expenses? It will be a blessing for Ireland, indeed, if Mr. Martin be returned; and if women are called to the work, how gladly would I work night and day to insure his return, were I now in Ireland! Or, that everyone who lives in Ireland may go to work and vote for John Martin, the true friend of Ireland, and organise for him a glorious victory! The only astonishment is that he has not long since been elected; for who is so well qualified to speak the mind of Ireland, as that venerated patriot? May God bless him! It does, indeed, send a thrill of pleasure, as the Nation says, through the heart that this selection should be made worthy of the country and the time. Excuse this from one who, perhaps, had no right to express an opinion, but who loves Ireland too well to be silent at such a moment. May God bless the man who votes for John Martin! -Yours faithfully, Caroline Queensberry."

Both sides were active on the ground in Longford as well, much of it supporting the opposition. A meeting was held on Friday, December 12th, at which it became clear that the Catholic Church authorities would do what they could to prevent John from being returned for Longford. A letter from Bishop McCabe was read to the crowd instructing all the local priests to urge their parishioners to elect Colonel Greville's son to Parliament. Another priest, Rev. Reynolds attempted to convince Martin supporters to withdraw his name from the election. In fact, someone sent a telegram to Dublin announcing John's withdrawal This fake message didn't deter John's supporters who were also hard at work in the area.

The next day about 2,000 Longford residents attended a meeting to support John's election, followed the day after by another impressive gathering in Edgeworthstown. Speeches were delivered from a window of the local hotel. Then the Martin supporters, marching behind a green flag, headed off toward the local chapel. Suddenly, Rev. Murray, a local priest, ran up to the flag bearer, grabbed the green flag he was carrying, and dragged the flag through the mud. Despite this provocation, no violence followed. More marches were planned for the following day as well.

George was following the election very closely. He reported that a letter was received in Newry about the election from a leading clergyman in Longford. "'We shall probably have John Martin returned for Longford. The priests who are working hard for Greville, have been hooted and abused in Longford. Edgeworthstown, and Granard. This is a glorious thing, and will show the Government what a miserable support they have gained in place of the loyal Protestants whom they have contemptuously cast off.'"

George also quoted a report in the *Cork Examiner* about the speeches that Mitchel and John had given at the Cooper Union. "'Mr. John Martin, who is travelling in the United States was present a short time since at a lecture upon 'Grattan and O'Brien,' delivered in New York by Mr. John Mitchel. Mr. Mitchel vehemently denounced the character and results of British rule in Ireland, and advocated the total separation of the two countries by force of arms. Mr. Martin, in a firm and temperate speech expressed his dissent from the latter view, and, while convinced that legislative independence was essential to the welfare of Ireland, he insisted that it should be accomplished by peaceful agencies, in which he still had confidence.'"

As the election drew nearer, confrontations between the supporters of John and Greville-Nugent became even more likely to produce violent encounters. At Granard, a large crowd of Martin supporters gathered to hear the stand-ins for John speak from a balcony in the center of town. Word of the event soon reached his opponents, and they too gathered in large numbers. Authorities took quick action to prevent a dangerous confrontation. First a magistrate read the riot act to quickly disperse the crowds from both sides. When that tactic failed, police put themselves between the two groups, loaded their rifles, fixed their bayonets and arranged their ranks so that troops were facing both groups. Order was quickly restored.

Nominations took place a week later in the Court House in Longford with the High Sheriff Philip O'Reilly presiding. The room was filled to overflowing, the din making the voices of speakers almost inaudible. Sheriff O'Reilly vainly begged voters on both sides to be respectful so that the speakers could be heard. Nomination speeches were made though few could hear them. Captain Greville-Nugent was nominated by John Maxwell, Esq. and Rev. James Reynolds. John's name was placed in nomination by John Murtagh, Esq. and seconded by John Quinn. The Sheriff asked for a vote by show on hands, following which he declared Greville-Nugent the winner. John's supporters immediately requested a poll. The following Monday was quickly selected for the voting.

George continued to follow the Longford election, realizing that his readers would be interested as well. He introduced them to the opposing candidate. Algernon Greville-Nugent was the son of the previous MP recently rewarded with promotion to the House of Lords. He was a Captain in the Guards, who had only recently become twenty-one. While Greville-Nugent had not previously shown any interest in politics, George believed that he too would be a Whig supporter.

George explained his interest in the election this way. "Resolved to put an end to the dictatorial bearing of the priesthood, 'the Nationalists' have brought forward Mr. John Martin. However many may differ from him on various subjects it is generally admitted that this gentleman has throughout his life, acted in a conscientious and straightforward manner in endeavouring to carry out what he conceived to be for the best interests of this country. As an opponent Captain Greville-Nugent will find him a most formidable one, and although Mr. Martin is at present on a visit in America, and necessarily absent, his friends and admirers are indefatigable in their exertions to secure his return, of which they are very sanguine. The result is looked forward to with even more interest than that of the recent election of Tipperary, because the issue really is whether the priests or the people are to have the selection of a representative for the country. The struggle is a most significant one, and a somewhat remarkable sign of the times."

Election day proved very dramatic. As was usual, supporters of both candidates attempted to get their voters to the polls early in the day, though by mid day, voting in Longford was very light. Though Longford was calm, rumors floated around town of problems in other parts of the district. "During the day the Martinites had to contend with the greatest possible difficulties. When a supporter entered any of the booths to poll, he was received with jeers and derision, and…were given to understand, either openly, covertly or in a jocular manner, according to their intelligence, that they were taking up a position in direct antagonism to that of their priests. On leaving the court-house again they were in some miraculous manner identified by the mob, and, if found, as in one or two instances, later in the evening, were attacked and beaten in a cowardly manner."

In the town of Ballymahon, the support for both candidates was almost equal. So it was here that confrontations were most intense. Around noon, voters who planned to support John gathered before attempting to vote. At the outskirts of town, they encountered a large number of Greville supporters and were forced to retreat. Though acting too late to prevent the expulsion of John's supporters, three magistrates summoned military and police to separate the two groups with orders to prevent anyone passing them armed with bludgeons or sticks.

The Martin supporters regrouped and attempted to enter from a different side of town, but again their efforts were foiled. However a group of Greville supporters were escorted to the voting site by British troops. They were pelted by a barrage of stones by the offended voters. Despite the provocation, the troops didn't respond. Angry confrontations continued throughout the day.

Bad as the situation was in Ballymahon, election day in Granard was even more frightening This was Martin territory, so the supporters of Greville-Nugent were brought from Longford town and other places, some from as far away as Cavan to interfere with the voting. Early in the day, these invaders kept out of sight, leaving the town to the control of another large military contingent. Before the Court House opened for voting, there was trouble. Some Greville supporters had sneaked inside, virtually taking control of the voting site. Martin supporters attacked with a barrage of stones, breaking all the windows in the building. Finally, the troops interfered and were able to clear a way for Martin supporters to get to their voting booths. So for a time, peace was restored, and voting began.

Around noon, another large contingent of Martin supporters arrived in town. The leaders of both groups of Martin supporters conferred on a plan of action. A group of about 200 young men with bludgeons split off from the main group and, moving behind houses, were able to come up behind the Greville supporters. As the main attack took place from the front, the Greville supporters, having apparently gotten word of the plan, fled to the surrounding fields with Martin supporters in pursuit.

The main confrontation was yet to take place. About an hour later, unbeknownst to the Martin supporters, another large group of Greville supporters had arrived from Longford. The Martinites seemed to succeed in pushing the Greville forces farther from town, but they only succeeded in pushing them to high ground. When the Martin forces tried to force them off the hill, they discovered that the unexpected reinforcements meant they were now outnumbered. After several failed attempts, they retreated to a hill opposite. For a time, the opposing voters hooted and hissed at each other.

The goal of the Martinites was to tempt the Greville forces to abandon the high ground to make an attack. In this effort they were successful. A pitched battle took place in the valley. Only then did the military intervene. About thirty mounted troops attempted to force the two groups apart, but it required additional troops, the reading of the riot act three times, and finally shooting into the crowds before the battle ended. One of John's supporters was wounded. This time calm lasted throughout the remaining hours that voting was underway.

When the official vote count was completed, Greville-Nugent won by 1,047 votes. John was badly defeated in all three towns, even in the Martin stronghold of Granard, where Greville had strangely received twice as many votes.

Reaction to the publication of the results was swift and negative. Daunt was shocked. "Good Heavens! To what a depth of degradation must men have descended who are capable of preferring a youth who cannot show a single deed done for Ireland—or one single personal claim on our political confidence to Mr. Martin, whose public life has been a continuous protest against the wicked suppression of our legislative independence and who has incurred imprisonment and exile in a cause which is dear to the millions of our countrymen at home and abroad."

Though Daunt was a Catholic himself, he turned in anger to the actions of the Longford priests. One of them had even warned his parishioners of the "vengeance of heaven on any one who opposed the will of the clergy. His cattle will die and his subsistence melt away."

One priest, Father O'Dwyer, made his agreement with Daunt public. "I cannot understand the attitude of my clerical brethren in Longford on this occasion. If Mr. Martin were a revolutionist, a republican or a political enthusiast, I should not wonder at their opposition to him. But John Martin is well known to be the very reverse of all this, and to be moreover, one of the most clear heads, single-hearted, devoted patriots in Ireland."

George provided his readers with a clear picture of his opinions on the election in a long leader. "The 'National' journals still continued to pour forth their lamentations on the result of the Longford election. They deplore the defeat of our neighbour, Mr. John Martin. And in their great chagrin and wrath they have directed their fierce attacks on the Roman Catholic clergy. They charge them with using the most illegal and violent means to prevent the electors voting according to their judgments and feelings." "We have referred to the baseless and horrible calumnies uttered against the supporters of Mr. Martin; we have alluded to the altar denunciations hurled against them, and the shameful threats of temporal and eternal penalties by which it was sought to terrify simple-minded and honest-hearted peasants from doing their duty to their country."

As Catholics had attended mass across the district the day before the election, they found that their priests had acquired copies of the voting lists. They called the names of each voter and instructed them on how they were to vote the next day. They were to appear at a designated time and place, so they could all proceed in a controlled fashion to vote under the supervision of their priests. Churches were thus being turned into a "tally-room for Greville-Nugent."

George found these charges shocking but not surprising. Priests had been inserting themselves into elections since Emancipation in 1829. This time, he was heartened by the bravery of Catholic laity. "There is a rising up a spirit of independence and love of liberty among our Roman Catholic countrymen. What they are beginning to assert as their rights, all Protestants in Ireland, indeed in every country, fully enjoy. Protestants owe allegiance to their clergy in spiritual things. They look with reverence to them for spiritual guidance and instruction. They submit to their spiritual authority as an ordinance of the most High. But, on the other hand, they will not suffer their clergy to bind them to vote for any particular Parliamentary candidate, they will not allow their clergy to drive them to the poll; they will not permit their churches to become electioneering tally rooms; they will not endure political harangues from the pulpit instead of Gospel sermons."

Clearly, George saw the post-election protests against the actions of the priests in Longford as a sign that Catholic laity were moving in a more independent direction, more in tune with the feelings of their Protestant neighbours. "Protestants leave their clergy to exercise the utmost freedom in the exercise of their electoral rights and privileges, while they will not tolerate any ecclesiastical authority despotically to control them in the enjoyment of their civil immunities. Now, what our Protestant countrymen thus enjoy, our Roman Catholic countrymen should enjoy also. We hold that they should be protected from all ecclesiastical authority that would rob them of their civil liberties, and hold them in its bondage as mere slaves."

§

While the Longford election was underway, John was invited to a grand banquet to be held in his honor by the Mayor of New York, A. Oakey Hall, and some of his fellow Irish rebels, John Mitchel and his son included. This event took place on January 22nd at Delmonico's. There was a star-studded group of prominent New Yorkers on the stage, led by Horace Greeley filling in for the mayor. The room was decorated with remembrances of Ireland. The United States flag was coupled with an Irish flag which hung above the chairman's chair. Also decorating the stage were the arms of Ireland with the words "Cead Mille Failta." The evening began with the reading of letters of regret from the President, the Chief Justice of the Supreme Court, and Generals George McClellan and Robert E. Lee. John must have been amazed that such important figures had been invited and that they had written responses.

Greeley introduced John. "He has been concerned and engaged in a long and earnest struggle for a great public object. He has been, in a very decided respect, a public man and now public men, especially in this age of remarkable venality and self seeking, are largely suspected always of working or of managing public causes for private ends. Always this suspicion goes with us through the earlier and perhaps the better part of our career. 'What is the man after?' people always ask (laughter) Even in the history of that Green Island which is brought so freshly before us tonight, it is recorded of one of her public men that he thanked God that he had a country to sell (laughter). Now I say it is something when we can be brought in connection with one whose falling or whose silvery hairs testify that he has passed beyond the reach of suspicion of the taunt of private purpose, and private or personal self-seeking in a public cause. The great apostle of the Gentiles in similar circumstance, was enabled to say and he had a right to say, 'I have fought a good fight. I have kept the faith.' Noble words to be said when every heart shows them and feels that there is in them but the simple and ever modest assertion of a truth. (applause) I feel that I may rightly claim for our friend, around whom we rally tonight that his character and his career have passed beyond the reaches of obloquy, beyond the reach of defamation. (great applause). Nobody can longer say, if anybody ever did say, that the objects and his reach of his career was some snug place, some office to be given or power to be given, or money to be given. (applause) This is all we know and all the world knows. Men may say, some of them, 'Well, he was mistaken;' others may say, 'Well, he has not succeeded;' But no one will ever say he was dishonest (applause, and cries of good, good) There are those who will say he has not succeeded, but I have a different theory of what is success. I believe that to have succeeded in supporting a great cause nobly and faithfully through a long and arduous career is victory though the cause may not have succeeded. (great applause). Others may have failed, he has not failed. His triumph is secure whether the cause succeeded or not (applause) Yes, a great cause is always sanctified and in the end its triumph is secured by the sufferings and the sacrifices of its heroes and martyrs. There is a cumulative force in such sacrifices and in time the cause itself wins through, the sanctity through the truth, through the reverence that has accumulated around the names of its great champions. (applause) Therefore, without claiming any more for him than I have claimed, I say that the career of our friend has been a true success. I have not looked into the future. I have not attempted to say what the future will do for the cause or the man. I only speak of what is already beyond the reach of fortune. I ask you then to join me in the toast--'Our guest John Martin."

John rose to "great applause and prolonged cheering" from the audience. He began by thanking Mr. Greeley and the audience for the words of welcome and hospitality. "Gentlemen, this is a festive occasion, and not a political meeting. The sentiment that has actuated many of you in honouring me with this banquet is not agreement with my particular opinions and aims in politics, but only respect for the patriotic character which you attribute to my motives, and for the unselfishness and adherence to principle which, you kindly say, have distinguished my political conduct. (cheers.) In this company there are men of different national origins and of different political sympathies. And I do not pretend that any of my kind hosts to-night, by entertaining me, commits himself to my sentiments as an Irish nationalist, or even to the Irish side in the national quarrel between my country and England. Just and blameless as I believe my political aspirations to be, legitimate as are the griefs of which my country complains against England, I do not understand you, gentlemen, as expressing by this compliment to me any opinion upon the questions between the two countries. Nor do I feel entitled to take this opportunity for arguing in vindication of my Irish national aims, and pleading for your support to the Irish national cause. I therefore abstain from describing these relations between my country and England which have caused so prodigious a migration from Ireland, and have rendered the Irish element proportionally the largest in the population of these American States. But I need not refrain from acknowledging that the hospitable reception which the flying masses of my fellow-countrymen have found in America has been a refuge to them from starvation, pauperism, idleness, degradation at home—from starvation in Ireland in the midst of plenty, from enforced idleness and pauperism, from the degradation of national slavery. Neither do I see any reason why I should not congratulate America upon the fact that her hospitable reception of the disinherited Irish has contributed largely to her own material progress and national strength. And yet the excessive and abnormal movement of population from Ireland has been made at heavy loss, moral and physical, to very many of the emigrants, as well as to the country whence they fled.

"Gentlemen, I have not tried to express my ideas of the height of national power already attained by these United States, and of the still more glorious national position which this country seems destined to attain, if virtue and patriotism prevail in its councils. So great themes are worthy of eloquent words, and I have not eloquence. I shall only say this much: Your national independence is secure against the hostility of any power of the world, or any combination of powers."

"Gentlemen, I must not occupy more of your time. May New York and Brooklyn flourish more and more! May you, who are my kind hosts to-night, live long and have many a better occasion for displaying such magnificent hospitality as this with which you entertain me."

John spent the rest of January in Brooklyn with the Mitchels. It was a special time for the old friends, to be together, and to argue and debate as they had across the earth. In the evenings the men smoked their pipes as they had for so many years. And the two couples played whist every evening. Hentie turned out to be the best player of the four.

Late in the month, the time had come when John and Hentie had once planned to return to Ireland. They were travelling again, not home to Ireland, instead traveling to Boston to visit the Mahons and other friends on their way to Canada for the longer visit they had promised his sister and family in Canada. When word of his visit reached Boston, he received an invitation to speak to the Irish community there. This didn't fit his plans, so he wrote a letter of regret to the organizers of the event.

"Dear Sir, I have received the very flattering and much-esteemed invitation, signed by yourself and a number of other 'Irishmen and sons of Irishmen,' resident in Boston. The unexpected and exceeding kindness which I meet in America from "Irishmen and the sons of Irishmen' gratifies me highly, but somewhat confuses me. My part of an Irish patriot has been comparatively an obscure one, and I did not suppose that many men here would know or care much about me personally. But I find to my delight that 'Irishmen and the sons of Irishmen' here watch the affairs of the dear old land of their sires so closely that even my humble career has been marked by them. With Kindest feelings towards my kindred here, and deep appreciation of their desire to make me 'feel good' (as you say in America), it is with reluctance that I beg leave to decline the offer of a banquet in Boston. But I shall be spending some days there very soon, and when I see you, if I learn that it will suit the views of my good friends, I shall try to arrange to come back before my departure from America, to lecture for the benefit of some cause in which they take a particular interest. Be so kind as to make my excuses and explanations to the members of your committee and the rest of my hospitable friends, and believe me, dear sir, sincerely yours, John Martin to PJ Flatley Esq. Another promoter of the invitation was Patrick Donahoe, founder of the important Catholic newspaper the *Pilot*. John did arrange to speak to them before he returned to Ireland.

John and Hentie stayed in the Boston area for almost three weeks. Much of that time, they spent with George Mahon and his family in Framingham. John was happy to introduce Hentie to his longtime friend. It was a pleasure for the two men to stroll around the countryside, conversing in person instead of through a long-distance correspondence. They also spent several days with friends of Hentie's from her years in Brooklyn who lived in the quaint old fishing town of Gloucester.

In mid-February, they headed west to Canada. Along the way, they stopped in Albany to visit a friend from Ireland, the son of a longtime tenant in Loughorne. "Our Albany host, who left Ireland with no more money than what paid the passage of his wife and himself to Albany, but with some knowledge of his trade of carpenter and much general intelligence and soundness, has become quite a rich man and lives in a fine house of his own. He is of the Orange Presbyterian stock and retains much of the traditional hatred and bullying spirit toward the Catholics. The 'Connaughtmen,' he thinks, have no right to set themselves up as equals of other men at Albany. Contemptuous toleration is good enough for them and they ought to be thankful for it—we had endless colloquies about our neighbors he and I and it was altogether a very interesting day that we spent with the family."

From Albany, they traveled quickly to Ontario where they spent three more weeks at his sister's home four miles outside London. The weather was very cold and snowy while they were there. For three days, it was so cold that John didn't "dare" go out except for brief outings to experience the intense cold. He loved the feel of the clear, crisp air. One day, the temperature on the warm side of the house was eight degrees below zero as the sun rose. They were kept busy despite the weather with numerous family gatherings and parties with family friends, experiencing the best food that Canadian cooks could provide.

They enjoyed fine health despite the cold. But when they returned to Brooklyn, after a hectic visit in Canada, they found Mitchel was still ailing. John was very concerned that "his constitution is broken down."

John was delighted to view the famous St. Patrick's Day parade from a window overlooking 5th Ave. When the last marchers had passed by, John went to the 9th annual dinner of the Knights of St. Patrick, again held at Delmonico's. The hall was decorated with red, white, blue and green streamers suspended from the chandeliers and walls. The windows were dressed with green curtains and gold cornices. The names of prominent Irish leaders were placed about the seats of each speaker. There was also a painting of Daniel O'Connell.

After a sumptuous dinner, Horace Greeley began the speeches. Then he introduced John, who spoke briefly. "It is very pleasant for me to be your guest and enjoy your hospitality and good fellowship, and it is more pleasant still to feel there is a higher and deeper and stronger sympathy between me and all of you than social enjoyment. Every one of you aspires after Irish national independence as his greatest earthly good. So does every men and boy of the thousands of members of Irish temperance or benefit societies, who for an hour and a half, passed in gallant procession before the window where I stood to admire and rejoice over them today. So do all the millions of Irish who this day in all the countries of the civilized world have met to honor the festival of our national Saint. The persecutions and misfortunes of many centuries have not prevailed to kill that aspiration—that faith in Irish nationality. The gates of hell shall not prevail against it. (applause).

"That the national independence of Ireland may soon come, let Irishmen labor at home and abroad, in each place by each way, and means as the circumstances of that place may render advisable. So I think we shall all do, and therefore I hopefully conclude with the words of your toast, "May the day of the accomplishment of our freedom be close at hand."

§

The time that John would spend in America was coming to an end. So his thoughts began to turn to events that had occurred in Ireland in the months that he had been away. Mitchel published John's observations in his paper near the end of March.

"The recent news from Ireland by mail and telegraph indicates a continual advance of the national cause. The Irish population in many ways shows itself more and more fixed in its determination never to consent to the English usurpation however overwhelming for the time may be the force of usurpers and however small the means at Ireland's command for resistance. The desire for Irish self-government spreads and strengthens among all classes and sects in Ireland. Upon the other side the English government and Parliament which some time ago proclaimed and protested calling all the world to witness that now at last, England repented of her cruel misdeeds toward the Irish people, and resolved henceforth to do justice and to let Ireland be ruled as a free country in accord with Irish ideas—the English Government and Parliament find themselves unable to keep on the mask of constitutional law any longer, and are obliged to appear before the world in their true character as rulers in Ireland by force alone." [through coercion laws]

Then he reflected on the meaning of the results of recent elections held in Ireland, including his own failed attempt. The situation had changed rapidly since the Longford election. Even potential candidates without sufficient funds to pay for an election and who have no support from patrons, were receiving enough support from local electors themselves to run for seats in Parliament. To make their voices heard, they were braving attacks from priests and the presence of armed troops. "I think that if a general election were to be held by ballot, even with the carefully constructed and arranged constituencies which English rule permits in order to keep up the pretence of a constitution, a large majority of national representatives would be returned."

In the new session of Parliament, Gladstone had introduced a bill to remedy the conflicts between landlords and tenants. John thought this might be, as many saw it, evidence of English good will. Certainly, some changes were needed to stem the flow of emigration out of Ireland caused in part by the longstanding conflicts between tenants and their landlords. But John didn't believe the current proposal was the solution to the problem. "To annul and abolish an English law for Ireland is good and gives relief. But to make an English law for Ireland never benefits Ireland. The evils which afflict the Irish population—the insecurity of tenure, the antipathy of landlord against tenant, the extermination of Irish families as if they were vermin, the agrarian murders which are the sad resource against a system of robbery and inhumanity—are far less the results of any particular English laws than the natural and necessary results of English rule itself. The existence of English rule is the cause of them. The removal of English rule will abolish them. While English rule continues, there cannot be a radical cure of the exceptional evils which afflict the Irish rural population, nor of any of the exceptional evils under which Ireland suffers. A radical cure can be affected only by taking Ireland out of the exceptional situation in which she lies and restoring her to national life and freedom."

John listed his objections to the current version of the legislation. "It does not give security of tenure, it does not prevent arbitrary ejection, it does not give the Tenant-right custom the force of law. It is calculated to embitter still more the relations between landlords and tenants by raising endless litigation between them; litigation in which the poor man will have the worst chance of eventual success, and it seeks to interpose the English Government (in the form of the new tribunal it creates) as a constantly present arbiter and mischief-maker between Irish tenants and Irish landlords. It offers temptations to landlords to evict tenants of farms held under the Tenant-right custom." To make matters worse, it established arbitration courts, which were useless to most tenants without the money to attain justice.

When great changes were to be made in Ireland, Parliament considered it prudent to have strong Coercion Acts in place. As usual, this one was marketed as for "protection of life and property in Ireland." But John pointed out that there were four murders committed in England for every one committed in Ireland. Yet England never considered it necessary to create such a law to protect life and property in England. This unfair treatment will only activate the Irish people and increase the demand for self-government. "And whenever that glorious day shall come, the English will, in my opinion, peacefully abdicate their usurped rule and peaceably yield us up our national right."

Before John left, he managed to schedule two more speeches. He did make the requested speech in Boston in the Music Hall on Monday, March 28th. Tickets cost 25 cents and 50 cents for reserved seats. The proceeds would go to help the families of the Irish political prisoners. The topic of his speech was "The Present Situation of the Irish National Cause."

John repeated his justification for a Nationalist movement in Ireland, much as he had in previous speeches. Ireland was governed against its wishes, but in accordance with the wishes and needs of England. Irish resources were sent to England to enrich the English. Whenever the Irish protested, however peacefully, the English instituted penal laws to optimize their control though the use of force. There was no equality between the two countries.

Still John believed that current conditions were changing around Europe that would soon make Irish ill-treatment unacceptable if England wished to continue holding a prominent leadership position around the world. "The national quarrel between England and Ireland is this: the people of Ireland do not enjoy possession of their own country, but only occupy it subject to the control of the people of England. The English by force of arms and by usurpation of the sovereign rights of Ireland, compel the people of Ireland to submit to laws made against their wishes to pay taxes without their own consent, and to yield up the rents, revenues, income and property of Ireland to the disposal of England.

"But the history of the English relation with Ireland is not of conquest and amalgamation of the victorious invaders with the Irish population. It is now a perpetual invasion lasting now for seven centuries—of an attempt at conquest never succeeding and which (please God!) never will succeed—of an international wound kept raw and bleeding generation after generation, age after age.

"But all the means employed for so many ages by the English for the purpose of getting quiet and full possession of Ireland—all the massacres, confiscations, devastations, exterminations, settlements, all their cunning acts to cheat, delude, divide, corrupt, brutalize educate their Irish subjects; to darken the Irish spirit and pervert the Irish intellect—all have failed. Impoverished, divided, discouraged, weakened, and very unhappy England has certainly succeeded in making her Irish subjects. But she has failed to reconcile them to her rule, she has failed to kill in their souls the sacred fire of freedom. She dare not to this day trust her usurping rule in Ireland without keeping her Irish subjects carefully disarmed, and their country occupied by a great military force."

There was one great hope in John's heart. As the election laws continued to change, new voters would support the idea of Irish independence that was growing "among all sects and classes." The religious antagonisms that had always divided the country were fading. "Moderation and firmness is our national demand, courage and prudence in sustaining it, will before long, by cooperation of the Irish at home and abroad, obtain the national freedom of Ireland. God grant it!"

John had hoped to get time for another visit with George Mahon and his family when he gave this speech in Boston. However, he had to return quickly to Brooklyn to fulfill a commitment to speak in Newark. Unwisely, John had given the organizers permission to set the date, and they had picked a time that conflicted with his plan to visit the Mahons before he left. So instead John went to Newark to speak at the Young Men's Catholic Institute, giving the same speech that he had given in Boston. It was the last speech he would give in America.

As the long trip to America neared an end, groups of supporters came by the Mitchel house in Brooklyn to say goodbye. A representative of the "Metropolitan Record," Mr. Mullally, visited with several others to read an address of farewell. They also presented him with a silver fruit stand with the date of the banquet and decorated with the coat of arms of the state of New York.

The Young Men's Catholic Institute before whom he had given his final address, sent a letter of goodbye. "The name of John Martin has long been familiar to exiled Irishmen in this western hemisphere, and the world over, because of his long suffering unselfish devotion to his and their native land; and none enjoyed more than the undersigned to know that whenever the opportunity presented itself during your short visit to our adopted country, the Irishmen resident here have not been unmindful of the valuable services rendered to the Green Ireland by honest John Martin.

"In this connection sir, will you permit us to express our regret that your visit to our country cannot be prolonged, nor your tour extended; and in this sentiment we are certain we express but the feelings of the masses of our exiled fellow-citizens in these United States, who would all be anxious to see and hear the sterling and unselfish patriot that has labored for over a quarter of a century for the cause of dear old Ireland…Go, as Ireland needs the assistance and presence of such men as you in these days of tribulation and renewed persecution—and carry with you the heartfelt aspirations of millions of Irish exiles, for the safe and speedy voyage of yourself and your estimable lady. That an all wise Providence may grant you prolonged years of health, and happiness to labor in the future as you have in the past, in the cause of long-suffering, long persecuted Ireland and that you may yet be spared to take part in the councils and government of your native land when Irishmen alone will make the laws by which they are governed, when you will again have your Parliament in College Green—in a word, when Ireland will be for the Irish and the Irish for Ireland." The letter was signed by the officers of the group.

John's departure was bittersweet. He suspected that these final hours with Mitchel would be their last together. He wished Mitchel could give up his newspaper work, thus prolonging his life by living quietly in Brooklyn. John and Hentie left New York on April 30th on the Inman lines 'City of Brooklyn' after seven months in America. As the ship steamed through the Narrows, and out toward the open Atlantic beyond, John knew he would never return.

After John had sailed, Mitchel published a letter that John had written as a farewell to the people who had treated him so kindly. "29 April 1870. Dear Sir. On the eve of my return home, after a visit of 7 months to America, I wish to say some words of farewell to the people of this country and especially those of them who are of Irish birth or descent. Circumstances have prevented me from traveling extensively through the country, and from satisfying my curiosity as to its natural features. But I have had much agreeable personal intercourse with the people and have received many tokens of their extraordinary and constant kindness. This kindness, when I received it from Americans not of Irish descent, I must attribute to the sympathy which such Americans entertain for the national cause of Ireland; for except as a faithful advocate of that cause, I possess no title to notice. The sentiment of Irish nationality, so fondly cherished by the Irish settlers in America, the idea of the Irish settlers that in showing favor to me they were honoring the Irish cause in the person of a humble but loyal follower of the cause is the sole motive for their kindness. Let me have the aid of your paper to convey my heartfelt thanks to my American friends, both those of Irish descent and those not of Irish descent and let me, through your columns, address to the American citizens of my own kindred a few parting words of advice concerning the great cause which they and Ireland and the Irish race all over the world desire to make triumphant.

"All good Irishmen (except those whose eyes have not yet been opened to the truth) see that Ireland is entitled to national self-government, that Ireland needs self-government, that it is the duty of Irishmen to labor for the deliverance of Ireland and her establishment as an independent nation. What are the forces that are opposed to the national right of Ireland and what are the forces that good Irishmen may bring together on Ireland's side? The force opposed to possession of our country, and makes such use of its produce and deals with its population as she thinks proper. It would be foolish to expect that a nation so selfish as England could be moved by considerations of generosity, or justice to relinquish any profitable possession. Only by direct force or else by operating otherwise upon the ideas of self-interest, can England be induced to give up her pretension to hold Ireland as a conquered province and treat the Irish as her bondsmen. If the population of Ireland were able to rise in arms, and if they resolved *as a nation* to rise in arms, they could have a perfect right to do so, for the purpose of expelling the English rule and establishing Irish national freedom, I believe my opinion upon that question in order to disabuse the minds of some people, who seem to assume that because I am a Repealer—because I have always with all my power advocated a peaceful and non-revolutionary settlement of our national quarrel with England—I therefore would deny the right of Ireland to draw the sword in her own just cause. And I wish it to be well understood that I do not counsel—nor have I ever counseled—appeals to England's mercy or any course of patriotic action which might imply a recognition of England's authority as existing otherwise than by unjust force.

"The population of Ireland are neither prepared nor inclined to rise in armed revolt. The circumstances in which the country is placed are such that without the protection of a sufficient foreign army, it would not be practicable for the people to provide themselves with arms and organize themselves as an armed body. In Ireland according to the common sense of the vast majority of the population rejects the idea of insurrections as utterly unsuited to the actual circumstances. And, moreover, considering that the object of national desire in Ireland has nothing in itself hurtful or hostile to the just rights of Englishmen, the vast majority of the Irish population persist in believing that it is possible to obtain that object without an actual war with England. And, lastly, the object of national desire in Ireland being simply self-government and needing for its realization only the removal and abolition of the English usurpation, the whole people of Ireland, but above all the popular clergy, anxiously wish to bring the country into possession of its national right without revolution."

As America receded behind them, John turned his concerns to what he would find when he returned home to Ireland. Under the terms of the new Coercion Act enacted while he was away, John would face arrest and long-term imprisonment without a trial if he said or wrote anything that the English government found offensive. He had come to believe that being elected to Parliament would be his best protection against such an arrest and imprisonment, which due to his age and health status could prove fatal. Despite his failure in Longford, John resolved to stand for election again should an opportunity arise.

Chapter 17

Member of Parliament
1870 – 1871

George was feeling very gloomy about events of the previous year as he began to compose his New Year message to his readers. "We have no hesitation in declaring that 1869 will be always looked back to as one of the blackest years in the history of Irish Protestantism. In the departed year our Legislature cast off its allegiance to the Great Ruler of nations, and, so far as Ireland is concerned, our state now repudiates and ignores all religion. This dreadful act of national apostasy from the Truth has already brought forth its fruit. Instead of the peace and concord we were promised as soon as our Protestant Churches should be bereft of their temporalities and placed 'on an equality' with Romanism and infidelity, we have been brought to the brink of revolution. The Government evidently have received authentic information of a Fenian outbreak. Our trade and commerce and manufactures have been brought to the lowest ebb. The gentry in the South and West are abandoning their homes to obtain safe asylums for their families in England. The state of the nation is deplorable."

Looking forward he saw nothing to brighten the new year either. "And it is to be feared that in the New Year our wretched, unprincipled Government will lend itself to carry out with high hand the unconstitutional Irish policy sketched for it by Cardinal Cullen, the virtual ruler at the present moment of this country. The design of Messrs. Gladstone and Bright is to hand over the nation to the domination of Ultramontanism. Mr. Gladstone will avenge himself on the Conservative party by striking many a heavy blow this year at Protestant ascendancy. Our Protestant landlords have the sword hanging over their heads; and the Papal Hierarchy are flushed with expectation at their having a grand haul out of the confiscated revenues of our noble Protestant University, and at their demands likely being virtually conceded for the establishment of an exclusive system of denominational education to be wholly under their 'supreme control.'"

The only hope that George could offer his readers was that the Gladstone administration would eventually come to an end. George wasn't willing to predict just when that would happen, but he was sure of one thing. "Concessions to Ultramontanism will come to an end. The cause of Truth everywhere will be triumphant. Our fatherland will yet be prosperous, enlightened, and free." In the meantime, there was something every Protestant could do to help. Every citizen must make the largest contributions they could afford to support their churches.

Besides facing new religious problems, Ireland also faced problems in two other areas. "Trade and commerce" were very depressed around Europe and America. Merchants were hoping that this problem was merely part of a periodic recession that should be expected and could be survived. Survival for Irish farmers might be impossible. Prices farmers got from their produce continued too low to meet costs. Of special concern in Newry was the outcome of the flax harvest. Sadly, the crop had been a failure in the previous autumn. Oat and wheat crops weren't much better. However, through most of Ireland, there were two stronger farm sectors. The potato crop had been bounteous, and prices received for sales of women's work, butter, fowl, pork and eggs had never been higher.

George pointed out an international bright spot. Europe and the colonies seemed to be at peace. George concluded with a bit of a pat on the back for the *Newry Telegraph.* "We are proud and thankful to say that this journal still retains its hold on the good will of the community. We heartily thank our subscribers and friends for their warm and generous support. The Telegraph, in the new year, will hold on its course perseveringly and without change. We abide by our old principles. We shall continue to support and defend our Protestant institutions and interest. We are Conservative, out-and-out.

"Grateful for past support, and confidently relying on the good-will of the public for the future, we wish all our readers—A Most Happy New Year."

There was another issue that George saw lurking ahead though he didn't mention it in his New Year's leader. A new effort to solve the stressful problems between tenants and landlords seemed to be on the agenda during the upcoming session of Parliament. Agitation for this legislation had begun in the southern parts of Ireland where tenants very much wished to have the rights of Ulster farmers extended to them. Those who had been holding meetings in the north, saw these southern efforts as "Radical and revolutionary." Participants had insulted landowners and spread "communistic" ideas. These agitators wanted to end the current customs of land ownership. But worst of all, from George's point of view, was the fact that at some of these meetings, Presbyterian ministers had appeared to offer their support for this major change.

When the government's intentions were revealed in the Queen's speech on February 10th, George felt his concerns were well founded. Five days later, when the legislation was introduced, his pessimistic outlook abruptly changed. He was surprised to discover the proposals were far different from what the supporters of tenant rights had been advocating with which George fiercely disagreed. The first cheering news was that Gladstone didn't intend to propose any measures on the touchy subject of "fixity of tenure." This was one of the major protections Ulster farmers enjoyed which southern farmers did not. Gladstone had apparently promised to extend this right throughout Ireland to attract strong Catholic support during the previous election. Nothing could have delighted George more than discovering that Gladstone intended to renege on this commitment.

When George wrote on the subject again, he applauded the legislation. "Public attention is mainly directed to the Government Land Bill. In the North there is a very general feeling that it is a fair and moderate measure. Conservatives and Liberals alike speak well of it. And we are glad to observe that in the highest circles men of all political parties approve of the general principle of the Bill, and of most of the details. Of course it admits of improvement, but on the whole the landlords of Ulster must feel that it is not of the confiscatory and revolutionary character that they might have anticipated, and in fact which they did anticipate from Mr. Gladstone's reckless statements made a year ago."

Initially, the legislation made quick progress in Parliament. The bill was not intended to "impose new relations or burdens upon the good landlords and said it would only oblige the bad ones to follow their practice." Ulster customs would not be extended beyond the boundaries of Ulster.

The rosy perspective of Ulster conservatives was somewhat dampened as opposition mounted. "The misguided people were led to believe that they were going to get the soil of the country into their own hands, and that the state would 'buy off' the Protestant landlords. Hence their storm of wrath now that they find the promised Land Bill is not a confiscatory, Communistic measure. The agitation against the Bill is increasing in the South and West." George predicted that opposition would only increase as debate moved forward.

The people of Ireland believed that problems for tenants in Ireland were worse than in other parts of Europe. George informed his readers that contrary to general local belief, the Irish tenants were not overcharged for their rent. He refuted another belief about Irish tenants. "A charge very frequently brought against Irish landlords is the number of evictions that they carry out, driving the struggling and industrious but unfortunate farmers out of their fatherland to be wanderers on the earth. This charge is a demonstrably false one." He offered no evidence for these assertions.

Sitting after sitting, members struggled to find enough votes on various amendments to pass the final product. One of the divisive provisions was the establishment of new land courts. Either landlord or tenant could take their disputes to court for resolution. However, this improvement was of little use to many Irish tenants who had no money to access such courts. Despite this lingering problem, the bill passed into the committee phase where the legislation would be examined line by line to prepare for final passage with a vote of 412 in favor, only 11 opposed.

§

The Landlord and Tenant bill still seemed to be moving safely toward final passage. But this progress slowed in the middle of March as protests swept across southern and western parts of Ireland. George informed his readers just what was happening there. "Bands of armed men, it appears, patrol particular districts, forcing farmers to swear oaths they impose, carrying away arms, and perpetrating acts of violence. Among the well-disposed and peaceable portion of the community in those disturbed districts there is great alarm, and, at the same time, they are filled with indignation because of the culpable heedlessness of the Government in regard to this deplorable state of matters. They feel that they have been deserted by the authorities by whom they should have been guarded, and by whom also the laws of the land should have been maintained and vindicated with firm hand."

There was conflict of a different kind in Newry though the causes were similar. George warned the Newry magistrates that the time had already passed for action in the matter. For several Sundays, a Catholic mob had gathered at the Corry Monument in central Newry to hassle and threaten Protestants as they went to one of the nearby churches. George demanded that police quickly disperse them, noting that police had been on hand the previous weekend, but just watched events as they unfolded. "We would not for a moment countenance any class of religionists being mobbed. And we feel assured that our respectable Roman Catholic townsmen feel in that respect as we do. But it is scarcely credible that in the town of Newry every Sabbath a Protestant cannot move through a Protestant neighbourhood without being assailed by an organized band of ruffians from a Roman Catholic district in a different part of the town."

George predicted what would happen if local magistrates ignored the provocation. "If there be a continuance of this outrage we dread that it will lead to deplorable consequences. The Protestants, not only of the town but of the neighbourhood, are determined that they shall not be subjected to further insult and injury. They will not tolerate any mob to maltreat their wives and children as they are going to or returning from their places of worship on God's day. If the authorities fail to protect them they declare they will protect themselves. Upon the authorities now rests a serious responsibility."

George concluded with an explanation of his personal religious thinking. "What a shame it is that our countrymen cannot learn to be at peace, no matter how widely they may differ as to faith or politics. Christianity is love. It smiles on no violence. Its agencies are all benign. The wretches who would support their religion by stone-throwing and such acts of violence prove either that they have no religion or that their religion is essentially a bad one."

Whether or not George's leader was the reason or not, authorities did take action, arresting some of the young boys who were disrupting the passage of Protestants to church. Local religious problems seemed resolved. George was also happy to inform his readers that the Landlord and Tenant Act would be set aside to allow Parliament to pass a new coercion law. Its provisions would allow police to seize all groups of men who were moving about after dark. A unique new feature allowed any citizen who had suffered financially from a sectarian outrage to be eligible for compensation. For certain crimes, trial by jury would be suspended, and all those accused of designated crimes would be tried before a judge, not a jury of their peers. Finally, the legislation would empower officials to arrest anyone speaking or writing sentiments officials didn't like. This could make John subject to arrest yet again.

Despite the increased powers this new bill would give government officials, George wasn't sure that even these harsh measures would be sufficient. "The scoundrels who have been covering the land with blood and violence must be struck down as with an iron hand. They are merciless wretches, and they should be dealt with mercilessly. The snakes must be scotched. We *must* have peace in Ireland, and perfect security for life and property. Things cannot be tolerated that have hitherto been overlooked. There are no causes in any way to justify disorder, violation of the laws, violence and murder. The great parties in the Legislature have now a grand opportunity of doing Ireland lasting good. Let them compel our professional agitators 'to set a watch on their foul and disloyal lips.'" George was supporting suppression of rights for opposition voices and newspapers that he would never want applied to the *Newry Telegraph*. He claimed his writings were exempt from the law, as what he wrote wouldn't "sow their bad seed broadcast among our excitable peasantry."

The fact that new coercive legislation was needed was proof to George of the failure of Gladstone's policies and legislation to bring peace to Ireland. "To stop agrarian crime and disloyalty, Ireland must be ruled as a part of the Empire, not as a separate nation. The people must be taught in the South and West that they must submit to the laws, and that offences will be punished heavily."

In fairness to his readers, George did note one feature of the bill which concerned him and might be concerning to his readers, the section that allowed for trials without juries. "But, under the circumstances, the proviso is needed. We highly approve of it. At the same time we trust that the Government may be induced to alter the system of trial by jury, adopting the Scotch system, which does not require a verdict from the whole of the jury, but only from a certain majority. That system would be found most effective in this country."

George wrote about the coercion bill again a few days later as it made quick progress through Parliament, informing his readers that the legislation had passed through committee and would soon be the law of the land. This progress prompted strong reactions from the nationalist newspapers. Editors were very angry with the Gladstone government about the entire bill, but especially about the clause that put them under threat of arrest and prosecution in a court without a jury. They claimed their writings were intended to be sufficiently inflammatory to challenge the current government. That was their right, even their obligation. Freedom of the press should never be subjected to the political whims of any government.

George couldn't deny that these editors were "earnest" men." But they were also rebels to their heart's core. If their power was in proportion to their desires, "the Queen's Government would be overthrown in Ireland before to-morrow, and a Republic would be proclaimed. And they are sanguine of success. They foolishly believe they will be able so to worry the British Government and people that at last they will cast them off and bid them rule themselves as they may; or, otherwise, they dream that should England become engaged in a war with France or with America, that they would, in that event have the succor of the foreign belligerent power to aid them in achieving their deliverance from British sway."

These dreams were clearly opposite to those that George had for the future of Ireland. And he firmly believed that his opinions and dreams would win in the end. "The predictions that were made in this journal in regard to the results of the Irish policy of Mr. Gladstone's Government have been fully realized. Foolish dreamers alleged that Mr. Gladstone's revolutionary measures would bring peace and prosperity to this nation, we were to have quite a millennium. Party strife was to cease. The Romish professional agitators were to find their trade and occupation gone. Law and order were to exercise the most benignant sway among us.

"We utterly disbelieved these predictions. We knew that they were baseless. We felt certain that the Government policy would be the curse of the country; that it would intensify, spread, and perpetuate religious strife; that it would set class against class; that, while it would embitter and exasperate the loyalists of the land, despoil their churches, and cast off the faith of the Reformation, it would not satisfy or appease the claimant Ultramontanes and Republicans, but, on the contrary, that it would incite them to make bolder and more arrogant demands. In every respect our predictions have come to pass. The Liberal journals have not a word to say in explanation of their vain boasting."

From George's perspective, none of the violence in Ireland would have happened if the Conservatives were in power. This was certainly why George took such a great interest in Newry elections and was so distressed by the victory of the Liberal William Kirk for Newry in the previous election. "Liberal Governments have been the curse of Ireland. But never had we a Government that has proved so baneful to our country as the present Liberal Government. Its Coercion Bill [Peace Preservation Act] is the fruit of its revolutionary policy. Mr. Gladstone's Administration will run its course, but the shorter that course be all the better will it prove for the best interests of the British Empire."

With final passage of the newest coercion bill still a few days away, George interrupted his coverage with sad news for many residents of Newry. Lord Robert Roden had died in Scotland. Though it wasn't mentioned in the extensive coverage of the death and funeral, many local residents remembered his involvement in the sectarian riots in Dolly's Brae in 1849. George also reported on the reaction to his death in the London papers. "They write of him as having been before the Legislature and the empire for more than half a century as a representative man. They all bear testimony to his exalted private worth, and to his rare excellence as a resident Irish landlord. The Radical journals, of course, unite with the Papal Press in designating him a fanatic, and an impractical Orange chief. The *Daily Telegraph* boasted that he lived to see his principles repudiated by the empire, and Orange ascendancy to be a thing of the past."

"Our London contemporary writes not without foundation for some of his boasting. There is no doubt that Radicalism is for the present all powerful in the House of Commons. There is no doubt that our National Church has been plundered and disestablished. There is no doubt that our nation, as such, has renounced Protestantism. There is no doubt that Cardinal Cullen exercises all powerful sway in Dublin Castle. There is no doubt that the loyal men of Ireland feel that the British Government has treated them harshly and as enemies. All these things Lord Roden lived to see and to deplore. But one thing his lordship did not see—namely, the loyal orange confederation destroyed. The Orangemen of Ireland are stronger to-day than ever they were, and the principles the Earl of Roden held and powerfully advocated they hold and they will never surrender them." George's warning proved prophetic.

Once the new Coercion Bill passed through Parliament, Gladstone returned to efforts to pass the Tenant Rights bill. One of the new amendments was particularly aggravating for George. It would actually achieve the main goal of the southern provinces of the country to extend the protections of the Ulster Custom to all of Ireland. When the amendment came up for a vote, it was soundly defeated, only 42 members actually supported it. George was delighted with this result. "It was a monstrous proposition. The custom never prevailed in the South or West, and the tenant farmers there have no claim to it. Landlords in many cases had purchased their estates in the other provinces with the express understanding that they were not subject to the Ulster Tenant Right; and on the properties of all the landowners it would have imposed a burden to which it would have been outrageous to subject them. The Government strongly opposed the amendment…The farmers of the North only have a claim to the system that has only had existence in the North."

Without much further delay, the bill moved on to the House of Lords for action, having passed through a third reading on May 20th. George didn't anticipate that there would be any significant changes and thought it would become law before the close of the session. He had analyzed the bill and had detected some who would benefit from its provisions. "We have no hesitation in saying that the Land Bill will benefit tenants under bad landlords. They will secure some compensation in case they should be arbitrarily evicted from their holdings, or that their rents should be raised exorbitantly."

Unfortunately, there were traps in the small print. Most Ulster tenants who leased their land from good landlords gained little from its provision. But they would soon discover the loss of a very prized privilege. Before passage of the legislation, tenants had a right to sell their leases at public auction, the value being determined by what buyers were willing to pay. Under the new law, "If tenants determine on leaving their holdings, their landlords, taking advantage of the provisions of the Act, will refuse to allow them to sell, calling upon them to appeal to the Land Courts to decide as to the amount of compensation they should receive; and the landlords will naturally say to the tenants: 'We are only following the course of action your own Land Bill has legalised.'

"We do not pretend to be prophets; but we venture to affirm that ninety out of every hundred of the farmers of Ulster will bitterly rue the passing of this Land Bill. It will eventually sweep away the old tenant right of Ulster."

Shortly before passage, George offered another caution. "We fervently hope that the Land Act will be all that its warmest admirers assert it will be. We do not believe it will be to the tenantry of Ulster any boon. It will be a grand 'feeder' for all attorneys practicing at Quarter Session Courts. It will be seen within a year whether or not is does not extinguish the most valuable element of our old Ulster Tenant Right–namely, the privilege of disposing of farms by public auction."

The Land Bill passed through the House of Lords on July 8th. However it took most of the rest of the session for both houses to negotiate the differences in their versions of the legislation. The Queen signed the Landlord and Tenant Act on August 1st.

§

The Longford election had seemed like a fairly routine corrupt Irish election. There was nothing usual either about John's supporters appealing the results to a Parliamentary committee for a hearing. However the subsequent investigation made a profound difference to Ireland and its future. The actions of the Priests, acting as political agents for Greville-Nugent, and threatening parishioners who defied their voting instructions, seemed to push Catholic laity to revolt. Perhaps the reason for this reaction was that most people in Ireland knew what a principled person John was, and how opposed he was to the Fenian movement. So when one of the priests referred to John as a Fenian, they knew that the priests were lying from their pulpits.

Rev. Patrick Fitzgerald of Cohlumbkill referred to John as "an Orangeman, a Fenian and a priest hunter—who would behead if he could all the priests and overturn all the Catholic institutions of the country." He hoped that a new coercion law would be enacted that would allow John and his supporters to be put in jail "where they might be allowed to rot—and rot they might, until the maggots and worms ate them, and after that, they would go to hell."

The revelations made public during the hearings provoked George to react. After the Longford hearings in Parliament were widely reported, he shared his observations with his Newry readers. He titled the new leader "A Strange Revolution." Then he explained the "revolution" he wished to write about. "WE have of late called attention to the extraordinary manifestation of a change of feeling on the part of many of the Roman Catholic laity toward the clergy of their own Church. Previously, they not only submitted to their ecclesiastical influence, but also to their political despotism." George was unwilling to criticize them for their submission in religious matters. "Within their own sphere of duty the functions of the clergy are of the most sacred character."

However, there was a long-standing problem in Ireland. "When the clergy of any denomination outstep their province, and by terrorism and acts of violence interfere with the laity in the discharge of their duties as citizens of the State then, we say, they subject themselves to the strongest condemnation."

George well understood that, like all citizens, Catholics had a right to exercise their rights to their own opinions as citizens, and to express them freely. "But if they would attempt to overawe the laity by personal attacks from the altar or the pulpit–if they threaten with excommunication from the privileges of the Church, and even from the enjoyment of heaven those who would exercise their electoral franchise contrary to their tyrannical commands—if they become the leaders of infuriated drunken mobs, whom they have lashed to fury and have maddened with drink—then we have no hesitation in declaring they have outraged their order, they have inflicted a great scandal on religion, they have made themselves intolerant despots, and they have subjected themselves to the reprobation of all right thinking men."

These actions of priests had been seen in two previous elections, one in Tipperary, one in Waterford. "The Roman Catholic priests in the South and West have gradually been driving the laity of their Church to rebel against their political despotism. They have begun to feel that they have an inalienable right to exercise their electoral privileges, and that their hierarchy and clergy have been treating them as 'dumb cattle,' driving them to the poll." "And at Longford the conflict between the priests and the people may be regarded as one of the most singular events of modern times in this country."

The conduct of the priests of Longford as revealed in the Parliamentary hearings "has made a terrible exposure of the priesthood." And George assured his readers that he wasn't the only person to have noticed this important trend. Surely Catholic laity had no obligation to follow the civic directions of priests who had shown themselves willing to engage in intimidation, and undue influence. Equally evil, the priests had taken large amounts of money from their churches to make their parishioners drunk. Altogether they took the role of "'electioneering agent'" according to the *Flag of Ireland.* The Longford priests were "'morally responsible for the sin, the drunkenness, the violence, the bloodshed, and the hatred which disgraced Longford.'"

Just to reinforce his point, George provided comments from another paper, the *Weekly News.* This paper lauded the actions of those in Longford who fought against the Greville supporters with nothing like equal resources. These Longford voters had less than the amount of money paid by the Greville forces for whiskey. "'The Longford patriot band fought Lord Greville's flowing thousands; fought altar desecration; fought unpriestly calumny and falsehood; fought an army of hired bludgeonmen; fought flooding bribery, corruption, drunkenness, debauchery, and murderous intimidation! Mark the fact revealed by all this!'"

These quotes that George picked out for his readers had come from Catholic newspapers. "We rejoice to see the laity asserting their rights. The movement will spread, and we anticipate from the extension of the movement the advancement of the best interests of our country."

The excessive corruption of the Irish elections, culminating with the Longford election, had stirred Parliament. Shortly after the Longford election, discussions began on a bill that would change the voting system from the open polling that had prevailed in Ireland for many generations to a secret ballot.

After the original idea was floated at the beginning of the session, nothing happened for most of the session. Just before adjournment, the subject reappeared. This time the presentation was made by Gladstone. The major reasons for the change were the threats and intimidation of opposing candidates displayed vividly in the Longford election. So even though John had taken no part personally in the election, his sterling character activated many of the Longford voters, and made the actions of the Greville forces by the Catholic leadership even more grievous. So in that rather indirect way, John had impelled the discussion of a new way of voting.

While George was greatly pleased at the growing resistance of the Catholic laity to voting directions delivered by their priests from the pulpit, he definitely opposed the government's solution to the problem, the secret ballot. He called the new governmental proposal "an extreme Radical scheme." This was a concept that all parties had objected to very strongly. "The system of vote by Ballot is a cowardly and dangerous system. Men are responsible to public opinion for the manner in which they exercise the franchise, and nothing of a secret character should screen them from that responsibility."

The secret ballot was the system of voting used in France and parts of Australia already, and it was therefore possible to see how such a system would work. George found from such evidence that the practice didn't enhance individual privacy. Indeed it only added to corruption. In Ireland, the power of the Catholic priests would make problems already obvious elsewhere even worse.

Despite the recent lessons of the Longford election and the Longford priests, George downplayed the idea that the same kind of coercion existed in Ulster. There pressure on voters would most likely come from the resident landlords not religious leaders. George felt that the Ulster landlords "have been much maligned. No doubt they have interfered to thwart the tremendous influence of the priests, but, after all, the tenantry, if left to themselves, would generally have voted as their landlords voted."

When the bill did come up in Parliament, George instructed his readers that "every Protestant in Ireland should use all his influence against the passing of the Ballot Bill. Its enactment would be a huge evil. The tide of Democracy is fast sweeping away the bulwarks of the British Constitution. The Revolutionists and Romanists have it all their own way now-a-days. We have at present to contend against overwhelming forces in the House of Commons who will bend and yield as their Dictator commands them. Meantime we must stand to our colours and endeavour to frustrate every assault of the enemy. The Conservatives of Ulster must rally together to meet the Vote by Ballot which is a revolutionary scheme, and they must urge on their representatives in the House of Commons to battle against it to the last."

§

Much had happened in Ireland while John was in America. Unfortunately, just a week after his return to Ireland in May, he caught a bad cold. As he struggled to recover, he had time to review events and write letters. "And colds these last few years are more serious troubles to me than they used to be. They render me very feeble and quite crush my little energy for the time."

For much of the summer, John settled in at home to watch local affairs as he recovered. There was much of personal interest to read in the pages of the *Telegraph*. John was feeling better by the time George sent a message to the Orangemen as the July 12th anniversary drew near.

"We have counseled the loyal Orangemen to submit to the laws of the land. That is still our earnest advice. But, at the same time, we shall never advise them to lie down–to be kicked and trodden over by their enemies. The Fenians have not been presented [prosecuted] for the processions in Dublin, in Cork, and Limerick; and we maintain that, if they have been permitted to do so with impunity, the Orangemen should not be molested in their peaceful processions on the approaching Twelfth, or, indeed, at any other time. We understand that the Orangemen intend to turn out in all their strength to assert their rights and to defy tyranny. Let the Government beware."

The Party Processions Act forbade marchers from displaying party flags or playing party music as groups moved along the public roads to their destinations. However, the law said nothing about what they could do when they arrived at rally locations. There they could still display their flags and play their music as they wished, allowing them to fully commemorate the great Protestant victories of the past. But as they celebrated, they should also take care not to offend any of their Catholic neighbours. Peace on this year's day of celebration was of particular importance as the government would be carefully watching.

The organizers of the Newry Orange celebration followed George's advice. This year, the celebration of local lodges was to be held at McGaffin's Corners in Donaghmore. One of the roads forming the intersection passed by the Harshaw house. The sound of the thumping drums would be clearly heard by Sarah and the two sons who lived there. The new editor of the *Newry Telegraph*, J. E. Finlay, sent a reporter to cover events.

Preparations had been underway for some weeks, as it seemed especially important to all the Orangemen and their supporters to make an impressive show in response to the new Party Processions legislation. Women supporters had been gathering for weeks to make sashes and rosettes, so their husbands, brothers, and lovers would make their support visible. However, even more important than these preparations was the weather. If the weather was cold and rainy, turnout would be reduced, and those who persisted in their plans would find their enthusiasm reduced.

On July 12th of 1870, the weather was everything that the Orangemen could hope for. When the participants rose early, they discovered that there was a cool breeze and bright blue sky. There would certainly be sun for the celebration, and yet the breeze would make everyone feel comfortable.

By 10 a.m., the brothers of several lodges had gathered at the Newry lodge on Downshire Road and formed up into marching order behind the Newry Protestant Band. As the Orangemen headed north along the old Dublin road, other lodges began to fall in behind the Newry contingent. After the Bessbrook and Mullaglass lodges joined their Newry brothers, the procession had grown to several hundred marchers. When everyone had joined, the line of marchers stretched out an entire mile.

When the marchers reached McGaffin's Corners, they found many local people waiting their arrival. The celebration site was on a slope, a perfect spot for the large convocation. At one side of the field a large platform had been erected to accommodate the speakers. It was almost 1:30 p.m. before the last lodge marched past the Donaghmore School that James Harshaw had worked so hard to create and arrived at the field. All in all, there were between four and five thousand marchers from thirteen lodges arrayed along the hillside with their supporters, ready for the speeches.

Around 2 p.m., the speakers climbed onto the stage. The crowd put aside their lunches and drinks to gather as close as possible to the platform to hear what inspirational speeches the leaders would provide them. The main speaker was the Rev. H. W. Lett. As he rose to speak, he was greeted with loud applause. Looking out at the large crowd, he told them he was very gratified to see that Orangeism was growing rapidly despite or perhaps because of the obstacles the government was placing before them. He regretted the government had burdened southern Catholics with the Coercion Act and were now intending to afflict the Protestants of Ulster with a new Party Processions Act. The government thought that Catholics and Orangemen would be pleased by one or the other of these bills. Rev. Lett saw these actions as "subjugating both."

To prove the growth of the Orange Party, he noted over 1,200 new members had joined local lodges in the last year. He hoped that the upcoming year would see a doubling of those numbers. Rev. Lett's speech was frequently interrupted with great cheering and applause.

When the last of the "thank you" speeches had been made, the crowd turned to enjoy the sham fight. Sham fights were held frequently in that same spot. There were several enactors, dressed in costumes appropriate to both sides. The men of William of Orange began the battle on the low ground, with King James II's troops holding the high ground. With great comic flair, the Williamite forces "fought" their way up the hill and routed their opponents.

With the field safely in control of William and his army, the participants, who had greatly enjoyed their day away from their customary hard work, formed up in their lodges and marched away. By the time the line neared Newry around 6 p.m., the Newry lodges were marching alone. They stopped at the main Orange Lodge for a good dinner, and a long evening of celebrating that lasted until early the next morning. British soldiers had been assigned to monitor events and maintain the peace had only one minor case of drunkenness that needed any intervention.

§

The Downpatrick Assizes took place a week later. One of the important items on the docket was whether or not to provide any financial compensation to farmers that had been harmed financially by a series of fires that were set in Donaghmore on the previous December 10th. The new Party Processions Act revision had made such payments possible for the first time. One of the men who had suffered loses was James Harshaw's son Andrew. The *Telegraph* reported that three farms in the area had been attacked on that same night. Andrew lost a stack of flax, and Joseph Clegg of Tullymurry had lost an out-building containing 2 heifers and a horse. A flax mill owned by John McMaster had also been set on fire. These three suspicious fires erupted at about the same time on Protestants' property leading the reporter to surmise that the perpetrators were Fenians or their supporters.

John McMaster wrote a letter of correction that appeared in the next edition of the *Telegraph.* He wanted to alert everyone that the perpetrators of his fire had nothing to do with the Fenians. In fact, the fire had resulted when one of his laborers had lit a fire in the boiling house, and then failed to properly extinguish it. The damage was very slight, and about two shillings would pay for the total damage.

The Presentment sessions hearing the complaints awarded Andrew £60 pounds for his ruined flax. Then the Court heard Joseph Clegg's presentation. He had suffered much greater damage than Andrew, losing three buildings, a barn, stable, and a byre and their contents, large quantities of grass seed, oats, harnesses, three cows, two calves, one horse, and some wheaten straw. Therefore, he was awarded greater damages, £150. A third Donaghmore farmer, Joseph Carswell, of Annaghbane lost two stacks of flax on that same fiery night. He received £75. No one was ever charged with these arson attacks.

Before farmers turned to bringing in the harvest, they gathered at the farming show organized by the Newry Union Farming Society and held in town on July 28th at the flax market. Farm shows had been more common before the famine when the Donaghmore Farming Society flourished. Sadly, this early group had ceased to exist some years before. So there was considerable interest in the new effort to give the country farmers an opportunity to show the results of their hard work. Strong support from the upper classes provided some hope that the new show would be successful and become an anticipated and important yearly event. Among those present this year were J. D. Gordon of Sheepbridge, Trevor Corry, Rev. Elliott, Hill Irvine, Meredith Chambre, and Robert Corbett of Lisnacreevy. John Martin, having finally recovered, attended as well. Fortunately, the weather was grand, so John didn't risk a relapse.

Andrew Harshaw won third prize in the best heifer in calf or in milk that was calved in 1868 for a calf named Lady Windsor. Andrew won first prize for the best heifer calved in 1869 for his short-horned heifer Cherry. He won other prizes as well, including a commendation for his Berkshire boar, The Colonel, and second for his Rouen drake and two ducks. John's brother David Martin entered a chestnut colt, which came in third place.

§

On July 19th, war had broken out between Prussia and France. John was very concerned as he had come to feel that France was a second home. Prussian forces moved quickly to defeat the French armies, capture Emperor Napoleon IV and establish a siege of Paris by September 19th.

Others in Ireland shared John's concerns. A group of these French supporters organized a meeting at the Rotunda on August 18th to form the Franco-Irish Ambulance Committee. Their goal was to raise enough money to fit out an ambulance to send to the war zone to provide humanitarian aid. John attended the meeting, reading a letter from Marshal McMahon, and then giving a speech supporting the idea. A delegation from France was on hand to encourage the Irish effort.

Two days later, the French delegation prepared to leave Dublin to return to France. From the balcony of the Shelburne Hotel, John provided farewell remarks. He concluded his comments with "Vive la France." He didn't realize these words would embroil him in another political controversy. The *Dublin Express* interpreted those words to actually mean "Up with the Irish Republic."

The *London Times* fed the controversy. John wrote a response to the *Times,* which was reprinted in some Irish papers. John told the paper that it "utterly and absurdly misinterprets" his comments. He was part of a group that had appeared on the balcony. He had actually asked those gathered in the street below to disperse so the French delegation could leave.

"Tis too much trouble you take to study my character at all. But it would save trouble to others, if you were to take care in judging me and deal only with my real words and deeds." First John took up the issue of disloyalty. He was not, contrary to the *Times* claims, telling his fellow citizens to be disloyal. He remained pledged to the Queen, but not to Parliament.

"We have made up our minds in Ireland that your policy towards us is adopted and regarded entirely from considerations of your own selfish interest and convenience. Whether you take measures to strike terror or to soothe and conciliate—whether you keep us 'in obedience' by brute force, or coax us with 'Better things' (by which you mean partial redress of some of the wrongs you have inflicted on us) we believe that you consider exclusively your own security, your own national profit, your own national reputation in Europe, your own temporary convenience.

"You refuse to let us be your equals, free as you are, owners and masters of our own country, as you are of yours. We shall never be content to be your subjects. Consider whether it is worse for you to insist in holding us subjects against our will. Alas! You talk of our hatred to you. What have we done against England? How have we shown hatred to the English? Can you specify any wrong we have ever done you? Have we pretended to rule you, to make laws for you, to tax you, to spend your taxes to disarm you, to treat you as our subjects and to revile you because you think proper to rule yourselves? Which people is it, the Irish or the English whose acts are acts of hatred to the other?"

Then John turned to the subject of the French delegation that led to the charges against him. "As to reception of French delegations. I am proud to belong to a people like the Irish, among whom the tradition of friendship is so faithfully pursued, who are so loyal in adversity, whose hearts are so deeply stirred by a generous sentiment and so little swayed by consideration of material interest. It was a purely disinterested expression of the sympathy of the Irish people for France, for the nation and not for any party of Frenchmen. If you and your countrymen cannot understand the reception in that sense, I think it is so much the worse for you and them.

"You are hopeful because you 'cannot but think that Irishmen are after all, human beings.' Try to confirm yourself in that view of the matter! Try to think that Irish men have the same national rights with Englishmen. Resign yourself and let your countrymen resign themselves to enjoy the rights of Englishmen without insisting any more upon depriving the people of Ireland of their rights. Thus you will cease to hate us, and we may commence to be your friends."

John received support from Irish papers. The *Freeman* wrote "Mr. Martin has written to the Times to correct his absurd misapprehension and though that journal devoted a lead to the honorable members letter, it characteristically omits all apology for its error."

Despite this diversion, the Irish Ambulance Committee continued working to outfit an ambulance and send health workers charged with administering aid "to the sick and wounded on the battlefield and in hospitals." All arrangements were soon completed. They successfully obtained wagons to use as ambulances, along with horses, uniforms and medical supplies.

The results of their planning were on display on October 7th in the Rotunda gardens. There were five wagons provided. "The medical volunteers were outfitted with uniforms consisting of blue flannel jackets with green facings and a red cross on the right arm. Personnel included one surgeon in chief, four assistant surgeons, thirty-two medical students and over two hundred young men of good character to assist." "Each member of the corps was given a blue woolen blouse, hat, rug, towel, goblet, plate, knife and fork and spoon, comb, satchel and prayer book."

A large crowd was on hand for the sendoff. Due to bad weather, the crossing into France was delayed, five days passing between their departure from Dublin and arrival at Havre. There they were given a grand reception before heading off to the front. Before the end of the year, the Irish ambulance had come under Prussian fire. They performed in a manner that would make their Irish sponsors proud.

§

While John had been in America, word began to circulate around Ireland that Irish nationalists were quietly discussing a new effort to acquire more rights for Ireland. John took note of what was happening in a letter he wrote to Daunt, as soon as he began to recover. He told Daunt who had already been involved in the early meetings that he had been invited to join the group.

The first major step to form an official organization to be named the Home Government Association took place in Dublin on July 21st to establish the rules needed to govern the organization. John wasn't there to participate, but he discussed the issue when he wrote to Daunt a few days later. He was quite distressed that the group was supporting the idea of a federal system with England and Scotland. John didn't think that the people of Ireland would support such an effort.

"I am afraid we repealers are permitting this committee for a time to misrepresent the real nationalist policy of the country. Many of the names upon their list of members (Yours, mine and a dozen others, I could pick out) are of men who would not consent to give the English on any pretence federalist or any other, the smallest control over our affairs. When I say, WE COULD NOT CONSENT, I mean that as individual citizens we would speak, vote, legitimately exert ourselves against any such thing; though we might loyally submit as good citizens to a federal arrangement, provided it were made by the deliberate act of the Irish legitimate authorities truly representing the national sentiment."

During the rest of the summer, additional meetings were held, but there was no great flood of either interest or membership. Press reports were generally opposed to the new effort for a variety of reasons. Parliament would never consent to have the majority Catholic Church become the new established church, something that well might happen if Irish affairs were directed by the Irish instead of England.

The *Express* reported that the members of the new group were already very divided in their goals. Some, like John, were totally opposed to English rule and wanted separation. Another group was willing to accept a limited form of self-government. A third faction would accept almost any step toward independence.

The same newspaper reported on a meeting held on the beginning of September. The editor wasn't impressed by what had taken place in the Round Room of the Rotunda. When the meeting began, the room was only half full, though the crowd size increased as the meeting proceeded. The reporter who covered the meeting saw it as another Repeal meeting with a few twists. The speakers could show nothing that an Irish Parliament could do to improve their current situation.

In fact, an Irish Parliament dominated by Catholics would be a disaster that no Protestant would likely support. Religious bigotry would sweep over the island. Jobs would be parceled out based on closeness to a Catholic priest. Then the reporter pronounced the last rites of the new Home Government Association. "It may bring out its resolutions, or occasionally shew signs of life in advertisements and circulars, but as to its influence it is dead and buried."

Still, the new group had gathered enough attention for George to offer his opinion. Not surprisingly, he wasn't in favor of the new group, though their stated goal was to unite all Irish no matter their religion. "Many who are true Irishmen at heart, anxious to promote the welfare of their native land, and ready to unite with their fellow-countrymen of different denominations in any practical project which does not involve a violation of principle, look with distrust upon a scheme which might make Ireland worse instead of better, by placing it under a new religious ascendancy."

The idea of a federal system of government was appealing to some Protestants, so the Home Government Association while preaching national unity was further dividing Protestants. Federalism wasn't a new idea, as it had been raised by Sharman Crawford a number of years earlier. There was little support for the plan then, and George anticipated only slight interest now. There might be possible benefits scattered among the drawbacks. Certainly Dublin would benefit greatly from the increased activity that was sure to result from local sessions of an Irish Parliament. This Parliament might even better understand Irish issues than the British Parliament did, railway issues for example. However, religious questions would be decided in favor of the majority. If the Catholic Church decided to move beyond the guarantee of religious equality now existing in Ireland and establish themselves as the official church in the new Parliament, what could the Protestants do?

After describing some of the various opinions expressed at the meeting, George concluded, "If Irishmen would honestly unite to promote national interests, some good might be done, but it is not very wise to shut one's eyes to the religious difficulty that is involved in the Home Government scheme."

John first appeared at a Home Government Association meeting on September 23rd. For the first time he met some men new to national activity, Dr. Shaw, and Dr. Galbraith of Trinity College among them. He also chatted with other members of the governing committee. He sat through a meeting that lasted over three hours, during which time, much of the discussion centered on organizational issues. John found the meeting "irksome." He didn't see many new members of "great and striking ability."

While John liked Isaac Butt who led the Home Government Association and found him a man of great ability, he had some serious flaws of character, which were problematic. He was notorious for his mishandling of his funds and womanizing. "He keeps himself continually in trouble and want, through his extravagance and negligence. I am very fond of the man, else I might not speak so angrily of the defects of his character."

Despite his reservations, John joined the new group, while making clear he still wished for Irish independence. "As to the question itself I am still of the opinion that the proper and desirable course for Ireland is simple repeal and subsequently such federal arrangements as our parliament, self-reformed under the influence of free Irish opinion, may consent to make. And in my mind *the less* connection of a political (or of any other) kind between our country and England the better."

The first formal meeting of the Home Government Association was held on October 6th at the group's office at 63 Grafton Street. The Lord Mayor of Dublin officiated. Despite the formal setting, the meeting was informal enough that anyone wishing to speak could speak.

John was one who took the opportunity. He had read Butt's pamphlet on a Federal system and liked what he read. In his remarks, he made clear how the new organization was different from others that he had been part of. "This movement, like all the national movements in which he had engaged in Ireland, was an attempt to unite all honest Irishmen—all patriotic men in Ireland on the only reasonable rational basis on which Irishmen could unite— that was the basis of his country (hear, hear). He believed, in order to make any movement a success, the only thing you have to do was to respect each other's differences of opinion. He gave his adhesion, formally to the Association and became a member of it, because this was a new attempt to unite nationalists of all shades in one national movement, and it was an attempt to make new converts to the doctrine and nationality. (hear, hear). Their members had thought fit to change their policy on certain matters and this change had the excellent effect of breaking down the wall of separation between the Irish people and of enabling good men, virtuous patriotic men, of a party that used to be called the Protestant Ascendency party to look their Catholic fellow-countrymen face to face, thereby bringing about a union for patriotic purposes. As a nationalist, pure and simple, he desired retaining of course, all his independent opinions and by his example to recommend it to the favorable attention of all men who were disposed to have the least confidence in his opinions. (hear, hear)."

This was the only meeting that John attended for most of the rest of the year. He had been stricken with yet another bad cold that kept him away from any public events.

Not surprisingly, George informed the people of Newry what was going on in Dublin. This new movement was apparently floundering as only twenty-seven members attended the first meeting. He noted how little agreement there was among the principal speakers. Under those conditions, a great amount of agitation would be required to generate any united interest in the group.

George believed the leaders of this group had little interest in actually creating a new movement but were really interested in obtaining well-paying jobs. "The real object will be to obtain seats in Parliament for a few, in order that they may obtain, not Federalism, but something for themselves. There have always been patriots of this stamp in Ireland, men ready to sell their country, so far as they can sell it, if they find a purchaser; but decidedly ready to sell themselves."

There was one major difference between the Home Government Association and other efforts that had been tried before. This time a group of upper class Protestants had joined. Some of these men had been moved to join the new group because of the passage of the disestablishment bill. As a result, they had come to believe that a united Irish organization was necessary to promote a unified Irish agenda. Mr. Butt had worked hard to create an organization they would embrace.

George acknowledged them. "Some of the members of the Home Government Association, though well-meaning men, influenced, we are sure, by the single desire to serve their country, are but deluded on this point. They cherish a confidence which has no solid basis and would disappoint them when the day of trial came. Federalism is an impracticable scheme, for it cannot succeed without the support of a majority of Irish members of Parliament. To obtain that the majority of electors must be Federalists. Is this to be expected, when it is admitted that the country does not desire Federalism, and requires to be converted by agitation? A federal Parliament would not succeed, unless the members were agreed; but would they agree any better than the Irish members of the Imperial Parliament? If Irish members were agreed, as Scotch members generally are in anything which concerns their country, Irish material interests would not be neglected, and there would not be a shadow of a reason for a Federal and subordinated Parliament."

Despite the presence of a number of Protestants, no consideration had been apparently taken to accommodate the feelings of the majority of Ulster Protestants. This substantial group hadn't been really heard on the church issue in the existing Parliament, and George didn't expect that the situation would change under any federal system. "It is idle to suppose that the religious battle is over. Rome will never be satisfied, unless so long as it serves her purpose, with religious equality. In the educational question which is coming on and other questions which will come on when the pear is ripe, Roman Catholic ascendancy will be aimed at. There may be liberal Roman Catholics in some other countries, but Ultramontanism rules in Ireland, and every man of ordinary foresight and common sense should grapple with it." So George informed his readers that Federalism "appears to be dying a natural death; it will never make much noise in the world."

Near the end of November, John had recovered enough to speak to a meeting of the Newry Catholic Young Men's Association in the Assembly Room of the Savings Bank. He had chosen as a subject "The Political Relations between Ireland and England." A large crowd was on hand to listen. He recounted for his audience a number of the historical events that had led to the current situation between the two countries. Many of the ideas were those that he had presented in previous speeches. However, because Parliament had passed the long-desired church disestablishment, he added an important new element this time. Even when England's intention towards the Irish were beneficent, their lack of understanding of the Irish produced a product which had negative side effects. He was hopeful that the time when Ireland was divided by religion was ending, recounting for the audience to great applause the names of Protestants who had led the fight for Irish independence, including John Mitchel.

§

As 1870 neared an end, John was experiencing changes in his personal life. The years of his guardianship of his brother Robert's children ended when Robert, the oldest of the children, reached his majority. John turned all the family responsibilities over to Robert and moved out of Kilbroney. First, he and Hentie visited with Hentie's sister and her husband, Hill Irvine, in Dromalane House in Newry. That visit gave them time to plan out where they would live next. His first thought was to build a small house at Loughorne, but Hentie didn't like that idea.

A month later they decided to rent a house in Seaview in Warrenpoint. By Christmas, they had settled into their new home. John was very happy with this change. This lovely line of homes was built on the edge of Carlingford Lough. He had but to walk across the street to get a good view of the lough with mountains on both sides. His new home wasn't far from Kilbroney, and with a railroad from the center of Warrenpoint into Newry, he had easy access to Newry and the rest of Ireland.

John was very content with his new freedom and new home, but concerned about the progress of the new organization, essentially agreeing with George's assessment. As he wrote to Daunt in a letter. "The Home Government Association, somehow does not advance. You could have pushed it forward; so probably could I. 'Tis a pity it does not move. There are really good patriots among its managers, and the whole scheme is genuinely patriotic."

John had a chance to test his improved access to transportation soon after his move to Seaview. He traveled to Dublin to preside at the dedication of a statue to Smith O'Brien and deliver the main address. There was a large crowd on hand to watch John unveil the statue at the 1 p.m. ceremony.

When John arrived, the crowd erupted with great cheering. He began by pointing out that erecting a monument to an Irish patriot was somewhat unusual. "Free peoples erect such monuments as this, and only such monuments to honor the memory of men of high talents and noble qualities, whose character and deeds gave renown to the name of their country, and who were loyal to the national cause of their country. But it has not been so in our country, because, unhappily our country is deprived of her national right of home government. The monuments which occupy the finest public places of the stately streets of Dublin are to the memory of men who have served England and won favor of England—the country to which ours is made subject. They are symbols of the haughty mastery of the English people over us, and of our servility or helplessness…It is only now that we begin to set up, in the public places of our capital, monuments to the memory of Irishmen distinguished for open and avowed patriotism—men like O'Brien, who devoted their lives to the task of redeeming Ireland from bondage, of replacing in Irish hands the scepter of national sovereignty, of restoring this ancient nation to her rightful rank among the free nations of the world—men, in short, who strove to bring the time when we shall be no more the subjects of the

English, but free men and their equals—the time when the English shall no longer make laws for us, and appoint officials over us, and consume our revenues and treat us, not as men, but as things to be used and abused at their pleasure—the happy time when we shall be free people."

John was still in Dublin when he was visited by a delegation from Meath who implored him to be their candidate for Parliament in an upcoming by-election. At first, John was not impressed. "I am bothered with PRIVATE solicitations to stand for Meath. And even if public invitations come, I hate to make a contest. So I shall offend and DISGUST enthusiastic political friends. But there is the scandal of the claims for expense in the Longford contest remaining some of them yet unsatisfied."

With the election just days away, John had little time to consider the invitation. Hentie certainly encouraged him to take this important step. Following subsequent conversations with the emissaries, he seemed somewhat more willing to enter the race. But he placed some conditions on his acceptance. The first was that they should understand that he had no money of his own to invest. And second that he demanded that the election be free of any violence, or threats, in short that the campaign would be totally free of the corruption of most Irish elections. The ambassadors readily accepted John's conditions, and again, for the second time in a year, John became a candidate for Parliament.

Once John made his agreement with the Meath electors, his involvement began quickly. John took the train to Meath from Dublin. He was met at the station with a band and many enthusiastic supporters. John was conducted through the town that had been decorated with arches that contained messages of welcome. The procession ended at the Court House where the nomination was to take place. The usual contingent of constabulary was on hand to keep order.

Patrick Brady of Navan put John into nomination. He proclaimed that he was honored to place John's name in nomination. "Some person had asked who was John Martin?–(A Voice–a patriot.) When John Mitchel was convicted and transported by a partisan judge, a perjured sheriff, and a packed jury, Mr. Martin was the man to step in and take his place. (Cheers) That man was able and willing yet, after twenty-two years, to try it again. He had the honour to propose Mr. Martin to represent this county. (Enthusiastic applause.)"

John began his speech with an apology to the voters of Meath. He had no property or background in Meath. If the voters there, found a person with local connections who really represented them well, he would step aside. Cries of "No no," spread through the crowd. However, he believed he shared the support for the national cause with the Meath voters.

This had been the case in Meath since the Monster Meeting in support of Daniel O'Connell had taken place there twenty-seven years before, attended by five times as many people as presently lived in the county. Beyond the vast reduction in the population, the people of Meath had come to understand that "nothing can serve the interests of Ireland, nothing can produce peace in Ireland, and nothing can enable this country to acquire a position of honour or safety but home government. (Cheers)"

Since John had personally lived through that time period, he explained a bit of the history for those who hadn't. "At that time the vast majority of the people of Ireland were for home government. Yet there was one important section of the Irish community that did not feel inclined to join in the national aspirations of the rest. I speak of the Protestants. I say that every honest Catholic who was a Repealer in '43 and '48 if he survives, is a Repealer to-day, and, if possible, more convinced of the value of home government, and more resolved for his part, so far as his influence can extend, never to let this country accept the position of a subject country to the English. (Cheers, and cries of 'Never.') In a country like ours, so richly endowed by God with all the means for supporting a great population in prosperity, in strength, in peace, and in safety, it is a disgrace to Irishmen if they will consent to a system which drags their country after England like a captured plundered prize at sea. We cannot bear it. (Cheers.)"

John needed to explain to the electors of Meath why he had agreed to seek to represent them in Parliament. "What I want to bring about is a state of things when Irishmen will not merely be in accord upon the questions which are fit subjects for legislation and government, but that they will take within their own hands the power to make their opinions facts, and to make their sentiments the rule and law of their own country and have the administration of that country. (Cheers.) It is for that reason I come forward, but fellow-countrymen, we never can do it in a foreign Parliament. (Cries of 'Never.') it is only in the Irish Parliament that the real opinions and the real sentiments of the Irishmen can control the legislation. It is only there that the material and moral interests of Ireland can prevail."

John concluded his appeal with emotion. "For my own part, the object of my life has been to advocate home government, to obtain self-government for Ireland by just means, and by any means that are necessary for that purpose. (Loud cheers.) But while I say that I would not shrink from the adoption of any means that might be necessary for obtaining our national right, I would deplore and I would feel the greatest reluctance myself to do any act that would cause civil strife or bloodshed for the attainment of that object. I think, in the present state of public opinion in Ireland, when the constituencies are so much enlarged that it will shortly be in the power of every constituency in Ireland to return men whose opinions accord with the electors and the people of the country upon that great question, and if you, my fellow-countrymen, elect me as representative for your noble county–(cries of 'We will')–because I am an Irish Nationalist, because I am for Repeal of the Union and home government, I think the example of your county will shortly be taken up and adopted by all the counties, and in all parts of Ireland."

Before leaving the stage, John asked that his followers show respect to his opponent. "Let me implore of you to grant me one request, and that is to hear Mr. Plunkett. (Cries of 'never,' and great confusion.) I demand fair play for my opponent. I do not want to be put in by intimidation. I shall only go in, if I go in at all, by the deliberate will of the people of Meath. (Cheers.)"

Most by-elections didn't attract attention beyond the local election district. However, this election turned out to be quite different. Not surprisingly, George wrote a long leader on the subject. George found what happened at the nomination quite unusual and he approved of what he had learned. "The nomination at Trim, on Monday, is a remarkable fact. Those assembled were almost all Roman Catholics, yet love of Ireland, mistaken though it be in the mode of carrying it out, asserted its ascendancy over love of Rome. Whatever may be the errors of the Nationalists, they are to be commended for their vindication of the rights of laymen to pursue an independent course in politics; in their determination to confine the clergy to their spiritual duties, not interfering with their rights as citizens, but not, permitting them to dictate in civil matters as if they possessed all the intelligence and all the power in the world; and in their love of country, in preference to attachment to an ecclesiastical scheme that would lord it not only over Ireland, but over the whole earth."

This election was supposed to be a walk-in for the priests' candidate, George Plunkett. John had appeared at "the eleventh hour," but it seemed that he might actually win. The local priests had promised that they would not repeat the outrageous actions from Longford that had so disturbed their Catholic parishioners. "The greatest enthusiasm was shown for Martin. A Roman Catholic priest, once popular, tried in vain to obtain a hearing. The Nationalists were orderly as well as powerful, for there was no occasion for the interference of police. When the Courthouse was entered Mr. Martin and his friends were received with 'Tremendous applause,' while the friends of Mr. Plunkett, who numbered very few, those few including several Roman Catholic clergymen, were received with 'boisterous groaning.' These are facts to which Mr. Gladstone and the Ultramontane faction would do well to take heed. The former need not suppose that by making bargains with Cardinal Cullen he will satisfy Ireland; and the latter need not imagine that any section of intelligent Irishmen will allow themselves to be made the slaves of a system that is politically and spiritually essentially tyrannical."

After a brief description of the speeches at the nomination, George returned to what he saw as the most remarkable part of this election campaign. "It is also remarkable that Mr. Martin, a stranger and a Protestant, met with such a reception in the centre of Ireland, which boasts of Tara's Hill, and is associated with old Irish royalty. The burden of his speech was home government, and few will deny that Ireland could be better governed, although there is a difference of opinion as to whether better government could be secured by a domestic Parliament, or by returning better members to the Imperial parliament. No one will call in question Mr. Martins' statement that Ireland is 'richly endowed by God with all the means of supporting a great population, in prosperity, in strength, in peace, and in safety.' But Ireland will never be well governed while statesmen make a game of politics, not studying what will promote the interests of the empire but what will best secure them office, and please their supporters. The material interests of Ireland–railways and other subjects–require attention, and yet these are neglected to throw a sop to this or that faction that happens for the time to be noisiest or most urgent. We are glad to hear from Mr. Martin that while home government is the object he aims at he 'would feel the greatest reluctance to do any act that would cause civil strife or bloodshed for the attainment of that object.' The greater part of the strife which is exerted in the country is produced by men who are not nationalists, but faction-mongers of different kind."

After the speeches, the electors were called upon to indicate their preference by a show of hands. George described what happened: "Mr. Martin had the show of hands in his favour, one report stating that 'a forest of hands were raised, many holding sticks or green leaves.' while only a few hands, including those of several Priests, were raised for Mr. Plunkett, 'amid tremendous booing and uproar.'" This led George to predict John would win, expecting the result to be a rebuff to Gladstone, that it would teach them that "nationalism still lives and is powerful."

The nomination for Parliament had taken place on Monday, January 2nd. Voting was set for Thursday. This didn't leave much time for John to campaign against a candidate who had been working hard in the district for weeks. While John intended to run a totally honest campaign, Plunkett intended to use all the campaign tricks usually employed to win elections, including threats and intimidation.

Plunkett looked to Dublin to find a mob of ruffians who were eager to make the trip into Meath during the campaign to threaten and beat John's supporters, something they would find enjoyable by itself. But they would also be paid, and offered whiskey and food in the bargain. So early in the morning, a group of about two hundred men arrived at the Broadstone Terminus to catch the 6 a.m. train to Meath.

The conductor wasn't pleased to see the kind of men he would have to deal with, so he attempted to persuade them to get off the train. As they were greatly looking forward to the anticipated fun, they refused. They assembled together in the last car of the train and refused to budge. When persuasion didn't work, the conductor executed a different plan. He moved about the car motioning riders not associated with the bludgeon men to move out of the car. In short order, only members of the Dublin mob were sitting in the rear car. With that accomplished, the conductor gave the signal for the train to move out of the station. The door to the car was closed, and the whistle in the engine announced the departure of the train. However, the last car didn't move. The conductor had disconnected the car from the rest of the train. Plunkett's muscle never left Dublin, ensuring that John's supporters remained unintimidated and undamaged.

Meanwhile, John set to work to meet the men of Meath in an attempt to catch up with his opponent. After the nomination at Trim, John spoke from a window in town to energize his supporters. Then he moved on to Navan to repeat his speech. On Tuesday, he traveled to Oldcastle and Kells. On Wednesday, he returned to Navan and spoke from a platform that had been erected there. On Thursday, his supporters were on hand as the polls opened, parading about the streets with banners containing advice, "Men of Meath do your duty." They intercepted all newcomers asking their political preference, cheering the Martin supporters and hooting at those supporting Plunkett. Most of the men coming into town seemed to be for Martin, or at least saw the wisdom of saying they were.

On the day of voting, John was still out working, making a trip in the bitter cold to Dulech and then back to Navan for the close of the polls. John wrote that he "was preserved from being crushed into jelly by the guardian arms of several very muscular Meathmen."

The government had assumed that there would be outbreaks of violence as the election results were announced. So a large force had been sent to Navan for the announcement. Three British units were on hand, the 17th Lancers, supplemented by the 70th, and a company of the 40th Foot. One hundred and twenty constables were on hand along with three resident magistrates. Any kind of violence could immediately be quelled.

When the polls closed, the books were turned over to the High Sheriff, who announced the results. John did particularly well in Navan and Trim. The only town that Plunkett carried was Dunshaughlin, his home area. Still John won handily. His total vote was 1,128 to Plunkett's 642, for a margin of 486. John Martin would be a member of Parliament.

With the results officially declared, John addressed his ecstatic supporters. He called the results, "The proudest position occupied by any public man in Ireland. (Cheers)." Then he made clear that he understood the unique and important achievement they had accomplished. "Such a victory, such a triumph as they had gained; the means by which it had been gained, and the circumstances under which it had been accomplished, were unexampled in Ireland for the last thirty years." Volunteers had honorably accomplished the election.

There was something else that made the election notable. "He was a Protestant, and a Catholic people had chosen him for their representative. He had no high rank, wealth, or conspicuous talents and accomplishments to recommend him, yet he had been invited by the people to represent them in Parliament. Among the many circumstances peculiar to that election there was one that he might mention; he had not asked one elector of Meath for his vote, and that the men who voted for him had done so of their own free choice. They knew that they could make no money by him; they knew from his political antecedents that he could not obtain a favour for them from the English Minister, who held the purse of Ireland, and disposed of her places of honour and emolument; they knew that they were performing an act of the highest self-abnegation by electing him."

John recognized the significance of the vote that the stalwart men of Meath had taken. He wished to make sure that they would understand and glory in their achievement. "All the newspapers of Dublin–he might say of Ireland–had referred to this triumph and had declared it to be one of the most significant events that had occurred in this country. The people of Meath had commissioned him to say in their name that they were not content to be at the feet of the people of England." He hoped that this election would promote unity across the spectrum of Irish political leaders.

John's desire that Meath voters savor their great accomplishment was one he allowed himself as well. "It is a wonderful wonder, this vote." John was the first supporter of the Home Government Association to win election to Parliament.

John was also right when he told his supporters that many newspapers would acknowledge the importance of this election. One of the papers to comment was the *Newry Telegraph*. George saw John's election as the lesser of two evils. It had destroyed the widely held myth that Catholics would never vote for a Protestant. "A majority of Roman Catholic electors opposed the priests, and their measures, snapped asunder old family ties, and elected an honest Northern Presbyterian, simply because, according to their views, he was best calculated to promote the interests of Ireland."

Many factors seemed to be against John's election beyond the religious affiliation of the voters, and the power of the Catholic Church. He had entered the campaign very late and insisted the election must be a totally honest one. Most newspapers had argued against him, declaring that his quest was hopeless. As George put it. "They could not even be ordinarily civil when discussing his claims. He was represented to be engaged in a hopeless contest. Yet he has succeeded, although no unfair means were had recourse to gain a victory. The election was conducted in exemplary peace."

George concluded his leader with praise for his old friend. "On the whole, we rejoice that Mr. John Martin has been returned for Meath. We are not Repealers, but we love our country, and we feel proud that the electors of Meath have been brave enough and strong enough to oppose and defeat a faction who prefer the interests of an ecclesiastical corporation to those of Ireland, and to defeat, at the same time, the servile tools of that faction–the Gladstone Government."

The news of the Meath results quickly reached John Mitchel in Brooklyn, and he wrote his opinion in his *Irish Citizen*. He thought that it would greatly benefit both English parties to have to face the honest man that they had dishonestly convicted and exiled. John responded with a message to Mitchel. "Were I with you now, I could, while the scenes of the contest are fresh on my memory, make you all laugh till your sides ached. Many things there were too, to make one cry with sympathy and admiration for the nobleness of soul and self-forgetting enthusiasm of our dear people." In a second letter, John made sure Mitchel understood how he felt. "It is all a little wearisome and creative of anxiety; for how I may succeed in making good use of this wonderful popular victory…I really ought to feel very proud; for such a victory, in such circumstances, and by such means, perhaps no other man in Ireland at present could have gained. But my pride is troubled by the responsibility."

Many newspapers around Ireland commented on the election as well. The *Drogheda Argus* editor wrote: "Throughout Ireland there is admiration and wonder at the glorious triumph won for Ireland. Wherever a Meathman breathes, whether at home, or in far America or Australia, there is that in what was accomplished on Thursday that will send the blood bounding through the veins to hear it, while his Irish heart beats faster and will make him proud to say he belongs to the premier county…This was no petty victory for a creed or party. It was one for all Ireland, one in which Irishmen of hitherto divided ranks happily combined on the common cause of country…not since O'Connell's return for Clare has a victory like this one been achieved so momentous in its effect. It will do for Home Rule what Clare did for emancipation."

The *Newry Reporter* also contained a glowing leader. "We are not aware of any election in Ireland for a long time the results of which will give more satisfaction. John Martin's name is synonymous of all that is honest in principle, and self-sacrificing in patriotism. There lives not to-day a more disinterested politician. He has lived, struggled and suffered for what he regarded rightly or wrongly, as the cause of Ireland. Others might trim and tamper and nicely adjust their 'patriotism' to suit ulterior and selfish ends, but John Martin never. Singular in purpose, he could be bold and direct, but nothing else. The innate nobility of his nature and the purity of his motives have long made him conspicuous, but the honor was reserved for the men of Meath to thus signally mark their appreciation of his consistency and worth."

John had suddenly become the most powerful nationalist leader in Ireland.

In 1866, John Martin met his friends John Mitchel and Father John Kenyon in Paris. They had formed their friendship opposing British rule of Ireland in the Young Ireland movement. Father Kenyon was so strongly against British rule of Ireland he was silenced by the church. This was the last meeting of the three before Kenyon died.

Chapter 18

The Lion's Den

1871

Supporters of winning candidates for Parliament frequently held banquets allowing them to gather together to savor their victories. Because of the importance, both symbolic and real, of the Meath election, John's supporters held just such a celebration at the Ancient Concert Rooms in Dublin in early February. The chairman of the event was William Shaw, MP for Bandon, and a Home Government Association leader. John sat between Shaw and his good friend Daunt. Other prominent leaders, both Catholic and Protestant sat at the head table.

After a sumptuous feast, the formal part of the celebration began as usual with a toast to the Queen. Next J. B. Murtagh drank to John's health, mentioning that John "was a native of the County of Down, a Presbyterian from the Black North, and a good Irishman."

John rose to give his speech of thanks to enthusiastic applause. It was a moment that he never could have imagined during the dreary days of exile in Bothwell and Paris. It was a moment he could not have foreseen when his Irish National League had ended in a barrage of rotten eggs. "I am proud of the almost unexampled honour done me by the noble people of Meath. I am proud of this demonstration of esteem from this great company of gentlemen, lately divided into contending parties, now all united in the one party of Ireland. (hear, hear). I love the favour and praise of my fellow-countrymen, though, looking back over the twenty-six years of my political life, I may truly say that I never uttered a statement nor did an act for the purpose of gaining popular favor and applause. But in my joy and triumph I am troubled by a bitter reflection – the something of bitterness…a rising up of strong pain in the very blooming of one's joy. This is my bitter reflection: that such popularity as mine, such respect and confidence freely bestowed by the general population of our country, is not enjoyed, is not earned by scarcely an individual of the highest class of Irish society." "Ah! How gladly, how loyally, our people would follow and honour such peers." John attributed this unnatural situation to English actions.

Next John spoke of the analysis of his election that had appeared in many newspapers. "I have been spoken of in some Irish papers as sort of Conservative–in others as a sort of Liberal. (laughter) Other editors had accused him of changing positions "from physical-force revolutionist" to seeking independence by "moral suasion."

However, John claimed not to have changed at all, and explained the Liberal vs. Conservative controversy. "In the true sense of...the words, it seems to me that I ever and always have been entirely a Liberal, and also entirely a conservative. (laughter) I would have all men equal before the law. I would have all men to enjoy the same civic franchises and rights as myself. I would have government based on the free consent of the governed. I would have religion and opinion free. I would not tyranise over men's consciences, nor deprive them of their civil rights – neither to do them harm nor to do them good. I suppose that is true liberalism. On the other hand, were I a citizen of a country possessing institutions established by the deliberate free will of the nation, I would reverently cherish those institutions – I would loyally defend them from violation – I would preserve, with the respect due to the memory of my fathers, whatever they had established and preserved for the public good." If different times required new changes, he would change them "with a tender hand." "Change for the love of change, I dislike and shrink from. I suppose then I am a genuine Conservative. (applause)"

George summed up the rest of John's speech. "He declared that there was not a man more sincerely anxious and desirous of adhering to a strictly peaceful course than he was. In 1848, notwithstanding his intense repugnance to bloodshed and civil war, he did expect a rebellion, and expected it not only with resignation, but with a feeling that it would be his duty, if it should break out, to take part in it with the people. The circumstances of Ireland at the time were such as seemed to him not only to justify but to command a loyal citizen to join in rebellion if his country determined on it. Having referred to the famine years, he said the condition of Ireland was so desperate at the time that it might well tempt parties to resort to desperate cures for a remedy. He thought his country was going to fight for its life, and he was resolved to take his part. (Cheers)"

The people of Ireland were in no position to revolt at that time. They were without weapons or food. "They did not dare the desperate venture of the contest with England, and England had the glory of triumphing very easily over her disarmed and half-starved subjects." But the situation in Ireland had changed. Since his return to Ireland from exile, he had "discouraged secret conspiracy and insurrectionary schemes, and had encouraged the union of all parties and nationalists upon a basis honourable to all–that of home government." Again he was silenced by enthusiastic cries of "hear, hear."

Next John explained his plans as a member of Parliament. First, he intended to encourage local Home Rule groups across the country. This would help create a union of nationalists. If this actually happened, he felt that Home Government would soon be strong enough across the whole country to control local governments. Furthermore, he would not vote for legislation that would help the government. He believed that only the action of the Fenians had propelled Gladstone to pass two laws, disestablishment and landlord and tenant reforms, to reduce some of the divisions that had split Ireland. These new laws, if carefully, and fairly carried out for a few years, would help persuade England to grant Ireland Home Rule without any disruption of Irish "social order," and "without becoming bad neighbours to the English."

John concluded with a heartfelt wish. "May all here to-night live to see the triumph of our national cause. (Loud applause)"

Everyone reveled in the happy memories of John's grand victory, celebrating until the early hours of the next day.

Surprisingly, George found the Dublin event impressive. Men of very different political beliefs sat down together in peace. John's speech generally supported unity as well. As to John being both liberal and conservative, George felt John was actually a fellow conservative. "From the explanation that he gives it appears, however, that he would be a Conservative if the institutions of the country were to his liking. He dislikes change for the love of change. He wishes to obtain for Ireland self-government by the united action of Irishmen of all classes and creeds, but he would obtain it 'if possible,' peacefully and without revolution. The words, 'if possible' diminish the value of the declaration. They show that the movement for home government might, in certain contingencies, lead to civil war."

But George strongly objected to John's statement that most constituencies favored home government. "Mr. Martin cannot be correct with respect to the constituencies of Ulster. They are patriotic in the right sense of the term; they would oppose Ultramontanism, but they will not prefer Nationalists to Protestants and Conservatives. As to the constituencies in the other provinces, they must be restrained by some tyrannical influences [priests] if they want Nationalists, and will not elect them."

§

Sir William Verner, whom Jenny Mitchel believed to be her grandfather, died at the beginning of February. This was the second great loss to Orange Protestants, which was followed in quick succession by the deaths of the Presbyterian stalwarts, Rev. Henry Cooke and Dr. Thomas Drew. On this sad occasion, the head of the Orange Order addressed a message to the members. It claimed that in time, the members of the Catholic Church will use their new freedom in Ireland to become Protestants. Then he supported this point of view with a mention of the recent election in Meath. "Union to promote the best interests of our common country is an object worthy of being sought. We should welcome, in this direction, any effort to throw off the influence of an Ultramontane priesthood on the part of our fellow-countrymen. It was for this reason we rejoiced when Mr. John Martin was returned for Meath. Irishmen should unite so far as is practicable. There is nothing to prevent Irishmen of different religions from uniting to promote the greatly neglected material interests of Ireland. But care should be taken lest in religious matters the Protestant minority be swamped by the Roman Catholic majority. There should be no union to promote Roman Catholic ascendancy."

Soon after the dinner, with the glorious event still on members' minds, the Home Government Association met in Dublin. Professor Galbraith, John's new Protestant friend, was still thinking of the dinner. With John in attendance he remarked, "Passing from that they remembered an occasion, not many hours past, when a numerous and brilliant assembly met to celebrate a great triumph of the National Cause in the County of Meath by the return to Parliament of Mr. John Martin, one of the honestest men within the four corners of the globe."

John returned home to Seaview on February 9th. "Then, I confess, I greatly enjoyed the triumph which my heart and conscience told me I had won by no unworthy thought, word or deed; and I loved to ruminate upon the beautiful and noble character of the Irish Catholic peasantry, my patrons. So I had frequent fits of luxurious laziness which my wife helped me just to enjoy."

A week later, he wrote a letter to Daunt. He recounted a chance meeting he had had with Galbraith on a street in Dublin. He told Daunt that he "liked the man well." However, he still had concerns about the potential problems that lay ahead for the association. He wasn't sure that it would be possible to imbue the organization "with the simple national spirit of the people."

Like other repealers, John and Daunt had compromised their preferred goals and affiliated themselves with supporters of a federal system. For his part, John would happily support a federal system designed by the Irish. But he was very doubtful about one tailored to obtain approval by the British Parliament. He also worried that the Butt and his most ideological supporters might force all members of the Association to submit to his interpretation of Federalism.

"No doubt the most subservient federal arrangement giving even so little relief from the tight grip of England upon our internal affairs – giving for example, merely the right to do our private bill business ourselves, and at home would be an improvement upon the Union. And if the English make any such relocations of our chains, give us any such bits of comparative liberty, we shall feel the better for them and be gratified – though not grateful. But we – the Irish people–cannot admit for a moment that we want or seek anything less than freedom and independence. We want and seek and intend to be equal to the English – aye, should we wait and suffer seven more centuries before we succeed."

There was one thought that kept John connected to the new group. "Perhaps I am not hopeful enough of the Association and its federalists. One should remember that many of these men are but recent converts to nationality and that their own examination and study of the whole question will probably educate them into thorough nationalists like ourselves. And a split in the association, or even the raising of a controversy among the members upon the questions which seems to me to lie between us and them, might tend to drive their minds back into the ways of their old prejudices."

Parliament had been in session since February 9th. Before John made his first trip to London after his election, he made a two day visit to Meath to talk to his constituents. Then he went home to Seaview until Wednesday March 1st when he and Hentie took passage from Warrenpoint to Liverpool. It was more convenient and cheaper than making the trip from Dublin. From there, they took a train to London. Once established in London, he entered Westminster as a member for the first time.

As a new member, John's background was of interest to many people. The editor of the "Heraldic and Biographical" records of the House of Commons had already written to enquire as to what coat of arms he was entitled to claim. John responded "I carry no arms! This is a proclaimed district."

On Wednesday, March 8th, John walked into the House of Commons, accompanied by John Maguire, MP from Cork City and Algernon Greville, MP from Westmeath, who introduced him to the members. John was given the oath by the Parliamentary secretary at the desk in the center of the room and then held a long conversation with the Speaker. John chose a seat on the opposition side, beyond the crosswalk under the Peers Gallery, far away from the Whig and Conservative leaders. His seat made his independent status clear. He would support neither the Whigs nor their Conservative opposition.

A few days later, John wrote Daunt recounting his experiences. "You will wonder how I get on in this strange place. I am here now for a week. I dislike it miserably. I see hardly anything to be done by a man of my sentiments in this House. And I wonder how patriotic and nationalist Irishmen can endure to attend it…as members. I think my proposed policy of such Irish members agreeing to stay away ought to harmonise with the feelings of all Irishmen here that are Irishman in heart and aspirations."

Despite his misgivings, John had little to complain about relative to his interactions with other members. "People are quite civil to me. A good many English members – mostly radicals, I think – have got themselves introduced to me. If I had half a dozen colleagues of my own mind or even one like the late G. H. Moore, [MP for Mayo who had died the previous year] – something good might be done."

§

Every March, elections took place in every Poor Law district to select a Guardian to take office the first day of April. This year John Harshaw was one of the candidates for the district of Ouley. He was opposed by a neighbor, Archibald Murdock. Among the townlands in this district were several that were owned by Lord Kilmorey and managed by a board of Trustees. The Trustees decided to take action to ensure that Harshaw would not win. They dispatched "Bailiffs and Runners" to all of their property to instruct voters that they must support Murdock. Harshaw was deemed "too Liberal."

Their efforts were successful. Harshaw lost. But John, rather like his father, refused to be silent after the injustice that he had suffered. He made his feelings quite clear in a letter he wrote to the *Telegraph*. "I would have gone in to [the Guardians] to act solely and entirely for the benefit of the ratepayers…against Toryism, Liberalism, Whiggery, landlordism, union rating etc. My defeat, if it can be called such is entirely to be attributed to landlord interference." In fact, John was surprised that the election had been so close.

"In the middle of the 19th century, in the face of the new Land Act, in these days of enlightenment and progress, I consider such conduct on the part of magistrates and *ex-officio* Guardians to be scandalous. Such doings are fit only for the 10th or 11th century. By their conduct, they don't consider the tenants capable of choosing their own Guardians. Talk not about civil liberty in the Ouley Division."

There were four divisions that were free to vote as they wished. All four of them voted strongly for him. "It is said by all parties if there had been no interference with the people five-sixths of the division would have voted for me." "Between Mr. Murdock and me, who are old friends, there is no controversy whatever, but to be defeated by such means is, in my estimation, a great honour."

§

Late on Tuesday evening May 16th, John rose to give his first speech in Parliament on a subject of great interest to his constituents, the new proposed Coercion Law that applied to Meath. Since he sat at one end of the chamber, Liberal and Conservative members had to crane their heads to watch him as he spoke. They seemed greatly interested to see this new member, who had carried off an extraordinary election victory.

John was very nervous. The sheer size and grandeur of the room, its soaring walls, heavily paneled with dark wood, made this historic space much more intimidating than any venue in which he had previously spoken. His words needed to project to the furthest corner. Fortunately, John possessed a voice that carried well so was easily audible to the members and contained a pleasing touch of Irish accent. While under the rules, members had to speak without notes, John had thought deeply about the issues he was addressing for a long time. He was hopeful that members would listen.

Everyone in the House, certainly including John, recognized that nothing John said would hinder the easy passage of the proposed bill. But John intended to educate the English as to what most Irish citizens thought. He would speak to the legislation, but he didn't intend to vote on the bill, for or against.

John didn't mince words. "Behold, sir, that it is the inalienable right of the Irish people to be bound only by the laws made by the Queen and Parliament of their own country. The Parliament of this kingdom took away the Parliament of my country, and it is true that for the last seventy years they have usurped the Government of my country, and that the people of Ireland, her Majesty's Irish subjects, yielding to superior force, have submitted to that usurpation, and have been ruled by the will of her Majesty's English subjects; but, sir, the Irish people and the Irish nation have never consented to that usurpation, and the right of Ireland to have a free Parliament of its own and a different Government from this country is as valid a principle of law in the present day as it was in 1783, when the English Parliament solemnly declared that right to be established and asserted forever." Many of the Irish members and some of the liberal English ones, interrupted with applause.

Then John turned to the legislation being debated. "This Bill being introduced by the Government, with the object of putting the people of Ireland under a new Coercion Bill–this Bill, being in fact, a new Coercion Bill, would be sure to have the support of a great majority of members on both sides of the House…when the question was to cast a new insult on the people of Ireland, they all with open handed liberality would bestow upon the Minister any power that in the very wantonness of despotism he might ask. (Hear, hear)

"It is very painful to be speaking my sentiments in this House, and I am thankful for the courtesy with which the House has listened to me so far. (Hear, hear) I will not trouble it long. I find, however, that the English feeling as represented in this Parliament still regards the people of my country as their Irish enemy. (no, no) A part of the Queen's subjects has, I contend, been ruled by exceptional legislation in every sense. Even when the measures have been what are called concessions to the Irish people, they were exceptional in this sense, that whereas the measures passed for England are always such as the wish of the majority of the English people demands, the measures passed for Ireland, are generally opposed to the opinions and desires of the majority of the people of that country. Therefore, I say that the language used in this debate and the tone of the English Press prove that I am not mistaken in this sad conclusion I have come to–that this nation still looks upon the Irish people as their Irish enemy." One member commented, "Very fine."

Then John gave his reasons for opposing the bill. "I think that the reasons against this Bill are, first and chief, and therefore sufficient if no other could be found–that it is an unjust law; next, that it is founded on false and treacherous allegations; then that it will not remove the causes of discontent and discord–that it will cause trouble and loss to innocent persons, and will thereby increase disaffection; and finally, that the true method in dealing with disorder–and I yielded to no man in declaring that order should be maintained–(hear, hear)–I say that the true method is not to suspend the Habeas Corpus, but to suspend the system of illegalities with which this Parliament and this Government rule my country."

The frequency and titles of coercion bills enacted by Parliament indicated that Ireland was more violent and lawless than England, "that the peace is more difficult to preserve in my country than in this. Now the fact is this, as is proved, that life is less insecure in my country than in England. (A laugh, and hear, hear) Yes, that crimes are both fewer in number and less atrocious morally than they are in England, and that it is quite as easy to preserve the peace in Ireland as it is in England, provided that the same measures be employed in both countries. I say that this Bill will not remove the causes of discontent and disorder. (Hear, hear)"

In Ireland, there were "particular reasons" for discontent, that differed from the causes of unrest that prevailed in many other countries, England included. These "reasons" explained why Irish citizens had violated the laws that England passed for them. England was pushing this new bill because they had failed to understand these "particular reasons." They had taken raw data for Westmeath on crime without doing any proper analysis.

John proceeded to provide that analysis, comparing Westmeath in Ireland and Chester county in England. In Westmeath, there had been 115 instances of "crimes and outrages" in a 14-month period. Out of this number 101 were threatening notices or intimidations. In total, there had been only three murders, and four attempted murders. During the same period of time, there had been 50 murders in Chester, allowing for the difference in population, that was a rate three times that of Westmeath. However, no one ever thought of applying a Coercion Law that suspended habeas corpus rights to any English country.

Next John took up another supposed justification for a new coercion law, problems bringing Irish criminals to justice. John refuted that claim with another comparison with England. During the last ten years, there had been 2,497 murders in England. Of these, only 237 murderers had been found and convicted, a conviction rate of one in ten, as John pointed out to the MPs who were still listening attentively to his speech. "If, then, the suspension of the Habeas Corpus is the proper means to employ for the detection of crime in Ireland, it seems to me that it might be employed with some advantage in England. (Hear, and laughter)"

The English government would never think of applying this remedy in England except in the case of a foreign war or enemy invasion. In Ireland, citizens had combined under different names for generations "ever since England had obtained possession of all the Irish territory in planting themselves on the soil of the country and had tried to exterminate the Irish population. Such combinations were natural under such circumstances, because the people felt that they were put outside the law, and they combined together for their protection."

So what should be done to solve the perceived problem? "I say that the proper way to detect and suppress the disorder in the County Westmeath is to cease for a time the present system of jury panels. Suspend your Disarming Act, and allow the population of that county to disarm themselves, (Hear, and laughter) allow the population of all Ireland, whom you call with bitter irony your fellow-subjects, to form themselves into Volunteer companies, and put under their charge the preservation of peace within their own hands."

The very notion of allowing the Irish to possess guns, which would allow them some protection of their own was laughable. The English government much preferred to have elements of the British Army maintaining, as best they could, the peace of Ireland. The suggestion produced a great stir throughout the Commons.

With time for this sitting running out, John had to conclude his remarks. "This Parliament, and the English Government have been ruling my country against law and in violation of the principle of the constitution for seventy years, and you are endeavouring now, by measures of conciliation to reconcile the people of Ireland to be your subjects. I and my countrymen are content to be subjects of the Queen, but not of the English nation; and the sooner the people of England make up their minds to look at the matter from that point of view the better it will be for them. The Irish are willing to be your friends and good neighbours, but they will not consent to be subject to you, and that is what they are to-day, subject not to the Queen but to England. It may seem to many members of this House the dream of an enthusiast, but I believe before very long that truth will be shouted into your ears by the people of Ireland as represented by your permission in this Parliament. If the English rule were to last seven hundred years longer I believe the Irish will keep up their love of freedom and their resolute adherence to their national rights."

George must have found it strange to be following the first speech in Parliament of a person whom he had known since they had met as young school boys. Certainly their paths had greatly diverged since those early years. Yet some of their early friendship showed through in the first words of George's leader on the speech. "Mr. John Martin, Member for Meath, cannot complain that he did not obtain a fair hearing in the Imperial Parliament. His gentlemanly bearing, his earnest, and impressive manner, and the conviction that, with all his errors, he is an honest politician, may be in his favour; but if Englishmen be such enemies to Ireland as he represents them to be, all these would not have secured him the patient and polite attention which he received."

Then George went on to attack every argument that John had offered. John had no right to speak for Ireland. Certainly control by the English government wasn't a usurpation. Indeed, George took that argument further than most Irish leaders would go. "We will not agree with him that the English Government is a usurpation. An Irish Parliament was a party to the Union, and Ireland as much governs England and Scotland as they govern Ireland."

George vehemently denied the majority of Irishmen were repealers. He didn't see any sense in the comparisons that John had made between the crime problems in Ireland and England. Putting guns in the hands of the people of Westmeath was not to be thought of.

Summing up his feelings, George maintained that the Protestants, not the Catholics of Westmeath and Meath, were harmed by the actions of Parliament. "Irish Protestants, remarkable for their loyalty, and attachment to British connection, have the greatest reason to complain. They and not the petty and pampered, though ungrateful, Roman Catholics, require better government, and they will yet obtain it, when Mr. Gladstone's reign, which promises to be short-lived, is over."

When Parliament convened on Friday May 19th, John rose at his seat to be recognized. "Mr. Speaker, I was interrupted in my remarks on the first day we were discussing this Bill by the rules of the House. I now wish to say a few words in addition to what I have already addressed to you. I shall try not to be long or to weary the House, but as one of the representatives of Meath County, I feel bound to make some remarks in respect of certain imputations cast upon the Sheriff and Sub-Sheriff of Meath, by Mr. Seed, the Crown Solicitor, and one of the witnesses relied upon, I believe, principally by the gentlemen who have introduced this measure called a Bill for the Protection of Life and Property in certain parts of Ireland."

John understood that the attack on the Meath officials had resulted from the Crown Solicitor's objection to how a jury panel in Meath had been selected. He proceeded to explain to the English members in detail just how that jury list had been selected and how it did conform to English laws. It was the responsibility of police to bring charges when they had suspects in a crime. Until they did their duty, there was nothing for a jury to be seated for.

There was another issue that was of great concern to John, the power the bill gave to suppress the press. "I admit that experience shows that the conduct of the Lord Lieutenant and of the Chief Secretary for Ireland has been temperate, considerate, and anything but cruel, because since August it has been in their power to ruin any Irish National journal at their pleasure if they found them writing anything of which they disapproved, and yet I have the pleasure of being able to state that they have not yet ruined any journalists in Ireland, though I cannot doubt the sentiments contained in the Irish National journals are very displeasing to them. The noble lord, in moving the second reading of the Bill, remarked that he thought the Irish National journals have been free enough, and perhaps he meant it. Notwithstanding that, the sword of Damocles is hanging over the head of each of the Irish National journalists who has still the courage to give utterance to his sentiments, but I do not like and I cannot reconcile myself to that state of things. I do not like that any Irish journalist, any more than an English journalist, should have to write his political sentiments under sufferance. I would wish every journalist in Ireland, whether advocating English or Irish interests to be free of the law, and to fear no man's displeasure. (Hear, hear)"

Before he yielded the floor, he argued that areas of comparative peace would be very negatively affected by the new Bill. John believed that current law could deal with any problems that had been raised to justify the new law. "I shall not further weary the House, but before I sit down I will say that there is a vast deal more that I should like to say upon this question, but I am aware that there is a moral as well as an intellectual gulf between me as a mere Irishman, expressing the sentiments of a vast majority of the people of Ireland, and those of the two countries." John was applauded as he resumed his seat. With John abstaining, the second reading of the bill passed by a vote of 293 to 11.

George wrote another editorial after John gave the second part of his speech though he proclaimed that there was nothing new in it to discuss. Instead he moved on to some of his favorite thoughts. Crime in Ribbon districts was different from that in England. Their ever-present threats made it impossible for any convictions to be obtained. "There may be a great gulf existing between England and Fenians, Ribbonmen, and Repealers, but there is no such gulf between it and Ireland generally, the small minority is a proof of this statement. The true friends of Ireland, who are also on good terms with

England, are the men who wish to suppress Ribbonism and all disturbing causes, and to remove all obstacles to Ireland's real prosperity."

George wasn't the only editor to include a review of John's first speech in Parliament, as he was famous across Great Britain. The *Nation,* reported, "The splendid speech he has just delivered is a weighty blow to the coercionists and to the whole system of fraud, hypocrisy and injustice on which they are proceeding while on the hearts of the Irish people its effect is most inspiring. It rings like a clarion note through this island, bidding the people be of cheer and summoning them to patriotic action. To that summons the country will make answer, and we have no doubt that renewed and vigorous action on behalf of the national causes throughout the length and breadth of Ireland will result from the fearless and able assault upon the enemies made by Mr. Martin in the House of Commons."

Newspapers in England reported on the event as well. The *Examiner* had surprising comments for its readers. "The interest expected in the House of Commons by the speech of Mr. Martin on the Westmeath bill was justified by the high character of the speaker as well as by the calm force of his statement. However mistaken Mr. Martin may be no one can doubt the purity of his motives. He is a most sincere patriot, and stands almost alone among Presbyterians as a champion of Irish nationalism…He is sent there not to vote but to protest, not to argue about Westmeath Bill but about the right of England to govern Ireland. He stated his case with the clearness and force arising from long meditation on the subject and profound convictions. He would revert to an Irish Parliament not constituted as it was in 1800, but a truly representative Parliament. He wishes Ireland to govern herself, subject to the nominal supremacy of the crown."

The *Globe* was impressed as well "There was something striking in the appearance of this ancient repealer, with his finely shaped head and intelligent face, standing up and warning the House of Commons that before long the agitation for the Repeal of the Union would be renewed more vigorously than ever. His voice too is pleasant to listen to and his manner is full of expression and earnestness."

As the coercion bill continued through committee, John tried again to warn the members that this bill would only have negative effects. On May 26th, he spoke again, responding to Prime Minister Gladstone's personal attack. "The hon. Member for Meath (Mr. John Martin) has come among us with certain stereotyped opinions which I venture to call antiquated for they are the inheritance of former people – they are the growth of circumstances that have passed away."

Gladstone charged John with a failure to exhibit "that flexibility of mind which would enable him to appreciate the full force of the efforts and…the sacrifice the British parliament has made for the sake of carrying the spirit of peace into Ireland and growing strength and unity to the Empire." "I tell the hon. Member for Meath we are not afraid to compete with him for the future confidence of Ireland. It is impossible that acts of justice and goodwill should not bear fruits. If we lose faith in human nature, we lose faith in all that enables us to meet adversity, or makes national prosperity worth having. We acted on the dearest principles of life and action when we professed our confidence in the people of Ireland, and when we ventured, even in these early days, to say we constantly received the most gratifying testimony of the effect that is being produced – in the minds and hearts of the people, by the recent Acts of the British Parliament."

John immediately rose to respond. He reminded Gladstone that Ireland had never asked England to manage its affairs, or to create laws very different from those enacted for Scotland or England. "The right hon. Gentleman (Mr. Gladstone) had seemed to challenge him as to the reception that would be given by the people of Ireland to his 'antiquated policies,' as he was pleased to term it. He was willing to accept the challenge of the right hon. Gentleman upon fair conditions. (Gladstone smiled.)"

"The right hon. Gentleman laughed – he hoped he would not sneer."

Gladstone apologized. "I beg the hon. Gentleman's pardon, I did not laugh at him, a smile is not a sneer."

John accepted the challenge to a competition on their different visions of the needs of Ireland under certain conditions. Gladstone should "suspend for one year the system of illegality by which Ireland was governed – the jury packing system, which had been the rule in all political trials so long as he had been able to observe public affairs in that country; let the rights of the constitution, as they existed in England and Scotland, be restored to Ireland; let the people of Ireland be entitled to have arms, to learn to use them, to form themselves into volunteer companies; let them have a free press; let that system be tried for 1 year, and it will be seen whether the policy of this measure was a wise and patriotic one to pursue, and whether, on the other hand, the confidence he felt in the ineradicable love of freedom of his countrymen would not turn out to be correct."

Before ending his response, John returned to one of the most galling aspects of the Bill. It allowed the Lord Lieutenant to seize any member of the press he deemed a threat and to hold them without trial for up to two years. The government maintained that this provision would deter criminal acts, that no harm would result to the innocent as the Lord Lieutenant "would know whom to imprison and whom to leave untouched."

John thanked members for their patience, but lamented the "gulf of mind that existed between the House and himself on this subject. The people of Ireland were perfectly willing to be the good friend of the people of England, but they would never consent to become their subjects – never! It would be the wiser part for the people of England to make friends of the people of Ireland and especially of the Catholic peasantry of that country, whom he knew to be the most inoffensive, the most gentle, the most forgiving, and the most moral population in Europe."

The *Telegraph* condensed the discussion for his readers. "At the session of the House of Commons on May 26, John Martin joined in the debate he already knew was lost. "Mr. Martin, as an opponent of the Bill took the opportunity afforded by the present stage of the proceeding of renewing his protest against a measure which was about to be exceptionally applied to Ireland. He gave the right honorable gentleman at the head of the Government credit for being actuated by the best intentions in governing the Irish people with a view to redressing their wrongs, so far as English interests would permit; but he complained of the present measure as both harsh and unnecessary, and as likely to produce a widespread feeling of discontent."

§

George followed the progress of the legislation from Dublin, sending off a leader to let his followers in Newry know how he felt. Though John maintained that the legislation was unnecessary, George contemptuously dismissed such a notion. "It is idle to assert that the measure is unnecessary, when it is now a well-known fact that the law in its ordinary course of administration has failed to convict Ribbon assassins; when the police cannot detect them; when the people, either from terror or sympathy, screen them; and when, for the same reasons, witnesses will not give evidence, if any Ribbonmen have been arrested, and juries will not convict. The statement that the Bill will cause great discontent and dissatisfaction throughout the whole of Ireland is not correct. It will not cause dissatisfaction to any who wish well to society, and desire that Ribbon murderers should not set the law at defiance, and upon a code of their own, destroy the peace, security and prosperity of any neighbourhood where their infernal system is in operation."

Then he turned directly to John "We are astonished that any member can have the audacity to oppose such a Bill, unless he can show a more effective method of suppressing the evil complained of." George also dismissed the idea that the legislation was in any way hostile. "Surely a law that proposes to protect the lives and properties of the Irish people is a friendly measure. It is even friendly to the Ribbonmen, for it may save some of them from an ignominious death on the scaffold."

One of the parts of the legislation most upsetting to John was most pleasing to George, the enhanced right of the government to arrest and imprison without trial writers and publications that challenged the government. An amendment to remove this clause from the bill had been introduced and defeated. George was very pleased with this result. "It is well that the attempt to omit the Press clauses in the Peace Preservation Act has failed. Those clauses only affect a portion of the Press which calls itself National; but which is really Fenian. Its articles, before the Act was passed, were calculated to do much mischief among an ignorant and excitable peasantry. The clauses in question, it appears, have had a good effect in moderating the language of the Nationalists, and therefore have been properly retained. The Bill may be considered now virtually passed, and it is to be hoped will have some effect in putting down sanguinary Ribbonism."

§

John and Hentie returned home to Warrenpoint when work on the coercion bill was finished. Once settled into his lovely seaside home, he wrote a letter to Daunt describing his experiences. He began by telling Daunt that he had intended to write of his experiences in Parliament while he was still in London. Yet, he never seemed able to put his intentions into action. "But it is the simple truth to say that I value your approval more highly than that of any other man living."

He explained his failure to write this way. "But, though I did carry on a very extensive and labourious correspondence all the time of my visit (which a little exceeded three weeks), and though the work of correspondence was a diversion to my terribly excited brain, I felt so lazy and exhausted always after writing the letters of obligation, and so craving social freedom and sympathy at my sister's lodging or at some other friends; that I did not write to you."

If there had been more members like Daunt, John was sure that Home Government would make good headway. Being the only Home Rule representative was difficult. However, he found a warm reception from other members of Parliament. "Not by any means that there are not good men among the actual Irish members. I confess I feared greatly that a bitter feeling would prevail among them against me, an indignant repudiation of the purer and manlier patriotic character attributed to me by many friends at the press. Well: it is not so. It may be partly my own instinctive aversion to such airs of superiority, but certainly the Irish members in general without being at all courted by me, seem to like me. Your heart would have been glad had you witnessed how loyally they cheered me on in my first speech, and how they crowded round me in congratulations when I came out of the House. The men's hearts are Irish you see, the poor fellows!"

Other Irish MPs were like John, men without great means. Since members of Parliament weren't paid, the expenses of attending Parliament weighed heavily upon them. They weren't to be blamed if they succumbed to offers of emoluments that would make life in London easier. "Ah! It is a sad state of things. But if we had half a dozen staunch respectable high-spirited men in the House, and a strong steady proud agitation outside, then it would not be difficult to bring over the whole body of Irish members to a proper stand for the country. And I am convinced the England of today – the House of Commons of today – will yield Repeal whenever we can lead members to take a proper stand."

Then John told Daunt about his famous first speech to Parliament. Despite positive reviews, John was not at all pleased himself. "As to my speeches they were partly little fragments of vast quantities of matter I had been preparing, partly in writing, partly in my restless brain; and partly improvisations. It is curious, but I am confident that I could make a clean DEBATE. When Mr. Gladstone spoke (on the motion for going into Committee on the Coercion Bill) and addressed the great part of his speech to me, I borrowed a pencil and applied myself to taking notes of this speech in order to reply. Unluckily the paper was the blue parliamentary papers of the

ORDERS OF THE DAY and the pencil was very pale, and when I rose in the dusk of the evening, I could not see a word of my notes. You can imagine how much a serious, shy, new member must be bothered by such an accident...I am confident, I could in the instant have given a crushing reply to every point of Mr. Gladstone's speech. In fact I plainly see that the man is absurdly over-rated as to ability. And so is Disraeli. And it is a very mediocre House altogether. But then I HATE it. I hate to contend in it. I find an invincible propensity to run away home as soon as I have a fair excuse."

As the first Home Rule member of Parliament, John had slipped into responsibilities that he assumed somewhat reluctantly, but still faithfully. At the end of June, the anniversary of the founding of the Home Government Association was held in the Round Room of the Rotunda in Dublin. Though John wasn't pleased with the progress the organization had made so far, he was pleased to see the large crowd that gathered to celebrate the occasion.

John arrived at 8 p.m. as the meeting was getting underway. The first speaker was the Rev. Haughton, a professor at Trinity College. He took the opportunity to praise John, as he offered the first resolution. "He had had the honour of a long acquaintance with his friend Mr. John Martin. (applause) He knew well his private worth, his social virtues, before he had the honour of agreeing with him, as he now did, in politics. (hear hear and applause) Mr. Martin's honesty of purpose had made him a convert to this cause. (applause)"

When John rose to read a letter that had been received from Australia, he was greeted with prolonged applause. He used the letter to document his strong belief that the Irish struggle for national rights would soon grow throughout the world. He urged the Americans who had come from Ireland to remember the unhappy status of the Irish still at home. He urged all supporters to follow the path of "constitutional agitation."

Writers for the *Express* were not impressed with this anniversary meeting. "The exotic doctrine is that moral force should alone used; but Mr. Martin hinted very plainly that this might not be the only pressure that would be put on the British Government; for, of course, he suggests that Irishmen at home, however, well disposed, could not be responsible for what was done by their countrymen in other parts of the world. The mask is now thrown off and everyone who chooses to use his eyes may see what is meant by Home Rule. It means, not Federalism, but Repeal, and the establishment of an 'Irish nationality.'"

John continued writing letters, and thereby spreading the goals of the Home Rule movement far beyond the sound of his voice. One of them reached the attention of the editor of the *Times* of London, who claimed that John had stated that the Irish people didn't care about disestablishment.

On the last day of June, John settled down in Seaview to write a response. He went right to the point. "Certainly the Irish people, myself included, are rejoiced at the overthrow of sectarian ascendency, and they feel that any mitigation of the system of robbery and extermination to which the rural people have been subject is a valuable relief. But we, I, do not forget that sectarian ascendency was imposed upon our country and maintained against our never-ceasing protests by England."

John then turned to the other law recently passed in Parliament to regulate the relations between landlords and tenants. "Far be it from me to say that all Irish landlords, or even the majority of them, have behaved toward their helpless tenantry in a spirit of cruelty and injustice…Any landlords who have abstained from oppressing their tenants did so, as it were, in spite of the teachings and suggestions of England."

He summed up his attitude toward the recent legislation designed to ease the grievances of the Irish. "I do not scorn any act of justice, nor do I undervalue any alleviation of oppression, no matter what motives may have caused them. If I live to become a free subject of the Queen, I shall welcome and applaud the restoration of my country's national right of self-government, even though the Act for repealing the Act of Union be passed reluctantly and grudgingly by the English Parliament. Mr. Gladstone and you seem to expect that the Irish people are to consent to remain slaves to the English people because the English have deigned to redress to some degree and extent flagrant wrongs to which they had compelled the Irish to submit. I think that is an unreasonable expectation.

"I must say that Mr. Gladstone's boast of confidence in the Irish people at the very moment he holds them disarmed, weak, under guard by great armies of soldiers and police, gagged by a press ukase, under the terror of the coercion bill of his own infliction, is incomprehensible to my simple mind or any hypothesis which attributes to the right honorable gentleman either justness of moral conception or appreciation of language. I think he does desire to redress some of the more serious and flagrant of Irish wrongs, resulting from the great system of wrong, which England has established by means of the Union of 1800, so far as the selfish interest of England may permit and in not much greater delay than the convenience of English Parliamentary business may require. But he (Mr. Gladstone) has no confidence in the Irish people, no respect for their rights and, in my opinion, no knowledge of their real character." This was the point that John was making that attracted the attention of the *Times*.

John closed by telling the popular London paper that he was puzzled to find that some now saw him as a competitor of the Prime Minister. "It is a strange political spectacle that of Mr. Gladstone declaring that 'he is not afraid to compete with me for the future confidence of Ireland.' He, a minister, with absolute power over my country, disposing of every place of power, honor and emolument in Ireland, commanding the army and police, holding the purse of Ireland, out of which he rewards his adherents, and with his two coercion bills to strike terror in those who may entertain my sentiments; and I, with neither money nor honors to buy support, banned because of my political sentiments, from office, honor or emolument of the state, a pariah in my own country, so far as the English rule can make me a pariah."

This letter, just as John wrote it, was published by the *Times*. The editor added a comment. He said that ordinarily, a letter like this would have been ignored or quickly discarded. But "Mr. John Martin belongs to a different type both moral and political, from most Irish nationalists of the present day, and though we regard that type as well nigh extinct, it was certainly very superior both to the rampant Fenianism and to the weak Federalism which have jointly succeeded to it. Moreover an Irish nationalist who enters the Imperial Parliament and takes part in its discussions even under protest, acquires thereby a claim to attention which does not belong to men who live recklessly propagating mistrust and hatred of England among Irish peasant farmers."

The editor went on to disagree with John in two specific areas. "The fallacy is that England under which personification all generations and all classes of Englishmen are lumped and confounded together – has been the willful, conscious and persistent enemy of 'Ireland' since the conquest of Henry II." As to John's view that the relationships between England and Ireland were harmful to Ireland, the editor on the surface seemed to agree. "Of course, if the union of a weaker nation with a stronger be ipso facto slavery, Ireland is enslaved." But while that same situation had once existed in Scotland, the Scotch were now proud to be English. Surely that would happen with Ireland as well.

John Mitchel wrote an approving article in his *Irish Citizen*. "Mr. Martin is following up vigorously his first assault upon British usurpation. The commanding position he has taken gives him the power for the present to breach the battlements of British public opinion through the press; and he has been using his advantage unsparingly. Having taken the Times by storm, he next turns upon the Echo which has had the hardihood to criticize his speeches."

The letter to the *Echo* to which Mitchel referred was on the subject of the freedom of the press. "While reports or rumors of Irish crimes being almost the exclusive and only intelligence the English public receives about Ireland, the effect produced is that my country is a very wicked country indeed. Our idea – probably you will consider it a misconception – is that England lately made a statute which authorizes your government to take and destroy the property of any Irish journalists whose writings it may dislike. You see, an Irish journalist must contend with unequal arms. The one combatant is weighted and shackled as it were, the other fights free."

However, since he wasn't a journalist, he could safely attempt to explain to the English the injustice of English treatment of Ireland. The people of England needed to hear the truth, that the Irish citizens didn't have the same constitutional rights that the people of the other areas of Great Britain enjoyed. "England, in the sovereign's name, has disarmed the people of Ireland and occupied the country with an army under English Command. England makes laws to bind the Irish people. England has taken possession of the Irish purse. England rules Ireland in all respects at her own will, and with a view to her own interests, against the wish of the inhabitants of Ireland. And…to their ruinous disadvantage…Well I must submit to your superior force so long as you may be able to maintain it. But if you think you have any other valid argument on your side, then I should like to know what it may be."

John didn't usually enjoy engaging in debate with newspapers. But he did enjoy the reactions that followed his election and first speech in Parliament. "I make no scruple to confess that I greatly enjoy the praises and approbation so very generally bestowed upon the speaker and the letters to the London *Times* and *Echo*."

Chapter 19

Home Rule

1871—1873

John continued to pour his limited energies into making the Home Government Association an increasingly important organization, too powerful for the English to ignore. In June, he had his first Home Rule colleague in Parliament, when Smyth was elected Member from Westmeath. "PJ Smyth, I trust, will do good as a nationalist MP. He is quite a clever speaker, quick, vehement, and often impressive. His fault (I think) is occasional capricious exasperation, and tendency to squat at rhetorical effects. As an Irish man, he has the root of the matter in him and he is proud and obstinate. On the other hand, he is crotchety, quarrelsome and suspicious, but not badly so." "Now I am going back to London at least for a few days in order to appear in the House with PJ Smyth and perhaps to say something in the debate if one be permitted on the new Irish jury Bill."

The Association needed positive publicity to attract new adherents. In early July, just after their first anniversary, the Association planned an appearance before the Dublin Corporation [City Council] to request support. There would be three speakers, John, Daunt and Galbraith. Together they represented an ecumenical shamrock, Presbyterian, Catholic, and Church of Ireland.

As Protestants marched throughout Ulster on Marching Day, the Home Government Association, met to announce that the Dublin Corporation would indeed hear their delegation on Tuesday July 18th. A wide range of officials, poor law guardians, street commissioners, and trade unions, were invited to attend.

The choice of speakers was widely applauded, and sure to attract great attention. Daunt was the Catholic representative. He had begun his life in politics as a strong supporter of Daniel O'Connell, and in his waning years, he was as "true in the evening of life to the land he loved and served in its morning and its noon."

John was described as a "Presbyterian well known and beloved throughout Ireland as a man of the most sincere patriotism and the most sterling honour." Galbraith, a professor at Trinity and a clergyman from the Church of Ireland, a scholar well known across Europe, was a newcomer to the cause of Irish nationalism. Leaders of the Association hoped his participation would indicate to Ulster Protestants that they need not fear joining Catholics to acquire more control of Irish affairs. Surely these three men, occupying the same stage, and pleading for the same cause would make a convincing case for the Association.

Shortly before noon on the appointed day, members of the Corporation assembled in committee room number one to don their official robes. The procession of Corporation members started promptly at noon. They seated themselves at a table near Daniel O'Connell's statue, and the Lord Mayor's chair. Outside this official area, important guests including officials from across the lower half of Ireland, representatives of many trades from silk weavers to book makers settled into their reserved seats. Respectable Dublin citizens, perhaps including George, crowded into the remaining space.

Daunt was the first to speak. He recounted the history of self-government in Ireland. He concluded his speech, "Our divisions, artfully fomented, lost strength to Pitt to crush our freedom. Our union will enable us to recover it." His presentation was received with loud and prolonged cheering.

John was the next to speak. Like Daunt before him, John was received with a great ovation. "I am proud, I am very proud—of the position that I occupy on this delegation and I feel it a very great honour and distinction to be banded together with the representative men of the Irish national aspiration for a quarter of a country, and the Irish representative men of the patriots that are now accepting the national political faith, and are determined to go through with it manfully." Again lusty cheers erupted.

John went on to directly address the Corporation. He had been chosen to represent a portion of the population that were educated people, "proud people who love freedom." And so, they wished religious freedom for every Irishman. Though the Home Rule movement had hopeful prospects, "some important powerful, influential portions of the community were averse to that agitation." That opposition, not withstanding, important Protestants were finally joining the national cause. As members of the Corporation could see by the presenters, and people attending, this religious division was decreasing allowing the chances of success to rise.

Recent action by Parliament showed the attitude of the English government was changing. The Government and the English people had begun to understand the unfair burdens that had been placed on Ireland by their attitudes and actions. They wished to make amends by removing them. The move toward Irish freedom was already underway.

"We must be as free as the English—we shall submit to no inferiority. We love our country and dare not have the head of that country lowered,—no, not one tittle." The audience interrupted John with shouts of "Hear, hear."

"Our country is smaller than England. But it must hold as high a role as England or any other country in the world." More enthusiastic cheering and loud applause caused John to pause again.

"I say not one word of this in threat or ill-will to the English—far be it for me to do so. It is not a threat to any man whom God has made equal with me to say—'I insist on my equality.' There is no ill-will in asking redress from a man who has wronged you. We ask the English for nothing that is theirs. We ask them only for what is our own, and I see great reason to hope that the actions which I trust will be taken by the Corporation to-day will afford a new strength to the cause of nationality." Again, John was forced to pause until the hearty shouting subsided.

John ended his speech with a summation for the Corporation. "I say that the action which I trust the Corporation will take to-day will virtually place the people of Ireland in the attitude of a nation peaceably, firmly and earnestly demanding their rights, and desiring a fair and just and an amicable settlement with the English." John resumed his seat to loud and prolonged cheering and applause.

The presentation to the Dublin Corporation concluded with Professor Galbraith recounting the history of the changing role of government. Then the members of the Corporation rose and made their ceremonial exit.

John, Daunt and some of their friends adjourned to the office of the *Nation* to share their thoughts on the day's events. During the conversation, the subject veered off to a discussion about lying. John repeated an opinion he had often heard from his friend Mitchel. He "divided liars into two classes, bad liars and good liars, bad liars being those who hesitate, who utter their inventions with some timid reserve, good liars being masters of the act who stop at nothing."

Hentie was present at the meeting as well. She was an impressive woman, not likely to sit primly in the back while men discussed important issues. So she felt totally free to participate in the discussion. Her view was somewhat different: "that some people lied themselves into such a condition of moral muddle as to be unconscious whether they were speaking truth or falsehood; that moral distinction was obliterated."

The Corporation's decision was almost unanimous, offering hearty support to the Association. Further the members voted to disseminate news of their action to all their town officials across the country who had attended the presentation. Only Alderman Sweeney resisted claiming that this was opposed to everything O'Connell had fought so hard to achieve, and what the people of Ireland actually wanted.

George was fierce in his attacks on the meeting and most of the speakers. He commented first that the meeting had taken place in front of a statue of Daniel O'Connell. "If the spirit of O'Connell could have surveyed the scene, we fear its composure would have been ruffled, seeing such pigmies, as compared with him, attempting an agitation."

Daunt's speech missed the point, being in reality less a speech supporting the Association's plans for federalism and more that of a Repealer. But he saved his harshest criticism for Professor Galbraith. He had told the Corporation that Protestants had nothing to fear from their Catholic neighbors. They should substitute trust and give up their fear. George was scornful of the notion. "Protestants do not fear it. [Catholic ascendency] They have shown on many occasions that they are no cowards; and if they were, to insult them by calling them so, is a bad way to bring them round to Home Rule views."

George concluded his lengthy leader with these words. "Protestants are not to be frightened by the bugbear of Irish disaffection. Their fathers weathered the gale in worse times, and their sons are not degenerate. If the Dublin Corporation, or a section of them be converted by the new agitators who have arisen, with no qualifications to agitate but self-conceit, the question of Home Rule will just be where it was."

Aside from a single mention that John was one of the speakers, George did not allude to him or critique a word John said.

§

While the Home Rule efforts continued in Dublin, the people of Newry and surrounding areas focused on their midsummer activities. The first was the annual agricultural meeting of the Newry Union Farming Society which took place in the flax market on July 5th. After weeks of effort preparing animals and produce for the fair, farmers enjoyed a friendly competition for awards with their friends and neighbors. James Harshaw would have enjoyed his family's success. His son-in-law, Archy Marshall, won one of the coveted awards, the first prize for a short-horned bull named Charlie. Son Andrew won a first prize as well for the best calf born in 1869 named Jessie and another first for the best heifer calved the next year named Cherry.

Both men won other prizes as well. Archy came in fourth for a short horned roan heifer named Fanny. Andrew got prizes for his calf Leinster, a Yorkshire sow, and a Dorking cock and hen. Farmers gathered together in the evening for a fine dinner at the Victoria Hotel.

Marching day came a week later and was celebrated in Mullaglass near Poyntzpass. One of the speakers was J. E. Finlay, the current editor of the *Newry Telegraph,* and an ardent Orangeman. Finlay told the large and enthusiastic crowd that the Orange Order was purely a defensive organization. He denied the validity of any anti-Catholic taunts, that the Protestant supporters should go back where they came from in peace.

In Finlay's eyes, anywhere Protestants might live was their country. "Protestants have the best right to use the language of patriotism for they have done something for their country, instead of contributing to make it poor and wretched...Yet persecution has been their lot for several years past...The days of arbitrary power are come back upon us. The late assaults upon Protestant liberty are scandalous. Liberal and Roman Catholic magistrates have dared to set up their proclamations as law, and a Government, that ought to protect loyal men who have violated no law, ordered their armed myrmidons to prevent a peaceable procession, thus doing the degrading work of a vile conspiracy to crush the Apprentice Boys of Derry, and espousing the cause of mobs of hungry Ribbonmen.

"We may have to struggle yet in this country for liberty of conscience and the right of private judgment, but if we think of the heroes of the Revolutions and the martyrs of the Reformation, we will not act ignobly, but leave behind us memories to which posterity will do honour."

Rev. McAllister of Ryans also spoke. "The Celtic Irish will never be united to England; we will never be separated...They will never give up their dogmas; and one hundredth of Protestant truth we will never yield...It was contrary to the very nature of things that the truth they held could commingle with error."

John seldom had much to say about the Orange marches. But he had made clear he believed that Orangemen and Catholics should be free to march and celebrate for any reason, the only restriction being that the marches must be peaceful. But too often Orange marches were enhanced by the possibility of a confrontation with Catholics. This mindset resulted from the kind of education that Protestants received. "The political education of Irish Protestants is at present very imperfect and unsatisfactory. They seem to read only such books and newspapers as are on the anti-Catholic and ordinarily the anti-Irish side. Much of their impressions of history are derived from grossly partial or lying books. But, in the state of legal equality in which all the Irish sects have just been placed, the ignorance and bigotry which ascendancy produced among Irish Protestants will pass away."

In the next edition of the *Newry Telegraph*, George had comments of his own. The Orangemen were united on a political agenda. They were strongly opposed to the Home Rule movement that John was working so hard to make a success. But that wasn't the topic that George lingered on. The Orange Order opposed the new Ballot Act (July 18, 1870) providing standard printed ballots to be cast in secret.

"Protestants have all the freedom of election which they wish or require. Open voting is the test of an honest elector. WE have known some in our experience who did not stand the test and whom the Ballot would have suited admirably, while we have known others who have stood the test; and although they may have experienced a little temporary petty persecution for doing right, they were protected by Providence better than any secret agency for screening knaves could have protected them, and they did not ultimately suffer. The man who advocated the Ballot should not be so inconsistent as to wear an orange ribbon, which is an open symbol of attachment to Protestant and Constitutional principles."

§

The Home Government Association moved quickly to build upon the support of Dublin leaders and the resulting publicity. Members would begin holding meetings in major cities around the country. While they understood that venturing very far into Ulster would activate Protestant opposition, they planned their first big meeting close enough to Ulster to infiltrate Ulster with information. The meeting was billed as a combined gathering of the citizens of Newry and Dundalk, citizens of Ulster and Leinster. It was held on Tuesday August 15th.

The Newry delegation arrived by train. At the station, they climbed onto hired carriages to drive them to the Fair Green where the meeting would be held. They were accompanied by bands and marchers waving banners. The leaders wore green bands on their hats with the words "Home Rule" written on them. Some wore green and orange rosettes. The Green had been fitted out with a platform for the speakers. Around 15,000 participants gathered as close as they could to hear John and other Home Rule leaders speak.

When John rose to give his remarks, the crowd cheered loudly, and waved their hats in the air in greeting. John began by telling everyone that he was very happy to see so many of his neighbors who had traveled down from Newry. He was also cheered to see so many young men in the crowd. "Men like himself had become bald and grey…had lost the fire…[and] were passing away." Fortunately "there were strong young men…with right hearts and principles, ready to take up the banner of Ireland and determined that it should at no distant time float proudly and freely over a proud, free and happy people." He was delighted that those on the platform represented the leaders of the future, from all religions.

George didn't find the meeting impressive when judged by the size of the crowd, and the importance of the people attending. He estimated that the crowd, which had been expected to reach 20,000 actually numbered nearer 5,000. Most local Catholic priests were missing as were most of the Dundalk Town Commissioners who had supposedly called the meeting. Most important to George, there were few Protestants on hand, and only a few respectable Catholics, and a single magistrate.

Before the next Home Rule meeting was scheduled, John had another exchange with the *Times*. The editor began by explaining the core problem with the Irish. "Other nations ally themselves with the strong and congratulate the successful. The chosen objects of Irish admiration and love are the improvident, the declining and the vanquished."

The Coercion law to which John had objected so vehemently was actually not an issue, as it wasn't being enforced. Then the editor attempted to explain what John meant when he spoke of England. "we—that is, the English nation—and every Englishman in particular, keep Ireland in subjection, hold her down designedly lower than England, crush her spirit and destroy her fortunes; he is therefore justified in speaking of us as a man speaks of an enemy with whom he neither expects nor desires amelioration." He claimed that there were citizens of both countries "whose feelings and words are not in harmony with the prevailing policy of this Empire which aims at equality of races and equal toleration of creeds, coercion won't work while conciliation may work slowly."

This was an editorial that John was not likely to ignore. The editor quoted John's response. "'Mr. Martin says *we* govern Ireland; *we* crush, diminish and degrade Ireland; *we* work her for our national interest and convenience as we should a beast of burden, or the creatures we keep for our food.'"

The *Times* editor responded. "What disgusts him beyond all bearing is to see a lot of fellows—the majority for ought he knows or cares—including ourselves, laboring for equality, unity and peace. He cannot provoke us to a good faction fight. But this little as Mr. Martin may see it is an admission that 'England' and 'The English' of his hereditary hatred, exist no more. He is running atilt against the shadow cast by his own figure on the fog before him…Those traditions are generally the thing of poetry and tale. In Ireland alone the past survives as a hideous spectre or foul fiend. That has to be laid somehow, but in itself it is an unsubstantial thing. The Ireland of these furious ravings has no existence. There is neither oppressor nor oppressed. We are all brothers and may again feel ourselves one family. Mr. Martin cannot but see this dread consummation and this it is that that stirs his indignation."

When the Home Government Association next met in at their headquarters at 63 Grafton Street, they celebrated the election of a third member to Parliament. A few weeks before, Isaac Butt had been elected by a constituency from Limerick. John spoke during the meeting. He said "he thought it was extremely likely that the sentiments he held with reference to that matter of political connection with England might not be held by the majority of his countrymen. He would be delighted to obey what might be the will of his country on that point as on every other."

John's support of a Federal arrangement with England rather than independence was a critical element of political success. Individual members couldn't expect that their ideas would always prevail. "He believed in order to make any movement a success, the only thing you have to do was respect each other's difference of opinion."

§

Another large Association gathering in Drogheda on the banks of the Boyne was John's last engagement for the rest of 1871. John was inactive, preferring to stay in Seaview with Hentie. He found he enjoyed tending the garden he had planted behind their home. And he took the hiatus to catch up on his correspondence with his friends. He told Mahon of his hopes for the future. "Were I to live long enough—say a dozen years—and don't lose what little ability I now have, 'tis likely that none of the Irishmen to whom you allude would at the end of that time have the face to call me a 'communist' and that nearly all of them would be won to my side."

Part of the reason for John's inactivity was the precarious state of his finances, something that John seldom mentioned except to such good friends as Mahon. The income that had allowed him to live the easy life of a member of the upper classes of Ireland was now far below what he needed to maintain his home in Warrenpoint, and pay the expenses of his stays in London. It was difficult for him to stay out of dishonorable debt. There was a certain irony in this situation, as John explained in his letter.

"Curious that it seems to me, recollecting my political proceedings since my return to Ireland, that is since the infliction of the income tax, as if I, John Martin, have actually been dissuaded from referring pointedly to that particular grievance of one subject condition, for the very reason that I whose entire income and means of life come from rents of land, am one of the Irishmen whose particular interests are especially affected by this tax. It seems to me as if a too great delicacy of feeling against using my own private injury as an argument in the national question has kept me from singling out the income tax as an illustration of the wrongs inflicted on my country by the

English rule. And yet there are Irishmen—landlords themselves, perhaps, but then big ones, receiving rentals to which mine is a beggarly affair in comparison—who regard me as a selfish political adventurer, looking to relieve and advantage myself and losses congenial with myself, but careless of any wrong to real landlords. Bother it all!"

Before he ended the long letter, John gave Mahon an update of Home Rule. "In Ireland certainly the Home Rule movement advances <u>slowly.</u> The ignorance and bigotry of the Presbyterians and a great part of the other Protestants are the great obstacles so far as the unbribed part of the population is concerned. Of course, the officials and trades in England...and such capitalists as think they make more money out of Ireland by help of the English rule than they could in freedom—work hard to keep the ignorant and bigoted Protestants on the English side."

§

The bigoted Protestants that John referred to in his letter would certainly not remain quiet in the face of a growing movement they deeply disliked. One of the very early opposition meetings took place in Poyntzpass, planned and carried out by the Orangemen of Armagh. Thirty-three Orange lodges from around the area gathered in the little village to indicate their opposition. Some marched over from the Donaghmore area, from Loughbrickland, the Glen, and Glascar Hill to join lodges from Tandragee and Gosford. Speakers proclaimed that Home Rule was revolution in disguise. If Home Rule were to be actually established, "it would be detrimental to the social and material interests of the county, that civil and religious freedom would be filtered by ultramontane despotism and commercial progress retarded by contentions and disorder."

John closed out the year with a letter to Daunt. John wished that Daunt would turn his talents to converting the "Ulster Protestant Liberals" by engaging in correspondence with some of the northern newspapers. This was an important task that John didn't feel equal to tackling. He had indeed tried his hand at that effort previously, exchanging letters and editorials with the editor of the *Northern Whig.* "My temper is too irritable, my cold haughtiness too chilling & my own energy, my fastidiousness at the vulgarity and lowness, combined with the self-conceit and high pretensions of the Whig editor (in particular) and those to whom he is a prophet and guide, too discouraging." This editor viewed John as a simple sycophant of his more talented friend John Mitchel, a perspective perpetuated by many historians.

John began the year 1872 as he had ended the previous year, with a letter to Daunt. He noted what a special year this was. "This year completes the seventh century since the English invasion began. Thank God! There are fine signs of a near release from the worst of its consequences. It is naturally a grief to you and to me that we are incapacitated or prevented from taking so active a part in the national agitations as the present temper of the people would gladly assign us. But it is a keen gratification to see this good work, which we both have tried to prepare, to advance, to purify and defend from what might soil or spoil it, now steadily progressing and receiving the aid and direction of worthy leaders. I have been much urged to attend the demonstration at Liverpool next Wednesday. But my private affairs are unaccommodating and my bodily energy hardly suffices for such proceeding so far from home."

George mentioned this new move of the Home Government Association into England and Scotland as well, referring to the Liverpool meeting about which John had written. This effort to expand into what might seem to be enemy territory didn't please George. The meeting would attract substantial numbers of the 100,000 Irish emigrants there. But they might also succeed in attracting some English converts as well. George speculated that the Home Rulers might become so annoying in England that the government would grant Ireland Home Rule just to silence them. He dismissed these new efforts. Home Rule was only a phrase around which a "motley group of politicians rally, but there is no real union among the parties…Above all, it is a piece of great folly to agitate for Home Rule in England."

Meetings and banquets continued across lower Ireland. In February two more Home Rulers were elected to Parliament: Blennerhassett in Kerry and Captain Nolan in Galway, though Nolan's victory was later overturned by the much-censured Judge Keogh. John attended some of these events. And George mentioned them in passing. He was more interested in covering the growing opposition to Home Rule in the Newry area. Following upon the meeting in Poyntzpass, another one was held in the Four-towns.

The main address in the Four-towns was given by James Harshaw's good friend Rev. Bryson, who was the minister of the Presbyterian church there. "There will always be different opinions on subjects affecting the political interests of our splendid country, but the idea of Home Rule is too utopian for any reasonable person to entertain…Ulster is too strong in the element of social intelligence, industry and prosperity, to give way to a movement of idleness and poverty."

George added more thoughts on the subject a couple of weeks later. "The question may be national in this sense—that it is calculated to injure the nation and therefore every man who wishes the nation to Prosper should oppose it." George saw that Home Rule might provide some benefits, but these should and could be achieved in other ways. But if John and his fellow members actually succeeded, Protestants would be subject to the oppressive whims of a Catholic government. This was the wrong time for such an effort, since Ireland had never been more prosperous than "at present, both in manufactures and in everything else."

As spring neared, John continued to participate in Home Rule meetings in Dublin, and to support Home Rule candidates when by-elections occurred. Despite his commitment and hard work, he was being attacked by some in the media for not being a good representative for the people of Meath. He continued to refuse to vote, even on what might be seen as important issues. John noticed the criticism and gave a brief response. If ever he got a letter from constituents stating that they were unsatisfied with his service, he would immediately resign.

When St. Patrick's Day arrived, John celebrated by traveling across the Irish Sea and giving his first Home Rule speech in Glasgow, Scotland. Though he arrived the day before the speech, many residents were on hand to greet him. There was a luxurious carriage drawn by four horses ready to take him to his hotel. It was preceded by a band and followed by a large number of happy Home Rulers. Supporters had also arranged to hold a banquet and concert before John's big speech.

The Home Rule event took place in the City Hall. Great pains had been taken to make it an exceptional event. The platform was decorated with banners, on one side that of St. Mengo, on the other side St. Patrick. The side walls were decorated with panels that said, "Cead Mille Failte," and "God Save Ireland." When John entered, the crowd rose to their feet, waving hats and handkerchiefs.

John was greatly affected by his reception. "I say that it is for this reason that I have been so long trusted and treated with wonderful indulgence and respect by my compatriots at home and abroad—because I have been a patriot of no party...I have been through all my course and with the help of God I shall remain of the Party of Ireland...It is true that by constitution and temperament, as well as by reflection and study, I am a moderate man—a man adverse to violence; a man that abhors violent revolution, and abhors it all the more from the view I have found of the character of my fellow-countrymen as to their strengths and their weaknesses, and as to every point in their characters; but I say that although I am and have been, as a politician, moderate almost to timidity, yet I can tell you of feelings that have stirred my breast before now and that sometimes stirs it even yet, in order to show how nearly the most moderate Irish patriot and Nationalist may approach the sentiments of the men who take most dangerous courses and suffer for these courses...I remember the horrors and the people dying of hunger, hundreds and thousands of families who had supported themselves, poorly as it might be, but respectably because independently and by their own industry, forced to become paupers. I remember also that hundreds of thousands of Irishmen were forced in the course of a few years to leave their native land to the extent of a fourth of the entire people. I thought upon all these things very bitterly, because I remembered that Ireland in each of those years produced enough food for the support of all the population..." He concluded that this history made it possible to understand nationalists who are more radical in views than he was.

A month later, John was trying to make another conversion to Home Rule, his dear friend John Mitchel. Mitchel had written an editorial in his New York newspaper, attacking Home Rule members who attended Parliament, and even worse, voted there. Mitchel claimed that this action showed they were willing to "aid and abet foreign rule" and abandon "the national course of Ireland."

John responded. "Alas! you have been long in exile from Ireland. You were carried away from the country when notwithstanding the raging famine, the national spirit and hope were yet unbroken. True, the national spirit and hope are now again arisen, high and strong. But the famine and the exodus, left the country long helpless and hopeless under the feet of England. And now this new national movement, which is steadily and fast obtaining the adhesion of the country, is not yet so universally recognized and organized as to enable the country by it to determine upon and adopt a policy such as lofty courage might suggest, and stern virtue might carry into effect…but I think we are on the way and sure to arrive at such a national position… No doubt there will be differences of opinion among patriotic men in Ireland when the question of Parliamentary policy comes to be seriously considered by the country. But even then no matter how great the differences, it will be unjust as well as mischievous to conclude that those men who do not hold our view are therefore treacherous or devious or in any respect less virtuous or less patriotic than ourselves. I am confident that you did not and do not intend to charge any of the Home Rule members with evil motives. But your words have been so understood in Ireland and it is therefore I venture to mention the subject."

§

In 1869, a very active group of Irish Nationalists had banded together to form an Amnesty Association to pressure for the immediate release of the Fenian prisoners. A riotous meeting in Newry, which George deplored as illegal, and a larger one held the next Sunday in Cabra, a small town outside Dublin, supplied sufficient pressure for the government to take action. Gradually prison doors opened, and Fenian prisoners were allowed to walk away as free men, as long as they promised to leave Ireland, not to return until such time as their sentences would have ended.

John O'Leary was freed in January 1871, and exiled, living then in Paris where he and John had first met. Despite the hostile attacks O'Leary had made on John during the existence of the Fenian newspaper, John continued to think of O'Leary as a "colleague and friend," though they had many differences. With O'Leary free, the two men began a correspondence.

On April 1, 1872, John wrote a letter about the contentious disagreement in Ireland about education. "You are a graver, sterner, or at least more severe character than I, and you seem much disposed to pessimism, while I try to excuse other men's faults by acknowledging to myself the many and ugly faults in my own conduct. But though there are differences between us that an ungenerous writer might exhibit as insuperable by or incompatible with friendship, the ungenerous writer would be absurdly mistaken."

With their friendship reestablished, John felt free to disagree with O'Leary on the subject of education, sure that O'Leary would respectfully consider what John believed. "For my part it is freedom I want for myself, and for every man, to educate our children (if we have any) as we wish or approve. I assume that every man who holds the Catholic faith or wills to belong to the Catholic religious community, therefore cares to educate his children as Catholics. So of Protestants. So of persons who decline to be attached to any Christian, or any religious community. What each man deems true and right for himself in faith and morals and knowledge, he will deem true and right for his children. If the whole people, in a state think proper and employ a part of their money in providing and regulating education that ought to be done so as not to deprive the individual parents of their rights or their freedom. And the denominational arrangement seems to me to be the only one which allows parents to exercise their right. I should much prefer to take the affair entirely and absolutely out of the hands of the state and leave it unto the voluntary control of the parents, associating themselves freely, or not associating themselves for the purpose as they may think proper."

There were many supporters for and against the existing integrated education with religious education being separate from other courses. But John restated a view of education that many from both sides of the issue would consider radical in the extreme. "In Ireland, Nationalists mean education by Britain, their ideas for their purpose. I am, besides a bitter unbeliever in the prevailing faith that literacy or school education is per se necessarily a good thing or a better thing than 'ignorance' of the school made knowledge. The child is learning always, whether employed in literacy lessons or not so employed. And the occupation of the child's time in literary lessons prevents some other lessons from reaching its mind and body. And it depends upon the comparative value of the one and the other sort of lessons and teaching in each case, whether the child is improved by being at school or not. And after, when the child has become a man, and has learned much of what schools and books teach him, it is <u>ignorance</u> he has learned rather than knowledge of the true and good!" Perhaps his ideas resulted from having his earliest education provided by his parents.

§

Home Rule meetings continued with John participating when he was able. But he was also very active in a behind-the-scenes discussion of tactics. In dispute and potentially divisive was how to advocate for Home Rule in Parliament. This was just the kind of key issue that John worried would blunt the effectiveness of nationalist organizations. The already elected Home Rule members sought a unified effort to force a discussion of Home Rule in Parliament. Isaac Butt was quite reluctant to take that major step. But John was firmly ensconced on the other side, actively pushing a debate.

"The present question of Englishmen as yet but dimly and imperfectly comprehend that the Irish national sentiment is <u>indestructible</u>. A Parliamentary debate may afford them the requisite instruction, and may enable such of them as prefer justice and safety to national spite to give their adhesion to our national cause. But though a few generous and far-seeing English politicians will probably be converted to our views by a Parliamentary debate upon Home Rule, we must not let ourselves be deluded so far as to expect that the English—the most selfish domineering and practical nation in the world—will ever admit the justice of our cause or consent to the restoration of the sovereign rights of Ireland which they have usurped to their profit, for simple respect for justice, or for any generous sentiment…In my opinion, the

English will be so convinced so soon as the Irish constituency elect a majority of Home Rulers and as soon as the Irish people (other parts of world) formally declare for Home Rule." As long as there was no consensus, this idea remained a debating point without any action being taken in Parliament.

At the end of May, George noted disturbing news. Rev. Baggot, Dean of Dromore, announced that he had joined the Home Rule movement. George warned any readers who might be tempted to follow the well-respected clergyman down what he saw as a destructive path. "The bone and sinew of the Home Rulers are Repealers, and worse. It is not Home Rule, but a strong conservative Government that is wanted to promote the material interests of Ireland."

Still George had to admit that Home Rule was gaining support as evidenced by the acquisition of such an important new convert. But he assured his readers that the vast majority of the people of Ulster needn't worry too much about Home Rule. The Presbyterians were still strongly opposed to the movement, and meetings were so sparsely attended as to be fairly judged a total failure.

§

In late spring, John had suffered another extensive illness, limiting his work to writing letters like the one to O'Leary. He wrote another to the *Newry Telegraph*. The editor of the paper had expressed strong approval of a new idea to extend rail transportation to areas as yet unserved. This was in keeping with the paper's long support of all rail projects.

This extension was the brainchild of a group of British capitalists, who wanted to build a tramway from Warrenpoint to Kilkeel. Though the project had already received approval, John did not intend to be silent. He objected to provisions that gave the company all rights to the existing road after the first year. How would local citizens be able to drive their carts and animals to Kilkeel? In addition, it would be an annoyance to all the people along the right of way who would be bothered by the noise.

If this company really wanted to build such a tramway, they should buy private land themselves and run the tram on it, leaving the public way open to the public. John warned, "Capital is like fire—a very valuable servant, but a most destructive master."

Editor Finlay objected to John's position. He agreed that "if it can be shown that the public would be injured, it should be opposed, but consideration of private interests should not be allowed to weigh in such a case." He accused John of making "no attempt to discuss the real question," rather indulging "his imagination." The citizens would be greatly benefited by "cheap, fast, transportation." It was an erroneous assumption "that present traffic will be driven off the road in favor of a monopoly." He concluded with a special dig at John. "Mr. Martin is merely supporting private interests—and very ineffectively—against the public good."

Finlay might have seen John's actions as "ineffective," but John prevailed. The tramway was never built.

The cattle show of the Newry Union Farming Society had quickly become an exciting local event leading up to Marching Day celebrations. As in the previous year, the show was held at the flax market. The competitors, officials, and attendees were blessed with fine weather.

When prizes were awarded, Andrew Harshaw was again very successful. He won 1st prize for the best heifer dropped in 1870, second for his short-horned heifer, Red Rose, 3rd prize for best calf of that spring for Admiral. Red Rose and Admiral were both short horned cows, but Andrew also got 1st and 2nd prizes for best spring calves that weren't short horned for Myrtle. To round out his wins, he came in 2nd and 3rd for the best cock and hen. Though there were certainly disappointments during the judging, Andrew must have viewed his successes as a tribute to his father's training.

John was sufficiently recovered to travel to London to "attend to his Parliamentary duties" in July. He was hoping to take part in a debate on actions of Judge Keogh in overturning the election of Captain Nolan. However, Parliamentary maneuvering delayed the debate until August. He did not linger in London, as he was very anxious to get home to Ireland to Warrenpoint, where Hentie was waiting.

Soon there would be a very special family gathering there. His sister Jane and one of her daughters were expected to arrive in Ireland around July 25th. Jane hadn't returned to Ireland since she had left for Canada over thirty years before, so she had much catching up to do. She had never met any of her brother Robert's seven children who were all growing up well and happy despite the loss of their parents. Her brother David lived in a grand house nearby with his wife and five children. Her sister Mary lived with her husband in Cork and because of the location, she would be the first to greet her returning sister and niece. It would be a wonderful family gathering.

So John was distressed that he would have to interrupt his time with his sister and family to return to London to participate in the debate that had been delayed for most of a month. He greatly loathed being in London especially when he very much wished to be in Ireland.

To make matters worse for John, the effort he hoped would have some positive results was unsuccessful. The session of Parliament was called to order at 4 p.m. But instead of getting to the main topic of discussion, minor issue after minor issue was brought up. The Prime Minister had promised to allow speeches promptly, so debate could end early in the evening. A dozen Irish members had signed up to speak against Judge Keogh, John being one of them.

Because Sir John Gray had made the motion to censure Keogh for bias, he spoke first. After Sir Gray had made his remarks, which lasted for an hour and a half, John rose to his feet to ask for recognition. Speaker after speaker was recognized, while John rose, waving his arms to attract attention to his side of the House in vain, even though he was aided by other members who kept calling attention to his efforts.

It was 2 a.m. the next morning before John was finally able to get recognition from the Speaker. By then the few remaining members in attendance were tired and some of them were "tipsy." Most of them had no interest in what John had planned to say. He had written out notes to ensure his speech would cover all his points, allowing him to glance at them for guidance before dropping them onto his seat. This planning was necessary as John well knew that reading a speech was against the rules of the Commons.

Unfortunately, a very drunk member had seated himself near John and was "whispering and muttering" in most distracting ways. As a result, John had to look at his notes more often than the speaker liked. Therefore, the Speaker interrupted and told John to put down his papers if he wanted to continue. This was irritating, as this rule was very unevenly enforced, and smacked of unfairness to John. This interruption brought jeers from Keogh supporters who really didn't want to listen to anything negative about the Judge.

John was very angry and pondered for a moment what his next step should be. He felt he had done sufficient planning that he could give a very powerful speech without the help of any notes. However, it wouldn't be the speech that he wanted to give on the Irish judicial system in general. John responded to the interruption and the jeering that followed. "I can assure this noisy and impatient assembly that its reluctance to hear me is not half as intense as my reluctance to address it." With those words, John resumed his seat.

When he had time to think over what he had done, he was most unhappy at his failure, even though he had managed to deliver the first part of his speech. So he resolved to send out copies of the speech to various newspapers, so his words might actually spread far beyond the Palace of Westminster. He first thought to send his speech to the *Echo,* whose editor had promised to publish whatever John wrote of Irish affairs. The speech was published there in two installments. With that business attended to, John immediately left London and headed home to rejoin the family festivities.

§

While John was happily enjoying relaxing with his family, George was watching the unfolding of the Home Rule movement and its effects locally. In late August, there was a murder in Newry that was laid at the feet of members of this new movement. A couple of weeks later, a group of Protestants were attacked by a Home Rule mob in Lisdrumgullion, which was just a mile and a half from Newry on the Armagh Road.

To reinforce his dismay at the Association, and the local hostilities it was creating, George wrote a leader on the subject. "If we were to judge from the talk that has expended on Home Rule lately in various places, it may be making progress in the North and this neighborhood. Home Rule is unfortunately associated chiefly with the use of the knife or the dagger—in one with fatal results. That is the way on which the rank and file of Home Rulers—whatever smooth phrases may be used at head-quarters—evince their anxiety to promote harmony among Irishmen. The mildest form in which Home Rule is put is objectionable, but there is no question that with the great majority of those that adhere to it, it is only a mask or a poor attempt at political masquerade. It is also evident that if Home Rule were obtained, it would only, like several legislative enactments during the last 40 years, be merely a stepping stone, a vantage ground, used to secure more extreme measures."

Once the summer was over and the family members had departed, John experienced another illness. He had intended to work for the Association and to support Home Rule candidates. His illness began the first of October. It was the middle of November before he could report "My health though improved and improving is still quite too feeble to let me attempt such a journey."

In a letter to Mahon, John explained his health situation. "It must be kept in mind that I am no chicken—I was 60 years old on the 8th September last. And never having had a robust constitution, it is no wonder if at such an age I begin to break down. And I am a nervous creature and though I find that I easily maintain a calm, patient manner in all my political botherations (in House of Commons, with Fenian wrong-headed but respectable good fellows &c &c) I suspect that such trials wear my strength pretty hard."

This time of ill health gave him an opportunity to think ahead about his goals for Ireland. He wished to solve the problems of land tenure without destroying landlords. He felt that this was the view of most farmers and tenants who were sometimes ill-treated by the owners of Irish land. When the Irish finally governed Ireland, landlords would become Irish as they learned to live under Irish laws. They would become Irish patriots rather than English subjects.

"After the cruelty and oppression which they have been the tools of England in long inflicting upon the peasantry, I think such treatment should be not merely just and generous. But moreover I know the Catholic Irish, I know their passionate pleasure in forgiveness & reconciliation. I believe they would love to maintain the landlord in ever greater social and political influence than might be wise and proper, just because they had been enemies, once the landlords became Irish patriots. And as to confiscation, I never met a sane nationalist who seemed to me to have an idea of it. No: that is for English not for Catholic Irish."

John was slow to regain his health. By the beginning of December he was able to move freely about the house. But he was far too feeble to travel to Dublin for an important meeting of the Home Government Association. Up to this point, they had been a sort of pressure group based in Dublin with loose ties to other groups appearing throughout Ireland and England.

This meeting was arranged to discuss whether or not the Association should become a more organized group, increasing efforts to become a more potent political force, resembling a real Irish political party. This was a daunting task for a group without much organized structure and less money. Their only funds came from the member dues of £1 a year. So before any great steps forward could be made, the funding problem had to be addressed.

Members who attended this meeting were asked without warning to pledge beyond their dues. Donations of £500 pounds were put on the table with an equal amount pledged. For the first time, the Association had operating funds. And for the first time, the Association would endorse and support candidates for Parliament.

The next step was to secure a managing secretary. With Catholic membership lagging below expectations, choosing a permanent secretary who would either be a Catholic, or someone pleasing to the Catholic Church, seemed prudent. There was one obvious candidate that would meet this need. From home, John immediately wrote to his friend Daunt and urged him to accept the post. With considerable reluctance, Daunt agreed.

Daunt had great affection for and trust in John, so he hoped that John would take a very active part to help move the Association to a more stable footing. John responded, "But don't persist in regarding me as an important individual among those gentlemen. My residence away from Dublin and the obstacles which keep me from making many or long journeys render me little more than a nominal member of the Council. I am always ready to give my opinion and advice, when consulted; but I can take but very little…part in the deliberations and proceedings of the Council."

§

By the end of February 1873, John was well enough to travel to London to attend the current sitting of Parliament, intending to stay until the Easter recess. The chief issue of this session was the University Bill for Ireland proposed by the Prime Minister and his Liberals. Essentially the legislation would put seven Irish universities under the control of a single board. No longer would each be independent. No longer would there be religious tests for professors or students. Trinity College would lose its special status and its endowment. John was strongly opposed, as were most Irish members. In the end, the bill didn't pass.

Though John was present, he didn't speak to the issue when the legislation came up for 2nd reading. John wasn't pleased that he had failed to speak, even though the benches emptied whenever an Irish MP rose to speak. "Neither to have spoken nor to have voted in so great a crisis was conduct to ruin the political reputation of an Irish representative."

His disappointment in his conduct led him to explore in his own mind whether or not he was pursuing the best approach in his service. "But it may be possible to strive here for the attainment of Home Rule for our country by a voting policy instead of my non-voting policy…No. if the representatives elected by Irish nationalist constituencies are to come to this house in order to serve the Irish national cause, they must appear here and act here as Irish nationalists and in no other capacity…They may resolve not to vote at all on any questions submitted to the house, except the question of repealing the Union Act of 1800 and making a new federal arrangement with the English, or they may prefer to vote upon every ministerial motion and always against the minister whether he be Liberal or Conservative. I see no objection to either of those courses of action." Ultimately, John concluded that his not-voting strategy was the proper course for him personally.

By the middle of April, John and Hentie had returned to Warrenpoint. He quickly wrote a letter of encouragement for Daunt's progress in his important position. "But I trust the occupation that you have as virtual director of the Association–or rather virtual missionary for bringing in members–keeps up your heart. You are doing good. Your very name attracts valuable support to the Association. And tends to give confidence in the movement. See how the priests are coming in! If now we had a good supply of young men of education, talent and virtuous ambition, the movement might immediately become vast and formidable. But emigration and competitive examinations leave Ireland a very short supply of young men fitted for the national work."

George continued to closely follow the actions of the Home Rule supporters, and from time to time, he wrote on the subject. He confessed to having trouble sorting out their goals. However, John's position was very clear to him. John wanted an Irish Parliament in Dublin, which would be totally independent of England. While George understood John's perspectives, he didn't agree. "Whatever the motto of the agitation, we ordinarily find in reality a monstrous hypocracy."

John was still in London when George had pronounced his opinion on Home Rule. If John actually read the editorial, he would have been unaffected by what George thought. Daunt had taken several important steps, one of them writing on the subject of financial relations between Ireland and England which was particularly interesting to both John and George. When the Home Rule Association had Daunt's paper published, John had passed copies on to several of his friends. "It is very desirable that all Irish members of Parliament and all Irishmen of considerable property should have the facts of England's money dealing with us, since she got the authority to take charge of our purse, forced upon their attention. If not for sake of sentiment–of the sentiment of justice, right, honour, dignity–yet for sake of material and money interest, Irishmen of property may be induced to contest for Home-rule."

This small action in no way compensated for his sense of failure as a Member of Parliament. When he was home in Warrenpoint, in bed or sitting by the fire in the evening smoking his pipe, he planned grand speeches in his mind. While he sat silently in the Commons, he would imagine how the issues under discussion would be handled in an Irish Parliament. "I thought I could overcome shyness, indignation, nervous irritability, all my own personal disqualifications as well as all the opposition of the House itself, and could do something as a member of the House to gratify my generous constituents and Patriotic Ireland in general, to gratify my own and my friends vanity to make the Irish question better and more favorably known to the world, and to dispose the English towards yielding peaceably to our national demand for restitution and justice."

John saw one solution to his continuing doubts. If there were more Home Rule members, they could act as a group. And such support would help him overcome what he felt were the character flaws he had been unable yet to overcome. As it was at the moment, he thought "the attendance of the Irish Home rule members in this parliament, is rather an obstacle to the progress and strength of the national movement."

§

Though John passed the summer in London, attending Parliament and occasionally offering brief remarks, he noted another problem. He saw that wealthy men were beginning to profess support for Home Rule. John feared that they were making "hollow professions of favor for the national and popular sentiment—just like gentlemen making love to women they intend to cheat." John would soon be deeply involved with just such an aristocrat.

John and Hentie didn't return to Seaview when they left London. They had had to give up the home they liked so much but could no longer afford. They would depend for a time on the hospitality of relatives and friends. They headed first to the west coast near Clifton. Both found it a very charming place to visit. After a brief visit, the couple took passage on a steamer that took them around the coast to Cork.

They didn't linger in Cork, but moved on to Bantry, where they stayed for three weeks with friends, enjoying excursions along the edges of the bay. John wanted to see if he could still climb after his ill health of the previous autumn. To test his stamina, he climbed Hungry Hill, which was about 2250 feet high. John described the view from the summit. "Magnificent indeed was the view from the top of ocean and bays and lakes and islands and mountain-range after mountain-range. It was a most brilliant summer day and the hottest one, perhaps, in our wretched last summer."

John and his male friends had another most pleasant outing. "We had (this is the men of our party) a grand voyage to Bearhaven and other distant parts of the Bay in a fishing hooker of 70 tons, whose owner and captain was a young gentleman of the neighbourhood—a huge, tall, handsome, kindly, innocent fellow—who seems to care for no more ambitious career. I wish I had a voyage all around the Irish coasts, stopping when and where we liked, in the same comfortable trawler and with the same pleasant company. Of course, we marked where Wolfe Tone lay on board the French man of war those terrible anxious days and nights." [in 1796 when a French invasion was aborted]

After John and Hentie left Bantry, they turned back to Cork for another three-week visit with more friends. From there they moved through Youghal, and Dungarvan to Waterford where they stayed an additional three weeks in "a great old semi-furnished country-home almost five miles SE of the city. These last hosts of ours seemed to consider themselves peculiarly entitled to entertain us, they being Meath people lately come to settle in the south." The people who were such kind hosts were Catholics.

It was while John and Hentie were on their travels around the south that John encountered the reality of fake supporters of Home Rule. John and Hentie were in Cork when they received word that Home Rule supporters in Tralee were in need of help. Daniel O'Donoghue, current head of a noble family, had indicated that he was planning to run for the Tralee seat as a Home Rule supporter in the next election. This was the same man who had failed to keep his commitment to John during the existence of the Irish National League. John knew O'Donoghue had left the Repeal movement to join forces with Gladstone and the liberals.

Strangely, the seat he was supposedly running for wouldn't be open until the next election. Yet, O'Donoghue followed the traditional steps of a campaign, publishing his platform in the local newspaper, and beginning a canvass. In this way, he would have a decided advantage when the next election was actually called.

John answered the appeal for help by writing a letter to the *Tralee Chronicle*. In it, he asked the voters to reject the O'Donoghue, though he was a "former political associate and personal friend." John explained his connections with the O'Donoghue to the voters of Tralee. Together they had decided to form the Irish National League to take up work of Repeal and confederation predating the Home Rule Association. O'Donoghue was well suited to lead in Irish politics. But he now supported the English rulers of Ireland. He helped the Lord Lieutenant oppress Irishmen by arbitrary arrest, unlimited impressments, and denial of trials.

There were only three hundred seven voters in Tralee. "Are they or the majority of them turned against Ireland to become content that their dear old country shall not be a nation, shall not have constitutional freedom, shall be under the foot of England, robbed, tortured and despised?...But I think the great majority of the people of Tralee, and I think of the 307 electors also, are like the people and the electors of the county of Kerry, Home Rulers and men determined to strive for the freedom and rights of Ireland. If so, let them say before God and man that they love their duty and country too well to allow any desertion of the national cause."

John recounted a conversation he had had with the O'Donoghue as the time the University bill was moving through Parliament. "Last spring at the time of the Irish University Bill, he one day sought me out in a lobby of the House and engaged me in a long conversation, the drift of which I guessed to be a desire on his part to return to his first love in politics and to rehabilitate himself with the Irish people. I spoke frankly to him as if Ireland so understood him, encouraging him with my opinion that if he sincerely returned to the National cause the people would perfectly forgive and receive him back to their hearts."

The same edition of the newspaper contained an editorial. "At a single bound the constituency rose to its feet the moment the danger became apparent, and its attitude of noble resistance has been sufficient of itself to fill its plotting enemies with dismay, and to send the wretched traitor, who sought to snatch a triumph from its hand, cowering back in shame and trepidation.

"The O'Donoghue has not dared to fulfill his swaggering boast and to risk the judgment of Tralee upon his political career. He may, indeed ere long, screw up his courage to that stretch of hardihood, but he has not ventured to do it yet. He has shrunk from even an attempt to redeem his declaration; and his threats and his promise to confront the patriotic men whose generosity he had abused, and whose trust he has betrayed, remain still unfulfilled."

But the O'Donoghue soon did appear in Tralee, moving about the district seeking votes. Tralee was in turmoil. When the O'Donoghue put up election posters, local Home Rulers tore them down. One of the posters was attached to a flag and hung from a second-floor window. Opponents doused it with flour and beer. Wherever he went, he needed police protection.

At one point, "the chieftain" went into a local pub. He held his hand out to a Tralee man sitting at the bar, drinking porter. He seized O'Donoghue's extended hand, and shook it vigorously. Then he told O'Donoghue, 'You wretched renegade, if I had a thousand votes I would not give you one."

The O'Donoghue had brought with him some bludgeon men from Killarney, but they were no match for the angry men of Tralee. When the O'Donoghue attempted to make a speech, his voice couldn't dent the thunder of hostile shouts. Even the members of the press who were in the front rows couldn't catch a word. Despite reality, the O'Donoghue decided to publish the remarks he couldn't deliver in Tralee in a number of newspapers, including some in London. Unfortunately, he decided to sprinkle in indications of cheers and laughter as though his words were being enthusiastically received by the voters. The men of Tralee were greatly amused.

Part of what he supposedly said was a direct and very personal attack on John. "It would be very hard to say anything disrespectful to that old gentleman because he always puts on the tone and manner of a grandfather, but he has addressed a letter to the newspaper. It contains some of the argumentary tricks, but a great deal of covert misinterpretations which I could fritter as easily as I could the spectacles which he puts on every morning when going to start himself. By his conduct in the House of Commons he has made himself ridiculous. At first he wants not power, but at last he pushed himself in. But what did he do when in there? Instead of taking his place and voting in most important questions, he cocks himself up amongst the girls in the gallery and gives a bird's-eye view of what he saw. I deny the right of those agitation species to use the name of O'Connell. What did he do for Mr. Martin himself? When he presented himself at the Repeal Association, he [O'Connell] ordered him to be turned out, and the one pound which he had proffered to be refunded to him and if he gave £1,000 he should not enter the Association."

John commented on the attack."There was nothing very offensive in his remarks on me, nothing downright malignant, only an attempt at sarcasm and jocularity. But his enemies made great use against him of the "abuse" (as they called it) of me, grossly exaggerating the offensive character of what he had written and calling on the people to resent his insolence towards such a nice person as myself. And in the letter I thought I perceived a *soupcon* of bullying—the man is capable of that—and, timid as I am, I never could stand bullying."

So John decided to make a personal visit to Tralee. "I went accordingly and had an amazing 24 hours of the Humerous of an Irish election contest. The whole town was 1 big public meeting, and very big fete and I was the man of the people, the conquering hero. I made 3 public speeches (all extempore) had 3 processions with bands and banners, ate 3 champagne feasts, all between 12 noon on 1 day and 9 a.m. next morning."

The *Cork Examiner* reported what John said in his speeches. "'I have already said my little say about this matter in a public letter, and I come here in person only because you repeatedly invited me, and because the O'Donoghue in a letter containing some personal reflections which probably he will someday be sorry for, seemed to challenge me to come here. (cheers) I don't like to mix up personal differences in public business. I don't wish to say a word personally of the O'Donoghue, but if I'm challenged to say what I think and what I propose to do, I will do, in the cause of Ireland. I am not afraid to do it. (cheers) I am an old man, I am a feeble man. I am not a man of talent, I pretend to no accomplishment whatever, but I have been I think I may say, now in my old age, pretty consistent and staunch to convictions (enthusiastic cheering) and if the O'Donoghue challenges me I publically say, old as I am, I am his man (enthusiastic cheering again and again renewed).'"

The men of Tralee responded with an address given on Monday night. (15th) "With feelings of joy and affection we bid you welcome to Tralee. We single you from amongst your honoured and trusted colleagues of the deputation, not alone because this is your 1st visit to the capitol of Kerry, but because of the circumstances which we cannot allude to without feelings too strong for utterance. With astonishment and indignation, we have read in some public journals a document which pretends to be a speech publically delivered or intended to be delivered in our midst containing a violent and unfounded attack on you by the man whom you and we once lauded. We ask you to believe that no man living would dare publically to insult you in this capital of a county that has recently given to Ireland a proud earnest of fidelity and patriotism. The men of Kerry are no strangers to the story of your sufferings and your sacrifices so nobly and uncomplainingly borne for the land of our love; not even amongst that detached tenantry who surrounded the dock in Green St., where you stood in chains for Ireland, not even amongst the true-hearted men of Meath who proudly selected, and enthusiastically returned you as their member. Nowhere amongst the millions of our race, who toil from pole to pole, is the story of your stainless life, of your unswerving consistency, more familiar than amongst the men who now surround you and their kindred throughout the glens and valleys of Kerry. Accept this welcome as our answer to the insult untruely said to have received the sanction of our presence and believe that the men of Tralee will answer it more practically when the day of election comes round."

John reported to his friends. "And the poor O'Donoghue never showed. I and the other deputies from the Home Rule Association were drawn by the people in carriages in spite of bodily resistance on my part; and the only party or person that appeared in the street for the O'Donoghue was a few wretched women manifestly of the *pave*. Nothing more is heard of office for the O'Donoghue or a vacancy in Tralee—I tell you all that both because it was an amusing and in the whole pleasant adventure of mine and because it may give you an idea of the intensity of the national feeling among the masses in the South."

However, when the general election was held in 1874, the O'Donoghue did manage to win a seat in Parliament.

Gravestones

George Henderson was buried in Mount Jerome cemetery in Dublin, along with his young daughter, to be followed by his wife and son.

John Martin was buried in the cemetery at St. Bartholomews Church (Church of Ireland).

James Harshaw was buried in the cemetery at Glascar Presbyterian Church.

Chapter 20

An Irish Political Party

1873 – 1875

On Saturday, November 1st, 1873, George wrote his last leader for the *Newry Telegraph*, severing his remaining tie with Newry and his former newspaper. After more than thirty years of devoted service to his family's newspaper, he was nearly 60, a good age to retire. The new editor was changing the editorial policy of the paper, diminishing the importance of editorials as times changed. However, when a subject attracted his attention, he would send a new leader to Newry, which the new editor seemed willing to publish.

John and Hentie took up residence in Dublin near Merrion Square when they returned from their adventures through the south of Ireland. "Mrs. Martin and I are in comfortable and cheap lodging (with a wild old Ulster Orange woman, somewhat civilized by eight years' service with the late Archbishop Whately) in Lower Mount St. WE are as it were 'in society' and it amuses me. Mrs. M. is right well enough in health and I well enough for my years. WE remain here at least till parliament opens. Our landlady is fond of us and we of her. And as I contemplate the humane and spiritual and entertaining character and instincts of this Ulster peasant of the Scotch stock I curse with rage at the Malignant Rule that sets the Ulster Presbyterian Orange peasantry at the throats of the Southern Celtic Catholic peasantry and teaches both the kindred Irish races to hate each other for English profit. But this is politics again." For a few months, John and George were again living in the same place.

Unfortunately, the move to Dublin had a negative effect on his health, as John soon suffered yet another attack of bronchitis. Much of each day, he spent reclining. But bronchitis wasn't his only health problem. Vision was also a problem. By evening, his eyes were very strained, making letter writing or reading difficult. However, John made sure that he attended an important meeting of the Home Rule Association in the Rotunda in Dublin. For three days in late November, members of the Association debated changes to the organization. To signify the altered organization that resulted, members changed the name of the organization to the Home Rule League. John was a member of the governing body. To support this new effort John left early in January for a tour of Home Rule groups in England.

Since one of the stops on this trip was in London, his activities drew the attention of the *London Standard*. The newspaper offered back-handed compliments to John for his direct approach to Home Rule. "He flourishes not the olive branch (like Butt), but the shillelagh, he hopes not to cajole but to intimidate us into concession. He does not expect to convert us to the wisdom of Home Rule by appealing to our benevolence, our sympathies, or our justice.

And he is right. Our benevolence revolts from the idea of handing over his country to the rule of rogues and fanatics. Our sympathy with our brothers by blood, race and religion forbids us to sacrifice them to their enemies; our sympathy for the better peasantry will not allow us to betray them to the sole guidance and rule of a hierarchy dependent upon the POPE, and subservient in all things to the interests not of Ireland, but of Rome."

The editor then accused John of damaging his cause. "Mr. Martin, with that straightforwardness which, if accompanied by common sense, would have cured him of Home Rule and other illusions, and which for want of common sense only makes him spoil the games of his adroiter colleagues, puts the claim of his party on a ground which at once exposes its absurdity."

John always argued that the Irish had never consented to the Union, and that the Irish were being governed by a foreign despotism, supported only by a minority of the Irish. The editor pointed out a fact, which John was all too familiar with, that Ireland was divided, "the smaller part being loyal and attached to the nation at large by every tie of interest, race, and religion, as well as by firm political allegiance." Their presence represented a powerful obstacle to John's beliefs that the Irish wanted independence.

When the editor shifted focus to the Catholic majority, there was a different argument. The Act of Union was designed to make them full citizens of England, removing them from their previous status as a conquered nation. So Catholics had a choice, recognize that they are a free part of a great empire or a conquered people, which England could treat as it pleased. "They must accept being part of the UK or conquered."

A few days after John returned to Dublin, the family suffered the unexpected death of one of its most important members. Robert Ross Todd, M. A., Clerk of the Crown for County Down and husband of John's sister Elizabeth, died. Robert had been working late in his office and was walking home around 2 a.m. Suddenly he collapsed just as he had reached Rutland Square. No one reported a body was lying there for a couple of hours, when a group coming home from a party found Robert lying on his side on the sidewalk. His watch chain had been pulled from his pocket, and the watch was missing. So, although there was £8 untouched in his pocket, it appeared a robbery had occurred. The revelers hurried to the nearest police station to summon help. By that time, help was no longer useful.

As this was a street death, and a possible robbery, an autopsy was ordered to determine whether foul play had been the cause of death. His doctor testified that Robert had suffered from some heart problems. The autopsy confirmed extensive problems with his heart. Though a robbery had occurred, it had apparently occurred after death. Because John was now a resident of Dublin, he could assist in all the funeral plans. Robert was buried on the main avenue of Mount Jerome Cemetery in Dublin where the most important Protestants of Dublin were buried.

John didn't have time to indulge his grief, as he had important work to do for the cause. John had become the secretary of the League. Not only did he have to create a functioning organization, but he had to prepare the League to support Home Rule candidates across Ireland in hopes that the group would be successful in the imminent elections. Unfortunately, Parliament dissolved earlier than expected at the end of January. Home Rule candidates scrambled to prepare their campaigns.

An important gathering of the League took place in the theater of the Mechanics Institute before the election. The theater was crowded by the time the 8 p.m. meeting began. Both the main floor and gallery were filled to overflowing. John presided and seconded one of the resolutions. The first resolution protested the suddenness of the elections. It was this amendment that John seconded. He maintained in his remarks that Home Rule had made great gains though they faced problems: "Money against them; Government influence against them; all the powers of the world, he might say, were against them. They would show at election that Ireland was for Home Rule."

For the first time in this election, Irish electors would vote in secret. Since this was a substantial change, newspapers began publishing articles to educate voters on the new voting procedures. The process seemed complicated and daunting. Elections would still be managed by local Sheriffs who would be responsible for erecting booths and for publishing placards telling voters where to vote. When voters entered the voting site, they were met by a presiding officer appointed by the local Sheriff, two assistant clerks, and agents for each candidate. The identification process involved matching the names voters provided with the names on the list of approved voters. An official stamp was placed on each ballot before clerks gave them to the voters. Once the ballots were stamped, voters entered private booths to identify their chosen candidate with an X made with the pen and ink provided. Ballots spoiled by any ink blot, stray mark, or missing the official stamp were discarded.

As actual voting occurred in different places on different days, final results weren't known for several days. John Martin won re-election for Meath by huge numbers. George wouldn't have been happy about the results in Newry as Lord Newry lost to a liberal candidate by four votes.

The election in Ireland was a great victory for Home Rule activists exceeding John's hopes that fifty members would win by nine seats. Although the Liberals won a majority of the popular vote, their margins declined, and their control of the House of Commons vanished. The Conservatives won a majority of seats, making Benjamin Disraeli Prime Minister with no need to rely on the Home Rule Party. George was certainly pleased with that result.

The Home Rule League held its March meeting in the round room of the Rotunda. At that meeting, the League began a new effort to attract attention from the British government and obtain funds for the League. John presented a large volume, bound in green leather and decorated with gold letters, the Irish National Roll, to the meeting.

The objective was to obtain 100,000 signatures, including women for the first time. Everyone who signed the book would be required to pay a shilling and commit themselves to two principles. The first was to swear before God and man that they would never consent to have Ireland controlled by any other country. The second was an affirmation that they were not insulting England but asking for their rights. Once Ireland was independent, they would be loyal friends to England.

John presented the idea behind the National Roll and the principles that underlay the project. He told the audience that "he was ready, if his people willed it to stand for his nation, to fight for it in the battlefield. He was ready, and he hoped the great majority of good Irishmen would also be ready. (hear, hear) to stand for the honour of the people, to stand for the name of Ireland, and Irishmen – to stand and to suffer any difficulties for their country's cause. They would never consent to be slaves. They had been slaves too long; in his mind they should not be slaves one day, one minute longer. When a people so numerous as the Irish, and so powerful as they might make themselves by proper organization, determined on being free, they would be free. (Loud cheers)"

John then became the first person to sign the Roll.

This new initiative was something that caught George's eye. Despite his retirement, he shot off a rare editorial, which was printed in the *Newry Telegraph*. He titled it "Repeal or Else. "Mr. John Martin, disdaining hypocritical utterances, has once more spoken with his natural voice and from the heart. Monday (2nd) witnessed another characteristic performance of the Home Rule League, on the metropolitan stage. There was enacted a new version of the well-known farce entitled 'Raising the Wind.' In the hey-day of Repeal, O'Connell had his Rent, and contrived to make a good thing of it. Patriotism is going a-begging afresh. Mr. Isaac Butt was said to have refused, on a late occasion, to permit the hat to be sent round on his own behoof. But, whether or not he had been so mawkish, or whether it was only temporarily he had practiced self-denial, he has now originated an appeal to the pocket, ostensibly in the interests of what passes for Nationality, and to bear the expense of keeping the agitation afoot."

George conceded that Home Rule had made impressive strides in a short period of time. They had "revolutionized the country" with very little funding. But there had been no discussion as to what effect more money would have on future steps. George thought it might be used for revolution. To support that interpretation, George quoted something that John had stated in his remarks at the launch of the National Roll. "For his own part he solemnly declared that his only desire was to see his country and England friendly neighbours, under the same sovereign; but while he said that he was ready and willing–if it was the will of the nation–'*to stand up for the rights of the people, in the battlefield,*' The candor of the avowal merits appreciative recognition. However, the mock heroic, in the case of one indentified with the Young Ireland of 1848, has a tendency to summon up, before the mind's eye a vision of Widow McCormick's immortalized cabbage garden and the Battle of Ballingarry so famous in song!"

The Home Rule League acquired an important new member at the March meeting. John introduced Charles Parnell to his fellow members and vouched for his support of Home Rule. He came from a patriotic family, his grandfather having been Sir John Parnell, who had given up his seat as chancellor of the Irish exchequer to join Grattan in his fight for Irish freedom. Immediately, A. M. Sullivan proposed that they support him in a by-election for a Dublin seat. This motion was unanimously approved. However, when the election was held ten days later, Parnell was defeated by nearly a thousand votes.

The next important step for the new Home Rule members for Ireland was to make their presence felt in Parliament. So Isaac Butt proposed an amendment to the Queen's speech that would support action on Irish Home Rule in an upcoming debate. In his long address, Butt explained that the Irish didn't enjoy the freedoms promised by the British Constitution and leaders in previous administrations.

A long discussion followed with opposition coming from the previous Prime Minister and the O'Donoghue, now new member from Tralee following his victory in the general election. Several of the new Home Rule members spoke in favor of the amendment. John was there but did not speak. When the division occurred, the amendment lost 50 to 314.

John reported on the event to Daunt. "Our moving an amendment on the address was, I think, a proper and almost necessary action. It has put us distinctly before the world as an Irish-national party, independent of and disconnected from all the English parties here. We are all COMMITTED to each other and before the country as such a party. For me, I am doing my best, and so intend to do even to the suppressing of my own personality as a politician–to unite and train and discipline the Home Rule members as the Irish National party. Circumstances, once every member feels it his duty to work here for the Irish cause, will gradually educate the men into the right idea of policy."

John did not linger in London, returning to his duties in Dublin before March ended. Behind him in London, the O'Donoghue wrote a letter rejecting Home Rule. "Agitation for Home Rule prevents Imperial Parliament from approaching the Irish question in a proper spirit."

John was working very hard to make the Home Rule League a truly national party, with Hentie's wise advice to help him. Still, he wasn't happy with his work as secretary. "I don't make a good secretary–and I had hoped that I would be. I have as yet made scarcely any progress towards bringing the League business into such order that I may efficiently and easily direct it. It is still a hand-to-mouth style of business with me. I even doubt whether my presence here is of any service to the League except for the reception of visitors at the offices and the courteous and proper answering of letters. All else of the Secretary work is done–and cleverly done–by the very active and intelligent assistant Secretary Mr. McAlister. I do not feel that I earn my salary."

Despite John's best efforts and their amazing election victories, transforming the Home Rule League into a powerful Irish political party was getting off to a somewhat rocky start. Not surprisingly, money remained a constant problem. The council of the organization seemed to enjoy spending more money than they had. John put his concerns into a letter to Daunt in April. "Perhaps you are not aware that the Council–quite needlessly, I think–hired new and additional rooms and employed an additional staff for the business of the National Roll. I protested against it on account of the expense, on account of the confusion it must introduce in our office business, and on account of my own strong feeling that the work might be done more effectively if left to me and the staff that I have. But no. Mr. Butt had wildly sanguine ideas about the raising, and at once, of a huge money income by the scheme. And so to do the work fast and well, he insisted upon a special Committee (of 13 I think) and a separate staff and separate rooms and an expensive machinery–and most provoking of all that I as Prime Minister should superintend and control and be responsible for all. I could only protest and warn." John asked Daunt to keep this information confidential.

Day-to-day spending was also a concern. Much as he had tried, John hadn't been able to even slow the outflow of their limited cash, a habit resulting from the emergency spending required to fund candidates in the early election. The committee had spent every penny as it came in. After the grand election victory, the spending had continued at a distressing pace. But that wasn't the only spending practice that concerned John. "And what wears me most is that much of our expenditures seems to be of very doubtful utility, while some labours of propagandism as well as of organization are neglected for want of money."

There was one large expenditure that disturbed him greatly. "Connected with this subject is my personal discontent with my position as a salaried office receiving so large a sum of League money as £3000 a year. I don't feel sure that I am worth my salary. I don't feel sure that the League can afford to pay me. I fear that I am influenced to hold the place by the consideration of the great relief and accommodation it is in my private circumstances to receive an addition to my scanty income of £2000 a year."

This salary problem was made worse by the fact that John had two positions that conflicted with each other. Now that there was a strong Home Rule representation in Parliament, he needed to pay much more attention to his duties there, yet he was greatly needed in the office in Dublin. He could choose to resign his seat in Parliament, but he felt strongly obligated to the people of Meath for their faithful support. He understood that his service in Parliament drained his income, while the position with the League provided a much more comfortable financial situation.

"You see I am in a puzzling dilemma. What I am thinking to do is to resign my office and salary at the end of this first quarter (30 April) and to move to London at that date and remain there till the end of this parliamentary

Session. In August, if the League then should want a Secretary and if I thought I might do League work worth the Salary, I might resume my secretaryship."

§

John had a keen eye and aptitude for analysis. He could see that some new Home Rule members of Parliament were supporters of the idea of Home Rule for Ireland under a Federal system more from an effort to catch the Home Rule tide sweeping the voters than from personal conviction. "Yet I am hopeful that when I die, the nationalists who will succeed us in the heavy and yet best beloved duty of striving for Ireland will not judge me to have failed in point of independence. God Help us all! We must go on in our own course, marked out for us by our own temper and characters."

Despite his recognition that Home Rule members must chart their own path, John was distressed that cracks in the party solidarity were already appearing, not from young members born after the famine, but by someone with long experience in the struggle for Irish independence, his longtime friend P.J. Smyth. Smyth wasn't a supporter of the federal concept, and still hoped for the total repeal he and John had supported for many years. Smyth didn't see his effort to turn the League away from federalism and toward repeal as a danger to the success of the organization. Rather he saw it as a tweaking of the current program. John saw it as an existential threat to the unity of the party.

"I am angry with Mr. Smyth. His object is more evil than good. At least he tries to bring on his country the immediate and terrible evil of disunion–of breaking up a great and powerful and steadily growing union of all the various parties of nationalists–and with no good object except the distant and not easily attainable one of reconstructing the nationalists on a basis such as he may lay down after clearing away the ruins of the one he desires to break down. The ways taken by Mr. Smyth in working at this work, I fear are unscrupulous and wicked."

While John hoped that Smyth's efforts would quickly fade away, he wasn't sure that would happen. "But he is so daring and active and persistent that he will gather a number of malcontent spirits and probably a fair [number of] thoroughly honest and well-intentioned patriots."

The day after recording these thoughts, John had concrete evidence that his worries were justified. He was working at the League headquarters when a gentleman came in who was a stranger to John. He handed John a letter requesting John to remove his name and those of his five sons from the membership roll. The reason for this action was hearing from Smyth that the federal system would leave Ireland forever subject to England. Nothing John could say changed the man's mind. "The man is honest and patriotic; but Mr. Smyth's daring rhetoric has got possession of his mind and has driven good sense away for the time. I surely envy Smyth the gain of so respectable a convert."

Despite Smyth's divisive efforts, John had hopes that an event scheduled for June 23rd would render Smyth's efforts ineffectual. On this date, the Home

Rule League would officially establish its members as an important presence in the House of Commons. Isaac Butt would propose an amendment to the Queen's speech that would initiate a full-scale discussion on the plans and goals of the Home Rule League.

"With respect to this very important step in our movement, what I am most anxious to have right is the wording of the resolution or resolutions, to be proposed to the 'House' as containing our national demand and offer...There will be very serious and anxious discussions among the Home-rule members before the words be determined on. [John participated in creating the wording.] Mr. Butt may be inclined to sacrifice something more than is right to his anxious desire for conciliating English opinion. But he will in the end accede to the deliberate opinion and judgment of the general body of his colleagues. For me I want, if possible, to have unanimity among the members as to the form and words of the motion but to have it such as clearly states Ireland's national right and clearly defines the terms on which the Irish people are content considering all they suffer in their actual situation and their inability to overthrow the superior material force of England and the circumstances of the geographical and political relation of their county to Britain and their connections with the English crown, to enter into a friendly federal arrangement."

This result appeared to be within reach as Home Rule members seemed to be getting on well during their first appearance in London. They clearly saw themselves as something different, a truly Irish party distinct from the current Whigs and Conservatives. They had set about getting to know each other. As part of this effort, they had initiated dinner gatherings of all the members every two weeks. John was also impressed with Butt's leadership. "Mr. Butt deserves praise for his careful leading and training of the party."

When the moment came for the Home Rule League to make its first presentation in Parliament, most of the members were on hand. Mr. Butt rose to speak for the League. He made a long speech outlining the problems that Ireland had endured through the laws that England had inflicted on them. The resolution that Butt presented didn't fulfill John's hopes. But what happened during the two days of debate was even more distressing.

"I must with shame and sorrow confess that when it closed I felt that our side had not the honors of it. To be sure this was partly owing to the impatience and bullying temper of the hostile majority who would listen to no more speaking after Disraeli sat down; and it was largely owing to the Government restricting our debate to two days (of seven hours each) where as the subject might well have occupied ten days. Moreover our adversaries appropriated to themselves more than eight of the fourteen hours we had." "But more than all that the English succeeded in PUTTING US ON OUR DEFENSE, instead of letting us put them and keep them on theirs, as we had a right to do & were bound in justice and policy to do." The debate soon bogged down in small details and methods instead of being "confined to principles and general purposes."

When the vote was taken, the motion of the Home Rule League lost 61 to 458.

§

The Cattle show in Newry was held at the Grain Market on Needham Street on July 9th. As usual, Andrew Harshaw was quite successful. His short-horned cows won three first prizes, and two seconds. He also won a first prize for his Berkshire sow.

However, the Cattle Show wasn't the big local news that prompted George to write another leader. His headline made the exciting announcement. "Arrival of Mr. John Mitchel in Newry." George went on to describe the unexpected return after years away. Mitchel arrived by train at the Dublin Bridge Station at half five where he was greeted by friends and family who escorted him to Ivy Cottage, his childhood home. It had since been incorporated into Dromalane House, which was owned by brother-in-law, Hill Irvine.

A placard had been posted in town, urging Newry citizens to welcome the man who had been in exile for twenty-six years. Around fifty locals gathered for that proper welcome. Some of them were given torches that lighted their way as they marched through Newry streets. A cannon on the steamer Amphion, which was anchored at the Canal Basin, fired a salute from its small canon. Mitchel must have greatly enjoyed the reception.

This was a happy gathering for the extended Mitchel family, John included. There were new family members for him to meet. And the two friends were together again. "I found Mitchel looking better on the whole than he looked 4 years ago…His constitution is manifestly broken down and he has not strength for any long sustained effort of either body or mind. But he is lively, very bright and cheerful and just now in a long broken dream of delight at the revisiting of his kindred and the scenes of his boyhood and early manhood, and at being in Ireland again. He will move about a little throughout Ireland and perhaps make a little tour of Scotland (where he has not yet been) seeing friends. He would run if vacancy occurred in Tipperary. Keeping low as any provocation could lead to arrest and death."

After Mitchel visited the North, he planned a two-week stay in Dublin to visit friends and introduce his daughter Isabelle to the sights of the city. Isabelle, the daughter born while Mitchel was in exile in Australia, was enjoying her first visit to Ireland. One of the people he very much wanted to meet was Smyth. Mitchel wrote him a letter from Newry to relay his plans. "I will be the guest of no 'Home Ruler' in Dublin, not even John Martin. In fact, I am savage against that helpless, driftless concern called Home Rule. And nearly as vicious against your 'Simple Repeal.'" However, if forced to choose, he would enlist beside Smyth. So he didn't stay with John and Hentie, instead hiring rooms of his own. Certainly, while Mitchel was in Dublin, he spent time with John and Hentie, enjoying their evening whist competitions. When the two men parted, both of them must have recognized that they would never meet again.

§

John spent the rest of the year in intense efforts to improve the organization of the League and to put it in a more stable financial position. He could see the potential to influence the people of Ireland and thereby perform a great service to the country. "But we are stopped for want of money." This situation prevailed though John believed that the country would be willing to provide the money that they needed to continue their work.

One of John's priorities was to prepare a realistic budget. "I calculate that this office ought to have at least £2,000 a year to enable it to do the work that is expected of it–say for salaries and wages, £800; for publications, £250; for lectures, meetings, advertisements £500; traveling expenses £250; rent, fire light &c. £200. Now in fact our income is at present barely £1000 net. I say net for the proceeds of the National Roll, coming in in driblets, are attended with expenses of postages &c which lessens them considerably.–Something needs to be done to give us an income of £2000 at least, but what thing?"

As 1874 came to an end, John took what steps he could to reduce expenses. He relocated League headquarters to less expensive rooms and cut back on the paid staff. In order to further reduce personnel costs, John considered eliminating his salary, working instead as an unpaid volunteer. He sent out reminder letters to members whose dues hadn't been paid in full. These steps provided some improvement in the League's financial situation. But still, the League was led by Butt, who had been endlessly bedeviled by spending money he didn't have for things he didn't need.

Perhaps these problems played a role in the health problems that inflicted John at the end of the year and the beginning of 1875. "There has been increased delicacy of health to cripple me. My chronic bronchitis was attended with difficult breathing and dyspepsia and some feebleness of body and depression or dullness of spirits. In short, I am growing old. And then certain private crosses and vexations render me less energetic to deal with the crosses and vexations that one must expect to meet with in the progress of a great and very difficult political movement such as this Irish national movement." However, as January progressed, John's health began to improve. He credited his recovery to the good care Hentie provided.

§

While he recovered, John had time to consider the problems of the League and his role as secretary. To improve the financial situation of the League and reduce his own growing health issues, John decided to resign as the League secretary. Members tried to convince him to remain by offering him more money, but he wouldn't be deterred from his decision. He felt much relieved when the decision had been made, as he always felt guilty for taking any money for his public service.

His resignation took effect in early February. He worked hard before his departure to put the League affairs in good order. So he watched with considerable distress a separation occurring in the Home Rule ranks. "The Irish members don't see eye to eye on any Parliamentary issue except Home

Rule." But now John could focus exclusively on the upcoming Parliamentary session and help forge unity in the Home Rule ranks.

Another somewhat unexpected event occurred that complicated John's plans for the new Parliamentary session. Before John had had time to go to London for the session, a news item of considerable local interest appeared in the *Telegraph*. John Mitchel was again running for Parliament from Tipperary. He had run for office from the same constituency during the general election the previous year and been soundly defeated. This time he planned to return to Ireland to compete for the seat. It was well known that he wasn't a supporter of the Home Rule League. Indeed he told electors that he would go to Parliament "unquestioned and unpledged."

George immediately wrote and sent off a new leader to the *Telegraph*. He began by explaining why this election in the south of the island was of interest to the people of Newry. "Whether or not the constituency of that thoroughly 'patriotic' County have a mind to send to the Imperial Parliament as their Representative any man who must needs be returned 'unquestioned and unpledged,' the mere election of John Mitchel would be, in effect, the affirmation by the electoral body of the principle that there ought to be no compromise such as is admittedly proposed by Mr. Isaac Butt and involved in his scheme. Regarded from this point of view, to the impending contest in the South an interest attaches which it would not otherwise possess in our sight."

A few weeks before returning to Ireland, Mitchel gave a speech in New York City that roundly condemned the Home Rule movement. John found the speech distressing. George noted it as well. "Recent utterances on an American platform clearly denote that neither time nor exile have in anywise altered the peculiar shape and spirit of the personal aims thus interpreted in 1848, or of that which was proclaimed as 'gospel' on the part of the present candidate for Tipperary. Dogmas such as those with which he is identified one would think sufficient to canonize him with the patriotism of the County that, not long since, gave token of its proclivities by electing a Kickham, whom the wrongs of a political martyr only endeared to popularity."

Kickham's election had been voided because of his conviction during the Fenian revolt. George believed that the same fate awaited Mitchel should he be elected over the other likely candidates. However, George found long-term benefits to the effort, at least for the people of Ulster. "By what mighty conjuration could there possibly be averted a conclusion lame and impotent, practically, although certainly not to be deprecated from a constitutional point of view, because tending to impose imposture and to give the Home Rule Association to see that their choice lies between unveiling 'veiled rebellion' and altogether abandoning a delusive and bootless agitation."

Mitchel's return to Ireland was big news in Ireland and England. The *Telegraph* shared some of these reports that the editor thought would be of interest to the readers of Newry. The *London Daily Express* reminded its readers that Mitchel had not completed his sentence for felony treason and was therefore subject to immediate arrest. Should that not happen, Mitchel would certainly not be allowed to take a seat in Parliament.

The *Daily News* article reported, "Whatever doubt may exist as to the real and ultimate aims of the active section of Home Rulers–there are among them moderate and honourable men who give respectability to an agitation which they are powerless to control–none at all exists as to the purpose with which Mr. Mitchel is now about to visit this country; and it accordingly becomes a serious question as to how far the Government would be justified in condoning this last escapade of an apostle of sedition. He comes to this country as an avowed agitator and apostle of sedition, abusing the clemency formerly shown him, and regardless even of the sentence which still hangs over him. As regards Mitchel himself, he is not a very formidable opponent; and the authorities were doubtless well-advised in overlooking his visit of last year, so long as he kept himself in obscurity. It may be doubted, however, now that Michel had put himself forward as an emissary of rebellion, whether it is desirable to leave the population of Ireland to imagine that the laws of this country are to be dared with impunity."

As Mitchel left New York, he sent his manifesto to Tipperary by telegram. In it, he told the electors that he was in favor of Home Rule along with the total overthrow of the established church, universal tenant rights, the abolition of ejectments, education of choice not funded by taxation. The problem with his declaration for Home Rule was that he had a different definition as to what Home Rule meant. To him it was total independence for Ireland.

John was disturbed by Mitchel's declaration for Home Rule, thinking that it would confuse voters. So he put his thoughts into a letter, which he gave Hentie to deliver when Mitchel landed.

"My dear John–I am writing this to be handed to you upon your arrival in Ireland. I want you to know at the outset and as clearly as I can make them known, such events and facts as you may be disposed to take into consideration in adopting your course as a candidate and also your course as a politician. Your long absence from Ireland, as well as your feeble health for the last four years, and my intimate connections with our home politics ever since I came back to Ireland in 1858, entitle me to think that I may serve you in this."

Continuing his letter, John explained that he would very much have enjoyed going to Cork to meet him as he arrived, and to assist in his canvass. However, since the strong attack on the Home Rule League that he had presented in the New York speech to which George referred, John thought it would be embarrassing for both of them if he participated in anyway. Instead, he would remain in London and participate in the Home Rule League actions in Parliament.

John then explained why he would support Mitchel for election. "You ask the compliment, and as the most eminent and worthy of Irish Nationalists living, you are entitled to it whatever be your intentions, whatever be the result of your coming, though the organization laboriously formed by the efforts of men who love Ireland as dearly as you (though they have not such claims as you to the honour) should be broken up and the bulk of the population and all the Nationalist parties now joined in National movement should be scattered again into powerless factions, still, still, I say, let John Mitchel be free to act as the highest and noblest of living Irish patriots.

"If I could believe that you come, to accept the Home Rule movement and to serve it, happy would I feel it for you, for me, for Ireland. Your days and mine would end in happiness. Our country would be in possession of in near prospect, of the best national settlement which circumstances render practicable – a settlement sufficient for her national honour and the happiness of her people. But I do not think you come to advocate and join our national movement. Your disrespectful remarks in your lecture deprived me of such a hope. What I do hope is that you come to treat the Home Rule movement with neutrality, not quite a respectful neutrality at the first, but still a fair neutrality."

Next John warned Mitchel that the people of various political opinions had joined the Home Rule cause because they believed that it was achievable and would represent a giant step toward Irish self-government. The electors of Tipperary would not be supporting him because they wanted to destroy the movement.

John concluded his long letter with these words. "I think I have said enough to acquaint you with my own view of the situation. I ask you to consider me as an *authority* on the actual state of Irish politics in Ireland. I think you do not distrust my *bona fides* whether towards you or towards Ireland."

By the time, Mitchel arrived in Queenstown, the Tipperary election had taken place. Since Mitchel was the only candidate, the outcome wasn't in doubt. So as Hentie and others welcomed him back to Ireland, he could enjoy his election triumph. However, Hentie reported her great concerns for Mitchel's health, that he was very feeble, that he was "very easily and sore tired, unfit for any active public work."

John relayed what she told him to his friend Daunt. "Poor Mitchel, I fear, is nearly through his tumbled earthly career...He is three years younger than I, poor fellow. It is a pity. A noble and splendid man. But it is something that he has had this triumph of his election by Tipperary and of forcing these wretched Government folks to tear their constitution to tatters in alarm about him."

The election celebrations were still underway when members of Parliament took the first steps to void the election. MP Hard Dyke made a motion in Parliament requesting the production of certain documents that Prime Minister Disraeli could use in the debate to overturn the election results. He requested certified copies of the records of Mitchel's trial and conviction, documents relating to his escape, dispatches from Governor Dennison of Van Diemen's Land concerning his ticket of leave. The Prime Minister then read his official Writ that he would move in Parliament a few days later. In it,

Disraeli recounted the offence, and Mitchel's failure to complete his sentence, and ordered a Writ for a new election in Tipperary.

Since most Irish members weren't at that session, the motion to discuss the voiding of the election passed by a vote of 174 to 13. John was one of the thirteen, and he immediately rose to request that additional documents be produced that included the composition of the jury, names of the jury, and a copy of the proceedings of the trial.

The Speaker informed John that his motion was out of order as he hadn't given notice. John immediately gave notice, so his motion could be discussed the next day.

At the sitting on the next day, John followed through on his actions. He requested the additional information he had referenced during the previous session. He then requested that all issues relative to Mitchel's actions except his renouncing of his ticket of leave be left to lawyers. This idea seemed confusing to Conservative leaders.

Then he proceeded to explain the terminating of Mitchel's parole himself. Mitchel had consulted his fellow prisoners about his plans, asking each of them whether or not escaping in the way he planned was a violation of parole. He wished to ensure that he was not sullying his honor by a violation of his previous commitment. They all responded in the affirmative in writing.

At that point, John was interrupted by laughter from the majority benches. He responded, "Honourable members might laugh, but he valued the laughter of no more importance than it was worth."

John concluded his remarks by pointing out to the members that he too was a member despite the fact that, if Mitchel had acted dishonourably to renounce his ticket of leave, he was the one responsible for approving Mitchel's action. Finally, he told members that he didn't care what they thought, and he didn't think that Mitchel did either.

Disraeli offered a firm defence of his writ. "Transportation involves arrest. Every lawyer and every law book will tell you that 'Transportation is not mere exile; it is carried out under statute; it involves the necessary discipline of imprisonment, however extended may be the bounds permitted by a license of the governor.'"

The motion of the Prime Minister was carried without division and a new election writ issued.

Mitchel immediately announced that he would run for the seat yet again. Indeed, he would run as many times as Parliament denied him the seat. John was very concerned about this plan. He felt that Mitchel had enjoyed his triumphant return to Ireland and election to Parliament. But if he continued to pursue the seat, the result would ultimately be the loss of a safe Home Rule seat.

With the new election date set for March 11th, John wrote Mitchel a letter from London to express his worries. But he made it clear that he would support Mitchel's decision. "For my own part, I should like best whatever you choose. And I should have expected you to claim for yourself to decide on the course to be taken as to this second election. So far as the *law* is concerned you know more of that than I. *If* you care to let law have influence on your action as to the seat, the best thing you could do would be to have an interview with Butt, who (I hear) is to be at Clonmel on Monday. Don't let personal feeling interfere. *He has none against you and never had.* Do what you think right."

Mitchel began to campaign again for the seat. To start the new effort, he gave an interview with a local reporter representing the *Manchester Guardian*. The interview was held at Sunday's Wells, an estate John frequently visited as well. The reporter thought that Mitchel looked very well despite rumours of ill health. As John had done before Parliament, Mitchel focussed the interview on his escape from exile. He pointed out that Lord Palmerston had pardoned John, Smith O'Brien, and O'Dogherty, referring to them as "honourable men" for keeping their word and enduring their punishment. "Their honour had been verified officially by the government. These men would not have endorsed his escape had it not been carried out with honour. That is a very important thing, for everybody knows Smith O'Brien. They know Martin and neither of these men would ever have spoken to me again if I had broken my parole.'"

While Mitchel was running again for the seat, John remained in London, preparing to make a speech there in Mitchel's behalf. John explained his plans to Daunt. "I am to speak tomorrow night on the Mitchel question, which I shall in my own way endeavour to use as an argument for Irish Home Rule. I want to speak very seriously and go to the utmost limit that the usage of the House permit in judging and condemning English rule in Ireland. And to do this well I ought to be well prepared and have my every word selected and weighed. Yet sensible as I am of the need of so preparing I have not yet written a line of my intended speech, though I hope to write it tonight."

John wasn't optimistic that his efforts would change anything. "I suppose the Government will succeed, one way or another in preventing Mitchel from being acknowledged as the legitimate representative for Tipperary. But they seem to have in their panic–fear that he was coming over to take the oath (Would to God he did take the oath of Allegiance & so become a Home-ruler or Repealer like the rest of us!) put themselves into an absurd position for the present."

On Friday, February 26th, John rose to give the speech he had told Daunt about in his letter. It was a powerful speech, and with his pleasant speaking voice and calm style, he was able to command the attention of Commons during a long speech.

"The question, I am about to raise will probably cause extreme impatience in the minds of English members, because they have the force overwhelmingly on their side. As an Irish member, however, I think it my duty to raise some of these very questions, and to call the attention of the English and Scotch members of this House to the manner and to the circumstances in which John Mitchel was made a felon under English rule; and in doing so I trust to the courtesy of the House for a fair hearing."

The "so-called trial was, as I shall venture to pronounce at the outset, a disgrace to English rule and the administration of the law in Ireland." John then proceeded to offer evidence to prove that the crime for which Mitchel was charged was for writing ideas that the British government didn't appreciate. Parliament had participated in the injustice to Mitchel by passing a law specifically providing the tools to convict Irish writers who supported that national cause. He recounted how the government had packed the jury with Protestant supporters of England. So Mitchel had been tried not by a jury of his peers, but rather a jury of his enemies. When John finished this part of his speech, members could have no doubt but that the British Constitution had been violated, and a grave injustice done.

"Now, I will not ask any English member to put it to himself what he would think if, in this country, a man were to be tried with all the forms of law, and pronounced to be a felon and sentenced to fourteen years transportation for speaking and writing the sentiments of seven-eighths of his countrymen. Thank God you are living under English rule and that rule is not a foreign rule to you. That solemn farce of justice was only a particularly flagrant case of the ordinary political trials in Ireland under English rule before and since."

John then pointed out the terrible situation in Ireland at the time of Mitchel's trial. "In 1845, the potato blight became very destructive, not only in Ireland, but over Western Europe. But it was only in Ireland, under English rule, that the potato blight resulted in famine. All the countries that had Home Rule were able to bear the loss of potatoes without a single death by starvation. Those countries, as well as Ireland, had great resources independent of the potato crop. Not one of those countries had greater facilities than Ireland in ports, canals, railroads and macadamized roads for receiving food and distributing it from place to place. And yet, under English rule, the potato blight in Ireland resulted in famine, famine raged for 6 consecutive years and the population of Ireland became less by almost 2,500,000." "A famine lasting for 6 consecutive years was never before heard of in the world. There is no account of such a famine in ancient or modern history. It was only possible in Ireland and under English rule.

"Under circumstances such as these and believing that the national Irish Parliament and Government of which Ireland had been deprived by the Union of 1800 could not be restored with consent of England, Mr. Mitchel became an advocate for separation and revolution. He concluded that it was the fixed determination of the English Government and nation, not to allow a national Parliament and constitutional freedom to exist in Ireland, and that the only hope for Ireland was separation from the English Crown. He thought it was better that the Irish people, disarmed and weak as they were, and their country in a state of military occupation by England, should die by fighting than endure famine any longer."

As John then turned to the new push for Home Rule that would prevent similar terrible tragedies in the future, he revealed in very personal terms how the famine had affected him personally. "I was in Ireland at the time. I witnessed the famine and saw all its miseries. It burned its marks into my breast, and they can never be totally removed."

"I was sent here as one of the 59 Irish representatives to advocate the cause of Home Rule. The Irish nation, by its legitimately appointed representatives, came here to ask for the restitution of their national Parliament. There would then be between the 2 countries a happy connection, which would make Her Majesty's subjects in Ireland as firmly attached to her Crown and Government as any of her subjects are. The Irish people offer that on the single foundation that the English shall do them justice and cease to do them wrong."

The situation in English governance had changed greatly over the intervening years. The English government had granted Home Rule to Canada and Australia, had expanded the right to vote, and instituted the secret ballot. Surely this was the time for Parliament to grant Home Rule to Ireland as well.

"It is reasonable to hope that with the feeling of responsibility arising from this change even their political situation, the English people will inquire into the relations which Ireland holds to England and the results of English rule in Ireland. I think it reasonable to hope that the conclusions at which the people of England will arrive, will be more just, more humane, more respectable for the name of England, and more happy for the people of Ireland."

John ended his speech with all the force he could muster. "As a consequence of the change in the foreign relations of England, it will henceforth be the desire of the English nation to act inoffensively toward all their neighbours, and to have united and contented subjects of the Crown in all Her Majesties three kingdoms. The common sense of the English people will before long convince them that Home Rule in Ireland can harm England no more than Home Rule in Canada or Australia. However, that may be, the wishes of the Irish people can now be declared by the legitimately elected representatives of Irish national sentiment. The Irish under these circumstances will not rebel or become separatist, but they never can consent to the deprivation of their national rights and their constitutional and civil freedom. Great will be the day when an English Prime Minister advises Her Majesty to restore the Irish Parliament and happy it will be for England and for Ireland when that day arrives."

John didn't enjoy speaking before Parliament. But he felt it his duty to do so. "Besides, I feel that hardly any of the other 59 might speak out so plainly to these English as myself and had ambition to perhaps raise the spirits of our men and let the English feel that we are not to be treated as worms that won't turn."

Reflecting on his speech before Parliament, John was satisfied for the first time with a presentation he had made there. "I have made one remarkable speech (26 Feb.) 45 minutes long to a perfectly still and attentive House, whose patience (considering their ignorance and prejudice) I cruelly tried.

They bore me all through with amazing courtesy and indeed earned my respect."

One of the other members told him afterwards, "There lives not another man, Irish or other from whom such a speech would have been so listened to by the House."

Meanwhile, the work of the Home Rule League continued with dark clouds rising. The split that John foresaw when P.J. Smyth withdrew did take place. At the end of February, Smyth renounced his membership in the League, and announced that he would bring in a bill for the complete Repeal of the Union.

Soon afterwards the League made the formal announcement that John had resigned his post as the League Secretary, becoming instead an honorary secretary. With his League work no longer distracting him, John intended to focus on serving his constituents in Meath. So he was on hand paying attention to his work in Parliament when another issue come up in which he had personal experience and great interest, the over-taxation of the Irish. A motion was made to have the government at least study the issue. The Conservative leadership resisted.

John had had suffered personally from the results of Irish taxation, so he was eager to speak on the issue before the government defeated it. "He had perceived that the consciences of some Englishmen were beginning to be touched. He had watched how eagerly they hung upon the words of the Chancellor of the Exchequer, seeking for some apology, some excuse, some explanation, anything that would satisfy them that it might be just to tax the people of one country 5s 3d in the pound, and of their own country 2s 6d only. There was another reason why the inquiry should be granted, and it was this– that the right hon. Gentleman had said–and a former Chancellor of the Exchequer had re-echoed his words that in fact Ireland in the matter of taxation was unduly favoured. Now, as an Irishman, he said he did not want to be unduly favoured. His countrymen would scorn to be unduly favoured."

With those words, John resumed his seat, watching quietly while the motion was withdrawn. Irish taxes would continue unchanged. John would not speak in Parliament again.

Chapter 21

Farewells

1875

The second Tipperary election was scheduled for March 11ᵗʰ. Just three minutes before nominations closed, a Conservative candidate came forth to oppose Mitchel. Should Mitchel's candidacy be voided, the new candidate would be declared the winner. That was indeed what happened. As John had anticipated, Mitchel's determination to run again despite his declining health would cost the Home Rule League another member.

Despite the unexpected opposition, Mitchel won by a vote of 3,114 to 746 for Moore. However, Mitchel wasn't in Tipperary to enjoy the victory, He was instead on a train from Cork to Dublin, cared for by Hentie. The trip was unexpected, so there were few people other than security forces on the train platform in Dublin to greet him. Press reports indicated that "Mr. Mitchel looks very weak, and has, it ought to be added, a ghastly complexion."

Mitchel and Hentie didn't remain long in Dublin. Two days later, they took the mid-day train north to Newry. Hentie helped him transfer to a carriage for the ride back to Dromalane. He sat in the drawing room for the rest of the day. Then he was helped up the stairs to the bedroom he had occupied as a child. He was never to leave it.

From there he wrote a letter to the voters of Tipperary to thank them for their support. It showed some of the old Mitchel fire. However, the letter he wrote to John in London was quite different. As John described it, "With many sighs and stoppages, he had written me a brief letter which I received in London on Thursday night. There was the old gaiety and the old earnestness of heart – he hoped soon to see me, – he sent his thanks to each member of Parliament...who had spoken out in the House on the National side in his case."

John continued his work in London. He also fulfilled a commitment to speak at a St. Patrick's Day event in Newcastle for the purpose of raising funds for the families of the remaining Fenian prisoners. While he had been ill recently, he felt sufficiently recovered to honor his commitment.

As always, John spoke from his heart about the need for Irish unity. "Until Irishmen thought of their country more and thought less of their private and personal factions and interests; until they manage to direct their faces and turn all their strength of their efforts against the common enemy – that was to say against the power that kept them in chains – they could not hope to make progress."

According to John, some progress was being made. Part of the reason for that progress was support from people like those in his audience. "What had taken place among the Irish in England and Scotland and in Ireland too, was proof that all parties of the Irish race who were patriotic – there were many parties, many differences of opinion, it would be a very dull world if there were not – were keeping their eyes up to that great object, the object that they should regard as a holy and heavenly one, the object of liberating their country...It was a good work and when men understood to try to do a good work they must work at it, they must do their best at it and leave the result to God."

Once that commitment had been fulfilled, John returned to London, spending much of the next day writing letters. The following day he went to Parliament to attend the session. It was there he received the telegram with the ominous black border. He did not have to open it to know what news it contained.

John immediately made plans for the sad trip home to Newry. Friends, knowing that he was just recovering from his latest bout of bronchitis, urged him to save his strength and remain at work in London. A.M. Sullivan, who was one of those friends, recounted the conversation. "It is too bad that I must go to Ireland. It may be thought strange and wonderful that I should say it while my dearly loved friend lies dead and it would be grievously misunderstood if I spoke out what I feel. But I would rather leave it to other hands to lay my friend in the grave, and to remain at my post to fight the Coercion Bill on Monday. I have given 30 years of labor to the national cause, and I have come now to feel like a soldier in a bayonet charge–my comrades on the right and left of me fall but I cannot turn aside–I must march on."

The trip was arduous. After a long passage across the Irish Sea on the night steamer, John arrived in Dublin. He paused to rest for a while with his sister Elizabeth before taking the train north to Newry. By the time Hentie met him at the Edward St. Station, plans for the funeral had already been completed. Hentie shared them with John as they drove to Dromalane. John had reservations about what he heard. The funeral was to take place just a couple of days later on Tuesday at 12:30 p.m. Mitchel would be buried beside his parents. John had hoped that the funeral would take place a bit later. He knew that there were many members of Parliament who would wish to attend, but who would be forced to remain in London for the important discussions underway there.

John immediately joined the family efforts to cope with the many details that had to be attended to in what would be a very important funeral. There were messages of condolence to respond to, a task which John could well handle. One of the letters he wrote was to P.J. Smyth. Apparently Smyth had indicated that he might not attend the funeral due to the important issues facing the House. Given John's own feelings, he had no trouble assuring Smyth and other members that remaining in London was the proper course. He informed Smyth of the plans, and his support for not having the grand Dublin funeral, which many Irish leaders were pushing for.

Then he shared reports of Mitchel's death, as Hentie had relayed them to him. "Every circumstance in the last day of the poor fellow has been pleasing for his friends to recollect and dwell upon. He was cheerful, happy, satisfied, and with his old quiet manner. He has had a happy end, seeming to wind up and finish his life in entire consistency with which had gone before of it. The face looks very beautiful now, youthful, bright, peaceful."

John acknowledged their political rupture. "However you and I have come to differ in politics and such things of late years, in this at least we are at one that we were always staunch friends to the noble Irishman that lies above where I write, his life well lived out, his task happily finished."

Once the news of Mitchel's death had been telegraphed around the world, newspapers began to publish their thoughts in editorials. John wrote a brief one of his own. "John Mitchel has died well, at home in Ireland, in his father's home, surrounded by his loving brother and sisters and other friends, after a nobly consistent life, crowned by the affectionate gratitude of the people he loved, and served triumphant in every respect but material force over his enemies."

George wrote a long leader on the death of a man he had known most of his life. He recounted in some detail the facts of his life. Then George acknowledged Mitchel's talents. "Mr. Mitchel wielded a pen of wondrous power, and he was surpassed by few as a pure and vigourous writer."

That skill didn't prepare him to lead a revolution, and another issue ensured his failure. Though his talk was always garnished with 'pikes and drums and wounds,' he had not the least taste for the practical part of war. He was a solicitor and a journalist, and knew nothing even of that most elementary kind of insurrection, street barricades, and was utterly unsuited by temperament or power to organise a real revolt."

However, George couldn't resist a parting comment revealing his own feelings toward Mitchel. "Death stepped in, and an eventful career was closed. Mr. Mitchel is gone to that 'bourne from whence no traveler returns,' and we hope the lessons of his mistaken life will not be lost upon the country." Other papers commented on the same two facts of Mitchel's life, his writing skills and his support for lost causes.

Placards were placed in shop windows in Newry announcing Mitchel's death. "Fellow-Townsmen! The member for Tipperary, The intrepid John Mitchel, Has expired. All Ireland mourns his loss, and will honour his memory. The men of Newry, amongst whom he spent his youth, and amongst whom he died in harness as he had lived, are, therefore, requested To assemble on the Fathom Line, At half-past eleven O'Clock, on Tuesday, and accompany to their last resting-place the remains of one who loved his country with unselfish devotion. By order of the [Catholic] Working Men's Club, The Secretary."

The funeral proceeded as proclaimed in the poster. Mitchel's body was placed in an oak casket, which was then carried into a hearse drawn by four horses. John was among the chief mourners. His brother David was one of the pall bearers. Many prominent leaders of Newry also attended.

The hearse and carriages turned onto the Dublin to Belfast Road, and proceeded down the hill toward Dublin Bridge, where large numbers of people joined the procession. Windows overlooking the line of march were filled with people attempting to witness the historic event. The sounds of hooves striking the pavement and the creak of carriage wheels alone interrupted the respectful silence of the crowds. The casket was unloaded and carried through the gate, and down the slope to the small cemetery where Mitchel's parents were already buried. The ruins of Reverent Mitchel's old Presbyterian church loomed over the scene. Rev. J. C. Nelson of Downpatrick delivered the eulogy. He had also officiated at the funeral of Mitchel's father many years before.

The remarks were almost a sermon and extended for many minutes. Part way through, John felt somewhat faint. He would have fallen to the ground, but for the quick action of William Mitchel who was standing beside him. William caught hold of him, and then supported him as they walked back up the hill to a carriage that hurried him back to Dromalane House. Hentie met the returning carriage and helped John up the steps and into the drawing room. She usually knew what to do to help John regain his strength whenever illness struck.

John's collapse was noted in the *Telegraph* two days later. "The excitement produced by the death and funeral of Mr. Michel proved too much for Mr. Martin, MP, and he was unable to remain for the close of the ceremony in the cemetery. We have learned that, although going on favourably, he is still in a very weak state of health."

Another report appeared in the next edition of the paper. "Since the day of Mr. Mitchel's funeral Mr. Martin, MP has been prostrated by an attack of bronchitis. Indeed, the report from Dromalane on Thursday was that he was dangerously ill. Yesterday, we were informed that there was no change for the better."

John had been taken to an upstairs bedroom. Chairs had been arranged near the fireplace, so John could remain in a reclining position, as he struggled for each breath. The life and death struggle continued for two more days after the alarming warning was first published. His friends around the world waited for news that he had again beaten back his lifelong affliction as he had so many times before.

However, near 9 a.m. on March 29th, the harsh sounds of his labored breathing, slowed. And then there was silence. Hentie held him as he slipped away. She was comforted for her shattering loss of husband and brother within a few short days by the presence of other family members. The loss of the lifelong friends in the same place and within a few days of each other, added greatly to the sorrow of the family and many Irish leaders who had known both men.

John's body was carried from the front bedroom, embalmed, and placed in a simple coffin in the front salon. The coffin remained open, so friends and colleagues could offer personal and private farewells. Many bent to kiss his brow and left in tears.

Friends vehemently argued that he should receive a national funeral in Dublin. Telegraphs to that effect flooded into Newry. The staff at the Newry Post Office was hard pressed to keep up with this traffic, printing out and dispatching telegraphs that contained over 5000 words total. Since John had expressed his wish to be buried in Donaghmore beside his parents, many of those picturing a grand funeral were to be disappointed.

Words of sympathy poured in to the family, some from absent friends, some from organizations, some from newspaper obituaries. The Home Rule League expressed their feelings clearly. "The council of the Home Rule League…solemnly expresses their deep sorrow at the death of their fellow member and honorary Secretary, John Martin MP for Meath; and at the same time desire to record the grateful remembrance in common with the people of Ireland, they now and ever must feel for the many noble sacrifices which throughout the course of an honourable and blameless life, he cheerfully made for his well beloved country."

The *Newry Reporter* featured the news in its leader the next day. "On yesterday morning at a quarter to nine o'clock, in the same house where his friend and compatriot expired ten days before, Mr. Martin calmly closed his eyes in death.

"Many who saw him on the day of Mr. Mitchel's funeral, borne away in a fainting state, from the graveyard to his carriage, said that he would not long survive his lifelong friend, and the gloomy prophecy has been too truly realized. It is not necessary that we should enter into any review of the public career of Mr. Martin. It is enough to say that, however people might differ as to his views on public questions, there was but one concurrent opinion as to the integrity of his motives, the purity of his life, and the goodness of his heart. No man could come into contact with John Martin without feeling that he was in a superior presence, without revering him for his truthfulness, and loving him for his amiability."

The *Newry Telegraph* contained a long leader on John's death, but George didn't write it. Instead the paper copied an obituary written by the London Correspondent of the *Belfast News-letter*. The Henderson family also owned this paper, so these were the views of one of John's opponents.

"'How singularly ignorant are frequently those who venture to instruct. The death of poor Mr. Martin, one of the members for Meath, has given the Times and Daily News an opportunity for writing an article upon him, professing to know a great deal, but really thoroughly misleading. The writer speaks of Mr. Martin as having no literary power, as being a person devoid of the graces of oratory, of the most elementary ideas of public speaking, of individuality and originality, and, in fact, as a person who was nothing more nor less than a sort of admiring aide-de-camp of his relative, the late Mr. Mitchel. Nothing could be more fallacious, so far, at least, as we at this side of the Channel are able to form an opinion. We never saw Mr. Martin until he came over as MP for the County of Meath. Those who had merely heard of him as the attached friend, co-rebel, and ardent sympathiser with John

Mitchel, expected a very different sort of person. But instead of a bellicose individual, with a loud voice, Celtic brogue, and violent demeanour and attitude, we beheld a mild, inoffensive elderly gentleman, with stooped shoulders and white hair, the organs of veneration and benevolence largely developed, a kindly voice and manner, moderate tone, and an earnest desire to conform to all respects to the rules and regulations of the assembly of which he was a unit. Indeed, Mr. Martin soon began to make friends in quarters where he little expected to find them.

"'One of the first persons who studied his character and formed an estimate of his qualities was the Speaker of the House of Commons. He, of course, had heard a good deal about Mr. Martin, as we all had, and when first informed that the dreaded member for Meath intended to address the Home Rulers, he at once expressed his readiness to give him an opportunity by 'calling' him. There were then three Mr. Martin's in the House, and the Speaker laying peculiar emphasis on the word 'John,' called upon 'Mr. John Martin.' When Mr. Martin rose every one listened with attention at first, and subsequently with interested surprise. They expected a very different sort of man and a very different sort of speech. But Mr. Martin was moderate, though firm, while the sincerity of his convictions (mistaken though they were) were so apparent that no one could for a moment associate him with the noisy, vain, conceited, and blatant agitators of the old Whig type, who for so many years had made the House of Commons the road to the attainment of their own selfish ends. English members who listened to Mr. Martin said to themselves, 'Here, at least, is a man with whom we can deal; we cannot, of course, agree with him, but he is evidently conscientious and sincere, a man of culture and a gentleman, not a noisy, vulgar, venal demagogue.'

"'The House of Commons is, of all places in the world, that in which a public man inevitably finds his level. The late Mr. Martin was no exception to the rule. He had not been in the House many weeks before he found his level, and that level was not one that either he or his friends had reason to be ashamed of. He was put down as an earnest and sincere, but ideal and mistaken, politician; and he was respected for the genuine and uncompromising manner in which he urged his opinions, while, at the same time, he admitted that he could not hope to make them acceptable to the vast majority of his hearers.

"'The last time he addressed the House he spoke with considerable dramatic power while repeating the lines commencing:- Alas! poor county. And when he concluded he was applauded, even by those who differed most widely with him. These were the last words he ever addressed to the Parliament of the United Kingdom.

"'It is not true, as asserted in the *Daily News*, that Mr. Martin contracted his fatal illness at the funeral of Mr. Mitchel. The proximate cause of the malady to which he succumbed was of earlier origin. For several days before the death of Mr. Mitchel, I observed that Mr. Martin was labouring under some form of pulmonary affliction. I saw him in his place in the House of Commons the day before he left London for the last time, and I was struck by his altered appearance. He seemed to have suddenly, as it were, lost flesh; his features assumed that alarming angularity of appearance that so often presages a fatal illness, and his voice had lost much of its power. I had a sort of presentiment that I should never see him again.

"The House of Commons will not readily forget John Martin, and I may be excused for expressing the hope that his successor may be equally inoffensive and amiable in his relations to it.'"

The *Irish Times* generally agreed with the comments from England. His speeches in Parliament were "characterized by clearness, directness, and honesty of purpose. The death of JOHN MARTIN–'honest,' 'truthful' JOHN MARTIN, is to the Home Rulers an irreparable loss. The character of the man gave prestige to any movement he decided to take part in."

A handful of editorials were negative. One claimed that John wouldn't even be remembered among the second-rate Irish leaders, another that John wasn't a man of any distinguish abilities, that he showed no sign of the intellectual abilities of other Irish leaders.

John's dear friend, Daunt recorded his feelings in his journal. "Returned home last week and was shocked and grieved to learn that my dear friend John Martin was no more. He was taken ill when attending the funeral of Mitchel near Newry, and never rallied. His death is a very serious loss to the Home Rulers, to whom his high character, his intelligence, and his great information on political subjects were of the highest advantage. A purer, more unselfish patriot never lived. Himself, an earnest Presbyterian, he had a generous and loving confidence in his Catholic countrymen. His enemies reproached him with the indiscretion of his conduct in 1848. The truth is that he, like Smith O'Brien, was driven to madness by the horrid spectacle of multitudes perishing of famine when the plentiful food their labour had provided was swept out of the country by the operation of the accursed union. And now the pure, noble spirit of our dear and revered friend has passed to its final account. May he rest in peace."

Despite the pressing business in Parliament that kept many of his colleagues in London, eight members felt honoring John more important than Parliamentary agendas. Large contingents from neighboring counties planned to attend along with John's constituents from Meath. Windows in Drogheda were darkened out of sorrow for John's passing. Delegations from Scotland and England too crossed the channel to honor their friend. "The funeral will, it is expected, be the largest demonstration seen in Ireland since the days of the great Liberator. And no other man, apart from O'Connell, more worthily deserves such a display than 'honest' John Martin."

Indeed, an estimated fifteen thousand people participated. Once again a sad line of black carriages and a hearse lined up in front of Dromalane House as John's coffin was carried with great tenderness from the drawing room, out the front door and then placed in the hearse. His new Home Rule friend, Rev. J. A. Galbraith was one of those who bore the burden of John's body and coffin. The chief mourners included the two young men for whom John had become a substitute father, many nephews and the sons of his late friend John Dillon. John Harshaw represented his Harshaw cousins.

The procession was led by a large delegation of clergymen of all faiths, walking two abreast down the driveway. The Dean of Dromore, Church of Ireland, Daniel Baggot, marched in the front ranks. Next came members of the various delegations, marching four across. Among them was Charles Stuart Parnell. The pallbearers walked beside the hearse, with the chief mourners walking behind.

The people of Newry lined the streets for John just as they had for his friend a few days earlier. The procession turned down the hill, crossed the bridge, and turned down Hill Street, taking John one more time past Dr. Henderson's school, where he had first met George Henderson, and John Mitchel, then past the *Telegraph* office. Sidewalks were packed with the grieving citizens of Newry. Others leaned out of every window above. They were respectfully silent, the only sounds coming from marching feet, the clatter of carriage wheels bumping over the cobblestone streets, and the thump of horses' hooves. When the cortege reached Kildare Street, it turned right, rejoining the main Belfast Road, passing the Court House and the home on Downshire Road where his sister Elizabeth had once lived, into the country beyond. As the town fell away behind them, the procession paused to allow the walkers to climb into waiting vehicles. The trail of mourners reached a mile in length.

The procession moved slowly northward to the Four Mile House. There it turned right for the last couple of miles to the church. When they reached the gate of St. Bartholomew's Church, the hearse and carriages stopped. The roads near the church were already crowded with local mourners. The coffin was removed and carried through the gates, up the walkway and onto the grass beside the church. Invited guests stood in the limited space next to the church. Those who had walked filled the street searching for vantage points in the roads and the hillside beyond the church wall.

Rev. John Elliott, who had officiated at James Harshaw's funeral, conducted the service. After a scripture reading, and general remarks on the joys of the new life that John was experiencing, he presented a fitting eulogy.

"And now, my beloved brethren, comforted by this blessed home in Jesus, it is our melancholy privilege to-day to unite in doing the last rites to our much beloved friend, Mr. John Martin. To us in this neighbourhood it is a source of much satisfaction that, after wandering over all seas and residing in almost all the habitable parts of the earth, he was by the good Lord our God brought home to die among his friends, and to be buried in his father's sepulcher. The Martin family have long occupied an important position in this neighbourhood, and I find their names often turning up in the registry and records of the Presbyterian Church, of which they were members. Many and interesting are the stories I have often heard from the lips of aged people, now gone, of the good and noble deeds of the father and the uncles of our dear friend whose remains we are now laying in the grave. His father was an excellent man, his mother an amiable woman, of great intellectual ability and of the deepest piety. In Mr. Martin's high sense of honour, in his spotless purity of life, in the transparent honesty of his character, in his tenderness and sympathy for all that was good and all that was human, we have the reflection of those noble qualities which smiled upon his infancy. He received the elements of his education in the little schoolroom which stands at the gate of this church, and often has he himself spoken to me with the fondest remembrance of those school days when many whose lives have been spent far apart sat on the same benches and read from the same books. The friendships formed in those early years have continued unbroken till death this day has snapped the bond. Men who differed entirely from Mr. Martin in politics never ceased to love him as a brother. The grave never closed over a man whose private virtues were of a higher order than those of John Martin–as a son, as the oldest brother in a very large family, as a father–more than a father–when death took away both parents, and threw a houseful of helpless orphans on his care. No wonder there is bitter sorrow among the poor and aged, and infirm in Loughorne to-day, for they have lost such a friend as is found only now and again at long intervals. The world knew nothing of Mr. Martin's charities. He seemed to tremble lest the right hand should know what the left was doing. 'When the ear heard him, then it blessed him, because he delivered the poor that cried, and the fatherless, and him that had none to help him. The blessing of him that was ready to perish came upon him, and he caused the widow's heart to sing for joy.' He was a father to the poor, and the cause which he knew not he searched out. As a landed proprietor, Ireland can name none better, very few equal."

"Among the saints and heroes whom Ireland has given to the world none was more remarkable for sincerity, for disinterestness, for real heroism. If ever any man loved his country, John Martin loved his. With him, love of country was a passion, which had taken complete possession of his soul. 'Its very dust to him was dear.' He loved its mountains and its valleys. He loved its caves and towers and ruins of a bygone glory, grand even in that desolation. He loved its people irrespective of creed or party."

"There was hardly a dry eye present, and the friends having taken a final leave of one whom they evidently loved with an affection almost too sacred for words to express here, turned sadly away, and John Martin was left to his long last home."

John's friends attempted to cope with his loss. His good friend A. M. Sullivan offered a fitting, final tribute bordered in black in the *Nation,* published on April 3rd.

"Unified through life, undivided in death, John Martin and John Mitchel sleep to-day almost side by side in the graveyards of Newry. Together, when youth was in their veins and hope was in their hearts, they entered the service of Ireland; together, in darker days, they endured the pains of banishment and the bitterness of exile; together–upon the same spot, within the same walls, almost in the same week–they looked their last upon the land of their birth. It is a gloomy time for Ireland. In the death of John Mitchel men saw the loss of the ablest pen, the boldest tongue, the keenest intellect that ever waged war scornful and victorious against the enemies of our race. In John Martin we mourn the truest, the purest, the most chivalrous, and the best of all the patriot band whose names are in the hearts of our people, and whose fame is the heritage of their country. The shafts of death pierced many a gallant Irish heart since Owen Roe died at Loughouter and Sarsfield fell at Landon: the muster-roll of Irish patriotism is swelled by a succession of names as noble and as honoured as ever lent luster to the struggles and the sufferings of a nation. Yet, while his patient fidelity, his earnestness, his utter unselfishness, his gentleness, his courage, and his zeal, are remembered, the name of John Martin will stand second in the estimation of his countrymen to few of the patriot leaders, soldiers or statesmen, orators or poets, 'You live for Erin's weal, but died for Erin's woe.'

"How pure, how tender, how noble in all its impulses that heart was which ceased to beat last Monday the present is not the time when we could tell. We can barely realize the fact that it throbs no more. Ever since the day when John Mitchel stood in the dock at Green-street John Martin has borne so prominent a part in Irish politics that we can scarcely conceive his place unfilled. Many of his associates of '48, when the hopes that inspired them had perished and the effort of the hour was over, retired despondent and disappointed from the cheerless arena, 'washed their hands' of Irish public life, and left the country and the cause to drift on without guidance or assistance. But it was not so with John Martin. His love of country was too fervent and deep-seated to be affected by failure or disappointment. His sympathy with his country-men was too ardent and generous to be neutralized by private interest. When the years of exile occasioned by his outspoken advocacy of the rights of Irishmen were over, he returned unconquered and unconquerable to the service of his country, giving to her cause the same patient earnestness, the same high sense of public duty, the same lofty instincts and indomitable spirit that had previously marked him out for government vengeance. Whoever might waver or falter, John Martin altered not. The storm of government persecution was not the only ordeal through which he was fated to pass. If he had the consolations, he had also the penalties of consistency; but public neglect and ingratitude, however much they might grieve his gentle nature, could not turn him from his course. The mists dissolved, the storms passed over, and John Martin was found standing where he stood. And then, when at length justice was done to his character and his labours, when gallant Meath rushed in a joyful procession, green as the leaves of the forest to place his name on the parliamentary roll, how little was he altered by the change. The applause of his countrymen was, indeed, dear to his ears; he loved the cries of welcome, the demonstrations of reverence and affection which greeted him wherever he turned; and yet, sooner than deviate one hair's breadth from what he conceived to be the line of duty and rectitude, he would see all that popularity pass away, just as to the same sense of right he had sacrificed years before his prospects, his home, and his liberty. And right well did his countrymen learn to appreciate that chivalrous love of principle. Never anywhere was there a leader in whose probity and rectitude greater confidence was reposed. His name alone was a sufficient guarantee for the character of any movement or undertaking. Whoever else might be imposed upon, 'Honest John Martin' could not be tampered with; and the ranks that *he* marched in could never stray. Thus it was that his spotless character and unswerving honesty came to be honoured in Ireland. So trusted and honoured, in the prime of his usefulness, he is gone from amongst us. The Bayard of Irish politics, free from pride, free from guile, free from fear, a purer or nobler citizen was never laid in an Irish grave.

"The tears of sorrow are soon effaced; the busy cares of life soon draw the last mourner from the tomb. The struggle which John Martin so gallantly shared in will continue, and others must try as best they can to fill the place he filled and lift the load he raised. His thoughtful face, his earnest gaze, his winning smile, we shall see no more. But the memory of John Martin will not die. 'By all his country's wishes blest,' his name will be spoken and his life and labours praised while the Irish race has a survivor. The reputation of such men as he, is not the property of a generation or of a century. Nor has he ended his service with his life. 'It is at the tombs of great men' says a recent writer, 'that succeeding generations kindle the lamp of patriotism;' and he is right. There is a sense in which we cannot say the dead are dead, or changed to us although they change. Through many a future year the lessons of John Martin's life will bear golden fruit; and from his quiet grave in Newry that clear, persuasive voice will ring upon the ears of his countrymen, exhorting them to the completion of the work to which the life of the dead patriot was devoted."

Well over a century has passed since that sad day. Still generations later, mourners make the sad pilgrimage to his grave to honor his service to Ireland, to cherish the example he left for political leaders to emulate, and to read the inscription on his tombstone. "John Martin, born 8th September, 1812; died 29th March, 1875. He lived for his country, suffered in her cause, pleaded for her wrongs, and died beloved and lamented by every true-hearted Irishman."

Henrietta Mitchel

Henrietta "Hentie" Mitchel was John Mitchel's sister. She married John Martin in November 1867. She survived both men.

Epilogue

After John wrote the letter to P. J. Smyth, advising him and the other Irish members of Parliament to remain in London instead of returning for Mitchel's funeral, he put down his pen and closed his writing desk. He wrote no more. The three Newry men had all ended their contributions to Irish history. People who had actually known these men gradually died taking personal memories of James Harshaw, John Martin, and George Henderson with them. But the story of their lives survived in their writings, in James's journals hidden in a bank vault in a small American town, in John's letters treasured by recipients until donated to Irish research facilities, and in bound copies of the *Newry Commercial Telegraph*. Almost one hundred and fifty years later, their writings are again ready for a different generation to read.

§

George survived John by seventeen years, but he left no additional public record. His last years weren't happy ones. One of two surviving children, a son, died while on duty with the British Navy. One son alone survived.

George not only endured terrible personal loss during his life, but also like John and James substantial financial losses. Emyvale, his Newry home, was a grand, two storied house large enough for a large family. But George died at his final residence, a small four room house at 14 Tivoli Terrace in Kingstown on October 22, 1892. George had bought his burial plot in Mount Jerome cemetery in July of 1890 for £5. It was near the outer wall of the cemetery grounds, far from the grand avenue where the important Protestants of Dublin were buried, including John Martin's sister Elizabeth. Apparently, that was all he could afford. There were no glowing obituaries to record his death.

George was survived by his second wife Catherine and his only living child James Ward. Catherine died two years later. His surviving son James married, but had no children to remember their grandfather. Like his siblings, he died while a young man in 1907. George's branch of the Henderson family had ended.

Henrietta Mitchel Martin lived many years after that sad March when she lost her brother and husband within a few short days. After John's death, she continued to write to George Mahon, recounting how difficult it was to endure life without John. She hoped that George would publish his correspondence with John, but she couldn't persuade him to take on the project. Instead, the letters were donated to the National Library in Dublin.

However, she kept moving forward, always busy. She taught young ladies to play the piano. For several years she was a governess in Italy. But she was always on hand to help when members of her family needed nursing. She remained a strong-willed woman who wouldn't allow her single status to limit her life. Her difficulties with the often roiling Atlantic didn't tie her to

Ireland. She traveled to New York to visit Jenny Mitchel. From there, she took a train across America, stopping to visit William Dillon on his ranch in Colorado, before visiting distant relatives in San Francisco. Then she crossed the Pacific to visit her sister Margaret Mitchel Irvine who had emigrated to Australia after the bankruptcy and death of her husband Hill Irvine.

In her later years, she returned to Ireland. She died on July 8, 1913 in the Donnybrook section of Dublin, and was buried beside her parents and brother in Newry. She had remained a widow for 38 years. The *Weekly Freeman's Journal* published an obituary. "She evinced the keenest interest in every movement that made for the realization of their ideals, and often contributed by her presence at their meetings to inspire the young men of a later generation with the resolve to persevere in the cause for which they toiled and suffered."

§

James Harshaw's widow, Sarah Kidd, lived 10 years after James, dying in 1877. She was spared witnessing the loss of the Harshaw land, acre by acre, and experiencing constables rampaging through Ringbane House, throwing all her cherished family possessions onto the road. She died three years before her youngest son Samuel, the beloved Absalom, died in Paterson NJ in 1880. Robert Hugh died soon after his older brother John in 1896. Willy died in 1902. James Jr. died in 1903. Andrew, the last surviving son, died May 19, 1906. Sarah Anne Megaw, the wee "chile," was the last survivor.

James had greatly loved daughter Mary's son James Alexander Harshaw Douglas. Just two years after James had died, James Alexander also lost his father, leaving him an orphan at age ten. Despite the family financial difficulties, he was able to graduate from Queen's University in 1879 with a degree in medicine. With his education behind him, he traveled to Australia, but returned to Ireland by 1884 and was then living nearby at the Glen. Sometime later, he moved to West Bromwich, Staffordshire, England. There he married Elizabeth Swift, and apparently practiced medicine. He died still a young man on November 10, 1897. He and his wife had no children.

James Alexander had many cousins who did marry and have children. Thus James has many descendents living today, some in America, some in Australia, but many still living near Donaghmore.

§

James had a major impact on the lives of friends and neighbors, and laborers who worked for him and his family. "Pat boy" (Patrick Kelly) whom James hired at a fair in Newry in 1860 and "nurse girl" (Catherine O'Hare) who cared for the newborn James Alexander Douglas when his mother died were two of them. After they fell in love and wished to marry, James did everything in his power to make their marriage happen.

When the young couple walked away from Ringbane, a happy life together seemed to be a big gamble, even though James generously paid them enough that they had sufficient money to travel to Canada or America. But they saved some of their money by making the less expensive trip to England. They settled in Thornley, in County Durham. There Pat had the option of working in the coal mines if he couldn't find employment on a farm. However, Pat had a special talent for working with horses, that James had quickly discovered, and found work as a horse trainer above ground on a local estate.

Pat and Catherine became parents of their first child, a son Thomas, a year later. Over the ensuing years, the couple became parents of nine more children, seven sons and three daughters. Unlike George and James, all their children lived to be adults

The Kellys left Thornley sometime in the early part of the 20th century and moved with their five unmarried children to Newcastle upon Tyne. There Pat and Catherine were able to retire in some comfort. Their daughter Elizabeth managed their home. They were supported by sons John who was a bricklayer for a construction company, Joseph who worked in the goods department of the railroad, and William who was an inspector of gun mountings at the Engineering Works. Their youngest child Norah was a school teacher.

Pat and Catherine were married for over 50 years before Pat died in 1912. Catherine outlived him by 3 years.

§

Neither John nor George lived to see the resolution of confounding issues that made life difficult for all three men. The land issue caused much hardship and many ejectments. It was finally resolved twenty eight years after John had died, in just the way he predicted. Parliament voted in 1903 to allow lease-holding farmers to gain title to their land by merely keeping current in their rent. Unfortunately, James Harshaw's children held no leases when the opportunity finally came.

The desperate poverty prevailing in the late years of the 19th century contributed to this sad situation. John and many of his fellow activists believed excessive taxation laid upon Irish landholders with the passage of the new income tax imposed in 1853 contributed to ever growing financial distress. Despite appeals to Parliament, members rejected this complaint. Finally, Parliament established a Financial Relations Commission in 1894. A final report was produced in 1896 which confirmed the Irish complaints that they were suffering taxation not allowed by the arrangements of the Act of Union. Ireland had been over-taxed by three million pounds a year since the enactment of the income tax in 1853. Parliament never offered to repay their debt. However, the law allowing Irish farmers to own their own property was designed to help assuage the unified outcry that followed the report.

§

John and George both thought deeply about the future of Ireland. John anticipated a day when England would grant Home Rule in Ireland because the majority of Irish citizens united to ask for it. George predicted that Ireland would be engulfed in civil war if home rule or any other version of independence were to be enacted by Parliament.

Both men were correct. The Home Rule forces forged a unified political party, the Irish Parliamentary Party, led by Charles Parnell, whom John had introduced to the Home Rule movement and who succeeded John as MP for Meath. His Irish party pressed Parliament for Home Rule. The Protestants of Ulster united in a roar of defiance. They created an armed fighting force, supported by an intensive smuggling operation to provide the necessary guns. They were ready for revolution. Just as the final push for Home Rule neared success, World War 1 broke out across Europe. Parliament delayed implementation of Home Rule until the end of the war.

By the time the final vote on Home Rule came in 1918, Parliament clearly saw the dangers of the civil war that George had always feared. The Home Rule legislation that was finally passed allowed Irishmen to vote on Home Rule, but those who opposed it in Ulster could take the option of seceding from the rest of Ireland.

In the general election of 1918, Sinn Fein, running on support of Home Rule, won 75% of the vote. The newly elected members immediately came to Dublin to set up their own unofficial Irish Parliament, just as John had pictured. The Protestants voted to withdraw, and establish a Home Rule government in the six counties on the northern edges of Ireland, carefully chosen to create a section of Ireland where Protestants predominated. While George hated the idea of Home Rule, he might well have endorsed Home Rule controlled by Protestants. Newry, along with Loughorne and Ringbane, remained part of Northern Ireland when the rest of Ireland became independent.

This division of the island, which neither John or George predicted, was followed by years of low-intensity civil war, just as George did predict. The most recent fighting, the Troubles, lasted thirty years, ending with the Easter Agreement in 1998.

The author will continue to relate the history of Newry in a blog that can be accessed at: http://duelingdragonsireland.blogspot.com.

Bibliography

This book is largely based on the writings of the three principals, James Harshaw, John Martin, and George Henderson. The journals kept by James Harshaw are in the Public Record Office of Northern Ireland in Belfast. Northern Ireland. The reference number there is D4149/1-7. The original documents have been filmed. These films are available at Bagnals Castle in Newry, Northern Ireland. In the United States, they are available at the New England Historical Genealogical Society in Boston Massachusetts at DA 995, D6 H37. A transcription is available from the following website: http://www.familysearch.org/search/catalogue/1827458 or from theMormon Library in Salt Lake City, Utah.

George Henderson wrote exclusively for the Newry Commercial Telegraph. Bound copies of the newspapers are available in many libraries. They are available on microfilm and hardcopy in the Reading Room of the National Library in Dublin. Microfilm editions up to the year 1867 are available at the Newry Public Library, Hill Street, Newry. Indexed newspapers through 1871 are also available online at the website of the British Newspaper Archive, https://www.britishnewspaperarchive.co.uk. This is a subscription service.

John Martin also kept a journal at various times in his life, portions of which survive. They are at the Public Record Office of Northern Ireland in Belfast, number D560. Transcriptions and additional Martin family information are online at www.theballards.net/Harshaw/Martin/Diary. Martin's letters and speeches have been published in various books or preserved at the manuscript section of the National Library in Dublin. The many newspaper sources are available at the British Newspaper Archive. This information will be referenced chapter by chapter. The text will make clear when the sources are either the *Telegraph* or the Harshaw Diaries.

Chapter 1.
John Martin's Journal, Part 3, 86-105.
Jail Journal, 208-218.
Chapter 2.
Weekly Dispatch. June 24, 1849.
Jail Journal, 221-2; 226-7; 230.
Wikipedia entry for Paul Cullen.
https://en.wikipedia.org/wiki/Paul_Cullen_(cardinal)
Letter of Thomas Meagher, undated; S 3226. National Library, Dublin.
Irish Exiles. 94.
Chapter 3.
Jail Journal, 243; 267-72; 278-291.

McManus, MS 3226. National Library, Dublin.
Wikipedia, Ecclesiastical Titles Act.
Irish Exiles, 98.
Chapter 4.
Irish Exiles, 116, 130.
Martin letter to O'Dogherty, August 16, 1853, MS 10,522. National Library, Dublin.
William Smith O'Brien Papers, MS 46/824/9, Part VII. National Library, Dublin.
Meagher Manuscript, MS 3224. National Library, Dublin.
The Nation, October 21, 1854.
Clyde Company Papers, 145, 230.
Chapter 5.
Recollections of Fenians, 60,
Wikipedia, Haussmann's renovation of Paris, section 4.
http://en.wikipedia.org/wiki/Hanssman%27s_renovation_of_Paris.
The Nation, October 28, 1854.
Martin letters to George Mahon, May 14, 1855; October 18, 1855. MS 22,190. National Library, Dublin.
Martin letters to Mahon, April 22, 1856; May 4, 1856; June 2, 1856; August 4, 1856. Letter with no date. MS 22,191. National Library, Dublin.
Chapter 6.
Martin letters to Mahon, January 21, 1857; February 1, 1857; September 29, 1857; October 11, 1857. MS 22,192. National Library, Dublin.
Martin letters to Mahon, April 24, 1858; August 6, 1858; October 6, 1858; November 7, 1858. National Library, Dublin.
Chapter 7.
No additional sources.
Chapter 8.
The Irishman, January 1, 1860; January 14, 1860; November 17, 1860; November 21, 1860; November 28, 1860; December 1, 1860; December 8, 1860; December 28, 1860.
Secret History, (Rutherford). 174-77; 181; 184-5; 187-99.
Recollections, (O'Leary). 152; 156; 158-9; 161-2.
Personal Narrative, (Denieffe). 166-7; 138.
The Nation, November 2, 1861; November 9, 1861; November 16, 1861; November 23, 1861.
The Irishman, November 8, 1862.
The Irish People, December 5, 1863.
Chapter 9.
The Nation, December 7, 1861; December 14, 1861; March 22, 1862.
Freeman Journal, March 18 1862.
Martin letter to Eva, September 25, 1862. MS 10,520. National Library, Dublin.
Chapter 10.

Daily Express, January 1, 1863.
The Irishman, January 10, 1863; April 25, 1863; May 30, 1863; June 20, 1863; August 1, 1863; August 31, 1863; October 17, 1863; October 24, 1863; October 31, 1863; November 7, 1863; November 14, 1863; November 21, 1863; November 28, 1863; December 13, 1863.
Pretty Jenny Mitchel, 192.
Martin letter to O'Brien, October 20, 1863. MS 8657. National Library, Dublin.
Wikipedia, Draft Riots, 1863.
http://en.wikipedia.org/wiki/New_York_City_draft_riots
Freeman Journal, May 11, 1863.
Irish People, December 12, 1863; December 19, 1863; December 26, 1863.
Chapter 11.
Irish People, January 9, 1864; January 30, 1864; February 27, 1864; March 5, 1864.
The Irishman, February 27, 1864; September 10, 1864; September 17, 1864; September 24, 1864.
Martin letter to Eva, July 18, 1864. MS 3226. National Library, Dublin.
The Nation, February 27, 1864; July 23, 1864; September 24, 1864.
Martin letter to Daunt, April 28, 1864. MS 8047. National Library, Dublin.
Kilkenny Journal, July 20, 1864.
Evening Freeman, August 9, 1864.
Chapter 12.
Irish People, September 17, 1864; January 14, 1865.
Freeman's Journal, January 4, 1865.
The Irishman, January 7, 1865.
The Nation, August 3, 2865; September 6, 65; March 21, 1865; February 10, 1866
Pretty Jenny Mitchel, 218-225.
Chapter 13.
Recollections (O'Leary), Vol. 2, 198.
Martin letter to Eva, no date. MS 10, 520. National Library, Dublin.
Martin letter to Daunt, September 18, 1865.
The Nation, February 10, 1866.
Young Ireland Manuscript, MS 3226. National Library, Dublin.
Freeman's Journal, August 8, 1866.
Chapter 14.
Martin letters to Mahon, January 11, 1867; January 25, 2868. MS 22, 197. National Library, Dublin.
The Nation, March 20, 1867; April 5, 1867; June 1, 1867.
Weekly News, April 27, 1867.
Martin letters to Daunt, July 31, 18678; December 13, 1867; February 2, 1868; February 27, 1868. MS 8047. National Library, Dublin.
Irish Citizen, December 21, 1867; January 3, 1868; March 21, 1868.

Mahon letter to Dr. Simpson, January 25, 1868. MS 22, 197. National Library, Dublin.

Prosecuted funeral. (Sullivan), 26, 29.

Chapter 15.

Martin letters to Daunt. June 19, 1868; July 16, 1868. MS 8047. National Library, Dublin.

Irish Citizen, July 18, 1868.

Martin letters to Mahon, January 5, 1868; September 30, 1868; November 14, 1868. MS22,198. National Library, Dublin.

Chapter 16.

Irish Citizen, April 27, 1869; May 23, 1869; June 19, 1869; June 26, 1869; July 3, 1869; July 27, 1869; November 1, 1869; December 7, 1869; December 25, 1869; January 27, 1870; March 9, 1870; March 26, 1870; April 7, 1870; April 14, 1870; May 7, 1870.

Martin letter to Daunt, June 9, 1869. MS 8047. National Library, Dublin.

Sillard, 215-16; 217-18.

The Nation, December 14, 1869.

Cork Examiner, December 14, 1869.

Chapter 17.

Martin letters to Daunt, May 17, 1870; June 6, 1870; July 26, 1870; August 6, 1870; September 23, 1870; October 7, 1870; October 10, 1870; November 4, 1870; December 18, 1870. MS 8047. National Library, Dublin.

Daily Express, July 22, 1870; August 24, 1870; August 26, 1870; August 30, 1870; October 7, 1870.

The Times, August 19, 1870; August 26, 1870; September 12, 1870.

Freeman's Journal, August 22, 1870; September 13, 1870; October 5, 1870; October 8, 1870; October 10, 1870; October 13, 1870; October 15, 1870; October 17, 1870; October 20, 1870; October 22, 1870; December 28, 1870.

Belfast News Letter, January 2, 1871; January 7, 1871.

Irish Citizen, January 14, 1871; February 4, 1871.

Chapter 18.

Martin letters to Daunt, February 18, 1871; February 19, 1871; March 14, 1871; June 8, 1871.

Irish Citizen, February 11, 1871; April 1, 1871; June 1, 1871; July 1, 1871.

Freeman's Journal, February 11, 1871; June 27, 1871.

Daily Express, January 21, 1871; June 17, 1871.

Newry Reporter, March 25, 1871.

Hansard, May 26, 1871, 1336-1346.

The Times, June 6, 1871.

Chapter 19.

Martin letters to O'Leary, May 23, 1871; April 1, 1872. MS5926. National Library, Dublin.

Freeman's Journal, June 27, 1871; July 12, 1871; July 18, 1871; July 19, 1871; July 21, 1871.

Martin letters to Daunt, July 19, 1871; December 1, 1871; January 1, 1871; December 1, 1871; January 1, 1871; February 14, 1873. MS8047. December 16, 1872. MS 8942. National Library, Dublin.
Irish Citizen, March 9, 1872; March 28, 1872; April 11, 1872.
The Nation, March 23, 1872; August 7, 1872; March 29, 1873; September 11, 1873; September 20, 1873.
Cork Daily Herald, September 15, 1873.
Chapter 20.
London Standard, January 7 1874; March 3, 1874.
Freeman's Journal, January 28, 1874; February 18, 1874; March 11, 1874; April, 1, 1874.
The Nation, January 31, 1874.
Daily Express, March 3, 1874.
Martin letters to Daunt, April 2, 1874; April 15, 1874; March 24, 1874; July 7, 1874; November 7, 1874; January 16, 1875. MS 8947. National Library, Dublin.
Martin letters to O'Leary, April 27, 1874; August 19, 1874. MS 5926. National Library, Dublin.
Life of John Mitchel, (William Dillon), Volume 2, 283, 285.
Sillard, 285-6, 288.
Chapter 21.
Martin letters to Mahon, January 4, 1875; March 10, 1875. MS 22,204. National Library, Dublin.
The Nation, April 3, 1875.
Martin letters to Daunt, January 16, 1875; Daunt addendum March 30, 1875.
Sillard, 265-270, 272, 283, 285-6, 287, 288.
Life of John Mitchel, (Dillon), 291-3, 299.
Hansard, March 12, 1875, Vol. 222, 1726.
Newry Reporter, March 30, 1875; April 1, 1875.

Additional Sources

Bardon, Jonathan. *The History of Ulster.* Blackstaff Press. 1992.
Brown, P.L. *Clyde Co. Papers. Vol. 6, 1854-58.* Oxford Press, London. 1968.
Cowan, Rev. J. Davison. *An Ancient Irish Parish Past and Present Being the Parish of Donaghmore County Down.* London. 1914.
Denieffe, Joseph. *A Personal Narrative of the Irish Revolutionary Brotherhood, Giving a Faithful report of the Principle Events from 1855 to 1867.* Gail Publishing Co. New York. 1906.
Dillon, William. *Life of John Mitchel.* London. 1888. Two volumes.
Elliott, Marianne. *The Catholics of Ulster, a History.* Basic Books. 2001.
Harshaw, James. *Diary of James Harshaw Donaghmore.* Volumes 3-7.
Kiernan, T.J. *The Irish Exiles in Australia.* Dublin. 1954.
MacManus, Seamas. *The Story of the Irish Race.* The Devin Adair Co., NY. 1975.

Partial Diary of John Martin. PRONI. D/560/3-6,

Mitchel, John. *Jail Journal*. Sphere Books Limited. London. 1983.

Murray, Alice Effie. *A History of the Commercial and Financial Relations Between England and Ireland from the Period of the Reformation*. P.S. King and Son. London. 1907.

O'Connor, Rebecca. *Pretty Jenny Mitchel Young Irelander*. The O'Connor Trust. Tucson, Arizona. 1988.

O'Leary, John. *Recollections of Fenians and Fenianism*. Downey and Co. Ltd. London. 1896. Two volumes.

Porter, J. C. *The Life and Times of Henry Cooke*. Ambassador Productions Limited. Belfast N. I. 1999.

Rutherford, John. *Secret History of the Fenian Conspiracy: Its Origins, Objects and Ramifications*. Kegan Paul and Co. London. 1877.

Salter, Henry Hyde. *On Asthma*. John Churchill. 1868.

Sillard, P. A. *The Life and Letters of John Martin*. Dublin 1893.

Sullivan, A.M. *The Prosecuted Funeral Procession*. 1868.

Thornley, David. *Isaac Butt and Home Rule*. MacGibbon & Kee. London. 1964.

Warren, Ira. *Warren's Household Physician*. Boston. 1889.

Young Irelanders: Exiles in Paradise. http:utas.edu.au/young-irelanders/home

Note on Transcriptions

Nineteenth century Irish authors wrote and spelled differently than twenty-first century Americans. James Harshaw had his own individual style. To convey these differences all the quotations from his diary and from the letters and articles of George Henderson and John Martin have been transcribed as is, with no attempt made to conform to current standards.

Illustration Credits

The illustrations in this book come from three sources:

Maps created for the book

The maps on pages v, vi, vii, and viii are the original work of David Robie, based on data from: http://openstreetmap.org.

Pictures and Photographs Owned by Individuals

The picture(s) of:
John Martin on page iii is owned by Wallace Beatty.

James Harshaw on page iv is owned by Walter Malcomson.

St. Bartholomews church on page 58 is owned by the author.

Handwriting samples of James Harshaw and John Martin on page 128 are owned by the author.

Harshaw house in Ringbane and the Emyvale house on page 150 are owned by the author.

Kilbroney on page 150 is owned by Adrian Murdock.

Dromalane and Seaview houses on page 322 are owned by the author.

Revs. Lindsay and Elliott on page 260 are owned by Adrian Murdock

Last Meeting on page 406 is owned by Adrian Murdock.

Gravestone of George Henderson on page 448 is owned by Maud Hamill.

Gravestones of John Martin and James Harshaw on page 448 are owned by the author.

Henrietta Mitchel Martin on page 474 is owned by Adrian Murdock.

Pictures from the Internet

The pictures of the Young Irelanders on page 4, the Fenian and Orange Order leaders on page 214, Cardinal Cullen on page 260, the British government leaders on page 282, and the Home Rulers on page 350 were obtained from the Wikimedia commons website. All are in the public domain because published in the 19th century.

The picture of the Donaghmore Presbyterian Church on page 58 is from the genealogy site of Ros Davies: "Ros Davies' Co. Down, Northern Ireland Family History Research Site"
http://rosdavies.com/PHOTOSwords/DonaghmoreAll.htm

Index

Abbreviations used in the index: aka-also known as; bro-brother; cont-continued; dau-daughter; dec.-deceased; Dr.-doctor; ed.-editor; elec-election; GH-George Henderson; HGA-Home Government Association; HRL-Home Rule League; INL-Irish National League; JH-James Harshaw; JM1-John Martin; JM2-John Mitchel; jr.-junior; m.-married; MP- Member of Parliament; OO-Orange Order; PM-Prime Minister; prby-presbytery; pub.-publisher; Rev.-Reverend; sis-sister; US-United States; VDL-Van Diemen's Land (Tasmania); VP-Vice President; YI- Young Irelanders

About the Author

Marjorie Harshaw was born in Minneapolis to a family of Irish origin. She spent her first years in a small town north of Washington DC, before moving to Andover Massachusetts. There she graduated from high school before studying English and Government at Tufts University.

After graduation, Marjorie married Eugene Robie. The couple lived in Virginia and West Virginia before returning to Massachusetts, where they settled in the small historic town of Ipswich, raised their six children and enjoyed visits from their ten grandchildren. Marjorie taught in the Ipswich public schools, establishing the Special Needs program at the secondary level. When she left teaching, she fulfilled a desire to run for public office, serving two terms on the Ipswich School Committee -- four years as its Chairman. She acted on her love of history and genealogy by serving many years on the Ipswich Historical Commission and researching her own family's history.

Marjorie's public writing career started with a weekly newspaper column on Irish history for the *Newry Democrat*. When she discovered a fascinating story of her family's connections to Irish history through much of the 19th century, she wrote her first book, *Dwelling Place of Dragons (2006)*. *Dueling Dragons: The Struggle for Ireland* concludes Marjorie's unique account of Irish history as experienced by her ancestors.

Back cover photo courtesy of Alice Bannon Robie.

CPSIA information can be obtained
at www.ICGtesting.com
Printed in the USA
LVHW011443300119
605809LV00018B/610